Adjustment and Personal Growth:
Seven Pathways

Adjustment and Personal Growth: Seven Pathways

SECOND EDITION

FRANK J. BRUNO

San Bernardino Valley College

JOHN WILEY & SONS

New York   Chichester   Brisbane   Toronto   Singapore

Cover painting by Edward A. Butler
Text and cover designed by Ann Marie Renzi

Library of Congress Cataloging in Publication Data:

Bruno, Frank Joe, 1930–
    Adjustment and personal growth.

    Re. ed. of: Human adjustment and personal growth.
c1977.
    Includes bibliographies and index.
    1. Adjustment (Psychology) 2. Self-actualization
(Psychology) I. Title.
BF335.B74 1983   155.2′5   82-8520
ISBN 0-471-09296-7   AACR2

Printed in the United States of America

10 9 8 7 6 5 4 3 2 1

For Jeanne

Preface

TO THE INSTRUCTOR

It is possible to organize an adjustment-growth textbook in one of several ways.

A widely employed approach is to organize the book around what might be called "arenas of life." Chapters are devoted to the challenges of college, career, marriage, childrearing, one's sexuality, and other domains of human concern. Advantages of this approach are that the book will be practical, relevant, and close to the problems of daily living. A drawback is the problem of redundancy. The same key principles are pertinent to various kinds of situations, and must reappear in more than one setting. However, there may be no appropriate place to adequately develop such subjects as unconscious motivation, defense mechanisms, behavior modification, assertiveness training, emotional self-control, biofeedback training, and the search for meaning in existence. The impact of these subjects is diluted when they are fragmented and spread throughout the book.

A second approach is to organize the book in terms of a principles orientation such as psychoanalysis, behavioral psychology, or humanistic psychology. By presenting a unified world view, systematic books often have a substantial impact on the thinking of the student. However, a difficulty with such textbooks is that many important concepts are simply left out. Also, their extreme bias may leave the student with the incorrect notion that there is one Royal Pathway toward greater adjustment and personal growth.

A third approach is to organize the book so that primary attention is given to principles and concepts. Books organized in this manner are eclectic, covering a wide spectrum of orientations toward adjustment and growth. This book utilizes the third approach. It has been my conviction that many of the principles and concepts of behavioral science may be construed as *psychological tools*, mental instruments by which we can more successfully cope with the challenges of human existence. Thus, in this book the emphasis is on these principles and concepts, including methods, management techniques, and coping devices by which persons effectively deal with the problems of day-to-day living. These psychological tools are illuminated by many examples drawn from all walks of human activity to provide a textbook with the breath of life in it. As such, *Adjustment and Personal Growth: Seven Pathways* (2nd Ed.) is intended to be both academically sound and practical.

TO THE STUDENT

The psychology of adjustment and personal growth is a subject of universal interest, an exciting field of study with many dimensions and applications. A survey of a number of college catalogs reveals that the following topics tend to be stressed in adjustment-growth courses.

Personality dynamics

Defense mechanisms

Emotional self-control

Psychotherapy

Modifying habits

Mental health

Human potentialities

Human relations

Self-understanding

Conceptions of normal and abnormal behavior

Applications to daily living

The preceding list gives you a preview of some of the subjects discussed in this book. All of the topics revolve around the core idea of leading a more gratifying and meaningful life—a unifying theme of this book.

Adjustment and Personal Growth: Seven Pathways (2nd Ed.) has been designed so that you may easily study its contents. Here are some of the book's distinctive features:

Seven principal pathways toward greater adjustment and growth are discussed. No one system is presented as having the Whole Truth. The book offers a wide spectrum of orientations, allowing you to use your own intelligence in making decisions about ideas that have the greatest personal value to you.

Each of the seven chapters devoted to a pathway contains a *Critique* section. Although the principal pathways are presented in generally favorable terms, the aim of the critiques is to help you strike a realistic balance between zealous acceptance or cynical rejection of a particular approach.

Two kinds of boxes appear in the book. These are titled *Contemporary Research* and *Application*. The *Contemporary Research* boxes highlight the way in which experiments, clinical data, or other kinds of studies relate to selected psychological concepts. The *Application* boxes make explicit connections between general principles and the way in which these principles can be used to enhance the quality of life.

Each chapter, with the exception of Chapter 1, ends with an *Applied Exploration* section. These sections are designed to be of practical value. They offer useful information and point toward the broader relevance of the concepts and principles discussed in the chapter.

Each important term appears in boldface type and is briefly defined the first time it is introduced. In addition, the principle or concept associated with the term is immediately clarified with a concrete example related to life. No term is allowed to stand in meaningless isolation without connections to reality.

Every chapter ends with a numbered summary highlighting key points.

There is an appendix toward the end of the book titled *Classifying Mental Disorders: An Introduction to the Diagnostic Categories in DSM-III.* (DSM-III stands for the *Diagnostic and Statistical Manual of the American Psychiatric Association,* Third Edition.) Although this is not an abnormal psychology textbook, there are enough references to mental disorders in the book so that you should have available the contemporary psychiatric nomenclature. You can use the appendix as a convenient reference when you are in doubt about the meaning of a clinical term.

All the principal terms appear in the *Glossary* toward the end of the book. You will find a formal definition given for each listed term.

There is an index at the end of the book, allowing for quick access to both subjects and persons.

In brief, an effort has been made to make *Adjustment and Personal Growth: Seven Pathways* (2nd Ed.) a book that you will find to be both worth studying and enjoyable to use. I wish you success in your study of this exciting field of psychology.

OF SEX AND ENGLISH USAGE

Of late it has become increasingly obvious to thinking persons that words such as "mankind" and such phrases as "the rise of modern man" are unfair, ignoring the self-evident fact that approximately half of the human beings on this Earth are women. Consequently, in this book I have replaced "mankind" with "humankind," and have made similar modifications whenever possible. There remains the stubborn problem of the *generic he,* the widespread use of the pronoun "he" to indicate both sexes.

The generic "he," like the word "mankind," contains a certain amount of inequity toward females. I have dealt with this problem in various ways. I have frequently used plural pronouns instead of singular pronouns; for example, a sentence such as, "The self-actualizing person maximizes his potentialities, and he will not waste his life," becomes "Self-actualizing persons maximize their potentialities, and they will not waste their lives." Also, examples in the book draw from the behavior of both sexes. In some instances, where I found it clumsy to use a plural pronoun, the generic "he" was retained in preference to the more cumbersome "he or she," or the alternative practice of randomly alternating hes and shes throughout the book.

Acknowledgments

A number of people have helped me to make *Adjustment and Personal Growth* (2nd Ed.) become a reality. My thanks are expressed to:

My wife Jeanne for our many meaningful discussions about adjustment and personal growth.

Ronald St. John for his confidence in the first edition.

Jack K. Burton for his help with the first edition and his confidence in the second edition.

Carol Luitjens for being a creative and supportive editor.

Connie Rende for providing able administrative assistance during the manuscript's first draft stage.

Pamela Bellet-Cassell for keeping things moving with able administrative assistance during the second draft and production stages.

Rosemary Wellner for enhancing the readability of the book through excellent copy editing.

Kathy Bendo for creative photographic research.

Jan M. Lavin for effectively supervising production.

Ann Marie Renzi for quality book design.

Rosemary Spurling for typing the manuscript.

R. C. Dixon-Robinson of the University of Wisconsin-Oshkosh, William J. Dibiase of Delaware County Community College, Bobby L. Jones of Diablo Valley College, Kathleen Kowal of the University of North Carolina at Wilmington, Gilbert Meyer of Illinois Valley Community College, and Joel D. West of Northern Michigan University for their thoughtful reviews of the manuscript and constructive suggestions for its improvement.

FRANK J. BRUNO

Contents

Special Features

A person walking a tightrope symbolizes the integral relationship between adjustment and growth, stability and change.

Chapter 1

PSYCHOLOGY, ADJUSTMENT, AND GROWTH

Overview

Imagine yourself in the following situation:

You are a single person invited to a party by a couple you have only recently met. You know only a few people at the party, and feel ill at ease. Most of the evening you don't quite know what to say to people. Your hostess introduces you to an attractive member of the opposite sex. The other individual makes clever small talk, and you try to be clever back—but you're convinced you're missing the mark. You feel your face getting red, your heart is beating faster than usual, and you wish you could crawl into a hole. Small talk continues for a while. Then the other person wanders off with some excuse, eventually showing an interest in someone else. You feel inadequate and very self-conscious. You leave the party early and feel that both you and it have been failures.

Is something wrong with the imagined you in the above paragraph? Do you have an anxiety disorder? Are you a troubled person? Do you need psychotherapy?

The odds are that the answer to these questions is *no.* In fact your experience is so basically human that it is commonplace. Many of us suffer from a certain amount of **situational shyness**, a lack of poise and self-confidence under a given set of circumstances. Social psychologist Philip G. Zimbardo conducted a survey on shyness and found that more than 80 percent of his subjects confessed to being shy some of the time. (Persons who suffer from **chronic shyness** in contrast to situational shyness have a long-standing prob-

Many of us suffer from a certain amount of situational shyness.

lem with shyness, and experience discomfort in almost all social situations. The incidence of chronic shyness is much smaller than situational shyness—about 25 percent in Zimbardo's survey.)

Problems such as shyness are simply a part of being alive. I conducted an informal survey with over 100 introductory psychology students. Two questions were asked: (1) Do you have any hang-ups or bad habits, and (2) If so, name at least one. In response to the first question, 94 percent said "Yes." In response to the second question, common problems identified were: Shyness, procrastination, nail-biting, smoking, overeating, excessive worry, depression, bad temper, poor self-image, and alcohol abuse. So we should not consider ourselves alone if we have one or two problems in adjusting to life.

One way to begin your study of adjustment and personal growth is to consider how you might answer the following questions:

Do you consider yourself a well-adjusted person?

Are you making the most of your talents and potentialities as a human being?

Do you feel you understand yourself?

Are there habits you want to break?

Are you living an authentic life?

Does life seem somewhat empty to you? Or does it seem to be filled with meaning?

The principal aims of this book are (1) to help you develop a deeper appreciation for the scope and implications of the preceding and related questions about human existence, (2) to point out ways you can find increasingly satisfactory answers to such questions, and (3) to establish some connection between abstract principles of adjustment and growth and the problems of your daily life. In brief, this book presents ideas that may contribute to a more rewarding life.

A concepts/principles book such as this one should be distinguished from the popular how-to book that offers categorical advice about living. This book presents no formulas for successful living. No single philosophy or point of view is argued as the Truth. Instead, the book is designed to give you quite a bit of information about what outstanding psychologists have had to say about adjustment and growth. The author hopes that the content of the book will stimulate you to think for yourself. Effective living is your responsibility and no psychologist, guru, or self-proclaimed wise man can take over that responsibility for you.

As you already know, the title of the book is *Adjustment and Personal Growth: Seven Pathways.* Later in this chapter you will find a discussion concerning the distinction between the concepts of adjustment and growth.

At this point, however, I want to stress the subtitle—*Seven Pathways.* In this book, seven general approaches to adjustment and growth are discussed. A chapter is devoted to each, and they are designated as follows:

1. Depth Psychology
2. Behavioral Psychology
3. Cognitive Psychology
4. Transactional Analysis
5. Psychotechnology
6. Existential-Humanistic Psychology
7. Transpersonal Psychology

The meaning and content of these approaches is, of course, the substance of this book. Therefore I will defer any discussion of the approaches themselves until the appropriate chapters. For now, the primary point to be made is that the book is eclectic—it does not see pathways toward adjustment and growth as mutually exclusive.

PSYCHOLOGY AND HUMAN BEINGS: SEEKING GREATER SELF-UNDERSTANDING

Psychology has become the most popular course on college campuses. And in bookstores across the nation, best-sellers such as *Born to Win, How to Get Whatever You Want Out of Life, Passages, Feeling Good,* and *The Sky's the Limit* fill the shelves. Why the interest in psychology? What do we expect to gain from studying it?

I have frequently asked students in introductory psychology classes what they expect from a psychology course. There are, of course, those who give a cynical reply: "Three college units." Sincere students, however, tend to give replies such as these:

"I want to find out what makes people tick."

"I want to know why I do things."

"I'm not getting along very well with my boyfriend. I want to get some ideas about how we can communicate better."

"I think I'm neurotic, and I want to find out what I can do about it."

It would seem that most students with a real interest in psychology seek greater self-understanding or greater understanding of other persons. Of course, these two goals are not mutually exclusive and many students have an active interest in both.

In the 1940s one of the best-selling books on popular psychology was *Peace of Mind* by Rabbi Joshua Loth Liebman. The book went through thirty printings in a relatively short time. More than a million copies of the book were printed in hardcover and paperback. What did Liebman offer? Here is an example:

> As we observe the growing hordes of neurotics and little tyrants, self-mutilators and self-slayers, that trail about the world, we realize that a new, more honest, and more dynamic map of man's troubled soul must be drawn before we can hope to explore this most tangled of terrains. Only one crayon can draw such a detailed map—and this is the crayon of modern psychology.
> . . . We learn to look upon our flaws and potentialities, and with searching fingers to probe out the causes of our failures, hates, and fears. We find out who we are! (pp. 7–8)

We find out who we are! What a promise! Perhaps those who write for Everyperson are too ambitious. Nonetheless, human beings seem to hunger for information that can help them live effective and meaningful lives. The popularity of modern psychology emanates from this hunger.

The Study of the Soul

The word **psychology** is a combination of two Greek works, **psyche** and **logos.** An informal translation of psychology into English is the "study of the soul." In much of Western classical philosophy, the soul and the body were thought to be distinct entities. Conscious awareness, personality, memory, and the mind itself were all associated with the soul, not the body. (The conscious mind, with its capacity for thought and reflection was believed to be an aspect of the soul.) The body was a thing or an object having no life without the soul. A useful metaphor for comprehending this point of view is to compare the human body with a toy mechanical doll. Imagine a doll that is activated by a battery; when the battery is in place the doll walks, and when the battery is taken out the doll does not walk. This was roughly the relationship between body and soul postulated by classical philosophy. The soul, like a battery, made the body move. (An animated cartoon is a moving cartoon; it is interesting to note that in several languages **anima** is the word for soul!)

Three giants of Western philosophy—Plato (427–347 B.C.), Saint Thomas Aquinas (1225–1274), and René Descartes (1596–1650)—did much to advance and establish the position that the soul is immortal, the body is mortal, and human existence arises from a combination of these two fundamentally different essences. *Dualism* is the word used to summarize the position that the body and soul are two distinct and different entities. The philosophy of dualism makes a science of psychology impossible. If the soul (and the mind) are members of a nonphysical realm, then precise explanation, prediction, and control of mental events is by definition impossible. This was a major theme in traditional Western philosophy and theology.

The Science of Behavior

The twentieth century brought a fresh definition of psychology. One definition that was at once both novel and brash was proposed by the father of behaviorism, John Broadus Watson, in the 1910s: *Psychology is the science of the behavior of organisms.* In one stroke Watson attempted to banish from psychology such traditional concepts as the human will and consciousness. Watson's attitude toward classical philosophy is well represented in these comments:

Before trying to understand the behaviorists' theory of thinking, won't the reader please pick up any introspective psychological text and read the chapter on thinking? Won't he then try to digest some of the pablum the philosophers have offered us on this all-important function? I have tried to understand it. I had to give it up. I believe the reader will give it up too.

. . . The behaviorist advances the view that what the psychologists have hitherto called thought is in short nothing but talking to ourselves. (p.176)

Watson felt that the traditional philosophical ideas applied to psychology led to circular arguments and meaningless debates. It was his desire to place psychology on a sound foundation of experimentation and observation. He was an extremist, and his call for a hard science of objective psychology had an electric effect on many of his contemporaries. He was elected president of the American Psychological Association in 1915, and his plea for cutting away philosophical deadwood has continued to reverberate to this day. The school of psychology called behaviorism has been a vigorous force in American psychology. Perhaps the most influential behaviorist of recent years has been B. F. Skinner. In the following quotation from his best-selling book *Beyond Freedom and Dignity* (1971), it is evident that he is an intellectual heir to Watson:

Almost all our major problems involve human behavior, and they cannot be solved by physical and biological technology alone. What is needed is a technology of behavior, but we have been slow to develop the science from which such a technology might be drawn. One difficulty is that almost all of what is called behavioral science continues to trace behavior to states of mind, feelings, traits of character, human nature and so on. (p.22)

The goals of psychology according to such thinkers as Watson and Skinner are to explain, predict, and control behavior. The traditional view of the individual as a creature with a mind and a will is dismissed as unscientific.

Inner and Outer

The follower of classical philosophical themes and the behaviorist live in different worlds. In spite of the impact of behaviorism, many sophisticated psychologists have returned to an emphasis on motifs suggested by Plato,

Aquinas, and others. The rise of existential-humanistic psychology in the past decade or so is one example. This rise has been called a "third force" in psychology (the other two forces are psychoanalysis and behaviorism). Existential-humanistic psychology affirms the commonsense notion that we are conscious, that we make real choices, and that we are much more than creatures of habit. It asserts that for fully functioning persons, life is what they make it, not something that happens to them. The writings of Abraham Maslow, Carl Rogers, Viktor Frankl, and others (discussed in Chapter 7) all have this common thread. For now, the point to be made is that the Third Force in psychology represents a partial return to the subjective psychology of early philosophy.

It seems to me that we are not compelled to make a choice between subjective psychology and objective psychology. Although they do represent different viewpoints, both are equally valid ones. The subjective psychologist is talking about the **inner world**, life as experienced. The objective psychologist is talking about the **outer world**, behavior as it presents itself to an observer. There is no necessity to take sides. There is no decision to be made about which viewpoint represents Ultimate Truth. One can draw from both viewpoints those concepts that are meaningful and useful, and one can apply them in appropriate contexts.

Some years ago the dean of American psychologists, William James, made a distinction between those who possess tough-minded temperaments and

Existential-humanistic psychology affirms the commonsense notion that we are conscious, that we make real choices, and that we are much more than creatures of habit.

those who possess tender-minded temperaments. Psychologists Heinz L. Ansbacher and Rowena R. Ansbacher write (1964):

The objective psychologist is apt to be tough-minded, the subjective psychologist tender-minded, and hence we can extend our list by adding James's description of his antithesis. (pp. 5–6)

[handwritten annotation: outer world ... inner world]

James points out that the individuals belonging to one category tend to have a low opinion of individuals belonging to the other category. This is unfortunate because we can learn a great deal under certain conditions from either point of view. As already indicated, I do not feel that a distinct choice must be made between the points of view.

In the following pages you will see both points of view underlying the specific ideas and concepts of different approaches to adjustment and personal growth. In many cases a theoretician or a school of psychology cannot be categorized easily as tough-minded or tender-minded, and we won't worry much about this difficulty. For example, Freud thought of himself as tough-minded. He saw psychoanalysis as an objective approach to the study of human behavior, with an emphasis on natural science and cause and effect principles. Watson, however, thought of Freud as tender-minded and saw psychoanalysis as a soft psychology with a set of mushy, poorly defined concepts. Who was right? If one has read enough of psychoanalysis, behaviorism, and philosophy, it is possible to engage in hours of entertaining discussion about the question. But if one wishes to call a halt to circular argumentation, it is essential to note that the question cannot be answered in a definitive way. Much of Freudian theory is based on Freud's solid observation of his patients, and much of Freudian theory is based on his self-analysis and interpretation of his own dreams. Thus psychoanalysis represents an amalgamation of objective and subjective points of view.

The inner and the outer points of view have something to reveal to each other, and as we approach our study of adjustment and personal growth we

THE TOUGH-MINDED	THE TENDER-MINDED
Empiricist (going by fact)	Rationalist (going by principles)
Sensationalistic	Intellectualistic
Materialistic	Idealistic
Pessimistic	Optimistic
Pluralistic (starting from parts, making of the whole a collection)	Monistic (starting from wholes, making much of the unity of things)
Irreligious	Religious
Hardheaded	Feeling
Fatalist	Free-willist
Skeptical	Dogmatical (Ansbacher & Ansbacher (1964), pp. 5–6)

will try to remember this. In this book psychology will be approached as both a natural science (tough-minded) and a mental science (tender-minded). It is my hope that this unified orientation will provide you with a broad spectrum of useful psychological concepts.

WHEN ADJUSTMENT FAILS: DIFFERING VIEWPOINTS

The poem *Richard Cory* by Edwin Arlington Robinson tells about a young gentlemen in a small town who is handsome, gracious, rich, and admired by all. The people in the town wish that they were in his place. The last four lines of the poem are:

So on we worked, and waited for the light,
And went without the meat, and cursed the bread;
And Richard Cory, one calm summer night,
*Went home and put a bullet through his head.**

What was Richard Cory's problem? We cannot tell; the author purposely does not give us enough information. Arlington seems to say between the lines, "Don't be taken in by what you see on the surface. Another person's in-

There are times when adjustment fails badly, when the individual's attempt to maintain a harmonious relationship with the world breaks down.

*"Richard Cory," *Selected Poems of Edwin Arlington Robinson,* 1931. Reprinted by permission of the Macmillan Co., New York.

ner world cannot be judged by his behavior." On the surface Richard Cory seems well-adjusted and content; below the surface, we surmise that he is in a state of despair.

In any event *Richard Cory* makes it amply clear that there are times when adjustment fails badly, when the individual's attempt to maintain a harmonious relationship with the world breaks down. (A formal definition of adjustment is presented in the last section of this chapter.) Serious failures in adjustment can take many forms. Clinical psychologists and psychiatrists speak of **mental disorders, abnormal behavior,** and **behavioral disorders.** These are all terms used to refer to patterns of behavior manifested by individuals when their coping abilities are unequal to life's demands.

Mental Disorders

This section will not present a complete listing of kinds of mental disorders. These are covered in detail in the appendix toward the end of the book, "Classifying Mental Disorders: An Introduction to the Diagnostic Categories in *DSM-III*." (*DSM-III* is an abbreviated form of *The Diagnostic and Statistical Manual of the American Psychiatric Association, Third Edition.*)

However, before we proceed, it would be a good idea to have a definition of the very general term **mental disorder** as well as definitions for a few basic kinds of mental disorders.

Here is how mental disorder is defined in *A Psychiatric Glossary*, a publication of the American Psychiatric Association (1980):

An illness with psychologic or behavioral manifestations and/or impairment in functioning due to a social, psychologic, genetic, physical/chemical, or biologic disturbance. The disorder is not limited to relations between the person and society. The illness is characterized by *symptoms* and/or impairment in functioning. (p.89)

In association with the general concept of mental disorders, let's identify at this point five commonly used terms: Organic mental disorders, psychotic disorders, personality disorders, anxiety disorders, and neurotic disorders.

Organic Mental Disorders   These disorders involve an actual brain disturbance. Possibilities include brain damage, biochemical imbalances, and hormonal imbalances.

Psychotic Disorders   When an individual takes leave of reality as most of us understand it, he or she is said to be suffering from a psychotic disorder. (The nature of what we refer to as "reality" is discussed in Chapter 8.) Characteristics of psychotic disorders include delusions (false ideas), hallucinations (the perception of something that has no actual presence), incoherence, mistrust, and illogical thinking.

Personality Disorders   These disorders are characterized by fixed and maladaptive behavioral traits. Attributes of personality disorders include behaviors that are immoral, impulsive, illegal, or just plain irritating to others. Persons with personality disorders often experience little subjective distress and don't necessarily see themselves in need of assistance and/or therapy.

Anxiety Disorders   The core of these disorders is, of course, captured in the very word **anxiety.** The quality we call anxiety is communicated by words such as **apprehension, tension, uneasiness,** and **dread.** Persons suffering from anxiety disorders describe their moods and feelings in terms of excessive worries about future outcomes. They also often suffer from **phobias,** fears without a reasonable basis.

Neurotic Disorders   In the past it would have been possible to define neurotic disorders as follows: Emotional disturbances characterized by inner conflict and anxiety. However, *DSM-III* does not have a single diagnostic category for neurotic disorders. Earlier versions of *The Diagnostic and Statistical Manual* did have such a category. But the revision published in 1980 by the American Psychiatric Association did away with it. Neurotic disorders have been broken up into five categories. One of these is **anxiety disorders,** already defined in the prior paragraph. The other four are: **affective, somatoform, dissociative,** and **psychosexual** disorders. (These terms are defined in the appendix.)

In view of the fact that the term **neurotic disorder** has played such an important part in the thinking of many theorists ranging from Sigmund Freud to Albert Ellis, it will be necessary to refer to it at various places. This should present no problem for us as long as we recognize that instead of indicating a precise clinical meaning it instead suggests a set of general problem regions in human adjustment including the old traditional meanings of emotional disturbance, inner conflict, and anxiety.

Keep two points in mind with regard to neurotic disorders: (1) The two terms, *anxiety disorders* and *neurotic disorders,* overlap to a certain extent, (2) Neurotic disorders do not exist as a single category in *DSM-III.*

The definitions offered in this section for kinds of mental disorders were brief and without examples. For a more complete treatment of mental disorders, with examples, you are referred to the appendix. The appendix, titled "Classifying Mental Disorders: An Introduction to the Diagnostic Categories in *DSM-III,*" can be turned to as a miniature dictionary whenever you have a problem with the language of mental disorders.

Let us now proceed to the question: How do we explain failures in adjustment? This question can be best answered by examining differing viewpoints. The four dominant viewpoints used by humankind over the years to explain mental disorders are (1) demonology, (2) the organic viewpoint, (3) the psychological viewpoint, and (4) the eclectic viewpoint.

Demonology

For many centuries demon possession has been a favorite way to explain mental disorders. In years gone by mental patients were whipped in the belief that this might chase the evil spirits out of them. **Exorcism**, a ritual casting out evil spirits, has been one way to "cure" mental disorders. Perhaps three-fourths of the world's population live in underdeveloped countries, and demon possession is still used by many groups of people to explain deviant behaviors. However, from the standpoint of contemporary psychology, demonology is seen as representative of a pre-scientific world view. Evil spirits, demons, and similar concepts represent **anthropomorphic thinking**, a kind of thinking that explains natural events in terms of humanlike attributes (i.e., evil spirits are much like evil human beings—they want to do you harm). An enlightened understanding of mental disorders requires that we seek explanations other than demon possession.

The Organic Viewpoint

The organic viewpoint explains mental disorders in terms of biological science. The assumption is that we are living organisms in the natural world, and that when something goes wrong with our behavior there must also be something wrong at a physical level. Possibilities include brain damage, genetic factors, and biochemical disturbances.

Brain Damage   It is possible for a mental disorder to be caused by an injury to or deterioration of the central nervous system. A wound to the head suffered in an accident or in combat may destroy part of the brain's cortex; this in turn may affect speech, thought, and moods. Or gradual brain damage may result due to abuse of alcohol or as a result of aging. Again, the personality may be adversely affected.

Genetic Factors   It is possible that an abnormal genetic pattern may reside behind some mental disorders. **Down's syndrome** (formerly **mongolism**) is caused by a chromosomal problem. One researcher postulates that schizophrenic disorders are due, in part, to an inherited brain defect that interferes with the brain's ability to process information (Meehl, 1962).

Biochemical Disturbances   It has been hypothesized that biochemical disturbances may play an important role in mental disorders. Too much or too little of important neurotransmitters may affect thought processes. (**Neurotransmitters** are chemicals used to send messages between neurons.) It has also been suggested that conditions such as **hypoglycemia**, chronic low blood sugar, may produce the symptoms of mental disorders. It has also been suggested that vitamin deficiencies may affect one's biochemistry. The principal focus has been on the B-complex vitamins (Lesser, 1980). It is asserted that a shortage of such vitamins affects the production of certain enzymes required by brain cells.

Speaking about the schizophrenic disorders, psychiatrist E. Fuller Torrey (1980) summarizes in a vivid way the conviction of those who favor an organic viewpoint to explain at least some mental disorders:

Within the last decade, research evidence has become overwhelming that schizophrenia is truly a brain disease and involves abnormalities of both brain structure and function. Psychiatrists who state otherwise have probably been on a prolonged sabbatical to Tibet and subscribing only to Popular Mechanics. *(p. 12)*

The Psychological Viewpoint

The psychological viewpoint explains mental disorders in terms of such concepts as **motives, thought processes, conditioned responses, habits, communication patterns,** and **inauthentic living.** The general psychological viewpoint is itself made up of a set of viewpoints including these: Psychodynamic, behavioral, cognitive, psychosocial, and humanistic approaches. (These viewpoints will be only briefly sketched here. Their elaboration forms much of the substance of the book in subsequent chapters.)

The Psychodynamic Viewpoint   The psychodynamic viewpoint focuses its attention on conflicting motives. The personality is seen as a battleground in which a kind of civil war takes place. A biological urge (e.g., a sexual impulse) may clash with a social norm (e.g., the moral thing to do), and in turn produce emotional distress and psychological symptoms. A key personality in the history of the psychodynamic viewpoint is Sigmund Freud, the father of psychoanalysis. A principal assumption of the psychodynamic viewpoint is that unconscious motivation plays an important role in human behavior. The psychodynamic viewpoint has been the dominant one in American psychiatry for many years, and it is still very influential.

The Behavioral Viewpoint   The behavioral viewpoint looks upon abnormal behavior in terms of the learning process. Chronic anxiety or chronic depression are viewed as maladaptive conditioned responses, ineffective ways the individual has learned to cope with difficult situations. The founders of behaviorism—men such as Ivan Pavlov, John Watson, and B. F. Skinner—had much to do with the prominence of the behavioral viewpoint.

The Cognitive Viewpoint   The cognitive viewpoint asserts that the conscious mind plays a significant role in mental disorders. The term **cognitive** refers to our higher thought processes—thinking, remembering, perceiving, solving problems, and making decisions. To **cogitate,** for example, means to give careful thought to something. The cognitive viewpoint assumes that irrational ideas and/or unclear thinking may cause emotional reactions such as excessive anxiety, inappropriate anger, or unwarranted depression. An early figure in the history of cognitive psychology was William James. He defined psychology as a mental science, thus placing an emphasis on the higher thought processes. Although cognitive psychology passed out of favor for many years, it has of late experienced a rebirth.

The Psychosocial Viewpoint The psychosocial viewpoint says that mental disorders are often reactions to interpersonal conflict. A family may use one of its members as a scapegoat for aggressive feelings, and this one member may be regarded as "sick." The psychosocial viewpoint would argue that it is the family that is "sick," not only the individual who displays symptoms.

There may be difficulties in communication in a marriage. And such difficulties may play a role in producing a depressive reaction in one or both of the marriage partners. A key figure in the history of the psychosocial viewpoint was the psychiatrist Harry Stack Sullivan. More recently, the psychosocial viewpoint makes its appearance in an approach known as transactional analysis (see Chapter 5).

The Humanistic Viewpoint The humanistic viewpoint asserts that what we call mental disorders arise from problems individuals have with attaining their highest human values. Some people have problems with **self-actualization.** (See the section on adjustment and personal growth toward the end of this chapter.) Others may be unable to find meaning in life. The humanistic viewpoint asserts that psychiatric labels are somewhat misleading. Many people who are excessively anxious or depressed are not so much sick as troubled. To a humanistic psychologist, the concept of the **troubled person** to a large extent replaces the concept of a mental patient. American humanistic psychology owes a debt to European existential philosophy. Existential philosophy stresses such themes as the worth of the individual and the importance of making responsible decisions in life. Examples of important personalities in humanistic psychology are Abraham Maslow and Carl Rogers (see Chapter 7).

The Eclectic Viewpoint

The eclectic viewpoint or **eclecticism** is what we might call a commonsense or middle-of-the-road approach. It asserts that at our present level of knowledge it is doubtful that one viewpoint is completely correct and says it all about mental disorders. It is more likely that each viewpoint makes a partial contribution to our overall understanding of failures in adjustment (see Table 1.1). Thus psychologists and psychiatrists who favor the eclectic viewpoint pick and choose among theories as they see fit when attempting to explain and understand the adjustment problems of a particular individual.

It is important to realize that even the organic and psychological viewpoints are not necessarily at odds with each other. In *The History of Psychiatry* by psychiatrists Franz G. Alexander and Sheldon T. Selesnick (1968), the

TABLE 1.1 VIEWPOINTS USED TO EXPLAIN MENTAL DISORDERS

Viewpoint	A Key Idea
Demonology	Evil spirits take possession of the person.
Organic Brain damage Genetic factors Biochemical	When something goes wrong with our behavior there is also something wrong at a biological level.
Psychological Psychodynamic Behavioral Cognitive Psychosocial Humanistic	Difficulties in psychological processes such as motivation, learning, thinking, and communicating are determining factors in mental disorders.
Eclectic	Each viewpoint makes a partial contribution to our overall understanding of failures in adjustment.

authors comment on the relationship of the organic and the psychological points of view:

Brain chemistry undoubtedly has a part in all mental processes, in all our strivings, learning, and ambitions, and also in our mental ailments. But brain chemistry cannot be isolated from man, from what is the core of his existence, his personality. Brain chemistry, indeed, can be altered by emotional stress, by anxiety, rage, fear, and hopelessness. (p. 34)

Thus we see the importance of avoiding an either-or way of thinking. Our overall understanding of mental disorders can obtain something of value from both the organic and psychological points of view. One approach does not cancel the other. An intelligent eclecticism has much to recommend it.

THERAPY: HELPING TROUBLED PERSONS

The roots of therapy for mental disorders extend beyond recorded history. Both anthropological studies of present-day primitive tribes and the excavations of archeologists suggest that some form of therapy has existed since the dawn of human existence. The shaman and the witch doctor play the role of therapist among prescientific people, which reveals an important trend underlying psychotherapy: **the magical trend.** Contemporary psychotherapy springs partly from a centuries-old belief in magic. To this day, many persons who go to a psychotherapist are unconsciously seeking some sort of magic from the therapist—he or she will be like Merlin the magician or Cinderella's fairy godmother and make their woes vanish by an esoteric ritual.

The peripheral belief in magic contributes to what is known as the **placebo effect** in therapy, a temporary improvement in the patient's symptoms caused by a momentary mobilization of his or her capacity to hope for the

Contemporary psychotherapy springs partly from a centuries-old belief in magic.

best (Frank, 1961). During the first few visits to a therapist, the patient often feels that "Everything is going to be OK now—I'm in good hands." But successful therapy often demands a contribution from the client. Psychotherapy in particular is a learning process, and patients can hardly expect beneficial results if they remain passive and psychologically inert. Some therapists might argue that the element of faith in magic is to some degree a necessary element in effective psychotherapy; however, few therapists would be willing to take the position that faith in magic is a sufficient condition for effective therapy. On the whole, contemporary therapy attempts to be both a rational and a scientific enterprise.

Psychiatrists, Psychoanalysts, and Clinical Psychologists

Before we proceed to discuss various kinds of therapy it might be well to draw distinctions among psychiatrists, psychoanalysts, and clinical psychologists. These three kinds of professional persons are often confused.

Psychiatrists are physicians, medical doctors who make the treatment of mental disorders their specialty. Although psychiatrists can and do practice psychotherapy, they also use various types of **somatic therapies**, therapies applied directly to the body for the purpose of alleviating the symptoms of mental disorders (see below).

Psychoanalysts are therapists who subscribe to Freudian or neo-Freudian assumptions. They base their approach on concepts such as unconscious motivation and ego defense mechanisms, subscribing essentially to the psychodynamic point of view. To be properly called a psychoanalyst the therapist should have completed an accredited training program offered by an established psychoanalytical association. Most psychoanalysts come from the ranks of psychiatrists. But not all; there are some psychologists who are psychoanalysts. Thus the term **psychoanalyst** crosses the boundaries of both psychiatry and psychology.

Clinical psychologists usually hold a doctorate in psychology (a Ph.D degree). (There are some exceptions. A relatively small percentage of qualified clinical psychologists hold a master's degree). The clinical psychologist is *not* a medical doctor, and may not prescribe drugs. The two principal functions of clinical psychologists are psychotherapy and psychological testing. Psychological testing in a clinical setting is undertaken for two principal reasons: (1) It is useful for diagnosing a patient's condition, and thus for suggesting appropriate lines of therapy, and (2) If a patient is hospitalized, the information from psychological tests may be helpful in making a sound decision about whether or not the patient is ready to be released. (Two principal kinds of psychological tests are intelligence tests and personality tests.)

Somatic Therapies

As noted above, **somatic therapies** are therapies applied directly to the body. The principal types of somatic therapy are (1) electroshock therapy, (2) chemotherapy, (3) psychosurgery, and (4) megavitamin therapy. **Electroshock therapy** involves inducing a convulsion similar to an epileptic seizure; the convulsion is induced by sending a small amount of electric current through the frontal lobes of the brain. A course of shock treatments may be prescribed for a person suffering from a severe depression with psychotic features (see the appendix).

Chemotherapy is based on the use of drugs as a form of treatment. Stimulants are sometimes used to improve a patient's mood; sedatives are often administered to calm mental patients. In the past two decades there has been a great increase in the use of **psychotherapeutic agents,** drugs that have a specific effect on psychotic, anxiety, and depressive disorders.

Psychosurgery is a broad term including lobotomy and electrical stimulation of the brain. In a **lobotomy,** the frontal lobes of the cortex are severed from the rest of a patient's brain. (Lobotomies are seldom performed; other kinds of somatic therapies have become preferred over lobotomies.) **Electrical stimulation of the brain (ESB)** is a subtle form of psychosurgery. Electrode implants are placed deep within the paleocortex ("old brain"), and it is possible, by applying small amounts of electric current to tiny areas, to affect emotions and behavior.

Megavitamin therapy is a regimen in which massive doses of selected vitamins are prescribed. It is applicable to both physical and psychological disorders. (Somatic therapies receive more detailed treatment in Chapter 6.)

Psychotherapy

Psychotherapy is the treatment of mental, emotional, and behavioral disorders by psychological methods. Psychological methods may include free association, habit-breaking techniques, hypnosis, and conversation. Most of these methods rely heavily on the fact that human beings can talk to each other, and psychotherapy has become known as "the talking cure." The word **psychotherapy** itself literally means "a healing of the self."

Let us distinguish four broad general modes of psychotherapy: (1) analytic therapies, (2) behavior therapies, (3) cognitive therapies, and (4) humanistic therapies. Like so many attempts at categorization, the categories overlap and are to some degree arbitrary. They are set up because they allow us to discriminate some major themes in psychotherapy.

Analytic therapies stress the concept of insight. There is something about oneself that is not completely understood. The assumption is that an analysis or interpretation of one's motivational structure will help one "see into" the deeper roots of a psychological-emotional problem. This "seeing into," or development of insight, is presumed to remove psychological material from an inaccessible unconscious level to a more accessible conscious level. The process is what has been described as "consciousness raising."

As an illustration of how analytic therapy might work, consider a client who has chronic ulcers. At one point in the therapy the client might remark, "I'm beginning to see things in a new way. I thought I was a nice person—liked everybody. I always got good marks in school for 'gets along well with others.' But I'm beginning to see that I've got a lot of bottled-up anger. There are a lot of things I want to tell my wife, but I don't let myself. I haven't even been letting myself think these things! Gads! There's so much about myself that I don't know. I'm just beginning to understand some of these things for the first time. I think my ulcers are aggravated by anger directed inwardly when it should really be directed outwardly." The client and the therapist will discuss such observations and attempt to evaluate them. At times the therapist may offer interpretations: "Do you think that maybe you were attracted to Mabel because she reminded you of your mother?" The basic assumption is that there is an unconscious level to mental life; a secondary assumption is that exploring this unconscious level is useful in freeing individuals from their inner struggles.

Behavior therapies tend to emphasize action instead of insight. The orientation tends to be tough-minded: "Get off your duff and do something about your problems!" (Such a statement would seldom be communicated to a client so bluntly; it is an implicit theme of the therapy, not an explicit directive.) The point of intervention is not the inner psychological struggle, but the observable behavior patterns. A behavior therapist will tend to be impatient with long-winded discussions about why this and why that; this therapist tends to be much more concerned with the question of how. "How is this undesirable behavior pattern maintained?" is a much more fruitful question for the behavior therapist than "Why did this undesirable behavior pattern come into existence?" The following exchange illustrates the orientation of the behavior therapist:

Client. I don't know why I smoke so much. I guess I've just got a weak ego or something. No willpower—I can't quit no matter how hard I try.

Therapist. Do you take coffee breaks at work? Do you usually smoke when you're taking a coffee break? And do you usually have coffee at the break?

Client. Yeah, I take breaks and I usually have coffee.

Therapist. OK. Let's try this: Tomorrow, when break time comes, go to a different place than the usual place. Or maybe take a ten-minute walk around the block. Don't drink any coffee—you're probably being cued by the coffee to light up. You're also probably being cued by the familiar place and the conversation of friends and the fact that some of them light up. Just take a walk by yourself for a few days and see if you can break the pattern. Let's make a start somewhere.

Client. It's worth a try.

Cognitive therapies place importance on clear thinking. The assumption of such therapies is that thoughts cause feelings. Thoughts that are illogical or irrational will produce emotional reactions that are both excessive and unwarranted. Extremes of anxiety, anger, depression, and other negative mood states may be linked to an individual's clouded thought processes.

For example, Michael has just been asked to give an oral book report. As he prepares to give his talk he finds that his heart is pounding and his palms are sweating, and he is aware that he is quite anxious. Why? He is thinking, "I wish the teacher hadn't asked me. If the class laughs, it'll be awful. I won't be able to stand it if they laugh at me. I won't be able to face anyone—any of my friends. I'm going to look like a fool. What if I stutter or something? I'd feel like killing myself!" Obviously, Michael's thought processes are inappropriate to the magnitude of the event. After all, he has merely been asked to give a small oral report, and not much is really at stake. But some people make a habit of **catastrophic thinking** (see Chapter 4), thinking in which they envision total disaster coming as the result of a single triggering event. The cognitive therapist helps persons suffering from excessive emotional reactions to examine the thought processes residing behind those reactions. The assumption made is that clear thinking can help to modify emotional reactions in a desirable direction.

Humanistic therapies tend to emphasize the importance of making the most of one's life. Two broad themes can be identified in humanistic therapies. One deals with the question, "What is my proper place in the scheme of things?" The other deals with the question, "What am I meant to be in terms of my talents and potentialities?" In humanistic therapies, a great deal of emphasis is placed on the principle of **becoming**, a growth-oriented concept. The assumption is that individuals who refuse to grow and who fail to make the most of their possibilities as human beings will suffer from **existential guilt**, the feeling that they have wasted their lives. To humanistic therapists, traditional neurotic disorders and other human disturbances are the result of some kind of interference with the capacity of the individual to grow and to become the person he or she was meant to be.

Humanistic therapies tend to reject the unconscious-conscious dichotomy of mental life made by the analytic therapies. Humanistic therapists regard the concept of an unconscious mental life as an abstraction and excess explanatory baggage. The emphasis is on the importance of the human capacity to make decisions as a tool for self-mobilization and self-realization. What is analyzed in the humanistic approach to adjustment and growth is not so much the relationship of elements within the mind, but the relationship of the person to life itself. (We will return to these themes in Chapter 7.)

The Effectiveness of Psychotherapy

In 1966 the experimental psychologist Hans J. Eysenck published a small book with the title *The Effects of Psychotherapy*. The book called into question the effectiveness of psychotherapy. Among its conclusions were these: (1) The methodology of outcome studies of psychotherapy is often poor. (2) The evidence in favor of the value of traditional psychoanalysis for treating neurotic disorders is questionable. Neurotic disorders tend to be self-limiting, and psychoanalysis is no more successful at treating them than other kinds of therapy. (3) Behavior therapies are probably more effective in treating neurotic disorders than traditional psychoanalysis is. (It should be noted that as early as 1952 Eysenck published material questioning the effectiveness of psychotherapy.)

The Effects of Psychotherapy does not simply attack the effectiveness of psychotherapy. The book contains discussions by seventeen therapists, including psychoanalysts. As you might expect, not all the therapists in the book agree with Eysenck's conclusions. The important point here is that the book stimulated a great deal of interest in research on the effectiveness of psychotherapy. And psychotherapists have taken a very close look at their profession.

What can we conclude today about the effectiveness of psychotherapy? Is it effective or is it not? The question cannot be answered with a simple *yes* or *no*. First, there are many kinds of psychotherapy. Second, more than one criterion or standard of improvement can be used. Third, the personality of the individual therapist may be an important factor. Fourth, the placebo effect often interferes with attempts to evaluate results.

Nonetheless, it can be said that more than one study suggests that psychotherapy is often effective. For example, a seven-year review of various kinds of data suggests the possibility that psychoanalysis may be particularly effective in treating various kinds of psychosomatic symptoms such as certain kinds of ulcers, headaches, and backaches (Greenberg & Fisher, 1978). In view of the fact that these kinds of symptoms are thought of in psychoanalytic therapy as being linked to neurotic anxiety, the review tends to lend some credence to the claims of psychoanalysis. Also, psychosomatic illness presents a major health problem (see Applied Exploration, Chapter 6, on behavioral medicine), and psychoanalytic therapy contributes to our attack on this problem.

And there is a good deal of evidence that certain kinds of behavior therapy have predictable and beneficial effects (Craighead, Kazdin, & Mahoney, 1976; Martin & Pear, 1978). Hostile critics of psychotherapy who say that it is next to worthless overstate their case. One the other hand, one cannot assert that psychotherapy is always helpful to troubled persons. A common-sense approach suggests that we accept a position somewhere between extreme viewpoints. As psychotherapy is practiced today, it is partly science, but also an art (Storr, 1980).

Theories of Personality

There is a close relationship between therapy and theories about the human personality. For example, around 400 B.C. Hippocrates (a Greek physician often called "the father of medicine") suggested that there are four basic kinds of personality types, which arise from varying amounts of body "humors" (fluids). A first type was said to be **sanguine**—a person who was optimistic and good-natured in temperament. An individual with ample amounts of blood fell into this category. A second personality type was described as **melancholic**—an individual with a tendency to be easily depressed. Such a person was presumably afflicted with excess amounts of black bile. A third type was called **choleric**—an individual who was easily excited to anger. This person was asserted to have just too much bile (no particular shade). The fourth type was the **phlegmatic** person—one who shows a considerable apathy toward life. Nothing is of much importance or interest to this person, and such an individual was thought to be overloaded with phlegm (mucus secretions of the nose and throat). You may laugh a bit at old Hippocrates, but his conclusions were based on the little information he could obtain. For example, is it not true that young men (optimistic and filled with great expectations) have a lot of red blood? And is it not true that someone dying of tuberculosis coughs up a lot of mucus and is rather uninterested in things that stimulate the attention of most people?

Psychotherapists often develop in-depth relationships with their clients. They may grow to feel that they have gathered powerful insights into the human condition. It seems almost inevitable that intelligent and creative therapists would develop general conceptions about what motivates people, what upsets people, and how people learn. Those with a talent for writing and for organizing their observations have reflected on their learnings and presented them to the world at large. Such individuals as Sigmund Freud, Carl Jung, Alfred Adler, Karen Horney, Erich Fromm, Carl Rogers, Viktor Frankl, Abraham Maslow, Rollo May and many, many others have formulated broad general conceptions of what it is to be a human being.

But no precise definition can be given to the terms **personality** or **personality theory**. The psychologist Gordon Allport once said, perhaps rather lightly, that "personality is what a man really is." This definition is a bit too circular for our purposes, however. At the risk of being a bit imprecise, I will attempt to define the concepts of both personality and personality theory.

Let us somewhat loosely define personality as a more or less stable set of traits, habits, and motivational predispositions characteristic of a particular individual. What we mean by personality is really a kind of consistency in behavior. If human behavior were not to some degree predictable, the concept of personality would not have arisen. Thus, if John has gotten into a number of fights in recent years, we may begin to think of his as "an aggressive character." We use the adjective "aggressive" to modify the noun "character" because we conceptualize him as "having" the trait of excessive aggression in his personality. Let us say that Jane has gotten a straight A average in college. We may see in her the motivational predisposition of "high need achievement." We thus say, "Jane is an ambitious person," and we have outlined a salient aspect of her personality. As you will see in Chapter 3, a critique of some value can be made of our conventional way of looking at human personality. Nonetheless, folk psychology—the psychology of daily usage—relies heavily on the commonsense approach to personality outlined in this paragraph.

Let us define a theory of personality as a set of concepts designed to explain the behavior of the whole human organism. The emphasis is on the word "whole." A theory of personality attempts to deal with the person as the individual actually lives in the world. The classical theories of personality are quite ambitious and often lay out, within one theory, explanations of human behavior and a philosophy of life.

It would be an error to think that all theories of personality derive from the clinical tradition of psychotherapy. Another major source of personality theories in American psychology is the tradition of experimental psychology. Although experimental psychology is often conceptualized as limited in its interest to molecular behavior, this is a mistaken impression. Experimental psychologists have been as ambitious in their theorizing as psychotherapists, and individuals like Clark L. Hull, Edward C. Tolman, John Dollard, Neal Miller, and B. F. Skinner are often identified as personality theorists. Indeed, the formerly sharp distinction between psychotherapy and experimental psychology is blurring today because so many of the findings from experimental psychology are becoming effective tools of psychotherapy. Also, research psychologists in university settings seem to be increasingly willing to attempt direct psychotherapy derived from the experimental, as opposed to the clinical, approach.

ADJUSTMENT AND GROWTH: OF HARMONY AND SELF-ACTUALIZATION

The opening pages of this chapter contained the question: "Do you consider yourself a well-adjusted person?" A second question was, "Are you making the most of your talents and potentialities as a human being?" The second question was intended to evoke your interest in a concept closely related to the concept of adjustment—the concept of personal growth. Although the concepts are closely related, they are not the same. Both are important, and it will be of value to examine their similarities and differences.

Adjustment

The *Dictionary of Behavioral Science* (Wolman, 1973) defines adjustment as follows:

Adjustment   1. A harmonious relationship with the environment involving the ability to satisfy most of one's needs and meet most of the demands, both physical and social, that are put upon one. 2. The variations and changes in behavior that are necessary to satisfy needs and meet demands so that one can establish a harmonious relationship with the environment.

The emphasis in the definition is on **harmony**. In practical terms, this means that you are adjusting if you eat when you are hungry, drink when you are thirsty, run when you are afraid, try to find shelter in a storm, seek relief from sexual tension, and avoid a disagreeable person. In all of these instances, you are coping with life in general; you are trying to survive.

This is the central theme of the concept of adjustment: A more or less harmonious relationship with the environment has been established when you find it relatively easy to survive on a day-to-day basis.

Personal Growth

The term **personal growth** as used in this book is intended to be synonymous with the concept of self-actualization. The *Dictionary of Behavioral Science* defines self-actualization as follows:

Self-actualization   1. (K. Goldstein) Striving toward completeness; fulfillment of one's potentialities. 2. (A. Maslow) Developing and fulfilling one's innate, positive potentialities.

Self-actualization refers to the fulfillment of one's potentialities.

The emphasis in the definition is on **fulfillment**. Clearly, in some cases the striving to fulfill one's potentialities may upset standing adjustments in one's life. Therefore we must not be glib and try to pass over adjustment and growth as if they were equivalent concepts. This is particularly important in view of the increasing emphasis on the concept of self-actualization in recent years.

Why bother with self-actualization at all? It is clear that moving forward does entail running risks. The psychologist Abraham H. Maslow was probably the one person most responsible for calling popular attention to the need for self-actualization. In *Toward a Psychology of Being* (1962), he has this to say:

Growth has not only rewards and pleasures but also many intrinsic pains and always will have. Each step forward is a step into the unfamiliar and is possibly dangerous. It also means giving up something familiar and good and satisfying. (p. 24)

So we see that there are risks in growth. However, Maslow argues, it is important that we concern ourselves with our need for self-actualization:

If this essential core (inner nature) of the person is frustrated, denied, or suppressed, sickness results. Sometimes in obvious forms, sometimes in subtle and devious forms, sometimes immediately, sometimes later. These psychological illnesses include many more than those listed by the American Psychiatric Association. For instance, the character disorders and disturbances are now far more important for the fate of the world than the classical neuroses or even psychoses. From this point of view, new kinds of illness are most dangerous, e.g., "the diminished or stunted person," i.e., the loss of any of the defining characteristics of humanness, or personhood, the failure to grow to one's potential, valuelessness, etc. (p. 181)

We now have the answer to our question: Why bother with self-actualization at all? The answer is that a person who does not try to make the most of his or her life runs the risk of falling into existential despair. There are risks in growth, as already noted. Less obviously, however, there are also risks in avoiding growth, refusing to act on one's talents, and rejecting opportunities when they present themselves. The person who clings like Linus to a psychological security blanket may someday regret his "safety first" policy. The eventual feeling that life has little meaning, that existence is empty, and that there is nothing really worth doing may turn out to be his "reward" for excessive caution. "Is this all there is?" asked a once popular song, reflecting the pervasiveness of what the psychiatrist Viktor Frankl has called the **existential vacuum**—a feeling of emptiness of existence. But for the person who is willing to run some of the risks inherent in a policy of personal growth, life is perceived as a challenge; the person has many constructive escapes from boredom and there is zest in living.

Stability and Change

Does a person have to make a choice between adjustment and self-actualization? Fortunately, for most of us the choice is not such a stark one. We must avoid categorical thinking, feeling that we have to choose one psychological box over another. The concept of adjustment represents stability in life; the concept of self-actualization represents change (and growth) in life. Consider as an analogy a tightrope walker. He or she must maintain balance on the rope to move forward successfully. Maintaining balance is analogous to the concept of growth. For most of us, this image of an integral relationship between stability and change is a preferable one to the image of stability and change as antagonistic forces. If we can keep the image of the tightrope walker in mind, we can see the value of the traditional concept of adjustment as well as the value of the more recent concept of self-actualization.

Concluding Remarks

We live in a rapidly changing world. The social critic Alvin Toffler (1971) coined the term **future shock** to indicate the stress reactions that can take place in people when change in a society is rapid.

In the three short decades between now and the twenty-first century, millions of ordinary, psychologically normal people will face an abrupt collision with the future. Citizens of the world's richest and most technologically advanced nations, many of them will find it increasingly painful to keep up with the incessant demand for change that characterizes our time. For them, the future will have arrived too soon. (p. 9)

As Toffler notes, many cannot adapt to changing times; others seem to thrive on change. If you must face change, certainly you would prefer to be among those who thrive on it. This book may not be able to show you how to thrive on change. (As noted in the opening pages, it is not a how-to book.) Nonetheless, it is my hope that some solid information is provided that will help you live a rewarding life in a painful-pleasurable world.

SUMMARY

1. The textbook is **eclectic**, that is, it does not see pathways toward adjustment and growth as mutually exclusive.
2. The word **psychology** is a combination of two Greek words, **psyche** and **logos**. An informal translation of psychology into English is the "study of the soul."
3. Watson defined psychology as the science of the behavior of organisms. The goals of psychology according to such thinkers as Watson and Skinner are to explain, predict, and control behavior.
4. The subjective psychologist is talking about the **inner world**, life as experienced. The objective psychologist is talking about the **outer world**, behavior as it presents itself to an observer.
5. William James made a distinction between those who possess **tough-minded temperaments** and those who possess **tender-minded temperaments**.
6. **Abnormal behavior, behavioral disorders,** and **mental disorders** are all terms used to refer to patterns of behavior manifested by individuals when their coping abilities are unequal to life's demands.
7. Mental disorders are categorized in **The Diagnostic and Statistical Manual of the American Psychiatric Association (DSM-III).** (See the appendix.)
8. For many centuries demon possession was a favorite way to explain mental disorders.
9. The organic viewpoint explains mental disorders in terms of biological science.
10. The psychological viewpoint explains mental disorders in terms of concepts such as **motives, thought processes, conditioned responses, habits, communication patterns,** and **inauthentic living.**
11. The eclectic viewpoint or **eclecticism** asserts that at our present level of knowledge it is doubtful that one viewpoint is completely correct and says it all about mental disorders.

12. The shaman and the witch doctor play the role of therapist among pre-scientific people, which reveals an important trend underlying psychotherapy: **the magical trend.**

13. The **placebo effect** is a temporary improvement in the patient's symptoms caused by a momentary mobilization of the individual's capacity to hope for the best.

14. It is important to draw distinctions among psychiatrists, psychoanalysts, and clinical psychologists.

15. Somatic therapies are therapies applied directly to the body.

16. **Psychotherapy** is the treatment of mental, emotional, and behavioral disorders by psychological methods.

17. There has been a substantial amount of debate concerning the effectiveness of psychotherapy. Questions concerning the effectiveness of psychotherapy cannot be answered with a simple *yes* or *no*.

18. There is a close relationship between therapy and theories about the human personality.

19. A theory of personality is a set of concepts designed to explain the behavior of the whole human organism.

20. In the definition of adjustment, the concept that receives principal emphasis is **harmony.**

21. The term **personal growth**, as used in this book, is intended to be synonymous with the concept of self-actualization.

Depth psychology asserts that, like inhabitants of an undersea world, many forces reside below the surface of consciousness.

Chapter 2

DEPTH PSYCHOLOGY: EXPLORING UNCONSCIOUS LEVELS

Overview

OUTLINE

KEY QUESTIONS

What is depth psychology?
Depth psychology focuses on unconscious mental processes. It asserts that there is a "lower" level to the personality, a level below the threshold of consciousness, and that this level is the scene of action for forbidden motives, painful memories, and disturbing ideas.

How do the principles of depth psychology relate to adjustment and growth?
Depth psychology views human problems as the result of lacks in self-understanding. A basic principle of depth psychology is that by gaining insight into one's own unconscious dynamics, the individual can attain freedom from their involuntary influence. The "normal" person is not under the excessive domination of invisible psychological agents.

Sigmund Freud died in 1939. In his obituary, which the *New York Times* published on September 24, Freud is quoted as having said, "The mind is an iceberg—it floats with only one-seventh of its bulk above water." In this short sentence Freud revealed the heart of his approach to psychology. This is why Freud's system and its derivatives are classified under the general heading of **depth psychology**. Depth psychology may be defined as any psychological system that places great emphasis on the assumption that most of our mental life takes place below the threshold of conscious awareness. The iceberg is utilized as a striking metaphor to convey the importance of unconscious forces in human behavior.

Freud is seldom thought of as a poet. And yet in the same *New York Times* obituary, the following words are attributed to him:

The conscious mind may be compared to a fountain playing in the sun and falling back into the great subterranean pool of the subconscious from which it rises.

Here Freud uses a different metaphor, that of a fountain, to illustrate his view of the mind as an active and living entity. It is clear from the fountain illustration that he did not think of "the unconscious" as a place or thing. Freud has often been accused of misplaced concreteness, making a process an object. One can find in the writing of many Freudians frequent references to the unconscious as it it were a territory or region. Such a notion was present in Freud's earlier writing, but his mature viewpoint was to think of the unconscious much more in terms of a process than of a thing. He preferred to use the word unconscious as an adjective; thus he spoke of unconscious mo-

Freud said that the mind is an iceberg.

tives, unconscious ideas, unconscious wishes, unconscious feelings, and so forth.

Before we go on, let me illustrate how the idea of unconscious factors in mental life can be used to explain human behavior. Assume that a man is away from home on a business trip. He spends a weekend away, and dashes off a postcard to his wife: "Having wonderful time, wish you were here." When he arrives home his wife is furious. She shows him the card. Much to his dismay he sees that he inadvertently left the *e* off the word "here." He finally convinces his wife that it was a meaningless error, that there was no time spent with another woman. He made the mistake because he was in a hurry and wrote the card rapidly. And in fact he was objectively innocent—there was no other woman. Freud, however, would have said that the error was not meaningless. It reveals the presence of an unconscious wish; unconsciously, the man wanted to be with another woman. But in terms of his particular self-concept, this was a forbidden wish. Therefore the wish was repressed, involuntarily shoved down by force to an unconscious level. The wish was not destroyed by repression; it made its existence known by causing the slip of the pen.

Perhaps you protest. The man was in a hurry. Are there no innocent errors that are just that—errors? Freud would reply that because the man was in a hurry proves nothing. It is precisely under such conditions that the censorship of unconscious elements becomes momentarily lax. They slip out and find some sort of route to a conscious level when one is off guard. As for innocent errors, Freud categorically denied them status. Freud adhered to the principle of **psychic determinism**, the assertion that all mental events have a cause.

It is important to note that not all contemporary researchers agree with Freud's explanation of behavioral errors. One line of investigation suggests that verbal slips and similar events are associated with a set of **cognitive factors**, factors having to do with conscious thought processes. Errors are thus explained in terms of accidents in the way the brain processes information (Norman, 1977). This explanation is quite close to the commonsense interpretation that some errors have little or no deeper significance. It is certainly possible that *some* errors reveal unconscious motives, as Freud asserted, and that others do not.

It would be incorrect to think that Freud was responsible for introducing the concept of an unconscious mental life to the Western world. The history of unconscious functioning can be traced through many centuries. More than three hundred years before the birth of Christ, Plato said that the soul of man has two divisions. The first division is the rational soul. It is with the rational soul that we think, reflect, analyze, evaluate, do arithmetic, and make decisions. The second division is the irrational soul. The irrational soul is the source of our appetites, our desires. The irrational soul is outside of conscious control; it is a blind force that gives impetus to our lives. As you can see, the irrational soul operated as a basically unconscious agent. In the thirteenth century, the great Roman Catholic theologian Saint Thomas Aquinas said that one of the powers of the human soul is the **nutritive power**, which gives human beings the capacity to grow, mature, and reproduce. This bears a strong resemblance to Plato's irrational soul. Both concepts are prototypes for Freud's more fully articulated concept of the id, an unconscious aspect of the human personality that is the source of our basic biological drives. (More will be said about the id later.)

Toward the latter part of the seventeenth century, the philosopher Gottfried Wilhelm Leibnitz proposed the concept of apperception. In contemporary terms, apperception would be equivalent to our concept of **subliminal perception,** the ability to record an event without conscious awareness. (See the research of Shevrin (1980), Box 2.1, for an example of subliminal perception.)

Immanuel Kant, a giant of German philosophy, accepted the doctrine of apperception and expanded on it. Writing in the eighteenth century, Kant said that the mind organizes experience through its power of apperception. Translated into contemporary language, this means that the world makes sense to us because we subconsciously organize it. We do not will it to be organized; it is not a voluntary process. It just seems to be quite proper and natural that event A precedes event B and thing X stands in front of thing Y. We think nothing of it; the perception of a world neatly ordered in terms of time and space seems effortless. This is what Kant meant by apperception or subconscious perception. He thus asserted that an important mental process takes place below the threshold of consciousness. That this can happen is a central assumption in Freud's system. This is particularly important in that Freud was certainly familiar with the basic outlines of Kantian philosophy.

In the early part of the nineteenth century, another German philosopher, Johann Friedrich Herbart, spoke of the **apperceptive mass**, a mental reservoir consisting of all our ideas and all our past experiences. Moment-to-moment experiences exist only briefly at a conscious level, then they sink below the **limen**, the threshold of consciousness, and become part of the apperceptive mass. According to Herbart, all meaning comes from our apperceptive mass. Thus the notion is important for educators. Suppose you tell a four-year-old child, "I'm going to teach you a little algebra. X + 3 = 5. Think it over. What do you think X equals?" The odds are that you are not going to get a sensible answer because the child has not yet acquired the concept of number; this concept is not part of his apperceptive mass (or in popular terms, his subconscious mind). Suppose, however, that you pose the same problem to an eight-year-old child. He has not studied algebra, but the problem is meaningful to him because he does have the concept of number stored in his apperceptive mass. He may very well give the correct answer. Herbart asserted that we store a great deal of important information at an unconscious level. This view is important in the Freudian system.

More important, Herbart wrote that ideas have energy and that certain ideas are compatible and others are incompatible. Thus Herbart laid down the outline of another assumption in Freud's thought, the assumption that ideas can fight each other—that there can be mental conflicts. Assume that a man has been raised with idea A, "Thou shalt not kill." He has also been raised with idea B, "One should be a patriot and do battle for one's country." The ideas are incompatible, and we have an example of a mental conflict. Assume that the conflict is intense, that he holds tightly to both ideas. The "solution" to such a conflict may come from an unconscious idea: "If I were paralyzed nobody would expect me to fight." The man might develop a conversion reaction, a neurotic response in which a conflict is resolved by converting it into a bodily symptom. He loses his ability to walk. It is essential to note that basic psychoanalytic doctrine postulates that the unconscious idea is really just that—unconscious. It is repressed and its content does not pass above the threshold of consciousness.

In the preceding few pages, an attempt has been made to establish the view that Freud did not invent or discover the existence of unconscious levels of mental functioning. This point is not made to downgrade Freud. On the contrary, Freud himself was aware of the contributions to his thought by philosophers and other psychologists. He saw himself as building on a solid tradition. His way of seeing human behavior was very much a part of what is called the *zeitgeist*, the mode of thinking of the times. Having noted this, we should also note that Freud was an original thinker. He modified existing concepts in ways that had an enormous impact on our view of ourselves.

PSYCHOANALYSIS: INSIGHTS ON THE COUCH

When the ordinary person thinks of psychoanalysis, he or she probably visualizes the patient reclining on a couch with the psychoanalyst sitting out of the patient's vision. This stereotype has been perpetuated by countless cartoons. One cartoon may show a duck dressed up like a man, lying on the couch and saying, "I don't know, doc. Lately I've developed a tremendous craving for milk and quackers." Another may find the psychiatrist commenting coldly to a skinny little man, "I've discovered your problem, Mr. Jones. You aren't suffering from an inferiority complex. You are inferior!" And there is the story of the female patient who says to her psychoanalyst, "Love me! Love me madly! I want only you! You're the man of my dreams!" The analyst smiles and says, "My dear, you are merely experiencing the transference phenomenon. This isn't real love, only an illusion. And furthermore it would not be professional for me to respond to your invitation. You see the many degrees on my wall representing my years of training. Indeed, I shouldn't even be lying here on the couch with you!" So we see that cartoons and jokes about patients and their analysts reveal a certain theme of hostility toward both. The jokes are usually putdowns of either the patient or the therapist. The general public has mixed positive-negative feelings about psychoanalysis.

The stereotype of the reclining patient is not in fact so farfetched. Classical psychoanalysis does imply insights on the couch. Freud had his patients recline and look away from him. There are theoretical reasons for this, but in addition it seems that Freud was a bit shy and found it painful to be stared at all day. *Inside Psychotherapy*, edited by Adelaide Bry (1972), is a book of interviews with various kinds of psychotherapists. One interviewee was psychoanalyst Van Buren O. Hammett, chairman of the Department of Psychiatry at Hahnemann Medical College in Philadelphia. In the following exchange, Miss Bry asks about the role of the couch in psychoanalysis:

Adelaide Bry. Does the patient now and then lie down on the traditional couch, and do you sit behind him?

Dr. Hammett. Yes—there are advantages to that. One is purely practical: it's a little more comfortable for both the patient and the doctor. You know, unless people are very fond of one another, or unless they're fighting, it's easier not to have to watch one another all the time while talking.

Adelaide Bry. I never thought of that before.

Dr. Hammett. It's more relaxed to just talk without watching the other person's face to see how you're being received, and this, incidentally, is the main reason for asking the patient to lie down and not see the doctor: so that he won't watch the doctor's face and change his thoughts according to what he sees or thinks he sees in the way of reaction in the doctor's face. So we try to remove that distraction, and the way we do this is to have the patient lie down, looking at the ceiling. (p. 37)

Freud once said that the therapist should be the opaque mirror on which patients can see themselves. The unobtrusive presence of the therapist is designed to facilitate the mirror function. There are other points of view, of course. Many contemporary psychotherapists prefer a face-to-face relationship with their clients.

Who Was Sigmund Freud?

Sigmund Freud was a man for all seasons. He was loved and hated, admired and despised. To some he was "the Master"; to others he was "that fool" or "that sex maniac" or, in his later years, "that dirty old man." He is widely regarded as one of the greatest thinkers of the twentieth century. He was a man with many friends and many enemies. Some of his early friends became disenchanted with Freud and fell away from his psychoanalytic circle; the two most prominent examples are Carl Jung and Alfred Adler. He was the most famous psychologist who ever lived, and yet he did not hold a university degree in psychology. He was a medical doctor, a specialist in neurology, and he developed his psychological theories from his work with neurotic patients. He never wanted to be a practitioner. As a young man he yearned for a university position as a researcher in physiology, but the low status of the Jews in Austria at the time made him unable to realize his dream of a career in pure science.

Freud was born in 1856 in the Austro-Hungarian Empire, and he died in London at the age of eighty-three. He spent most of his years as a practicing physician in Vienna, Austria. He was finally convinced to leave his beloved Vienna toward the end of his life, fleeing the anti-Semitism of the Nazis. His old age was marred by his flight to London and cancer of the mouth; for several years he wore a painful prosthetic device that gave him an artificial palate. In spite of the pain and the great difficulties in speaking, he saw some patients until shortly before he died.

Freud was the first child of a "May–September" marriage. His mother was considerably younger than Freud's father; she was his second wife. Freud was born with a thick shock of black hair, the sign of a prophet among Jewish people. Freud's mother took this sign seriously and treated him throughout his development as a special person. His brothers and sisters referred to him as "the little genius." One of Freud's major theoretical conceptions is the Oedipus complex, which involves guilt over sexual attraction to the parent of the opposite sex. It seems clear enough now that some of the theory arises from his own romantic attachment to his mother. She was young when Freud was born, retained her beauty for many years, and always treated Freud like a crown prince. Indeed, Freud maintained a close relationship with her as long as she lived, visiting her at least once a week.

Sigmund Freud was the father of psychoanalysis.

A major influence on Freud's thinking was the doctrine of **antivitalism**, as proposed by that giant of German physiology and physics, Hermann Ludwig Ferdinand von Helmholtz. The doctrine of antivitalism asserts that to explain the existence of life, it is not necessary to postulate the presence within living things of some special force, such as a soul or a "vital energy." Life is explained by the interaction of known electrochemical reactions. A major proponent of this point of view was the physiologist Ernest Brücke, and Freud was one of his most devoted students.

From his early years Freud thought of himself as a natural scientist, and he always sought cause-and-effect explanations (Sulloway, 1979). Thus we can see why he was so dedicated to the principle of psychic determinism; mental events are like any other events—they are caused and follow lawful principles. One of Freud's discoveries in Brücke's laboratory was the anesthetic properties of cocaine. A few drops in the eye made painless eye surgery possible. Freud published his findings, but somehow early fame passed him by. Another man publishing at the same time was credited with discovering the value of cocaine. This was one of Freud's greatest disappointments in life.

Turning from pure to applied science, Freud graduated from medical school at the age of twenty-five. He spent a period of time in postgraduate study in France with the famous neurologist Jean Martin Charcot. Charcot had great skill as a hypnotist and demonstrated to his students that some persons who seemed to have neurological problems were actually suffering from a **hysterical neurosis**, a condition in which individuals display the symptoms of neurological impairment. For example, they seem to be deaf, blind, or paralyzed. (The contemporary term recommended by *DSM-III* to identify this condition is **conversion disorder**.) Under hypnosis, however, Charcot was able to relieve their symptoms temporarily, thus demonstrating that some sort of psychological, emotional, or personality disturbance was the real cause of their difficulties. Freud was impressed by Charcot and his demonstrations, and the idea grew in Freud that unconscious forces played a part in hysteria.

Another idea thrown out rather carelessly by Charcot impressed Freud— the idea that neuroses have a sexual origin. Freud was at a party at Charcot's home, and a discussion arose about a young married woman who suffered from neurotic reactions. There was reason to suspect her husband of either impotence or great sexual awkwardness. In *The Passions of the Mind*, a biographical novel about Freud by Irving Stone (1971), an exchange at the party between Charcot and a colleague is dramatized:

"*Are you suggesting, Monsieur Charcot, that the wife's illness could have been caused by the husband's condition?*"

Charcot cried with great vitality: "But in this kind of case it's always a question of the genitals . . . always . . . always . . . always."

Sigmund was astonished. He watched Charcot wrap his arms around his stomach and jump up and down with insistence. (p. 188)

[handwritten margin note: synonomous]

This incident is said to have had a great impact on Freud's thinking. The importance of frustrations and distortions in the sexual drive play an important part in the Freudian theory of neurosis.

As a young and struggling physician in Vienna, Freud was befriended by the successful Dr. Josef Breuer. Breuer sent Freud patients, discussed cases with him, and lent him money. Like Charcot, Breuer also had an enormous impact on Freud's early theorizing. One of Breuer's patients was a young woman named Bertha Pappenheim (Freeman, 1980). When Freud and Breuer subsequently wrote her case history, they protected her identity. (In the annals of psychoanalysis she is famous as "Anna O.") Bertha suffered from a variety of neurotic symptoms. Breuer discovered that her symptoms could be greatly alleviated by encouraging her to talk freely under hypnosis. Breuer called his treatment the "talking cure." Bertha herself nicknamed it "chimney sweeping." The things she revealed were filled with emotional content; she experienced distress and cried as she spoke. Breuer and Freud worked together on the theory of why the talking cure worked and called the emotional release an **abreaction**, a reliving of painful emotional experiences. They theorized that the abreaction was essential for improvement; the pent-up feelings associated with key experiences had to be discharged.

Freud was anxious to publish the result of their research, but Breuer was reluctant. There were certain problems. For one thing, Bertha's conflicts revolved around sexual feeling for her dead father. For another, during the treatment Bertha went through a phase in which she fell in love with Breuer. In straitlaced Vienna of the late nineteenth century, such an occurrence would be considered extremely shocking and unmentionable. Breuer feared for his reputation; he wanted to keep his lucrative private practice thriving and not run risks. Freud, of course, had less to lose. He was not yet established and wanted to make a reputation. Also, he was more willing than Breuer to shock the establishment. As it worked out, Freud was able to convince Breuer that they should publish jointly *The Case of Anna O.* and other investigations. Breuer, however, did not pursue his early leads, gradually withdrew from Freud, and detached himself from psychoanalysis. It is ironic that the man who introduced Freud to the talking cure and the effects of abreaction fell into relative obscurity.

Freud was a family man. He married Martha Bernays and fathered six children. One of his children, Anna, became a famous psychoanalyst in her own right. The Freud family spent many years in a large apartment, and Freud saw his patients in one of its rooms. Freud's sister-in-law lived with the family, and it has been claimed that Freud had an affair with her. In an interview with Theodor Reik (1972), a psychoanalyst and one of Freud's closest friends, this was denied:

Reik.   *Freud talked about his work to his sister-in-law, whom I knew quite well. He made some trips with her. She was much younger than Mrs. Freud, and there were suspicions that he had an affair with her. Nothing of the kind. I don't believe it. Freud had a certain puritanical trend in his nature. (p. 48)*

Freud worked in relative obscurity for many years. His ultimately influential book *The Interpretation of Dreams* was published in 1900, when Freud was forty-four years old. The first printing was small, and several years passed before all the copies sold. Freud continued writing and lecturing, however, and his ideas began to capture the imagination of many laymen and some professionals. By 1909 he had achieved sufficient fame to be invited to give a series of lectures at Clark University in Massachusetts. He traveled to the United States by ship with the psychiatrist Carl Jung, who had become an advocate of psychoanalysis. The lectures at Clark University are generally regarded as the key event marking the transition of psychoanalysis from a local Austrian phenomenon to a way of thinking that gained worldwide recognition.

Only one year later the International Psychoanalytic Association was founded and Carl Jung was named its president, not Sigmund Freud! But this was at Freud's request. He was still concerned about psychoanalysis being perceived as a strictly Jewish phenomenon. Jung was a Christian, Swiss, and the son of a clergyman; Freud felt that Jung's credentials were impeccable. It was one of Freud's major disappointments in life when, a few years later, Jung resigned as president of the association and detached himself from the Freudians. By now, however, the association had gathered strength and momentum. Psychoanalysis was on its way.

Unconscious Aspects of Mental Life

Alan M. is a high school English teacher. For three years he has been working on a novel and has been revising it for several months. It is complete, but he resists sending it to a publisher. His wife encourages him to submit the novel. She thinks it is excellent and that it will become a best-seller. Finally Alan gathers his courage and takes the novel to the post office. He sends it to a leading New York publisher. Much to his surprise, the package containing the novel appears at his home two days later! Alan can't help laughing when he sees that the mailing container is not addressed to the publisher but to his own home address! He had inadvertently sent the book to himself. How would psychoanalysis explain the error? Freud would have said that Alan's ego was threatened by having to face the reality that the novel may be rejected. It is more pleasant to live in a world of fantasy and imagine oneself a best-selling author than to confront the realization that perhaps no publisher will actually want the manuscript. The act of mailing the novel sets the stage for the following unconscious thought: "I wish I didn't have to face this. I don't want to run the risk of having my work turned down." The mailing error is a response to the unconscious wish, and its purpose is to defend the ego against the potential harshness of the real world.

Freud used the word **unconscious** in two ways. First, it was used as a noun; the unconscious is a region of the mind. Second, it was used as an adjective; there are unconscious ideas, unconscious motives, and unconscious memories. Let's elaborate on these two usages.

In 1915 Freud published a paper called "The Unconscious." In this paper he presents the unconscious as a region of the mind. He postulated that the human mind is divided into a system conscious and a system unconscious. The **system conscious** functions on the basis of the secondary process, the mental process by which we are in contact with reality, think logically, and make rational decisions. The **system unconscious** functions on the basis of the primary process, the mental process by which ideas have nonrational connections. In the system unconscious, wishes, magic, and egocentricity reign supreme. Thus when a liquor company tells you that "successful people drink XYZ whiskey," it is appealing to your system unconscious. The primary process happily associates, on a nonrational basis, a human desire such as success and a particular brand of liquor.

The magical thinking of the system unconscious produces the following conclusion: "If I drink XYZ whiskey, I will be successful." The system uncon-

The system unconscious is a kind of Alice-in-Wonderland region of the mind where A doesn't have to come before B and where wishing can make it so.

scious is a kind of Alice-in-Wonderland region of the mind where A doesn't have to come before B and where wishing can make it so.

Freud divided the system conscious into two subsystems: the **perceptual-conscious** and the **preconscious**. The perceptual-conscious refers to whatever you are aware of right now. Let us say you have a corn on your foot and, at the moment, you are painfully aware of how much it hurts. Then the idea "it hurts" and the pain associated with the idea are the content of consciousness; the idea and the feeling are "in" the region of the mind called the perceptual-conscious.

The preconscious refers to a region of the mind just below the conscious surface. Its contents consist of any ideas or feelings that can be made to enter the perceptual-conscious by an act of will. Let us say that Irene is asked her date of birth. She answers, "February 4, 1940." The date was stored in the preconscious and was brought into the perceptual-conscious by a voluntary act of remembering. It will sink back into the preconscious region after a short residence in the perceptual-conscious. Thus the preconscious is a large storehouse of memories and useful information. It is parallel to what is called "the subconscious mind" in popular psychology. It is also identical to what Herbart and pre-Freudian thinkers called the apperceptive mass. Freud's description of the preconscious was not particularly original, nor did he claim that it was. It was merely included as part of the whole of his formal theorizing about the structure of the mind. The really important addition by Freud is his conception of the unconscious as a region of the mind containing repressed ideas.

To Freud, the content of the unconscious consisted of ideas and motives unacceptable to the conscious personality. He said that ideas in the unconscious are in a state of repression, a process by which a psychological force opposes certain ideas and shoves them down into the nether territory of the unconscious. This is why Freud's psychology is sometimes called a **dynamic psychology**—ideas within the mind push and shove each other about. They struggle with each other for survival. It is crucial to realize that the ideas in the unconscious are dynamically repressed, not merely forgotten. Sometimes this is spoken of as **motivated forgetting**, a kind of forgetting that takes place because it serves the needs of the conscious ego.

To illustrate, say that Mary R. considers herself, on a conscious level, a good wife, mother, and part-time nurse. Her ego demands that nothing intrude on this self-concept. She was raised in a strict family having a conservative set of moral values. The thought of divorce is unthinkable, something no decent woman would do. Further assume that her husband has an authoritarian personality; he is forever putting her in her place, telling her what to do, criticizing her character, and in general treating her like a child. A tremendous resentment toward her husband begins to grow within Mary. Although she may think, "I'd like to kill him," the thought is quickly repressed.

2.1   CONTEMPORARY RESEARCH: UNCONSCIOUS MENTAL ACTIVITY AND THE BRAIN

The doctrine that we have an unconscious mental life is a key one for psychoanalysis, and it is one of those ideas that has been much debated among psychologists. William James thought that the idea of unconscious mental activity was somewhat whimsical. The behaviorist John Watson made a mockery of Freud's teachings. More recently, humanistic psychologists have tended to discount Freud's emphasis on the significance of unconscious motives. So Freud's propositions about the existence of an unconscious mental life seem to stand on shaky ground.

The evidence in favor of the hypothesis that indeed some mental activity is unconscious comes mainly from clinical work in psychoanalysis. Slips of the tongue or pen, meaningful accidents, dream interpretation, abreaction, defense mechanisms, and the recovery of childhood memories are the kind of evidence brought forth by Freud and the psychoanalysts to support their hypothesis. However, the evidence is indirect, and unconscious mental life remains an inferred construct, not an experimental discovery.

Freud himself was aware that unconscious mental life was a construction, a hypothesis. And he was unhappy with this state of affairs. As you will recall, his early training was in physiology, and all of his life he dreamed of

It does not fit in with the thought "I'm a loving wife." But the repressed idea does its dirty work in her life nonetheless. Perhaps Mary is an excellent cook. Perhaps her husband is overweight and suffers from hypertension, and his physician has told him to cut down on starchy foods and desserts. But Mary just can't help herself. She keeps cooking in the old ways, refusing to learn to make lighter meals. Indeed, she keeps right on experimenting with new desserts. Behind Mary's back one family friend remarks, "She is killing him with her oven." Mary is behaving in a destructive manner, but because she is repressing her hostility toward her husband, she is able to be destructive and live with herself.

"Very sick!" you say. Yes, and these are just the kinds a patterns in human behavior that are the concern of psychoanalysis—the "sickness" of everyday life. To Freud, the average person does not control his life fully with his conscious ego. Instead, he is "lived" by unknown and uncontrollable forces from the unconscious. Freud, however, was not without hope. The aim of psychoanalysis is to explore the unconscious and bring repressed ideas up to a conscious level. Then they are presumed to lose their destructive power.

finding physiological support for psychological constructions. In his early years he tried to make explicit connections between neuron firing patterns in the brain and mental life, but gave up because of lack of sufficient experimental data.

Freud would have been pleased to learn that there is now some experimental data supporting the hypothesis that we have an unconscious mental life. Physiological psychologist Howard Shevrin (1980) reports he has conducted experiments measuring the brain's electrical responses to various kinds of subliminal messages. Words or pictures are flashed on a screen for just a thousandth of a second, below the threshold of conscious recognition of the stimulus. Nonetheless, subsequent testing of the subjects suggests that they unconsciously recognized the stimulus. For example, if a picture of a bee is flashed on the screen, free association brings forth more words such as "bug" or "sting" or "honey" than to the subliminal presentation of a geometric form. (Note that Shevrin has used Freud's method of free association with good results.)

Shevrin feels that he has accumulated a certain amount of hard empirical evidence in favor of the proposition that we have an unconscious mental life. He says, "The experiments suggest that the brain is fairly humming with unconscious thoughts and emotions that shape what we pay attention to and what we tend to repress—to use the psychoanalytic term." (Shevrin, 1980, p. 128). Freud would have welcomed Shevrin's findings!

The Structure of Personality

In 1923 Freud published a book called *The Ego and the Id*. This book is one of the central psychoanalytic documents, and it contains the outlines of Freud's theory of personality. It also contains a revision of his theory of the unconscious. The 1915 view described in the previous section was modified in an important way, to be described shortly.

Freud theorized that each of us has a basic component to our personality that is present at birth. He called this basic component the id (see Figure 2.1). (In German the term "das Es" was used, which merely means "the it." Id is the Latin word for it. The term and its use were not Freud's invention. In *The Ego and the Id*, he credits the concept to a German physician, Georg Groddeck. Freud also notes that the term goes back to the philosopher Nietzsche.) According to Freud, the id never leaves us. It is our deepest self, our primal self. The id is the source of our basic biological drives: hunger, thirst, pain avoidance, temperature regulation, reflex action, sex, and aggression. The last two drives, sex and aggression, play an important part in psychoanalytic

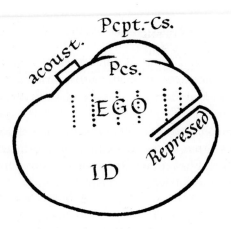

FIGURE 2.1 Freud explored the structure of the human personality and made this drawing to indicate the relationship of the id and the ego to unconscious and conscious levels of mental life. (Note that the drawing does not include the superego.)

thinking. These are the two drives subject to the greatest amount of repression from civilization; more will be said about this point later.

The id has sometimes been called the Frankenstein monster within the personality. This is a correct analogy if we think of Frankenstein's monster as neither good nor bad, but devoid of morality. Thus if an adult human organism were pure id, he would stomp about and take whatever he wanted without regard for the rights of others. He wouldn't wait patiently in a school cafeteria line; he would shove others aside and grab his food without paying. If he saw an attractive female and craved sexual relations, he would knock her down and proceed to rape her. Obviously, the individual would not last long as a free person; he would be quickly apprehended and treated as a mental patient. Thus a human being must learn to control the id if he or she is to live and function in the world. The crucial characteristic of the id is captured if we say it is pleasure-oriented.

When a baby is born, its personality is pure id. With development, though, the infant learns that the world is often a frustrating place. Certain things cannot be obtained in an instant on demand. The infant must wait to have diapers changed, to be fed, to be picked up. Later he will find that he can't obtain certain things directly; he has to make a detour. He has to learn to walk, to talk, to feed and dress himself, and so forth. Thus a part of the personality that may be called the ego is formed. The ego is the I, or the conscious center of the personality. Its aim is to try to meet the demands of the id within the constraints imposed by external reality. Assume that a preschooler sees some candy on a high shelf. From the id's point of view, there is nothing but the pure wish, "I want the candy." As far as the id is concerned, "Let's just fly right up there." Indeed, one might observe a young preschooler jumping up and down in frustration before the shelf, stretching for something that can't be reached. An older preschooler, however, might drag a chair to a spot below the candy, climb up on the chair, and solve the problem. Thus the ego has been brought into action in service of the id.

One of the functions of the ego is **reality-testing**. Human beings, whether adults or children, often want to see how far they can go without getting into trouble or hurting themselves. This can be particularly important in raising children. Sometimes when children are being willful and unreasonable, they are trying to find out the practical boundaries of their allowable worlds. Parents who cannot resist the child's persistence and "cave in" against their better judgment do the child a disservice. The child may get a mistaken concept of what is safe or what is appropriate. In a famous passage from *The Ego and the Id*, Freud compared the id to a horse and the ego to its rider:

The functional importance of the ego is manifested in the fact that normally control over the approaches to motility devolves upon it. Thus in its relation to the id it is like a man on horseback, who has to hold in check the superior strength of the horse; with this difference, that the rider tries to do so with his own strength while the ego uses borrowed forces. The analogy may be carried a little further. Often a rider, if he is not to be parted from his horse, is obliged to guide it where it wants to go; so in the same way the ego is in the habit of transforming the id's will into action as if it were its own. (p. 25)

Briefly, the ego is that part of the human personality that is reality oriented. It tries to accommodate the demands of the id by taking into account practical obstacles in the external world, the world outside the mind and body. In essence the ego says to the id, "Wait a bit, you impulsive child. I'll find a way to get you what you want." The ego exists in service of the id; it is its agent. Thus if a person's personality were only id and ego, the individual would be, in colloquial terms, a "con-artist," a "wheeler-dealer," or "someone who plays all the angles." In clinical terms the individual would be said to have a character disorder (not a neurosis), and a label such as "sociopath" or "psychopath" would be used. The cold-blooded person who seems to have no heart would fall into the general category we are describing. Of course, it is doubtful that there are pure types, people with only an id and an ego. We are exaggerating to make the point that human existence seems to demand some sort of value-morality principle.

This third demand is satisfied by the third major component of the human personality structure, which Freud called the **superego**. The superego is that aspect of the personality that orients itself toward abstract concepts of good and bad, right and wrong, decency and indecency. When a child is growing up it is not enough that he or she learn practical ways of satisfying the id's wishes. Parents also send various messages that certain actions are shameful. Assume that Sarah, a pre-school child, has been told not to take cookies from the cookie jar. When mother is out of the room, the child ignores the prohibition and tries to steal the cookies. The ego is functioning in service of the id. It has made the child wait until mother is out of sight. But there is no superego yet. Nothing inside Sarah is saying, "It's wrong. Don't do it." This comes with development. The child is caught with her hand in the cookie jar when mother comes back into the kitchen. She says, "You naughty child! I told you not to take any cookies! You should be ashamed of yourself." Perhaps she spanks the child, or perhaps she sends her to her room. In either event the mother's behavior is designed to make the child feel ashamed.

The word shame refers to what is felt when one is caught doing something that others judge to be wrong or bad. The person who is caught feels discredited and awkward. Assume that Sarah has been caught stealing cookies ten times and has experienced shame ten times. The eleventh time she looks at the cookie jar, starts to walk toward it, and begins to anticipate the feeling of shame. It is unpleasant and she is beginning to think twice about whether she should take the cookies. If her mother has been consistent in catching her and shaming her, she almost certainly feels the enterprise is doomed to failure. It is as if her mother is in her head, saying, "Don't take the cookie, Sarah. If you do, you are a bad girl." The superego is forming. She is beginning to feel guilt for thinking about a forbidden action. Say that she overrides the voice of her budding superego and steals the cookies anyway. After the cookies are eaten, she feels bad—and it isn't from a stomachache; she is feeling bad because she feels guilty. Perhaps she even goes to her mother and blubbers, "I stole the cookies." She confesses crime to get relief from the nasty feeling of guilt that is poisoning her existence. Once she is punished and subsequently forgiven by mother, she no longer feels guilty. The word *guilt* refers to what is felt when one has internalized the standards of external agents and uses these standards to judge oneself. Shame and guilt are closely related. Shame is the result of external judgments; guilt is the result of internal judgments. Guilt feelings have their origin in earlier shame experiences.

We can see from the example of Sarah and the cookie jar a prototype of how a child develops a superego out of the ego. The ego must not only learn ways of accommodating itself to the practical limits of time and space; it must also learn ways of accommodating itself to the abstract values of its culture. For a human being to be accepted by parents, relatives, and peers, the individual must hold approximately the same values they do. We call such a person **socialized**; a socialized person is a full-fledged member of the surrounding culture. If the person happens to be a headhunter, then it is the right thing to do to hunt the heads of enemies of the tribe. If the individual lives in a communist country, then it is the right thing to do to be frugal and look down on people who want to own large amounts of real estate. If the person is an American, then it is right to be ambitious and to own property.

The superego itself can be divided into two subagents. The first of these is designated the **ego ideal**. The ego ideal sets an individual's level of aspiration. It presents him with a mental picture of what he should do with his life, or what he might become. Freud felt that the ego ideal is created by the attitudes and beliefs of the person's parents. The cliché example would be the Jewish mother who "brainwashes" her son: "You were meant to be a doctor. I feel it in my soul. I feel it in my bones. You are such a bright, talented boy. Don't waste these things!" Such statements may form the ego ideal of becoming a doctor within the child. Thus we get the "my son the doctor" syndrome. Freud notes that he himself was an example of just such a self-fulfilling prophecy.

The second subagent of the superego is the conscience. The ego ideal is a plus factor; it says what ought to be strived for. The conscience is a negative factor; it says what ought not be done. The conscience sets up inhibitions, restraints within the individual against taking certain kinds of action. The voice of conscience says, "Stop! Don't do it! That's a sin! That's bad! That's nasty! That's dirty! That's immoral! You're no good if you do that!" People with strict superegos that set a high moral tone often find it difficult to act with flexibility and spontaneity. Their consciences are like straitjackets. They are too inhibited; there are too many internal frustrations. As already noted, a superego is probably necessary for one to be what is termed a "socialized person." But it is probably better for both the individual and society if the superego is more like a comfortable coat than a straitjacket.

It would be an error to think that only the conscience can act like a straitjacket. The positive side of the superego, the ego ideal, can also be too rigid, demanding too much of the person. Theodore I. Rubin, a practicing psychoanalyst, provides an example from his own analysis:

In psychoanalytic treatment, I learned a great deal about myself that I had no previous idea about at all. This included many emotional problems and confusions as well as much about human substance, too. But despite these quite valid and important insights, my depression and despair went on and on and I began to feel that I never really would get better. I became aware that I was, in fact, psychologically beating myself unmercifully. I realized that much of the beating came from a false, perfectionistic, impossibly exalted image of myself. I felt that in falling from this image I had descended to considerably less than a subhuman status. (p. 13)

He explains how he learned to stop berating himself, to simply let go and let be what would be, to relax and not make such a great effort to put his life together; he came out of his depression. Some of us have grand expectations based on an unrealistic ego ideal. The frustration that results from failing to attain our impossible dreams can result in depression if we are not wise enough to revise our standards to a more realistic level, as Rubin did. In psychoanalytic terms, the superego must be tempered by a strong, reality-oriented ego.

In the previous few pages, we have been describing Freud's final view of the structure of personality: The personality is made up of three substructures: the id, the ego, and the superego. There is no longer such a structure as the unconscious. In this final view of human personality, Freud no longer spoke of the unconscious as a place in the mind. He now proposed that the word "unconscious" be used to refer to a *quality* of mental life. Thus unconscious wishes, unconscious ideas, unconscious memories may exist, but not wishes in the unconscious, ideas in the unconscious, memories in the unconscious. Instead, Freud proposed that repressed wishes, ideas, and memories become a part of the id. The id operates in terms of the magical, fantasy-oriented primary process. Thus repressed elements of mental life are subject to the same distortions, the same nonrational connections that Freud had spoken of for years.

In spite of Freud's suggestion, many contemporary psychoanalysts still speak of the unconscious as if it were a place in the mind. Apparently this usage has a certain attraction and utility. Freud's early theorizing is retained along with his conception of the id, ego, and superego. Thus we can say that the word "unconscious" in depth psychology has acquired two meanings: (1) It is used in a substantive sense to indicate a region of the mind; it is used as a noun when one speaks of the unconscious. (2) It is used in a dynamic sense to indicate a quality of mental life; it is used as an adjective when one speaks of unconscious wishes, ideas, and memories. Let us note again that Freud's final preference was for the second usage.

Human Development

Psychoanalysis stresses human development, the growth of the personality over time. It has already been noted, for example, how the ego grows out of the id as the id is faced with the problems of the external world. Now let us turn our attention to another aspect of human development, the maturation of the sexual drive. Freud felt this was a particularly important subject because he was convinced it had a great deal to do with basic character types in people. The theory I will describe is called a **psychosexual theory** because it has to do with the simultaneous development of the personality and the sexual drive. A central concept in the theory is **libido**, which Freud defined as "psychosexual energy." Psychosexual energy is the force that resides behind our mental life and our sexual life. It arises from the basic metabolism of the body. It is not, however, a measurable physical energy; libido is a psychological concept. As a concept, libido is a bit vague and escapes precise definition. If you can imagine a diffuse energy that is associated at once with both mental life and sexual life, you have a rough image of what Freud meant by libido.

Freud theorized that infants and children have a sexual life of sorts. Their sexual life is described as **pregenital**, a sexual life that takes its pleasures in ways that precede adult heterosexual relations. The development during the pregenital period is merely a forerunner of adult sexuality and bears only a small resemblance to it. When Freud said that infants and children have a sex life, this is what he meant: They go through developmental stages that build toward genital sexuality. But the character of childhood sexuality is more quickly understood if the word *sensual* is substituted for *sexual*. During the early years the child does seek and experience sensuous gratification, and these experiences play a formative role in adult sexual life. The sensuous gratification is received via the three principal **erotogenic**, or **erogenous**, zones of the body, zones that are particularly rich in nerve endings responsive to touch. These are the oral, the anal, and the genital areas.

During the first twelve to eighteen months of life, the libido is presumed to be concentrated in the oral area: This is the **oral stage**. The infant gets a great deal of gratification out of sucking and putting things in the mouth. The pleasure received from such activities is "sexual" in the broadest possible sense—the activities bring sensuous gratification by stimulating an erogenous zone. Parents can testify that it is often difficult to wean a child from the breast or the bottle; many parents complain of what they consider an inordinate amount of thumb-sucking in a child. All these behaviors are indicators of the gratification infants receive from oral stimulation.

During the next eighteen months to the third year of life, the libido moves out of the oral zone and concentrates itself in the anal zone: This is the **anal stage**. Now the infant gets principal erotic gratification from sensations associated with this region. The voluntary control of the retention and expulsion of fecal matter is learned during the anal stage, and the acquisition of this kind of bodily self-control gives the child a great deal of pleasure. It may also be noted that during the toilet-training period, the child can "get back" at punitive parents. Not having a bowel movement at the right time or having one

The oral stage is associated with infancy.

at the wrong time (or in the wrong place) are events that send some parents into states of great emotional agitation.

The time period from about the third year of life to the sixth year of life is designated as the **phallic stage**. Libido moves from the anal area and concentrates itself in the phallus. (The male phallus is the penis and the female phallus is the clitoris.) The word *phallus* should not be confused with the term *external genitalia* (the external genitalia include the phallus and other sexual structures). During the phallic stage, the child receives great bodily pleasure from masturbating. It should be noted that such masturbation is merely the prototype of adolescent masturbation. The child does not masturbate to orgasm; instead the phallus fills with blood and becomes firm for a time during autostimulation. When Freud first proposed the existence of childhood masturbation, he was scoffed at by many of his fellow physicians. Today we know that Freud was partly wrong and partly right. He thought that childhood masturbation was universal, but he apparently was incorrect about this. Contemporary studies suggest that about 60 percent of children engage in childhood masturbation. Freud was thus partly correct in that childhood masturbation does take place and is common.

The famous **Oedipus complex** comes into being during the phallic stage. The boy is said to develop a sexual yearning for his mother. In classical Freudian theory, this was thought to be a full-blown incest fantasy. The boy feels guilty about his forbidden wish, and he develops another fantasy—the fear that his father will somehow cut off his genital organs as punishment for wanting to have sex with his own mother. This leads to **castration anxiety**. Anxiety about castration is too high a price to pay for maintaining the incest fantasy, and the whole conflict is repressed to an unconscious level. The Oedipus conflict is psychologically useful to the boy in that it fosters an identification of the son with the father. It is a case of, "If you can't lick your enemies, join them." The son controls his castration anxiety by unconsciously associating his own ego with the ego of the father. Guilt about forbidden sexual impulses and the self-control of such guilt play a crucial role in the formation of the superego, the internal agent of social control. The socialized boy feels, at a conscious level, that the idea of sexual relations with his own mother is disgusting.

What I have said about the boy can also be applied to the girl. The girl has an incest fantasy about the father. She also experiences guilt and repression. The associated complex is sometimes called the **Electra complex**. The term "Oedipus complex" is often used to refer to either males or females, however.

The repression of sexual impulses during the sixth year of life leads to the fourth stage of psychosexual development, the **latency stage**. The latency stage lasts from about the sixth to the twelfth year. This time period is sometimes referred to as "the golden years of childhood." These are the elementary school years. During these prepubertal years there is much running, playing, and constructive activity. In our culture, boys tend to develop interests in such areas as scouting, model-building, baseball, and so forth. Girls tend to develop interests in such areas as dancing, sewing, cooking, and so forth. Avoiding the current debate over to what extent these sex-role patterns are innate or learned, the simple point is being made that the prepubertal child has no apparent interest in sex per se. His or her interest seems to turn outward toward the larger world. Children during this period show a tremendous intellectual vitality and interest in learning about their environment. To Freud, this was evidence of **sublimation,** a process in which direct sexual expression of libido is repressed and reappears in modified form as a general interest in the wider world.

The final stage of development is called the **genital stage** (see Figure 2.2). This stage begins at approximately the twelfth or thirteenth year of life. The mature adult who has developed the capacity to work and to love is in the genital stage. It is the optimal stage of development, and not all adults can be said to have reached it. Genital sexuality implies more than self-oriented pleasure. The oral, anal, and phallic stages are **narcissistic;** the pleasures of sex are aimed solely at the self. The genital personality takes pleasure in giving pleasure. He or she cares about the sexual experience of the other person. More than this, the genital personality can care about others beyond the sexual domain.

The path of personality development is seldom smooth. **Emotional traumas,** painful psychological events, can cause the unfolding of the psychosexual stages to become distorted. (Also, overindulgence during a stage is sometimes postulated to produce distortions.) Freud spoke of **fixations,** meaning that the libido or part of the libido can get "stuck" at one of the infantile stages. Thus a person who was weaned too quickly or was punished for thumb-sucking as an infant may develop oral fixations, seeking unconsciously to return again and again to forbidden pleasures. Such an individual has an **oral character** and may be inordinately fond of such oral gratifications as talking, smoking, and eating. The oral mode may also be generalized. For example, the oral personality may be gullible—the person is willing to "swallow anything." Or, he may be fond of saying sarcastic things—his words "bite" others and hurt them.

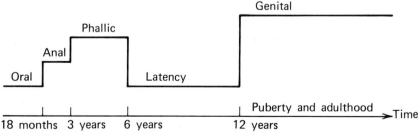

FIGURE 2.2   The five psychosexual stages proposed by Freud.

Emotional conflicts between parent and child over toilet-training may produce anal fixations. When these fixations are generalized and form part of an adult's life-style, the adult is said to have an anal character. Two basic kinds of anal characters are postulated. The **anal-expulsive character** is described as a disorderly and defiant person; the individual gets a great deal of satisfaction out of "making a mess." The person who actually enjoys being cruel to others would fall into this category. The **anal-retentive character** is described as a stingy and excessively orderly person; this individual gets a great deal of satisfaction out of "not giving" and "holding back." (Such a person may also have actual problems with constipation; he is forever taking laxatives in a vain attempt to unclog himself. A psychoanalyst would say that he needs to become emotionally unclogged first.) The famous miser Scrooge, in Dickens' *A Christmas Carol*, captures the image of the concept of the anal character.

Emotional conflicts taking place during the phallic stage of development may also produce fixations, and it is possible to postulate a **phallic character**. Such an individual might have unresolved conflicts over masturbation and incest wishes. The phallic character is unable to give others real love, only synthetic love; such persons exhibit behavior that has the appearance of caring but lacks the inner core of real concern. This is revealed by not meeting others' needs at crucial times and by discounting others' evaluations. Psychoanalytic theory hypothesizes that phallic fixations play a role in homosexuality.

It is, of course, absurd to speak of pure types. If the psychoanalytic conceptions have any value, that value resides in terms of dominant and minor themes in the human personality. It is far too constricting to say, "Jim is obviously an anal-retentive character. He's so damn tight with his money!" and thus act as if one has explained the whole person. But it may be of value to realize that Jim shows traits that may be partly but not completely, grasped in terms of Freud's developmental theory.

Defense Mechanisms

One of the more useful concepts of psychoanalysis for explaining behavior is the concept of **ego defense**, a tendency of the ego to distort its perception of reality in favor of the fantasy-oriented wishes of the id (see Figure 2.3). Briefly, the ego protects itself against "the slings and arrows of outrageous fortune." It should be understood that the defense mechanisms to be described "kick into action" automatically. They are not willed; one does not say, "Now I think I will use a defense mechanism and defend my ego." That is why they are called **mechanisms**; like the parts of a machine, they operate in fixed and predictable ways.

Repression The most important defense mechanism is **repression**, a tendency of the ego to shove down anxiety-arousing information to unconscious levels of the personality structure. As we have already seen, Freud theorized that the Oedipus complex is "solved" for most individuals by repression. He also said that we have a general amnesia for many events of early childhood because we repress memories that are too painful.

A person who has the tendency to criticize others "for their own good" may in fact be doing so out of hostility. There is a wish to inflict pain on others, but this is unacceptable to the ego. It is necessary to think "I am a nice person." Thus the destructive wish is repressed and becomes an unconscious motive; the unconscious motive reappears in the guise of a critical do-gooder.

"But surely people cannot be so blind to themselves!" one may protest. "A hostile person must realize he is hostile." There is some validity to the protest. The person using the defense mechanism does in a sense know; however, repression implies that *he does not know that he knows*. If this sounds abstruse, the whole thing can be made much less complicated by saying "Human beings have a tremendous capacity for kidding themselves."

Reaction Formation   What has just been described not only defines repression; it also captures the essence of a defense mechanism called **reaction formation**. This is a tendency for repressed motives to emerge on the conscious side as mirror opposites of their repressed cousins.

Regression   The defense mechanism called **regression** is associated with the concept of fixation in one of the pregenital stages of development. The literal meaning of regress is "to go back." Under stress, persons have a tendency to go back to behavior patterns that brought comfort at an earlier age. A person with oral fixations, for example, may eat large quantities of food when

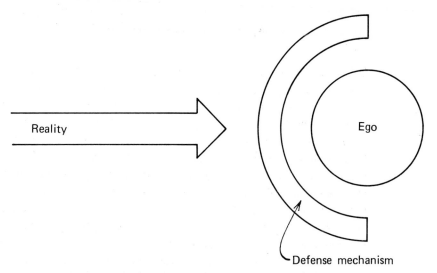

FIGURE 2.3   The function of an ego defense mechanism. Like a shield, the defense mechanism protects the ego from the harsher aspects of reality.

frustrated. I know one man who goes on eating binges when he has an argument with his wife and feels temporarily unloved. In general, we can speculate that the greater the stress, the greater the regression. There are numerous reports of prisoners of war who became so demoralized that they regressed to infantile levels. Under such conditions, formerly brave individuals have been known to urinate and soil themselves as if they were babies. There are reports of others who curled up into fetal positions and sucked their thumbs. On a more familiar level, almost any of us may cry like children if our frustration, pain, or anxiety is great enough.

Rationalization   Say that you are studying for an important examination. A friend calls and invites you to a party. You are in a state of conflict. You know realistically that if you don't study this evening you will probably turn in a poor performance on tomorrow's exam. On the other hand, you have a strong desire to go to the party (a certain member of the opposite sex to whom you are attracted is probably going to be a guest). Then the thought comes into your mind, "I've been studying too hard. I need to get out and relax a little, unwind a bit. It would do me good." You reply to your friend, "OK. I'll see you in a half hour," and you go to the party. What has happened? You have rationalized your behavior. The defense mechanism called **rationalization** is used when the real motive for one's behavior is unacceptable to the ego. The real motive is replaced with a cover motive. The cover motive makes it possible to behave in what seems to be good faith with one's conscience. In the above case, the real motive for going to the party was simply to have a good time. But this unadorned motive is unacceptable to the ego. "If that's your only reason for going, you should stay home and study" says a small voice within. The ego now becomes a cosmetic expert and "fixes up" the motive so it becomes prettier. "You're really going to relax and unwind. All work and no play makes Jack a dull boy." Now one is going to the party for a virtuous purpose.

Compensation   The defense mechanism known as **compensation** is used to defend against feelings of inferiority. The cliché example is, of course, the dictator who holds the power of life and death over millions of people. It turns out he is a short man, only five feet, four inches tall. His craving for power arises from an unconscious desire to be a big man and show others that, at least psychologically, he "stands above them." Or take the case of Grace. She has an auditory loss, and must wear a hearing aid. She is, however, a straight A student and holds a student body office. She is compensating for feelings of inadequacy associated with her sensory difficulty by proving she is an adequate person. Another example is provided by Horace. He is overweight and has difficulties in his social relations with young women. Yet he is the star comedian of his class; he is often surrounded by an audience that is both laughing with and at him. Through the mechanism of compensation, he is making himself feel more worthwhile.

Human beings can be handicapped in many ways. If the handicap is not so severe that the individual is completely incapacitated, it can sometimes be turned to a sort of advantage. Countless numbers of people with real or imagined deficiencies have used the mechanism of compensation to convince themselves and others that they have value as human beings.

Identification   Horace is not only a comedian. He is also a comic book fan. His favorite comic books are the ones about the adventures of such super-heroes as Superman, Batman, and Luke Skywalker. This interest reveals Horace's use of the defense mechanism called **identification**. When people use identification, they unconsciously associate their egos with the ego of an admired person. As a consequence, they pick up feelings of competence or power by association. Many of us identify with movie stars, sports heroes, and other famous people. Our own deflated egos are pumped up and made to swell to greater size through the identification process.

Fantasy   Closely related to the defense mechanism of identification is the defense mechanism of **fantasy**. When we fantasize, we usually use our imaginations to create mental pictures in which we visualize our fondest dreams coming true. The transient daydream is familiar to almost everyone. In these daydreams, we may take revenge on someone who has wronged us; we may succeed in love with someone who in reality is not interested in us; we may see ourselves overcoming personal inadequacies; or we may find ourselves acting out forbidden sexual impulses. Perhaps you are familiar with James Thurber's *The Secret Life of Walter Mitty*. Mitty was a submissive husband who was constantly being pushed around by his wife. In his daydreams, however, he saw himself in various heroic roles. His fantasy life was extremely important to him. It was his method of maintaining self-respect and surviving the harshness of his real life. cannot cope

Displacement   The philosopher Aristotle is credited with the following statement: "Anybody can become angry—that is easy; but to be angry with the right person, and in the right degree, and at the right time, and for the right purpose, and in the right way—that is not within everybody's power and it is not easy." Aristotle's statement is pertinent to the defense mechanism known as **displacement**. Displacement takes place when an individual places on one person an emotional reaction that should properly be placed on another. A husband who is angry with his boss may come home and pick a fight with his wife. We say, "He takes out his anger on her" or "She is the scapegoat for his aggressions." Assume that Laureen, a college professor, has just had a serious disagreement with a colleague. She may go into her next class and give students sarcastic answers when they ask questions. Her punitive approach to teaching reveals her underlying anger.

Projection   Projection is a defense mechanism in which a person actually perceives the external world in terms of his or her own personal emotional conflicts. The person takes reality to be the equivalent of his or her own somewhat distorted conception of it. A particular man may be ambitious and overly willing to take advantage of others to foster his own financial success. Such a person may think "You've really got to watch out for people nowadays. They all want to use you and manipulate you." Of course, it is he himself who is the wheeler-dealer and the manipulator. But such a self-image is threatening to the ego. He protects his ego by his perception that "they" are the ones with the reprehensible motives.

Although other defense mechanisms exist, the ones listed are perhaps sufficient to convey the general theme that human beings have many self-deceptive ways of maintaining self-esteem (see Table 2.1). The professional psychological consensus seems to be that when used in moderation, the defense mechanisms play a positive role in coping with life (Lazarus & Launier, 1978). They are crutches, though, and—like physical crutches—they should not be used when one can function without them. One of the values of knowing about defense mechanisms is that such knowledge alerts us to their possible misuse.

The Meaning of Dreams

Freud believed that dreams have meaning, that they are symbolic messages from the unconscious level and reveal the existence of unconscious wishes. Freud distinguished a minimum of two levels to every dream: the **manifest level** and the **latent level**. The manifest level refers to the actual content of the dream, the images the dreamer experiences. The latent level refers to what the dream is about, what the dream means. One could say that the manifest level is the superficial, or false, layer of the dream and that the latent level is the deep, or real, layer of the dream (Freud, 1900).

The reason the dream has two layers is that the latent level is unacceptable to the ego. It contains impulses that are disagreeable to the conscious self. Thus the latent material is distorted, by what Freud called the **dream work**, into a set of events that seem relatively innocent to the conscious mind. The purpose of symbolism in dreams is to act as a mask or cover for the real meaning of the dream. Freud further theorized that most dreams concern either sex or aggression. These, he proposed, are the two impulses most subject to repression in society.

One of Freud's patients, an unmarried adolescent girl, reported a dream in which she saw herself in the nude riding a horse through the forest. The girl was a virgin. Freud had her give associations to the images of the dream (the manifest content), and her associations revealed that the horse made her think of the male phallus. The up-and-down motion of the horse made her think of sexual intercourse. (Such associations do not necessarily occur in

TABLE 2.1   REPRESENTATIVE DEFENSE MECHANISMS

Mechanism	A Key Feature
Repression	Shoving down anxiety-arousing information to unconscious levels of the personality structure.
Reaction formation	Repressed motives emerging on the conscious side as mirror opposites of their original form.
Regression	Going back to behavior patterns that brought comfort at an earlier age.
Rationalization	Replacing a real motive for behavior with a more acceptable cover motive.
Compensation	Defending against feelings of inferiority by taking action designed to enhance one's sense of self-esteem.
Identification	Associating one's ego with the ego of an admired person.
Fantasy	Using the imagination to create mental pictures in which one visualizes his or her fondest dreams coming true. [cannot cope]
Displacement	Placing on a second person (or animal or inanimate object) an emotional reaction that properly should have been placed on a first source.
Projection	Perceiving the external world in terms of one's own personal emotional conflicts.

one step; there may be several links before the last link of the chain is reached.) Freud interpreted the dream as meaning that the girl wished to have sexual intercourse (the latent content). Because she was a "good" girl and unmarried, such a wish was unacceptable to her conscious ego. To maintain a positive self-image, it was necessary for her to have her fantasy of sexual intercourse in disguised form. Perhaps this all seems rather farfetched. But keep in mind that Freud was working in the climate of a prudish and Victorian society. Adolescent girls from the "better" families in 1910 in Vienna were not supposed to have "animal cravings." Under these conditions, one can appreciate that Freud's interpretation is not too unlikely.

Assume that a man dreams he is a knight in rusty armor, having a sword-fight with another knight. With his sword, the first knight penetrates the armor of the second knight, and the second knight screams out—not in pain but in ecstasy! The Freudian interpretation of such a dream might be that the dreamer has a repressed wish for homosexual relations. He is wearing rusty armor because homosexuality is a "low" or "deteriorated" act. The sword is a symbol for the male phallus, and the penetration of the sword into the body represents penetration by the penis. That the second knight screams out in ecstasy reveals the fantasy-oriented quality of the dream. When a person is pierced by a sword he certainly does not experience ecstasy.

One can see that the Freudian conception of dreams is associated with the defense mechanism of fantasy. Dreams are more powerful fantasies than those we allow ourselves in a waking state. Like conscious fantasy, they are defensive; they maintain our self-esteem while allowing us to express conflicting emotions.

But what about dreams that contain little or no symbolism? Don't people have frank sexual dreams? Don't people often express their hostilities directly in dreams? The answer to these questions is yes. Thus one of the problems with the Freudian theory of dreams is that it makes a certain kind of dream, a heavily symbolized dream, a universal type. This is probably because Freud derived his data from patients. It is plausible to suppose that a neurotic person who has many repressed conflicts would find it necessary to dream in symbols to censor real meanings. A more normal person, however, might not have such a need; consequently, many of his dreams might be more explicit. That so many people do report symbolical dreams, however, suggests the generality of neurotic trends in human behavior.

Freud's trailblazing investigation of dreams is widely recognized as an important contribution to human understanding. For example, the psychoanalyst Erich Fromm, one quick to note many of Freud's limitations, had these kind words to say: "If Freud had not created a theory of neurosis and a method of therapy he would still be one of the most outstanding figures in the science of man because he discovered the art of dream interpretation." (Fromm, 1980, p. 70)

Therapy

The basic tool of traditional psychoanalytic therapy is **free association**. The patient reclines on a couch and is told to say aloud anything at all that comes to his or her mind. This is to be done without inhibition, without conscious censorship, and without regard to logical order. The instruction to free associate is called the **fundamental rule** of psychoanalysis. It is not particularly easy to consistently observe the fundamental rule, and most patients have to spend a period of time learning to free associate successfully. The reason the fundamental rule is difficult to learn is the tendency toward ego defense. Thus the psychoanalytic patient often offers **resistances**, blocks that thwart honest self-disclosure. For example, while free associating, a woman patient may have an image of her therapist sitting on the toilet while she is thinking "He seems so kingly. But he sits on an ordinary 'throne' like anyone else." Perhaps she dismisses this as an unimportant image, not worthy of repeating to the therapist. But the dismissal itself is a defense against the awkward feeling that would come to her if she repeated her thoughts to the therapist. It is not until patients have come to trust their therapists and feel accepted by them that they are willing to free associate without reservation.

DRAWING BY OPIE; ©1972 THE NEW YORKER MAGAZINE, INC.

"Did you miss me on your vacation?"

IMP.

cause for everything we say & do

Freud saw free association as the major road to repressed material. Remember that he believed in the principle of **psychic determinism,** the view that **all mental acts have a meaning.** Thus he believed that seemingly random associations actually have a common thread and that if this thread is followed to its end, one will discover the core element in a particular personal problem.

To illustrate, assume that a male patient is having a great deal of difficulty in his marital relationship. He feels his wife is a shrew and tries to dominate him. He is asked to free associate to the word "wife." " 'Wife' for some reason makes me think of words like 'kitchen,' 'sink,' 'bread,' 'knife,' and 'butter.' Now I'm seeing my own mother standing in the kitchen and she's chewing me out for something, like she always did. I'm thinking that she was a real put-down artist and I'm wondering why she always loved my brother Tommy more than she loved me. Now I'm thinking of a day in the park with my mother. The sun was shining and I was about six years old and we had a good time. For some reason I had her all to myself—no brothers or sisters around. But I don't remember many good times with her, and I never really learned how to talk with her. Now I'm seeing my Dad standing next to her—

but he's an invisible man! Don't ask me how I can see him when he's invisible. Maybe he's not invisible—he's sort of transparent or something. She hits him and he shatters into a million pieces like glass."

A classical psychoanalytic approach would suggest that the patient's associations to his wife have led him back to his relationship with his mother and his perception of her relationship with his father. His present conflict with his own wife is probably a compulsive repetition of old problems that have never been resolved adequately. In psychoanalysis, he can work through some of these psychological leftovers and explore some new ways of interacting with a female.

The basic principle of growth in psychoanalysis is **insight**, which may be defined as "seeing into" the essence of a problem. It is the well-known "ah-hah!" phenomenon. We are trying to solve a problem—can't get it, can't get it—and then "click!" something happens and things fall into place. A patient in therapy may declare, "Now I see why I always had trouble with my officers in the Army and why I'm always on the outs with teachers, bosses, and even ministers. It all goes back to dear old dad and the way he treated me—like I was some kind of puppet or something. I had to strangle my rage and act like I loved it when he ordered me around. As an adult, I'm trying to prove to every 'father' I meet that I'm not a puppet—that I'm a living person!"

Early psychoanalytic work stressed the concept of **abreaction**. An abreaction takes place when a patient remembers an emotional trauma (with an emphasis on childhood memories) and "relives" the event *with feeling*. The patient thus discharges stored-up negative emotions and at the same time transfers the painful memory from an unconscious to a conscious level. The present-day psychoanalyst does not reject the importance of abreaction, but feels that abreactions are not the key to longterm personal growth. The majority of contemporary analysts place greater emphasis on **ego analysis**, an approach that scrutinizes the patient's defense mechanism, ways of relating to other people, and mode of adjusting to reality. The aim of ego analysis is to help the patient build **ego strength**. A person with a high level of ego strength is well oriented in time and space, knows the practical limits of his or her capacities, is able to make good working compromises between the fantasy-oriented demands of the id and the morality-oriented demands of the superego, and in general is able to cope effectively with life's challenges.

Another major concept in psychoanalytic therapy is the **transference relationship**. The theory of psychoanalytic therapy proposes that patients tend to transfer to the therapist feelings held in childhood toward their parents. In many cases the therapist becomes a kind of symbolic parent. Thus patients have been known to express a strong emotional attachment to their therapists, professing, for instance, great affection. To the traditional Freudian, such an attachment on the part of patients does not arise out of reality-oriented considerations. Instead, it arises out of the fantasy-oriented images of the primal self, the wishful id. For example, the patient may be looking for a love that he or she feels was never adequately forthcoming from one or both parents. It is the therapist's responsibility to recognize the existence of a transference relationship and to eventually interpret it to the patient.

It is also possible for the therapist to use the relationship in a constructive way during the patient's psychoanalysis. The therapist does not allow the client to act on the transference feelings; this would be giving in to the fantasy-oriented id and would take the patient away from reality. The therapist may, however, rely on the transference to a certain extent as a means of energizing the therapy. As long as the patient sees the therapist as a parental figure, the possibility exists that the therapist has a greater impact on the patient than if he or she is seen as just another person. Up to a point, the emotional attachment of the patient to the therapist may have a place. It is crucial in a successful psychoanalysis, however, that the transference not go too far and that it be analyzed for what it is before the termination of therapy. When the transference relationship has been analyzed and accepted by the patient, the traditional psychoanalytic case is closed.

Not all schools of psychotherapy accept the use or the fostering of the transference relationship. Specifically, Adlerian therapy, transactional analysis, and client-centered therapy would all look down on the fostering of a transference relationship. These schools of psychotherapy would prefer an adult-adult relationship with the client. They would criticize classical psychoanalysis as encouraging a parent-child relationship and thus undermining the client's capacity for self-sufficiency. The classical analyst would answer that these criticisms are valid only if the transference is not analyzed and finally revealed for what it is. The responsible Freudian does not allow the patient to leave analysis with a therapist hang-up.

The most important assumption of psychoanalytic therapy is that psychological material that is available at a conscious level can be dealt with in a rational fashion. The work of therapy is seen much as a "dredging" operation in which repressed material is brought up from the darkness of the unconscious domain to the light of the conscious domain. Thus the principal orientation of psychoanalysis is as old as the ancient dictum "Know thyself."

There has been much debate about the effectiveness of psychoanalysis. Outcome studies have yielded conflicting results. However, a seven-year review of various kinds of data suggests the possibility that psychoanalysis may be particularly effective in treating various kinds of psychosomatic symptoms such as certain kinds of ulcers, headaches, and backaches (Greenberg & Fisher, 1978). In view of the fact that these kinds of symptoms are thought of in psychoanalytic therapy as being linked to neurotic anxiety, the review tends to lend some credence to the claims of psychoanalysis. Also, psychosomatic illness presents a major health problem (see the applied exploration section on behavioral medicine at the end of Chapter 6), and psychoanalytic therapy contributes to our attack on this problem.

2.2   APPLICATION: IN SEARCH OF SELF-UNDERSTANDING

Psychoanalysis is not a set of prescriptions about living. Freud never wrote a how-to book. And yet in reading psychoanalysis, one gets the powerful feeling that there are applications one can make to the process of living. What psychoanalysis emphasizes is the importance of self-understanding. As noted in the text, implicit in psychoanalysis is the ancient dictum "Know thyself."

How can psychoanalysis aid us in the search for greater self-understanding and a better life? Several possibilities exist.

Many people find that extensive reading of the works of Freud and other depth psychologists is a mind-expanding activity. (The same claim can, of course, be made for reading in general.) The writings of Freud have been quite popular, and you will have no trouble finding some of his books in inexpensive paperback formats. If psychoanalysis speaks strongly to you, you will gain from your reading a broader perspective on life and a different perception of the human condition. It is expected that these larger orientations will be life enhancing and contribute to more effective living.

Most of us are curious about our motivations. We like to have an answer to the question, "Why do I do the things I do?" The subject of motivation is

ANALYTICAL PSYCHOLOGY: DIGGING DEEPER

In *Memories, Dreams, Reflections,* the psychiatrist Carl Jung comments (1972):

Among the so-called neurotics of our day there are a good many who in other ages would not have been neurotic—that is, divided against themselves. If they had lived in a period and in a milieu in which man was still linked by myth with the world of his ancestors, and thus with nature truly experienced and not merely seen from outside, they would have been spared this division within themselves. (pp. 143–144)

This statement captures the central theme of Jung's **analytical psychology**, an approach that asserts there is a deeper and more primitive layer of the mind than the unconscious level postulated by Freud. We return to this point of view in the following pages since it is an approach that requires augmentation to acquire greater meaning. For the present, let us identify Carl Jung.

the particular strength of psychoanalysis, and a knowledge of it makes you feel you are not a mystery to yourself. If you accept the doctrine of unconscious motivation, much that was previously opaque about your behavior becomes transparent. You feel you have insight into the deeper sources of your actions. No one likes to feel that he or she is pushed and pulled by invisible and nameless psychological forces. Psychoanalysis shines a spotlight on these forces and gives them names.

Being aware of defense mechanisms can be helpful in avoiding self-deception. It can contribute to taking responsibility for your own behavior to say to yourself something such as, "Who am I kidding? I'm just rationalizing so I can take the easy way out."

A knowledge of psychoanalysis tends to make us more tolerant of the behavior of others. People who see behavior in largely deterministic terms and who explain the behavior of others in terms of childhood experience, unconscious motives, and ego defense mechanisms will not tend to be blaming persons. They may think "Oh, what fools we mortals be." But they will not think "When a person suffers it's his own fault. Anyone who wants to can use willpower to help himself if he really wants to." The student of psychoanalysis recognizes that this is somewhat like shouting to a person sinking in quicksand, "Quick! Reach down to your bootstraps and tug! You can pull yourself out!"

Who was Carl Jung?

Carl Jung was a Swiss psychiatrist who was born in 1875 and died in 1961. His childhood years were characterized by an interest in the same kinds of subjects that make up the body of analytical psychology: myth, magic, religion—the subjective and "unscientific" domain of human existence. From his early years, Jung had an interest in finding the meeting ground between the rational and the irrational worlds. Jung's father was a Swiss Reform pastor, and he seems to have been a man who had a cold-blooded approach to religion. Jung could not accept his father's rather technical approach to God, and much of Jung's search as a man was for a deep and meaningful relationship with the Universe (Fordham, 1966).

For a time Jung was a student of Freud. As you already know from the previous section, Jung was the first president of the International Psychoanalytic Association. Perhaps too much has been made out of the Freud–Jung relationship, however. Jung was a psychiatrist before he met Freud, had

Carl Jung was one of the principal founders of depth psychology.

already done important word-association experiments, and had formulated theories about mental complexes. The work done after his break with Freud is original and independent of Freudian influence; it would be unfair to Jung to see him as always standing in Freud's shadow. In proper perspective, we would have to say that Freud was the father of depth psychology. But Jung was one of its principal founders and is generally considered to have been a giant of the field (Bennet, 1966).

Carl Jung was a scientist. Carl Jung was a mystic. If these two statements strike you as contradictory, Jung would have commented that your thinking takes arbitrary categories too seriously. It is perfectly possible for a person to be at once both a scientist and mystic. Much of Jung's work was devoted to showing how superficial opposites could be united to form a meaningful whole. Thus it is possible to say of Jung that he was a scientist-mystic.

The Collective Unconscious

Jung accepted the Freudian unconscious. He agreed that there was a layer of the personality that consisted of repressed ideas. Jung designated this layer the **personal unconscious**. But Jung also said that there is a deeper layer to the human personality—the **collective unconscious**. The collective unconscious is impersonal—we all have the same collective unconscious. Its contents are the residual memories of the human race. These memories are based on more or less similar experiences had by all peoples in all times and places since the dawn of human existence. These oft-repeated experiences have somehow made a deep and permanent impression on the human mind. These enduring patterns Jung terms **archetypes** (pronounced "ar-ke-types").

By postulating the existence of archetypes, Jung was in essence saying that the human mind is much more than a blank slate at birth. We have inborn behavioral predispositions. Archetypes are for humans what instincts are for animals. Like an instinct, the archetype guides behavior and tells us what to do in certain circumstances. A particular set of circumstances will cause us to "plug into" a particular archetype. Once we are in the grips of the archetype, our behavior becomes robotlike; the archetype takes over and for a period of time determines the course of events. The archetypes make up the inner core of human nature, and it was Jung's view that we need to know our archetypes if we do not wish to be controlled blindly by them.

Jung felt that Western men and women are alienated from their deepest nature, that they do not have a creative contact with the archetypes. As a consequence, they place too much trust on conscious reason and are "sitting ducks" when an emotion-arousing set of circumstances activates an archetype. A familiar example is provided by the rise to power of a dictator in a country beset by economic woes. A figure comes forth who promises to cure everything. He rants and raves and presents "solutions" to the country's great crises. The emotional state of the populace is such that an archetype is activated. This archetype could be called the Rescuer or the Hero or the Saviour. The dictator quickly becomes a demigod. He acquires all the attributes of the age-old archetypes. He will lead the people out of the wilderness of their problems, he will defeat enemies both inside and outside the country, and he will have at his disposal great powers. The dictator's success is based on the ancient wish of a group of people to follow a leader who is all-knowing and all-wise. If, for a time, a dictator is perceived as an archetypal figure, he has it made.

The archetypes can also operate at an individual level. Say that Tom falls in love with Julie. He is on cloud nine, head over heels in love with her. She is Miss Perfect, everything he ever wanted in a woman. When he thinks of their future together he can visualize only bliss and unadulterated happiness. Somehow Julie has enabled Tom to plug into the archetype represented by such familiar symbols as Cinderella, Snow White, and Miss America. Note that Cinderella, Snow White, and Miss America are not themselves archetypes. They are **symbols**, figures presented at a conscious level that stand for the underlying archetype. In this case the underlying archetype might be called the Beautiful One. In the grips of the archetype of the Beautiful One, Tim has obviously taken leave of his senses. His behavior has become robotlike, programmed by the attributes of the archetype.

Before we proceed, let us discuss the plausibility of the existence of archetypes. Many psychologists have rejected the Jungian archetypes and the collective unconscious because the two seem to demand the acceptance of an outmoded evolutionary theory, **Lamarckian inheritance**—the doctrine that experiences affecting the individual can be directly transmitted through the germ plasm to that individual's children. To illustrate, assume that a man is a weight lifter and builds up powerful muscles. Lamarckian inheritance would say that this man will have children with powerful muscles. Modern biologists are convinced that the evolutionary process does not work in such a crude and obvious way. It is more likely that changes in a species over time are determined by the processes of mutation (spontaneous changes in genetic structure) and natural selection (survival of the fittest). Thus it seems absurd to many individuals who know something about modern biology and contemporary evolutionary theory that there can be "racial memories" in the form of archetypes.

Jung did not, however, pin the existence of the archetypes on the doctrine of Lamarckian inheritance. The way the archetypes arose was not the central issue for him. He felt that their presence was documented amply by the way human beings behave and, in particular, by the themes that reappear in myth and folklore. If modern biology cannot explain how archetypes come to be, this was a problem for modern biology, not a problem for Jungian theory.

Perhaps a compromise position is possible. First, if we think of the archetypes not as specific memories, but as *patterns*, it is possible to see how the human brain and nervous system might have certain kinds of predispositions; these predispositions could easily fit within the framework of mutation and natural selection. Second, we must realize that an archetype is a concept, an abstraction that is utilized to explain sets of events. As such, concepts are neither true nor false. It is a basic error to argue over the reality of concepts. They are like tools; they are either useful or useless. If they are useful, they should be retained. If they are useless, they should be discarded. A number of psychologists and other thinkers have found that Jungian archetypes have a degree of utility in certain contexts; thus one might agree that for some behaviors they have both explanatory and predictive power. One may use the concept of the archetype as a working hypothesis without asserting that it represents the Truth.

Kinds of Archetypes

Archetypes may be classified as falling into three broad categories: (1) personifications, (2) processes of the world, and (3) systems of the self.

Personifications   Examples of personifications are the Hero, the Wise Old Man, the Earth Mother, the Evil One, and the Beautiful One. The same personifications appear and reappear in myth, folklore, fairy tales, novels, plays, movies, television dramas, and comic books. Consider the Wise Old Man. The archetype suggests a kindly soul with great vision and magical (or at least semimagical) powers. Specific symbolizations of the Wise Old Man are Merlin the Magician (King Arthur's "godparent"), Shazam (the ancient one who gave Billy Batson the power to turn into Captain Marvel), and Marcus Welby, M.D. An obvious example of the Earth Mother is Mother Nature; a somewhat less obvious example is Betty Crocker. Sentimental songs about mother and the kind of mother portrayed in Mother's Day cards are stimuli that evoke the archetype of the Earth Mother—a good mother who will stroke us and nurse us for as long as we wish. Satan, the intelligent alien from Planet X who seeks to destroy the Earth, the mad professor who confronts Superman, and the bad guy in a Western all symbolize the archetype of the Evil One.

Processes of the World   It was Jung's contention that eons of experience with processes of nature also gave rise to certain kinds of archtypes in humankind. These archetypes represent processes of the world; examples are Rebirth, Sunrise and Sunset, and the Circle. Specific symbolizations of the archetype of Rebirth can take many forms and may sometimes seem quite remote from the archetype. A relatively risky one-week trip down a river with straits and rapids may symbolize, for some people, a death and rebirth of the spirit. They come out of such an adventure feeling that they have a new lease on life. Jung said that for modern man such returns to nature may well connect with the ancient archetypes of Birth and Death in the broadest sense. Actual birth is itself a "water trip" down a narrow passageway; the river trip provides an obvious parallel for the collective unconscious.

Another symbol for the archetype of Rebirth would be skydiving. As the person plunges toward earth, a feeling of death may close in; when the parachute flowers overhead, the sense of being reborn takes over. It could be argued that, from a Jungian standpoint, the exhilaration of such sports arises from the activation of the archetype of Rebirth. More obvious and familiar examples of symbols for Rebirth than the ones already given are the Phoenix rising from the ashes, Igor Stravinsky's *Rites of Spring*, pagan festivals marking the beginning of new seasons, and the Resurrection.

Many familiar symbols portray the archetype of Sunrise and Sunset. The Japanese flag uses the symbol of the rising sun. Many Americans worship at Easter Sunday sunrise services. The Pueblo Indians in New Mexico believe in Father Sun; their religion requires that they pray and thus help the Father across the sky each day to save the world from darkness. In the musical *Fiddler on the Roof*, the central character, Tevye, and his wife, Golde, sing:

Is this the little girl I carried?
Is this the little boy at play?
I don't remember growing older,
When did they?

Sunrise, Sunset,
Sunrise, Sunset
Swiftly flow the days;

Seedlings turn overnight to sunflow'rs,
Blossoming even as we gaze. *

The tendency of many processes of nature to bring into existence circular and spherical structures gives rise to the archetype of the Circle. An example of such a process is the tendency of a soap bubble to form a sphere. The planets, including Earth itself, and the sun are spheres (note also that the planets travel in more or less circular orbits). There is magic in the circular form. In alchemy and magic, a circle is used for casting spells. On an everyday level, the wedding band is a circle symbolizing wholeness and unity—aspects of the archetype of the Circle. The following poem by Edwin Markham invokes the power of the circle:

He drew a circle that shut me out,
Heretic, rebel, thing to flout.

But love and I had the wit to win,
We drew a circle that took him in. †

Would it not seem odd to you if the poem used the phrase "a square that shut me out"? The square does not connect with the collective unconscious. Jung was fond of pointing out the universal appearance of mandalas, circular figures—often elaborate—divided into four quadrants. Indeed, mandala is a Sanskrit work meaning a circle and has the specific connotation of a magic circle. The mandala tends to appear in cultures greatly separated by space and time. It was Jung's contention that these were spontaneous appearances, not arising from communication between cultures. Although the possibility of cultural transmission can always be advanced, Jung felt that this interpretation of the mandala (and other symbols representing archetypes) was far-fetched. He felt it was much more plausible and had much more meaning to think in terms of intrinsic processes in all people. In any event, one can find many examples of the mandala in different cultures. The ground plans of many temples in the East are based on the mandala, and the mandala appears in the form of pictures in Eastern temples. On the American continent, the mandala was used by the Plains Indians. *Black Elk Speaks* (Neihardt, 1961), the life story of a holy man of the Oglala Sioux, contains the following passage:

You have noticed that everything an Indian does is in a circle, and that is because the Power of the World always works in circles, and everything tries to be round. In the old days when we were a strong and happy people, all our power came to us from the sacred hoop of the nation, and so long as the hoop was unbroken, the people flourished. The flowering tree was the living center of the hoop, and the circle of the four quarters nourished it. The east gave peace and light, the south gave warmth, the west gave rain, and the north with its cold and mighty wind gave strength and endurance. . . . Birds make their nests in circles, for theirs is the same religion as ours. (pp, 39–40).

The sacred hoop of the Sioux, with its four quadrants, was clearly a mandala.

Systems of the Self   The third broad category of archetypes refers to systems of the self, such as the Anima and Animus, the Persona, the Shadow, and the Self. The Anima and the Animus refer, respectively, to the female and the male personalities in all of us. The Anima is nurturing, tender, and intuitive; the Animus is aggressive, tough, and practical. In the female the Anima is dominant and the Animus is recessive, and in the male the Animus is dominant and the Anima is recessive. But every individual, regardless of objective sex, has both archetypes. One of life's principal tasks is to acknowledge the existence of both archetypes and bring their opposing tendencies together for a meaningful synthesis. Say that one woman has acknowledged only her Anima. She takes care of her home, loves her husband and children, and is a good cook. But she goes to pieces in the face of adversity, hates to leave her home for more than a few hours at a time, will not learn to drive a car, blushes when she hears an off-color joke, and never takes the sexual initiative with her husband. By not acknowledging her Animus, she falls far short of being a whole person. On the other hand, let us say that another woman has psychologically "become a man." Her Animus reigns supreme, and her Anima is denied. Here we have the sterotype of the militant feminist who curses like a deckhand, speaks frequently of "male pigs," and complains of universal sexism. If she is married, she is the dominant one in the marriage; her husband is a meek and passive person who tries to make his behavior conform to her wishes.

The male may be subject to the same imbalances in the relationship between his Anima and Animus. The male who tries to repress his Anima completely tends to be an extroverted gogetter. He rejects shows of emotion and attempts to remain stolid in the face of adversity. In the business world, he thinks in terms of dog-eat-dog and conceptualizes success in terms of a battlefield. If he is married, he refuses to do any of the things around the home that are usually the wife's task. He won't change the baby's diapers, wash dishes, vacuum, or dust. This would be true even if his wife were fatigued or clearly operating under a time pressure. He distinguishes between women's work and men's work, and never the twain shall meet. He will, in all likelihood, be handy with tools; carpentry, painting, and yard maintenance are all perceived as masculine tasks, and these do not threaten his self-image as a real man's man. His relationship with his children will entail difficulties revolving around his tendency to be authoritarian with them; it will be hard for such a man to develop emotional closeness with his children. He is of the old school, which grants the father an exalted status in the household.

Now imagine a different situation. Another man has a dominant Anima and a recessive Animus. Such a man will speak softly, have difficulty asserting himself, and may display female mannerisms in his walk and speech. He will hate to do any kind of rough or dirty work. The idea of getting into a fight and getting cut or bruised is abhorrent. His interests will be in the fine arts—music, painting, sculpture, and literature. He will be looked down on as a sissy and a fool by the man with a highly dominant Animus. Our society appears to have much less tolerance for the femalelike man than for the malelike woman. Although both types receive their share of hostility, the femalelike man receives more, probably because traditional male roles have tended to receive more status than traditional female ones. Thus the woman who mimics male behavior seems to take a psychological step up; however, the male who mimics female behavior seems to be taking a psychological step down.

The Persona is the public self, the social role an individual has chosen to play. The mask worn by a Greek actor was called a *persona*, and it designated the actor's role in the drama. One's Persona is thought to be one's mask. The Persona (1) defines how a person is to act in certain situations and (2) provides a disguise for real thoughts and feelings. The Persona thus acts like a "skin" between the inner self and the outer world. As such, the Persona is as necessary as the physical skin that covers the human body. It is a protection, and without it the ego would be naked in the world. Jung did not believe it was possible to be absolutely authentic and a "transparent self" in all one's human relations. On the other hand, he did feel that trouble arises for the individual when he makes the mistake of identifying his ego with his Persona. Such an individual thinks that his inner being is identical with his social role, and this is a mistake. For example, the judge who continues to play the part of powerful magistrate with his wife, with his children, and with his friends fails to recognize that the sober demeanor of the professional judge is a role that fits nicely in the courtroom and is, of course, expected in the setting. When he is with his family, however, a different role should be played. When people are unable to be flexible, we often have an inner reaction toward them such as, "Oh, come off it" or "I wish he would get off his high horse."

The minister's wife who is all smiles and kindness we take to be a "wonderful person with a heart of gold." We forget that this is her social role. Any other behavior might strike us as deviant or odd. If she departs too sharply from the behaviors defined by the role, members of the congregation are apt to gossip and say, "She's gone crazy!" In *Two Essays on Analytical Psychology*, Jung writes (1953):

Society expects, and indeed must expect, every individual to play the part assigned to him as perfectly as possible, so that a man who is a parson . . . must at all times . . . play the role of parson in a flawless manner. Society demands this as a kind of surety: each must stand at his post, here a cobbler, there a poet. No man is expected to be both . . . that would be "odd." Such a man would be "different" from other people, not quite reliable. In the academic world he would be a dilettante, in politics an "unpredictable" quantity, in religion a free-thinker—in short, he would always be suspected of unreliability and incompetence, because society is persuaded that only the cobbler who is not a poet can supply workmanlike shoes. (p. 48)

In Jung's statement, one can detect a note of frustration with conventional society. Social roles are necessary, but they should not act like straitjackets that inhibit the growth of the whole person. Unfortunately, social roles do just that for many people.

The **Shadow** is the animal side of the human personality. (The archetype of the Shadow is similar to Freud's concept of the id.) The Shadow is a kind of inferior being within each person. Robert Louis Stevenson's novel *Dr. Jekyll and Mr. Hyde* captures well the archetype of the Shadow. Mr Hyde is ev-

The Story of Dr. Jekyll and Mr. Hyde captures well the archetype of the Shadow. (Spencer Tracy is shown in a scene from the movie.)

2.3 CONTEMPORARY RESEARCH: HIGH AND LOW SELF-MONITORING

Additional understanding of Jung's concept of the Persona and the way in which public masks determine behavior is given by the research of social psychologist Mark Snyder (1979). Employing a twenty-five item questionnaire, the Self-Monitoring Scale, it is possible to distinguish high self-monitoring individuals from low self-monitoring ones.

High self-monitoring individuals are very aware of how they act in social situations. They work at the impression they make on others, are alert to signals from others such as approval or disapproval of their behavior, and monitor their actions accordingly. Thus they are constantly fine-tuning their performance in response to social feedback. These individuals are uncomfortable with excessive amounts of self-disclosure.

Low self-monitoring individuals, on the other hand, are more autonomous in social situations. They are likely to say what they actually think and feel without overconcern for the opinion of others. Such individuals seldom put on a show in order to impress or entertain, and tend not to be the center of attention.

In terms of Jung's concept of the Persona, it is clearly the high self-monitoring individuals who use the Persona to distinct social advantage. They feel that the impression they make on others is of sufficient importance that they are willing to mold their social selves to fit the demands of a situation. Low self-monitoring individuals are closer to what existential philosophers and humanistic psychologists call authentic living (see Chapter 7). They resist having their behavior shaped by the reactions of others.

It is possible to make value judgments and say that one pole of the self-monitoring continuum is better than the other. Jung seems to feel that the use of the Persona is natural. He therefore would not look down on people who demonstrate high self-monitoring behavior. Humanistic psychologists stress the value of authentic living, and tend to feel that the use of social masks is undesirable. The research of Snyder opens up the possibility that we should avoid value judgments. Perhaps both high and low self-monitoring individuals are following tendencies that are the most comfortable for them. And it is reasonable to suggest that there is room for both kinds of persons in a complex social world.

erything that Dr. Jekyll is not. Dr. Jekyll is decent, kind, altruistic, law abiding, and so forth; Mr Hyde is immoral, cruel, selfish, and cares nothing for the law. The perennial fascination of Stevenson's novel may be that many of us see an undiscovered self reflected in the behavior of Mr. Hyde. He is a monster, but we are nonetheless intrigued. A popular radio series of the 1940s about an invisible detective was called *The Shadow*. The show opened with a mocking laugh, and the Shadow said, "Who knows what evil lurks in the hearts of men? The Shadow knows!" And then the mocking laugh was repeated. This captures rather accurately what Jung had in mind with his concept of the Shadow—one wonders if the author of the series was familiar with Jungian theory. (Jung's views were presented and well known long before the 1940s.) Or perhaps the author chose the image of the Shadow for the same reason that Jung chose it: There is a self that resides in the darkness.

It was Jung's view that denial is not the proper way to handle the Shadow. Many persons are horrified by the Shadow when they get a glimpse of it, and they quickly repress it into the unconscious. Jung felt that the Shadow should be acknowledged, even welcomed, and integrated into the whole personality. When this is done, the Shadow becomes a source of creativity, and there is no risk of being taken over and destroyed by the Shadow. On the other hand, if the Shadow is completely blocked in its expression, it will find ways of kicking up and creating trouble. There are many possibilities: nightmares, chronic anxiety, episodes of irrationality, and so forth. Over and over in Jung we find the point of view expressed that opposites should be united to form a higher whole.

The archetype of the **Self** represents the whole person. Let us defer our consideration of the Self for a few pages. We will return to this archetype in the discussion under the heading "The Individuation Process."

Types of Persons

The idea that there are different types of persons is centuries old. You will recall from Chapter 1 that more than two thousand years ago Hippocrates designated four different kinds of personalities. Jung also designated personality types, and he felt that such a classification scheme could be of value in understanding ourselves and others.

The most well-known dichotomy from Jungian theory is the distinction between the extrovert and the introvert. This distinction has become part of popular psychology and is familiar to millions of people from articles in magazines and newspapers. Unfortunately, popularizations of Jung's work do not do justice to the richness and complexity of his thought. His approach to personality types was not based so much on a static classification scheme as it was on a recognition of dominant and recessive processes in the individual. To clarify, Jung postulated that the human personality takes an orientation toward the world that is either outgoing or ingoing. The basic orientation is called the individual's **attitude**.

If an individual has an extroverted attitude, the person tends to have a dominant interest in the outside world as opposed to the inner world of thought and the mind. It is a cliché to suppose that all extroverts are talkative and popular. In many instances this may be the case. A practical person who likes to make a living with his hands, enjoys using tools, and takes satisfaction in completing a physical task, however, would also be an extroverted type. Practical inventors would thus also be considered extroverted types. On the other hand, the introverted type tends to be interested in philosophical discourse, abstract issues, and such subjects as mathematics.

Jung felt that the basic attitude is built into the individual. It is innate, not learned. Family life and the environment can modify the basic attitude, but the foundation nonetheless remains. This point of view has been repugnant to American psychology, which has leaned heavily on the Lockean tradition of the **tabula rasa**. (The British philosopher John Locke taught that the mind at birth is a *tabula rasa*, or blank slate containing no inborn ideas.) In the past decade, however, there has been a partial return to accepting the idea of inborn differences in personality traits. Research evidence suggests that some infants are more stolid than others. Such findings bear a partial resemblance to Jung's notion of inborn types.

In addition to the attitudes of extroversion and introversion, Jung postulated **psychological functions**—processes by which the conscious mind orients itself toward the outer world and the inner world. Jung designated four functions: **thinking, feeling, sensation,** and **intuition**. He arranged these into two sets of opposed pairs: thinking versus feeling and sensation versus intuition (see Figure 2.4). Thinking and feeling are called the "rational functions" because they are used primarily to evaluate ideas. When an individual attempts to make an evaluation of an idea in terms of other ideas, the person will use logic and abstract concepts; he or she may be said to be using the thinking function. Say that another individual evaluates the same idea in terms of the pleasant or unpleasant feelings the idea evokes within him; such a person would be using the feeling function.

Sensation and intuition are called the "irrational functions"; the designation irrational is merely meant to imply that these functions have little to do with conventional thought processes. Sensation and intuition both refer to *knowing about*. Assume that one individual is convinced that all we can know about the world is what we see, taste, touch, smell, or hear. This philosophical position corresponds to what is called **empiricism**, the doctrine that all man's knowledge comes in through the sense organs. Such an individual takes the position, "I'm from Missouri. You've got to show me." On the other hand, say that another individual is intrigued by meditation and the teachings of the mystics. Such a person might be convinced that through the power of intuition, one could be aware of all sorts of things not available through the sense organs. A belief in the possibility of psi phenomena, such as extrasensory perception and telepathy, would give status to the intuitive function.

Jung contended that we all use the complete set of attitudes and functions, that no one is either a pure extrovert or a pure introvert and no one is either a pure thinking type or a pure feeling type. Nonetheless, there is a tendency within us to develop habitual modes of preference. Consequently Jung would contend that there are types, even though the types are far from pure. The problem for the individual arises when the person has become too lopsided in depending on one of the attitudes or functions. Adjustment and growth would imply bringing the opposing pairs into better harmony. One should, for example, recognize that thinking and feeling are only superficially opposed. Both have their place and purpose in the well-balanced personality.

Dream Analysis

Like Freud, Jung believed that dreams have meaning. And also like Freud, Jung agreed that dreams are messages from unconscious levels of the personality. Unlike Freud, however, Jung did not believe that the aim of the symbols in a dream is to act as a disguise or cover for the real meaning of the dream. On the contrary, the symbol appears in the dream because the symbol is rich in connotative meaning. When someone seems dense and cannot grasp an explanation, we sometimes say, "Do you want me to draw you a picture?" The implication is that a picture has the capacity to make things obvious. To Jung, a dream is an attempt on the part of the deeper self to send

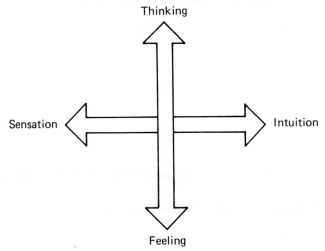

FIGURE 2.4 Jung designated four psychological functions arranged into two sets of opposed pairs.

important clarifying messages to the conscious self. A dream is a projection of "motion pictures" into the conscious mind from the unconscious mind. The pictures aim to *inform*, not conceal or distort.

Because Jung accepted the personal unconscious of Freud, it was also acceptable to Jung that some dreams had to do with personal conflicts, repressed desires, sexual problems, and aggressive themes. Jung felt, however, that some dreams also emanated from the collective unconscious. Such dreams contain an archetypal content—they speak the "wisdom of the ages." These dreams seem to glow in the mind and are long remembered in consciousness as somehow being of great importance. These "glowing" dreams Jung referred to as **numinous dreams**. One example is a dream that sends a warning to the dreamer that the person has taken a wrong path in life, which will lead to possible disaster. Another numinous dream may have a positive motif; it may show the dreamer what he might be able to do with his life if he were to act on his highest aspirations and best talents.

One of my students had a numinous dream in which a kindly magician turned him from a snake into an angel. The magician, the snake, and the angel are all symbols for familiar archetypes. A Jungian interpretation of the dream would suggest that the dreamer is trying to go from a "lower" to a "higher" status in life; it also suggests that he feels he has the potential to make such a transformation. Like Cinderella, however, he is waiting for someone else to do the job for him. But I hasten to add that such an interpretation is risky without knowing quite a bit about the dreamer's circumstances in life and without having heard a series of dreams from the dreamer. Jung emphasized the importance of collecting a series of dreams and searching out common patterns in dreams over a time span.

Freud's method of dream analysis called for the dreamer to free associate to the elements of the dream. Jung rejected this approach. He felt that random associations to the content of a dream led one away from the dream message itself. Of course, free associations do lead somewhere; Jung contended that they always lead one back to the same set of predictable Freudian concepts. The dreamer is led to the Oedipus or Electra complex, infantile oral or anal trauma, and so forth. Thus, following the Freudian method, the unique meaning of the dream for the individual is destroyed. He finds himself at the end of his dream-analysis journey in the same place as all other dreamers. Thus he has got nowhere. He might as well read a textbook on Freudian theory as analyze his own dream.

Instead of free association, Jung used a method that may be called **amplification**, which requires that the individual use his or her creative imagination and elaborate and augment the symbols in a dream. This may be done in a variety of ways: by daydreaming and consciously fantasizing, by taking up oils and painting a picture, by writing a story that augments the dream symbols, and so forth. Jung felt that in this way one is drawn into the inner meaning of the dream and properly identifies with it.

2.4   APPLICATION: EXPLORING YOUR DREAMS

Freud, Jung, and many other psychologists have felt that dreams are messages from an unconscious level of the human personality to the conscious self. The question arises: Can you explore your dreams on your own?

If you adopt a Freudian position, the answer tends to be negative. Dreams conceal and distort unconscious wishes. There is a great deal of repression of the meaning of the dream, creating the division between the latent content and the manifest content. Therefore the meaning of the dream is not easily given up, and the help of a psychoanalyst is probably required. However, even given Freud's assumptions, it might be possible to free associate in writing to the various elements of a dream and catch some glimpse of its meaning.

If you adopt a Jungian position, it would seem quite reasonable that you can explore dreams on your own. You will recall that Jung felt that dreams are meant to be revealing. The unconscious chooses the dream symbols because of their great meaning, not because of their disguise value. If you adopt the Jungian view, there is no reason why you should not be able to draw quite a bit of meaning from your dreams. The method you would follow is direct. Keep a notebook of your dreams. Record as much of a dream as you can remember immediately after awakening. The remembered content of dreams tends to be quickly lost and quickly distorted with the passage of time. Then use Jung's method of amplification. Let your imagination elaborate and augment the images in the dream. As noted earlier in the chapter, this can be done in a variety of ways: By daydreaming and consciously fantasizing, by drawing or painting pictures, by writing a story or a poem, and so forth. As you produce material ask yourself such questions as: What does this mean? What message is my unconscious sending to me?

You would be ill advised to plunge ahead with dream interpretation if all you know about it is what you have read in this textbook. The methods described here are not blanket recommendations for all readers. However, if the general line of self-investigation described above interests you, I refer you to the original writings of Freud and Jung. In addition, you would probably find *The Meaning of Dreams*, by Calvin S. Hall (1966), a useful book. He subscribes to the dream series method of Jung and gives many clues to what various kinds of dreams seem to be saying to the dreamer. Also, *Dream Power*, by Ann Faraday (1973), presents a broad spectrum of approaches to dream meanings.

Jung's approach to dreams still exerts an influence on contemporary psychology. For example, the psychoanalyst Charles Rycroft (1979) presents an approach to the study of dreams in which dreams are understood in terms of an extension of imaginative activity. While his approach is by no means identical to Jung's, there are distinct similarities.

It should be understood that while the modern study of dreams may begin with pioneers such as Freud and Jung, not all contemporary researchers agree with the directions suggested by depth psychology. Some investigators feel that dreams have been overinterpreted. For example, researchers J. Allan Hobson and Robert W. McCarley propose an **activation-synthesis hypothesis**, suggesting that the "main event" at night is the activity of neurons in the brain. Dreams represent an attempt to make sense out of sometimes uncoordinated and contradictory messages arising from somewhat arbitrary central nervous system activity (Kiester, 1980). This does not mean that dreams are meaningless. But it does suggest that perhaps depth psychology has made an excessive case for their importance.

dreams biological (physiological reactions)

The Individuation Process

The phrase **individuation process** was used by Jung to indicate a process of psychological growth within the person, a tendency to become whole within oneself. In his later years, he said that the process of individuation had to become the central concept in his particular approach to psychology. Many people live in a state of self-alienation, divided within themselves. The Animus in a man may be at war with his Anima; or the Anima in a woman may be at war with her Animus. There is a tendency to attach too much importance to the conscious ego and think that is the whole personality; troubled persons try to handle the Shadow and other archetypes that represent their deepest human nature by the brute method of repression. Such inner tactics only aggravate the state of self-alienation.

To overcome self-alienation and attain psychological wholeness, Jung felt that the task of the individual was to become acquainted with the contents of his or her personal and collective unconscious. Jung felt that this was a slow process of personal maturation, not something that could happen overnight. The emphasis is on process, not instant awakening. The individuation process is thus a natural process, an inherent tendency in people—not something reserved for those in psychotherapy.

The task of individuation is to overcome the arbitrary polarity of opposites within the personality. The Anima must make peace with the Animus. The emotional content of the archetypes of the collective unconscious must be acknowledged at a conscious level. In particular, the ego is no longer taken to be the center of the personality. Jung argued that the ego is a false center; it is the center of a self-alienated personality. In this kind of troubled personality, the Shadow is an undiscovered self. In the individuated person-

imp.

(margin handwriting: individualized persons — self actualized)

ality, the ego and the Shadow have overcome their age-old enmity and have learned to live at peace with one another. Thus a new center emerges, and this center is none other than the Self. The Self is the real person, the person that one was always meant to be. Individuated persons are thus relaxed and spontaneous and free to live a rewarding life because they are truly themselves.

In *Two Essays on Analytical Psychology*, Jung writes (1953):

> *Individuation means becoming a single, homogeneous being, and insofar as "individuality" embraces our innermost, last, and incomparable uniqueness; it also implies becoming one's own self. We could therefore translate individuation as "coming to selfhood" or "self-realization." (p. 171)*

It is important to stress that because individuation refers to a process, there is almost always room for more growth in the individual. It is probably better to speak of persons who are well along the path of individuation than it is to speak of a completely individuated person. As long as a person is alive, regions of the self to be explored remain.

PSYCHOANALYSIS RECONSIDERED: THE VIEWS OF A GENTLE REBEL

Jung's break with Freud was distressing to both men. Others remained somewhat more faithful to Freud's basic assumptions, but revised psychoanalysis in important ways. These individuals, known as neo-Freudians (i.e., "new" Freudians), might be called "rebels in the ranks." (Two of these thinkers, Harry Stack Sullivan and Erich Fromm, will be discussed subsequently.) Major attention to this section will be given to Karen Horney, called by psychiatrist Jack L. Rubins (1978) a "gentle rebel of psychoanalysis."

Who Was Karen Horney?

Karen Horney was one of the most influential thinkers in the psychoanalytic movement. During the 1930s and 1940s she exerted a substantial amount of influence on the course of psychoanalysis in the United States. She was one of the principal founders of the American Institute of Psychoanalysis in New York. Her biographer, the same Jack L. Rubins cited above, describes his impression of her the first time he heard her lecture: "An aura of youthfulness— or perhaps more accurately, of agelessness—hung over her. I judged her to be about fifty, though I later learned she had passed sixty." (p. 2)

Horney was born in Germany, in 1885, and received training there as both a medical doctor and a psychoanalyst. She was active for a number of years in the prestigious Berlin Institute, one of the pioneer organizations in the psychoanalytic movement. In 1932 when she was forty-seven years old, Horney came to the United States and began her career anew. She saw patients, gave

Karen Horney was one of the most influential thinkers in the psychoanalytic movement.

lectures, wrote books, and made her distinctive views known. The Karen Horney Clinic in New York remains a distinguished organization. She died in 1952 at the age of sixty-seven.

The two principal assumptions of Freudian psychology retained by Horney were (1) the validity of psychic determinism, and (2) the importance of an unconscious mental life. Beyond these two assumptions, she felt free to reconsider and revise some of Freud's principal ideas. Horney believed that neurotic disorders were not primarily the result of defects in psychosexual development (as did Freud); rather, she felt they were much more the result of defects in **psychosocial development**, the development of a child's relationship to significant other persons in his or her life. For example, it is not too difficult to imagine how cold and rejecting parents or parents incapable of giving sound guidance might produce disturbed children. Stressing the importance of such social factors in contrast to biological factors as she did, we can understand why Horney rejected Freud's version of the Oedipus complex. To Horney, the child in the family does not have a blatant incest wish. The child wishes to have the status and power of the parent of the same sex. Thus a boy may have a guilt-ridden wish to displace the father from his proper station and take over his role. But the sexual drive plays little part in the conflict.

Horney was one of the pioneer contributors to the psychology of women. One of Freud's most frequently quoted remarks is "Biology is destiny." In this remark Freud implied that gender determines a woman's role in society, thus placing somewhat arbitrary limits on the capacities of women. Horney protested Freud's emphasis on biological factors, insisting that cultural factors were even more important. She might have said, "Culture is destiny." A woman lives out a traditional sexual role to a large extent because she is expected to by her family and by society in general. And Horney indicated that the family is to a large extent a mirror of the larger society. In her own life as a medical doctor, a psychoanalyst, and an author Horney followed a course of action that was unpopular for women in the early part of this century.

Basic Anxiety and Neurotic Needs

According to Horney, an infant is born with a need for security. If, during one's early years, this need is not adequately met by the family, a condition of basic anxiety may arise. **Basic anxiety** may be thought of as a persistent underlying feeling that one is alone and helpless in a hostile world (Horney, 1937). The feeling may be present in an adult. One may argue that the feeling is without merit. One can insist that the adult in question has a loving family and friends. But the feeling is beyond logic, having its roots in misunderstandings within the family during a person's developmental years. Indeed, the feeling of basic anxiety in an adult may be unverbalized and covered up in many ways. That is why it is thought of as belonging to the unconscious level of mental life. The person tries to cope with the feeling of basic anxiety by developing neurotic needs, needs designed to control and minimize one's feeling of insecurity. Horney (1937) identified ten of these needs. The individual with a large core of basic anxiety may demonstrate a neurotic need:

1. For affection and approval.
2. For a partner who will dominate a relationship.
3. To keep life constricted and "safe."
4. For power.
5. To achieve personal gain by exploiting other people.
6. For prestige.
7. For admiration from other people.
8. For grand achievements.
9. To be self-sufficient and independent.
10. For perfection, infallibility, and unassailability.

It is important to realize that in one sense all these needs are "normal." It is only when they are excessive, compulsive, and energized by a core of basic anxiety that they may be thought of as neurotic. For example, take neurotic need number 1. It is certainly normal to seek affection and approval from one's partner in a marriage. But let's say that one member of a couple becomes depressed and pouts if the other member does not say, "I love you" at least once a day. Such a demand seems excessive, manipulative, and would be what Horney means by a neurotic need.

Let's take another example. Say that Oscar is an ambitious business executive. Is he motivated by a neurotic need for power? It depends. If he is hardworking, keeps reasonable hours, spends time with his family on weekends and evenings, and seems to have things in balance, we might argue that any need for power that he exhibits through his business activity is within normal limits. However, say that he uses his position as "the boss" to dominate and insult his employees. At home he is also a tyrant. His excuse is that he "is tired" and can't be civil. One begins to suspect that he is more than just an ambitious businessman. He seeks power over others as a way of coping with his own feelings of insecurity.

Horney (1945) eventually summarized the list of ten neurotic needs into a cluster of three: (1) movement toward other persons, (2) movement away from other persons, and (3) movement against other persons. These movements she called **neurotic trends**. The three neurotic trends produce three personality types: (1) the compliant type, (2) the detached type, and (3) the aggressive type.

The **compliant type** moves toward other people by being friendly, agreeable, and cheerful. Such people are often talkative and outgoing. The **detached type** moves away from other persons by being aloof, quiet, and reserved. Such people often seem to be cold and unfriendly. The **aggressive type** moves against people by being loud, insulting, and demanding. These are not pure types, of course. And many subtle variations may exist. For example, an aggressive type may learn to cover aggression by a superficial sweetness—thus aggressively manipulating and using others in the name of niceness. Also, it is important to realize that these types can only be considered to represent neurotic trends if they are taken to an excessive degree. If the person is compulsively locked into one of the personality types, one might be willing to see this as reflecting a core of basic anxiety. Most of us will see ourselves mirrored to some degree in Horney's types. This does not mean that we are all neurotic wrecks.

Sides of the Self

The core of basic anxiety residing in neurotic persons tends to produce an idealized self. The **idealized self** is a perfectionistic image, the self that one feels one ought to become. It is often created by the demands and expectations of one's family, and may not represent the emotional needs of the true self. The **true self** might be defined as the self that one was "born to become." It is that self that maximizes one's unique abilities, interests, and aptitudes. It is what people mean when they speak of "the real me." In persons who utilize neurotic needs to cope with basic anxiety, the true self may be repressed and only half-perceived. A compromise is made in many of us between the idealized self and the true self. The compromise is termed the **actual self**, the self that is brought forth and presented to the world at large (see Figure 2.5).

The compromise between the idealized self and the true self may be visualized as an overlap. If the overlap is fairly large, the person may be said to be well-adjusted. There is a high level of agreement between his deepest desires and what he feels he ought to do. However, if the overlap is fairly small, the person may be thought of as troubled or neurotic. (Horney tended to use the word "neurotic" as a generic term covering a broad spectrum of behavioral disorders.)

Alex provides an example of a troubled person. As a boy he showed quite a bit of drawing talent, and was encouraged to pursue a career as an artist by several of his teachers. Alex himself was enthusiastic about following up on his talent. But his parents discouraged art as a vocation. They felt it was impractical and that jobs would be hard to come by. Instead, Alex's parents insisted that Alex become an accountant and go into business with an uncle who was already a successful accountant. A compliant type, Alex was anxious to please his parents. He submerged his talent and his desires, and majored in accounting in college. At thirty-five years of age Alex is married, makes a good income, has two children, and owns a pleasant home. But he is depressed much of the time. Why? In accordance with Horney's formulation, he has denied the true self in favor of the idealized self. The actual self that he has brought forth is one that doesn't contain enough overlap between the idealized self and the true self. He is an unenthusiastic accountant who dimly recognizes that he should be doing something else with his life.

Self-Realization

Although she thought of herself as a psychoanalyst, Horney's method of therapy relied as much or more on confrontation as it did on Freud's method of free association. She was concerned as much with the present as the past,

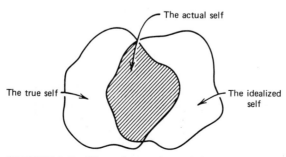

FIGURE 2.5   The relationship of the three selves postulated by Karen Horney. The actual self represents an overlap of the true and idealized selves. It is the actual self that is presented to the world at large.

and encouraged patients to take a hard look at their neurotic styles of coping. She indicated that neurotic styles are vicious circles amplifying themselves. Thus the more one is overly compliant as a way of blocking basic anxiety, the more one relies on compliance. The coping method strengthens itself and tends to become a fixed trait of character.

The way out of the trap is to take a realistic look at oneself as if in a psychological mirror. The therapist functions somewhat as this mirror, giving interpretations of behavior and explaining to patients just how they are using this or that neurotic method of coping. If Alex was one of Horney's patients, he probably would be encouraged to get back in touch with his true self. Conversations with the therapist would reveal his boyhood dreams. He might be encouraged to take some art courses in the evening, and the possibility of art as a career would be at least considered as an option. Even if Alex did not earn his living as an artist, he might receive a great deal of gratification by developing his skills. The process of learning and growing is self-rewarding, and is in line with the needs of the true self. By getting in touch with his true self, Alex might be able to bring forth into the world a happier and less troubled actual self.

Horney spoke of self-realization, and the concept is implicit in the case of Alex given above. **Self-realization** may be defined as making an optimal compromise between the inner urgings of the true self and the demands of the idealized self. One can't completely ignore the expectations of one's family and of society. On the other hand, one must also attend to the famous line from Shakespeare's *Hamlet*: "To thine own self be true."

In summary, Horney was a psychoanalyst who accepted Freud's emphasis on psychic determinism and the importance of an unconscious mental life. However, she placed greater emphasis on social and cultural factors than Freud did. Her formulations concerning neurotic needs as ways of coping with basic anxiety were illuminating. Her ideas concerning the three sides of the self and self-realization were important contributions to personality theory.

NEO-FREUDIANS: FREETHINKERS OF PSYCHOANALYSIS

It is reported that the motion picture producer Samuel Goldwyn once said to author Garson Kanin, "I hear that you are a very clever genius." The exaltation implied by the statement's redundant quality can readily be applied to Freud. And yet, although Freud was "a very clever genius," few psychologists take the position that the whole story of psychology was told by Freud. As we have seen, Horney felt free to revise Freud's views as she saw fit. Many completely reject the entire Freudian apparatus consisting of id, ego, superego, defense mechanisms, unconscious motivation, and so forth. Behavioral psychology (discussed in Chapter 3) disassociates itself completely from Freudian psychology; in many ways it tends to be actively hostile toward it.

Some investigators accept many of the general proposals of Freudian theory, but reject many of its specific conclusions. These thinkers, as noted in the previous section, are termed **neo-Freudians**. These individuals are the freethinkers of psychoanalysis, forming their opinions independently and challenging dogmatic assumptions. The psychoanalytic tradition has produced a number of these individuals. Carl Jung was one. Karen Horney was another. Still another was Alfred Adler (see Chapter 7).

It is beyond the scope of this book to identify every free-thinker of psychoanalysis. (*A History of Psychoanalysis* by Reuben Fine (1979) is 686 pages long.) Instead, two neo-Freudians, Harry Stack Sullivan and Erich Fromm, have been selected for inclusion. Before we proceed, we should note that two common threads unite Horney, Sullivan, and Fromm. The first thread is a common agreement on the importance of the unconscious level of the human personality. The second unifying thread is an emphasis on social factors in development as opposed to Freud's emphasis on biological factors.

Harry Stack Sullivan

Harry Stack Sullivan (1892–1949) was a psychiatrist who did a great deal of work with schizophrenic patients. He placed much emphasis on the role played by **interpersonal processes** in human behavior, which refer to the psychological-emotional exchanges we have with other persons (Sullivan, 1953). As Horney noted, these are particularly important when we are growing up. But Sullivan is of particular interest to us in that he stresses the continuing significance of human relations in the present. He felt that the basic unit of analysis for understanding the person was not the person himself, but *the individual's exchanges with other persons*. To Sullivan, a person is not disturbed in a vacuum. It is a question of *who* is involved in the person's disturbance. Let us not elaborate the point now. Sullivan is generally recognized as an important precursor to transactional analysis (Chapter 5), which views personal problems in terms of disturbed human relations; the importance of Sullivan's thesis will become evident when transactional analysis is discussed.

It may be of some value at this point, though, to introduce at least one other important idea of Sullivan's. He spoke of **dynamisms** in the human personality. A dynamism is similar to the more familiar concept of "habit" or "trait." But the concept of dynamism stresses the importance of habitual reactions to *other* people. Thus a dynamism may be thought of as a programmed response to persons falling within a given category. Susan might always find her heart melting if a man who is tall, dark, and handsome talks to her; Tom, a white man, may always feel hostile when he is talking to a black man; Donald may find himself becoming angry whenever a salesperson approaches him in a department store. These are all examples of dynamisms, and they are all unreflective responses—the person does not think through his or her behavior. Thus dynamisms tend to give human relations a mechanical quality that leaves much to be desired.

Erich Fromm

Erich Fromm was born in 1900 and studied psychoanalysis at the Psychoanalytic Institute in Berlin. In 1972 Fromm published *The Anatomy of Human Destructiveness*, a book that sets forth many of his ideas in their most developed form. Alienation is a major theme in Fromm's writings. To be alienated is to be an outsider. Of course, one cannot be alienated without reference to something or someone else. Alienation is always alienation from.

To Fromm, modern men and women exhibit excessive alienation from two important realms: (1) nature, and (2) other people. We of the Western world are alienated from nature because we do not see ourselves as part of nature; rather, we see ourselves as its conqueror. We use and abuse the earth for our vast technology and think ourselves masters of the world. We must learn to realize that we are really one with nature to guarantee our long-term survival of this planet. Fromm says we are alienated from other people in a consumer society because we have to use each other to "make sales" and "get ahead." Thus people get trampled on and become mere things or objects within the waste-oriented culture. The forces described by Fromm tend to produce neurotic reactions in people and make it difficult for them to live deeply satisfying lives.

Fromm suggests that one of our most powerful needs, a need that is uniquely human, is our need for **relatedness**. The need for relatedness is the need to care for others and feel cared for in return. Personal growth, in Fromm's view, would imply the capacity to overcome alienation and find relatedness. His ideas are closely related to existential-humanistic psychology (Chapter 7).

CRITIQUE

To illustrate the kinds of attacks that can be made on depth psychology, here is a quotation from *Doctor Freud* by biographer Emil Ludwig (1973):

The constant restatement of Freud's themes, the growing acceptance of them by bandwagon-climbers, both professional and lay, does not prove his theories. Not one general thesis advanced by Freud is actually proven in the scientific sense to this day—as any honest psychoanalyst would be the first to admit. But today his teachings operate to undermine effort, especially among young people—to excuse weakness often masquerading as passivity—and to make ignorant folk contemptuous of the cultural treasures accumulated by Mankind down the ages. Seducing all manner of men from the simplest to the most enlightened. Freud's opium endangers our generation. (p. 35)

It is possible to throw all sorts of critical stones at depth psychology. It is far from being an unassailable citadel. On the contrary, it is really quite easy to find numerous weak spots in what at first seems to be a formidable fortress of theory. It is not my purpose, however, to attack and "destroy" depth psychology or any other model for adjustment and growth. The aim of the Critique sections in this chapter and in Chapters 3 through 8 is to help you gain the broadest possible perspective on the psychologies discussed in this book; each Critique may be thought of an outline that is filled in by the content of the other chapters. You should look at each school of thought with the proverbial grain of salt. A bit of doubt will help restrain you from getting carried away and giving all your credence to a particular way of thinking.

The following are some difficulties associated with depth psychology.

1. The concepts of depth psychology are "mushy." Freud, Jung, and the other depth psychologists tend to use large global concepts such as the id, the ego, the superego, the Shadow, the Self, the collective unconscious, the real self, and so forth. These concepts are not well anchored in antecedent and consequent events. It is difficult to point a finger at exactly what events in a person's life history modify these large global agents within the person. It is also difficult to specify precisely what behaviors are being "caused" by the inner agents. Harsh critics would argue that the inner agents of the depth psychologists really represent nothing more than a new demonology. Everything is explained by word magic, by reference to a variety of wonderful and powerful forces within the human personality. To such critics, the problem of depth psychology is not that it does not explain enough; on the contrary, it explains too much.

2. The conclusions of depth psychology are based on clinical data, not on the experimental method. In a proper experiment various conditions must be met. Subjects should be randomly assigned to a control condition and to an experimental condition. Data should be objectively gathered, with an effort to protect against biases of perception. Quantitative data are preferred because they allow for a statistical analysis. The giants of depth psychology—Freud and Jung—did none of these things. They observed patients, their own patients, in private practice. Their sample was not randomly selected, there were no control observations, and no statistical analysis was made. Thus the principal method of depth psychology, the clinical method, is a weak method that does not meet the rigorous demands of hard science. As a consequence, the "discoveries" of depth psychology are not really discoveries; they are interesting hypotheses that require further verification.

3. Depth psychology tends to perpetuate dualistic thinking. Plato, some thinkers contend, made the error of arbitrarily dividing the whole person into a mind and a body as if these two aspects of the individual were separate realities. Freud makes the same error when he divides the personality into two realms, conscious and unconscious, and proceeds to treat these two domains as distinct entities. Jung perpetuates the same kind of error when he

speaks of the collective unconscious mind and the conscious mind. Horney also utilizes a dualistic model of personality when she writes about the true self and the idealized self. A softer criticism would be that the error of the depth psychologists is not so much that they use dualistic models, but that they act as if they were working with discovered realities instead of useful abstractions. The distinction between the unconscious and the conscious may be used as a convenient tool for self-exploration, but it should be recognized that the tool is manufactured by the mind of man. It should, of course, be noted that the aim of depth psychology is to overcome arbitrary opposites within the human personality. Thus in the long run, depth psychology also rejects dualism.

4. Existential thinkers charge that depth psychology is modeled too much after the natural sciences in that it places great stress on cause and effect. You will recall that Freud was a strict determinist: Nothing happens in the mind that is not caused. This, claim existential authors, is not the fabric of our experience. We experience ourselves much of the time as self-moving agents. Our inner reality is not determinism; our inner reality reveals a world where choices are made and there is responsibility for action. Interestingly, you would not find the same charge leveled by behavioral psychologists. They would contend that depth psychology fails because it is not sufficiently rigorous and does not come up to the ideals of natural science. Thus depth psychology is caught between existential thinkers who claim it is too much of a natural science and behavioral psychologists who claim it is not enough of a natural science.

5. Humanistic psychologists contend that Freud and Jung place too much emphasis on the human being's animal nature. Freud's id and Jung's Shadow are representations of basic biological drives. Both Freud and Jung make the set of inborn biological drives the foundation of the human personality. Good manners, ordinary politeness, and so forth represent a thin veneer of civilization—the superego for Freud and the Persona for Jung. Ask yourself this question: Do you believe that biological drives are the only inborn drives? We will return to this question in Chapter 7, where we discuss existential-humanistic psychology.

6. In connection with the criticism that depth psychology overemphasizes our animal nature, it can be argued that Freud in particular made too much of sex and aggression. Although it may be reasonably contended that civilization subjects these drives to a substantial amount of repression and modification, it can hardly be contended that they are the only important themes in human existence. Freud's error was that he made the sexual and aggressive motifs universal explanations of neurotic reactions. This was one of Jung's basic criticisms of Freudian theory. There are other great drives in life. Alfred Adler proposes an inborn will to power in human beings. Viktor Frankl speaks of the will to meaning. Abraham Maslow postulates an inborn urge toward self-actualization. And Jung himself postulates an innate striving

toward psychological wholeness (the individuation process). The frustration of any of these impulses can be associated with neurotic reactions. But we should continue to recognize that the frustration of sexual and aggressive drives remains one of the common factors behind neurotic reactions.

7. Classical psychoanalytic therapy is slow and expensive. A fully qualified psychiatrist of Freudian persuasion charges patients in the vicinity of fifty dollars per session. If you paid the therapist only one visit per week (and many patients go two or three times per week), it would cost about two hundred dollars a month to see a psychoanalyst. A full-scale psychoanalysis takes three to five years; thus the cost of a complete psychoanalysis ranges from seven thousand to twelve thousand dollars! Psychoanalysis is hardly the treatment of choice for the majority of persons with personal problems. Thus the value of psychoanalysis resides not in its capacity to treat a limited number of persons, but in whatever light it can shed on the human condition and in whatever ideas can be adapted from it by eclectic psychotherapists.

It would be possible to go on at much greater length regarding the various problems with depth psychology. But by now you certainly catch the trend the criticisms would take, and there is no point in belaboring the obvious. In spite of the many competent criticisms leveled against it, the edifice of depth psychology remains. Granted, it stands with a few large holes and many small ones in it. But it stands all the same. We would be rash and somewhat foolish if we declared, "Oh, depth psychology is just a lot of mumbo jumbo about the unconscious and sex. Freud was a dirty old man, and Jung was a mystic. Let's get to more scientific matters if we want to understand ourselves." My position is that we have a great deal to learn from depth psychology; its concepts are psychological tools that can help us in our daily adjustment and personal growth.

Depth psychology assumes that you have an unconscious mental life. The ancient dictum "Know thyself" captures the essence of what depth psychology is all about. This dictim is augmented and presented with particular impact in "The Stranger in the Pumpkin," by the poet John Ciardi:

The stranger in the pumpkin said:
"It's all dark inside your head
What a dullard you must be!
Without light how can you see?
Don't you know that heads should shine
From deep inside themselves—like mine?
Well, don't stand there in a pout
With that dark dome sticking out—
it makes me sick to look at it!
*Go and get your candle lit!"**

Go and get your candle lit! That is what depth psychology tells you to do.

We started this chapter with Freud's statement that the mind is an iceberg, floating with only one-seventh of its bulk above the water. Extending Freud's metaphor, depth psychology attempts to give us a radar capable of revealing the hidden outline of the iceberg. Such information may make it possible for us to steer clear of hidden dangers that interfere with living a full and rich life.

SUMMARY

1. A quotation attributed to Freud is, "The mind is an iceberg—it floats with only one-seventh of its bulk above water."
2. Freud adhered to the principle of **psychic determinism**, the assertion that all mental events have a cause.
3. Leibnitz's concept of **apperception** is equivalent to our concept of subliminal perception.
4. Herbart spoke of the **apperceptive mass**, a mental reservoir consisting of all our ideas and all our past experiences.
5. The doctrine of **antivitalism** asserts that life can be explained by the interaction of known electrochemical reactions.
6. Hysterics display the symptoms of neurological impairment, but they are not neurologically impaired.
7. The **primary process** refers to an unconscious mental process by which ideas have nonrational connections.
8. The concept of **repression** is sometimes referred to as "motivated forgetting."
9. According to Freud, the basic component of the personality present at birth is the **id**. It is said to be our deepest self, our primal self, and the source of our basic biological drives.
10. The **ego** is the *I*, or the conscious center of the personality. It is reality-oriented.
11. The **superego** is the aspect of the personality that orients itself toward abstract concepts of good and bad, right and wrong, decency and indecency. In brief, it is morality-oriented.
12. Freud defined **libido** as "psychosexual energy."
13. The five stages of psychosexual development proposed by Freud are: **oral**, **anal**, **phallic**, **latency**, and **genital**.
14. According to Freud, the **Oedipus complex** comes into being as a way of coping with incest fantasies.
15. **Ego defense mechanisms** represent a tendency of the ego to distort its perception of reality in favor of the fantasy-oriented wishes of the id.
16. Freud distinguished a minimum of two levels to every dream: the **manifest level** and the **latent level**.

17. The basic tool of traditional psychoanalytic therapy is **free association**.

18. Jung said that the **collective unconscious** is a very deep layer of the personality. It is said to contain enduring patterns called **archetypes**.

19. Archetypes may be classified as falling into three broad categories: (1) personifications, (2) processes of the world, and (3) systems of the self.

20. The **Anima** and the **Animus** refer, respectively, to the female and male personalities in all of us.

21. The **Persona** is the public self, the social role an individual has chosen to play.

22. The **Shadow** is the animal side of the human personality.

23. **Extroversion** and **introversion** are reflections of what Jung designated as the individual's **attitude**.

24. Jung designated four **psychological functions**: thinking, feeling, sensation, and intuition.

25. Jung believed that a symbol appears in a dream because a symbol is often rich in connotative meaning. Instead of free association, Jung used a method of dream analysis called **amplification**.

26. The phrase **individuation process** was used by Jung to indicate a process of psychological growth within the person, a tendency to become whole within oneself.

27. Horney felt that neurotic disorders were largely the result of defects in **psychosocial development**, the development of a child's relationship to significant other persons in the child's life.

28. According to Horney, **basic anxiety** is a persistent underlying feeling that one is alone and helpless in a hostile world.

29. Horney drew up a list of ten neurotic needs. She also said that the list of ten needs could be summarized into a cluster of three: (1) movement toward other persons, (2) movement away from other persons, and (3) movement against other persons.

30. According to Horney, the **idealized self** is a perfectionistic image. The **true self** is the self that one was "born to become." The **actual self** is the self that is brought forth and presented to the world at large.

31. Horney encouraged patients to take a hard look at their neurotic styles of coping.

32. According to Horney, **self-realization** represents making an optimal compromise between the inner urgings of the true self and the demands of the idealized self.

33. Harry Stack Sullivan placed emphasis on the role played by **interpersonal processes** in human behavior.

34. Sullivan's concept of a **dynamism** is very similar to the more familiar concept of "habit" or "trait."

35. To Erich Fromm, modern men and women exhibit excessive alienation from two important realms: (1) nature, and (2) other people.

Applied Exploration

STUDYING HUMAN SEXUALITY: FROM FREUD TO MASTERS AND JOHNSON

The writer Thyra Samter Winslow made the comment "platonic love is love from the neck up." This witty comment brings a smile to the lips and suggests that nonplatonic love, or sexual love, is love from the neck down. And that's probably the way some people think about sexual activity. However, any distinction we might care to make between the mind (i.e., above the neck) and the body (i.e., below the neck) when discussing human sexuality is, of course, arbitrary. Sexual responsiveness involves the whole person. And that is the approach we will take in this section.

The reason for including a discussion of human sexuality in a book on adjustment and personal growth is quickly apparent. A great many couples experience various kinds of distress in their sexual relationships. Complaints vary from fairly serious problems to differing levels of sexual desire. Understanding the nature of sexual behavior, including sexual difficulties, is of substantial value to all of us.

Freud was one of the early researchers into the sexual aspects of human behavior. You will recall, for example, that his theory of development was a psychosexual theory. In his clinical work he dealt with a variety of sexual complaints. He formulated explanations of why sexual difficulties occur and how they might be treated with psychoanalysis. Other famous figures in the history of sexual research include Havelock Ellis, Alfred C. Kinsey, and the team of William H. Masters and Virginia E. Johnson.

Ellis was an English psychologist and a contemporary of Freud's. He wrote a seven-volume work titled *Studies in the Psychology of Sex* (1897–1928), and did much to encourage the scientific investigation of human sexual behavior. Kinsey was a zoologist who with co-workers interviewed thousands of persons about their sex lives. He was the director of the Institute for Sex Research at Indiana State University, and co-authored *Sexual Behavior in the Human Male* (1948) and *Sexual Behavior in the Human Female* (1953). These books provided important statistics and dispelled many myths about sexual behavior.

Masters and Johnson are associated with the Center for the Study of Sex Education of the University of Pennsylvania Medical School. Their *Human Sexual Response* (1966) brought them fame. It was the first book to report detailed investigations into the physiological responses taking place during sexual arousal and orgasm. Various measurements utilizing heart rate, body temperature, respirations, skin changes, and muscle contractions were made on volunteers who were willing to engage in sexual activity in a laboratory setting. Most of what we know about the physiology of the sexual response cycle is based on their work.

The Sexual Response Cycle

The research of Masters and Johnson indicates that the human sexual response cycle takes place in four stages: (1) excitement, (2) plateau, (3) orgasm, and (4) resolution (see Figure 2.6). The **excitement** stage may be induced by a variety of physical and psychological stimuli. The particular appearance of another person, a smell (e.g., the odor of a special perfume), a touch, or a thought may all be triggers for excitement. The **plateau** stage is a prolonged period of sexual arousal. During the plateau phase the person is said to be "fully stimulated." Heart rate and blood pressure are both elevated. Some subjects exhibit a **skin flush**, a rose-colored mottling caused by vascular reaction; the skin flush is more typical of women than men. The plateau stage may be brief or prolonged, and is to some extent under one's control.

Orgasm is experienced as the height of sexual pleasure. The orgasm itself is brief, lasting about three to ten seconds. (Although the duration can be somewhat longer in some women.) In males, the bladder muscles contract, compressor muscles around the urethra relax, and semen is ejaculated. In

Excitement is the first stage of the sexual response cycle.

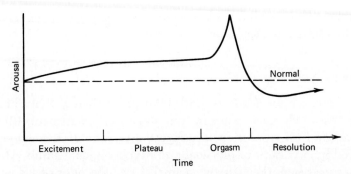

FIGURE 2.6 The four basic stages of the sexual response cycle according to Masters and Johnson. (Adapted from Masters and Johnson, 1966.)

women, involuntary rhythmic contractions take place in the **orgasmic platform**, an area designated by Masters and Johnson. The area includes primarily the walls of the outer third of the vagina. Contractions occur during orgasm at the rate of about one per second. The **pubococcygeus muscle (PC muscle)** surrounding the vaginal channel seems to be an important muscle involved in the rhythmic contractions associated with orgasm. Other muscles may participate in the orgasm. For example, there may be involuntary contractions of the sphincter muscles of the rectum.

The **resolution** stage is the fourth and final stage of the sexual response cycle. Heart rate and blood pressure return to normal levels. The sex flush fades. Various muscles relax. The individual experiences a relief from tension and a sense of satisfaction.

The length of the sexual response cycle varies somewhat between the sexes. The average male takes between three to four minutes to complete the cycle. The average woman takes between ten to twenty minutes. This difference in typical timing can make for problems in a sexual relationship, and these will be commented on subsequently. However, it is important to note that Kinsey and his associates (1953) reported that when stimulation to the vaginal and clitoral area is provided by hand, an electric vibrator, or oral-genital contact, a female can often attain an orgasm in about four minutes. It seems that the difference in typical time required to reach orgasm is not so much a function of a fixed physiological process as it is a function of how stimulation is provided. The act of sexual intercourse does not tend to bring females to a climax as rapidly as it does for males.

Male Sexual Disorders

Men have a reputation for being sexual machines. The healthy male is supposedly always close to ready for a sexual experience. Such a concept may form part of a particular male's masculine image. But machines stop or break down, and men are not immune to sexual disorders by any means. It will reward us to become familiar with the principal ways in which the male sexual response may be disturbed.

Primary Impotence   Primary impotence refers to a condition in which the male has never been able to have an erection adequate for sexual intercourse. This is a fairly rare problem. (The word **impotence** itself means "lack of power.")

Secondary Impotence   Secondary impotence refers to a condition in which the male has had successful sexual intercourse at least once. Often the male has had intercourse many times, and then a problem develops. A male is said to be suffering from secondary impotence when he has an inadequate erection for intercourse twenty-five percent or more of the time.

Although impotence of either the primary or secondary kind is usually explained in terms of psychological and emotional factors, it is possible for either kind to be due to organic factors. Erectile capacity depends on a substantial flow of blood to the penis. Thus in men who are suffering from cardiovascular disease (e.g., hardening of the arteries), there may be inadequate blood supply to the penis (Rosenfeld, 1981).

Premature Ejaculation   If a man regularly has an ejaculation before his sexual partner has an orgasm, he is said to be suffering from premature ejaculation. The condition may be explained in several ways. A psychodynamic explanation suggests that premature ejaculation is a form of passive-aggression. The male who is hostile to his partner may punish her by leaving her unsatisfied. He can excuse himself by saying, "I couldn't help it." On the other hand, premature ejaculation can also be the result of excitement. A young male who is very stimulated by his partner may find it quite difficult to prolong the plateau stage of the sexual response cycle. Healthy males can run through the cycle in about three or four minutes, and females are likely to take ten to twenty minutes to reach orgasm. In view of these facts, it is clear that men often have an orgasm before women have theirs because of these built-in time differences. Ways to compensate for this common difficulty are discussed under the heading of *Coping and Therapy*.

Ejaculatory Incompetence   Ejaculatory incompetence refers to a condition in which the male finds it difficult or impossible to ejaculate when his penis is in the vagina. He may have an erection adequate for intercourse, but finds himself unable to complete intercourse by means of having an orgasm. This is a fairly rare problem.

Female Sexual Disorders

There has been much talk during the twentieth century about "frigid women," women who are "cold" and unresponsive to sexual stimulation. The term frigidity has no clinical or psychiatric meaning. It is a popular term used to inaccurately describe various kinds of female sexual disorders. In truth, there are very few women incapable of sexual arousal. Most women can become excited under appropriate circumstances and with optimal stimulation. Masters and Johnson estimate that about ninety-five percent of women have orgasmic capacity. Nonetheless, there are various ways in which the female sexual response can be disturbed. Some of the principal ways are described below.

Primary Orgasmic Dysfunction   Primary orgasmic dysfunction refers to a condition in which a woman has never had an orgasm, and seems unable to have one. She cannot go beyond the plateau phase either in sexual intercourse or during masturbation. "True" cases of primary orgasmic dysfunction are rare in view of the estimate that about ninety-five percent of women have orgasmic capacity. Just because a woman has never had an orgasm during sexual intercourse does not mean that she is suffering from primary orgasmic dysfunction. Her partner may ejaculate prematurely, or she may not receive enough adequate stimulation. If she can masturbate to a climax, she does not suffer from primary orgasmic dysfunction.

Situational Orgasmic Dysfunction   Women with situational orgasmic dysfunction have had at least one orgasm. The orgasm could have been induced by either intercourse or masturbation. If a woman rarely has an orgasm with her sexual partner, she can be said to be suffering from situational orgasmic dysfunction. Kinsey and his co-workers (1953) estimated that about 30 percent of women do not experience an orgasm during their first year of marriage. Reliable up-do-date statistics are hard to come by. Many contemporary surveys are of questionable value. Let's make the optimistic assumption that more women presently experience an orgasm during their first year of marriage than in the 1950s. Let's also assume that as women build up sexual experience in a marriage or in a nonmarried sexual relationship they are more likely to have an orgasm. Even with these optimistic assumptions it is clear that situational orgasmic dysfunction is a very common problem.

In the context of a discussion of orgasmic dysfunction it should be noted that Freud made a formal distinction between a clitoral orgasm and a vaginal orgasm. A **clitoral orgasm** was identified as one induced by stimulation of the clitoris. (The **clitoris** is the organ in the female that is parallel in structure to the penis in the male. It is rich in nerve endings and highly sensitive to stimulation.) A **vaginal orgasm** was identified as one induced by sexual intercourse alone without manual or other stimulation of the clitoris. Freud felt that a clitoral orgasm was inferior to a vaginal orgasm, indicating emotional immaturity on the part of the female.

It now appears that Freud's distinction between the clitoral orgasm and the vaginal orgasm was an inaccurate one. The research of Masters and Johnson indicates that there is only one orgasm. The physiological response is the same whether it is induced primarily by clitoral stimulation, vaginal stimulation, or a combination of both. Indeed, it appears that the clitoris is the basic female sexual organ, and that when an orgasm is induced through sexual intercourse alone it is because the clitoris and its associated network of nerves are being adequately stimulated. This is important information for both women and men to know. A woman should not feel that she is in any way inadequate because she requires additional stimulation to the clitoris or surrounding area to reach an orgasm. Many women fall into this category.

Vaginismus   Vaginismus is a disorder in which the vaginal opening involuntary closes making penetration by the male difficult or next to impossible. It is essentially a muscle spasm. Causes of vaginismus are assumed in most cases to be linked to psychological and emotional factors. For example, a woman married to a man who suffers from premature ejaculation may find herself involuntarily rejecting his attempts at intercourse. Or a woman with strong religious inhibitions may find herself unable to relax sufficiently to engage in intercourse (Lehrman, 1976).

Coping and Therapy

From the descriptions of the primary sexual disorders given above it should be evident that in milder instances of the disorders a couple can sometimes cope effectively by a combined application of knowledge and common sense. Here are some examples.

Vernon sometimes has a problem maintaining an erection during intercourse. If he takes the attitude, "It can happen to anyone," this will be a healthy approach. If his partner is supportive and imposes no pressure, the problem will not be magnified. When both members of a couple recognize that a man is not a sex machine, but a fallible human being, anxiety about sexual performance is reduced.

Charles tends to have premature ejaculations. He is young, healthy, has a high sexual drive, and the premature ejaculations are probably due to these factors. He and his wife work out a pattern of sexual activity in which Charles provides her clitoral area with manual stimulation prior to penetration. Sometimes she has her climax before intercourse begins. Then they can relax and both enjoy intercourse knowing she has already had an orgasm. At other times masturbatory techniques bring her to the threshold of orgasm, and she reaches her climax shortly after penetration.

Glenda has a difficult time reaching a climax from intercourse alone. If no adjustments are made, she will be one of those who is said to suffer from situational orgasmic dysfunction. However, she can easily masturbate to an orgasm. Therefore she instructs her husband in the manual approach required to bring her to a climax. He is sensitive and willing to accommodate her. She has orgasms with him on a regular basis.

If common sense efforts fail, or if a sexual disorder is more severe, therapy is available. Early attempts to treat sexual disorders often favored a psychoanalytic approach, and the individual with a problem was usually seen alone. The focus of treatment was on insight into unconscious emotional conflicts. Although sometimes helpful, the psychoanalytic approach often met with limited success.

More recently, a behavioral approach to sex therapy has come into prominence. This is the approach favored by Masters and Johnson. The focus of treatment is on *how* the sexual disorder can be modified, not the emotional history of *why* the disorder exists. It is a practical down-to-earth approach, and more than one couple has been helped to cope effectively with sexual disorders. Note that in the last sentence the word *couple* appeared. Masters and Johnson treat the couple, not the individual. The assumption is that a sexual disorder often reflects disturbances in a relationship. The focus of the sex therapy used by Masters and Johnson is on the kind of adjustment skills described in the earlier examples, on the reduction of anxiety, and on the release of unnecessary inhibitions.

Masters and Johnson are not without their critics. As in most areas of research, there is controversy over methods and the implications of findings. For example, clinical psychologists Bernie Zilbergeld and Michael Evans feel there are flaws in Masters and Johnson's research methods and in their reporting of data (1980). Others feel that a combination of psychoanalytic and behavioral methods can be used effectively in therapy (Kaplan, 1974). Controversies aside, it is clear that quite a bit of progress has been made in the understanding and treatment of sexual disorders. There is substantial hope for couples who experience difficulties in their sexual relationship.

In summary, famous figures in the history of sexual research include Sigmund Freud, Havelock Ellis, Alfred C. Kinsey, and the team of William H. Masters and Virginia E. Johnson. The human sexual response cycle takes place in four stages: (1) excitement, (2) plateau, (3) orgasm, and (4) resolution. Male sexual disorders include primary impotence, secondary impotence, premature ejaculation, and ejaculatory incompetence. Female sexual disorders include primary orgasmic dysfunction, situational orgasmic dysfunction, and vaginismus. In milder instances of the sexual disorders, a couple can sometimes cope effectively by a combined application of knowledge and common sense. If commonsense efforts fail, or if a sexual disorder is quite severe, therapy offers hope.

Behavioral psychology sees human problems as the result of learned error tendencies.

Chapter 3

BEHAVIORAL PSYCHOLOGY: NEW HABITS FOR OLD HABITS

Overview

OUTLINE

KEY QUESTIONS

What is behavioral psychology?

Behavioral psychology is an approach that emphasizes the **learning process**. It calls attention to such concepts as **habits** and **conditioned responses**. The subject matter of behavioral psychology is behavior *itself*, not the mind (the subject matter of classical psychology). Thus behavioral psychology tends to downgrade such concepts as the ego, unconscious motives, and defense mechanisms—the stock-in-trade of depth psychology.

How do the principles of behavioral psychology relate to adjustment and growth?

Behavioral psychology sees human problems as the result of **learned error tendencies**. Just as these tendencies were learned, they can be unlearned. This point of view can be applied with equal facility to overt behavior (e.g., chronic nail biting) or to covert behavior (e.g., excessive anxiety). Thus for the behavioral psychologist, the prime pathway toward adjustment and growth is learning new and more effective ways to behave.

Adjustment and growth through the self-modification of behavior is an increasingly dominant theme of behavioral psychology. But the idea is far from new. Consider this poem written more than sixty years ago by John Boyle O'Reilly:

How shall I a habit break?
As you did that habit make.
As you gathered, you must lose;
As you yielded, now refuse.
Thread by thread the strands we twist
Till they bind us, neck and wrist.
Tread by thread the patient hand
Must untwine, ere free we stand.
As we builded, stone by stone,
We must toil, unhelped, alone,
Till the wall is overthrown. *

Contemporary behavioral psychologists would be able to agree with only parts of O'Reilly's poem. They might agree with the "thread by thread" image, which could be taken as a metaphor for the hypothesis that a set of related conditioned responses taken together make up a larger habit. Implicit in the poem, however, is the traditional concept of *will power*; the idea of resolution is crucial to O'Reilly's method. Behavioral psychologists would reject this approach to habit breaking. Indeed, the very idea of "breaking" habits is poor language usage to behavioral psychologists. They would much prefer to speak of modifying behavior or unlearning habits. The advantages of this second approach over the breaking approach will become evident as we progress in this chapter.

O'Reilly's poem does at least reveal that the concept of habit has been around for a long time. The role of habits in human behavior is important. Many people feel that they are slaves to undesirable habits, but they do not know how to free themselves and find a more independent existence.

Of course, habits are not all bad. We need them to function smoothly, to do countless everyday things with a minimum of conscious thought. If professional pianists had to think consciously of where to put each finger, they would be unable to give any attention to their interpretations of the music. The simultaneously desirable and undesirable aspects of habits are well expressed by author Colin Wilson in *New Pathways in Psychology* (1972):

I am writing this on an electric typewriter. When I learned to type, I had to do it painfully and with much nervous wear and tear. But at a certain stage, a miracle occurred, and this complicated operation was "learned" by a useful robot whom I concealed in my subconscious mind. Now I only have to think about what I want to say: my robot secretary does the typing. He is really very useful. He also drives the

---

*Copyright 1913 by John Boyle O'Reilly. "How Shall I a Habit Break?" from *Selected Poems*. Reprinted by permission of the publisher, P. J. Kennedy & Sons, New York.

We need habits in order to function smoothly, to do countless everyday things with a minimum of conscious thought.

car for me, speaks French (not very well), and occasionally gives lectures in American universities.

He has one enormous disadvantage. If I discover a new symphony that moves me deeply, or a poem or a painting, this bloody robot promptly insists on getting in on the act. And when I listen to the symphony for the third time, he begins to listen to it automatically, and I lose all pleasure. He is most annoying when I am tired, because then he tends to take over most of my functions without even asking me. I have even caught him making love to my wife. (p. 4)

Wilson's "robot" is a powerful metaphor for conveying that in many ways everyone's life becomes routinized and much behavior becomes semiautomatic. If this is the case, and if it is unavoidable, the question becomes: How may we keep our advantageous habits and rid ourselves of (or modify) our disadvantageous ones? The balance of this chapter concerns itself with answering this question.

DESENSITIZATION: FIGHTING FEARS WITH FANTASY

One of the principal symptoms of neurosis is **chronic anxiety**, which may be defined as a perpetual state of alarm. The person with chronic anxiety is afraid of his own shadow, a worrywart. He feels that something terrible is going to happen—but he isn't quite sure what. A dark cloud seems to hang over his head. The most prescribed drug in the United States today is Valium, a tranquilizer designed to help individuals cope with unwanted emotional reactions such as chronic anxiety. We begin to realize the great frequency with which unwanted emotional reactions occur when we consider that about 60 million prescriptions are written for Valium (diazepam) each year! And Librium (chlordiazepoxide), also used to treat anxiety, is prescribed about 10 million times per year (Graedon, 1980).

Is there a better way to cope with negative emotional reactions? Behavioral psychologists think so, and the method called **systematic desensitization** is the treatment they specify. Desensitization is a method by which an individual *learns* to respond differently to fear-arousing and anxiety-arousing stimuli.

Classical Conditioning

Before we deal specifically with the method known as systematic desensitization, it would be of some advantage to examine its theoretical basis. One of the principal roots of desensitization is in the work of the Russian physiologist Ivan Pavlov, who made most of his great discoveries about animal conditioning in the early part of this century. He earned a Nobel Prize in 1904 for his work on the functions of the digestive glands, prior to his interest in conditioned reflexes.

It is said that Pavlov's interest in the phenomena of conditioning began when he made a chance observation. He noticed that his experimental dogs salivated when they heard the footsteps in the corridor of the man who was about to feed them. They did not salivate when they heard unfamiliar foot-

Ivan Pavlov did pioneer research on classical conditioning.

steps. In ordinary parlance, we might say that the animals were using the footsteps as a cue and were anticipating being fed. Pavlov found it fascinating that an auditory stimulus could produce a reaction in the salivary glands, and he termed the saliva produced in response to the footsteps "psychic secretion." He decided that it was a phenomenon worthy of investigation.

To make an orderly study of psychic secretions, Pavlov placed a typical experimental dog in a restraining harness. Meat powder was placed in the dog's mouth, and the dog quite naturally salivated to the meat powder. In this instance the meat powder is referred to as an **unconditioned stimulus**, a stimulus to which an unlearned response potential exists in the organism. It is assumed that this unlearned response potential is inborn and that it forms the foundation on which learned responses can be built. The salivary response to the meat powder is termed an **unconditioned response** or an unlearned response.

Now suppose that a dog is in its harness and it has already been established that the dog responds properly to meat powder. What would happen if we provided the dog with a signal that meat powder would be presented soon? Almost everyone has heard of "Pavlov's bell," an auditory stimulus pre-

Both animals and human beings acquire conditioned responses.

sented before the presentation of meat powder. In actuality, Pavlov used a simple tone as the auditory stimulus. With a tone generator he could control precisely the pitch, the amplitude, and the duration of the auditory stimulus. Such considerations became quite important as Pavlov's research progressed.

Assume that the tone is sounded and a few moments later meat powder is placed in the dog's mouth. Assume that this is done many times. These would be considered **training trials**, associated presentations of the tone and the meat powder. After a number of training trials, the dog is ready for a **test trial**, a presentation of the tone alone without meat powder. If the dog salivates to the tone alone, the tone has become a **conditioned stimulus**, or a stimulus to which there is a learned response. The learned response itself (salivation to the sound of the tone) is termed a **conditioned response** (see Figure 3.1). Although the response to the meat powder is the production of saliva, and the response to the tone is also the production of saliva, the unconditioned response and the conditioned response should not be considered as identities. This point will become clearer and its importance will emerge when we discuss aversive conditioning. For now, note that the saliva produced in response to the meat powder is greater in quantity and more viscous than the saliva produced in response to the tone.

A number of phenomena of classical conditioning studied by Pavlov merit consideration. Each of these bears a distinct relationship to the systematic desensitization approach to be discussed later. One of the most important phenomena of classical conditioning is **extinction**, which takes place when an organism ceases to respond to the conditioned stimulus. Say that at some point the experimenter decides that salivating to the bell is a "bad habit." How would the experimenter "cure" the dog of its affliction? The easiest and most reliable method of extinguishing a conditioned response, if the experimenter has total control, is merely to present the conditioned stimulus over and over again without the backup of the unconditioned stimulus. In other words, the dog hears the tone many times without getting fed. In time, salivating to the tone will stop. Thus we can see that extinction is essentially the **unlearning** of a response pattern, not a forgetting of the response pattern.

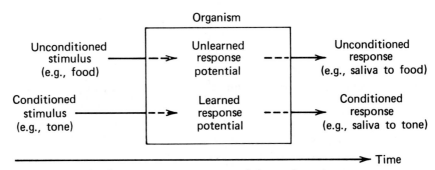

FIGURE 3.1 A schematic representation of classical conditioning.

Assume that a dog has been through a successful series of extinction trials, and it no longer salivates to the tone. Allow the dog a break, or rest period, of several days. Now bring it back into the laboratory and expose it to the tone. What happens? The dog salivates. This kind of response pattern is called **spontaneous recovery**—the reappearance after a rest period of a conditioned response previously extinguished. Spontaneous recovery is often explained by psychologists by postulating a two-factor theory of extinction. During extinction trials, some actual unlearning takes place. Thus the first factor in extinction is the intended one, unlearning. But if extinction trials are too close to each other in time (i.e., if trials are not sufficiently spaced), a second factor such as fatigue or boredom tends to build up in the animal. This fatigue or boredom factor artificially suppresses the extinction response. It is an artifact of the experimental setup, and it creates the illusion that more extinction has taken place than is actually the case. It is further postulated that fatigue or boredom dissipates spontaneously between trials, and thus a rest period allows for the reappearance of the conditioned response.

The phenomenon of spontaneous recovery is particularly important to remember in connection with human habit modification. You may think you have kicked a habit and later are dismayed to find that the habit has abruptly returned. As with animals, human beings often have to go through the process of habit extinction several times before extinction is complete.

Say we are working with a dog that has a strong conditioned response to a tone. No attempt has been made to extinguish the response; on the contrary, we are interested in variations that can occur when a strong and well-established conditioned response exists in an animal. Say we raise the pitch of the tone slightly. The animal has received all its conditioning trials on a tone of a standard pitch, but is now confronted with a slight variation in the stimulus. What will happen? The dog will salivate to the changed tone, but not as much as to the original tone. This phenomenon is called **stimulus generalization**. It can be demonstrated that if the tone is raised or lowered from an original standard tone, the animal will show progressive decrements in magnitude of its conditioned response on either side of the standard tone. If this is graphed, the resultant function on a graph is called a **stimulus generalization gradient**.

In brief, the phenomenon of stimulus generalization tells us that the experimental animal can detect similarities and differences. We may thus define stimulus generalization as the capacity of an organism to respond to stimuli that are similar to an original conditioned stimulus by exhibiting a fractional component of the original conditioned response. As you will see, this principle plays an important role in systematic desensitization with human beings.

Assume that a dog has been trained to salivate to a conditioned stimulus. The question now arises: Could the conditioned stimulus serve as the foundation stimulus for a conditioning chain? To be explicit, say that the dog is shown a circle projected on a screen. This presentation is followed quickly by the sounding of the tone. The dog receives many such pairings of the circle and the bell. Obviously, if we do too much of this, the dog will extinguish its response to the tone. So from time to time it is necessary to pair the tone with food. At no time is the circle paired with food, however. The circle is associated with the tone, which is associated with food. Assuming that the animal has had repeated pairings of the circle with the tone, will the animal salivate on a test trial when presented with the circle and no tone? It certainly will, and this reaction is known as **higher-order conditioning**.

In brief, higher-order conditioning may be defined as a learned response to a second conditioned stimulus in which the learning is reinforced by a first conditioned stimulus, not by an unconditioned stimulus.

Dogs are not capable of building very long higher-order conditioning chains. Human beings, however, are capable of doing so, presumably because of their neocortex, or "new brain." Pavlov considered the extensive use of language in human beings an example of a higher-order conditioning chain. We are capable of giving emotional reactions to words almost as if they were physically present entities. This is evident in the polygraph test, in which pulse rate, galvanic skin response, and other autonomic indicators change as a response to questions posed by the examiner. It is also implicit in the bit of children's folklore that proclaims, "Sticks and stones may break my bones, but words will never hurt me." It is precisely because words can inflict psychological hurt that we feel it necessary to set up a "countervoodoo." Pavlov considered words a "second signaling system" in humans. Words are obviously the main tool used in every form of verbal psychotherapy, and they are used in systematic desensitization to evoke mental images in place of actual stimuli.

Say that a dog has been conditioned to salivate to the sight of a circle projected on a screen. Further assume that the animal has been trained to inhibit salivation when a narrow ellipse is projected on the screen. What will happen when the projected circle is elongated just a bit? The dog will salivate because of stimulus generalization. What will happen if the narrow ellipse is thickened just a bit? The dog will inhibit salivation, also because of stimulus generalization. What will happen if we show the dog a figure that resides between the circle and the ellipse? Here we have a paradoxical situation. Two stimulus generalization gradients cross, and the animal doesn't know what to do. The stimulus seems to say, "Salivate—don't salivate."

If the animal receives many presentations of such a stimulus, it will cease to be a willing experimental subject. The dog will snap at its trainer, froth at the mouth, urinate when the confusing stimulus is shown, and so forth. The animal is "mad," or has "gone crazy." Pavlov termed this response pattern **experimental neurosis** and considered it a model that provides a partial explanation for human disturbances. In recent years, such thinkers as Gregory Bateson (1978) and R. D. Laing (1970) have postulated the psychological "double bind" as an important factor in psychotic disorders. Note that

Pavlov's disturbed dogs were placed in a double bind in which a reasonable choice could not be made.

Aversive Conditioning

Aversive conditioning is readily conceptualized as a special case of classical conditioning that takes place when the unconditioned stimulus is "unpleasant" or "punitive." At a behavioral level, an aversive stimulus is one that an animal tends to escape from. An example of aversive conditioning is provided by an experiment conducted by Notterman, Schoenfeld, and Bersh (1952). The subjects were human beings. A typical subject sat quietly in a chair for ninety minutes while his heart rate was monitored by an electrocardiograph to establish a heart-rate baseline. Then the subject received a moderate and brief electric shock to his hand. As a response, the heart rate increased. In this case, electric shock is the unconditioned stimulus and heart-rate increase is the unconditioned response.

After it was established that there was an unconditioned response to shock, the subject heard a tone just prior to being shocked. The tone and shock were paired eleven times, and then a test trial was held in which the tone alone was presented. There was a heart-rate *reduction* to the tone alone. You will recall that the heart rate speeded up after the shock. In this experiment, the tone is the conditioned stimulus and the heart-rate reduction is the conditioned response. The findings of this experiment illustrate why a conditioned response should not be thought of as identical to an unconditioned response. There are similarities, of course. Both responses have something to do with heart rate. Thus we can say that there are similarities and differences between conditioned and unconditioned responses to paired stimuli, but the responses are not identities. Also, the experiment provides a clear-cut case of the relative ease with which a human being can be conditioned.

Aversion therapy applies the principles of aversive conditioning to psychotherapy. In aversion therapy, the cues that trigger an undesirable behavior pattern are paired with some noxious stimulus. After a sufficient number of pairings, the cue creates anxiety or some other kind of negative emotional reaction (e.g., nausea), and the subject may opt for a different kind of behavior than the familiar and unwanted one. In *Behavior Control*, psychologist Perry London notes (1969):

Conditioned avoidance can also be used to reduce the pleasure of behavior patterns that patients wish to get rid of. To free a man of homosexual desires, for example, the electric shock is connected with pictures of nude males. Each time the patient is aroused by a picture, he is shocked, till eventually the pleasure of the picture is destroyed by coupling it with pain. The resulting "unlust" generalizes to real-life situations where he faces homosexual stimulation. (p. 75)

Antabuse therapy, a form of aversion therapy, is an increasingly popular means of treating alcoholic patients. When a patient is taking antabuse, he or she feels no ill effects from the antabuse itself. If the person takes a drink, however, the mixture of alcohol and antabuse in the body releases a toxin into the blood. The toxin produces dramatic reactions: nausea, vomiting, dizziness, hyperventilation, an increase in blood pressure, flushing of the skin, and an increase in heart rate. If the patient has experienced one or several such untoward reactions, the mere sight of a drink is likely to create anxiety and cause nausea.

Aversion therapy has been used with several kinds of behavior problems including distress associated with unwanted homosexual arousal, alcoholism, smoking, and overeating. Is aversion therapy ethical? Many persons object to aversion therapy on the grounds that therapists have no right to shock people or determine for them what is "right" behavior. If homosexual arousal is wanted by the individual, it is certainly an intrusion on the person's existence to insist that he or she undergo aversion therapy. But if the person is distressed by the arousal, seeks therapy, and feels willing to undergo aversion therapy as a matter of choice, there would appear to be no ethical issue. But it could be argued that even the person who voluntarily seeks therapy for unwanted homosexual arousal has been pressured into it by the generally negative view that society takes of homosexual behavior. Thus the gay liberationist would say that even self-referred persons are victims of an unfree world.

In the case of patients who overeat, there would certainly seem to be no ethical objection to aversion therapy if they are willing subjects. Even in this area of treatment, though, there are those who decry the efforts of psychotherapists—a small but vocal group of overweight persons who might be called "fat liberationists." They argue that "fat is beautiful" and that some people are born to be fat. Again, they see the larger society as a watchdog that unfairly imposes arbitrary standards of appearance and conduct.

As you can see, there are no easy answers to questions about what kind of therapy is appropriate and who it is appropriate for. The debate continues. In the case of aversion therapy, the debate is brought to a head because there is a general loathing in a democratic society to use punitive means to control behavior. For one thing, these means may have undesirable side effects, such as anxiety and suppressed anger. These side effects may occur even when the aversion therapy is chosen voluntarily. Also, it is not farfetched to imagine that such side effects may be complicating factors in stress-induced illnesses. Consequently substantial care must be exercised in the application of aversion therapy.

Aversion therapy seems to point toward a "brave new world" in which human beings are reduced to robots. Such fears are in all probability greatly exaggerated. Nonetheless, if aversion therapy is to be used, a minimum safeguard should continue to be the consent and cooperation of the patient.

Systematic Desensitization

The father of systematic desensitization is generally acknowledged to be Joseph Wolpe. His already classic book *Psychotherapy by Reciprocal Inhibition*, published in 1958, describes how a behavioral psychologist can approach personal problems along avenues not traveled by traditional psychotherapists. Wolpe was greatly impressed by the writings of Pavlov and was influenced strongly by the learning theorist Clark L. Hull's *Principles of Behavior* (1943). Wolpe's work represents imaginative adaptations of the principles espoused by Pavlov and Hill, however. Thus it should be considered as significant and original in its own right.

The first principle underlying systematic desensitization is easily grasped. Imagine yourself at a swimming pool. You stick a toe into the water and withdraw it. "It's too cold to go in!" you declare. A companion who is already in the water calls out, "Nonsense. Just jump in! The water's fine!" You get up your courage and take the plunge. In a few minutes, you are happily splashing around and the water is just right. What has happened? You have gotten used to the water, you have adapted. The word **desensitization** could be used: You have desensitized to the low temperature, and it is no longer capable of evoking a response. This familiar behavioral phenomenon is the foundation stone of Wolpe's systematic desensitization method.

Let's apply the method to a personal problem. Suppose a client has a fear of flying. Further suppose that this is a great inconvenience to him. He is employed by a corporation and will be promoted to an important position if he demonstrates a willingness to travel around the country on short trips when required to do so. He is highly motivated to earn the promotion and thus has a strong incentive to overcome his phobia. Further assume that he does not appear to be grossly maladjusted otherwise. Such an individual would probably make an optimal candidate for systematic desensitization of his flying phobia.

Countless numbers of people have a phobia of flying, but they have no strong and evident incentive to overcome it. Such individuals would not present themselves for therapy. Again, behavior therapy is not designed to "cure" everybody of everything. It is a question of the person being distressed by a behavior pattern or an emotional reaction that is the necessary condition for effective psychotherapy. The necessary condition is not the same as the sufficient condition. If it were, all people who are unhappy with themselves could cure themselves by just wishing to be cured. It is because the sufficient conditions for effective psychotherapy are open to question that there are so many modes of psychotherapy in existence. In any event, assuming that the person who has a fear of flying meets the conditions we have set forth, therapy can proceed.

A first step would be to have the client make a list of fear-producing situations. He is then asked to rank-order the list, placing the least fearful situation first and the most fearful situation last. A typical list might look like this:

1. Reading an aviation magazine.
2. Seeing a movie about flying.
3. Building a model airplane.
4. Having coffee in an airport coffee shop
5. Talking to a ticket clerk about taking a trip.
6. Watching airplanes take off and land.
7. Having a flight attendant take me on a tour of a parked airplane.
8. Talking to the captain of a jet airliner and being shown the control room.
9. Sitting in one of the seats, fastening the safety belt—with the assurance that the plane will not take off.
10. Being in the plane while it taxis from one spot to another.
11. Being in the plane when it takes off.
12. Looking out the window while flying.

The desensitization therapist then trains the client to deeply relax his muscles. Once the client is capable of deep relaxation, the first and least offensive stimulus situation is described by the therapist in such a way as to induce vivid mental images. If the client indicates anxiety, the therapist stops describing situations from the list. Instead, he again induces deep relaxation. This procedure is repeated over and over again until the client is able to tolerate without anxiety presentations that suggest actual flight in an airplane. Of course, the entire desensitization procedure generally requires a number of sessions; from ten to fifteen sessions tend to be typical.

The term **reciprocal inhibition** is used by Wolpe to indicate the importance of relaxation to his form of treatment. If a person is deeply relaxed, he is not anxious. Thus relaxation is a behavioral response that is antagonistic to anxiety. If fearful stimuli—real or imagined—can be produced when a client is in a state of relaxation, the relaxation response will "fight" the anxiety response. This antagonism between the two responses will weaken the association between the fearful stimulus and the involuntary anxiety reaction. In the same way that water is used to fight fire, Wolpe uses relaxation to fight anxiety. This is what is meant by reciprocal inhibition.

Wolpe also cites Hull's principle of **reactive inhibition** and gives it a major role in explaining the effects of systematic desensitization. You will recall that the principle of reactive inhibition was already introduced in connection with classical conditioning. Hull theorized that it is a temporary fatiguelike process and that it acts to "hold back" a response. In view of the contention that reactive inhibition spontaneously dissipates between trials, however, deconditioning is seldom complete in one session. That is why there is a spontaneous recovery of symptoms from one treatment to the next and why a number of sessions are required before extinction of a symptom is complete.

But the real importance of reactive inhibition in desensitization is as follows: Although reactive inhibition dissipates with rest, it leaves a permanent residual called **conditioned inhibition**—a learned tendency to not respond. According to Hull, it accounts for permanent extinction effects. Drawing on Hullian learning theory, Wolpe theorized that every time a stimulus is used to produce anxiety without actual pain or injury, a small but permanent tendency builds up to not respond to that stimulus with the usual anxiety. In brief, systematic desensitization is an extinction procedure. In the same way that Pavlov's dogs unlearned salivary responses to tones, human subjects unlearn anxiety responses to fearful stimuli.

The importance of the concept of stimulus generalization is also evident in systematic desensitization. This is what the word "systematic" refers to. Stimuli are picked that are far down the line on the stimulus generalization gradient, stimuli that evoke a "weak" anxiety response. As these anxiety responses are extinguished, the subject is moved closer and closer to the central conditioned stimulus.

Also take note of the tremendous importance of higher-order conditioning in systematic desensitization. The therapist uses words—not actual stimuli—to produce anxiety responses. It is because of the capacity of human beings to respond to symbols with strong emotional reactions that systematic desensitization is possible as a form of verbal psychotherapy. Our capacity to give emotional responses to symbols is an example of higher-order conditioning. Would systematic desensitization be more effective if actual stimuli were used? For example, if the man with the fear of flying were instructed to actually go to an airport coffee shop, talk to a ticket agent, take a tour of a parked airplane, and so forth—would this be preferable to an office procedure? Many experiments have been designed to answer this question. The answer seems to be that fantasy induction is as effective—perhaps more effective—than actual stimulus exposure. There are apparently at least two reasons for this. First, in an office setting, patients can be relaxed when their anxiety levels get too high. The principle of reciprocal inhibition can be readily used. In actual situations, all sorts of irrelevant stimuli may also produce anxiety and little or no deconditioning will take place. Second, a much greater range of stimuli can be produced in fantasy than is practical in reality. Limitations of time and money make it difficult to expose the client to all the situations that can be generated readily by the fantasy method.

Systematic desensitization is appropriate for a large range of neurotic reactions and symptoms. It is particularly useful for individuals who suffer from untoward psychosomatic reactions: hypertension, ulcers, muscle spasms, hyperventilation, tachycardia (excessively rapid beating of the heart), overfrequency of urination, and so forth. It can be useful to identify the stimuli

3.1   CONTEMPORARY RESEARCH: EVALUATING SYSTEMATIC DESENSITIZATION

In evaluating systematic desensitization, two questions are critical: (1) Does systematic desensitization merely replace one symptom with another? (2) Is systematic desensitization more effective than other forms of therapy?

Symptom Removal   It has been charged that systematic desensitization removes a symptom without treating the symptom's underlying cause. It is asserted that this may result in symptom substitution. For example, a person cured of compulsive nail biting might develop a facial tic. The logic is that perhaps a chronic state of anxiety or nervous tension needs an outlet in the form of a symptom. Wolpe (1974) surveyed 249 cases of neuroses and phobias treated by desensitization. He reported that from 10 to 15 years after treatment only 4 of the 249 patients acquired new symptoms. These kinds of results suggest that systematic desensitization does more than merely replace one symptom with another.

Effectiveness   Wolpe (1981) asserts that systematic desensitization is more effective than other forms of therapy. He says that many therapies report 40 to 50 percent recovery rates; so he takes this range as a standard. Systematic desensitization has to report even higher rates of recovery to consider it more effective than other therapies.

In one of Wolpe's studies of his own work, somewhat more than 200 clients were treated, and they received an average of 30 sessions of therapy each. Eighty-nine percent improved. Among the criteria used by Wolpe to evaluate improvement were: (1) Improvement in symptoms, (2) increased productiveness at work, (3) enhanced sexual function and enjoyment, and (4) better interpersonal relationships.

Outside of Wolpe's own evaluations, there is a good deal of data to suggest that systematic desensitization has reliable beneficial results (Craighead, Kazdin, & Mahoney, 1976; Martin & Pear, 1978). Wolpe (1981, p. 153) summarizes a large amount of research on systematic desensitization (i.e., "behavior therapy" in the following quote) with these words:

Alone among the systems of psychotherapy, behavior therapy yields a percentage of recoveries significantly above the baseline: 80 to 90 percent of patients are either apparently cured or much improved after an average of twenty-five to thirty sessions.

It would appear that research on systematic desensitization offers encouraging answers to the two questions asked at the opening of this box.

associated with these reactions and then put the client through the systematic desensitization procedure.

A problem arises when the anxiety is said to be "free floating." Persons with free-floating anxiety seem to walk about with a dark cloud over their heads. Nothing in particular seems to be the source of their anxiety. The behavior therapist views free-floating anxiety as understandable in terms of stimulus generalization. The individual with free-floating anxiety has generalized his or her original fears to almost anything and everything. The therapist can help the client define a few stimuli or situations that invoke anxiety. The desensitization procedure can be applied to these first, and then other stimuli can be dealt with. By this procedure, free-floating anxiety will decrease gradually.

In this section, systematic desensitization has been associated with the treatment of anxiety and phobic reactions. But, can systematic desensitization be used to treat other negative emotional conditions? For example, can it be used to help persons who suffer from chronic anger or chronic depression? The answer is a qualified yes. We have to assume that the individual's anger or depression is perceived by himself as out of proportion to his life circumstances. We also have to assume that the potential client is sufficiently distressed by his anger or depression to be motivated to cooperate with the therapist. Given these assumptions, desensitization therapy can be applied to anger and depression.

To illustrate, relaxation is not antagonistic only to anxiety; it is also antagonistic to anger. Thus the client with chronic anger can be desensitized by alternating relaxation techniques with descriptions of situations that produce unreasonable anger. To illustrate further, happiness is antagonistic to depression. Using relaxation techniques and descriptions of memories and events that arouse feelings of serenity and happiness, the therapist can induce an emotional state that is antagonistic to depression. This positive emotional state can be alternated with descriptions of situations that generate unwarranted depression. Thus a gradual desensitization to the kinds of stimuli and situations that produce out-of-proportion depression takes place.

Implosive Therapy

From what you have just read, you are aware that systematic desensitization is a careful, step-by-step procedure. In particular, the anxiety of the client is never permitted to mount to high levels. Is there a more rapid and effective way to desensitize people? Would clients be able to tolerate vivid descriptions of horrible scenes that produce an "implosion" of anxiety? The researcher and therapist Thomas G. Stampfl (1967) thinks so. He has done a considerable amount of work with **implosive therapy**, a form of therapy designed to bring a client's anxiety to a maximal level. Like Wolpe, Stampfl constructs a hierarchy of fearful situations with the client. Unlike Wolpe, Stampfl may present descriptions of high anxiety items before the client has completely extinguished the anxiety response to low-key items. Basically, Stampfl believes that clients, in the safety of the office, can tolerate high levels of anxiety. After all, they basically know they are safe. On one level is the vivid fantasy. On a second level is the conscious awareness that the whole thing is imaginary. Stampfl feels that the client can push things ahead at a somewhat more rapid pace than is conventional with systematic desensitization.

It is also the convention in systematic desensitization that the worst does not happen in the fantasy. The airplane takes off and lands successfully. After all, we want to cure the client of his fear of flying, not make him more fearful. Thus it would seem that word pictures portraying positive outcomes would be the common-sense way of proceeding in therapy. But Stampfl believes that extinction of anxiety occurs because of repeated presentations of anxiety-arousing stimuli in a safe environment. This being the case, it would make sense to produce super-anxiety-arousing stimuli. Logically, they would have greater extinction power. To illustrate, an implosive therapist might present a client who has a fear of flying with the following fantasy-inducing description:

Well, at last you're flying. The plane is aloft, and you are thinking, "Hey, this isn't so bad after all. What was I afraid of all those years?" Then suddenly there is a sharp jolt, and you look out the window. One of the jet motors has ripped off and there is a gaping hole in the wing. The rest of the passengers now realize what has happened, and panic is spreading fast. People are screaming. The stewardess is at the microphone begging people to remain calm, but no one is listening to her. Suddenly there is an explosion, and the whole left wing is on fire! The fire is spreading to the passenger compartment, and you will be burned to death or suffocate in a few minutes. The plane begins to spin crazily and nosedives toward Earth. You see the ground rushing up at supersonic speed. Now the fire has reached the people. You see the stewardess holding onto a seat to keep from falling, and her clothes are on fire. The flames are searing her face, burning her flesh. You think, "She was so pretty." Then you realize the flames have reached you. You feel a wetness on your legs and realize that you have involuntarily urinated out of terror. You try to scream, but your panic is so complete that you are paralyzed. There is nothing you can do to help yourself. You are completely helpless, and you face certain disaster as the plane continues on its reckless course to destruction.

Such a description hardly seems calculated to help a person overcome a fear of flying. But the contrary seems to be the case. With repeated exposures to scenes of horror and disaster, the scenes lose their power to evoke anxiety. The first few times clients force themselves to go along with such scenes, they do experience the implosion of anxiety; their pulses race, their hands grow damp, their mouths go dry, they feel faint, and so forth. Within a number of sessions, however, they build up a tolerance for the portrayal of doom and become able to face their fears with equanimity.

It somehow seems difficult to accept that fantasy techniques could have potent deconditioning effects. But, it should be remembered, phobic clients are responding more to their own fantasies than to real situations. It is their own imaginings that give them trouble. Otherwise, their responses would not be considered out of proportion or inappropriate. On the eve of World War II, Franklin Delano Roosevelt declared, "We have nothing to fear but fear itself." Similarly, it could be said that persons with chronic anxiety fear fear itself. Systematic desensitization and implosive therapy turn the tendency to ruminate about fears on its head, and by this method anxiety is made to defeat itself.

BEHAVIOR MODIFICATION: SHAPING ACTIONS

The following statement is credited to the Chinese sage Confucius: "Life is really simple, but men insist on making it complicated." This statement could almost be the slogan of the behavior modifiers.

In *About Behaviorism*, the foremost contemporary advocate for behavioral psychology, B. F. Skinner (1974), observes:

In the traditional mentalistic view . . . a person is a member of the human species who behaves as he does because of many internal characteristics or possessions, among them sensations, habits, intelligence, opinions, dreams, personalities, moods, decisions, fantasies, skills, percepts, thoughts, virtues, intentions, abilities, instincts, daydreams, incentives, acts of will, joy, compassion, perceptual defenses, beliefs, complexes, expectancies, urges, choice, drives, ideas, responsibilities, elation, memories, needs, wisdom, wants, a death instinct, a sense of duty, sublimation, impulses, capacities, purposes, wishes, an id, repressed fears, a sense of shame, extraversion, images, knowledge, interests, information, a superego, propositions, experiences, attitudes, conflicts, meanings, reaction formations, a will to live, consciousness, anxiety, depression, fear, reason, libido, psychic energy, reminiscences, inhibitions, and mental illnesses.

. . . No one has ever directly modified any of the mental activities or traits listed above. . . . When a devotee of mentalism confesses that "we have not learned much about these problems in somewhat over two thousand years of reflective thought," we may ask why reflective thought has not sooner come under suspicion. Behavior modification, although still in its infancy, has been successful, whereas mentalistic approaches continue to fail. (pp. 207–209)

And what do behavior modifiers offer in place of the worn-out mentalistic baggage? They offer the laws of conditioning and the principle of reinforcement. The principle of reinforcement notes that actions are shaped by their consequences. For example, if, when two-year-old Billy whines and screams, mother comes running to him, and if he seems to be whining and screaming more and more these days, we may infer that her behavior is augmenting the frequency of his whines and screams. Or suppose that a quiet young man begins to date a lively young woman. Whenever he speaks, she brightens and makes eye contact with him. On dates, he finds himself becoming increasingly talkative; eye contact is reinforcing talking behavior. Note that the behaviorist studiously avoids explanations that refer to the inner world of the organism. The behaviorist would not say, "The young man enjoys her attention, and he decides to do more talking." What the young man "enjoys" and "decides" are irrelevant and part of the mentalistic domain.

The principle of reinforcement leads to the concept of a **reinforcer**. We can see from the prior examples that a reinforcer is a stimulus that increases the probability that a certain class of behavior will occur. If mother-comes-running tends to increase the probability that Billy will whine and scream, mother-comes-running is a reinforcer. If eye contact from a young woman tends to increase the probability that a young man will talk, eye contact is a reinforcer. Technical distinctions between kinds of reinforcers will be reserved for a later section of this chapter.

Instrumental Conditioning

Earlier in this chapter, classical conditioning was defined and discussed at some length. We are now ready to explore a different kind of conditioning, **instrumental conditioning**, which takes place when an organism learns that certain actions will produce certain results. A common example from experimental psychology is the rat who is taught to run a maze for food. Running the maze correctly is an instrumental action for the rat; it is a way of obtaining food. Correct maze-running can be thought of as a conditioned response. Note that in instrumental conditioning, the conditioned response has an effect. This is not the case in classical conditioning. If the dog does or does not salivate, it receives its food (the reinforcer). In instrumental conditioning, however, if the organism does not exhibit the conditioned response, no reinforcement is forthcoming. This is an important difference between classical and instrumental conditioning, and it has practical implications.

The distinction suggests that classical conditioning is more appropriate for understanding how we learn emotional responses (e.g., changes in heart rate, skin moisture, and blood pressure) and that instrumental conditioning is more appropriate for understanding how we acquire overt behavioral patterns (e.g., tying a shoelace, steering a car, speaking, walking, and writing). The distinction is to some extent a distinction between **passive** and **active** modes of behavior. The emotional response is passive in that it seems to have no particular effect on one's immediate world; in classical philosophy and traditional psychology, it is thought of as **involuntary**. The overt behavioral pattern, in contrast, is traditionally thought of as **voluntary**; it would seem to be only common sense that one moves one's body about by using one's mind and will. Not so, says the behavioral psychologist. The mind and the will are useless concepts. A person moves his or her body about because of what the person has learned and the ways in which that learning has been reinforced. In brief, *all* behavior is conditioned.

One of the first psychologists to study instrumental conditioning in substantial detail was Edward L. Thorndike (1874–1949), who is justly famous for his research into trial-and-error learning. Imagine that you are a visitor at Thorndike's psychological laboratory at Teachers College of Columbia University in the early 1900s. Thorndike places before you a puzzle-box for cats. The apparatus contains a string leading to a door via a pulley arrangement. If the cat pulls the string in the right place, the door will spring open and the cat may escape from the confines of the box to a bowl of waiting food. Thorndike places a cat in the box, the cat immediately reaches out and claws the string in the right place, escapes, and starts eating. The whole process is complete in minutes. "Pretty smart cat," you say. "It knows what's going on! It understood the way the string is connected to the door. I guess that shows you cats are pretty clever and can figure thing out."

Thorndike would disagree with your analysis. He would point out that the cat you saw was a cat who had been placed in the puzzle-box many times. The first time the cat was placed in the puzzle-box, it made many random movements, most of them irrelevant to the problem. It clawed the string as one of its random actions, and it escaped more by chance than by intelligence. But each time the cat was placed in the box some learning took place. Little by little—with many ups and downs in its learning curve—the cat became quite adept at escaping. When the cat was placed before you, it appeared to have intelligence, insight, and thought power—attributes you gave the cat. Pavlov, Thorndike, and other behaviorists have disdainfully referred to explanations of animal behavior in terms of human consciousness as **anthropomorphism** (i.e., having the form or structure of humans).

Thorndike (1911) theorized that responses in the cat's repertoire that were successful were "stamped in" the cat's nervous system. Those that were unsuccessful were "stamped out." What agent or force accounts for the stamping in and stamping out processes? Basically, Thorndike believed, organisms operate on the basis of **hedonism**, the view that pleasure and pain are the main factors in motivation. This is the same view of human motivation that was postulated by Aristotle more than two thousand years ago. Thus if an action leads to a state of **satisfaction**, it is preserved by the organism. Thorndike called this principle the **law of effect**. This law was the precursor to the contemporary principle of reinforcement. The important difference between Thorndike and such contemporary behavioral psychologists as B. F. Skinner is this: The contemporary behavioral psychologist does not speculate that the organism feels "satisfaction" when it receives a positive reinforcer. From a formal point of view, the inner world of the organism's experience is off limits for the behaviorist. The behaviorist is interested in the functional relations between reinforcers and actions, not the thoughts, feelings, and perceptions of the subject. (The term **behavioral psychologist** in this paragraph refers to radical behaviorists. **Radical behaviorism** should be distinguished from **moderate behaviorism**. See the paragraph below.)

Behaviorism has been a vigorous movement within American psychology. Thorndike was really the dean of American behaviorism, although he was not a self-labeled behaviorist. We might refer to him as an objective psychologist; he made no issue of swinging the sword that divides experience from behavior. John B. Watson (1878–1958), as you already know, is considered the father of behaviorism. In the 1910s, he created such a stir among psychologists that he was elected president of the American Psychological Association. His most important thesis was that behavior cannot be explained by making references to **consciousness**. This reflects the view known as **radical behaviorism**. Usually when the unadorned world **behaviorism** appears it refers to radical behaviorism, the kind of behaviorism advocated by Watson and Skinner. More recently, **moderate behaviorism** has made an appearance. Moderate behaviorists are willing to allow that thinking is a kind of behavior. Thus they have introduced the concept of consciousness into behavioral psychology. So it becomes important henceforth to keep in mind the distinction between radical behaviorism and moderate behaviorism. (See the section on cognitive behavior modification later in this chapter.)

Three important figures in the history of American behaviorism are Clark L. Hull, Edward C. Tolman, and Edwin R. Guthrie. Clark L. Hull (1884–1952) was the giant of learning theory in the United States for at least two decades. His great emphasis was on the importance of two theoretical constructs: **drive** and **habit**. The spring that energizes the behavior of an organism is its inherited set of biological drives. Habits are learned by their association with reduced drives. For example, if a hungry rat learns to turn right in a maze to obtain food, and if a reduction in the intensity of the hunger drive is the result, the animal learns to associate the response of turning right (the habit) with drive reduction (less hunger). Thus Hull's theory of behavior and learning is often called a **drive-reduction theory**.

Edward C. Tolman (1886–1959) was the gadfly of the behavioristic movement. Although he considered himself a behaviorist, he labeled his approach "purposive behaviorism" (which tends to suggest that organisms are conscious and that there is some sort of meaning to their actions). Many of his experiments were designed deliberately to embarrass the Hullians. For example, Tolman hypothesized that learning can take place without drive reduction. He and his students conducted a series of experiments in which nonhungry rats were permitted to wander through mazes without food as bait. The rats actively explored the mazes. Subsequently, the rats were placed in the mazes in a state of hunger, and food was placed in a goal-box. Within a few trials, the rats ran the maze with a minimum of errors. When the exploration group's performance was compared with the performance of a group that did not have the exploration experience, it was clear that the rats had been learning the maze while they were randomly exploring it. Tolman referred to this phenomenon as **latent learning,** learning that takes place without reinforcement and lays dormant until it is ready to be used.

Assuming that the human learning process is in some ways similar to the rat learning process, the doctrine of latent learning suggests that we are making connections and storing information almost all the time—even when there is no explicit reinforcer involved. The parlor game "trivia," in which a person is asked all sorts of random questions, provides an illustration: What is Superman's secret identity? Who was the male star in *Gone with the Wind*? Name the three men who traveled with Dorothy in the *Wizard of Oz*. Usually we can answer many of these questions, which suggests the tremendous scope of the learning process.

Edwin R. Guthrie (1886–1959) stressed the importance of **contiguity** in learning. Things that are contiguous are adjacent to each other; they are touching or in contact. Thus if two stimuli are presented to an organism at the same time, the stimuli are "touching" in time and space and they tend to be associated. Familiar examples are the associations we make between thunder and lightning, bread and butter, parent and child, wind and rain, ham and eggs, wife and husband, car and road, and saw and wood. Similarly, if a stimulus is followed closely in time by a response, the stimulus and response become associated—thus forming habit patterns. Familiar examples are the associations we make between seeing a red light and stepping on the brake, hearing a buzzer go on and turning off the oven, hearing a bell and picking up the telephone receiver, and being touched on the back of the shoulder and turning in the direction of the touch.

Guthrie's emphasis on the importance of contiguity in learning was based on a rich tradition of philosophical observation. We have already observed that Aristotle wrote of the importance of the principle of hedonism; he also noted the importance of contiguity in the learning process. In the 1600s and 1700s, the British philosophers John Locke, George Berkeley, and David Hume made the association of ideas a cornerstone of their thinking. Guthrie's contribution resided in his ability to demonstrate the implications, generality, and power of the principle of contiguity. In particular, he developed a number of practical suggestions that are useful when a person is trying to extinguish an unwanted habit pattern. We will return to these suggestions in the section titled "Self-Modification of Behavior."

B. F. Skinner and Operant Conditioning

Who is B. F. Skinner? (The "B. F." stands for Burrhus Frederic, but these names do not appear on his book covers.) Skinner was born in 1904 in Susquehanna, Pennsylvania. Skinner's ambition in college was to be a writer and novelist. In a sense, this ambition has never left him. He has written one novel, *Walden II* (1948), a utopian tale based on his views of human behavior. He has also written and published a number of books that explain his basic psychological position. Skinner has demonstrated a substantial amount of inventive productivity. He designed a special crib for one of his infants, called the "air-crib." The air-crib provides a controlled environment for an infant: The temperature is just right, there are no unwanted drafts, the air circulates properly, and so forth. The infant can stay in the crib without blankets or diapers, thus allowing freedom of movement and eliminating diaper rash.

In World War II Skinner developed a guided missile system using a trio of pigeons pecking simultaneously at a visual target. The pigeons were reliable "pilots," and the system worked beautifully. The Pentagon did not share Skinner's visionary power, however, and the system was never put into operation.

One of Skinner's inventions that has become operational is the widely used teaching machine. Through a learning program, the teaching machine presents material to students in step-by-step fashion. Students are required to make responses. If students make the correct response, they are reinforced by being presented with the next frame. If they make an incorrect response, the program's forward motion is delayed until the correct response is made. The material is presented in such a way that students will make a minimum of errors and a maximum of correct responses. In traditional terms we would say that students are thus made to feel good about themselves, the many small successes improve their self-images, they develop a feeling of competence as students, and so forth. Skinner avoids such explanations. The important thing is what happens on an observable level. If the material is presented in a certain way, and if students become more effective learners as a

B. F. Skinner is well known for his research on operant conditioning.

consequence, that is all that is important. No hypothetical explanations in terms of inner processes are necessary.

Skinner is widely considered to be the arch-behaviorist of the twentieth century. His admirers call him the "Newton of psychology." But his detractors feel he has a cold-blooded and mechanical view of humans and claim that his view of human beings as creatures who lack a conscious mind or an inner autonomy is degrading and destructive.

Skinner's most important invention is the **instrumental conditioning apparatus**, informally referred to as the "Skinner box." The basic version of the Skinner box was built in the 1930s for conditioning experiments with rats. The box is nothing more than a simple cubicle with a lever sticking out of one wall. Below the lever is a food cup. Outside the box is a food bin loaded with pellets. When the lever is pressed, a pellet is released through a tube into the food cup. A food-deprived rat will usually learn to press the lever at a fairly high rate. (Note that Skinner refers to the rat as food deprived, not hungry; he does this to stay as much as possible at the objective level of discourse.)

The Behavior of Organisms was published in 1938, and it sets forth Skinner's first experiments and his basic behavioral system. Skinner refers to his brand of conditioning as operant to suggest that the instrumental behavior of the organism operates on the environment to produce a change in its environment. The environment shapes the behavior of the organism, and the organism in turn shapes its immediate environment. The word operant is used the same way the word operator is used in mathematics. A plus sign, for example, is an operator because it can transform the independent numbers two and three into a five. Similarly, all organisms learn to use various kinds of operants to transform their local worlds. Henceforth the terms **instrumental conditioning** and **operant conditioning** will be used interchangeably. When a rat presses a lever to obtain food, the behavior can be called either an operant or an instrumental act.

Skinner was largely responsible for the distinction made between classical conditioning and instrumental conditioning. In *The Behavior of Organisms*, he designated Pavlov's kind of conditioning as respondent behavior, behavior in which a stimulus produces a response. He noted that this kind of behavior is elicited by a known stimulus. The kind of conditioning studied in the Skinner box, operant behavior, is emitted by the organism, and the stimulus for the behavior is unknown. For this reason operant behavior has been traditionally thought of as mysterious, incomprehensible, and under the influence of free will. Skinner contended that the traditional point of view merely represented a case of murky thinking and that, indeed, operant behavior could be conceptualized as being controlled by stimuli. This brings us to one of the most important concepts in operant conditioning, the discriminative stimulus.

A **discriminative stimulus** is a stimulus that provides an organism with information that an operant act is presently paying off or not paying off. To illustrate, say that a rat in a Skinner box has been trained to press the lever for pellets of food. Now let us place a small light in the box. When the light is on, lever-pressing brings pellets. When the light is off, lever-pressing is a useless activity—no pellets are forthcoming. Soon the rat will press the lever when the light is on and ignore it when the light is off. The light has become a discriminative stimulus, and it "controls" the behavior of the rat. The experimenter can use the light in the same way that a puppeteer uses a string to control a puppet. Viewed from outside the box, it is clear that the rat lacks automony over its own behavior. The experimenter turns the light on, and the rat presses the lever. The experimenter turns the light off, and the rat ceases.

Similarly, Skinner feels that there are many discriminative stimuli that control human behavior, countless cues that set the stage for operant acts. If the cues are present, the behavior takes place. If the cues are absent, the behavior is also absent. One of the most obvious examples would be a high school in which the students are conditioned to go to class when the bell rings. A less obvious example would be provided by "body language," in which a girl's way of sitting next to a boy says, "It's OK to kiss me." The bell and the girl's way of sitting are discriminative stimuli that set the stage for certain kinds of operant actions. The discriminative stimulus in operant conditioning is the equivalent to the conditioned stimulus in classical conditioning.

Kinds of Reinforcers

It has already been noted that a reinforcer is a stimulus that increases the probability of occurrence of a certain class of behavior. If a pellet of food increases the likelihood that a rat will press a lever, then a pellet of food is a reinforcer for the rat. If a nickel or dime increases the likelihood that little Billy will hang up his clothes, then a coin is a reinforcer for little Billy. If the words from a wife, "Great meal, honey," increase the likelihood that her husband will try to maintain and even improve the quality of his cooking, then the particular phrase is a reinforcer for that husband. A distinction of some value is made between a **reward** and a **reinforcer**. A reward is defined subjectively; it is what the giver thinks is of value to the organism. Rewards often backfire and have effects opposed to those intended by the giver. A reinforcer, in contrast, by definition cannot backfire. It is defined objectively and is discovered in an empirical way by observing the organism's responses to various kinds of stimuli. This distinction can be useful to beleaguered parents who feel that "nothing works." It is quite possible that they are trying to use inappropriate reinforcers based on what would be reinforcing to them, not what is reinforcing to the child.

A **positive reinforcer** is different from a **negative reinforcer**. A positive reinforcer follows an instrumental action. The instrumental action is a means of obtaining the positive reinforcer. The examples already given of pressing a lever to obtain food, hanging up clothes to obtain a coin, and so forth fit the concept of positive reinforcement. A negative reinforcer precedes an instrumental action, and the instrumental action is a means of avoiding or escaping from the negative reinforcer. Say that a rat is placed in a box that is marked off into two areas. Area A contains an electrified floor and is painted black. Area B is a safe area and is painted white. Whenever the rat wanders into the black area A, it is shocked. The rat scurries about and escapes into the safe, white area B. If the experimenter places the rat in the box directly on area A, the rat will run to area B. If the experimenter places the rat in the box directly on area B, the rat will avoid area A. In this illustration, shock is a negative reinforcer because it strengthens the likelihood of escape from and avoidance of area A. Escape and avoidance are both operants, or instrumental acts, designed to eliminate shock from the rat's environment.

What has just been described is called **avoidance conditioning**, in which an organism learns on cue to avoid contact with a particular kind of stimulus. The cue or discriminative stimulus in this case is the brightness dimension; a black stimulus says, "Run." Avoidance conditioning is similar to the earlier described aversive conditioning. Avoidance conditioning is instrumental in nature, however; the organism is active and can do something about the situation. In aversive conditioning, the organism is passive and helpless.

One of the interesting features of avoidance conditioning is that it is slow to extinguish. If the shock grid is disconnected from its power source, this will bring about extinction slowly—if at all. The rat has learned to avoid shock. It does not sit around and wait to see if the experimenter has suddenly decided to become kindly. A formal Skinnerian analysis of avoidance conditioning would preclude using such a word as **anxiety** to explain the rat's behavior; the radical behaviorist considers this a mentalism. Nonetheless, one could say that the rat runs away from the black stimulus because it feels anxiety. Whey does the rat feel anxiety? Because it associates the black stimulus with pain.

Indeed, this is precisely the position of the learning theorists John Dollard and Neal Miller. In *Personality and Psychotherapy* (1950), they contend that many neurotic disorders in human beings may be thought of as conditioned avoidance responses. In view of the observation that chronic anxiety is often associated with neurosis, Dollard and Miller's contention seems tenable. Thinking of neurotic disorders in this manner also helps us to understand why they persist year after year. The neurotic individual's anxiety is functional; it is an alarm reaction that helps the person avoid psychological pain. Like the rat, the individual is not about to find out if certain stimuli are no longer hurting. The person is going to get out of a situation while the getting out is good. That certain stimuli, persons, and situations have long ago lost their pain-inducing power is something the neurotic person finds difficult to learn.

Negative reinforcement and punishment are easily confused because both utilize aversive stimuli (see Figure 3.2). But there is an important difference between them. As already noted, a negative reinforcer precedes an instrumental action. In the case of punishment, the aversive stimulus follows the instrumental action. If a rat presses a lever, and receives an electric shock for its efforts, the shock is a punitive stimulus. The behavioral effects of negative reinforcement are quite different. As we have seen, behavior learned to escape from or avoid negative reinforcers is quite slow to extinguish. On the other hand, it is difficult to use punishment as a tool to extinguish a well-established instrumental response. Say that a rat has been reinforced with pellets of food many times for lever-pressing. We know we can bring about eventual extinction of the instrumental responses by the simple principle of nonreinforcement. If the lever stops paying off, the rat will in time stop pressing it at a high rate.

Can we speed up the extinction process by using punishment? W. K. Estes (1944) made an in-depth study of this question and concluded that punishment temporarily suppresses a well-established operant but does not extinguish it. Estes suggested that in the long run the organism must be allowed to emit its quota of nonreinforced operants before the operant is fully extinguished. Other research (Solomon, 1964) suggests that punishment may sometimes be effective in hastening extinctions. If punishment is used, it is most effective when it is (1) immediate, (2) consistent, and (3) allows an appropriate new behavior to be positively reinforced (Martin & Poland, 1980).

From a practical point of view it is clear that the effects of punishment on extinction are often disappointing. Parents who try to punish their children for such "bad habits" as thumbsucking, stealing money, talking back, and so forth often find that the punishment has a temporary effect. The behavior often goes underground, the child becomes resentful, and the unwanted behavior bursts forth again stronger than ever. Similarly, penal institutions

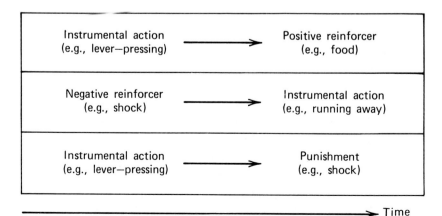

FIGURE 3.2   A schematic representation of the differences among positive reinforcers, negative reinforcers, and punishment.

3.2 CONTEMPORARY RESEARCH: LEARNED HELPLESSNESS

The adverse effects of punishment, pain, and failure have been studied in a series of experiments on learned helplessness (Seligman, 1975). **Learned helplessness** takes place when an organism generalizes its actual helplessness in a first situation and acts helpless in a second situation. The point is, of course, that it may not actually be helpless in the second situation.

Here is a description on a typical experiment on learned helplessness. During a training phase, rats in Group A are placed in a restraining harness and subjected to inescapable electrical shocks. No matter how they struggle, they must endure the pain. Rats in Group B are subjected to the same electrical shocks. But they are provided with the opportunity to jump to a safe side. So they learn that their efforts meet with success. (Each rat is trained on an individual basis.) During the test phase of the experiment, rats from both groups are placed one by one in a tank of deep water. Most rats selected from Group A give up immediately and sink to the bottom. They will drown unless rescued. They have learned to be helpless. Most rats selected from Group B will swim for hours and will not drown until they are physically exhausted.

The rat experiment is dramatic. But it is important to realize that human beings are also subject to learned helplessness (Bugelski & Graziano, 1980). Say that you received an F in algebra in the tenth grade. Perhaps you now avoid all mathematics courses in college. Or say that you have been used and abused by a member of the opposite sex. Now you avoid forming a new relationship. The important thing to remember is that when we learn to be helpless, *we are not actually helpless in the second situation*. We are inappropriately confusing the second situation with the first one. Understanding the way in which learned helplessness works can, to some extent, free us from its effects.

that attempt to "shape up" prisoners by various punitive measure more often than not find that the measures bring about superficial conformity for a time. But in the long run, there may be great discontent, riots, and little real behavioral change in the prisoners. In brief, there is evidence that too much punishment often has the effect of making the punished organism more aggressive (Azrin, 1972).

Do not conclude from the preceding paragraph that aversive stimuli and negative reinforcement have no place in the training of organisms. On the contrary, if the negative stimulus precedes the action, and if the action can reduce the intensity of the negative stimulus, then the organism will learn. To

"Go ahead, Dad . . . release all that hatred and resentment. It's good to get it out of your system."

give a rough analogy, say that a teenage boy has just received his driver's license. His father can say, "Son, you don't have unlimited use of the car. Driving is a right that has to be earned. You have to earn the money for the gas and oil you use, and you have to pay your pro-rata share of the insurance. Before you can start driving the family car around, I want you to make a down payment on your share of the insurance." This hard-line approach is analogous to the principle of negative reinforcement. The teenager can do something about his negative condition. His instrumental actions will bring about a reduction in "car-use-deprivation."

Contrast this first case with another family in which, on receipt of a driver's license, the teenage son begins to drive the car about at his own discretion. Say that he gets into a minor accident and badly dents a fender. Now the father gets angry and decides to punish his son. "You're grounded for two weeks. Hand over your driver's license until you can learn to be responsible. I want to teach you a lesson." This procedure will make the teenager resentful and is of questionable instructional value. Training via negative reinforcement appears to have substantial advantages over training via punishment.

It is not always easy to tell what will be a reinforcer for a particular organism. A major contribution to solving the problem of discovering effective reinforcers has been made by David Premack (1959). Premack has noted that behavior can be used to reinforce behavior. If behavior A is a high probability behavior, and If behavior B is a low probability behavior, then behavior A can be used to reinforce behavior B. Say that eight-year-old Susan has a low probability of doing her homework on her own. On the other hand, left to her own devices, there is a high probability that she will roller skate. She need not be allowed free behavior in which she is eventually punished for not studying. Using Premack's principle, her parents would insist that she do her homework first, then roller skate. Thus studying behavior is reinforced by its association with a positive reinforcer, being allowed to roller skate.

In *Behaviorism in Everyday Life*, behavioral psychologist Howard Rachlin (1980) writes about lower-valued behavior and higher-valued behavior as a basic distinction. (This distinction is roughly equivalent to Premack's distinction between low probability and high probability behavior.) Rachlin notes that when a lower-valued behavior comes first we have a case of reinforcement. He gives this example: eating too much pie and getting a stomachache later is punishment. Painting a fence and getting pie for it is reinforcement. Rachlin says (1980, p. 141), "It depends on which comes first, the worse act (effort or pain) or the better act (eating the pie)."

One of the interesting aspects of reinforcement is the effect different schedules of reinforcement have on extinction. Let us distinguish *continuous reinforcement* from *partial reinforcement*. Continuous reinforcement suggests a one-to-one relationship between the instrumental response and the reinforcer. If a rat presses a lever once, it receives one pellet for its efforts. Partial reinforcement suggests any situation in which there are more instrumental responses performed than reinforcers obtained. If a rat has to press a lever three times in a row to obtain one pellet of food, this would be one kind of partial reinforcement. Assume that rat A has learned to lever-press at a high rate under conditions of continuous reinforcement. Rat B has also learned to lever-press at about the same high rate under conditions of partial reinforcement. Now let us stop reinforcing both rats for lever-pressing. Which rat will have the faster rate of extinction? The answer is the rat that received continuous reinforcement, rat A. Organisms that learn instrumental responses under conditions of partial reinforcement show greater resistance to extinction than organisms trained under conditions of continuous reinforcement. The phenomenon is called the **partial reinforcement effect**.

When first noted, the partial reinforcement effect gave learning theorists quite a pause. For example, Hull's principle that habit strength is a direct function of reinforced trials was discarded. The partial reinforcement effect revealed that an organism with *less total reinforcement* than another organism could have a stronger habit than the greatly reinforced organism. Many theories have been proposed to account for the partial reinforcement effect. For example, there is the **unit-response hypothesis**: Perhaps the organism perceives a set of instrumental responses as a unit or, psychologically, one response. Another example is the **frustration hypothesis**: Perhaps an organism that receives partial reinforcement builds up more tolerance to frustration and thus has more resistance to extinction—is willing to perform longer without reinforcement. Still another example is the **expectancy hypothesis**: The organism that expects to get reinforced every time for an instrumental response will not persist if reinforcement is not forthcoming. An organism trained under conditions of partial reinforcement does not expect to be steadily reinforced and thus continues to produce operants even when there is no reinforcement. One more example is the **discrimination hypothesis**: Perhaps an organism that has been trained under continuous reinforcement can more readily discriminate that a nonreinforcement condition now exists than can an organism trained under conditions of partial reinforcement. To the organism trained under continuous reinforcement, the switch to nonreinforcement is like the change from black to white. To the organism trained under partial reinforcement, the switch to nonreinforcement is like the change from one shade of gray to another shade of gray; it has trouble telling the two shades of gray apart.

The multiplicity of theories offered to explain one isolated phenomenon in learning theory has been noted here to illustrate how many different theoretical constructions it is possible to offer to account for one behavioral phenomenon. For this reason Skinner and the radical behaviorists have no patience with any theory that proposes to explain behavior by processes that go on within the organism. Skinner has little interest in the various theories of partial reinforcement. As far as he is concerned, it is far more fruitful to study the functional relationships between behavior and reinforcement than it is to speculate on the why of such relationships. From a formal point of view, he takes the position that we are quite well off if we think of organisms as stuffed with cotton; then we don't have to bother with elaborate explanations of hypothetical inner processes.

In any event, the partial reinforcement effect has profound implications for behavior modification. Say that a parent wants to train a preschooler to wash his hands before dinner. Should the parent praise, give attention to, or otherwise reinforce the desired instrumental response (handwashing) every single time? This might be useful to get the desired behavior started. But in the long run the behavior will be much more likely to remain a permanent part of the child's repertoire if it is acquired under conditions of partial reinforcement. Keep in mind that classical philosophers and Western tradition have for centuries looked on instrumental behavior as springing from some deep and inaccessible source within the organism. Skinner turned this orthodox view on its head. One of the powerful arguments used to support the view that instrumental behavior is indeed a form of conditioning is the fact that most of the phenomena of classical conditioning, such as extinction, stimulus generalization, and higher-order conditioning, have operant parallels. Working from the premise that instrumental behavior can be understood in conditioning terms, it is possible to make a number of applications to practical situations.

3.3   APPLICATION: BEHAVIOR MODIFICATION AND DISCIPLINE

There are many ways to apply behavior modification. One of the ways that has gained a certain amount of prominence is in its application to child-rearing practices. A number of books for parents and teachers explain how to use the techniques of operant conditioning in disciplining children; one is *How to Make Johnny Want to Obey* by psychologist Stephen Beltz (1971). The faith of the behavioral psychologist is revealed in the title of the book and in the following quotation:

This is a book about how to motivate children. It doesn't attempt to tell you what to teach Johnny or what Johnny should do. It tells you how to get him to do what you, the parent, want him to do. (p. v)

Another book with a behavioral approach, *Successful Parenthood* by psychologist Wesley Becker and coauthor Janis Becker (1974), defends the rights of parents to use behavior modification with their children:

Adults who take a scientifically based approach to the care of children are often attacked for not caring about children by those who call themselves "child-oriented," or "humanistically-oriented." An attitude exists that to use scientific knowledge is imcompatible with being a "good" human being. It can be argued, however, that effective care and caring can only exist when parents know ahead of time how their actions will affect their children; that is, when parents know enough about the learning process to anticipate the effects of their behavior on their children. (p. 1)

One of the main uses of behavior modification in the classroom is the management of unruly children. To illustrate, Lloyd Homme (1970), a consulting behavioral psychologist, was called in to help a teacher manage a difficult group of children. He observed that there was a great deal of spontaneous running and screaming and decided to make use of Premack's principle. Time out to run and scream could be earned by sitting still and paying attention. He shaped and augmented attentive behavior gradually in this manner. In *Behavior Mod* by Philip J. Hilts (1974), Homme is quoted as saying, "We were in control to the extent that we were able to teach everything in about one month that we could discover was ordinarily taught in the first grade."

One of the meanings of the word **discipline** is education. And a *disciple* is one who receives the teaching of another. So it is clear that when behavior modifiers speak of the discipline of children they are speaking in terms of practical applications of the learning process. They see themselves not as judges of children, but their effective teachers. And they encourage parents to take the same practical approach to disciplining their own children.

SELF-MODIFICATION OF BEHAVIOR: BECOMING YOUR OWN PYGMALION

The ancient tale of Pygmalion has fascinated humankind for centuries. In its oldest form, Pygmalion was a sculptor of Cyprus who fell in love with the statue of a lovely female that he had created. He prayed to Venus, asking the goddess to give life to the inert stone. The statue came to life and Pygmalion married her. The George Bernard Shaw play *Pygmalion* and its musical version *My Fair Lady* use the Pygmalion theme. The crude Eliza Doolittle is transformed into a charming young woman by Professor Higgins and his training methods.

The Pygmalion theme fits nicely with the concept of behavior modification. The sculptor shapes the stone. Professor Higgins shapes the person. In a corresponding fashion, the behavior modifier looks on the organism's behavior as a "clay" to be shaped by the control of cues (discriminative stimuli) and reinforcers. Skinner himself uses the term **shaping** when he "molds" behavior

In *My Fair Lady*, based on the play *Pygmalion*, the crude Eliza Doolittle is transformed into a charming young woman by Professor Higgins and his training methods.

in the desired direction by reinforcing successive approximations of the desired behavior.

The question arises: Can you become your own Pygmalion? Can you, by applying behavior modification techniques to yourself, eliminate unwanted behavior patterns and augment desirable behavior patterns? The answer seems to be yes, within limits. Assuming a strong incentive to make a behavioral change, and assuming a basic knowledge of behavioral principles, there are times when a person can succeed in extinguishing a bad habit or acquiring a good habit by his or her own efforts.

There is a bit of a paradox in the behavioral psychologist's use of the word "self" in the phrase **self-modification of behavior**. If the organism has no mind and no world of inner experience, how can it have a self? The self is usually thought of as an inner agent, the person within. This concept does not square well with radical behaviorism. Also, the concept of self-modification of behavior seems to imply that an organism can be subject and object at the same time. The person can be both Skinner and the rat in the box! Absurd as this may seem, we do in fact seem to have some such capacity. Orthodox psychology uses such terms as **reflection**, **introspection**, **insight**, and so forth to deal with this peculiar human talent.

The behavior modifier sidesteps the issues by avoiding loaded words having to do with consciousness. Nonetheless, it seems to some thinkers that buried in the concept of self-modification of behavior is the old and venerated idea of human consciousness. They contend that only a self-conscious organism can be capable of self-modification of behavior. Whatever the case, the behavioral psychologists have much to offer in the way of practical suggestions. If we do not concern ourselves with philosophical niceties for the moment, it is possible to rally around the flag of behaviorism and follow it into some interesting psychological territories.

Cue management

Cue management refers to the control of discriminative stimuli. You will recall that discriminative stimuli set the stage for operant behavior. They inform the organism that a situation is presently reinforcing or nonreinforcing. In the case of humans, many situations and persons cue behavior. Numerous examples can be provided. For example, one alcoholic may drink only when he is alone in his apartment. The empty apartment has become the discriminative stimulus that sets the stage for drinking behavior. Another alcoholic may drink only when she is in a crowded bar with her friends. The crowded bar has become the discriminative stimulus for her instrumental behavior. A third alcoholic may have a drinking buddy. The presence of this second individual is required for the excessive consumption of alcohol to take place. All these individuals might be able to develop practical strategies for managing the cues that set drinking behavior in motion. The first person might find a roommate, the second person might avoid crowded bars, the third person might break off his relationship with his drinking buddy. In operant terms, such cue management would be likely to reduce the rate of responding (frequency of drinking), and some progress would be made with the alcohol problem.

Say that John has a smoking problem. He smokes over two packs of cigarettes a day. Further assume that he has a strong incentive to cut down: His physician has informed him that he is suffering from hypertension. Applying the principle of cue management, John can make a list of the situations that cue off smoking behavior. A partial list might look something like this:

1. Getting up in the morning. The first thing I do—before I even get my pajamas off—is have a cigarette while sitting on the edge of the bed.
2. Coffee breaks. I take at least two a day and smoke with the other workers.
3. Bowling. Whenever I go bowling, I smoke like a fiend.
4. After a meal. I usually stay in the chair at the table and relax with a cigarette and a cup of coffee.

Obviously, there would be more items on the list. Taking only these items, however, John might now ask himself this question: "How can I eliminate, avoid, or suppress these cues?" There are many possibilities. He could get out of bed on the nonhabitual side, take off his pajamas immediately, and go brush his teeth each morning—thus avoiding the situation that sets the stage for his first cigarette. He might take a short walk during coffee breaks instead of socializing. He might avoid the bowling alley for a few weeks; or he could play fewer games when he does bowl; or he could go less often; or he might take up a different sport. He should avoid staying in the chair after a meal is over. As soon as he is done eating, he could rise and engage himself in some other activity. John would be ill advised to attempt to manage all these cues at once. His best plan would be to make a list of cues relevant to smoking behavior and to work on restructuring one or two at a time.

A common problem among college students is difficulty with studying. The behavioral psychologist Israel Goldiamond (1971), worked with a young woman who had study problems. The student complained of feeling sleepy when she was at her desk. Goldiamond's first recommendation was that she replace a forty-watt bulb with a better one. His second recommendation was that she turn her desk away from her bed. Goldiamond further suggested that if the girl wanted to write a letter during her study time, she should leave the desk and write the letter in the kitchen. If she wanted to read a comic book, she should leave her desk and read in the kitchen. If she wanted to daydream, she should get up from the desk and do the daydreaming elsewhere. When at her desk, she was to do her schoolwork. In a rather amusing exchange between Goldiamond and the young lady, the difference between the traditional view of human freedom and the view of the behaviorist is revealed:

This girl had previously had a course in behavioral analysis and said, "I know what you're up to. You want that desk to assume stimulus control over me. I'm not going to let any piece of wood run my life for me."

"On the contrary," I said, "you want that desk to run you. It is you who decided when to put yourself under the control of your desk. It is like having a sharpened knife in a drawer. You decide when to use it; but when you want it, it is ready."

The first week the plan was carried out, the young woman spent only ten minutes at her desk. But she studied for that ten minutes. Eventually she reported that she spent three hours a day at the desk for four straight weeks; she had never done this previously.

The principle of cue management can be generalized to the self-modification of almost any behavioral problem. For another illustration, Goldiamond worked with a young man who overate. Goldiamond notes that food is seldom the cue that sets off eating behavior. In our society food is usually in a cupboard, a refrigerator, a box, and so forth. Television watching, time of day, being with friends, restaurant signs, and other stimuli tend to assume stimulus control over our behavior. Goldiamond advised the young man to find ways of making food, and only food, control his eating behavior. The client was advised not to fight the urge to eat, to eat whenever he wanted to. But he was to give food his complete attention when he ate: he was to put the food on a plate, turn off the television set, and not study or read while eating. Thus television and other cues would lose their power to start sequences of behavior leading to eating. Goldiamond reports that the young man stopped eating between meals within one week. "You've taken the fun out of it," he commented to Goldiamond. Goldiamond saw the young man about three months after he had stopped coming to therapy. The young man had lost quite a bit of weight, and he told Goldiamond that he no longer needed a therapist to help him deal with his problems. He felt in charge of himself.

Reinforcement Management

In the self-modification of behavior, **reinforcement management** is fully as important as cue management. Unwanted behavior patterns can be eliminated or their frequency of occurrence reduced by the method of nonreinforcement. Correspondingly, desirable behavior patterns can be amplified by reinforcement. This is the basic approach used to extinguish and/or build habits in lower organisms, and the approach can be generalized readily to human behavior. Self-application of the principle of reinforcement management for unwanted behaviors involves asking yourself, "What is the payoff of this bad habit? What am I getting out of it? How can I get the same reinforcement value in a more constructive way?" Similarly, for wanted behaviors, you ask yourself, "How can I arrange things so that the desirable behavior will be strengthened by some kind of payoff? What can I make it earn that I really want?"

Let us return to John, the person with the smoking problem. John can ask himself these questions: "What is reinforcing my smoking behavior? What am I getting out of it?" An incomplete list of responses to the question might look like this:

1. Oral gratification. I like to put things in my mouth.
2. Gives me something to do—keeps my hands busy. I often get restless and a bit bored when I socialize.
3. Smoking helps me unwind when I'm tense. It seems to relax me.

Now John has to ask himself how he can obtain approximately the same reinforcement value out of his behavior without smoking. There are a number of possibilities. To illustrate, John could obtain oral gratification by eating, talking, drinking, or chewing his nails whenever he feels like smoking. He could carry with him at all times a package of gum or a roll of mints; these could be used as oral substitutes for cigarettes. John could keep his hands busy in a variety of ways other than lighting cigarettes. Greek men, for example, carry "worry beads" that they take out and manipulate when they get a bit restless. In our society, worry beads are not the fashion with men. But other, rather similar, behaviors might be more or less acceptable. For example, one can fold a small piece of paper into various forms, twist and untwist a paper-clip, or doodle. This may all sound a bit silly, but if you will actually observe people talking to each other in such places as coffee shops and snack bars, you will note many of these behaviors taking place. They generally tend to occur without any particular planning, but the person who is trying to avoid smoking a cigarette can use these "busy-hand" behaviors deliberately. Finally, John can seek other ways to induce relaxation. He might decide to take a hot bath every day on arriving home from work. Or he could become interested in meditation (more will be said about that in Chapter 8).

The main point is that roughly the same reinforcement value can be obtained by a variety of instrumental responses. In Skinnerian terms, a person doesn't have to keep pressing the same old lever to get the same old pellet.

Let us return to Goldiamond's young woman with the study problem. She has a behavior pattern that requires a positive reinforcement procedure, not an extinction procedure. How can she reinforce studying at her desk? It might seem offhand that the good grades she would get for organized study habits would be sufficient reinforcers to maintain the desired behavior. For some people this might be so. For many students, however, the grade is too remote a goal. A more immediate reinforcer is required. For such students, Premack's principle can be useful. Goldiamond's client might ascertain that studying is a low-probability behavior and that television watching is a high-probability behavior. Now she could decide to make television watching contingent on studying. For example, she could "reward" a half hour of study with a half hour of "guilt-free" television viewing. It is important when such an arrangement is made to have the recreational activity follow the "responsible" activity. The instrumental behavior should be seen as the way in which the payoff was earned. This will have the effect of strengthening the instrumental behavior, in this case the likelihood of staying at a desk and studying. Almost anything she wants to do or wants to buy can be used to reinforce study behavior. If, for example, there is a magazine she wants to buy, she might make the purchase of the magazine contingent on remaining at her desk for a specified time period.

A close relationship exists between the concept of feedback and reinforcement. Feedback takes place when performance information is returned to a system or an organism. A guided missile can be kept on a correct course by the feedback principle. A radar system can be used to let the missile know if it is on target or off target. Positive feedback says to the missile, "Yes, you're on target." Negative feedback says to the missile, "No, you're off target." Constant corrections based on the positive and negative feedback keep the missile heading in the right direction.

Similarly, feedback is important in the behavior of organisms. In the psychology of human learning, a phrase used to communicate the feedback principle is **knowledge of results**. It is difficult to learn anything if you cannot know the results of what you are doing. If, for example, you tried to learn to shoot a bow and arrow with your eyes blindfolded, it is doubtful that you would ever develop much accuracy. For human beings, it seems that feedback or knowledge of results is reinforcing; we seek it when we are learning. In the self-modification of behavior, this tendency can be turned to an advantage.

Behavior modifiers often advise their clients to keep an accurate record of the behavior they are trying to change. John, the smoker, could keep a daily tally of the number of cigarettes he smokes. The girl with the study problem could keep a daily record of the amount of time spent at her desk. The young man with an eating problem could record everything he eats. This kind of recordkeeping has the effect of giving people a high-quality feedback. It lets them know how they're doing, and it helps them to keep their bearings.

Anything that can augment the feedback can be helpful. For this reason a number of behavior therapists are having their clients use behavior-counters. The behavior-counter is similar to a golf stroke-counter. It is usually worn on the wrist, counts up to ninety-nine, and can be reset at the wearer's convenience. The behavior-counter lends itself particularly well to behaviors that can be counted easily, such as cigarette smoking. I have used the behavior-counter on an exploratory basis with several overweight clients and have had mixed success. Clients were told to count each mouthful of food or beverage having caloric value. One obese young man started using the behavior-counter with great enthusiasm, became hostile to the whole idea within a few days, and discontinued using it. A young woman used it with great success while simultaneously using other behavioral strategies and lost twenty pounds. The young man was more than one hundred pounds overweight, and the young woman was only about twenty-five pounds overweight. A depth psychologist would probably be willing to speculate that super-obese persons have more unconscious resistance to behavior modification techniques than those with a less severe problem. Thus we see that although the principle of feedback is important in learning, the way it can be used in the self-modification of behavior depends to a large extent on individual differences.

Classical Habit-Breaking Methods

In his book *The Psychology of Learning* (1935), the behaviorist E. R. Guthrie formulated several methods for breaking undesirable habits. They have worn well with time and can be used to improve the likelihood of a self-modification program's success. Guthrie's basic rule of habit-breaking is to "find cues that initiate the action . . . and practice another response to those cues."

As a practical example of what Guthrie means, let us return to the subject of child guidance. Say that Nancy comes into the house every day, takes off her coat, and tosses it on the sofa. Her mother sees the coat, becomes irritated, and tells Nancy to hang up her coat. This has been going on for some time and is a well-established behavioral sequence. Nancy's mother feels exasperated. "Why can't that child learn?" Guthrie points out that the child has learned, and she has learned well. An obedient child, she has learned to get her coat and hang it up when her mother tells her to do so. She has not, of course, learned to enter the front door and hang up her coat. But she has not been cued to do so by her mother.

Guthrie suggests that to eliminate the undesirable behavior pattern, the child should be cued differently. When the child errs and throws her coat on the sofa, she should be told to put her coat back on, go outside, then close the door behind her. Now she should open the door, come in, take off her coat, and hang it up. In this manner the correct cue becomes associated with the correct behavior. The front door is the cue for entering. The behavior of entering is the cue for taking off the coat. Behavior or a response can be a cue for a next response; there is a chain of cues and responses here in which responses to cues become cues themselves. Taking off the coat is the cue for hanging it up, and so forth. Guthrie's concept is valuable not only in child training; it is also useful when we decide to train ourselves (i.e., embark on an attempt at self-modification of behavior).

Several of Guthrie's methods of eliminating undesirable habits are described on the following page.

The Method of Incompatible Responses   The object of this method is to make responses to the habit's cues that are antagonistic to the habit, and make it difficult to perform the habit. As an example, say that a girl has a nail-biting problem. One cue for nail biting is television watching; another cue is identified as "being restless" or "being bored." The girl could decide to keep a nail file handy and file her nails whenever she is cued to bite them. The act of filing the nails is incompatible with the act of biting them. The more desirable act becomes a new habit attached to the old cues.

As another example, say that a mother comes to the conclusion that she has developed a bad habit of screaming at her children when they are disorderly. She also decides that the children are insensitive to her loud voice; they turn a deaf ear. She may, using the method of incompatible responses, decide to write short messages on slips of paper and hand them to the children instead of screaming at them. It is just possible that such an approach may be more attention getting than the screaming and will also be helpful in extinguishing the habit.

Cue Toleration   The cue toleration method, proposed by Guthrie in 1935, is similar to Wolpe's much more recent method of systematic desensitization. One difference is that in the cue toleration method, the actual stimuli are used in contrast to imaginary stimuli. A second difference is that in Guthrie's cue toleration method, annoying emotional reactions are only slightly aroused. To illustrate the cue toleration method, Guthrie gives the example of the way the U. S. Army prefers to break horses. First a light blanket is placed on the horse's back. When the animal is completely adapted to carrying a light blanket, a second blanket is added. After further adaptation, a light sack of grain is added; then a heavier sack. This gradation procedure continues until the horse can tolerate the weight of a saddle. At no point is the horse aroused to anger, allowed to buck, and so forth. The whole procedure is painless and reliable. It is slow and requires patience, however.

The cue toleration method can be applied in the self-modification of human behavior in many ways. For example, I know a man who reduced a long-standing fear of dogs by buying a Doberman pinscher puppy and raising it to adulthood. He wasn't afraid of the puppy, and as the puppy grew up he still wasn't afraid of it. The whole process was so gradual that his fear was never aroused. Was he less afraid of dogs in general? Yes, the procedure resulted in generalization. He is somewhat more afraid of dogs than the hypothetical average person, but much less afraid than he once was.

A person with a smoking problem may say, I can't stand to be with friends who smoke and not smoke myself." The presence of smoking friends is a cue that has become conditioned to the smoking response. Such a person might ask, "Can I stand to wait one minute before I light up?" If the answer is yes, this much delay can be self-imposed at first. The self-imposed delay can be extended after one week to two minutes. Week by week the delay can be

3.4   APPLICATION: NEGATIVE PRACTICE

Knight Dunlap, a psychologist who did a great deal of research on human learning, published a book in 1932 called *Habits: Their Making and Unmaking*. He notes that for some forms of learning, "the occurrence of a response lessens the probability that on the recurrence of the same stimulus-pattern, the same response will recur." (p. 78) This observation led to one of the classical habit-breaking methods, negative practice. **Negative practice** requires the voluntary and conscious performance of the error tendencies in the unwanted habit.

An intuitive understanding of negative practice is shown by the father who lets his school-age son smoke cigarettes until he "turns green." Similarly, a person with a smoking problem might double or triple cigarette consumption for several days until the thought of a cigarette makes him ill.

Persons suffering from various kinds of tics often find negative practice helpful. Say that Herbert has a disconcerting tic—some of his face and neck muscles contract involuntarily. This is particularly embarrassing in social situations. Using the method of negative practice, he might spend two ten-minute sessions per day in front of the mirror in his bathroom consciously contracting the muscles involved in the tic. This procedure will tend to have a short-run effect of producing some fatigue in the muscles used in the tic, thus reducing the likelihood of the tic's spontaneous occurrence. As a long-run habit-breaking method, it seems that some kind of voluntary control over the muscles is gained, which also reduces the spontaneous appearance of the tic.

An irritating spelling error can also be corrected by the use of exhaustion. Say that you tend to misspell the word recommend. You spell it r-e-c-c-o-m-e-n-d. You have looked it up many times, each time checking to see if it has one c and two m's or two c's and one m. Using negative practice, you could write the word *incorrectly* twenty or thirty times, each time saying to yourself, "This is *not* the right way to spell it." When you come to the word again, you are very unlikely to make the error involuntarily.

Negative practice can be quite useful in the self-modification of behavior. If you have a habit you want to break, ask yourself if there is any practical way that you can voluntarily and consciously practice the error tendencies involved in the habit. If there is, you might find that negative practice is a method you can put to good use.

continued until the person may eventually be able to tolerate a whole fifteen-minute coffee break in the company of others.

Similarly, a person with an eating problem may find ways to impose small delays on eating in the presence of conditioned cues. For example, an overweight homemaker may report a problem with eating between meals, particularly when she is alone in the house. I have sometimes suggested to such women that a three-minute egg timer can be used to impose a delay between whatever cues them to eat and the eating response itself. First the person learns to tolerate a three-minute delay. This in itself is a success experience. It shows her that some degree of self-modification of behavior is possible; the case is not hopeless. With practice, the delay can be increased to the point where the conditioned cues no longer evoke the response. At this point the habit is broken or, in somewhat more precise language, extinguished.

As you can tell from the preceding material, there are many ways the self-modification of behavior can be accomplished successfully. It is one of the capacities of the human organism that one can sometimes be one's own Pygmalion.

COGNITIVE BEHAVIOR MODIFICATION: IS THINKING A KIND OF BEHAVIOR?

Imagine yourself sitting in a chair reading a book. You turn a page. Is this behavior? This question presents no problem. We'll agree that turning a page can be thought of as behavior. Let's say you next start to think about what you are reading. Is your thinking also a kind of behavior? This second question is not as easy to answer as the first one, and it has important implications for behavioral psychology.

Viewpoints on Behavior

The behavior modification methods discussed in the previous sections focus on **overt behavior**, behavior that is observable. This reflects the emphasis of the principal founders of behaviorism—persons such as Pavlov, Thorndike, Watson, and Skinner. When the unadorned word **behavior** is used, it is usually observable behavior that is being referred to. It is possible to define behavior narrowly as any observable action of the organism. This is traditional, and is the viewpoint associated with radical behaviorism. You will recall that radical behaviorism asserts that it is not necessary to introduce the concept of consciousness to explain, predict, or control behavior.

However, moderate behaviorists assert that any response or activity—public or private—can be thought of as behavior. Thus to a moderate behaviorist thinking is a kind of behavior. It is **covert behavior**, behavior that is hidden or unobservable to an external observer. Thinking is this kind of behavior. You *know* when and what you are thinking even if others do not. A

Turning a page when you are reading a book is clearly behavior. However, is the thinking you do as you read also a kind of behavior?

thought can even be identified as an operant if it has some eventual consequence. For example, say you think, "I'm going to sharpen the pencil." Then you actually carry out the action of sharpening the pencil. It can be argued that your thought has the status of a **covert operant**, an operant hidden within you—but an operant nonetheless. It has been suggested that this kind of operant be called a **coverant** (Homme, 1970). The argument runs that a coverant, or covert operant, is subject to the laws of learning. It can be acquired or extinguished or modified like any other behavior.

This brings us to the view in behavioral psychology known as **cognitive behavior modification**. The word *cognition* refers to knowing or awareness, and includes thinking. (The familiar word *recognize* literally means to "know again.") Thus cognitive behavior modification is an approach in which thought itself is shaped. It is assumed by cognitive behavior modifiers that a thought often precedes an overt action. So cognitive behavior modifiers make thoughts themselves the object of their intervention.

It should be noted that this section on cognitive behavior modification anticipates to a certain extent the material in Chapter 4, "Cognitive Psychology: The Power of Clear Thinking"; it could have been introduced in that chapter or, as it is, in this one. The choice was somewhat arbitrary. It is included here because it is associated with behavioral psychology and arises from the tradition of behaviorism. Also, the emphasis in cognitive behavior modification is on *learning*, the principal focus of behavioral psychology. But in fact the gap between behavioral psychology and cognitive psychology has been closed to some extent by the introduction into behavioral psychology of cognitive behavior modification.

Training Methods

The practical side of cognitive behavior modification resides in its training methods. These are useful in behavior therapy and also in the self-modification of behavior (Meichenbaum, 1977; Mahoney, 1980). Some training methods are identified below.

Stress-Inoculation Training   Stress-inoculation training involves preparing oneself ahead of time to cope with a stressful situation. Let's say that Maria is to be interviewed tomorrow for an important new job. The situation will be stressful, and she is understandably apprehensive about the forthcoming interview. Using stress-inoculation training, Maria can do a number of things. She can visualize the outcome of the interview in positive terms: the interviewer likes her and things go well. She can mentally review how well prepared she is for the position she is applying for. She can realize that she doesn't have to totally eliminate anxiety, just keep it within reasonable bounds. These and similar procedures will "inoculate" her ahead of time and help her cope successfully with the interview.

Cognitive Restructuring   Cognitive restructuring refers to changing the form and content of one's ideas. Common sense tells us that our ideas may affect both our emotional states and our behavior. Say that Leroy has the persistent thought, "You can't trust women." It is almost inevitable that he will be edgy in the presence of women and have a hard time establishing a close affectional bond with a woman. If he can learn to change his thought to the more rational, "Some women can be trusted and some women can't," this should have a beneficial impact on his relations with the opposite sex. Cognitive restructuring is dealt with at further length in Chapter 4, and it will not be elaborated on here.

Gradation   Gradation is defined as dividing a difficult challenge into small, manageable steps and coping with them one at a time (Mahoney, 1980). Say that David has been assigned a term paper in his biology class. He feels overwhelmed by the assignment, even though he has ten weeks to do it. Using gradation, he would list the small steps involved in completing the assignment: (1) Choose an interesting topic from the list of topics presented by the instructor, (2) do some background reading on the topic, (3) make up a file of references and notes on index cards, (4) obtain a standard term paper style manual, (5) draw up a topical outline for the paper, (6) decide on the length of the paper, (7) write a rough draft of the paper, (8) set the paper aside for a

3.5 APPLICATION: SELF-INSTRUCTIONAL TRAINING

It has been observed that children often talk out loud to themselves before they do things. This is particularly true of pre-schoolers. They give themselves instructions such as, "I've got to hold the pencil in my right hand," or "I'm going to put the red book on top of the yellow book." Evidence suggests that these overt statements drop out and eventually become thoughts. So an older child, or an adult, simply thinks, "I'm going to put the red book on top of the yellow book" without announcing it for the whole world to hear.

If there exists behavior that you seek to modify, it may be helpful to return briefly to the talking out loud stage. Say that you want to cut down on impulsive purchases made at the supermarket. As you drive to the store, you can say to yourself out loud, "I'm only going to buy things on my shopping list today." In other words you give yourself overt instructions. If you do this often enough, you will become conditioned to think the self-instructional thoughts without a voluntary effort.

It has been jokingly observed by some critics of cognitive behavior modification that only pre-schoolers and mental patients talk to themselves. So it is probably prudent to use self-instructional training when alone. It is also possible to mutter, whisper or write yourself notes as alternative forms of self-instruction.

few days before editing it, (9) revise and edit the paper as one imagines the instructor might edit it, (10) write the final draft. Although the assignment "Write a term paper" might seem overwhelming, it does not seem nearly as overwhelming when it is broken down into a series of small steps.

Thought Stopping   Thought stopping requires that one call a halt to an unproductive chain of thought. Say that Nadine has been divorced for two years. Sometimes she finds herself thinking, "I wish Harry had tried to communicate more when we were married. If only he had been less stubborn. I really loved him, but he was insensitive. I wish I could turn back the clock and we could try again." Nadine has found that thoughts like this depress her. Harry has left the state and is in reality out of her life. So when she begins to run off an unproductive chain of thought she visualizes a stop sign with the big capital letters STOP! Or she visualizes a policeman's hand and a whistle blowing, both calling a halt to her pointless ruminations.

Scarlett O'Hara, the heroine of *Gone With the Wind*, was an expert at thought stopping. In more than one place in the novel she says, "I won't think about that now. I'll think about it tomorrow." She stops self-pitying thoughts and gets on with the business of living.

Thought Substitution   Thought substitution is a skill that can be used to augment thought stopping. When a thought has been stopped it is often useful to substitute a thought that is antagonistic to it. For example, Nadine (see above) can voluntarily think, "Wishing won't make it so. I'm not going to spend my life thinking about things that might have been. I'm better off facing facts and moving on." Sometimes one can introduce a distracting thought. For example, one can mentally recite a favorite poem or song.

CRITIQUE

In spite of its success and popularity, behavioral psychology is far from problem-free. There is something about the behavioral approach that seems to make certain kinds of people start "frothing at the mouth" and making noises like mad dogs. The tender-minded person who has great hopes for humanity tends to detest the kind of psychologist who explains human behavior by drawing parallels with salivating dogs, lever-pressing rats, and pecking pigeons. Those who are hostile to behavioral psychology have presented a number of challenges to its authority. Let us examine some of these challenges. It is important to note that most of the challenges listed below pertain primarily to radical behaviorism, which denies the importance of consciousness, *not* to cognitive behavior modification, which allows that consciousness and thought are important aspects of human behavior.

1. Radical behaviorism grossly oversimplifies the nature of human existence. In *The Ghost in the Machine*, Arthur Koestler (1967), a well-known author and social philosopher, writes:

Behaviourism is indeed a kind of flat-earth view of the mind. Or to change the metaphor: it has replaced the anthropomorphic fallacy—ascribing to animals human faculties and sentiments—with the opposite fallacy: denying man faculties not found in lower animals; it has substituted for the erstwhile anthropomorphic view of the rat, a ratomorphic view of man. . . . Its declared aim, "to predict and to control human activity as physical scientists control and manipulate other natural phenomena," sounds as nasty as it is naive. Werner Heisenberg, one of the greatest living physical scientists, has laconically declared: "Nature is unpredictable"; it seems rather absurd to deny the living organism even that degree of unpredictability which quantum physics accord to inanimate nature. (p. 17)

Behaviorists would reply that one aim of science is to simplify complex phenomena. It could also be argued that even if total prediction and control of behavior is impractical, partial prediction and control is a realistic goal.

2. Behavioral psychology in general and radical behaviorism in particular deny the existence of free will. Thinkers in theological, existential, and humanistic traditions take behaviorists to task for their position on free will. It

is argued by the more tender-minded thinkers that to deny free will is absurd. We experience ourselves as free; a primary datum of human existence is our inner awareness of the capacity to make decisions and choices. This criticism of behaviorism is implicit in Koestler's reference to the physicist Heisenberg. Heisenberg's principle of indeterminacy in physics is often cited as evidence in favor of the existence of a free will in humans. Sophisticated behavioral psychologists respond to their critics by saying that they are not making statements about Ultimate Reality; they do not pretend to be metaphysicians. They are talking about the here and the now, what can be measured and observed. Under these conditions, they feel that the predictability of human behavior is an excellent **working hypothesis**. In terms of the modification of behavior, it is possible to get more mileage out of a conditioning approach than a free-will approach.

3. Radical behaviorism denies the importance of consciousness. This seems like some sort of joke. We all know we are conscious. Critics of behaviorism assert that behaviorists must be idiots or malicious villains to try to take away from human beings so precious a possession as consciousness. Advocates of behaviorism could again talk about the working hypothesis versus Ultimate Reality. They would point out that behaviorists feel it is more fruitful from a scientific point of view to do research and sometimes therapy as if the organism were not self-aware. Acknowledging the consciousness of the organism takes behavioral scientists in the wrong direction. It takes them away from the functional analysis of behavior in terms of the physical and social environment. Instead, they end up in the head, heart, or soul of the individual—making the person the prime cause of his or her behavior. To behaviorists this is a serious error and a major problem with explanations of behavior in terms of such familiar concepts as free will and consciousness. For these reasons, radical behaviorists adopt the formal position that the organism is not conscious.

4. Behaviorists are quick to charge other schools of psychology with sloppy thinking. Behaviorists themselves, however, tend to be sloppy when they start counseling others. Their elegant ideas are often left behind when it comes to doing practical work with troubled clients. For example, Wolpe draws from Pavlovian and Hullian theory for his concept of desensitization. But Pavlov and Hull worked with actual stimuli; Wolpe works with imaginary stimuli. There seems to be a world of difference. Indeed, doesn't the use of imaginary stimuli and fantasy imply that the subject is conscious? "I'm confused!" cries out the beginning student. To clarify the situation, let us note that there are behaviorists and then there are behaviorists. In other words, behaviorism is not itself a unitary and completely consistent approach. It is true that radical behaviorists would not speak of imaginary stimuli and/or fantasy images. But as the behavioral approach has matured, many behaviorists, particularly behavior therapists, have tended to seek a middle ground. Thus we might speak of a large group of therapists who are

soft behaviorists, not radical behaviorists. The mellow group find it useful, particularly when talking to clients, to use familiar mentalistic concepts.

5. The concept of reinforcement is said to be circular. The hostile critic makes a mockery of the behaviorist's view of reinforcement. "Why does the organism do what it does? Because it is reinforced for doing it. When is a stimulus designated a reinforcer? When the organism does what it does to get it!" Ergo, declares the critic, reinforcement is an empty concept. This charge is more clever than accurate. Anyone who has seen the concept of reinforcement applied in an experimental laboratory or in practical settings with troubled children or disturbed mental patients can hardly deny that reinforcement is a powerful concept. Its application has observable effects. Actually, the problem of circularity seems to be a pseudoproblem arising from the unfortunate way reinforcement is usually defined: any stimulus that increases the probability of a response. The definition seems to make behavior fold back on itself. If, instead, we keep in mind that "a response" really means a *response category*—such as pressing a lever—we break out of the circularity. The reinforcer follows act 1; this increases the probability not of act 1 but of act 2.

It should also be noted that Premack's principle of using a more probable behavior to reinforce a less probable one has done much to undermine the charge that reinforcement is a circular concept. Premack's formulation does not define a reinforcer in terms of its effects, but in terms of behavioral relationships. This is a substantial advance and a contribution to the theory of reinforcement.

6. Behaviorism has no larger vision of humankind. This charge is basically accurate. Behavioral psychology sees the human being as an organism to be conditioned, not as a person seeking to lead a life of meaning. There is no concept of a "higher" destiny for the individual. The traditional glorification of man in myth and fable as a hero and as a creature with a higher purpose is implicitly rejected by the behaviorist. If you find the behaviorists' restricted view of human existence distasteful, you can still take out of behavioral psychology those elements that you find useful. In my view, there is much of value in behavioral psychology even if one does not completely agree with the basic premises. We are free to abstract from the behavioral system whatever we find of worth. Rejecting everything behaviorists have to say because one is a humanist is like "throwing the baby away with the bathwater."

7. Aversive therapy, one kind of behavior therapy, is said to dehumanize the client. The individual is shocked, receives Antabuse, or is in some other way made to feel uncomfortable for undesirable behavior. "You can't rehumanize a person by treating him like an animal," says an opponent of behavior therapy. The behavior therapist answers, "On the whole, these individuals seek the therapy themselves. We don't impose it on them." This point was discussed at some length earlier in the chapter.

8. The parent who raises a child by using behavior modification techniques is not an authentic parent. He or she is manipulating the child and using bribes to control behavior. Behaviorists answer that all parents use some form of manipulation in raising children. It is only a question of what methods have the greatest effectiveness. Furthermore, an important distinction is made between a bribe and a reinforcer. A bribe is usually given to get a child to stop an undesirable behavior; thus a bribe is a form of blackmail and teaches a child to become a blackmail artist. As such, behaviorists are against bribes. A reinforcer, on the other hand, is given to get a child to *maintain* or *augment* desirable behavior. Thus reinforcers have long-run beneficial consequences in socializing the child.

It is possible to fire a number of gunshots at behavioral psychology. But for every shot fired, the behaviorists have an answering salvo. When the smoke of battle clears, we see that neither the behaviorists nor their detractors have won the field. Each side commands a goodly portion of the terrain. Behavioral psychology was, is, and will be for some time to come a dominant influence in American psychology.

A Spanish proverb observes, "Habits are at first cobwebs, then cables." Behavioral psychology takes the optimistic viewpoint that the cables making up unwanted habits can be unwound strand by strand. Continuing the metaphor, behavioral psychology also asserts that we can, strand by strand, build the strong cables of wanted habits in ourselves and in our children. It is evident that the basic principles of learning have many direct applications to the human condition.

SUMMARY

1. Adjustment and growth through the **self-modification of behavior** is an increasingly dominant theme of behavioral psychology.
2. **Systematic desensitization** is a method by which the individual learns to respond differently to fear-arousing and anxiety-arousing stimuli.
3. A **conditioned stimulus** is a stimulus that evokes a learned response.
4. **Spontaneous recovery** refers to the reappearance after a rest period of a conditioned response previously extinguished.
5. The phenomenon of **stimulus generalization** refers primarily to the ability of organisms to detect similarities.
6. Pavlov demonstrated that it is possible to produce what he termed **experimental neuroses** in dogs.
7. In **aversion therapy**, the cues that trigger an undesirable behavior pattern are paired with a noxious stimulus.
8. The principle of **reciprocal inhibition** takes advantage of the antagonism of relaxation and anxiety.
9. **Implosive therapy** brings a client's anxiety to a maximal level.

10. A **reinforcer** is a stimulus that increases the probability that a certain class of behavior will occur.

11. **Instrumental conditioning** takes place when an organism learns that certain actions will produce certain results.

12. Thorndike said that if an action leads to a state of satisfaction, it is preserved by the organism; he called this principle the **law of effect**.

13. Hull's theory of behavior and learning is often called a **drive-reduction theory**.

14. According to Tolman, **latent learning** takes place without reinforcement and lays dormant until it is ready to be used.

15. If two stimuli are presented to an organism at the same time, they are said to be **contiguous**.

16. Skinner refers to his brand of conditioning as **operant** to suggest that the instrumental behavior of the organism operates on the environment to produce a change in its environment.

17. A **discriminative stimulus** provides an organism with information that an operant act is presently paying off or not paying off.

18. A **positive reinforcer** follows an instrumental action. A **negative reinforcer** precedes an instrumental action.

19. Negative reinforcement and punishment are sometimes confused because both utilize aversive stimuli. As noted above, a negative reinforcer *precedes* an instrumental action. In the case of punishment, the aversive stimulus *follows* the instrumental action.

20. The **partial reinforcement effect** refers to the general finding that organisms learning instrumental responses under conditions of partial or intermittent reinforcement show greater resistance to extinction than organisms trained under conditions of continuous reinforcement.

21. Behavior modification has made inroads into child-rearing practices.

22. In the self-modification of behavior, **cue management** refers to one's obtaining better control of discriminative stimuli setting the stage for habitual behaviors.

23. **Reinforcement management** requires that one pay attention to the consequences or pay-offs associated with one's behavior.

24. The **method of incompatible responses** requires making responses to a habit's cues that are antagonistic to the habit, that make it difficult to perform the habit. Ex. filing instead of biting nails.

25. The **cue toleration** method proposed by Guthrie is similar to Wolpe's method of systematic desensitization. but no contact w/actual stimuli

26. **Overt behavior** is behavior that is observable.

27. A **covert operant** or a **coverant** is an operant hidden within the organism. such as thinking

28. **Cognitive behavior modification** takes the position that thinking is a kind of behavior.

Applied Exploration

ASSERTIVENESS TRAINING: THE WORM TURNS

The phrase "the worm turns" tends to evoke the following scenario: Harriet Shrew is married to Casper Milquetoast. It is Saturday morning. Casper wants to watch a ball game, have a beer, and relax after a hard week at the office. Harriet has a list of chores for him.

Harriet. I want you to mow the lawn and wash the windows today, Casper.
Casper. Yes, dear.
Harriet. And after that, I want you to clean the oven.
Casper. Yes, dear.
Harriet. And after that . . .
Suddenly a low moan escapes from Casper's lips.
Harriet. What's wrong dear?
Casper begins to shout and scream a list of obscenities at Harriet.
Harriet (shocked). Casper, this isn't like you! What's happened?
Casper (triumphantly). Sometimes the worm turns!

Terry Paulson (1974) of the Fuller Graduate School of Psychology in California wrote an assertiveness training syllabus for his students. He opens the syllabus with this quotation from the musical about Charlie Brown and the Peanuts gang:

You're a good man, Charlie Brown!
You're a prince, and a prince could be a king.
With a heart such as yours you could open any door—
*If only you weren't so wishy-washy!**

What is Assertiveness Training?

The term **assertiveness training** is used to refer to a program of learning designed to increase a person's competence in dealing with other human beings (Bugelski & Graziano, 1980). Courses in assertiveness training are becoming increasingly popular and are being offered at various colleges, universities, and counseling centers throughout the country. The emphasis in assertiveness training is on **skills** and on putting these skills into action (Alberti, 1980). There is a minimum of emphasis on the analytic concept of insight. Thus assertiveness training has come to be classified as a variant of behavioral psychology. As such, it can also be thought of as another approach to the self-modification of behavior.

*Clark Gesner, *You're a Good Man Charlie Brown.* Copyright 1965, 1967 by Jeremy Music, Inc., 15 West 44th St., New York, N.Y. and reprinted by its permission.

The theory of assertiveness training is based on the hypothesis that many people suffer from anxiety, depression, and similar unhappy reactions because they are unable to stand up for their rights. Such persons tend toward the neurotic direction. Their problem is that they are **oversocialized**. The distinction between the undersocialized and the oversocialized person is presented clearly in *Sense and Nonsense in Psychology* by H. J. Eysenck (1957), a British experimental psychologist. Eysenck contends that the undersocialized person, a person with little respect for the law and the rights of others, tends to develop problems referred to as character disorders (see Chapter 1). The oversocialized person, on the other hand, is too concerned with the letter of the law and what he or she conceives to be the rights of others. The individual is too inhibited, too correct, too shy, too timid, too vigilant, and so forth. The antidote for such a person involves recommendations that release inhibitions and encourage the person to become somewhat more spontaneous. As you can see, Casper Milquetoast and Charlie Brown fit within the category of the oversocialized person.

Eysenck ties undersocialization and oversocialization to innate characteristics of the person. He notes that some people are more conditionable than others. Those that are least conditionable are those having a propensity toward extraversion; the most conditionable ones are those having a propensity toward introversion. Although there does indeed seem to be increasing evidence that traits of temperament are to some degree intrinsic to the indi-

Assertiveness training is a program of learning designed to increase a person's competence in dealing with other human beings.

vidual, we should not forget the tremendous importance of the whole socialization process. If parents are passive, emotionally uninvolved, and/or psychologically absent, it is possible that this may be a source of undersocialization. If parents are authoritarian, place great stress on being polite and doing the right thing, and make children purchase affection via their demeanor, this can be a major route toward oversocialization.

This, of course, is an environmental theory. There is no inherent incompatibility between a genetic theory and an environmental theory. It is easy to imagine how a "born introvert" could be raised in a family that reinforces "being proper." Such a person might be over-oversocialized and, as a consequence, have a double-loading in the neurotic direction. In any event, the faith of the behavioral psychologist is that some degree of learning and unlearning can take place in adulthood. The oversocialized person can engage in a program of systematic assertiveness training and overcome many personal problems.

An important distinction should be made between assertiveness and aggression. The two are easily confused, and the oversocialized person—in an effort to become more assertive—may be in danger of becoming too aggressive. It is helpful to imagine a passive-aggressive continuum. The left end of the continuum represents passivity in human relations; the right end of the continuum represents aggression in human relations; and the middle of the continuum represents assertiveness in human relations. The person who habitually gives the passive response in dealings with other people is variously classified as a "dishrag," a "jellyfish," a "spineless wonder," a "self-sacrificing martyr," and so forth. The person who habitually gives the aggressive response in dealings with other people is variously classified as "a dirty dog," "a rat," "a hostile person," "a put-down artist," a "stinker," and so forth. The assertive response is, on the other hand, "just right." It seeks the middle ground between passivity and aggression and permits the person to stand up for himself without putting other individuals down.

In *Don't Say Yes When You Want To Say No*, Herbert Fensterheim, a New York City behavior therapist, and Jean Baer (1975), his wife and co-author, clarify the distinction between assertiveness and aggression. Here is one example from their book:

Madge and Rose work as secretaries in a two-girl insurance office. Three times a week, Madge leaves early to see her psychiatrist. Rose has to answer the phone and finish the day's work. She doesn't really mind the extra labor; she does have an increasing feeling that the situation is unfair.

Unassertive: *Not wanting to interfere with Madge's psychiatric sessions, Rose keeps quiet. Tension mounts. Rose decides she should look for another job.*

Aggressive: *Rose fights with Madge and says things like "I'm tired of doing your work"* . . . *"This office isn't a nice place anymore because you take advantage of me"* . . . *"Better stop seeing the doctor, or I'll tell the boss about you."*

Assertive: *Rose brings the subject up for discussion with "We have a problem. What can we do about it?" They discuss possible solutions, such as Madge coming in earlier and doing work ahead, or trying to change her analytic time to an evening hour. (pp. 30–31)*

As you can see, the assertive response is a graded response, the happy medium between passivity and aggression. As such, it should bring optimal results in human relations. As psychiatrist Willard Gaylin (1979) points out, most of us don't like to feel used. When we feel used we experience feelings of outrage, shame, hurt, and resentment. Assertiveness training is designed to help persons avoid being used by others.

A guide to assertive behavior titled *Your Perfect Right* by Robert E. Alberti and Michael L. Emmons (1978) contains a chart (p. 10) that summarizes the relationship between different behavior patterns and one's feelings (see Table 3.1).

Assertiveness Skills

It is the conviction of behavior therapists who offer assertiveness training that inhibited persons can acquire assertiveness skills and put them into action before they feel the self-confidence of the already assertive person.

TABLE 3.1   THE RELATIONSHIP BETWEEN BEHAVIOR PATTERNS AND FEELINGS*

	Nonassertive Behavior	Aggressive Behavior	Assertive Behavior
	Self-denying	Self-enhancing at the expense of another	Self-enhancing
	Inhibited	Expressive	Expressive
As Actor	Hurt, anxious	Depreciates others	Feels good about self
	Allows others to choose	Chooses for others	Chooses for self
	Does not achieve desired goal	Achieves desired goal by hurting others	May achieve desired goal
	Guilty or angry	Self-denying	Self-enhancing
As Acted Upon	Depreciates actor	Hurt, defensive, humiliated	Expressive
	Achieves desired goal at actor's expense	Does not achieve desired goal	May achieve desired goal

*Robert E. Alberti and Michael L. Emmons. *Your Perfect Right*. Copyright 1978. Reprinted by permission of publisher, Impact, San Luis Obispo, Calif.

The working hypothesis is that feelings can follow from actions. The common-sense view that feelings always precede actions is disputed by behavior therapists. They cite the James-Lange hypothesis, formulated around the turn of the century by William James and the Danish physiologist Carl Lange. These two thinkers noted that common sense tells us that when we see a bear we run because we are afraid. They also note that we feel fear because we run, however. The act of running stirs up our nervous system. The runner's heart pounds, respirations increase, and all these sensations augment the feeling of fear. Actions feed back to the organism information that changes the moment-to-moment feeling. Consequently, behavior therapists argue, passive individuals need not wait until they have acquired insight into the roots of their passivity before starting to assert themselves. On the contrary, they can rid themselves of their chronic passivity by consciously learning and practicing assertive skills. Some of the assertiveness skills frequently discussed by behavior therapists are as follows.

Feeling Talk   Feeling talk is one of the oldest of the systematic assertiveness skills. It was first identified and discussed by Andrew Salter, therapist and hostile critic of psychoanalysis, in his book *Conditioned Reflex Therapy* (1949). He argues that the neurotic person suffers from excessive inhibition—the individual "holds back" too much. The person needs to express feelings and act more decisively. As one technique for reducing inhibition, Salter recommends that the timid person more openly express feelings. Such a person should state feelings of dislike, approval, relief, impatience, discomfort, appreciation, curiosity, skepticism, amazement, anticipation, confidence, contentment, regret, love, anguish, and surprise. A few examples of feeling talk given by Salter are:

"I don't like this pie."

"That shade of green is perfect for you."

"I cried when he came home safely."

"You can't do this to me!"

"Excuse me, but I was here first."

"You don't expect me to believe that, do you?"

"Say it again, I like it." (p. 98)

In connection with feeling talk, Salter also suggests the associated technique of the *deliberate* use of the word *I* with great frequency. "I am angry about . . ." "I saw that movie and . . ." "I wish I could . . ." "I think . . ." The fear expressed by the inhibited person when he or she hears about the techniques of feeling talk and the conscious use of the word *I* is that the person will either lose self-control or be thought of as conceited. Salter argues that these are false fears. Feeling talk and the more frequent use of the word *I* are skills designed to counterbalance the excessive inhibition of the oversocial-ized person.

Broken Record   Broken record is an assertiveness skill that involves calm repetition of one's position. It can be used in a negative sense or in a positive sense—for saying no to an unreasonable request or for asserting one's own wishes. One of the concepts that goes with broken record is that the user should not be sidetracked into explanations of his position. He simply re-peats his position over and over again. The argument is that his feelings about the matter are legitimate simply because he has them, not because they can be demonstrated to be rational.

An example of the negative use of broken record can be given in connec-tion with dealing with a salesman:

Salesman. This is the finest life insurance policy ever offered by the Galaxy Insur-ance Company.
Prospect. I'm sorry. I don't want any insurance.
Salesman. But don't you want to protect your wife and children in the case of your death?
Prospect. Maybe I wasn't clear. I don't want any insurance today.
Salesman. Let me ask you a question. How much insurance do you have now? Do you have a group policy where you work?
Prospect. As I said, I really don't want any insurance today.
Salesman (getting frustrated). Are you aware of the new changes in the social secu-rity laws? May I explain the law changes to you? You will find the information of value even if you don't buy insurance.
Prospect. No thanks. Let me repeat, I just don't want to buy any insurance.
Salesman. OK. I guess you don't want to buy any insurance today.
Prospect. That's right.

To illustrate the positive use of broken record, imagine a situation in which a wife wants to see a particular movie and the husband is showing no interest. Keep in mind that she has determined already in her mind that it is fair and proper that he take her. Last week she went to see a science-fiction movie he wanted to see. Now she feels it's her turn to see a love story. Also, note that broken record is not manipulative. She is being honest about her feeling, asserting herself, not playing the angles, and not trying to trick her husband:

Wife. I want to go see *Jane Eyre Remarries.*
Husband. I'm tired tonight.
Wife. That's OK. We can go tomorrow night or the night after that. It's playing until Wednesday.
Husband. Why do you want to see that corny movie?
Wife. I just want to see it. That's all.
Husband. Yeah. But it stars Judy Morningstar. She can't act her way out of a paper bag.

Wife. Honey, I just want to see it. That's all.
Husband. Don't you think you'd rather go see *Frankenstein Lands on the Planet of the Apes*?
Wife. No, I want to see *Jane Eyre Remarries*.
Husband. I hear it got terrible reviews.
Wife. I don't care. I want to see it.
Husband. You really want to see it, huh?
Wife. Yes. I want to see it.
Husband. Well, OK. When do you want to go?
Wife. Tonight if you're not too tired. I really want to see it.
Husband. Well, OK. I guess I'm not too tired.
Wife. Thanks, honey.

Fogging   In *When I Say No, I Feel Guilty* by Manuel J. Smith (1975), the following definition is given of the assertiveness skill called "fogging"

A skill that teaches acceptance of manipulative criticism by calmly acknowledging to your critic the probability that there may be some truth in what he says, yet allows you to remain your own judge of what you do. Clinical effect after practice: Allows you to receive criticism comfortably without becoming anxious or defensive, while giving no reward to those using manipulative criticism. (p. 301)

Fogging is particularly useful when dealing with a nagging person. Parents, husbands, wives, relatives, and others in positions of great or small authority may fall into patterns of criticizing behavior. Smith gives the following example of a daughter using the fogging technique with a critical mother:

Mother. Sally, you know how important looking good is to a young girl who wants to meet a nice man and get married. If you keep staying out late so often and don't get enough sleep, you won't look good. You don't want that to happen, do you?

Sally. You're right, Mom. What you say makes sense, so when I feel the need I'll get in early enough. (p. 98)

Smith notes that Sally can augment the assertion by adding at various times such statements as, "But I wouldn't stay up so late worrying about me if I were you" or "But I'm not worried about it."

In his assertiveness training syllabus, Paulson notes that fogging is useful in that it makes the person under critical attack a small target. The essence of the skill resides in agreeing without making a behavioral promise. Paulson suggests that the fogger use placating and nondefensive statements. Examples he gives are as follows:

"You're absolutely right. I should never do that."

"That's a good point."

"I really should try to be more serious."

"I can't understand why I have been so insensitive."

"I really should do that." (p. 7)

Feeling talk, broken record, and fogging are just three of the assertiveness skills taught by behavior therapists. If you are interested in learning more about systematic assertiveness skills, the books cited in this section are good starting places. All the skills, however, revolve around the central point made at the beginning of our discussion of assertiveness training: The thesis is that, in Salter's language, many people suffer from a "well-bred" neurosis. They are too inhibited, hold back feelings, and are oversocialized. Behavior therapists contend that the conscious practice of assertive behavior is a specific corrective remedy for socially inhibited persons.

Aristotle said that the human being is the thinking animal.

Chapter 4

COGNITIVE PSYCHOLOGY: THE POWER OF CLEAR THINKING

Overview

OUTLINE

KEY QUESTIONS

What is cognitive psychology?

Cognitive psychology represents a point of view that emphasizes the **thinking process**. Its central concerns are decision-making, logic, and how we form judgments. A cognitive approach to a personal problem implies the use of sound reasoning to reach an optimal solution to the problem. The focus is on the application of clear thinking to life's challenges.

How do the principles of cognitive psychology relate to adjustment and growth?

Proponents of the cognitive approach assert that people who have trained themselves to think more clearly and more realistically have at least two advantages over less-well-trained persons. First, they will suffer less from undesirable emotional reactions. They will have better coping mechanisms and will thus be somewhat less susceptible to emotionally induced illnesses. Second, they will plan ahead in a realistic manner, which will enable them to avoid some of life's worst blind alleys. They will do more than stumble through existence.

Aristotle called man the thinking animal, suggesting that human beings are the only life form on the planet Earth capable of rational thought. Indeed, the very term **homo sapiens**—our self-proclaimed label—means wise man. Before we proceed too far with our flattering view of people as rational creatures, it is best that we hesitate a moment to consider that people are not always rational. In an article called "The Rationalizing Animal," social psychologist Elliot Aronson comments (1973, p. 46), "Man likes to think of himself as a rational animal. However, it is more true that man is a *rationalizing* animal, that he attempts to appear reasonable to himself and to others."

In the novel *Of Human Bondage* by W. Somerset Maugham, the central character, Philip, is confronted by the decision of his friend, Hayward, to volunteer for overseas combat. To Philip, the decision seems unlike Hayward. It is totally against Hayward's stated philosophy of life:

Philip was silent. He felt rather silly. He understood that Hayward was being driven by an uneasiness in his soul which he could not account for. Some power within him made it seem necessary to go and fight for his country. It was strange, since he [Hayward] considered patriotism no more than a prejudice, and flattering himself on his cosmopolitanism, he had looked upon England as a place of exile. His countrymen in the mass wounded his susceptibilities. Philip wondered what it was that made people do things which were so contrary to all their theories of life. It would have been reasonable for Hayward to stand aside and watch with a smile while the barbarians slaughtered one another. It looked as though men were puppets in the hands of an unknown force, which drove them to do this and that; and sometimes they used their reason to justify their actions; and when this was impossible they did the actions in despite of reason. (p. 452)

Is man a rational animal? Or is man an irrational animal? The answer can only be that man is a rational-irrational animal. There are times when we use intelligent thought to plan ahead, and there are times when we use reason to justify our actions. The proponents of cognitive psychology discussed in this chapter clearly recognize the tendency of human beings to misuse the thinking process. Indeed, this is, in a sense, their whole point. They feel that although the great mass of people think in murky ways, it is possible to learn new and more effective ways of thinking. They assert that most persons have the potential for clear thinking, but it must be brought forth by specific kinds of educational procedures.

The study of thinking is itself a large subject that covers such diverse areas as concept formation, language acquisition, and problem-solving. It is not the aim of this chapter to offer a general survey of the many facets of the human thinking process. Instead, the goal is the limited one of exploring those approaches specifically designed to enhance adjustment and growth.

Before we proceed to the topics of this chapter, however, some mention should be made of the work of Jean Piaget, the Swiss researcher who has made great contributions to our understanding of the development of human thought from childhood to adulthood. It would be possible to write a sub-

During the preoperational period a child's consciousness is dominated by stimulus-bound, anthropomorphic, and egocentric thinking.

stantial section on Piaget, but I will limit myself to a few observations of particular relevance to clear thinking. Piaget's research provides ample evidence that the consciousness of children is dominated by **stimulus-bound**, **anthropomorphic**, and **egocentric** thinking. Piaget (1926) speaks of a stage of mental development termed the **period of preoperational thought** and notes that it lasts, roughly, from the age of two to the age of seven.

A child's thinking is stimulus-bound when he makes his evaluations on the basis of one and only one outstanding aspect of a stimulus situation. For example, a child may think that a narrow glass with a high water level contains more liquid than a squat glass with a low water level. The squat glass may in fact contain more liquid, but the child responds to the height of the water level alone as the basis of his decision. A child's thinking is anthropomorphic when he perceives processes of nature in human terms. For example, a child may think that the wind is a person and that the leaves are blowing wildly today because Mr. Wind is angry about something. A child's thinking is egocentric when he can see no point of view but his own. For example, say that a very young child is looking at a picture book. You ask the child, "Can I see the picture?" The child may very well show you the back of the book, holding the picture in such a way that his own view is improved. He thinks that if he can see it more clearly, so can you.

As the child matures, he passes from the period of preoperational thought through an intermediary stage called the **period of concrete operations**. This stage lasts from roughly the age of seven to the age of twelve. During the period of concrete operations, the child elaborates his capacity for symbolical thought and becomes more flexible in his thinking. Finally, the child arrives at the last stage of mental development, the **period of formal operations**. This period begins roughly at age twelve and lasts throughout adulthood. The term *formal operations* is chosen to imply that the mature adult has a number of high-level cognitive capacities. He can reflect, analyze, form concepts at a high level of abstraction, philosophize, and can think about thinking.

But the point of my exposition is to suggest that human beings make it to the stage of formal operations in varying degrees. Many of us carry forward into adult life a substantial number of the ways of thought common to the preoperational child. It is not at all unusual to find adults who try to cope with their problems with the outmoded mental tools of children, using stimulus-bound, anthropomorphic, or egocentric thinking. One way of conceptualizing the ideas presented in this chapter is to think of them as psychological catalysts capable of helping a person move increasingly in the direction of Piaget's designation of formal operations. Briefly, the ideas in this chapter are designed to enhance an individual's capacity for clear thinking.

GENERAL SEMANTICS: THE MAP IS NOT THE TERRITORY

The field of investigation called **general semantics** was the brainchild of a Polish count named Alfred Korzybski (1879–1950). General semantics is an approach to adjustment and growth that asserts that human beings can become more psychologically and emotionally competent if they make an effort to improve their language environment. The phrase "the map is not the territory" was frequently repeated by Korzybski (1958) to indicate that the human nervous system is not external reality.

Korzybski argued that a person would be "crazy" if he or she thought a map was identical and an actual physical territory. The map is a guide to the territory, but it leaves much out and may contain errors. Similarly, the human nervous system is a "map" to the external world, but it clearly is not the external world itself. This is an obvious distinction, once made. But Korzybski argued that it is a distinction few people make. He suggested that most people take the ideas in their heads to be identical with the real world. This, he insisted is a great error and leads to all sorts of defective thinking.

The Word is Not the Thing

And how are the "maps" in our heads "drawn"? Korzybski's answer was that they are drawn by language. To change the metaphor, think of the brain as a computer. The computer is programmed by a special language, such as Fortran. If the language is accurate and congruent with reality, the "thinking" of the computer will be realistic. If the language is inaccurate, sloppy, or otherwise defective, the thinking of the computer will be similarly inaccurate. Korzybski's thesis was that our brains are programmed by ordinary, everyday language and that ordinary, everyday language contains a host of built-in defects because conventional language is nonmathematical and arose from the thought processes of prescientific people. Archaic and outmoded ways of thinking are retained as residuals in the language patterns of daily usage.

Korzybski felt that a giant step forward could be made in the domain of clear thinking if we would only recognize that the language we use to represent reality to ourselves is not reality itself. A basic slogan of general semantics is "the word is not the thing." Korzybski states (1958):

If we start, for instance, with a statement that "a word is not the object spoken about," and someone tries to deny that, he would have to produce an actual physical object which would be the word—impossible of performance, even in asylums for the "mentally" ill. (p. 10)

Let us attempt to provide a lucid example of what Korzybski had in mind. When a child is very young, a parent does a great deal of naming of objects: "This is a spoon." "This is a dog." "This is a saltshaker." These sentences seem harmless enough. Korzybski noted, however, that they contain what he called the "is" of identity. The use of the word *is* suggests an identity between the word and the thing and sets up an early confusion in the child's nervous system. "Absurd!" you say. "It is all so innocent!"

"Not so absurd!" says Korzybski. Let's see where the "is" of identity leads. As long as the "is" of identity is used to refer to things that can be pointed at, there is no great problem. Words that refer to things that can be pointed at are called **extensional** words. Such words refer to direct perceptual givens, such as spoon, dog, and saltshaker. But the human language is replete with another category of words: the **intensional words**, and they refer to things that cannot be pointed at. They have no external referent, but exist as processes in the human nervous system. Nonetheless, conventional language has objectified these processes, and they appear in dictionaries as nouns—just as if they too were things. A few examples are *anger, love, beauty, hunger, curiosity, frustration, hope, ecstasy,* and *decency.*

Two friends are standing before a painting in an art gallery. "It's beautiful!" exclaims person A. "No, it's not," protests person B. "It's ugly!" They then begin arguing over whether the painting "is" beautiful or ugly. The way out of the argument is for the individuals involved to recognize that neither beauty nor ugliness are properties of the painting, but perceptual judgments made by human beings. Beauty and ugliness are in the human nervous system, not in the painting. Thus person A can say, "I sure think that looks beautiful!" or "I would call that a beautiful painting," and person B can issue his or her own opinion—"I would call it ugly"; but there is no foolish argument over whether the painting "is" beautiful. General semantics asserts that it would be a good idea to say, to even very young children, "We call this a dog" or "This is called a saltshaker" to avoid the error of the "is" of identity.

A couple has come to a marriage counselor in great distress. "What seems to be the problem?" asks the counselor. "He doesn't love me any more," says the wife. "That's not true!" says the husband. "I do love you!"

"No you don't," she protests.

"Yes I do," he insists.

"Then why don't you phone me when you're going to be late for dinner?"

"What's that got to do with love? Don't I always bring home the paycheck?"

"What's that got to do with love?" she asks.

A general semanticist would point out that this couple is using the word *love* as if it were a thing. Implicit in their argument is the "is" of identity. Love "is" something—but they aren't sure what! Korzybski would point out that the word *love* refers to a concept, an abstraction without a direct referent in the external world. Thus the couple's argument can only be circular. They need to recognize that there can be more than one concept of love, and that both concepts can be equally valid.

Semantic Reactions

Semantics is often defined as the study of the meaning of words. Korzybski invented the term **general semantics** to suggest the idea that the effects of word meanings are not limited to conscious awareness, that they have generalizing, or "spreading," effects on human emotions. The term **semantic reaction** is used to refer to an emotional response to a word. Words can make us happy, sad, angry, frustrated, anxious, or depressed. One of the aims of general semantics is to free people from the direct emotional control of words.

An illustration of the concept of semantic reactions is provided by S. I. Hayakawa (1963), an advocate of general semantics, in an article titled "How Words Change Our Lives."

People suffering from . . . prejudices seem to have in their brains an uninsulated spot which, when touched by such words as "capitalist," "boss," "striker," "scab," "Democrat," "Republican," "socialized medicine," and other such loaded terms, results in an immediate short circuit, often with a blowing of fuses.

Korzybski called such short-circuited responses "identification reactions." He used the word "identification" in a special sense; he meant that persons given to such fixed patterns of response identify (that is, treat as identical all occurrences of a given word or symbol; they identify all the different cases that fall under the same name). Thus, if one has hostile identification reactions to "women drivers," then all women who drive cars are "identical" in their incompetence. (pp. 9–10)

The terms **identification reactions** and **semantic reactions** are more or less interchangeable. It was, as noted already, Korzybski's contention that emotional responses to words take place because of the tendency to treat all members of a class—things with the same name—as identical.

The author Stuart Chase has done much to popularize general semantics. His book, *The Tyranny of Words* (1966), contains an excellent illustration of how semantic reactions are formed:

> *Take the word "bad." It probably arose to express a vague feeling of dislike. Rather than go to the trouble of describing the characteristics one did not like in an animal or plot of soil, one said, "It is bad." All right, a useful short cut. Then the word was made into a substantive, "badness." At this abstraction level, it became something ominous and menacing in its own right. One had better not be associated with badness. Badness was incorporated into rigid standards of judgment, especially moral judgment: "This girl is bad." The statement implies that she is wholly bad, a veritable chunk of badness. But she may also be a charming girl, kind to children, kind to her parents, and perhaps overkind to her young man. To cast her out of society as "bad" is the result of a false, one-valued or two-valued appraisal. Adequately to judge this girl, we must make a many-valued appraisal; we must know her other characteristics, the circumstances of the environment in which she was brought up, the status of the moral code at the place and time of the alleged badness, and something about the economic and social prejudices of the judge who calls her "bad." (pp. 77–78)*

It does not seem to be the thesis of general semantics that we should dispense with emotions. The person trained to think in the general semantics way does not become a cold-blooded robot. The idea is to free one from false and inappropriate emotional reactions, reactions that plunge one into excessive anger or out-of-proportion depression.

Basic Errors

Korzybski contended that the thinking of the average person is riddled with basic errors. He said that most of us are unsane—not sane and not insane. The term "unsane" was chosen to call attention to the fact that our thinking is not completely delusional, but that it has a rather poor fit with reality as revealed by modern science. For this reason, Korzybski titled his major work *Science and Sanity*. The remainder of this section discusses some of the basic errors noted by Korzbyski.

Our Logic Tends to be Two-valued The ancient Greeks placed great emphasis on classification as the basis of science, and Aristotle carried the importance of the concept of classes to a fine art in his system of logic. Aristotle said that a thing either does or does not belong to a class. An animal is either a fish or a not-fish; a person is either a man or a woman; an individual is either tall or short. A close look at our language reveals many built-in polarities: good-bad, right-wrong, yes-no, up-down, alive-dead, big-small, decent-indecent, success-failure, and so forth. For the sake of simplicity, thinking in two-valued terms can be referred to as **either-or thinking** or **black-white thinking**. The point is that either-or thinking does not do justice to the realities of existence. For example, a man may go bankrupt and think, "I'm a failure." But is this not artificial, two-valued thinking? He may have been a success as a parent, as a husband, as a friend. Is he justified in over-simplifying his existence with two-valued logic?

Korzybski called the two-valued logic of ordinary language **aristotelian** to distinguish it from the multivalued logic—a logic with shades of grey—taught by general semantics. The system of logic advocated by general semantics is called **non-aristotelian**; it calls attention to the fact that many events and processes in nature take place on a gradient having many points. To the general semanticist, a person's height is not adequately described by saying, "He is tall." It is far better to say he is five feet, nine inches, or five feet, eleven inches, or six feet, two inches.

We Make the Error of Treating Space-time Events as Things   An apple is a fairly solid example of a "thing." Or is it? Once the apple was small and green; now it is red and ripe; in a few days it will be shriveled and decaying. What seems to be a solid object "is" in reality a process of growth and decay taking place as an event in space and time. A somewhat more lucid example is provided by the word "wave." We look at the ocean and say, "There is a wave coming to shore." "Wave" has the status of a noun and is treated as a thing. But it is evident to us that the wave is temporary and is changing all the time. Clearly, the wave represents a process and is not a thing or an object. Similarly, notes Korzybski, all so-called things are better thought of as space-time events. Note that Korzybski does not say an apple "is" a space-time event, which would be to fall into the trap of the "is" of identity and to make general semantics equivalent to reality; this would be to make the map the territory. The conception of an apple or other "thing" as a space-time event is merely the most adequate conception available, but it is not identical to reality itself.

And what is the value of all this in practical terms? Just this: We too are space-time events. We speak of ourselves as if we were permanent and un-changing objects. "She is a pretty girl," says a young man. She "is" a pretty girl? Does the young man stop to think that the girl may change with time, that she may gain weight, that she may not be pretty when she is forty or fifty years old? "Tom is so well built!" exclaims a young lady. He "is" well built? Will he be well built forever? Perhaps he will have a potbelly in ten years. All this may seem rather obvious and too negative. But the point is that important decisions are often made without conscious recognition that people do change, that what seems permanent today is often gone to-morrow.

I know of a woman who often referred to her husband as "good old Harry—he's my Rock of Gibraltar." When Harry died suddenly of a heart at-

General semantics reminds us that the person is a changing space-time event, not a permanent unchanging thing. (Actor James Cagney in the 1930s and in the 1980s.)

tack, she went into a state of emotional shock. She protested to her relatives, "He's not dead!" and "This can't happen to me!" and "I don't believe it!" Korzybski would say that the woman had failed to recognize that Harry was, like all perceptual objects, not a "thing" but a process. Harry, like the apple and the wave, may be also thought of as a space-time event. He was an infant once, then a child, then an adolescent, then a young adult, then a mature man, and then an organism that died of a heart attack. Such possibilities are in the cards from the very beginning, and it is "unsane" to refer to a human being as "a Rock of Gibraltar" or anything else that suggests absolute permanence.

Korzybski suggested that we remind ourselves of the transient and changing quality of persons and things by dates. For example, we could speak of Harry 1964, Harry 1972, Harry 1975, and so forth.

We Incorrectly Treat Members of a Category as Identities   We would find it hard to function without perceptual and conceptual categories. In *A Study of Thinking* by Bruner, Goodnow, and Austin (1956), it is pointed out that the foundation of concept formation revolves around the process of classification. They say, "By categorizing as equivalent discriminably different events, the organism *reduces the complexity of its environment*. It is reasonably clear 'how' this is accomplished. It involves the abstraction and use of defining properties in terms of which groupings can be made." (p. 12)

Unfortunately, the advantage gained by the reduction of complexity is undermined to some extent by the "unsane" idea that there are no differences of importance among members of a group. A person may say, "Teenagers don't respect adults nowadays." But what about *this* teenager? She has a high B average, helps her mother around the house, baby-sits for extra money, and seems to be liked by adults. Someone may comment, "Black people are lazy." But what about *this* black man? He has a profession, supports a wife and two children, mows his lawn every Saturday, and so forth. "Jews are stingy," someone comments. But what about *this* Jewish person? He donates to charity, pays the prices asked by merchants, and has never owned his own business. If we make the mistake of treating members of a group as identities, we will be in for some rude semantic shocks when we encounter discrepancies from our expectancies. Even such a simple statement as "Apples are sweet" can cause trouble. What about *this* apple? You bit into it expecting the familiar sweet taste, and it is sour! This is a bit of a shock. Korzybski warned that we should be careful to avoid building up false expectancies based on the error of identity.

Korzybski suggested that we remind ourselves of the nonidentity of members of a class by the use of index numbers. For example, we could speak of $apple_1$, $apple_2$, $apple_3$, and so forth; we could speak of $teenager_1$, $teenager_2$, $teenager_3$, and so forth. This kind of self-alerting would be likely to reduce the impact of annoying semantic reactions—we would experience fewer rude awakenings.

Conventional language usage overdefines terms by intension and underdefines terms by extension. You will recall that intensional words refer to things that cannot be pointed at; thus the term **intension** by itself refers to events taking place within the individual. You will also recall that extensional words refer to things that can be pointed at; thus the term **extension** by itself refers to events taking place in the external world. With this introduction, consider the following quotation from Korzybski's *Science and Sanity* (1958):

The dictionaries define "house" as a "building for human habitation or occupation," etc. Let us imagine that we buy a house; this buying is an extensional activity, usually with some consequences. If we orient ourselves by intension we are really buying a definition, although we may even inspect the house, which may appear desirable, etc. Then suppose we move into the house with our furniture and the whole house collapses because termites have destroyed all the wood, leaving only a shell, perhaps satisfying to the eye. Does the verbal definition of the house correspond to the extensional facts? Of course not. It becomes obvious then that by intension the term "house" was over-defined, or over-limited, while by extension, or actual facts, it was hopelessly under-defined as many important characteristics were left out. In no dictionary definition of a "house" is the possibility of termites mentioned. (p. iii)

Stated informally, we overdefine a term by intension when we use a word to "see" things that are not there (e.g., perceiving a house to be sturdy that is not in fact sturdy). We underdefine a term by extension when our belief in a word makes us fail to see things that are there (e.g., missing the presence of termites).

Korzybski asserted, "Different maladjusted, neurotics, psychotics, etc., orient themselves by intension most of the time." The disturbed person is likely to evaluate by overdefinition. He or she believes in words and not extensional facts. As a corrective procedure designed to remind ourselves that most words are underdefined in extensional terms, Korzybski suggested we make liberal use of "etc." (et cetera), which may mean "and others" or "and the rest" or "and so forth." Etc. reminds us that much has been left unsaid. (You will note that the quotations from Korzybski use etc. It is also interesting to observe that the journal of general semantics is called ETC.)

We Create Verbal Divisions where No Divisions Exist in Fact Language has produced conceptual categories that have no extensional referents. Familiar examples are mind and body, and space and time. It is hardly possible to point at a mind without a body or a body without a mind. Mind and body are concepts of some convenience, and we may want to make a distinction for certain purposes. But we should remember that they are not separated in nature; they are separated only in our thought processes. Space and time provide another illustration. In *People in Quandaries*, Wendell Johnson (1946), an advocate of general semantics, observes, "To speak of space and time is to imply it is possible to demonstrate something nowhere at some time, or somewhere at no time!" (p. 214) Physics underwent a great crisis around the turn of the century, and this crisis was caused partly by physicists speaking of space and time as completely different entities. The Einsteinian revolution brought a new picture of the universe, and in the special theory of relativity it is necessary to speak of space-time, not space and time.

The unfortunate tendency to make arbitrary divisions such as mind and body can have real and undesirable consequences. Say that a man is suffering from ulcers. His physician says he has a medical problem. He is producing too much gastric juice, and the excess secretions are eating a hole in his stomach. His psychologist says he has a mental problem. He worries too much, is hyperanxious, and has to learn to relax. His physician treats him with drugs, and his psychologist treats him with psychotherapy. Perhaps the two professionals communicate little with each other; they may even be a bit hostile to each other's approach. Is the man's problem mental or physical? Is it a "mind" or a "body" problem? Obviously, the man's problem should not be divided arbitrarily into either a mental or a physical domain. He has a mind-body problem. He is a whole organism and deserves to be treated as such. Ideally, the professionals involved should have open communications with each other and work out a coordinated treatment program.

Love and hate are examples of intensional words that are divided arbitrarily. A client speaking to a counselor may say, "Sometimes I think I love my husband madly. Then there are times I feel that I hate him. I just can't figure myself out. Do I love him or hate him?" The problem, according to general semantics, is the attempt to make verbal categories out of a total emotional

4.1   APPLICATION: USING EXTENSIONAL DEVICES

Korzybski recommended that we frequently remind ourselves that the world cannot be chopped up into static categories, that there is growth and change, that our knowledge is far from complete, and that nothing is identical to anything else. To remind ourselves of these items, he recommended that we use **extensional devices**, practical techniques designed to orient us toward the external world of our senses as opposed to the internal world of abstract ideas. These devices are summarized as follows:.

1. **Indexes**. Apple$_1$ is not apple$_2$ is not apple$_3$, etc. Teenager$_1$ is not teenager$_2$ is not teenager$_3$, etc.

2. **Dates**. The United States$_{1930}$ is not the United States$_{1975}$, etc. Adam$_{1960}$ is not Adam$_{1965}$ is not Adam$_{1975}$, etc.

3. **Etc. (et cetera)**. Etc. is used to represent non-allness. It was used in No. 1 and No. 2 to suggest that the examples given are incomplete. It could also be used in the following manner: "Mary is a great cook, etc." This is done to suggest that Mary is not completely captured and understood by saying she is a great cook. She may also be a poor seamstress, an effective parent, a good driver, a mediocre golfer, a loving wife, etc.

4. **Quotation marks**. Quotation marks are used to indicate that a certain word should be qualified and does not mean precisely what it seems to mean. As an example, consider the "is" of identity. The quotation marks are placed around the word *is* to suggest nonidentity between two terms in the same sentence. "This *is* a delicious cheesecake," we normally say. Korzybski says that what we really mean is, "This cheesecake tastes delicious *to me*." It may not taste delicious to someone else. If we insist on using the "is" of identity, Korzybski suggests that we at least put quotation marks around it.

5. **Hyphens**. Korzybski suggests that we speak of space-time instead of space and time, mind-body, not mind and body, etc. In the opening pages of this chapter, the two questions were asked: Is man a rational animal? Or is man an irrational animal? The verbal split created by the questions was healed by the use of the hyphen: The questions were answered by saying that man is a rational-irrational animal.

It is clear that the extensive use of the extensional devices in writing or speech would be cumbersome. On the practical level, it is mainly a matter of awareness. You can imagine or visualize using the extensional devices in connection with your thought, speech, or writing. If this is done on a fairly regular basis, Korzybski asserts that you will be less victimized by adverse and destructive psychological-emotional responses to words and their meanings.

process. Love and hate do not "exist" outside our skins, like a table and a chair. They are at best two aspects of one internal process. Thus the client might be advised to speak of a love-hate relationship toward her husband to help her recognize the ambivalent quality of her feelings.

As you have already noted, the general semantics device for healing arbitrary verbal divisions is the hyphen. Korzybski advised that whenever possible we speak of mind-body instead of mind and body, space-time instead of space and time, love-hate instead of love and hate, and so forth.

RATIONAL-EMOTIVE THERAPY: EMOTIONAL SELF-CONTROL

Like general semantics, rational-emotive therapy is designed to prevent the suffering produced by unnecessary emotional reactions. The elimination of excessive guilt, anger, and anxiety is the goal of rational-emotive therapy. Although the term **therapy** is used as a convention, the father of rational-emotive therapy, New York psychologist Albert Ellis, notes that he would prefer a less loaded term, such as **emotional education**, for his system. It is clear from his writings that Ellis conceives of rational-emotive therapy as having broad general applicability to the problems of life. Rational-emotive therapy is a more recent discipline than general semantics. In *Humanistic Psychotherapy: The Rational-Emotive Approach* (1973), Ellis acknowledges the relationship of rational-emotive therapy to general semantics:

RET [rational-emotive therapy], like the science of psychology itself and like the discipline of general semantics, as set forth by Alfred Korzybski, particularly teaches the client how to discriminate more clearly between sense and non-sense, fiction and reality, superstition and science. (p. 63)

Irrational Ideas

Ellis contends that excessive guilt, anger, and anxiety are the result of various irrational beliefs. These irrational beliefs are *consciously* held by people, and they make themselves sick by repeating the ideas over and over again to themselves. Thus one factor in emotional illness is the pattern of **self-indoctrination** with false notions. Rational-emotive therapists are not passive when they work with clients. They are active, and they aggressively attack unrealistic notions when they hear them.

Ellis believes that human beings suffer largely because they confuse desires with needs. People say, "I have to have a new dress," "I need to go on a vacation," "I've just got to have a date with Jill," "I just can't live another minute without a drink," and so on. They make their wishes into demands, and they feel miserable if they cannot make their wishes come true. Ellis contends that

Albert Ellis is the father of rational-emotive therapy.

it is an irrational idea to think that wishes must come true or life will not be worth living.

The Ellis theory of human suffering revolves around man's cognitive capacities. People think, they have conscious ideas, and it is these conscious ideas that lead to emotional reactions. That is why rational-emotional therapy is sometimes designated as a **cognitive-emotional system**, a system in which thoughts lead to feelings. Say that a young woman thinks to herself, "I just won't be able to endure it if Bill ever leaves me." Suppose that her relationship with Bill is somehow terminated. If she really believes that she must have Bill to endure existence, she will be plunged into depression. Ellis contends that her extreme unhappiness in the present is produced by her earlier unrealistic assumption that life without Bill would not be worth living. The termination of a relationship could, of course, be the occasion for some sadness; but it is seldom the end of the world that some people make it into. There is a distinction between being merely unhappy and being desperately unhappy. Mere unhappiness is rational; desperate unhappiness is more often than not irrational.

According to Ellis, people who suffer from chronic negative emotional states do a lot of **catastrophic thinking**. They are like Chicken Little. An acorn hit him on the head and he declared, "The sky is falling!" Similarly, the anxiety-prone person sees an odd skin discoloration and thinks "I've got cancer!" Or this individual hears a squeak from the wheel while driving and thinks "The car is falling apart!" Or the person fails an examination and thinks "I'll never graduate from college!" The basis of catastrophic thinking is the logical error of **overgeneralizing**, making a single instance of a phenomenon serve as the predictor for a whole set of phenomena. The anxiety-prone person needs to be reminded of the proverb "One swallow doesn't make a summer." To overgeneralize is to make a blunder in one's thinking, and Ellis asserts that we should make a conscious effort to avoid such blunders.

Another emphasis of rational-emotive therapy is on **long-range hedonism**. Ellis has no argument with a basically hedonistic attitude toward life, the view that pleasure is good and that it is an important end in itself. He contends, however, that much suffering is the result of short-range hedonism—living mainly for immediate gratification. Say that someone drinks too much tonight. When a companion tries to stop him, he declares, "Live today, for tomorrow we may die!" The next day he has a terrible hangover and regrets the indiscretion of the previous night. As the psychologist O. Hobart Mowrer aptly commented, "The trouble with the live today for tomorrow we may die philosophy is that we usually don't die tomorrow!" The rational-emotive philosophy teaches that one should attempt to maximize one's total happiness, not just the pleasure of the moment.

In *Humanistic Psychotherapy*, Ellis (1973) summarizes the cardinal irrational ideas that lie behind extreme emotional reactions as follows:

1. The idea that it is a dire necessity for an adult human to be loved or approved by virtually every significant other person in his life.
2. The idea that one should be thoroughly competent, adequate, and achieving in all possible respects to consider oneself worthwhile.
3. The idea that certain people are bad, wicked, or villainous and that they should be severely blamed and punished for their villainy.
4. The idea that it is awful and catastrophic when things are not the way one would like them to be.
5. The idea that human unhappiness is externally caused and that people have little or no ability to control their errors and disturbances.
6. The idea that it is easier to avoid than to face life's difficulties and self-responsibilities.
7. The idea that one's past history is an all-important determiner of one's present behavior and that because something once strongly affected one's life, it should indefinitely affect it. (p. 37)

It is evident that the rational-emotive approach has much in common with the doctrine of stoicism as taught by the Greek philosopher Zeno. The Stoics believed that a wise person should be guided by reason and should train himself to be detached from pleasure and pain. Ellis concedes his debt to the Stoics and views the current rational-emotive conceptions as systematic elaborations of Zeno's basic insights. Ellis, however, does not seem to be as extreme as the Stoics. They taught indifference to all emotions; Ellis, instead, teaches indifference to destructive emotions that arise from irrational ideas.

ABCs of Emotional Self-Control

Ellis believes that emotional self-control is possible, that a person need not be the slave of capricious inner storms. Perhaps the term **emotional freedom** would be in some ways be preferable to the more familiar term **emotional self-control**; Ellis's idea is to help people find freedom from the constraints of excessive and unnecessary emotions. Toward this end, Ellis proposes a systematic approach called the ABCs of rational-emotive therapy. The ABCs are a convenient device for remembering the basic outlines of the system.

Point A   Ellis says that at point A there is some event that starts an emotion-producing change. This event actually takes place; it is in the real world. For convenience, this event can be called "activity," "action," or "agent." Numerous examples can be given: A person has a fight with a spouse, fails a test, loses a job, is kept waiting by a friend, is disappointed by a child's choice of spouse, and so forth. Any one of the examples can be the real-world agent that presses the starter button for one's emotion-generating motor.

Point B   At point B, the person has a belief about the activity, action, or agent. If the person has a rational belief, there is no problem. For example, a person may think, "It is irritating that Mary and I had to fight this morning," or "It is annoying that Jim wants to become an accountant instead of a dentist." These are rational thoughts; they reflect an appropriate orientation to reality. Life's disappointments and frustrations should be accepted as irritating, annoying, and so forth.

But the person who is controlled by emotions tends to escalate his or her belief system beyond the realistic level. Thus at Point B the person has an irrational belief. He or she thinks "It is awful that Mary and I had to fight this morning," or "It is a catastrophe that Jim wants to become an accountant instead of the wonderful dentist I always dreamed he would become." Ellis argues that an irrational belief cannot be sustained by the facts of life. Such beliefs refer to events that are seldom awful or catastrophic, but merely inconvenient.

Point C   Point C represents the consequence of a belief. If the belief is rational, the consequence will be an emotion that is appropriate to the situation. If the belief is irrational, however, the emotion will be something such as excessive guilt, anxiety, depression, or anger. A person who makes a habit out of thinking in terms of irrational beliefs tends to be prone to feelings of self-pity and psychosomatic reactions, such as ulcers and high blood pressure. Such individuals are highly defensive and have a great deal of difficulty in seeing their own mistakes. Ellis notes (1973):

And he generally experiences what we call "disturbed," "neurotic," or "overreactive" symptoms. His actions and feelings at Point C are inappropriate to the situation that

4.2   APPLICATION: AVOIDING PERFECTIONISM

One of the important themes in the rational-emotive approach is the teaching that many of us suffer needlessly because we expect too much of ourselves. You will recall that one of the cardinal irrational ideas residing behind extreme emotional reactions is this one: The idea that one should be thoroughly competent, adequate, and achieving in all possible respects to consider oneself worthwhile. Ellis contends that a person who holds this idea or some version of it is bound to experience low self-esteem no matter what the person's objective accomplishments in life.

From the point of view of family or friends, these individuals may be quite successful. From the person's own point of view, he or she has not lived up to their possibilities. Their internal standards are simply too high—so high that they are unrealistic; and when these people fail to reach their own high standards, they must pay the price in the way of low self-esteem. Ellis thus attacks perfectionism about the self; living one's life by a doctrine of perfectionism is just one more irrational idea to Ellis. It is an idea that does not fit with reality. Any objective analysis of human existence reveals that people are not perfect.

Our understanding of the way in which a perfectionistic outlook on life can lower self-esteem can be enhanced by reference to the concept of **cognitive dissonance**, a term introduced by Leon Festinger (1957), a social psychologist. When you hold at least two contradictory conscious ideas, a state of cognitive dissonance exists. It is possible to apply the concept of cognitive dissonance to areas such as understanding the self-concept (Aronson, 1980).

is occurring or may occur at Point B, because they are based on magical demands regarding the way he and the universe presumably ought to be. (p. 58)

Point D   To points A, B, and C, Ellis adds a point D (see Table 4.1). This is a point not usually added by the typical person. Most of us accept our emotional states uncritically. The feeling at point C is one that we deem to be legitimate simply because it is ours. Ellis vigorously attacks the view that all emotions are legitimate. Point D stands for **dispute**, and Ellis contends that the key to emotional education resides in the capacity to energetically challenge the irrational beliefs of point B. Thus a person can ask, "Why is it awful that Mary and I had to fight this morning?" There is some likelihood that the answer will be, "Well, it's not really awful. It's irritating, and it will upset my day for a few hours, but I'm sure to get over it soon enough." Or a parent

In the context of Ellis' work, it seems fairly evident that a common idea such as "I ought to be accomplishing twice as much as I'm actually accomplishing" is in the direction of perfectionism. It is dissonant with the idea "I'm working night and day. I'm doing all I can." If a person does in fact consciously hold two such contradictory ideas at the same time, it is easy to see why the individual will experience distress and have a poor self-concept.

Ellis takes the position that you have intrinsic value to yourself just because you exist and for no other reason. From the inner point of view, aliveness equals worthiness. There is no answer to the question "What am I worth?" Ellis notes that the tendency of most persons to rate themselves in terms of deeds or acts works only if a person is performing well. But in time you may become less praiseworthy. For example, most of us grow older and eventually less competent. What then? Do we become progressively less worthwhile? The answer is yes if we rate our internal existence in terms of external capacities. The answer is no if we rate ourselves as worthwhile independent of external capacities.

Ellis says that if you must rate anything, rate behavior—not the internal self. It is rational to think "I failed the test. I'm going to study harder for the next one." It is irrational to think "I failed the test. I'm a jerk." The first way of thinking is problem oriented and will lead to practical solutions. The second way of thinking is blame oriented and will lead to feelings of worthlessness.

For the reasons indicated in this box, Ellis advises us to avoid perfectionism.

TABLE 4.1   THE ABC SYSTEM OF EMOTIONAL SELF-CONTROL

Point	Stands for	A Key Feature
A	Activating Event	An emotion-producing change takes place in the observable world.
B	Belief	The person may have either a rational belief or an irrational one.
C	Consequence	If the belief is rational, the emotion will be appropriate. If the belief is irrational, the emotion will be inappropriate and excessive.
D	Dispute	The person energetically challenges an irrational belief at point B.

may ask, "Why is it a catastrophe that Jim wants to become an accountant instead of a dentist?" A realistic attempt to answer the question may produce these sorts of thoughts: "It's not a catastrophe." "I won't starve. He won't starve." "He's still affectionate toward me." "I've been placing all my emotional chips in one bowl and that's nonsense." "I still think it's annoying that he won't take my advice. But it is hardly a catastrophe."

The vigorous dispute of irrational beliefs at point D is not designed to replace negative emotional states with bliss. The goal is more limited: The idea is to bring the emotions into balance, to make them appropriate to one's life circumstances. Ellis understands that human beings will have emotional reactions. He only argues that the level of emotional response should be graded to fit the facts of existence. The emotional slave is hyperemotional. The Ellis ABC system is designed to introduce a corrective element into the domain of human feeling.

Ellis has written a number of books for the average reader. In one of these, *A Guide to Rational Living* (1961), Ellis and his co-author Robert A. Harper give the following advice:

Combat the idea that it is terrible, horrible and catastrophic when things are not going the way you would like them to go. When conditions are not the way you would prefer them to be, calmly and determinedly try to change them for the better; and when, for the moment, they cannot be changed, the only sane thing to do is quietly accept them (and wait and plan for the time when they finally can be changed). The greater your loss or frustration is, the more philosophic you must be in regard to it; the more you must accept the fact that it is bad and undesirable—but not catastrophic or unbearable. (p. 186)

This quotation contains the essence of the ABC system for emotional self-control.

REALITY THERAPY: BECOMING A RESPONSIBLE PERSON

The father of reality therapy is William Glasser, a California-based psychiatrist. Early in his career he became disenchanted with the treatment of clients by classical Freudian methods and began developing a treatment approach based on other tenets. His innovations have become reality therapy. Reality therapy has been used in a variety of settings, including institutions for the treatment of disturbed adolescents, mental hospitals, and private practice. It is clear from Glasser's writings that he sees reality therapy as not only a system of treatment, but as a practical set of guidelines for living. In an article co-authored by fellow psychiatrist and reality therapist Leonard M. Zunin (1973), the following observations are made:

. . . Reality Therapy is applied not only to the problems of people who are extremely irresponsible and incompetent, but also . . . it can be applied to daily living. It is not a therapy exclusively for the "mentally ill," incompetent, disturbed, or emo-

tionally upset; it is a system of ideas which can help anyone learn to gain successful identity and to help others to do so. Reality Therapy is readily understandable and it may be applied to anyone who understands these principles without prolonged, specific training other than the application of effort, sensitivity, and common sense. (p. 292)

Reality therapy is included in this chapter on cognitive psychology because, like general semantics and rational-emotive therapy, it emphasizes clear thinking and the long-run aspects of behavior. The foreword to Glasser's book *Reality Therapy* was written by O. Hobart Mowrer, a noted learning theorist and a former president of the American Psychological Association. In that foreword, Mowrer suggests that an action can be called "unrealistic" if it gives temporary satisfaction, but a substantial amount of ultimate pain and suffering. On the other hand, an action can be called "realistic" if it yields ultimate satisfaction, even if there is some immediate work or inconvenience required. Mowrer observes, "In the final analysis, it is the capacity to choose wisely between these two types of behavior that we call reason" (p. xviii). Thus we see at the outset that reality therapy places a heavy burden on the faculty of reason, the potential capacity of human beings to lead a life of intelligent action.

Basic Assumptions

The central assumption of reality therapy is that one can have a rewarding life only by living a responsible life. The essence of responsibility, and of facing reality, is finding effective ways to meet our psychological needs. Glasser (1965) specifies two basic psychological needs:

1. The need to love and be loved.
2. The need to feel that we are worthwhile to ourselves and others. (p. 9)

It is important to comprehend that Glasser's concept of responsibility includes responsibility to oneself. Glasser feels that irresponsibility, either to oneself or someone else, is the common thread running through all behavioral problems.

In addition to the central assumption concerning responsibility, reality therapy makes a set of corollary assumptions.

1. Reality therapy rejects the value of traditional psychiatric categories such as anxiety, personality, and psychotic disorders. These tend to categorize and stereotype people and lead away from understanding the person and his or her problems. The problem is "explained" by the label; human difficulties are "understood" in terms of word magic instead of processes. To Glasser, the conventional clinical pigeonholes are only descriptions of various forms of irresponsibility—nothing more.

2. The term **mental health** is itself of dubious value because it tends to suggest that there is something organically "wrong" with troubled persons.

Glasser, as a physician, notes that a tiny fraction of so-called mental disturbances may be caused by known biochemical disorders or brain damage. He feels, however, that in the majority of cases it would be better to substitute *responsible* for "mental health" and *irresponsible* for "mental illness."

3. The present and the future are more important than the past. Reality therapy rejects the emphasis of classical psychoanalysis on examining a person's past history. Instead, the philosophy of reality therapy asserts that the important thing in therapy or in daily living is to focus one's attention on the here and the now and where the immediate circumstances of one's existence are leading. If anything is to be analyzed, it is the relationship of the person to the person's life situation, not to the meaning of events in the past. Thus we may characterize reality therapy as *present/future-oriented* in contrast to *past-oriented*.

4. Insight into unconscious motives is not essential for change. There is greater stress in reality therapy on conscious problems than on unconscious conflicts. One of the pet peeves of the reality therapist is the tendency of people to refer to unconscious motives as excuses for irresponsible behavior. For example, a young man may say, "I guess I just have a lot of repressed hostility toward my father. Maybe that's why I can't turn in assignments on time. Unconsciously, when I reject Professor Smith I also reject my father." Glasser says that this kind of "insight" may be interesting, but it unfortunately makes allowances for irresponsible behavior. The reality therapist insists that behavioral change can *precede* insight. A person can decide consciously to act responsibly because it is in his or her best interest. Later, as a more effective person, the individual may reflect and understand why he or she once acted in an irresponsible manner. Within this framework, insight into unconscious motives is perceived as a kind of psychological excess baggage not having a great deal of importance.

5. Values and moral principles are important in daily living. Reality therapy holds that it is appropriate to think in terms of right and wrong. When people cannot fulfill their needs, their behavior is "wrong." One's task is to confront one's total behavior and *judge for oneself* the quality of one's life. Glasser notes that his approach to morality might not stand the test of scholarly debate with the great moral philosophers of the world, but he feels his approach is practical. He observes:

We believe that almost all behavior which leads to fulfilling our needs within the bounds of reality is right, or good, or moral behavior, according to the following definition: When a man acts in such a way that he gives and receives love, and feels worthwhile to himself and others, his behavior is right or moral. (p. 57)

This is why people must do the "right" thing, why they must conform with their own internal standards. It is the way in which a person feels worthwhile.

6. We grow as persons by setting up definite plans and following through with the plans. Of course, a plan is not supposed to be a straitjacket, and some flexibility should be built into the plan. But people need goals, they need something to work for. People without plans just drift, flounder about, and become demoralized. Mowrer, commenting on this aspect of reality therapy, makes an interesting point in his foreword to *Reality Therapy*. He distinguishes between *tragedy* and *folly*. Irresponsible persons are fond of saying such things as "I knew a guy who went to school for years, never had any fun, was waiting to get married, and then he got killed in an auto accident. What was the point? He should have lived when he had the chance!" Mowrer says that such a comment points to the potential tragedy in human existence. But what is the alternative? If one lives only for the present, and if one continues to live, the individual will experience a substantial amount of long-term suffering.

Facing Reality

Glasser contends that it is essential for us to face reality. It is the only way we can meet our basic psychological needs, our needs for love and a sense of worth. Every chronically unhappy person suffers from the same basic lack: the inability to satisfy fundamental needs. Glasser notes that all troubled and troublesome persons deny the reality of the world around them:

Some break the law, denying the rules of society; some claim their neighbors are plotting against them, denying the improbability of such behavior. Some are afraid of crowded places, close quarters, airplanes, or elevators, yet they freely admit the irrationality of their fears. Millions drink to blot out the inadequacy they feel but that need not exist if they could learn to be different; and far too many people choose suicide rather than face the reality that they could solve their problems by more responsible behavior. (p. 6)

You can see from the preceding quotation that Glasser places the responsibility squarely on the individual's shoulders. This may seem harsh. A person may say, "But my mother screamed at me when I was a child, always put me down. That's why I have such a bad self-image. I keep thinking I'm a dumb kid who can't do anything right." Glasser has little patience with such statements. He feels that looking backward can supply a sufferer with endless fuel to keep the engine of irresponsibility turning. Recall that reality therapy is present/future-oriented. The reality therapist says, "You have a brain. You can learn. Put the past behind you and decide now to lead a responsible life."

To illustrate how the principles of reality therapy can operate in the case of a particular person, let me briefly relate the story of Dee, one of Glasser's clients. Dee was twenty-five years old, the mother of two children born out of wedlock. The children had been given up for adoption, and Dee had also had several abortions. When she came to Glasser, she was living with a man for whom she had little real affection. Dee had a number of positive qualities. She was intelligent, interested in education, and had a warm feeling for people.

Glasser saw Dee for about one year. The two of them battled steadily. Dee tried to prove to Glasser that any change in her way of life was impossible. Glasser confronted her with the idea that she had a choice, a *real* choice. It was up to her to decide if she wanted to go on with her old ways or take a new path. Essentially, Glasser helped Dee to see that there was no real payoff in giving into the impulse and/or pleasure of the moment. The payoffs worth talking about all resided in forgoing some of the fun of the present and making some plans for the future. One of the things Glasser helped Dee to see was that she could not meet her need for love through indiscriminate sexual activity; such behavior was destroying Dee's hope of ever feeling worthwhile.

Dee eventually went on to finish high school and junior college. She entered the University of California on a scholarship and was preparing to teach in a junior college at the time Glasser wrote about her in *Reality Therapy*. By becoming responsible to herself, Dee was able to turn her life around and discover deeper satisfactions.

Controlling Perception

In his recent work, Glasser (1981) has become interested in the important role that perception plays in adjustment. The subject of perception has traditionally been an important one in the study of cognitive psychology. **Perception** refers to being aware of both the external and internal world in organized and/or meaningful terms.

Glasser has found great value in the formulations of William T. Powers, a student of cybernetics. **Cybernetics** is the science that deals with the control of systems (e.g., computers). Distinct applications of cybernetic insights can be made to the behavior of organisms. Specifically, Powers suggests that human beings have a strong tendency to control the inputs to their perceptual systems. Put in more familiar terms, we try to control what we see, hear, and otherwise sense so that we will construct a perceptual world that satisfies our personal expectations. The purpose of much human behavior thus becomes to control perception. The three key words here are **behavior, control**, and **perception**. As a consequence, Glasser speaks in short-hand terms of **BCP psychology**, adapting Powers' formulations to reality therapy.

According to BCP psychology, one of the reasons people suffer is because of **perceptual error**. Perceptual error takes place when there is a gap between what is **expected** (i.e., demanded, wanted, or wished for) and what is **observed** (i.e., perceived). We can reduce suffering by changing what is expected or by changing what is observed. Either kind of change, in the right

Perception plays an important role in adjustment and behavior.

direction, can close the gap. As noted above, the usual effort is in the direction of changing what is observed. Thus we attempt to control perception by controlling input.

For example, say that Graham marries Blanche. He thinks of himself as the head of the household, and says to his friends, "I want an old-fashioned marriage." One of his expectations is that Blanche will have a home-cooked meal for him every night when he comes home from work. Let's say that Blanche is willing enough to prepare a home-cooked meal many nights, but not every night. She has a job too, and finds it difficult to satisfy Graham one hundred percent. Now Graham will experience perceptual error. If Blanche "fails" him infrequently, he will experience a small perceptual error. If Blanche "fails" him often, he will experience a large perceptual error. Let's say that Blanche "fails" him fairly often.

Now Graham will begin to experience a substantial amount of distress. He will experience anger, and will feel that it is caused by something that Blanche is doing to him. Glasser disagrees. He argues that Graham is **angering**, meaning that he is actively creating his own anger. *It is something he is doing to himself.* How will Graham cope with the large perceptual error? If he is typical, he will try to get Blanche to change her behavior; that is, he will control for input. (Blanche's behavior can be thought of as input to Graham's perceptual system.) He will complain, pout, express his anger, or call Blanche names. This is often counterproductive. If Blanche resists, as well she may, he will experience even larger perceptual error. Graham may then escalate his attempts to get Blanche to change her behavior. And a vicious circle has been created. Although the example is much simplified, the basic pattern is valid enough. It is out of such patterns that divorces are eventually made.

How else can Graham deal with his perceptual error? He can modify what is expected. He can ask himself, "Is it reasonable that I demand a home-cooked meal *every* night?" If the answer to this question is *no*, as it is likely to be, he will reduce his perceptual error. And he will stop angering himself. But let's not be too optimistic about all this. One of the reasons therapists stay in business is because many people are very unlikely to question the validity of their own expectations.

A step called **evaluation** was a standard part of reality therapy before the introduction of BCP psychology (Bassin, 1980). In evaluation, the therapist asks, "Is this behavior doing you any good? Do you think it's the best choice open to you? Is it in your best interests?" BCP psychology formalizes the importance of evaluation, giving it greater status in the process of therapy.

In his book on BCP psychology, *Stations of the Mind*, Glasser (1981, p. 117) comments, "It follows logically that if we believe our in-the-head world is the external or real world, then we also make the mistake of thinking that our world is the same as your world and everyone's world." He further notes that it is an almost universal mistake to think that our world is the real world. As you can see, these observations of Glasser's are very similar to Korzybski's contention that the map (i.e., the thought pattern) is not the territory (i.e., reality). This is an often repeated theme in the cognitive approach to adjustment and growth. And it will reappear in the following section on cognitive therapy.

COGNITIVE THERAPY: IN SEARCH OF AUTOMATIC THOUGHTS

Cognitive therapy is one of the more recent developments in the application of cognitive psychology to the problems of adjustment and growth. It is similar in some respects to cognitive behavior modification (see Chapter 2) and Ellis' rational-emotive therapy. However, cognitive therapy has distinctive features of its own that merit exposition. Aaron T. Beck, professor of psychiatry at the University of Pennsylvania School of Medicine, is the principal author of cognitive therapy.

What Is Cognitive Therapy?

 Cognitive therapy helps troubled persons search out certain maladaptive automatic thoughts, suggesting ways to replace them with realistic thoughts. A key assumption is that maladaptive automatic thoughts reside behind many emotional disorders. The concept of automatic thoughts is a key one in cognitive therapy. **Automatic thoughts** appear spontaneously and are very rapid, coming and going quickly. They are conscious, but often so fleeting that they are not given much status or notice. Nonetheless they can have important emotional impacts. They occur *prior* to emotional reactions, and are their principal cause. For example, one of Beck's patients was afraid of dogs (Beck, 1976). The patient felt anxious even if the dog was chained, fenced in, or too small to really worry about. The patient was unable to account for his obviously excessive anxiety reaction. Beck advised him to pay attention to any thoughts that passed through his consciousness the next time he observed a dog. At the next appointment the patient reported that every time he saw a dog he had the automatic thought, "It's going to bite me." This automatic thought was the cause of the patient's anxiety. The patient said that he even felt anxious when he saw a miniature poodle. He observed, "I realized how ridiculous it was to think that a small poodle could hurt me."

Beck notes four characteristics associated with automatic thoughts. First, they are *discrete*. They are well-formulated and specific (e.g., "The dog is going to bite me). Second, they are regarded as *plausible*. They may seem unreasonable or irrational to others, but the person doing the automatic thinking tends to accept the automatic thoughts without criticism. Cognitive therapy aims to correct this, of course, by training the patient to evaluate the quality of these automatic thoughts. Third, they are *autonomous*. The thoughts have an involuntary quality; they seem to be generated by themselves. Because of this third characteristic they are called "automatic." Fourth, they are *idiosyncratic*. The thoughts are peculiar to the individual. They are the person's own oddity or quirk. Nonetheless, patients with a given problem (e.g., depression) tend to have somewhat similar automatic thoughts.

A fear of dogs may be associated with the automatic thought "It's going to bite me."

Before proceeding to examine other aspects of cognitive therapy it is important to note that cognitive therapy has its roots in prior psychological research. The similarity of cognitive therapy to cognitive behavior modification and Ellis' rational-emotive therapy has already been noted. In addition, cognitive therapy is linked to the work of the personality theorist George A. Kelly. Kelly was associated with the clinical psychology programs at several major universities for a number of years, and was active as a psychotherapist. One of the most important ideas formulated by Kelly in his theory of personality was the idea of a personal construct (Kelly, 1955). A **personal construct** is a conceptual category, a way of perceiving one's world. It involves assumptions derived from one's limited personal experiences, and on the basis of these assumptions we construe the world we live in to be a certain way. Personal experiences may include warnings by parents, information acquired by reading, and gossip. Thus a personal construct may often be limited, distorted, or based on false assumptions. A personal construct may reside behind an automatic thought. For example, if a person has the personal construct "All dogs are dangerous" it is easy to see why the person might have the automatic thought on seeing any dog "It's going to bite me." Similarly, if Johanna has the personal construct "All men are untrustworthy" it is easy to see why she might have the automatic thought "He wants to take advantage of me" when a man shows an interest in her.

Cognitive Content of Emotional Disorders

One of the more interesting features of cognitive therapy is its ability to zero in on the typical cognitive content associated with a fairly standard set of emotional disorders. (**Cognitive content** refers to conscious ideas and automatic thoughts.) Beck's list (1976) of emotional disorders is modified slightly here to bring it into agreement with the DSM-III nomenclature (see the appendix). Disorders identified are hypomanic disorder, generalized anxiety disorder, phobic disorders, paranoid disorder, conversion disorder, obsessive compulsive disorder, and dysthymic disorder (or depressive neurosis).

Hypomanic Disorder   The person suffering from a hypomanic disorder often manifests an expansive and elevated mood. He or she is too optimistic, has unrealistic expectations, and becomes irritated when contradicted. Cognitive content includes such ideas as "I'm the greatest" or "I can lick the world" or "This invention is going to make me a millionaire in one year."

Generalized Anxiety Disorder   The generalized anxiety disorder is to be distinguished from phobic disorders. Beck notes that patients with an anxiety disorder perceive danger in situations that *cannot be easily avoided*. Persons with phobic disorders experience anxiety in *avoidable situations*. Thus a person with a generalized anxiety disorder may perceive danger arbitrarily when engaged in almost any normal activity. A knock at the door might produce the automatic thought "That might be a burglar." An automobile back-firing might produce the automatic thought "A sniper is shooting at my car." Rain clouds might produce the automatic thought "Maybe there will be a flood and my house will be destroyed."

Phobic Disorders   As indicated above, persons with phobic disorders experience anxiety in avoidable situations. Therefore, in most cases, the situations are avoided. If the situation is approached or cannot be avoided, the automatic thoughts start up. Examples are: "If I go for a plane trip, the plane might crash and I'll be killed," or "If I climb that ladder, I might fall off and have a brain concussion," or "If a black cat crosses my path, I'm bound to have bad luck," or "If the car goes through the tunnel, the tunnel will collapse and suffocate me."

Paranoid Disorder   Persons with a paranoid disorder feel that others are abusing them or interfering with their goals in life. There is a strong feeling that others are unfair, that injustices are taking place. Beck says that the main theme in automatic thoughts is "I am right, everyone else is wrong." Other examples of automatic thoughts are "They're out to get me," or "Everybody takes advantage of me," or "Nobody will give me a break."

Conversion Disorder   An older term for the conversion disorder is hysterical reaction. The conversion disorder, or hysterical reaction, is characterized by a loss of physical functioning, suggesting an organic problem. The patient may experience such automatic thoughts as, "I'm blind," or "I can't hear anything," or "I can't walk," or "My hand is numb." (It is important to realize that the conversion disorder is *not* an organic problem. Often the physical difficulty conforms more to the patient's imagination than to biological fact.)

Obsessive Compulsive Disorder   The obsessive compulsive disorder may be characterized by either obsessions or compulsions. **Obsessions** are recurrent ideas that seem to intrude uninvited on one's consciousness. Examples of such ideas are "I wonder if I turned off the stove before I left the house" or "Maybe I'm going to get leukemia. Bill has leukemia and I touched his robe when I visited him at the hospital." **Compulsions** are repetitive and stereo-typed behaviors designed to reduce the anxiety associated with obsessions. Thus one might think "If I tap the steering wheel three times with my right hand and three times with my left hand and then three times again with my right hand that means I turned off the stove before I left the house and everything will be all right." Or "If I drive around the block of the hospital where Bill is staying four times without looking at the hospital, being careful to stare straight ahead, I won't get leukemia like Bill."

Dysthymic Disorder or Depressive Neurosis   One of the prominent characteristics of a dysthymic disorder, or depressive neurosis, is a loss of interest or pleasure in almost all of one's usual activities and pastimes. Familiar terms

4.3   CONTEMPORARY RESEARCH: COGNITIVE THERAPY COMPARED WITH ANTIDEPRESSANT DRUG THERAPY

One of the principal treatments for depression is antidepressant drug therapy. Is there any evidence comparing the effects of cognitive therapy and antidepressant drug therapy? The question is important because the treatment of various mental disorders with drugs has attained substantial status. Direct comparisons of psychological treatments with drug treatments are desirable.

The psychiatrist David D. Burns (1980) describes a study conducted at the Center for Cognitive Therapy at the University of Pennsylvania Medical Center. Forty-four patients defined as severely depressed were assigned at random to a cognitive therapy group and a drug therapy group. Members of each group received only one type of therapy in order to clearly distinguish the effects of the two kinds of therapy. The course of treatment was twelve weeks.

Psychological tests were administered before and after therapy. The results of these tests were the bases for evaluations of the effectiveness of the two kinds of therapy. The psychologists who gave the tests were not the therapists in the study. This was done to assure an objective evaluation of the results.

The results of the study favored cognitive therapy, and they were impressive. (There were small differences in the sizes of the two groups. The cogni-

such as "sad," "blue," "down in the dumps," and "low" convey the meaning associated with this disorder. (The term **dysthymic disorder** is the one preferred by DSM-III. However, DSM-III also recognizes the usage **depressive neurosis**. In view of the fact that the second usage is more familiar, and also that Beck speaks of depression in his writing, the single term **depressive neurosis** or simply **depression** will be used in this section.) Beck notes that persons suffering from a depressive neurosis feel they have lost something they consider essential to happiness or tranquility.

Beck says that depression is characterized by what he calls a **cognitive triad**. Beck says (1976, p. 84) that the cognitive triad contains three elements: "A negative conception of the self, a negative interpretation of life experiences, and a nihilistic view of the future." Let's translate each element in the triad into the kinds of automatic thoughts they might produce. A negative conception of the self might produce such thoughts as "I'm not as smart as other people," or "I'm ugly," or "Nobody likes me." A negative interpretation of life experiences might produce such thoughts as "My family was too poor

tive therapy group had 19 subjects, and the antidepressant drug group had 25.) The number who recovered completely at the end of twelve weeks in the cognitive therapy group was 15, or seventy-nine percent. The number who recovered completely at the end of twelve weeks in the antidepressant drug group was 5, or twenty percent. The difference between the two groups is both large and significant.

Follow-up tests during the year after active treatment suggest that on the whole the cognitive therapy group maintained its gains over the drug group.

We now have an answer to the question asked at the opening of this box. Yes, there is evidence comparing the effects of cognitive therapy with antidepressant drug therapy. And the study described suggests that cognitive therapy is a highly effective treatment for depression. In fact, quite a bit of work has been done in the application of cognitive therapy to the treatment of depressed persons. And it is encouraging to note that more than one outcome study suggests that cognitive therapy is effective in the treatment of depression (Rush, 1980).

In order to strike a balance, it should be noted that psychiatrists Paul H. Wender and Donald F. Klein, authors of *Mind, Mood, and Medicine* (1981), indicate their reservations about the adequacy of studies such as the one reported here showing a low effectiveness for antidepressant agents. They say that numerous other studies have demonstrated the specific benefits of these agents.

to give me a good education," or "I wasted too much time in the Army," or "Most of my college professors were boring." A nihilistic view of the future might produce such thoughts as "I'll never get anywhere," or "I know my marriage will eventually end in a divorce," or "This job is just a dead end."

Techniques

In order to accomplish its primary goal of helping the individual to think more clearly, cognitive therapy has developed a set of specific techniques. These techniques can be utilized in both therapy and daily life to reduce the negative impact of maladaptive automatic thoughts. Some of the principal techniques are identified below.

Recognizing Automatic Thoughts   It is possible with some effort and training to acquire a greater ability to recognize automatic thoughts. It is important to pinpoint the thought and say to oneself, "I just had the thought that nobody likes me." Now one is in a much better position to evaluate the automatic thought.

Filling in the Blank   Automatic thoughts often flash so quickly into and out of one's consciousness that there seems to be a blank between stimulus and response. An example of this was provided by the patient who felt anxious when he saw a dog. The formula seemed to be *see dog = feel anxious*. The patient was asked by Beck to "fill in the blank" between stimulus and response, and the patient then noted he was having the automatic thought, "It's going to bite me."

   Beck (1976, p. 241) gives the example of a college student who "avoided public gatherings because of inexplicable feelings of shame, anxiety, and sadness in these situations." When the student filled in the blank between the situation and the emotional response he found he was having thoughts such as "Nobody will want to talk to me," or "They think I look pathetic," or "I'm just a misfit."

Distancing   With repeated observations one becomes able to look at automatic thoughts more objectively. This phenomenon is known as **distancing**. As distancing takes place, one grows to realize that one's thoughts are not identical to reality. (In Korzybski's terms, the map [i.e., the thought pattern] is not the territory [i.e., reality]).

Decentering   Decentering requires that one recognize that many things that happen have no personal meaning. In other words, it is important to realize that one is not the center of the world. Pre-schoolers often think that everything revolves around them. You will recall that earlier in the chapter it was noted that Piaget used the word **egocentric** to describe this kind of thinking. Persons with emotional disorders often manifest an egocentric attitude in their thoughts, and decentering is required to help them. Beck gives the example of a graduate student on his way to take an important oral examination. When the student slipped and fell he thought, "The snow has been put there so that I would fall." The student then noted that others were falling too and that cars were skidding on the icy road. He was thus able to decenter and reduce some of his anxiety about the examination.

CRITIQUE

On the whole, cognitive psychology appeals to common sense. It is difficult to take issue with the basic point that clear thinking is of value in making decisions and in formulating plans. The guidelines presented by the thinkers discussed in this chapter are certainly of substantial practical value. Nonetheless, it is possible to take issue with certain general assumptions and specific conclusions made by Korzybski, Ellis, Glasser, and Beck.

1. Two of the major forces in modern psychology, psychoanalysis and behaviorism, tend to downplay the significance of reason. As you already know, psychoanalysis stresses the importance of unconscious motives. It sees the power of consciousness as weak when up against the forces of unconsciousness. Radical behaviorism, of course, gives no credence at all on a formal level to the importance of conscious thought and the use of enlightened reason. The behaviorist sees reason as a poor weapon against entrenched conditioned reflexes and habits. To the extent that a psychoanalyst or a moderate behaviorist might allow for the importance of reason, it would be only as an *indirect* agent of change, not as a direct agent. In other words, reason can be used as a "thin entering wedge" that sets about to upset the apple cart of unconscious motives or old habits. But it can seldom be used successfully in head-to-head confrontation with the profound processes of motivation or learning. The advocate of cognitive psychology, on the other hand, seems to suggest that reason can sometimes be used like a hot knife, cutting as if through butter the resistance offered by irrational wishes and undesirable habits.

2. In some ways general semantics seems to perpetuate the very either-or thinking it deplores. Korzybski sets up two-valued categories such as **sane** and **unsane, aristotelian** and **non-aristotelian**. This is peculiar in that general semantics is supposed to be a multivalued system of thought.

3. Perhaps Korzybski is too hard on ordinary language. He would almost seem to suggest that our conventional vocabulary has no extensional devices built into it. But it can be contended that a number of reality-orienting arrows are built into orthodox grammar. For example, adjectives are often used to indicate gradients as opposed to dichotomies. We do not use only the twofold classes *tall* and *short*. We speak of people as being very tall, medium tall, extremely short, and so forth. The very word **gradient** is itself a part of ordinary English, thus suggesting the common recognition that not all events and things present themselves as dualities. Perhaps the *use* of ordinary language should be criticized, not ordinary language itself.

4. The link between thinking as a cause and emotions as an effect is not as well established as those who favor cognitive psychology would suggest. There is a relationship, of course. The history of laboratory experiments on emotion supports a number of theories of emotion, and the role of thought in reference to emotion is not completely clear. We could just as well say that emotion is a cause of thought as say that thought is a cause of emotion. Indeed, this very point is sometimes recognized by cognitive psychology. (See the applied exploration at the end of this chapter in which a cognitive distortion called **emotional reasoning** is identified.) However, it tends not to be emphasized. It is also possible to tag actions, instead of thoughts, as a cause of feelings, as assertiveness training does. The most accurate statement would seem to be that thoughts, actions, and feelings all interact in a com-

plex relationship in which no one element can consistently be identified as cause and another as effect. This does not discredit the contentions of the cognitive approach, but it does dampen a bit any tendency to unreservedly accept reason as the absolute king of the psychological jungle.

5. Rational-emotive therapy and reality therapy have an important point of disagreement. Rational-emotive therapy teaches that self-evaluation is unnecessary, that we do not have to judge our inner being on the basis of accomplishments measured against social standards. We are worth something to ourselves merely because we exist. The tendency toward self-evaluation is learned, and it can be unlearned. Reality therapy, on the other hand, argues that the royal road to self-esteem is discovered by setting standards and living up to them. It is inevitable that we will judge ourselves. Thus it is essential that we be at least responsible to our own values. It is not easy to reconcile these two points of view. They seem to be based on entirely different assumptions. Rational-emotive therapy looks on self-evaluation as a learned tendency, a part of the socialization process. Reality therapy seems to suggest that self-evaluation is an innate tendency, an inborn process that is part of all of us. I will not attempt a glib reconciliation of the two points of view. It is an issue you may prefer to think through for yourself.

6. Reality therapy makes a single concept—the concept of responsibility—do too much work. If a person is responsible, he or she will enjoy mental health and sense of self-worth. Glasser goes so far as to equate mental illness with irresponsibility. This may be going a bit too far. So much is explained by pinning all of the person's behavior on the responsibility-irresponsibility dimension that nothing is explained. What is the source of the person's capacity for responsibility? Orthodox psychology would point to a person's learning history, family experiences, social opportunities, and so forth. Glasser seems to brush all this aside, making the person the prime cause of his or her own behavior. Even if we accept the doctrine that it is a cop-out to blame parents, unconscious motives, or whatever else for one's problems, it is probably going too far to totally dispense with environmental factors as having relevance for explaining behavior. Skinner, for example, would probably say that irresponsibility is just one more mentalism. For Skinner, the ultimate sources from which behavior springs are to be found in the environment—not within the skin of the individual. If we wish to adopt ideas from both behavioristic psychology and reality therapy, we may adopt the rather complex model that persons have **partial responsibility** for their actions. If you feel that there is some truth in both orientations, you are stuck with having to live with a paradoxical model of human nature.

7. General semantics, rational-emotive therapy, and cognitive therapy tend to place a little too much emphasis on thinking, and not quite enough emphasis on doing. One almost gets the impression from reading authors who take the cognitive approach that thinking will make it so. But after clear

thinking takes place realistic action is often required. This point is not, of course, entirely missed by thinkers who emphasize cognitive aspects of human behavior. But they seem to focus a bit too much on the role that thinking plays in causing emotions, and not enough on the role that thinking plays in determining overt actions. (Note that the criticism in this paragraph has been withheld from reality therapy, which does stress both responsible action and realistic thinking.)

In spite of some of the difficulties noted, cognitive psychology holds together fairly well. As one reads the writings of Korzybski, Ellis, Glasser, Beck, or their followers, one receives the strong impression that these are thoughtful persons of goodwill. As already noted, most of their ideas make a strong appeal to common sense.

There are those who mistrust reason. The famous *Rubáiyát* of Omar Khayyám, twelfth-century Persian poet and astronomer, proclaimed the importance of extracting as much joy as possible from the present moment. In the following quotation from Edward Fitzgerald's translation (1946) of the *Rubáiyát* into English, a direct attack is made on reason:

You know, my friends, with
what a brave carouse
I made a second marriage in
my house;
Divorced old barren reason
from my bed.
And took the daughter of the
vine to spouse.

The "daughter of the vine" is wine and is meant to symbolize joyful living—eating, drinking, merrymaking, and lovemaking. Khayyám prefers this to "old barren reason."

By way of contrast, let us consider the view of Kahlil Gibran (1958), a Lebanese poet. Writing in the twentieth century, Gibran had this to say about reason:

When Reason speaks to you, hearken to what she says, and you shall be saved. Make good use of her utterances, and you shall be as one armed. For the Lord has given you no better guide than Reason, no stronger arm than Reason. When Reason speaks to your inmost self, you are proof against Desire. For Reason is a prudent minister, a loyal guide, and a wise counsellor. Reason is light in darkness, as anger is darkness amidst light. Be wise—let Reason, not Impulse, be your guide. (p. 53)

We do not have to make a stark choice between living by desire and living by reason. It is possible to make compromises, to extract some joy from the present while at the same time planning ahead. This seems to be the course recommended by the advocates of reason.

SUMMARY

General semantics

1. Aristotle called man the thinking animal, suggesting that human beings are the only life form on the planet Earth capable of rational thought.
2. The proponents of cognitive psychology feel that although the great mass of people think in murky ways, it is possible to learn new and more effective ways of thinking.
3. Piaget's research provides ample evidence that the consciousness of children is dominated by **stimulus-bound, anthropomorphic**, and **egocentric thinking**.
4. The phrase "the map is not the territory" was used by Korzybski to indicate that the human nervous system is not external reality.
5. According to Korzybski, the "is" of identity tends to make us confuse words and things. This is summarized in his expression "The word is not the thing."
6. The term **general semantics** is used to suggest the idea that the effects of word meanings are not limited to conscious awareness, that they have generalizing, or "spreading," effects on human emotions.
7. Korzybski contended that the thinking of the average person is riddled with basic errors. Some of the basic errors noted by Korzybski were: *apple , wave* two-valued logic, treating space-time events as things, treating members of a category as identities, overdefining terms by intention and underdefining terms by extension, and creating verbal distinctions where no distinctions exist in fact.
8. **Extensional devices** are practical techniques designed to orient us toward the external world of our senses as opposed to the internal world of abstract ideas. Five devices identified in the textbook are: (1) indexes, (2) dates, (3) etc. (et cetera), (4) quotation marks, and (5) hyphens.

Rational-emotive therapy

9. Albert Ellis conceives of **rational-emotive therapy** as a kind of emotional education.
10. Ellis contends that excessive guilt, anger, and anxiety are the result of various irrational beliefs.
11. **Catastrophic thinking** involves the logical error of overgeneralizing, making a single instance of a phenomenon serve as the predictor for a whole set of phenomena.
12. Rational-emotive therapy emphasizes the value of **long-range hedonism**, maximizing one's *total* happiness, not just the pleasure of the moment.
13. Ellis proposes a systematic approach to emotional self-control called the **ABCs of rational-emotive therapy**. *A* stands for activity, action, or agent. *B* stands for belief. *C* stands for consequence.
14. To points *A, B,* and *C,* Ellis adds a point *D*. Point *D* stands for dispute.

15. Ellis contends that perfectionism, a tendency to expect too much of oneself, can lead to low self-esteem.

16. **Cognitive dissonance** takes place when you hold at least two contradictory conscious ideas.

17. The central assumption of **reality therapy** is that one can have a rewarding life only by living a responsible life.

18. Glasser specifies two basic psychological needs: (1) The need to love and be loved, and (2) the need to feel that we are worthwhile to ourselves and others.

19. Reality therapy rejects the value of traditional psychiatric categories such as anxiety, personality, and psychotic disorders.

20. Reality therapy indicates that in the majority of cases it would be better to substitute **responsible** for "mental health" and **irresponsible** for "mental illness."

21. Reality therapy asserts that the present and the future are more important than the past.

22. Reality therapy asserts that insights into unconscious motives is not essential for change.

23. Glasser contends that it is essential for us to face reality. He indicates that it is the only way we can meet our basic psychological needs.

24. Glasser has found great value in the formulations of William T. Powers, a student of cybernetics. Glasser and Powers write of **BCP psychology**, standing for behavior, control, and perception.

25. **Cognitive therapy** helps troubled persons search out certain maladaptive automatic thoughts. **Automatic thoughts** appear spontaneously and are very rapid, coming and going quickly.

26. Beck, the author of cognitive therapy, notes four characteristics of automatic thoughts: They are *discrete, plausible, autonomous,* and *idiosyncratic.*

27. According to Kelly, a **personal construct** is a conceptual category, a way of perceiving one's world.

28. One of the more interesting features of cognitive therapy is its ability to zero in on the typical cognitive content associated with a fairly standard set of emotional disorders.

29. According to Beck, depression is characterized by what he calls a **cognitive triad**. The cognitive triad contains three elements: "A negative conception of the self, a negative interpretation of life, and a nihilistic view of the future."

30. Some of the principal techniques of cognitive therapy include recognizing automatic thoughts, filling in the blank, distancing, and decentering.

Applied Exploration

COGNITIVE DISTORTIONS: RECOGNIZING WARPED THINKING

Imagine looking at yourself in a funhouse mirror. Your head is swollen, your feet are shrunken, your stomach sticks out, and your fingers look as long as breadsticks. The image is still you, but it is bent all out of shape—distorted. Thinking can be like looking into a funhouse mirror. Cognitive distortions, or warped thoughts, can cause us to see reality in odd ways. This theme is not new, of course. It has been implicit in the whole of Chapter 4. However, it is useful to collect a set of common cognitive distortions for convenient reference. The list presented here is adapted from the work of the psychiatrist David D. Burns (1980). The list is inspired primarily by Beck's work with cognitive therapy, and overlaps to some extent with the points made by Ellis

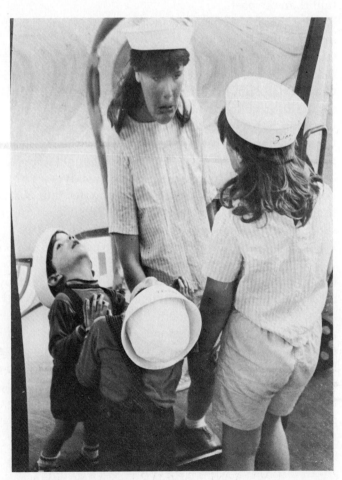

Cognitive distortions can be like looking into a fun house mirror.

Go Over

and Korzybski. If we can recognize common cognitive distortions in ourselves and others, it will contribute to our adjustment and growth.

All-or-Nothing Thinking   All-or-nothing thinking can also be called "either-or thinking" or "black and white" thinking. All-or-nothing thinking tends to sort all events and experiences into two categories. A person is short or tall, smart or dumb, good or bad, a success or a failure. Say that Hector is fired from his job. He thinks "I'm a failure." And this thought will make him feel depressed. He is ignoring the fact that he is a success in other areas: as a husband, as a father, and as a son.

Overgeneralization   To overgeneralize is to extend a judgment or an evaluation beyond reasonable bounds. Say that Meryl goes on a trip and is robbed in California. When she tells friends about her trip she says, "Everybody in California is a thief." Stuart has a bad experience with a person with red hair. "Watch out for people with red hair," he warns others.

Mental Filter   Mental filter involves selecting one negative detail out of a set of stimuli, paying too much attention to it. Say that Isman is eating dinner with Melba in a good restaurant. They are kept waiting ten minutes too long by the waiter before they can place their order. Isman thinks, "The evening is ruined." He has failed to note that Melba is in a good mood, the food itself is excellent when it arrives, and the coffee is hot.

Disqualifying the Positive   When a person disqualifies the positive, he or she tends to discount or minimize any good aspects of a situation. To illustrate, in the example given above of Isman and Melba eating dinner, let's say that Melba comments, "The steak is so tender and juicy, Isman. Don't you think so?" (Maybe she is trying to improve his mood.) Isman answers, "I've had better."

Jumping to Conclusions   Jumping to conclusions involves making a quick adverse evaluation without adequate information. Sebastion asks Judith for a date next Saturday night, and she answers that she has a prior engagement. Sebastion concludes, "She doesn't like me." Ward is an unpublished author. As he puts a manuscript in the mail, he thinks, "What's the use? I know it will be rejected."

Magnification or Minimization   Magnification involves making too much out of one's own failures and someone else's successes. Ramona and Idelle are competing for an important promotion to supervisor. Both are interviewed and seriously considered by their employer. Idelle gets the position and Ramona is passed over. Ramona thinks, "Idelle is so clever and pretty. I'm so ugly and stupid."

Minimization is the opposite of magnification. When we minimize we tend to discount our own accomplishments or abilities. Similarly, we may tend to discount another person's failures or shortcomings. Yvette receives an A on the first important examination in a biology course. She thinks, "It's just luck. I won't be able to keep it up." On learning that her friend Sabrina received a C on the same exam, Yvette thinks, "You can bet that's the first and last C Sabrina will get in this course. She must have been sick or something the day of the exam."

Emotional Reasoning Emotional reasoning takes place when one's judgment is clouded by a mood or a feeling. Sterling has just had a disagreement with a superior at work. He goes out to lunch in a black mood. When he is presented with the check by the waitress, he thinks, "Will you look at how much they want for a lousy hamburger and a few greasy fries? They're overcharging me! Everybody wants to rip you off these days!" On a different day, in a better mood, he might have thought the food was satisfactory and the charge was reasonable.

Burton is going through a bitter divorce action. He thinks about his wife, "Gloria is trying to ruin me. She wants to take me for everything I've got." An objective observer would say that Gloria merely wants her fair share of the community property and reasonable child support payments.

Should Statements Should statements are forms of mental self-pressure characterized by words such as **should**, **ought**, and **must**. If overused, they tend to generate guilt and depression, particularly if we find ourselves unable to live up to their moralistic demand. Neda visits her aging mother once a week even though she must drive two hours to do it. Neda's mother complains that Neda should visit more often. After a visit, on her way home, Neda thinks, "I *should* visit more often." In fact she visits as often as is practical.

Elfreda looks at herself in the mirror and decides she is getting fat. She thinks "I *ought* to go on a diet." But she doesn't. Although she doesn't really need to go on a diet, the ought statement makes her feel that she is failing herself.

Saxon is a good student. He usually earns A's or B's in his courses. But he thinks, "I *must* study more. I *ought* to be getting straight A's." He makes himself depressed by focusing on his failures instead of his successes.

Personal Labeling Personal labeling involves attaching a negative name to ourselves or others. We usually pick out one characteristic and make an oversimplified judgment. It is as if our whole personality, or the other individual's whole personality, is no more complex than the negative name. Alfonso goes out on a date with Deanna. The date goes badly, and Alfonso feels he has made a bad impression. After the date is over, Alfonso thinks "I'm a *fool*." It is not uncommon to think "I'm a *jerk*" or "I'm a *loser*" when one is disappointed in one's own performance.

Similarly, we may attach negative personal labels to others. We may think "He's a *slob*," or "She's a *bitch*" when the other person fails to live up to our expectations.

Personalization   Personalization is a cognitive distortion in which we tend to take responsibility for another person's failures, lack of success, or otherwise disappointing behavior. Margaret's sixteen year-old son, Steven, is experimenting with drugs. Upset by Steven's behavior, Margaret thinks "I must be doing something wrong. I've failed him as a mother." Burns makes a distinction between **influence** and **control**. It is true that Margaret has some influence over Steven's behavior, and she should make an effort to exert that influence. But it is a fantasy for Margaret to think that she can have absolute control over Steven's behavior.

Briefly, cognitive distortions cause us to see reality in odd ways. In addition, they can produce unwanted and unnecessary negative emotional reactions. This section presented a list of cognitive distortions adapted from the work of the psychiatrist David D. Burns. Cognitive distortions identified were all-or-nothing thinking, overgeneralization, mental filter, disqualifying the positive, jumping to conclusions, magnification or minimization, emotional reasoning, should statements, personal labeling, and personalization.

Transactional analysis is designed to enhance our understanding of how people communicate.

Chapter 5

TRANSACTIONAL ANALYSIS: OF STROKES AND GAMES

Overview

OUTLINE

KEY QUESTIONS

What is transactional analysis?
Transactional analysis is a coherent system of concepts designed to enhance our understanding of how people communicate. The emphasis in transactional analysis is on **interpersonal behavior**, behavior involving two or more people. Transactional analysis also studies how we communicate with ourselves within ourselves, however. This aspect is referred to as **structural analysis**, and it forms the foundation for transactional analysis proper.

How do the principles of transactional analysis relate to adjustment and growth?
Transactional analysis asserts that human beings have a strong tendency to fall into self-defeating patterns of living. **Rackets**, **games**, and **losing scripts** are some of the terms used to suggest these patterns. The aim of transactional analysis is to help us attain greater personal autonomy and intimacy.

Consider the following dialogue:

Tom. I don't know how I'm going to keep up my grades and keep my job too. It looks like I'm going to get a D or an F in statistics the way it's going. Got any ideas?
Sue. Why don't you go to bed an hour earlier every night? Then you can get up bright and early and study.
Tom. No, that wouldn't work. I can't relax if I go to bed too early. I've got to unwind with a little TV.
Sue. Well, maybe you could drop one of your courses. Then you could put more effort into statistics.
Tom. I hate to do that. I counted on completing twelve units this semester.
Sue. I know! Let's just cut out the weekend visiting for the rest of the semester. That'll give you plenty of time to study.
Tom. Are you kidding? Do you want to lose all our friends?
Sue. Well, maybe your boss would be willing to cut your hours from twenty to fifteen—that would give you five extra hours to study.
Tom. No, I don't think he would. Besides, we need all the bread we can get.
Sue. Well, why don't you get a tutor for statistics?
Tom. No, I don't think so.

The preceding dialogue illustrates a game identified by transactional analysis as **Why Don't You, Yes But.** (The concept of a game receives a formal definition later in the chapter. For now, think of a game as a manipulative give-and-take between at least two people.) Tom's statement of his problem would appear to be an adult request for problem-solving suggestions. In actuality, it is a psychological trap designed to put down Sue. Tom's ulterior goal is to feel superior to Sue. In the language of transactional analysis, he seeks to be one up, to be in a position of psychological power. If he succeeds, Sue is one down, in a position of psychological weakness. The seemingly innocent conversation between them in actuality reveals a power struggle initiated by Tom to prove to himself and to Sue that he is the dominant one in their relationship. It is said that *Why Don't You, Yes But* was the first game identified by Eric Berne, the father of transactional analysis. (It is not, however, the basic game. That is identified as **Mine Is Better Than Yours.** More will be said about this game later.)

As noted in Chapter 2, the psychiatrist Harry Stack Sullivan is generally recognized as an important precursor to transactional analysis. Sullivan's idea here well developed in the 1930s, about thirty years before the publication of Eric Berne's best-selling *Games People Play* (1964).

The psychiatrist Thomas A. Harris, one of the founders of the Institute of Transactional Analysis, notes in the preface of *I'm OK—You're OK* (1967) that he first heard the term "interpersonal transactions" under the tutelage of Sullivan. The focus of Sullivan's theorizing was to emphasize the idea that a personal problem has its source in confused and confusing human relations. The problem is not "in" the person. If the problem "is" anywhere, it is "in" the pattern of communication between two or more persons. It is this basic insight that provided the seed from which transactional analysis grew.

WHO WAS ERIC BERNE?

In an article by writer Hugh Gardner, Eric Berne is referred to as oracle, scientist, healer, humorist, and poet of Everyman's destiny. Never, says Gardner, did he have so much fun with his neuroses as when he read what Berne wrote about them. Gardner says:

There were times in my reading when I actually jumped on my feet, so flush with Berne's insights that had the man been within my reach, I probably would have kissed him right then and there on that magnificent cerebral cortex of his. (p. 25)

Eric Berne was born in 1910 and died in 1970. He received his M.D. degree in Canada in 1935 and subsequently trained as a psychiatrist at the Yale University School of Medicine. He was married twice and was the father of four children. Fatherhood was an important element in Berne's life; he believed that many parents turn children into **frogs**, children who suffer from low self-esteem. Berne believed that children are born **princes** or **princesses**, that is, children who have a high self-esteem. When Berne separated from his first wife, he moved to Carmel, California. He began to work in both Carmel and nearby San Francisco. As Berne's ideas on transactional analysis formed, he gathered a group of followers. For a number of years he met with a small group of psychiatrists, psychologists, counselors, and social workers interested in expanding his basic formulations. These informal seminars led to the

Eric Berne was the father of transactional analysis.

eventual formation of the International Transactional Analysis Association and the *Transactional Analysis Journal*.

Berne placed a great deal of emphasis on the concept of "cure" as opposed to "making progress" or "getting better." He was suspicious of psychiatrists who kept patients in long-term therapy, who spoke in terms of slow progress. Such psychiatrists, Berne believed, cater to the patient's unconscious wish to remain locked into old patterns. Berne was also impatient with preoccupation with the *why* of behavior. Constantly asking, "Why do I do this?" or "Why am I this way?" places the sufferer on a mental merry-go-round to nowhere. Berne instead said to his patients, "Why don't you get better first, and then find out why afterward?"

It is important to note that Berne spent a substantial period of his life training to be an orthodox Freudian psychoanalyst. Although he eventually broke with the psychoanalytic establishment, he had a high regard for Freudian theory. Many concepts in transactional analysis have their roots in ideas espoused by Freud and other psychoanalysts. For example, Berne's formulation of Child, Adult, and Parent ego states is similar to Freud's concept of the id, the ego, and the superego. This is not to say that Berne was not a brilliant and original thinker. But it is best to realize that his work has its place within a certain tradition of psychological thinking.

Berne rose to national prominence in 1964 with the phenomenally successful *Games People Play*. For two years the book was at the top of the nation's best-seller lists. It still sells briskly in its paperback version. It has inspired other best-selling books on transactional analysis, such as *I'm OK—You're OK* by Thomas Harris (1967) and *Born to Win* by Muriel James and Dorothy Jongeward (1971). Berne himself was surprised by the popular success of *Games People Play* because it was aimed at a basically professional audience. But Berne's writing and ideas appealed to Everyman. His writing is sprinkled with such colloquialisms as *frog, prince, game, stroke, one up,* and so forth in place of ponderous and self-important psychological terminology. Although the heavy use of colloquialisms gave Berne's writing a "flashy" appearance, it was not Berne's intention to write a superficial "pop psychology." He was adamant about the value of colloquial terminology. The following comment is from *Games People Play*:

As I have tried to show elsewhere in discussing colloquial epithets, a whole page of learned polysyllables may not convey as much as the statement that a certain woman is a bitch, or that a certain man is a jerk. (p. 71)

As already noted, Berne died in 1970, of a heart attack. Claude Steiner, a close associate of Berne's, says in his book, *Scripts People Live* (1974) that he is convinced that Berne himself was living out an unconscious life plan that called for his death of a heart attack in his sixties. Steiner notes that in Berne's books the only cause of death ever mentioned is coronary heart disease.

Berne's father died of a heart attack when Berne was eleven years old; Berne's mother, like Berne, died of a heart attack when she was sixty years old. Steiner says, "I believe that he had a limited life-expectancy script which he lived out just as planned" (p. 19). Such a statement is, of course, highly speculative. Nonetheless, it is provocative.

Berne's intellectual child, transactional analysis, is a robust adolescent now. Although Berne himself is dead, the interest in transactional analysis has not died with him.

THE THREE EGO STATES: WAYS WE EXPERIENCE OURSELVES

The English poet William Wordsworth made the famous comment: "The child is father of the man." The children we once were contributed to the adults we are today, and those children are retained in our adult personalities in some form. Eric Berne's formulations expand greatly on these observations. According to him, as adults we have three potential ego states: the Child, the Parent, and the Adult (see Figure 5.1). You will notice that the terms are capitalized. This is done to distinguish them from a living child, parent, or adult. The term **ego states** is used to indicate that from time to time we actually experience ourselves as acting like children, parents, or adults (Berne, 1966). We "enter into" an ego state as we might enter a room.

The Child

Berne identifies the Child ego state as a set of emotional "recordings" carried forward from childhood. The feelings we felt as children we are capable of reexperiencing in the present. Transactional analysis makes heavy use of a

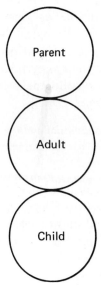

FIGURE 5.1   The basic structure of the personality according to Eric Berne.

variety of metaphors to present its case and clarify its meaning. Thus it is said that something pushes your Child "button" and an old "tape" starts playing. For example, say that a married man was a bully when he was a child. When anyone frustrated him, he began pushing and shoving. Now he is having an argument with his wife, and feels frustrated. He begins to push and shove her about the kitchen, copying the behavior of the little bully he was in grammar school. His wife's behavior pushed his Child button, and he entered his Child ego state. His Child is now determining his behavior, not his thinking Adult.

Of course, husbands are not the only ones who may enter the Child ego state when quarreling with their spouses. Let us say that a particular wife tended to pout and cry as a child when her parents didn't let her have her way. Now, as an adult, her husband may be objecting to plans she made for the weekend without consulting him. She may enter her Child ego state, pouting and crying as she did when she was an actual child.

Many examples can be given of ways we enter the Child. An adult riding the roller coaster at an amusement park may take on the behavior characteristics of a child. Body posture and facial expressions mimic the way the person acted when he was younger. The person may use speech patterns that were popular when he was a child: "Whee! This is keen!" For all practical purposes, this adult has temporarily become a child. He has "lost himself," we say. Transactional analysts would simply say that he is in his Child ego state.

According to Berne, the Child may be divided into three levels: (1) the Adapted Child, (2) the Rebellious Child, and (3) the Natural Child (see Figure 5.2). The Adapted Child represents the part of the Child that conforms, adapts to society's rules, and tries to please Mommy and Daddy. The question immediately arises: "Why does the child try to adapt at all? Why is it so desperately important to please Mommy and Daddy?" The answer given by Berne is, essentially, that human beings have a powerful inborn craving for affection. Berne cites the research of Harry Harlow with infant monkeys, which demonstrated that personality development is grossly distorted when the infant monkey is reared in social isolation without mother love. Berne also cites the research of René Spitz with infants reared in orphanages; Spitz

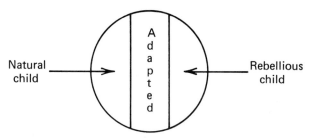

FIGURE 5.2 The three levels of the Child ego state.

demonstrated that ignored infants—infants in a state of psychological-emotional deprivation—developed poorly and had high death rates. As the child grows older, the need for affection translates itself into a **recognition hunger**, a need to have others confirm one's presence and existence. Thus it is common for children to say, "Look at me!" when they do something. As adults, we also want to be recognized.

The preceding observations are captured by the transactional analysis term **stroke**, which is any act that recognizes the presence of another person. An infant is being stroked when diapers are being changed, when being fed, or when being tickled. In terms of the conditioning process, it is presumed that symbolic expressions of attention become associated with actual physical stroking and are eventually capable of replacing it to some degree. Thus an adult is being stroked when someone says, "Hello," when someone listens to a story, when someone says, "Do you think it will rain today?" Any form of human recognition has stroke value.

The Adapted Child, then, is the aspect of the Child that earns strokes. If a child's parents are the kind of people who demand that the child be "nice" in order to earn strokes, if strokes are almost always conditional, if affection must be "purchased" by actions, that child will become an adult with an overdeveloped Adapted Child. This would be the kind of person who is supersweet, too goody-goody, and excessively polite. In conventional psychological language, such a person would exhibit neurotic trends.

Let us turn to the second level of the Child identified by Berne, the Rebellious Child. The Rebellious Child also develops out of the human need for strokes. Assume that a child's parents are the kind of people who notice the child only when he is acting up. The child is psychologically invisible until he breaks something, says a four-letter word, wets his bed, brings home a poor report card, irritates the neighbors, or engages in any other kind of behavior that automatically commands attention. The parents are forced to notice the child by his acts of rebellion. By noticing the child, they stroke him. Although they may hit, shout, scream, or become irrational, these are still strokes. They represent some form of attention, some form of recognition; and anything that makes the parents acknowledge the child's existence is better than nothing. When parents become punitive in words or actions, such strokes are called **negative strokes**. Transactional analysis asserts that negative strokes reinforce the formation of the Rebellious Child.

In an illustrated book titled *T.A. for Tots* by psychologist Alvin Freed (1973), positive strokes are called **warm fuzzies** and negative strokes are called **cold pricklies**. The thesis is that we prefer warm fuzzies, but will take cold pricklies if we have to. Cold pricklies are better than nothing, and many children and adults are forced to survive on an emotional diet of cold pricklies. If a child has the kind of parents who withhold warm fuzzies, and if they give cold pricklies when the child is being a nuisance, that child will become an adult with an overdeveloped Rebellious Child. This would be the kind of person who always places himself first, has little affection for others, tends to be highly impulsive, has a hard time waiting for gratification, often breaks rules, and in general tends to "have a chip on his or her shoulder." In conventional psychological language, such a person would exhibit the traits associated with character disorders.

Let us now turn to the third level of the Child identified by Berne, the Natural Child. The growth of the Natural Child is also fostered by strokes—positive strokes. In addition, these strokes do not have to be earned by "being nice" or by acting in such-and-such a way. Assume that a child is fortunate enough to have parents who give the child quite a lot of spontaneous affection and attention. They like to play with the child, talk to the child, and go places with the child. The child does not have to either earn positive strokes by acting in a particular way nor demand negative strokes by becoming a nuisance. Parents who foster the development of the Natural Child give the child a great deal of unconditional stroking, stroking that is not tied to some sort of explicit behavior on the child's part. Unconditional stroking acts on the Natural Child like sunshine acts on a plant. The Natural Child thrives on the warmth of love freely given.

If a child has the kind of parents who give the child a great many unconditional positive strokes as he or she is growing up, that child will become an adult with a well-developed Natural Child. This would be the kind of person who has high self-esteem, likes other people, is autonomous without being a lawbreaker, and is capable of participating in intimate (game-free) human relationships. In conventional psychological language, such a person would exhibit the attributes associated with the healthy personality.

The growth of the Natural Child is fostered by unconditional positive strokes.

To Berne, adults with an overdeveloped Adapted Child or Rebellious Child were victims of poor parenting. They had been converted from princes or princesses into frogs. Adults with a well-developed Natural Child retain their birthright. They remain princes and princesses.

All this may seem a bit hard on parents, but Berne believed that the experiences of childhood are the prime determiners of the human personality. During the child's formative years, before he can think for himself, the parents shape the child's development. Of course Berne recognized that many children are raised by single parents, stepparents, foster parents, counselors in institutions, and so forth. Such parent surrogates may be loosely labeled "parents" if they have the kind of impact on the child's development usually associated with natural parents.

The Parent

Berne describes the Parent ego state as having certain similarities to the Child ego state. Like the Child, the Parent also consists of a set of "recordings" carried forward from childhood. The Parent recordings often have to do with "oughts" and "shoulds." The Parent represents our incorporation of our parents' values, and our personal moral code is based on Parent recordings. We "hear" our parents or parental figures saying, "A penny saved is a penny earned," or "You should always go to church on Sunday," or "Work hard and be thrifty," or "You're never going to amount to anything," or "You're going to be famous someday." The part of the Parent that moralizes and issues advice is called the Controlling Parent. The Parent has another aspect, the Nurturing Parent. Thus the Parent has two levels (see Figure 5.3).

The Controlling Parent is an inner judge. It acts as a watchdog of our behavior and says such things as, "You really shouldn't be taking a second helping of dessert; you ought to lose weight," or "You're really a jerk! How could you have gotten a D on that test?" or "You're a failure! You had a good chance and you blew it!" When we blame ourselves, when we criticize ourselves, when we deplore our own behavior, it is the Parent speaking down to the Child that produces inner bad feelings.

The Controlling Parent is also an outer judge. When our Parent button is pushed, we enter the Parent ego state and look down our noses at other people. To illustrate, say that a middle-aged businessman and his wife are driving down the highway in their air-conditioned Cadillac. They pass a young couple hitchhiking. The girl is braless, and the boy has long hair. The businessman mutters, "Darn hippies! Why don't they clean up and get to work—do something useful with their lives?" His wife replies, "They're disgusting. And did you see the girl? What a brazen hussy—revolting!" Both the businessman and his wife are speaking out of the Controlling Parent. The sight of the young couple pushed their respective Parent buttons, and they ran off some old tapes. When we are in the Controlling Parent, the words that come out of our mouths represent, not thought, *but what we were taught*. It is as if we were robots, reciting old moral lessons. The person who is critical of others is an individual who is often prone to enter his Controlling Parent.

The Controlling Parent is the agent of society. Its aim is to "keep us in line" and force us to conform to the norms of the behavior expected of us. Its concern is primarily with the survival of groups to which we may belong, not individual survival. The Controlling Parent seeks to make us resemble good members of an ant colony. We are to do our duty, place others first, and ignore our own feelings. A certain amount of Controlling Parent is probably necessary for a person to become socialized. A person with an overdeveloped Controlling Parent, however, will tend to also have an overdeveloped Adapted Child. Such a person will be too socialized for his or her own good. This person will tend to be uptight, prone to emotionally induced illness, and unable to just relax and have some fun. He or she will take things too seriously and will lack a spontaneous sense of humor.

The other level of the Parent is the Nurturing Parent. The function of the Nurturing Parent is to provide strokes. Like the Controlling Parent, the Nurturing Parent has its inner and outer aspects. The Nurturing Parent is aimed inward when a person strokes himself. Self-praise would be an example of the inward function of the Nurturing Parent. A person might make a success of a task and give himself a mental pat on the back, saying to himself, "A job well done." The Nurturing Parent is aimed outward when a person strokes someone else. Giving children recognition for their real accomplishments would have its source in the Nurturing Parent. Also, a person with a well-developed Nurturing Parent is capable of genuine concern for the welfare of others, whether they be children or adults. People with a large Nurturing Parent can give other people strokes freely without necessarily demanding strokes in return. Their philosophy is not "If you scratch my back, I'll scratch yours," but "I'll scratch your back because I like to see you feeling good." A well-developed Nurturing Parent is an important component of the healthy personality.

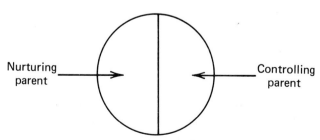

FIGURE 5.3 The two levels of the Parent ego state.

The Adult

The Adult ego state is the computer of the personality. Its function is to be rational, plan ahead, and take reality into account. It has no feeling of its own, and an actual adult whose personality is all Adult would be a human iceberg. The science-fiction character Mr. Spock of the Star Trek series is the caricature of a person who can think but who has no feeling. The Adult begins to form in early childhood, differentiating itself from the Child and the Parent. You must not confuse the term Adult with an actual adult. Thus a child of five can be said to have an Adult, although this child is not yet an actual adult. This is merely another way of saying that the child has some capacity to think for himself.

In some adults, the Adult is not sufficiently discriminated from the Child and the Parent. Transactional analysis speaks of such a situation as **contamination** (Forman and Ramsburg, 1978). A person can have an Adult that is contaminated by the Child, an Adult that is contaminated by the Parent, or an Adult that is contaminated by both the Child and the Parent. Say that Bill's Adult is contaminated by his Child (see Figure 5.4). He tends to be impulsive, inappropriate in social situations, and selfish. His Adult and his Child are mixed up with each other, and he has a hard time acting with appropriate maturity. Say that Susan's Adult is contaminated by the Child. In her case, imagine that the Child has almost completely swamped the Adult. Susan tends to exhibit the traits we associate with some psychotic reactions—silliness, flights of fantasy, disorientation, and so forth.

Now assume that Tom's Adult is contaminated by his Parent (see Figure 5.5). He tends to be hard on himself and others; he owns his own business, works ten to twelve hours a day, six days a week; and he seldom takes a vacation. In many ways he is mimicking his father, who used to be fond of saying, "Early to bed, early to rise, makes a man healthy, wealthy, and wise." Tom also tends to be prejudicial in his thinking. "The Republican party is the only true American party," he has said many times. But he has never really thought about this statement; he was raised a Republican, and he is parroting what he heard as a child.

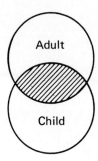

FIGURE 5.4   An example of contamination. In this case the Adult is contaminated by the Child.

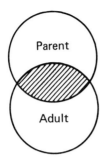

FIGURE 5.5 Another example of contamination. In this case the Adult is contaminated by the Parent.

Say that Karen's Adult is contaminated by both the Child and the Parent. Such a state may be defined as **double contamination** (see Figure 5.6). Karen has a hard time thinking for herself. She is a slave to the ideas implanted into her head by her parents and other authority figures. At the same time, she tends to make decisions on an emotional basis. Recently she was a guest at a dinner party and was offered a rich dessert by the hostess. Karen is over-weight, and she is always talking about losing weight. In response to the rich dessert, her Parent proclaimed, "It isn't polite to say no." Her Child shouted, "I want it!" Her Adult, heavily contaminated by the Parent and the Child, made no clear expression of its opinion. Karen took the cake and ate it rapidly. Her behavior was unthinking and programmed—determined by messages from the Parent and the Child.

In contrast with contamination of the Adult by a particular ego state, transactional analysis identifies a condition known as **blockage**. Blockage takes place when there is a barrier between one ego state and the Adult. To illustrate, Linda's Adult is contaminated by her Parent, but there is a block between her Adult and her Child (see Figure 5.7). Linda is the martyr-home-maker-superwoman, holding a demanding job, constantly cleaning house, running errands for her husband and children, cooking elaborate dinners,

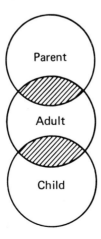

FIGURE 5.6 An example of double contamination. In this case the Adult is contaminated by both the Parent and the Child.

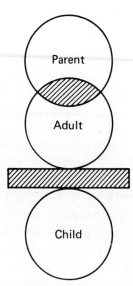

FIGURE 5.7 An example in which the Adult is contaminated by the Parent and there is a block between the Child and the Adult.

and responsible to a fault. She leads a joyless existence, however. There simply isn't any fun in her life; she seldom relaxes or laughs spontaneously. Her potentially happy Child has been locked away in a psychological freezer. In Linda's case, there is a block between her Adult and her Child.

A second kind of blockage takes place when there is a barrier between the Adult and the Parent. From the point of view of civilized living, this kind of blockage is of more concern than the first. To illustrate, Pete's Adult is contaminated by his Child, and there is a block between his Adult and his Parent (see Figure 5.8). Pete's parents were much too harsh and punitive. Pete's father used to whip the boy with a leather belt for minor infractions of parental law. Pete's mother was a slapper, and she had little emotional self-control.

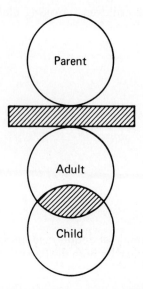

FIGURE 5.8 An example in which the Adult is contaminated by the Child and there is a block between the Parent and the Adult.

Pete's parents were once investigated for child abuse, but they were not prosecuted. Pete preserved his psychological existence by insulating himself emotionally from his parents. He stopped caring about what they thought or felt or wanted of him. Thus Pete was unable to internalize the little his parents had to give him in the way of human values. Speaking of people like Pete, Harris comments in *I'm OK—You're OK* (1967):

He excludes the painful Parent, but he also excludes what little "good" there is in the Parent. Such a person does not have available to his current transactions any tapes which supply data having to do with social control, appropriate "shoulds" and "should nots," cultural norms, or what, in one sense, may be referred to as conscience. His behavior is dominated by his Child, which through the contaminated Adult manipulates other people to his own ends. (p. 103)

A third kind of blockage occurs when there are two psychological barriers, one between the Parent and the Adult and the other between the Child and the Adult (see Figure 5.9). In such a case, the Adult is not functioning at all. The person is either in a Parent ego state or in a Child ego state. Transactional analysis associates this condition with psychosis. The person with a blocked-out Adult cannot think for himself, is not capable of rational action, and is not oriented toward reality. We speak of such people as "crazy," "nuts," "weird," "screwballs," and so forth. Not all such people are in mental hospitals, but many are. Countless examples of the person with a nonfunctioning Adult could be drawn from hospital case reports. As a brief illustration, let us again refer to Harris. He offers the case of a female patient in a mental hospital "whose singing of tent-meeting hymns (Parent) was inter-

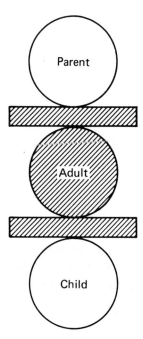

FIGURE 5.9   In the case of double blockage, the Adult is out of commission.

5.1   CONTEMPORARY RESEARCH: EGOGRAMS

Based on clinical research, an innovative application of the concept of ego states has been proposed by psychiatrist John M. Dusay, author of *Egograms* (1977). Dusay was associated with Berne and his early seminars on transactional analysis. Dusay (1977, p. 3) defines an **egogram** as "a bar graph showing the relationship of the parts of the personality to each other and the amount of psychological energy emanating outward." He indicates that each person has a unique egogram profile. The egogram is constructed in a conversation between the therapist and the client. Dusay notes that it is based on intuition, and is born of the cooperation between the "feeling" and "thinking" sides of the individual.

An egogram is constructed by drawing a horizontal line on a piece of paper. There are five equal spaces reserved, from left to right, for Critical Parent (CP), Nurturing Parent (NP), Adult (A), Free Child (FC), and Adapted Child (AC). (Note that Dusay's designations deviate slightly from prior terminology used here. He uses "Critical Parent" instead of "Controlling Parent," "Free Child" instead of "Natural Child," and there is no category in the egogram, as presented by Dusay, for Rebellious Child.)

A vertical column is drawn above each of the ego state labels to indicate the magnitude of the role that a given ego state seems to play in one's personality. The relative heights of the columns provide a graphic display of the interactions of the five ego states.

A typical egogram is presented in Figure 5.10 for a person we will call Clara. The large Critical Parent suggests that Clara is very self-demanding. The small Nurturing Parent suggests that she has a difficult time giving or receiving unconditional affection, praise, or recognition. The large Adult sug-

spersed with obscenities relating to body functions (Child)." Harris states (1967):

The content was bizarre, but seemed to replay an old Parent-Child conflict between good and bad, should and should not, salvation and damnation. The content of these verbal productions quickly revealed a great deal about her Parent and Child. The fact that her Adult was gone indicated the severity of the conflict (p. 105)

What we have been discussing in the past few pages is formally termed **structural analysis**. Structural analysis is the study of how the three ego states—Parent, Adult, and Child—relate to each other in a single individual. Structural analysis forms the theoretical foundation for transactional analy-

gests she is responsible, logical, and rational. The small Free Child suggests she has a difficult time just letting go and having some fun; being spontaneous and relaxed is a problem for her. The large Adapted Child suggests she has a great need for affection and recognition, and attempts to earn these by "being good" and "doing the right thing." Note that the large Critical Parent and the small Free Child are logical reciprocals of each other. So are the small Nurturing Parent and the large Adapted Child.

One purpose of egograms is to advance our general understanding of personality structure. A second purpose is to help individuals see their own personality structures in meaningful ways. Dusay asserts that this in turn can lead to creative action and personal growth.

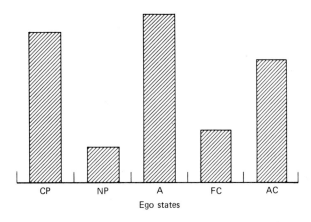

FIGURE 5.10   An egogram for a person we will call Clara. CP = Controlling Parent, NP = Nurturing Parent, A = Adult, FC = Free Child, and AC = Adapted Child.

sis proper, the study of how two or more persons communicate with each other.

TRANSACTIONS: LOOKING FOR STROKES

A transaction is defined by Berne as the unit of social intercourse. As such, a transaction always contains a transactional stimulus and a transactional response. You say, "Hello" to a friend you pass in the hallway; the friend responds by saying "Hello" to you. This is an illustration of a simple transaction. Your "Hello" was the transactional stimulus. His "Hello" was the transactional response. Transactions need not be at a verbal level. Say that

Tom sees a pretty girl in the school cafeteria and he would like to get acquainted. Tom smiles at her. She sticks out her tongue at him. Their behaviors also represent a transaction with a stimulus and a response.

Why do we engage in transactions? Berne's answer is that they provide us with strokes. Strokes satisfy the human need for some sort of affection. By being recognized and paid attention to, our affectional drive is gratified. As already noted, strokes may be positive or negative. Although we tend to prefer positive strokes, we will accept negative strokes in preference to no strokes at all. To the transactional analyst, this observation offers an explanation of why people often maintain destructive relationships for long periods of time.

Complementary Transactions

If all transactions between human beings were complementary, this would be a rather bland world. The **complementary transaction** is defined as a no-conflict transaction. On the transactional analysis diagrams, the lines representing the transactional stimulus and the transactional response are parallel (see Figure 5.11). So long as this condition is met, the transaction is complementary. The following are some examples of complementary transactions.

Parent-Parent

Husband. The governor of this state is a jerk! Why can't he get the bums off of welfare?
Wife. I hate to see our tax money go to support a bunch of shameless unwed mothers.

Mother 1. The Smith children are so poorly mannered. I hate to have them play with my children.
Mother 2. I know! The other day I saw Billy Smith picking his nose while he was eating an ice cream cone.

The Parent-Parent transaction often represents an exchange of prejudices. As such, it does not indicate an expression of thought on the part of the speakers; instead, it serves as a pleasant pastime.

Child-Child

Husband. Hey, this is great fun! I haven't been on a roller coaster in years.
Wife. Oh, it's so scary way up here!

Mother. I know I'm on a diet, but I'm going to cheat just this once and have a hot fudge sundae. What do you say, Susan? Would you like to stop at a coffee shop for a treat?
Child. Oh boy! Sounds great!

Child 1 (watching cartoon). Ha-ha-ha! Bugs Bunny is so funny!
Child 2. Ha-ha-ha! I think so too!

Friend 1. I'm really depressed today.
Friend 2. I know what you mean. Things are really getting me down too.

The Child-Child transaction tends to be an exchange at emotional level. The feeling expressed can be positive or negative, as indicated in the preceding examples.

Adult-Adult

Boyfriend. Should I pick you up at seven?
Girlfriend. No, it would be better for me if you came over about eight.

Student. What is the length of one meter?
Teacher. A meter is 39.37 inches.

Husband. Honey, where's my favorite blue shirt?
Wife. I put it in the front closet—between two white shirts.

Child 1. Can you come out and play?
Child 2. No, Mom says I have to wash up for dinner.

Prospect. I'm not interested in the savings aspect of life insurance, just the protection aspect.
Salesman. Then you would be interested in a straight-term policy, not an endowment policy.

Mother. I expect you to make your own bed every day.
Child. Do I have to do it before I go to school, or can it wait until I come home?

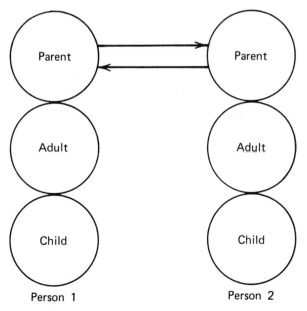

FIGURE 5.11 An example of a complementary transaction. The diagram illustrates a Parent-Parent transaction.

The Adult-Adult transaction tends to be nonemotional and reality oriented. Its purpose is to make a decision, solve a problem, or exchange information. As you can see from the preceding examples, Adult-Adult exchanges can take place between children and between a parent and a child. The transaction is Adult-Adult if it is out of the Adult ego states. The person's status as an actual parent, child, or adult has nothing to do with categorizing a transaction.

Parent-Child

Husband. You never clean this house! It's beginning to look like a pigpen!
Wife (tearfully). I'm sorry, honey. I'm going to try to do better.

Wife. I'm ashamed of you, Fred Jones! Do you realize that you drank like a pig tonight?
Husband. You're right, sweetheart. I'm such a fool. You know I'm weak when it comes to alcohol. Please forgive me.

Mother. You've become a very irresponsible boy, Jimmy. You never pick up your clothes on your own—I always have to tell you.
Son. Please don't be mad at me, Momma. I'll pick them up right away.

Teacher. This essay is sloppy and completely without organization.
Student (hanging head). Yes, ma'am. I'm sorry.

Boss. Is this the way you wipe off a table? Are you a busboy or a zombie? My two-year-old son could get a table cleaner than this.
Employee. Yes, sir. I'm sorry.

Mother (listening to her daughter play the piano). That was fantastic, Julie! You have great talent.
Daughter. Gee! Thanks, Mom.

Boyfriend. You look just great in that dress—terrific!
Girlfriend. Wow! I'm so happy you like it, Bill.

Parent-Child transactions tend to represent either criticism or praise. If the transactional stimulus is out of the person's Controlling Parent, the aim of the speaker is to put down the listener and to be one up himself. If the transactional stimulus comes out of the person's Nurturing Parent, the aim of the speaker is to stroke the listener's Child. Parent-Child transactions are identified as complementary because the person in the Child position agrees with the statements made by the person in the Parent position.

Crossed Transactions

A crossed transaction takes place when there is conflict between two or more people. On a transactional analysis diagram, the lines representing the transactional stimulus and the transactional response cross (see Figure 5.12). The following are some examples of crossed transactions.

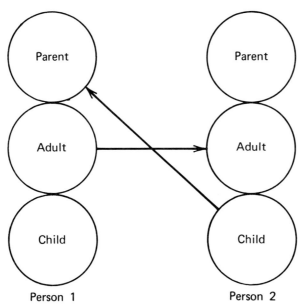

FIGURE 5.12 An example of a crossed transaction. The diagram illustrates an Adult-Adult, Child-Parent transaction.

Adult-Adult, Child-Parent

Teacher. What is seven times eight, Suzie?
Student. It's too hard! Why do you keep picking on me?

Husband. Honey, I'd like to explain my life insurance policies to you.
Wife. Oh, this is so boring! Why do you have to force me to think about things I don't want to think about?

A crossed transaction takes place when there is conflict between two or more people.

Adult-Adult, Parent-Child

Son. What time is it, Mom?
Mother. You're a pest.

Employee. Can I have off next Tuesday?
Boss. You've been asking for too many privileges, Harry. It's about time you realized that we keep our noses to the old grindstone around here.

Husband. Why is the gas tank almost empty? Didn't you have time to stop for gas?
Wife. You're irresponsible too. You didn't put your socks in the clothes hamper today. I always have to pick up after you, just like a little kid.

Parent-Child, Parent-Child

Husband. You never clean this house! It's beginning to look like a pigpen!
Wife. And you never clean the yard! You should get out there right now and start working on it.

Mother. You've become a very irresponsible boy, Jimmy. You never pick up your clothes on your own—I always have to tell you.
Son. You don't do what you're supposed to either. I keep asking for pancakes for breakfast, and all you give me is cold cereal. You're lazier than I am!

Parent-Child, Adult-Adult

Husband. You never clean this house! It's beginning to look like a pigpen!
Wife. Billy was sick with the flu today.

Wife. I'm ashamed of you, Fred Jones! Do you realize that you drank like a pig tonight?
Husband. I'm going to call Alcoholics Anonymous and get some help.

Teacher. This essay is sloppy and completely without organization.
Student. I'm going to get some books on composition and study them. And I'm going to get a tutor.

As already noted, the crossed transaction represents conflict. It also represents a break in communication. As such, however, it is not "all bad." There are times when a crossed transaction is preferable to a complementary transaction. Transactional analysis notes that when someone addresses your Child from their Parent, one strong tendency is to accept the Child position and engage in a complementary transaction. If you do this, you will feel put down. The other strong tendency is to "flip" from the Child to the Parent. If you then address the other person's Child from your Parent, you will have a harsh crossed transaction (Parent-Child, Parent-Child). The optimal response when addressed Parent-Child would seem to be to come back Adult-Adult. Although this too represents a crossed transaction, it is a fairly moderate one. There may be some confrontation, but it is realistic confrontation.

Ulterior Transactions

Berne identifies **ulterior transactions** as those involving the activity of more than two ego states simultaneously. Ulterior transactions contain a hidden message, and they underlie most games. Ulterior transactions have a hidden aim or purpose and as such are the real troublemakers of human communication. There are two levels to ulterior transactions: (1) the social level and (2) the psychological level (see Table 5.1). The social level contains the manifest message, a message that is being communicated in an obvious sense. The psychological level contains the latent message, a message that hides behind the surface message. The latent message is often the "real" message contained within the transaction.

Two kinds of ulterior transactions are identified by transactional analysis: (1) angular transactions and (2) duplex transactions. An angular transaction involves three ego states in two persons (see Figure 5.13). Say that an automobile salesperson is talking to a customer. The salesperson says, "The Hornet-X is the top of our line, but the payments are probably more than you can afford." To simplify what may be an involved set of transactions, say that at some point the customer says, "I'll buy it." What has happened? The salesperson has spoken from his own Adult to two ego states in the customer, the customer's Adult and the customer's Child. The salesman's messages at the social level are Adult-Adult. They state facts. The Hornet-X is the top of the line. And it is true that the customer's financial resources will be strained if the person buys the Hornet-X. The salesman is also, however,

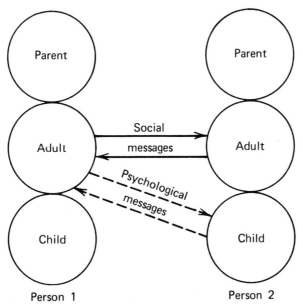

FIGURE 5.13 An example of an angular transaction.

5.2   APPLICATION: LOOKING FOR HIDDEN MEANINGS

If we take the transactional analysis concept of ulterior messages seriously, we will be on the alert for hidden meanings in the statements, remarks, questions, and requests of other people. Psychologist Gerald Smith (1977) has written a whole book called *Hidden Meanings* in which a number of ulterior messages are catalogued and described. Examples are given of ulterior transactions between lovers, parent and child, friends, and associates and acquaintances.

Let's expand a bit on just one category, hidden meanings between friends. As Smith points out, friendship offers an opportunity for talking openly and directly. Unfortunately, too often friends hide behind a verbal camouflage. For example, a friend says to you, "Are you tired?" On the surface this seems to be a solicitous inquiry. However, say that your friend has been trying to get your attention in a conversation, and you have been acting bored. Then the question's hidden meaning may very well be, "I'm exasperated with you."

You have just had a disappointment or a financial reversal. Maybe it's your fault; maybe it's not. A friend glibly advises, "I think you should ask yourself what you can learn from this experience." The hidden meaning is, "I wouldn't have done such a stupid thing." The friend is gloating with superiority.

Perhaps a friend criticizes you. You try to explain that you don't agree with the criticism. You are told, "Don't be so defensive." The hidden message

TABLE 5.1   KINDS OF TRANSACTIONS

Kind	Diagram	A Key Aspect
Complementary	Parallel lines	No conflict between person 1 and person 2.
Crossed	Crossed lines	Conflict between person 1 and person 2.
Ulterior	Social level represented with a solid line. Psychological level represented with a dashed line.	The transaction has two levels. The social level contains the manifest message. The psychological level contains a hidden message.

sending a message from his Adult to the customer's Child. This unspoken message taunts the customer. It says, "The other kids can have toys you can't have." The unspoken message "hooks the Child" of the customer, makes the

is that you lack objectivity about yourself; it also insultingly suggests that you don't really know your own mind.

The value of decoding messages and looking for hidden meanings is that you find out what another person really intends by his or her remarks. Sometimes this can be very useful to you. You don't go forward on a false basis, and choices are open to you. You can respond directly to the hidden meaning, ignore it, or cope with it in some other way. But you know what you are responding to, and don't feel that you are shadow boxing.

For instance, say that you have decided that the hidden meaning of "Are you tired?" is "I'm exasperated with you."(Remember, your friend has been trying to get your attention and you have been acting bored.) You can say, "I know I might seem bored. But please don't take offense. I really *am* very tired." Or you might respond only to the surface message and say, "No, I'm not tired." Thus you seem to ignore the hidden meaning. But you don't really ignore it in your actions. You put a greater effort into looking interested in the conversation.

Although it can be of value to be aware of hidden meanings, it should be remembered that not all messages have hidden meanings. You can develop too much mistrust and suspicion, constantly thinking, "What did he mean by that remark?" or "Just what is she getting at?" Let's decide that a message has a hidden meaning only if some strong clue in the other person's facial expression, tone of voice, or other body language suggests that there is one.

Child feel an emotion such as envy, and as such plays a potent part in the customer's decision.

A duplex ulterior transaction involves four ego states in two persons (see Figure 5.14). Berne (1964) offers a simple flirtation as an example of a duplex transaction:

Cowboy. Come and see the barn.
Visitor. I've loved barns ever since I was a little girl. (p. 33)

At the social level, the cowboy's Adult is addressing the visitor's Adult, politely inviting her to see a building. But the hidden message from his Child to her Child is "Let's have some fun." Her Child is apparently saying, "I'd like to have some fun too."

Duplex transactions can take on a variety of patterns. Oftentimes there are Parent-Child messages involved. Harris (1967) offers the following example:

Husband says to wife, "Where did you hide the can opener?" The main stimulus is Adult in that it seeks objective information. But there is a secondary communication

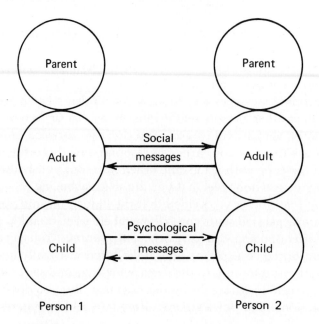

FIGURE 5.14   An example of a duplex transaction.

in the word hide. (Your housekeeping is a mystery to me. We'd go broke if I were as disorganized as you. If I could once, just once, find something where it belongs!) This is Parent. It is a thinly veiled criticism. (p. 89)

The analysis of transactions is designed to throw a spotlight on the processes of social intercourse. Berne assumes that there are many hidden snares in human communication and that we are somewhat better off when we know something about where and what these snares are.

THE FOUR EXISTENTIAL POSITIONS: ARE YOU OK?

Berne's view that we are all born princes or princesses and that early childhood experiences with parents and authority figures often turn us into frogs has given rise to the analysis of basic outlooks on life. These outlooks are called **existential positions**, stances we take toward ourselves and our relationships with others. Four basic positions are identified: (1) I'm not OK—You're OK, (2) I'm OK—You're not OK, (3) I'm not OK—You're not OK, and (4) I'm OK—You're OK.

I'm Not OK—You're OK

"I'm not OK—you're OK" is a kind of shorthand for saying that some people suffer from low self-esteem and see others as having traits they themselves lack. Such people tend to view themselves as incompetent, unintelligent, not pretty, not handsome, lacking in creativity, unpopular, uncoordinated, or otherwise inferior. If a person is convinced that she is unintelligent, she sees the planet as populated with hordes of people brighter than she is. If a man has become convinced that he is not handsome, he lives in a psychological world where everyone seems to be handsomer than he is.

Inferiority feelings often have little or no relationship to actual inferiorities. A bright person may be convinced that she is not bright. An attractive man may be sure that he is unattractive. These are matters of self-image—matters that have to do with subjective perceptions, not external reality. This is the point at which Berne's notion of royalty turning into frogs comes into play. The infant is born feeling OK. The growing child will feel OK too if the parents can give unconditional strokes and refrain from being hypercritical. Unfortunately, many parents have a big Controlling Parent, and this Controlling Parent does untold damage to the child's developing self-image. The destructive parent makes many **attributions**, statements to the child that he or she has such and such personality characteristics. "You're lazy," or "You're rude," or "You're stubborn just like your father," or "Stop being such a clod," or "You're dumb," or "I never thought a child of mine would have such straight hair" are a few examples of ways in which children are made to feel bad about themselves.

Sometimes attributions are unspoken. The criticism is hidden in an ulterior message. To illustrate, Joan read a book called *Between Parent and Child* by Haim Ginott (1969). In that book, Ginott recommends that children be given a choice in matters that affect them. Joan decided this was sound advice and told herself that from now on she was going to allow her five-year-old daughter Carol to do more thinking for herself. A short time later they were in a children's dress shop. Joan found only two dresses whe would consider buying for Carol, one pink and one yellow. She had a strong private preference for the yellow dress, but she was determined to allow Carol to do some thinking for herself. She told Carol, "You can have the dress you like better." This was a message from Joan's Adult to her child's Adult. Delightedly, Carol rapidly picked the pink dress. Immediately Joan's face took on an icy look; her posture became rigid. Her facial expression and body posture said, "You have very poor judgement." This message was from Joan's Controlling Parent to Carol's Child.

Joan was following the letter of Ginott's advice, but she was unable to enter into the spirit of the advice. Under these conditions, she was sending her daughter a confusing message. Transactional analysis asserts that if there is a pattern of similar experiences, a child such as Carol will develop, as part of her self-image, the idea "I have poor taste in clothes"—even if her mother never says so at a verbal level.

A traditionalist would identify the person in the I'm not OK—you're OK position as having neurotic patterns of behavior or an anxiety disorder. But transactional analysis prefers not to use conventional psychological labels. The important thing, according to transactional analysis, is not to assign the word "neurotic" to someone, but to understand the underlying process. By recognizing the interpersonal pattern that is typical of "neurosis," there is some possibility of breaking free from the pattern.

It should be noted that transactional analysis sees the majority of people in the I'm not OK—you're OK position. The argument is that the vast majority of parents tend to be overcontrolling. They use put-downs, attributions, and ulterior messages as their way of socializing the child. Also, their strokes are conditional; affection must be earned. Thus Berne saw the vast majority of individuals in the one down position, struggling to overcome feelings of inferiority traceable to early childhood experiences.

I'm OK—You're Not OK

The person in the I'm OK—you're not OK position feels that he is superior to other people and that, consequently, he has a right to use others for his own ends. He looks down on others as "worms," "cruds," "jerks," "saps," "dummies," "pigeons," or "suckers." The conscious position is one of smug self-confidence. But it is clear that in some cases this is a mask or a pose designed to cover up inferiority feelings. The person in this position tends to behave in an undersocialized manner. He may be a common criminal, breaking the law to reach his goals. More commonly, however, he would be a criminal from a moral, but not a legal, point of view. He knows what he can get away with. Thus he becomes what is variously described as a "con artist," "wheeler-dealer," "manipulator," "fast-talker," "supersalesman," or "make-out artist." The existence of so many slang terms for people who behave out of the second position suggests the common recognition of such persons.

The roots of the second position were described earlier in this chapter. You will recall the transactional analysis formulation of the person with a big Rebellious Child. It is theorized that such persons had to force their parents to pay attention to them by acts of rebellion. Thus persons in the second position probably got their strokes in the form of punishment. If the punishment was excessive or unfair, it tended to reinforce the I'm OK—you're not OK position. The child thought, "It's not fair. They had no right to do that to me. My parents are a couple of cruds." According to transactional analysis, a pattern of harsh punishment tends to backfire. Instead of socializing the child, it sends the child into the basically antisocial second position. The traditionalist would associate personality disorders with the second position.

I'm Not OK—You're Not OK

People in the I'm not OK—you're not OK position feel that they are inferior in some way. At the same time they also feel that other people are defective in some way. Others are incompetent, have bad intentions, or are conspirators. This third position is a position of no self-trust and no trust of others.

Thus it is the "sickest" of the life positions. A person in the third position is likely to exhibit highly inappropriate behavior from a conventional point of view. Slang terms used to describe people in the third position are "crazy," "screwy," "nuts," "cracked," "goofy," "dizzy," and so forth. The existence of so many slang terms is significant because it suggests the reality of the third life position. Slang terms arise in response to a need for an everyday descriptive language. In traditional terms, persons in the third position would be associated with various kinds of psychotic disorders.

How do people get into the third position? We must realize that traditional psychologists and psychiatrists see psychotic disorders in terms of a complex interplay of genetic, biochemical, and psychological factors. Transactional analysis concentrates only on the psychological factors. From a transactional analysis point of view, we can infer that persons who in adulthood have arrived at the unfortunate I'm not OK—you're not OK position were subjected to an extra heavy dose of destructive parent-child transactions during early childhood. The parents seldom came on "straight." Ulterior messages were the rule of the day. Slated colloquially, the transactional analyst would say, "Crazy people were talked to and dealt with in crazy ways when they were kids. They are victims—scapegoats of Mom and Dad's hang-ups." Using Berne's metaphor of the royal person turning into a frog, we could say that people in the third position were not only turned into frogs; they were turned into superfrogs by the superbad magic of mixed-up parents.

I'm OK—You're OK

A person in the I'm OK—you're OK position is in the healthiest life position. He feels that he is reasonably competent and that life is worth living. He also feels that other people are, on the whole, friendly and likeable. He trusts himself and others. His stance toward others is reminiscent of Will Roger's remark, "I never met a man I didn't like." He looks for the best in others, not the worst. The individual in the fourth position does not think of others before meeting them as superior, inferior, or untrustworthy; such prejudices arise from the traces of early experiences recorded in the Parent and the Child ego states. The person in the fourth position operates out of his Adult, being open to information arising from the present and evaluating people as he goes along. He thus forms his conclusions about others from his transactions with them, not from old transactions with his parents and parental figures.

Is the fourth position just too good to be true? Maybe people who are trusting are less intelligent or just more gullible than others. Julian B. Rotter, a former president of the American Psychological Association, makes distinction between high trusters and low trusters on the basis of a psychological test. Research conducted by Rotter (1980) suggests that high trusters are neither less intelligent nor more gullible than other people. On the whole, they appear to be happier and more likeable than low trusters. Thus Rotter's work lends credence to the assertion of transactional analysis that the I'm OK—you're OK position is a highly desirable one.

How does a person get into the fortunate fourth position? There is some controversy among transactional analysts about the correct answer. Harris feels that the fourth position is arrived at only by a conscious decision. The early childhood experience always places us in one of the first three "down" positions. The only way out is to realize that there is an "up" position, to recognize its merit, and to choose to be in it. Steiner feels that the fourth position is the natural position, the individual's birthright. It is the destructive transactions with insensitive and unloving parents that shove us into one of the first three positions. The difference between Steiner's and Harris's view point is that Harris feels early childhood experiences inevitably place the child in the down position and make the child feel not OK. No matter how loving or understanding the parents are, the child must develop not OK feelings because he or she in fact knows less than adults, is incompetent compared to adults, is smaller than adults, and so forth. Steiner's position is that early childhood experiences do not inevitably place the child in the down position; a child can be saved from going into one of the unhealthy positions by a rich diet of unconditional strokes and constructive transactions. In other words, the prince or princess does not have to become a frog. Steiner's position would seem to be closer to transactional analysis as originally formulated by Berne.

Perhaps there is more congruence between the Harris and Steiner viewpoints than might be apparent on the surface. Both men would certainly agree that tremendous numbers of people wind up as adults in one of the three down positions. Although Harris would say this is inevitable, and Steiner would say it is not inevitable, the practical question becomes: How does a person move from an unhealthy life position to a healthy life position? There is no categorical answer to this question. The various pathways to adjustment and growth discussed in this book represent different answers to the question. The specific answer given by Harris was already noted: The person must comprehend the value of the healthy life position and make a conscious choice to accept it. In addition, we can say that implicit in transactional analysis is the suggestion that a knowledge of ego states, transactional patterns, games, and life scripts will give a person the self-awareness required to reach the I'm OK—you're OK life position.

PLAYING GAMES: DISGUISED MEANINGS AND MANIPULATIVE PLOYS

Berne's best-selling book *Games People Play* had so much general impact that it even inspired a popular song by the same title:

Oh, the games people play now,
Ev'ry night and ev'ry day now.

Never meanin' what they say, now
Never sayin' what they mean. . . . *

The lyric captures to some degree what Berne had in mind when he used the word game. He saw a game in terms of disguised meanings and manipulative ploys. In *Games People Play*, Berne writes:

A game is an ongoing series of complementary ulterior transactions progressing to a well-defined, predictable outcome. Descriptively it is a recurring set of transactions, often repetitious, superficially plausible, with a concealed motivation; or, more colloquially, a series of moves with a snare, or "gimmick." (p. 48)

It is important to realize that Berne was using the word "game" in a serious way. A game may not be fun or even enjoyable. It is often self-destructive and destructive toward others. A game is called a game because it is played by a set of rules. In games played for fun, these rules are usually well defined and made explicit. In serious life games, the rules are often poorly defined and are seldom explicit. Nonetheless, the rules are there; and they are known by the players at a psychological level. Thus the word "game" was chosen by Berne to refer to complex sets of transactions having predictable outcomes.

Time

Why do people play games? The answer has to do with time. People are alive and they must spend their time on Earth in some way. There thus arises, according to Berne, a need to structure time. Some form must be given to existence. Berne says that the need to structure time arises from three underlying hungers: (1) stimulus hunger, (2) recognition hunger, and (3) structure hunger. **Stimulus hunger** represents itself as the craving for some kind of sensory input. We want to see things, hear voices and music, taste foods, smell odors, touch objects and other people. Prisoners hate solitary confinement because of the sensory isolation. **Recognition hunger** represents itself as the craving for some kind of human attention. The infant needs the cuddling and embraces of nurturing parents. The adult needs other people to say "Hello" and to give some sort of audience for the person's behavior. **Structure hunger** represents itself as the craving for something to do or somewhere to go. We feel restless if the day, the week, or life itself seems formless. Games help us satisfy all three hungers. No matter how destructive a game is, it provides us with a certain amount of stimulation, recognition, and structure.

Games are not the only way people structure time. In *Games People Play* and *What Do You Say after You Say Hello?* (1972), Berne gives a slightly different list of ways in which people structure time. Let us use the second book as our guide. It was published about eight years after the first book, not long

*Joe South, "Games People Play." Copyright 1968 by Lowery Music Co., Inc., Atlanta, GA. Used by permission. International Copyright secured. All rights reserved.

before Berne's death. Thus it reveals his developed thought on the subject of time structuring. In *What Do You Say after You Say Hello?*, Berne identifies five basic ways the majority of people structure time for the short run. (Structuring time for the long run is associated with scripts; scripts are the subject of the next major section of this chapter.) The five basic ways are (1) withdrawal, (2) rituals, (3) activities, (4) pastimes, and (5) games.

The concept of **withdrawal** states that the first basic choice we make in relating to others is "to play or not to play." We can engage in social interaction, or we can refuse to interact. Withdrawal is common. Berne gives as examples the behavior of people on a subway train and group therapy with withdrawn schizophrenics. Another illustration is provided by the **autistic child**, a child who manifests little interest in relating to other human beings. Still another illustration is provided by the shy adolescent girl who refuses all dates with boys; she is withdrawing from a particular area of her life.

A **ritual** consists of a series of predictable complementary transactions. A ritual may be formal or informal. A Roman Catholic Mass would be an example of a formal ritual. On the other hand, a dinner guest leaving a friend's home would be expected to participate in an informal ritual in which the person thanks the host, says how much he or she enjoyed the dinner, and makes some reference to inviting the host over soon. The proper host would be expected to say how much he or she enjoyed the guest's company, would be glad to accept an invitation to the guest's home, and so forth. This at-the-door leavetaking ritual might take several minutes and is an important part of the evening's behavior. The purpose of rituals is not to exchange information, but to exchange strokes. Each smile, nod, and word of approval is a stroke.

An **activity** is a form of social interaction in which the transactions are programmed by the nature of the material with which people are working. In other words, a situation or a task tells two or more people how to act together. The word "work" is often used in association with activities. Two friends working on a car, a husband and wife working on their income tax return, and two students working on arithmetic problems together provide illustrations of human beings engaged in activities. Like rituals, activities provide a fairly safe way of obtaining strokes.

Slightly riskier than rituals and activities are **pastimes**. Pastimes are a step on the way to games; they represent an intermediary concept between rituals and activities on the one hand and games on the other hand. A pastime may be defined as a series of complementary transactions having to do with a particular subject. As such, a pastime exhibits semiritualistic characteristics. Pastimes are most likely to be manifest at social gatherings; people tend to feel awkward just staring at each other or at their feet. So they search for subjects of general interest and make comments to fill in the void that would otherwise exist. Like games, pastimes may be named. A few names given by Berne are "PTA," "Psychiatry," "Ever Been," "What Became," "General Motors," "Kitchen," and "Wardrobe." Here is an illustration of two people playing "Ever Been":

Person 1. Have you ever been to Italy?
Person 2. No, but I've always wanted to go.
Person 1. We went last summer. It was fabulous.
Person 2. Oh, do I envy you. Did you visit Rome?
Person 1. Yes, and was it fantastic!
Person 2. That's terrific. Tell me, have you ever been to Hawaii?
Person 1. No, but I've always wanted to go.
Person 2. Well, we managed to go last year, and . . .

Trading Stamps and Rackets

After pastimes, there are games. Games are thus the fifth way the majority of people structure time for the short run. The concept of a game was defined a few pages earlier. The essential characteristic of a game is that at least two people manipulate each other for personal and ulterior ends. Before discussing specific kinds of games, it might be useful to introduce two concepts not previously discussed: **psychological trading stamps** and **rackets**. They play an important part in games.

The notion of a psychological trading stamp in transactional analysis is similar to the actual trading stamps given by merchants. Stamps can be redeemed for various kinds of "goodies." Similarly, psychological trading stamps can be "cashed" for various kinds of feelings. Also, like actual stamps, psychological stamps come in various colors. Two basic colors are brown and gold: Brown stamps are associated with bad feelings, gold stamps with good feelings. It should be understood that not all people are stamp collectors, although transactional analysis clearly implies that most are. People in the healthy I'm OK—you're OK position would have little need to collect psychological stamps. People in one of the three down positions would be likely to collect stamps. Say that Martha is a habitual brown stamp collector, which means that when she is offended by someone else she collects a favorite bad feeling, such as anger. At a certain point she may feel that she wants to cash in her brown anger stamps for a prize. The prize may be a "free" temper tantrum. The word "free" is used because Martha feels justified in throwing her temper tantrum. Another person might save up to several books of brown stamps and feel entitled to a guilt-free divorce.

Gold stamps are collected when a person is praised, given a medal, receives a five-year pin, or is otherwise recognized. Like brown stamps, gold stamps are traded in for the right to engage in guilt-free behavior. If Neal, an employee, has recently received a five-year pin, he might phone in sick one day, rationalizing that he has earned the time off. If eight year-old Jinny has just been given a gold star by a piano teacher for playing a piece particularly well, she might "goof off" for a few days. We say, "She is resting on her laurels." Some people who have collected many books of gold stamps may just

Gold stamps are collected when a person is praised or is otherwise recognized.

stop working for life. Such might be the case of a great champion. He may have collected so many gold stamps in his twenties and thirties that in his forties and fifties he feels entitled to get fat and be half drunk most of the time. Thus transactional analysis asserts that the collection of and trading in of gold stamps can be just as "sick" as dealing in brown stamps. Again, it is argued that the person in the life-enhancing I'm OK—you're OK position has little need to deal in stamps, either brown or gold.

Transactional analysts say that the individual tends to have a favorite kind of stamp he or she collects. Cashing in pages or books of stamps is really a form of self-indulgence. The pattern that is peculiar to the particular individual is called a **racket**. Rackets tend to be associated with such negative feelings as inferiority, anxiety, hostility, and guilt. In *What Do You Say after You Say Hello?*, Berne defines a racket as follows:

A racket, then, is a feeling, out of all possible feelings, that is habitually turned on by a given person as his payoff in the games he plays. (p. 139)

We see now one of the major reasons people play manipulative and destructive life games. According to Berne, a major aim is to engage in self-indulgent rackets. The other major aim of game-playing is to consolidate one's position. For example, if a person feels I'm not OK—you're OK, he seeks to prove to himself that this is true.

Kinds of Games

Transactional analysis identifies many kinds of games. In addition to the basic category of life games, there are marital games, party games, sexual games, underworld games, consulting room games, and good games. Furthermore, within each category a number of games can be specified. In *Games People Play*, Berne labels and describes more than thirty-five games. And new games have been identified since the publication of *Games People Play*. It is not within the scope of this book to make an exhaustive list of games. Instead, a few games will be named and described to illustrate the way games operate in daily living, according to transactional analysis.

Mine Is Better Than Yours   It was noted earlier in this chapter that "Mine Is Better Than Yours" is the basic game of all the games. The reason is that it best represents the raw power struggle between two or more persons. The aim of the game is to be one up, to place the other person in the one down position, and to consequently obtain a bit of relief from the I'm not OK—you're OK position. The game is evident in preschoolers: "My toy is better than your toy." The game is also evident in school-age children. "I got an A on the test and you only got a C," says Vernon to Edward. "Yeah? So what? I can run faster than you," says Edward to Vernon. "Mine Is Better Than Yours" becomes a full-fledged game when played between intimates. For example, let us say that Al and Jane are a married couple. Both are students working toward higher degrees. They tend to discount each other's achievements, constantly trying to outshine each other. Consequently, they receive little positive stroking in their relationship. Under such conditions, "Mine Is Better Than Yours" is a "sick" game leading nowhere in the long run.

If It Weren't for You   Berne identifies "If It Weren't for You" as a game early in *Games People Play*. He says it is the most common game played by married persons. The game frequently appears in the form of a submissive wife complaining about a domineering husband. She expresses, sometimes to her husband and sometimes to others, that if it weren't for him she might have had a wonderful career or might have realized her art talent or whatever. She blames him for inhibiting her, holding her down, keeping her from realizing her potentialities.

Berne argues that in such a game the husband is performing a real service for the wife, however. Berne notes that the husband forbids her to do something she is deeply afraid of and prevents her from becoming aware of her fears. The wife is really the central figure in the game, and the game is played between the couple primarily because of her unconscious aim to find a justification for her inability to live up to her potentialities as a person. The husband in this game is essentially a fall guy or patsy.

There is, of course, no reason why "If It Weren't for You" can't be turned around in a particular marriage. The husband may be the one who blames his wife for his lack of success, for example. "She stopped me from going into business" or "I would have gone back to school if she had been for it" are typical male laments. The game can also be played between two business partners: "I wanted to expand when interest rates were low. This one store could have been a whole chain. But Joe was against it." Thus we see that the game "If It Weren't for You" can be played by many people under a variety of conditions.

Alcoholic   Transactional analysts tend to regard alcoholism as neither incurable nor a disease. Indeed, the very term "alcoholic" has a different meaning within the context of transactional analysis. In *Games People Play*, Berne says:

In game analysis there is no such thing as alcoholism or "an alcoholic," but there is a role called the Alcoholic in a certain type of game. If a biochemical or physiological abnormality is the prime mover in excessive drinking—and that is still open to some question—then its study belongs in the field of internal medicine. Game analysis is interested in something quite different—the kinds of social transactions that are related to such excesses. Hence the game "Alcoholic." (p. 72)

The two principal players in the game "Alcoholic" are the Alcoholic and the Persecutor. The surface motives for excessive drinking vary with the individual. "I drink to escape from my worries." "I drink just because I like it." "A few stiff drinks are the only thing that relax me when I'm uptight. Then I just seem to lose control." "I drink because I'm depressed." These and other reasons are examples of verbalizations offered by excessive drinkers as explanations of their behavior. Transactional analysts doubt the validity of these stated purposes, however. They see a deeper theme running through the excessive use of alcohol: self-castigation. In game analysis, the Alcoholic is seen as a person who carries around a heavy load of guilt. He is greatly disappointed in himself as a person. The real payoff in the game "Alcoholic" comes when he is having a hangover and his spouse or other significant person takes on the role of Persecutor, heaping abuse on his head. When this happens, the Alcoholic experiences substantial psychological torment. He thus pays some of the price for his past transgressions or failures and in turn feels less guilty about them. Thus we see that the Persecutor is really the Alcoholic's patsy, playing into his hands and reinforcing the pattern of excessive drinking in the long run.

Psychotherapist and transactional analyst Claude M. Steiner has deepened and expanded Berne's insights concerning the social role of Alcoholic. In *Healing Alcoholism*, Steiner (1979) reaffirms that alcoholism is neither incurable nor a disease. He sees it in terms of several factors: a bad habit, a game, a life script, and a decision. (The concept of a life script is discussed in the next section.) Steiner places the responsibility for excessive drinking in the individual's own hands, and shows the person ways in which to become more autonomous and in turn cope effectively with a tendency to abuse alcohol.

Frigid Woman   "Frigid Woman" is categorized as a marital game. Like "Alcoholism," transactional analysis sees "frigidity" in terms of a role, that role of Frigid Woman. The Frigid Woman is provocative; she teases the male in various ways until he is aroused enough to make an advance. Then she rejects him with accusations that he is little more than an animal and that he is not interested in her as a person—only as a sex object. She is motivated by an unconscious fear of sexual intimacy. The ulterior aim of the game on her part is vindication. She proves to herself that she is a Proper Wife and he is an Inconsiderate Husband. The husband participates in the game because unconsciously he is just as afraid of sexual intimacy as his wife is. The game can, of course, be turned around. Some couples play a game of "Frigid Man"; but Berne argues that this is less common than "Frigid Woman."

Ain't It Awful   "Ain't It Awful" is classified as a party game. As people become well acquainted, particularly in a given social circle, games begin to make their appearance at get-togethers. "Ain't It Awful" can be broken down into several versions. One of the versions is "Nowadays." It usually consists of a set of Parent-Parent transactions in which the players exchange put-downs of other people.

"Nowadays all teenagers take drugs," says the first player.

"I know. It's just shocking! And the moral decadence!" exclaims the second player.

"Yes! The son of the people next door has one of these vans. And he has girls in it until all hours in the morning."

"My sister's daughter goes out with boys who own vans. I know for a fact what she is doing. In my day we had a name for girls like that."

Persons play "Nowadays" from a form of self-righteous stance. Their remarks tend to be punitive and vicious. The more punitive and vicious the remarks, the more likely it is that the players unconsciously envy those they criticize. The social message emanating from the Parent is, "Ain't it awful." But the psychological message emanating from the Child is "I wish I could do it."

Uproar   The game "uproar" is classified as a sexual game. In its most common version, it is played between an authoritarian father and his adolescent daughter. The father plays the role of Judge, finding much fault with his daughter. This leads to anger, and perhaps the girl goes to her bedroom and slams the door. Or they may go to their respective bedrooms and slam the doors. In any event, the slamming of bedroom doors is symbolical. In *Games People Play*, Berne comments:

"Uproar" offers a distressing but effective solution to the sexual problems that arise between fathers and teenage daughters in certain households. Often they can only

live in the same house together if they are angry at each other, and the slamming doors emphasize for each of them the fact that they have separate bedrooms. (p. 130)

In brief, transactional analysis sees "Uproar" as a way two relatives who experience a forbidden sexual attraction keep themselves from reaching the point of sexual intimacy.

Cops and Robbers   "Cops and Robbers" is classified as an underworld game. Some habitual criminals lead a life of crime for profit. They are law-breakers because they have found a way to make substantial sums of money, and they find numerous ways to avoid prison. Such people are not playing the game of "Cops and Robbers." The protagonist in "Cops and Robbers" is described by Berne as a "compulsive loser." His Child really wants to get caught. He rarely earns large sums of money from his criminal activities. He plays the role of Robber to seek reassurance. Reassurance may be interpreted as a form of stroking in which parental figures say, "We care enough about you to stop you." The Robber's Child is saying from the psychological level, "You must catch me." Those who play roles such as Cop or Judge are happy to oblige.

I'm Only Trying To Help You   "I'm Only Trying To Help You" is catego-rized as a consulting room game. It is played between such professionals as social workers, psychotherapists, and attorneys and their respective clients. The person playing the role of Helper is the hard player in the game, and the person playing the role of Client is his or her patsy. The Helper's ulterior mo-tive is to prove to himself that people are ungrateful and disappointing. The Helper strenuously works at making suggestions, none of which seem to work. One day the Client may get angry and pour forth bitter criticisms of the Helper. The Helper is bewildered. His words or expression convey the message to the Client, "But I was only trying to help you!" The bewilderment and psychological pain of the Helper are his payoffs for playing the game. Berne feels that a Helper is a person with masochistic tendencies, seeking punishment to relieve chronic feelings of guilt. It is important to note that not all professionals and their clients play "I'm Only Trying To Help You." The legitimate helper who charges a fair fee for services rendered, does not raise false expectations in his or her clients, and relates on an Adult-Adult basis must be distinguished from the game-playing Helper.

Cavalier   Most games are "bad" because they involve ulterior motives, ma-nipulation, and exploitation of at least one of the players (the patsy) by the other player. It is not easy to find "good" games. A good game also involves ulterior motives and a certain degree of manipulation, or it is not a game in transactional analysis terms. A good game is one in which the players are not hurt or used and in which one or both players derive some benefit. "Cava-lier" is an example of a good game.

The game "Cavalier" is played between a man who adopts the role of Poet and a woman who adopts the role of Appreciative Subject. The Poet must be a man who is not under sexual pressure. He may be an older man, a man with a satisfactory marriage, or a celibate content with his state. In brief, the Poet and the Appreciative Subject do not have sexual designs on each other. Within the bounds of good taste, the Poet seeks out numerous opportunities to admire, praise, and flattter the female in question. He is eloquent. She in turn reinforces his behavior with responsive appreciation. Their joint aim is mutual admiration, and that is why they play the game.

The Drama Triangle

Our understanding of games can be enhanced by looking at them in the light of the **drama triangle**, or **game triangle**, as formulated by Stephen B. Karpman (1968). The concept of the drama triangle asserts that in a large percentage of games there is a triangular relationship between the participants such that they play the social roles of Persecutor, Rescuer, and Victim (see Figure 5.15). For an example, let's return to the game called "If It Weren't for You." You will recall that Berne says this is the most common game played by married persons, and that the game frequently appears in the form of a submissive wife complaining about a domineering husband. Let's see how the drama triangle can shed a light on this game. Say that Vicky is the submissive wife, and occupies the position of Victim. Vicky's husband, Jeremy, is the domineering husband, and occupies the position of Persecutor. Vicky's mother, Edwina, takes many phone calls from Vicky in which she listens at length to Vicky's problems with Jeremy. She decides to take it on herself to set Jeremy straight, calls him at work, and gives him a lecture about how he has to stop mistreating her daughter. So Edwina takes the position of Rescuer.

One of the most important points to understand about the drama triangle is that the positions can make abrupt switches, and the players in the game can quite suddenly begin playing different social roles (Karpman, 1968; Woollams & Brown, 1979). For example, Jeremy may feel like a Victim when Edwina lectures him. He comes home from work and admits to Vicky that Edwina's phone call both angered and depressed him. Now Vicky decides that she must rescue Jeremy from his bad feelings; she phones her mother and

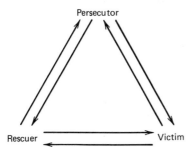

FIGURE 5.15 Karpman's drama triangle. The arrows go both ways between social roles to indicate that the participants in the drama can switch positions.

5.3 APPLICATION: ENDING THE GAMES

Are we doomed like chess pieces to play games for life? The answer given by Berne and other transactional analysts is *no*. People need not go on playing games indefinitely. The purpose of game analysis is to shine a spotlight on games, reveal their hidden nature, and thus make it possible for people to give up destructive transactional patterns.

Say that you are the principal player in a game. Once you recognize the nature of your social role in the game, you can ask yourself, "Do I want to keep playing this part? Is this the real me, or is it just a cardboard character going through stale moves to achieve ulterior aims?" Understanding the ways in which you instigate and continue the game, you can use your Adult ego state to decide to stop the game.

Perhaps you are the patsy in a game, and you discover that you have been allowing the principal player to manipulate and victimize you. You can ask yourself, "Do I want to keep on being a patsy? How can I stop the other person from conning me?" Berne felt that every game contained both a thesis and an antithesis. The **thesis** is the general pattern of the game, including the social roles, standard moves, and predictable payoffs. The **antithesis** is the "game stopper," a principle that will disrupt the pattern of the game. One of its main effects is to undercut a payoff. If you discover that you are the patsy in a game, and want to stop the game, the introduction of the antithesis can have powerful effects.

bawls her out for interfering in her marriage. After all, Vicky never asked Edwina to get into the act and talk to Jeremy. So now Vicky has become Jeremy's Rescuer and her mother's Persecutor. And now poor Edwina who was a Rescuer only a few hours ago has suddenly become the Victim. The drama triangle and the sudden switches that can take place in social roles are patterns of action that often take place in games.

LIFE SCRIPTS: YOUR FATE IS NOT IN YOUR STARS

Long before the appearance of Eric Berne and transactional analysis, Shakespeare penned these well-known lines:

All the world's a stage,
And all the men and women merely players:
They have their exits and their entrances;
And one man in his time plays many parts . . .

(*As You Like It*, Act II)

Let's return, for example, to the game "If It Weren't for You." Say that you are the fall guy or patsy. The other person is blaming you for his lack of success in some area of life. You continue the game if you play the social role of a demanding person. If you insist on restricting the other's options and choices, you will continue to be blamed. Messages from you such as "Don't you dare!" or "Over my dead body," or "I won't let you," keep the game going.

If, on the other hand, you want to invoke the game antithesis, let go and give permission. Say, "It's all right with me," or "Go ahead," or "I don't mind." Now the other person cannot turn on you and blame you if he or she fails to achieve stated goals. You are not the barrier. As noted earlier, the antithesis undercuts a payoff. The other player loses the psychological security of failing without responsibility.

Let's face it. Ending games is not easy. Sometimes you may very well prefer to continue playing the game for certain satisfactions it brings to you. Perhaps for these reasons much of Berne's writing about games had an exceedingly pessimistic tone. However, he was a long-range optimist. He believed in the power of human awareness. By comprehending the nature of games, by seeing the way rackets work, by recognizing the roles that we play in games, by invoking the antithesis, it is possible for some of us to proceed to a better existence beyond games.

Shakespeare clearly reveals in these lines a view of human nature that finds its parallel in the current formulations of transactional analysis. Specifically, transactional analysis asserts that we not only tend to live by games, but we also tend to live by **scripts**. A script is defined as an unconscious life plan.

In another play by Shakespeare, *Romeo and Juliet*, the two central characters are referred to as "star-crossed lovers." This implies that their personal destinies can be understood in astrological terms, a view popular in both Shakespeare's time and ours. Transactional analysis, however, does not see one's life script in terms of an impersonal fate determined by planetary bodies. On the contrary, the life script is the person's own choice. It represents a **decision** made in early childhood out of the Child ego state. As such, it is difficult to change. Nonetheless, because it does represent a decision, it is something for which the person must take responsibility if he or she wishes to modify it.

Kinds of Scripts

You will recall that games are one of the ways that people structure time for the short run. Scripts represent a way that people structure time for the long run. As already noted, a script represents an unconscious life plan adopted by the Child ego state. According to Berne, the script is adopted in early childhood. If it is a losing script—and many are—at least one of the child's parents was functioning much like a witch or an ogre in a fairy tale, "hexing" the child and making him feel that he was destined to be a loser. The child was made to feel that he was not lovable or competent, and this turned him into a frog. The frog-child then made a statement to himself such as "I'll never amount to anything no matter how hard I try," "I'll hurt them someday the way they're hurting me," or "If they think I'm crazy, then I'll just be crazy." One of these thoughts, depending on the particular child, represents a decision to live life in a certain way. This decision is the **script protocol**, a crude image of the way the future will be. In adulthood, the script protocol is replaced with the **shooting script**, complete in dramatic detail and filled out with a cast of characters.

In *What Do You Say after You Say Hello?*, Berne sets up a basic script typology. He says that there are (1) winning scripts, (2) nonwinning scripts, and (3) losing scripts. Persons who have adopted **winning scripts** are called princes and princesses. They will accomplish their goals in life. To illustrate, if a winner's script calls for retiring by age forty, earning an M.D. degree, or marrying the prettiest girl in town, he will do it. Persons who have adopted **nonwinning scripts** stand somewhere between royalty and frogs. They are the also-rans, the at-leasters. To illustrate, say that Tom sets out to have $100,000 saved by the age of forty. When he is forty, he has saved $10,000 and he can say, "Well, at least I saved $10,000." Persons who have adopted **losing scripts** are called frogs. They do not reach their goals in life. Berne observes, "The typical, classical loser is the man who makes himself suffer sickness or damage for no good cause" (p. 205).

In *Scripts People Live* (1974), Steiner expands on Berne's concept of the losing script and notes that in his own study of unhappy life-styles, three kinds of losing scripts seem to stand out: (1) the depression, or no love, script, (2) the madness, or no mind, script, and (3) the drug addition, or no joy, script. Persons living out a **depression script** experience a chronic lack of adequate stroking. The theme of their life is lovelessness, and they often feel unworthy of love. In extreme cases, the depression script may end in suicide. Persons living out a **madness script** suffer from a chronic fear that they will go crazy. Some persons in the grips of a madness script are eventually hospitalized; others are relatively incompetent and have a difficult time coping with the problems of daily living. Persons living out a **drug addiction script** may be dependent on such obvious drugs as alcohol or heroin, or they may rely heavily on the drugs found in coffee, aspirin, and sedatives. The aim of chronic drug-taking is to block feelings, to dim one's awareness that life is a joyless affair.

Steiner notes that the three losing scripts are not necessarily mutually exclusive. A person can suffer from a mixture of two or even three scripts in which one of the scripts forms a major theme and the other one or two form minor themes. Steiner also notes that in everyday life many of the persons acting from a losing script live it out in what is described as a **banal manifestation**, meaning a version of the script that is nondramatic—a rather dull and featureless version of what might have been an exciting and tragic script. Illustrations given by Steiner of banal manifestations are the spinster or bachelor, the cigarette-and-coffee-addicted unhappy person, or the individual who is almost always in a crisis because of an inability to manage ordinary problems.

Script Variations

Scripts can vary in ways other than along the winning-losing dimension. Two principal script variations from the basic script are (1) the counterscript and (2) the antiscript. The **counterscript** represents the social message sent by a parent, parents, or parental figures. It is what a child was told to do in words, as opposed to what the child was programmed to do by ulterior psychological messages. The counterscript represents the "oughts" and the "shoulds" of the Right Path and, consequently, may be taken only half-seriously by the Child ego state of a person who has adopted a losing script. For example, assume that Albert is a chronic alcoholic. His script calls for him to drink himself to death. His counterscript calls for him to abstain from alcohol forever. From time to time he makes a presumably iron resolution to never touch a drop of liquor again. He may observe the resolution for days, weeks, or longer. But he feels like a puppet acting out a farce, and at a deeper level he knows he will eventually return to the bottle. While he is "being good" he is living out the counterscript. The counterscript provides a bit of temporary relief from the script, and it makes the individual's life less featureless; but it is not to be taken seriously. It is just a lull in the action.

The **antiscript** is the mirror image of the script. Say that a person has become aware that he has a particular kind of script. He says, "I don't want to play the role the script calls for." He then decides to oppose every instruction in the script. If the script says "Stop," he goes. If the script says "Speak," he is quiet. If the script says "Be polite," he is nasty. If the script says "Work hard and make a lot of money," he quits his job and joins a commune. He may delude himself that he has freed himself from the script, but this is an illusion. The script is still determining everything he does.

AUTONOMY AND INTIMACY

The principal goals of transactional analysis are autonomy and intimacy for the individual. Within the context of transactional analysis, **autonomy** may be defined as game-free and script-free living. The autonomous person tends to be nonmanipulative in personal relations. The individual is not a put-down artist. He or she does not live life like a character in a play, rigidly acting out unconscious directives as if a hypnotized subject. At this point it should be noted that living out a winning script is not the same as script-free living. A script is by definition an unconscious life plan. Thus even a winning script may be a kind of straitjacket that confines a person to a narrow set of acceptable behaviors. A person with a winning script is programmed to be top dog, to achieve his or her goals, and so forth. Thus, in a sense, having a winning script is not quite the same thing as being a "real" winner. A real winner is a person who has broken free from the script. He or she is not living out of unconscious script directives, but out of conscious decisions. This is not to say that a person without a script has no plans and no goals. On the contrary, the individual has flexible plans and realistic goals made out of the person's thinking Adult, not his or her irrational Child.

The other principal goal of transactional analysis, **intimacy**, is defined by Berne in *What Do You Say after You Say Hello?* as follows: "A game-free exchange of emotional expression without exploitation" (p. 443). The concept of intimacy is particularly important when it is applied to the way we relate to **significant others**—parents, husbands, wives, children, and close friends. When there is intimacy in a relationship, there is mutual respect for each in-

One of the principal goals of transactional analysis is intimacy.

dividual's status as a real person. Berne saw intimacy as a function of the Natural Child. Thus autonomy and intimacy are closely related. The autonomous person, living in a game-free and script-free way, liberates his or her Natural Child. The liberated Natural Child finds intimacy a rewarding way of life.

CRITIQUE

Transactional analysis has become one of the most widespread systems used for understanding the communication process between two or more people. It has tremendous popularity. Books on transactional analysis have sold millions of copies to persons in all walks of life. Transactional analysis should not be accepted and used without any critical reservation whatsoever, however. The following are some thoughts to consider.

1. A large number of psychologists remain relatively unimpressed by transactional analysis. A common comment is, "Transactional analysis is just warmed-over psychoanalysis." It is certainly correct that much of transactional analysis grew directly out of psychoanalysis. Berne's concept of ulterior aims is approximately the same as Freud's idea of unconscious motivation. Berne's formulation of the Parent, Adult, and Child is detected by many critics as a copy of Freud's superego, ego, and id. Berne argued that there are important differences. The Parent, Adult, and Child are ego states: thus they are *directly experienced* by the person. The superego, ego and id are abstract concepts; they are hypothetical constructions *about* the person. In spite of Berne's protests, the similarities between the Parent, Adult, and Child and the superego, ego, and id seem to outweigh the differences. The charge that transactional analysis is just warmed-over psychoanalysis seems somewhat appropriate when applied to structural analysis, the analysis of ego states. It seems unfair, though, when directed at transactional analysis proper. The idea that one person's ego states communicate with the ego states of other persons is not evident in the writings of Freud or his followers. Their primary concern was with processes within the individual, not the dialogue between two or more persons. It is in the area of interpersonal communications that transactional analysis makes its original contributions.

2. Transactional analysis itself can become a game. Berne himself warned against this danger. A person may learn and use most of the jargon of transactional analysis as an elaborate way of avoiding legitimate insight. He or she talks at length *about* autonomy and intimacy, but never becomes autonomous or intimate. The person intellectualizes transactional analysis to such a degree that it is of no service to the person's quest for greater adjustment and growth.

3. Transactional analysis lends itself readily to those who wish to exploit others. Persons of ill will who seek to manipulate other people may use the concepts of transactional analysis to further their own selfish aims. Steiner calls attention to this hazard in *Scripts People Live*. The hazard is hardly the

fault of transactional analysis itself. A knife can be wielded by a thug or by a surgeon. Like the knife, transactional analysis can cut two ways, depending on the intentions of the user. But it is important to realize that in certain people's hands, transactional analysis may have adverse effects.

4. The heavy use of slang by transactional analysts has led some thinkers to see transactional analysis as a slick, superficial psychology. The slang terms do indeed seem to encourage an oversimplified either-or kind of thinking. People are either frogs or princes. They are either getting positive strokes or negative strokes. They are either game-bound or game-free. They are either script-bound or script-free. They are either one up or are one down. Parents are either nurturing parents or they are witches and ogres. The reflective reader of transactional analysis will realize that slang terms and two-valued logic are used because they have impact. They make the system more accessible to people with a limited background in psychology. Berne felt that more was gained than was lost by presenting ideas in sharp black-and-white images as opposed to shades of gray. This is a debatable point. From a practical point of view, however, we should be cognizant that gradients usually underlie two-valued terminology. For example, persons cannot be classified simply as frogs or princes. The frog image is invoked to suggest low self-esteem. The prince and princess image is invoked to suggest high self-esteem. Self-esteem can be conceptualized as a gradient with low self-esteem at one end and high self-esteem at the other, with an infinite number of points in between. An individual may have low self-esteem, slightly below average self-esteem, moderate self-esteem, somewhat higher than average self-esteem, and so forth. The actual person defies a label such as frog or prince.

5. Perhaps transactional analysis overemphasizes the importance of early childhood. Reading Berne and his followers, one would think that human destiny is determined by the time a child is five or six years of age. In contrast to Berne's formulations, several lines of research suggest that the school-age years (from about six to twelve years of age) are of particular importance in shaping one's sense of competence versus one's sense of inferiority. Also, experiences with peers appear to be of enormous importance during the adolescent period. These experiences have a great deal to do with the development of one's identity and one's capacity for intimacy. Berne overlooks the role of later childhood and adolescence in personality development. Even if experiences during the first five or six years of life may have more impact than the subsequent years of development, it seems an oversimplification to give the early years as much weight as Berne gives them.

6. Is Berne too hard on parents? Thomas C. Oden, author of *Game Free: The Meaning of Intimacy* (1974) writes:

Although Berne denies that he is being unkind to parents, the logic of his language and the force of his rhetoric lands almost without exception on the side of children against parents. Always the parenting voice is the witch, devil, ogre, or pig.

At a time when actual parents and children are having tough times communicating on the same wavelength, TA comes on with what to many seems to be a steady put-down of the necessary constraining parent inputs into the formulation of consciousness. (p. 87)

Oden goes on to note that Berne does in fact distinguish between the Controlling Parent and the Nurturing Parent. Berne is not, of course, critical of all parents, just those parents who set up irrational injunctions for their children. Oden observes, however, that in the heat of rhetoric the crucial distinction between the Controlling Parent and the Nurturing Parent tends to get lost.

7. Transactional analysts are against clinical namecalling. They say that they consider it insulting to label people with such terms as "neurotic" or "psychotic" or to say that certain people have character disorders. Yet transactional analysts do not hesitate to coin a new form of namecalling in which people are referred to as bitches, jerks, witches, ogres, winners, losers, frogs, princes, and princesses. Although it may be complimentary to refer to someone as a winner, a prince, or a princess, it is not insulting to refer to someone else as a bitch, jerk, witch, ogre, loser, or frog?

8. Like most approaches to more effective living derived from clinical experience, transactional analysis does not derive its conclusions from rigorous experimental designs. There is a general consensus among psychologists that the clinical method is a weak method. Thus observations derived from the clinical method should be looked on more as hypotheses than as facts. Unfortunately, Berne and his followers tend to use a fact-oriented language, which gives readers the feeling that they are reading about the one and only system for understanding human behavior.

The foregoing critique does not discredit transactional analysis, but simply points out some problems with it. In spite of these problems, transactional analysis remains a useful psychological tool. It is a coherent system for clarifying communication processes within and between ourselves. It throws a spotlight on ulterior games and unconscious scripts, suggesting ways of breaking free from these often destructive patterns. It tells us that we are basically OK as persons, that we are meant to be real winners. And it indicates that movement in the direction of greater autonomy and greater intimacy is desirable.

SUMMARY

1. In the language of transactional analysis, the person who is one up is in a position of psychological power.
2. The psychiatrist Harry Stack Sullivan is generally recognized as an important precursor to transactional analysis.
3. Eric Berne was the father of transactional analysis.

4. The three ego states identified by transactional analysis are the Child, the Parent, and the Adult.
5. The Child ego state may be divided into three levels: (1) The Adapted Child, (2) The Rebellious Child, and (3) The Natural Child.
6. The Parent ego state may be divided into two levels: (1) The Nurturing Parent, and (2) The Controlling Parent.
7. The Adult ego state is the computer of the personality.
8. **Contamination** of the Adult takes place when the Adult is not sufficiently discriminated from the Child, the Parent, or both. Blockage of the Adult takes place when there is a barrier between at least one ego state and the Adult.
9. An **egogram** is a bar graph showing the relationship and size of the ego states relative to each other.
10. According to Berne, a **transaction** is the unit of social intercourse.
11. The **complementary transaction** is defined as a no-conflict transaction.
12. A **crossed transaction** takes place when there is conflict between two or more people.
13. An **ulterior transaction** involves the activity of more than two ego states simultaneously. Such a transaction contains a hidden message.
14. The four **existential positions** identified by transactional analysis are: (1) I'm not OK—You're OK, (2) I'm OK—You're not OK, (3) I'm not OK—You're not OK, and (4) I'm OK—You're OK.
15. "I'm not OK—You're OK" is a kind of shorthand for saying that some people suffer from low self-esteem and see others as having traits they themselves lack.
16. "I'm OK—You're not OK" is a position in which the individual feels that he or she is superior to other people and that, consequently, he or she has a right to use others for his or her own ends.
17. "I'm not OK—You're not OK" is a position in which the individual feels inferior in some way to others. At the same time the person also feels that other people are defective in some way.
18. The "I'm OK—You're OK" position is the healthiest life position. The person in this position tends to trust both himself and others.
19. According to Berne, a **game** is an ongoing series of complementary ulterior transactions progressing to a well-defined outcome.
20. Berne says that the need to structure time arises from three underlying hungers: (1) stimulus hunger, (2) recognition hunger, and (3) structure hunger.
21. A psychological **trading stamp** can be "cashed" for various kinds of feelings.
22. A **racket** is feeling that is habitually turned on by a person as his or her payoff in a game.
23. Berne identifies a number of games. Examples are **Mine Is Better Than Yours, If It Weren't for You, Alcoholic, Frigid Woman, Ain't It Awful,**

Uproar, Cops and Robbers, I'm Only Trying to Help You, and **Cavalier.**

24. Karpman's **drama triangle** asserts that in a large percentage of games there is a triangular relationship between the participants such that they play the social roles of Persecutor, Rescuer, and Victim.

25. A **script** represents an unconscious life plan adopted by the Child ego state.

26. Berne set up a basic script typology consisting of (1) winning scripts, (2) nonwinning scripts, and (3) losing scripts.

27. According to Steiner, three kinds of losing scripts seem to stand out: (1) the depression, or no love, script, (2) the madness, or no mind, script, and (3) the drug addiction, or no joy, script.

28. Two principal script variations from the basic script are (1) the counterscript and (2) the antiscript.

29. **Autonomy** refers to game-free and script-free living.

30. **Intimacy**, as defined by Berne, refers to "a game-free exchange of emotional expression without exploitation."

Applied Exploration

EFFECTIVE COMMUNICATION: UNDERSTANDING EACH OTHER

The humorist Mike Nichols once said, "You'll never really know what I mean and I'll never know exactly what you mean." The remark is closer to being sad than funny. We have already seen in Chapter 5 ways in which the communication process can go wrong, and how this can be damaging to human relationships. Murphy's Law says, "If anything can go wrong, it will." And, indeed, there sometimes seems to be a kind of Murphy's Law of Communication saying, "If a message can be misunderstood, it will be." However, the situation is really not this dismal. There are things that can be done to enhance effective communication. This exploration seeks to build forward on the ideas already presented in connection with transactional analysis.

Why Communicate?

"Why Communicate?" may sound like an obvious question. Maybe an easy answer comes to your mind. However, it is asked here as a device to explore the goals of the communication process. Common goals are: (1) to explain a point of view, (2) To share experiences, (3) To change another person's attitude, (4) To sell something, (5) To express affection, (6) To resolve a difference or settle a dispute, and (7) To overcome feelings of isolation and alienation. These are all answers to the question, "Why communicate?" As already noted, the communication process sometimes breaks down. Author Milton Mayer remarked, "I have never been able to understand why it is that just because I am unintelligible nobody understands me." Again, the remark is funny. And, again, it is sad. When someone misunderstands us we feel frustrated; and the emotional distance between us increases.

Sometimes we expect too much of the communication process. Effective communication can't resolve every difference or dispute between people. For example, a husband and wife may be at legitimate cross purposes because they have different values. Sam isn't interested in saving much money for the future. He wants to "fly now and pay later." He is confident that his retirement plan is enough of a nest egg. Sam's wife, Violet, places a high premium on thrift. She thinks they should save twenty percent of the couple's income "for a rainy day." They bicker often about spending and saving money. It is possible that the money squabbles are shams for latent aggressions, a power struggle between the two, and other psychological processes. However, it is also possible that they *do* clearly communicate. And, as already noted, they simply have different values.

No, clear and effective communication can't solve every problem. That is far too idealistic. But it can clarify the nature of a problem. It can move people down the right road toward a solution. And, sometimes, it can reveal that there are *not* differences in values, but simply superficial disagreements. Thus it pays us to seek ways to become more effective communicators.

The communication process sometimes breaks down.

Skills

A productive way to approach effective communication is to think in terms of **communication skills**, conscious ways one can improve the quality of messages both sent and received. The communication skills identified below are adapted from a number of sources including Haim G. Ginott's *Between Parent and Child* (1969), Thomas Gordon's *Parent Effectiveness Training* (1970), Ernst G. Beier and Evans G. Valens' *People-Reading* (1975), George R. Bach and Ronald M. Deutsch's *Stop! You're Driving Me Crazy* (1979), and Stan Woollams and Michael Brown's *The Total Handbook of Transactional Analysis* (1979). The skills discussed apply to many relationships such as parent and child, employer and employee, boy friend and girl friend, general friendships, and husband and wife.

Make Eye Contact   It is a good general principle to make frequent eye contact when either stating a point or listening to someone make one. When you are saying something, you seem much more assertive when you make eye contact. When you are listening, the other person will feel you are paying attention. However, it is important to realize that unrelieved eye contact can be a strain. So eye contact should be spontaneously broken from time to time.

Criticize an Action, but not the Personality   If you feel that you must be critical, it is probably a good idea to keep your criticism at a concrete level. Don't hit below the belt and tell the other person what a fool or how irresponsible he or she is. A person's actions are fairly concrete; the personality is more abstract. For example, Joyce is angry at her husband Warner because he promised to help her clean house on Saturday; instead, he is watching the football game on television. She is tempted to say, "You know, Warner, you're such a lazy thing! All you ever do is sit around and watch television." (Note that laziness can be thought of as a personality trait.) Warner is bound to feel insulted and put down. He will think, "I'm not lazy! I worked hard all week!" Instead, let's hope that Joyce, even if she is somewhat upset, limits her criticism to something such as "You promised to help me clean house. I work all week too. And I don't think it's fair for you to back out of your promise." This is harsh enough. And it sticks to the facts. If Warner actually made the promise, he can hardly deny it. And he may say, "I'm sorry, honey. You're right. I did promise, didn't I?"

Praise an Action, but not the Personality   The guideline for criticism applies equally well to praise. It would seem that praise is always good. But we can lay it on too thick. Let's return to Joyce and Warner. Say that he helps her clean house. He washes the floor, vacuums, and dusts the furniture. This takes him about two hours. In an effort to reinforce his behavior, Joyce gushes, "Oh, Darling, I'm so lucky to have a husband like you. You're just the greatest. All my girl friends envy me so much." It is doubtful that this kind of extravagent praise will actually make Warner feel very good about helping Joyce. He may think "She's always trying to butter me up to get me to help out." And he may feel manipulated. It will be better if Joyce simply says something such as, "Thanks honey. I appreciate your help. And the floor looks great!"

Respect Feelings   In order to protect another person's self-esteem it is important to respect his or her feelings. We often tend to discount another person's feelings by overriding them or by saying, "That's silly," or "That's nothing." When we do this the other individual feels put down and reduced in value, and this response impairs the relationship. Say that Sharon and Melody are friends. Sharon is complaining to Melody that she is depressed because her boy friend, Tyrone, hasn't called her in two weeks. Melody says, "You're silly to let him get you down. A pretty girl like you can get guys better than Tyrone any day of the week. He's not much." Sharon feels offended. She loves Tyrone and hopes to marry him someday. She has also been made to feel that she has poor judgment in loving Tyrone. It would have been much better if Melody had respected Sharon's feelings by saying, "I know it hurts when somebody you love ignores you."

Use Active Listening   When we use active listening we do more than hear words. We "hear" the emotional message behind the words. We **decode** a surface message into its real meaning. Here is an example from *Parent Effectiveness Training* by Thomas Gordon (1970):

Child: Daddy, when you were a boy what did you like in a girl? What made you really like a girl?
Parent: Sounds like you're wondering what you need to get boys to like you, is that right?
Child: Yeah. For some reason they don't seem to like me and I don't know why. (p. 53)

If the father in the example had not used active listening and decoded his daughter's questions, he might have answered, "What made me really like a girl was when she had a winning personality. And I have to admit I really went for blondes too—tall ones." Or he might have given any number of equally irrelevant answers, answers that did not touch on the concern behind the daughter's question. Gordon comments (1970):

In active listening, then, the receiver tries to understand what it is the sender is feeling or what his message means. Then he puts his understanding into his own words (code) and feeds it back for the sender's verification. The receiver does not send a message of his own—such as an evaluation, opinion, advice, logic, analysis, or question. He feeds back only what he feels the sender's message meant—nothing more, nothing less. (p. 53)

We can see that active listening is a way of fostering understanding between people. And it is certainly not limited to parent-child relationships.

Use I-messages to Express Emotions Some of us have the misguided idea that in order to preserve the quality of a relationship we should always be on our very best behavior. People with this notion are hesitant to express emotions such as anxiety, depression, or anger. They think that a strong emotion will "rock the boat" and blow the relationship apart. However, if an emotion is expressed properly without insulting the other person, it has a place in most relationships. Emotions can usually be expressed quite adequately by remembering to send **I-messages** instead of **you-messages**. A you-message assigns blame for your feeling to the other person, and is likely to be resented. Examples of such messages are "You're worrying me to death," or "Your behavior depresses me," or "You are always making me angry." In contrast, an I-message states what you are feeling just as firmly, but with less hostility. Examples of the preferred I-messages are "I'm worried," or "I'm depressed," or "I'm angry." The other person can hardly deny the existence of your feeling and say, for example, "No, you're not worried." But he or she can certainly say in response to a you-message, "You're wrong to blame me for your worry."

Don't Stockpile Complaints It is wise to express complaints and grievances from time to time instead of saving them for one big blow-up. One can say as one goes along, "I've been waiting for twenty minutes," or "I was expecting something for my birthday," or "The bathroom was a mess this morning!" These kinds of small complaints, although unpleasant, at least have the advantage of clearing the air. If one waits for weeks or months to complain about another person's irritating ways, one might end up shouting generalizations such as, "You always keep me waiting," or "You're such a slob." And you're back to criticizing the other individual's personality and using you-messages.

Be Credible In order to be credible, or believable, it is important to speak from a foundation of correct information. Some people make all sorts of interesting and remarkable statements, but when we get to know them we realize that half of what they say is nonsense. And we then begin to lose respect for almost any remark or opinion they may express. Miles is having lunch with his friends and they are talking about health problems. Miles volunteers the interesting observation, "It takes 250,000 virus to cover the period at the end of a sentence." His companions find the statement provocative, and one asks, "Where can I look that up?" If Miles says, "Gee, I don't know. I think I heard it on a game show," he loses credibility. If instead he says, "I found it in *The Random House Encyclopedia* in the section of microbiology," he will gain credibility. Our reputation as poorly informed or well-informed people becomes a part of the image that others have of us. And it affects our ability to communicate with them.

Don't Send Ulterior Messages with a Double Meaning   Ulterior messages have already been discussed earlier in Chapter 5 in the context of ulterior transactions. An **ulterior message** is one with two levels. At the social level something "nice" or appropriate or kind is said. At the psychological level there is often an element of rejection, a put down, or a discount. In *Stop! You're Driving Me Crazy* by George R. Bach and Ronald M. Deutsch (1979, p. 10) the example is given of a husband who stops his wife when she starts to take the trash cans out one morning. They had argued the night before and the husband, Dick, is trying to be solicitous. The trash cans are too heavy for Martha, his wife. It is his job to do such things. Dick goes to work and Martha notices later that the trash collectors have passed by and Dick has not put out the trash.

Bach and Deutsch point out that Dick is sending a double message:

Message One: *I want to protect you by doing the heavy work. So I will take care of the trash.*

Message Two: *If you want to take the trash cans out, take them. You don't take care of me, so I don't take care of you. (p. 12)*

These kinds of ulterior messages with a double meaning are said to be destructive to a relationship or simply "crazymaking."

Briefly, there are many ways in which the communication process can go wrong. Fortunately, there are specific learnable skills that can enhance effective communication and in turn our understanding of each other. Skills identified in this exploration were: (1) Make eye contact, (2) Criticize an action, but not the personality, (3) Praise an action, but not the personality, (4) Respect feelings, (5) Use active listening, (6) Use I-messages to express emotions, (7) Don't stockpile complaints, (8) Be credible, and (9) Don't send ulterior messages with a double meaning.

Does nutrition have a relationship to mental health?

Chapter 6

PSYCHOTECHNOLOGY: FROM PSYCHOSURGERY TO BIOFEEDBACK

Overview

OUTLINE

KEY QUESTIONS

What is Psychotechnology?
The word **technology** taken by itself means applied science. Thus the best translation of psychotechnology into a meaningful phrase would be "applied behavioral science." In general terms, psychotechnology suggests a wide domain of exploration in which the orthodox distinctions among psychology, the physical sciences, and the biological sciences become blurred.

How does psychotechnology relate to adjustment and growth?
Advocates of psychotechnology point to its useful features. Persons prone to violence, worry, depression, or hyperactivity may find relief from their conditions through psychosurgery, drugs, or changes in diet. Individuals with chronic migraine headaches, hypertension, and other psychosomatic problems can sometimes learn to reduce the impact of these problems via biofeedback training. Also, some researchers believe that psychotechnology can be used to greatly augment human abilities. Critics of psychotechnology, however, point to its many possibilities for abuse and arbitrary behavior control.

Psychotechnology is as new as today's headlines and as old as the dawn of civilization. *The Egyptian*, a highly popular novel in the late 1940s written by Mika Waltari, tells the tale of Sinuhe, physician to the Pharaoh. The action takes place about three thousand years ago, and yet brain surgery is described. Sinuhe is called on to relieve the distress of a man who constantly hears the roar of the sea in his ears, who is "given to swooning," and who suffers from excruciating pains in his head. The novel is written in the first person, and Sinuhe describes the brain surgery as follows:

I tapped him with the hammer at different points, and he made no sign until suddenly he cried out and fell to the ground senseless. I concluded from this that I had found the spot where it would be best to open his skull.

. . . I began my work. Slitting up the scalp, I stanched the copious bleeding with red-hot irons, though I was uneasy at the agony this caused him. . . . I had given him plentiful draughts of wine in which narcotics were dissolved so that his eyes protruded like those of a dead fish and he was cheerfully disposed. Next I opened the bone as carefully as I could with the instruments I had at my disposal, and he never even fainted but drew a deep breath and told me it already eased him when I removed the piece of bone. Now my heart rejoiced, for just where I had opened his head either the devil or the spirit of disease had laid its egg. . . . It was red and hideous and the size of a swallow's egg. With the utmost care I removed it, burning away all that held it to the brain. . . . I closed the skull with a silver plate and stitched the scalp over it, and the patient never lost consciousness at any time. When I had finished, he rose and walked about and thanked me with all his heart, for he no longer heard the terrible roar in his ears, and the pains also had ceased. (pp. 140–141)

The passage from *The Egyptian*, presumably a well-researched novel, is instructive in several ways. It suggests that perceptual delusions, such as a roaring in the ears, can be caused by a diseased brain. It proposes that the ancient Egyptians did more than drill holes in the skull to "let out evil spirits." Possibly they understood something about the removal of brain tumors. It notes that **trepanning**, making a perforation in the skull, is an ancient art. And, lastly, the patient was conscious during the surgery! This may seem farfetched, but it is not. Patients are sometimes conscious during modern brain surgery. For example, the famous neurosurgeon Wilder Penfield performed numerous operations on sufferers from epilepsy in the 1930s and 1940s. During the course of the operations, he stimulated the brains of his conscious subjects with electrodes. Such stimulation often produced experiences of sights or sound within the subject; sometimes the patient experienced a vivid recall of memories. Other points of stimulation produced motor movements, such as the involuntary clenching of a fist. Penfield was not merely using his patients as guinea pigs. Their reports were valuable feedback to him; they guided his hand. Fortunately, Penfield systematically collected his observations, and his findings have played a large part in the con-

Trepanning, making a perforation in the skull, is an ancient art.

temporary mapping of the motor and sensory areas of the cortex in human beings (Penfield & Rasmussen, 1950).

In contemporary times, psychotechnology has had several precursors. One set of precursors was the **shock therapies**, therapies in which the treatment involves sending the organism into a state of shock by electrical or chemical means. Shock therapies played an important role in the development of psychotechnology because their wholesale use for several decades in mental hospitals paved the road for other psychotechnological applications.

There are three principal forms of shock therapy: (1) Metrazol therapy, (2) insulin coma therapy, and (3) electroconvulsive therapy. **Metrazol therapy** utilizes Metrazol, a drug prepared from camphor, to induce convulsions. The method was pioneered by L. J. Meduna in the mid-1930s. Metrazol therapy never won a large following. It is of historical interest in that it stimulated the search for other ways of inducing seizures. **Insulin coma therapy** is another method of inducing a state of shock by chemical means. The patient is injected with insulin. This burns up blood sugar at a rapid rate, and the patient goes into a state of shock. The patient is left in a coma and watched closely for about one hour. Then the patient is brought out of the coma by an injection of glucose. The method was developed by Manfred Sakel, also in the 1930s.

Why did Meduna, Sakel, and other psychiatrists seek to induce seizures in mental patients? The answer is based on their day-to-day observations, not on an elaborate psychological theory. It was noted that epileptic patients, patients subject to involuntary seizures, were seldom psychotic. There seemed to be a relationship between mood and nervous system "storms." It was also noted that following accidental insulin comas, diabetic schizophrenic patients sometimes improved psychologically. Consequently it was reasoned that the artificial induction of shock might be an effective treatment for psychosis.

By far the most widespread form of shock therapy was and is **electroconvulsive therapy**, a form of treatment in which an electric current is briefly passed through the frontal lobes of the brain. This induces a **grand mal seizure**, a large convulsion similar to the kind manifested by epileptic persons. Electroconvulsive therapy was introduced in 1937 by two Italian psychiatrists, Ugo Cerletti and Lucia Bini. It is reported in an article by psychiatrist Robert L. Taylor (1975, p. 7) that their first electroconvulsive patient said after coming out of his seizure, "Non una seconda! Mort fera." ("Don't give me a second treatment. It's going to kill me.") His statement expresses the fear shared by most patients of having their brains "zapped" by electricity.

The principal value of electroconvulsive therapy appears to be its use in cases of psychotic depression, particularly when the patient is suicidal. Advocates of electroconvulsive therapy also recommend it for breaking up bizarre patterns of action, thought, or perception.

Unfortunately, electroconvulsive therapy lends itself to a substantial amount of questionable use. In *The Making of a Psychiatrist*, an autobiographical account by psychiatrist David S. Viscott (1972), is a chapter titled "Quacks, or Nobody's Perfect But . . . ." In it, Viscott takes his colleagues to task for the excessive application of electroconvulsive therapy. He argues that various organic conditions can produce symptoms that mimic psychotic reactions. Such patients cannot benefit from shock treatments. He says:

One afternoon I became extremely upset thinking about all of this. I went down to my car and not knowing what else to do I drove to the zoo. At least this zoo wasn't disguised as a hospital. I bought two bags of peanuts, one for the elephant and one for me. . . .

It's not that I don't believe in electroshock. I do, but I think its use is limited. I simply had no idea EST was being abused this much. (p. 360)

Viscott's dismay is shared by others. For example, neurologist John Friedberg has written a book called *Shock Treatment Is Not Good for Your Brain* (1976) in which he says that shock treatment is a horrible mistake. And research indicates that one major side effect of electroconvulsive therapy is some memory loss (Loftus, 1980). Concern exists about the potential for abuse in electroconvulsive therapy and similar treatments. We will return to this point in the critique section of this chapter. For now, let us take a close-up look at key aspects of psychotechnology.

PSYCHOSURGERY: WILL SOCIETY BECOME PSYCHOCIVILIZED?

Visualize the following train of action: A man is standing in a bullring in Spain, facing a charging bull. The man is unarmed. He holds a small radio transmitter in his hands. Before the bull can reach him, the man presses a button on the radio transmitter. The radio message activates an electrode planted deep in the bull's brain, and the bull stops in his tracks! Is this science-fiction, a glimpse of the psychotechnology of the future? No, the demonstration actually took place a few years ago. The man was the Yale Medical School neurophysiologist, José Delgado.

Delgado has done a substantial amount of research on electrical stimulation of the brain and is the author of *Physical Control of the Mind: Toward a Psychocivilized Society* (1969). We will return to Delgado and his work in a few pages. The material in the following section is applicable only to serious and/or chronic behavioral disturbances, not to the common problems of adjustment faced by most people in daily living.

Early Psychosurgery

As already noted, it is possible to stretch the history of psychosurgery back to the ancient Egyptians. But the story of modern psychosurgery begins in 1935 with the work of the Portuguese physician Egas Moniz. Moniz was impressed by research reports that severance of the frontal lobes of the brain calmed a chimpanzee prone to violent temper tantrums. Moniz decided to try the same kind of brain surgery on hostile and aggressive mental patients. Thus was born the **lobotomy**, a surgical procedure in which the connections between the frontal lobes of the cortex are severed from the subcortex. This, of course, makes the frontal lobes nonfunctional. It has been hypothesized that the frontal lobes of the cortex have a great deal to do with the higher thought processes in humans. Thus mental patients who are "thinking too hard for their own good" may be pacified by a lobotomy. The crude theory of lobotomy seems to be that hyperthought, or mental overactivity, tends to make certain mental patients hostile, assaultive, aggressive, uncontrollable, compulsive, depressed, and so forth.

The medical colleagues Walter Freeman and James Watts (1950) jointly introduced the lobotomy to the United States in 1936. By the 1940s lobotomies were a firmly established form of psychiatric treatment; thousands of lobotomies were performed during the 1940s. They were performed primarily on patients who were aggressive and assaultive, but their use was not limited to such patients. All types of patients received lobotomies, including those with such symptoms as compulsion or depression.

By the early 1950s the proverbial honeymoon was over. Lobotomy patients were not "cured" of mental illness and restored to normalcy. Often, they were more impulsive, unable to plan for the future, and had fragmented self-images. As one patient's wife complained, "You have removed the devil in him, but you have also destroyed his soul." The lobotomy patient often loses a coherent sense of self, the feeling that one is basically the same person one was yesterday. The appearance of tranquilizers on the psychiatric scene also contributed to the growing disenchantment with the lobotomy procedure. Behavior control of mental patients with drugs was obviously a less drastic procedure than cutting into their brains. Lobotomies have fallen into disrepute and are seldom performed today. As we will see presently, however, more sophisticated forms of psychosurgery are emerging.

Electrical Stimulation of the Brain

To appreciate the nature of modern psychosurgery, it is important to know something about research that utilizes a procedure known as **electrical stimulation of the brain (ESB)**. ESB requires that tiny holes be drilled in the skull of the subject. Electrodes (insulated wires with small uninsulated tips) are inserted through the holes, pushed through brain tissue, and implanted in selected areas of the brain (Lubar, 1981). Electrodes can be cemented to the skull with an exposed plug. Thus the subject can be connected or disconnected to a source of current at the researcher's convenience.

The electrodes are usually implanted in various regions of the subcortex and brain stem, which are often hypothesized as being the site of primal drives and basic emotions. Sending small amounts of current through the electrodes to specified regions of the brain stimulates neurons of that region to "fire," and various nervous system pathways are consequently activated. The subject, particularly an animal subject, can be made into a "puppet" controlled by the electricity.

To illustrate, let me cite the research, initiated in the 1920s, of the Swiss physiologist Walter R. Hess. Hess, the first researcher to use ESB, implanted electrodes in a cat's hypothalamus, a region of the subcortex just above the brain stem. When Hess sent a mild current through a selected electrode, the cat acted as if an enemy were present. It went through a patterned fright reaction—spitting, growling, and arching its back. Repeated stimulation of the same brain region elicited the same pattern over and over. Hess experimented with more than one cat, of course. Indeed, his work with chemical and electrical stimulation of the brain eventually earned him a Nobel Prize. Hess found that by stimulating different regions of the subcortex, each region only a slight distance removed from another region, it was possible to induce a variety of responses in his experimental cats.

A dramatic example of the power of ESB is provided by the research of James Olds and Peter Milner (1954). They reported on ESB of the septal area and nearby regions of the rat brain. The Olds and Milner setup was unique. For the first time, the experimental rat was allowed to stimulate its own brain. The rat was placed in a Skinner box. Whenever it pressed the box's bar, a small amount of current was delivered to the rat's septal area. Thus a new concept in ESB research was introduced: self-stimulation of the brain. It was discovered that a specific region of the septal area was highly reinforcing, and this region has been nicknamed "the pleasure center." A rat allowed to self-stimulate its own pleasure center may press the bar as many as seven thousand times in a single hour! Many rats will engage in this behavior for hours on end, often dropping of exhaustion eventually.

In one experiment, Olds trained rats to cross a shock grid to obtain food. When the grid was electrified, the rats would starve to death before crossing the grid to eat. When given the opportunity to cross an electrified grid to reach a self-stimulation bar, however, the rats scampered across it. The motive to engage in self-stimulation was stronger than the hunger motive!

Other researchers have explored what might be called "pain centers." In 1954 José Delgado, Neal Miller, and W. W. Roberts (1954) reported an experiment that suggested that the amygdalae are triggers for the experience of pain. The **amygdalae** are small brain structures located near the hypothalamus. There is a right amygdala and a left amygdala, one located in each hemisphere of the brain. When a chimpanzee has one of its amygdalae stimulated, the chimpanzee grimaces and acts as if it has been whipped.

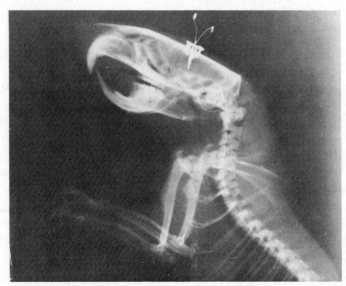

Electrical stimulation of the brain requires electrode implantation.

The research on ESB of the amygdalae has reached an advanced stage. A device called the **stimoceiver** has been perfected; it is an electrode-radio unit implant that receives activating messages and transmits information about brain states. A chimpanzee with a stimoceiver becomes a receiving-transmitting organism without wires.

Paddy, one of Delgado's experimental subjects, is such a chimpanzee. When he began to act in an aggressive manner, a nearby computer noted that the electroencephalogram patterns from Paddy's amygdalae were displaying brief bursts of intense activity. The computer automatically sent a signal that activated the stimoceiver, and Paddy was quickly pacified. His aggressive impulse was inhibited before he had a chance to act on it. The potential for behavior control of the stimoceiver-computer combination is enormous.

ESB with Human Beings

The Terminal Man by physician-author Michael Crichton (1972) tells the story of Harry Benson, an epileptic patient prone to violence, and how a surgical team outfits him with a computerized stimoceiver. Whenever Harry starts to go into a violence-epilepsy pattern, the computer directs the stimoceiver to deliver a short pulse of current to Harry's pleasure center. The resulting pleasant experience aborts the unwanted brain-behavior pattern. Unfortunately, Harry—like Olds's rats—seeks to continue to produce the pleasurable stimulation. The epileptic pattern is the instrumental response that brings the current to the pleasure center. So Harry begins to produce more and more seizures, and the stimoceiver-brain system goes wild. *The Terminal Man* is usually dismissed as "just science fiction." But how close does it come to reality? The answer is: *The Terminal Man* does not go far beyond actual psychosurgery that has taken place with human beings.

The problem with doing ESB research with human beings is that it evokes passionate emotional responses and raises a considerable number of moral-ethical questions. Hostile critics of ESB often think of the brain as an inviolable organ, and they see no value in ESB research. Indeed, they feel that the whole area of ESB research is fraught with potential dangers for humanity. We will not evade the moral-ethical problems raised by ESB and other forms of psychotechnology, but let us wait until the critique section of this chapter to make an evaluation. For now, we will simply establish the existence of ESB with human beings by presenting a few illustrations of actual work that has been done.

"I guess, Doctor, that your electricity is stronger than my will." This statement was made to Delgado by a human subject who had electrode implants. When Delgado applied current to a certain subcortical region, the man's hand closed. Delgado asked the subject to try to keep his hand open when the current was applied, and he couldn't do it. Thus he made the statement that his will was weaker than ESB. Delgado notes that ESB always overwhelms the will of human subjects if a sufficiently intense current is applied! He has demonstrated with more than one human subject the power of ESB over conscious intention. In a great many cases of ESB-induced behavior, the subjects rationalize their behavior after the fact. They justify their actions, offering to Delgado superficial "cover" explanations for their behavior.

Pioneering research conducted by Robert Heath (1963), a psychiatrist at the Tulane University School of Medicine in New Orleans, illustrates potential applications of ESB with psychiatric patients. Two of his patients are identified as Patient No. B-7 and Patient No. B-10. Heath gave the patients themselves the power to push the buttons that operate implanted electrodes. Thus he spoke of **self-stimulation** of the brain. The patients, not a remote computer, stimulate their own brains.

Patient No. B-7 was twenty-eight years old. One of his main problems was **narcolepsy**, an involuntary tendency to fall asleep at inappropriate times. He had not responded to standard treatments. Fourteen electrodes were implanted in various brain regions. Three buttons operated the electrodes, and the patient wore the operating unit on a belt. It should be understood that the patient had a severe case of narcolepsy. Heath states that within seconds the patient would go from an alert state to a deep sleep.

Patient No. B-7 wore the stimulator for seventeen weeks. Whenever he felt unwanted sleep approaching, he would press one of the three buttons. It soon developed that he pressed only one of the buttons, the one that stimulated the septal region of his brain. This is the same region self-stimulated by Olds's rats. Patient No. B-7 found that stimulation of the septal region kept him from falling asleep. The feeling he got from ESB was like the feeling of an approaching orgasm, although a climax was not reached. Perhaps this explains why self-stimulation of the septal region tends to occur at a high rate. The anticipation of great pleasure is evoked, but the peak is not achieved.

Patient No. B-10 was twenty-five years old and suffered from **psychomotor epilepsy**, a form of epilepsy in which the "seizure" takes a peculiar form: The patient is conscious, but lacks voluntary control over his or her actions. The patient may see or hear things, steal items of value impulsively, walk for hours, or become violent. (Crichton's *Terminal Man* suffered from a form of psychomotor epilepsy.) Patient B-10 tended to engage in brief episodes of uncontrolled impulsive behavior. Heath reports that fifty-one electrodes were implanted into seventeen brain sites. Like patient No. B-7, patient No. B-10 was outfitted with a portable belt-stimulator that permitted him to send a brief current to various self-selected sites. And also like Patient No. B-7, Patient No. B-10 reported pleasurable sexlike feelings from stimulation of the septal area. This, however, for Patient No. B-10 was not the most frequently stimulated brain region. Another region, one that seemed to bring back an elusive memory, was preferred. Both Patient No. B-7 and Patient No. B-10 achieved partial control over their problems with the use of self-controlled ESB.

6.1   APPLICATION: USES OF ESB

The range of potential uses of ESB is quite great. It is possible to indicate a wide range of clinical applications and future possibilities (Delgado, 1969; Restak, 1979; Calvin and Ojemann, 1980). Here is a brief listing:

1. *Localization of tumors.* ESB can be used to pinpoint the location of tumors without opening the skull.

2. *Treatment of Parkinson's disease.* "Freezing" certain areas of the thalamus is a form of brain surgery used to treat Parkinson's disease. With the use of ESB techniques, it is possible to avoid the destruction of important motor pathways during surgery.

3. *Treatment of pain.* Intractable pain, such as the pain of certain cancer victims, can be partially controlled with ESB to selected brain sites.

4. *Control of severe mental disturbances.* Anxiety, fear, compulsive obsessions, and aggressive behavior are among the symptoms Delgado associates with severe mental disturbances. He notes that the use of ESB to treat the listed symptoms is controversial. Delgado (1969) comments, "Some investigators report a remarkable therapeutic success in obsessive patients; others are more skeptical about the usefulness of depth electrodes and electrocoagulations in treating mental illness." (p. 199)

5. *Control of tremors.* ESB can be used to help control the severe tremors associated with mulitple sclerosis. Patients can operate a self-stimulation ESB unit to attain partial control over their involuntary movements.

6. *Treatment of anorexia nervosa.* The treatment of **anorexia nervosa**, a condition in which patients lose appetite and may starve to death, is presented by Delgado as a possible application. With ESB, a patient may self-stimulate an excitatory region of the hypothalamus associated with hunger.

Heath's research has continued. In one article (Heath, 1977), he used the interesting term **brain pacemaker**, and described its use in the modulation of emotion. The possibility exists that erratic personal behavior (e.g., overly impulsive or aggressive behavior) can be regulated with a brain pacemaker in somewhat the same way that a heart pacemaker regulates erratic heart action.

The English poet John Milton wrote, in *Paradise Lost*:

The mind is its own place,
and in itself
Can make a heaven of hell, a
hell of heaven.

Delgado makes a similar comparison. One of the chapters of *Physical Control of the Mind* is titled "Hell and Heaven within the Brain." In another chapter, Delgado uses the phrase "magic window" in referring to electrode implants. ESB gives us a deeper glimpse into that poetic heaven-hell described by Milton.

NUTRITION: FOOD FOR THOUGHT

What does nutrition have to do with psychology? Just this: Remember that the psychotechnologist first and foremost sees a human being as an organism. An organism is made up of living cells. The brain is the principal organ of what we call mental or psychological phenomena—thinking, remembering, reflecting, and so forth. These processes can be no more "healthy" than the health of the organism in which they take place. In other words, we are what we eat in the most complete sense. Our bodies and our thought processes are so closely associated that distinctions between the two domains are primarily linguistic conveniences, not physical realities. Food is literally "food for thought."

Perhaps humankind recognizes a profound connection between personality and food. Have you ever noticed the number of food words that we commonly use to describe the human personality? *The Pocket Dictionary of American Slang* lists many of these words. Here are just a few: A *top banana* is a comedian in a burlesque show; an *egghead* is an intellectual; a *peach* is a pretty girl; *honey* refers to one's beloved; a *nut* is an insane or crazy person; a *cold fish* is someone who is too reserved or withdrawn; and a *big cheese* is an important person. Also, folklore provides many associations between traits of character and food. For example, some people believe that oysters increase a person's sex drive. Others say that fish is "brain food." And a Zen koan teases us with this question: When does the food you eat become you?

Protein and the Brain

When does the food you eat become you? There is no categorical answer. There is general agreement, however, that the food you eat does eventually become you. (At least it becomes that aspect of you that is you-the-organism.) Consequently, it is important to attain some understanding of the way food relates to the development and health of the organism. It would be beyond the scope of this book to explore all the ways nutrition relates to health. But it is appropriate to give some attention to those aspects of nutrition that are most closely related to dimensions of human behavior. Let us first take a look at the relationship between protein and the brain.

One of the principal ways of categorizing foods is to identify them as proteins, carbohydrates, and fats. **Proteins** are the principal "building blocks" of the muscles and body organs. **Carbohydrates** and **fats** are fuel; they "burn" and supply us with energy. The brain is made up mainly of protein. Children who do not receive sufficient protein during their developing years cannot have as large or as physically healthy a brain as they might have had. In turn, they will exhibit less general intelligence as a consequence of their stunted brains.

Adults also need a steady supply of protein to maintain and rebuild their bodies and their brains. There is evidence that a protein intake inadequate in **tryptophan**, one of the essential amino acids, can adversely affect the levels of a neurotransmitter in the brain such as serotonin (Restak, 1979). If serotonin levels fall below a critical point, it is reasonable to infer that the capacity for clear thinking would be to some degree impaired. (Incidentally, milk is a particularly rich source of tryptophan.)

Are the world's people getting enough protein? If depends on the country you're talking about. The United States and the industrialized nations in general have adequate protein supplies. But about one-half of the countries of the world are spoken of as "underdeveloped countries." In *The Population Bomb* by biologist Paul Ehrlich (1968), it is stated that half the people of the world are undernourished or malnourished. Such people and their children have little hope of reaching relatively normal levels of intellectual functioning.

Nutritional problems exist even in the United States. In the preceding paragraph, a distinction is made between **undernourished** and **malnourished**. According to Ehrlich, an undernourished person does not get enough food; in contrast, a malnourished person does not have a properly balanced diet. In an affluent country such as the United States, it is possible for a family to have enough money to eat well. Yet, because of an ignorance of the basic facts of nutrition, its members may be malnourished.

To illustrate, in many families sugar cereals are purchased for and eaten by children. The protein content of such cereals is about 4 percent. If, by some stretch of the imagination, a child had to live on sugar cereals alone, the child would be severely malnourished—even if he or she got enough calories. Generally, we need a minimum of about 14 percent protein to avoid malnourishment. Fortunately, adding milk to a bowl of sugar cereal brings the total protein content of the breakfast to about 14 percent. Whole grain cereals have about 14 percent protein, and adding milk to them brings the protein content to about 25 percent. Millions of people in the world's underdeveloped countries subsist on about 8 percent protein, not enough for proper physical and mental health.

The richest sources of protein are meat, fish, and meat by-products such as milk, eggs, and cheese. In the developed countries, these have been the favorite mainstays of a protein-rich diet. With rising food costs and less availability of the high-protein foods, however, we are faced with a problem: How can we obtain an adequate protein supply from less expensive and more available foods? To answer this question, it is important to know about th principle of **protein complementarity**, the fact that one protein can supplement another one. Protein is a complex food made up of **amino acids**, complex organic molecules that are the building blocks of protein itself. Meat, fish, and meat by-products tend to contain most of the important amino acids. (Eggs are almost a "perfect" protein food, containing almost all the amino acids.)

If a person is forced to live on grains and various kinds of legumes, such as beans, getting all the essential amino acids can be a problem. This is where the principle of protein complementarity comes in. In *Diet for a Small Planet*, Frances Moore Lappé (1971) points out that beans eaten with wheat equal a nearly complete protein in terms of amino acids. The important point is that beans and wheat have *different* amino acids. Eaten together at the same meal, they enhance each other. Understanding and utilizing such principles as protein complementarity can help us avoid protein malnourishment.

All the body organs depend on a steady supply of high-quality protein. Our principal concern here is with the brain, however. The brain, like the other organs, needs protein in the proper quantity and of the proper quality for continued efficiency. The capacity for clear thinking is related to getting enough protein. It is important in childhood; and it continues to be important in adulthood.

Low Blood Sugar or a Mental Disorder?

Bernard R. is a thirty-three-year-old stockbroker. Lately he has been complaining of depression and insomnia. He is irritable and has difficulty concentrating on his work. Sharon C. is a twenty-eight-year-old lawyer. Recently she has found herself prone to unaccountable anxiety and crying spells. She has never before had any serious problem with muscle pains, but now she has developed a chronic backache. What is wrong with Bernard and Sharon? Are they suffering from mental disorders, particularly of what used to be called (prior to DSM-III) the "neurotic" variety? It would certainly seem so from the presenting symptoms. But some researchers who study the relationship of nutrition to behavior claim that a condition of chronic low blood sugar can produce symptoms that mimic certain mental disorders (Lesser, 1980). Although we should not dispense with the orthodox psychological approach to understanding "neurotic" disorders, it is certainly a tenable hypothesis that an undetermined number of persons with depression, insomnia, anxiety, and similar symptoms are actually victims of chronic low-blood sugar.

The technical label for chronic low blood sugar is **hypoglycemia**; it may have several causes. For example, a tumor in the pancreas gland may induce the gland to secrete too much insulin. The oversecretion of insulin too quickly oxidizes the blood sugar, and blood sugar concentrations may fall far below normal. The victim of this condition may, in extreme cases, go into a state of coma; too much insulin can induce a coma. Most victims of hypoglycemia, however, do not suffer from a tumor in the pancreas gland. Thus there is a kind of hypoglycemia that has come to be called **functional hypoglycemia**, hypoglycemia not caused by a detectable organic condition. Seale Harris, the pioneer researcher on hypoglycemia, indicated in the 1930s that he believed hypoglycemia was more common than diabetes, its opposite pathological condition. Indeed, it has been suggested that years of low-grade hypoglycemia may precede a diabetic condition.

Some nutritionists and physicians (Abrahamson & Pezet, 1971; Saunders & Ross, 1980) suggest that functional hypoglycemia is a common condition and that it underlies many symptoms mistakenly taken to be "neurotic" disorders. A more recent line of research (Hudspeth, 1980) indicates that the oversecretion of insulin by some people has a direct and disruptive effect on the brain's ability to conduct electrical impulses. Abnormalities in electroencephalographic records (EEG) are found in people who oversecrete insulin. If either low blood sugar or the oversecretion of insulin is a problem, what can be done to correct the situation?

In either case, it is proposed that **refined carbohydrates**, primarily highly processed flour and sugar, overstimulate the pancreas gland to secrete insulin. Refined carbohydrates are digested quickly and assimilated into the blood stream as sugar. The brain is constantly scanning blood sugar levels. When the blood sugar level is too high, the brain sends a message to the pancreas to secrete insulin to burn up the excess sugar. If the blood sugar "spikes"

Eating too much sugar is associated with hypoglycemia and the oversecretion of insulin.

6.2 CONTEMPORARY RESEARCH: ORTHOMOLECULAR PSYCHIATRY

The Greek word **orthos** means "right." Thus **orthomolecular psychiatry** is an approach to mental health in which it is deemed important for mental patients to receive the "right molecules." In practice, this refers to **megavitamin therapy**, a regimen that prescribes massive doses of selected vitamins for a patient.

The current high level of interest in orthomolecular psychiatry was initially sparked by Linus Pauling, a famous biochemist and Nobel laureate. In 1968 Pauling published an article on megavitamins in *Science* magazine. In 1973 he and David Hawkins, a psysician, coauthored a book titled *Orthomolecular Psychiatry*.

The theory behind megavitamin therapy is that mental disorientation is caused by a deficiency in certain enzymes. These enzymes are needed to carry out crucial chemical reactions that take place at the level of the brain cells. Megavitamins help the suffering individual overcome an enzyme deficiency by acting as catalysts. They facilitate enzyme production. The emphasis in megavitamin therapy is on the B-complex vitamins, which are believed to be crucial ones (Lesser, 1980).

The relationship of sugar intake to orthomolecular psychiatry is noteworthy. Research biochemist Richard Passwater writes (1975, p. 48), "Sugar-restricted diets are used in megavitamin therapy for schizophrenia because sucrose unnecessarily consumes valuable nicotinamide during its metabolism." Nicotinamide is a coenzyme (part of an enzyme), and it is formed by vitamin B_3 (niacinamide or nicotinic acid). Briefly, sugar "uses up" the products of vitamin B_3. Thus refined sugar is tagged as a culprit again. It was hypothesized earlier that a high sugar intake might contribute to hypoglycemia and symp-

(i.e., rises too high too fast), the brain's alarm message is too strong and the pancreas overreacts, thus oxidizing too much sugar and sending the individual into a low blood sugar state. Paradoxically, eating too much sugar produces a low blood sugar condition! It also induces the oversecretion of insulin.

It is argued that citizens of the United States and England are massive users of refined carbohydrates, and this may be the source of much functional hypoglycemia. John Yudkin, a professor of nutrition and dietetics at Queen Elizabeth College of London University and author of *Sweet and Dangerous*

toms that mimic neurotic disorders. Now it is suggested that sugar depletes the body of the products of vitamin B_3, products essential for efficient functioning of the central nervous system. It should be mentioned that the nutritionists who are down on sugar are not critical of **fructose**, the natural sugar found in fruits. They are concerned about **sucrose**, refined sugar.

What about people who are not hospitalized, people who are "normal"? The implication is clear in the writings on orthomolecular psychiatry that "What is sauce for the goose is sauce for the gander." The line between normal and abnormal is often hard to find, and many people who are not hospitalized as out-and-out mental patients may suffer some symptoms of mental disorientation because of poor nutrition. It is thus concluded that proper nutrition is important for all of us, not just for people branded with labels such as "schizophrenic disorder."

One of the unfortunate side effects of the enthusiasm for orthomolecular psychiatry has been the tendency of some people to self-prescribe massive doses of vitamins. It is one thing to eat correctly and to take some vitamins judiciously—it is quite another to embark on an unsupervised megavitamin regimen. People often say, "Oh well, it does no harm. It all goes out in the urine. So the worst that can happen is that you'll have expensive urine." This is not completely true. In the first place, not all vitamins are water soluble, and their excessive intake may be toxic. In the second place, even water-soluble vitamins may have adverse effects if consumed in great quantities. The simple truth is that the long-run effects of years of taking megavitamins is unknown. Megavitamin therapy is a treatment, not a way of life.

Advocates of orthomolecular psychiatry make grand claims for their approach. They speak of emptying mental wards, restoring shattered lives, bringing families together again, and saving taxpayers millions of dollars in mental hospital bills. There are less enthusiastic voices, as we will see in the critique section of this chapter.

(1972), states that the average American and Briton eat two pounds of sugar or more a week! He comments:

> One of the reasons why some people find it difficult to accept that on average Americans and Britons eat two pounds of sugar or more a week is that they think only of the sugar that is brought into the home as visible sugar. But an increasing proportion of sugars is now bought already made up into foods by the manufacturer.
>
> Industrial sugar goes to the factory and comes to us in the form of candy, ice cream, soft drinks, cakes, cookies, and nowadays also in a very wide range of other items, especially the fancily packaged "convenience foods." (p. 47)

If a person suspects that he or she is suffering from hypoglycemia, the person should consult with a physician. If in turn the physician suspects the presence of hypoglycemia, the physician will order a **glucose-tolerance test**, a six-hour test in which the blood is sampled for sugar content at regular intervals. When an individual is found to suffer from functional hypoglycemia, a diet that restricts refined carbohydrates is often recommended. The patient is also asked to reduce intake of caffeine and alcohol; these are said to stimulate the pancreas. And the individual is encouraged to take in an adequate amount of protein.

For our purposes, it is important to observe that the claim of a relationship between neurotic symptoms and chronic low blood sugar makes us appreciate that the division between "psychological problems" and "medical problems" is to some degree arbitrary.

Artificial Food Flavors and Colors

Ralph Nader and "Nader's Raiders," consumer advocates, have called the American way of eating "the chemical feast." They are referring, of course, to the many substances added to our foods. In particular, it has been suggested that artificial food flavors and colors play an important role in the behavior of **hyperkinetic children**, children who strongly manifest such characteristics as impulsivity, distractability, excitability, and perceptual and motor coordination problems. Such children are also said to be resistant to discipline and to be domineering in their social behavior.

Several theories have been expounded to account for hyperkinesis in children. The first theory advanced was that hyperkinetic children suffer from **minimal brain damage**, a condition in which the nervous system damage is so slight that the child incorrectly seems to be organically normal. Another theory is that most hyperkinetic children are basically of sound body, but their unique behavior is caused by inborn temperamental differences. This theory is presented by Paul H. Wender, a professor of psychiatry on the staff of the College of Medicine at the University of Utah, in his book *The Hyperactive Child* (1973). He asserts that the majority of hyperkinetic children are not brain-damaged. A third theory is that the term "hyperkinetic child" is a wastebasket term that includes a host of possible states. Sydney Walker, III (1974), a neuropsychiatrist, asserts that a variety of conditions ranging from hypoglycemia to heart problems may underlie hyperactive behavior.

The leading advocate of the principal theory that concerns us in this section is Benjamin Feingold, a pediatrician and allergist. In *Why Your Child Is Hyperactive* Feingold (1974) presents the thesis that artificial food flavors and colors play an important role in hyperactivity. Feingold does not indict food preservatives as culprits, with the possible exception of butylated hydroxytoluene (BHT), an antioxidant used in many foods; he says that an occasional child may show a reaction to BHT. Essentially, Feingold's theory is an allergic-reaction theory. Hyperkinesis results as a side effect of allergic reactions to artificial flavors and colors. Feingold's work has created a substantial amount of interest, and he was invited to testify before Senator Edward Kennedy's Subcommittee on Health.

Feingold asserts that the problem of hyperactive children has reached epidemic proportions. Several sources place the estimated percentage of hyperactive children between 10 and 15 percent of the children in the United States. Converted to numbers, these percentages suggest about five million children. These figures are probably too high, however. The Department of Health, Education, and Welfare estimates that about 10 percent of the nation's children are emotionally handicapped. This percentage includes problems other than hyperkinesis (e.g., autism, schizophrenia, mental retardation, etc.). Nonetheless, the number of children that get tagged with the label "hyperkinetic" is large. A December 1975 edition of *People Weekly* contains an interview with Feingold. Asked about the upsurge in the problem of hyperkinesis, he comments:

I correlate this increase with the increased consumption of food chemicals and in particular the artificial colors and flavors, of which there are 1,500 to 1,800 on the market. If you project a graph for the estimated incidence of hyperkinesis and then compare it with the Standard and Poor's table for the dollar value of soft drinks over the past decade, you'll find it is identical. Circumstantial evidence, but interesting. (p. 65)

There is also the clear implication in Feingold's work that adults are not immune to the effects of artificial colors and flavors. Irritability, restlessness, and various symptoms associated with neurotic reactions may be related to the ingestion of these substances. Feingold's approach may be classified as a variety of orthomolecular psychiatry. The usual approach to orthomolecular psychiatry is "Let's get the right substances *into* the organism"; Feingold's theme is "Let's get the wrong substances *out* of the organism."

The saying "You are what you eat" is a familiar one. The nutritionist would add, "You think and behave as you eat." This section on nutrition has revealed the possible links between protein intake and brain functioning, sugar usage and hypoglycemia, megavitamin therapy and mental illness, and artificial colors and flavors and hyperkinesis. Many of the statements about nutrition and behavior should be accepted only at the level of provocative hypotheses, not established facts. Nonetheless, it is clear that the disciplines of nutrition and psychology have something to say to each other.

DRUGS: THE TRANQUILIZED MIND

The following excerpt is from an article titled "Coping with Depression" by Matt Clark in a 1975 issue of *Newsweek*.

Carl Schwartz, a 61-year-old New York lawyer, spent nearly 40 years swinging between the highs and lows of endogenous manic-depressive illness. "I literally enjoyed the manic phases," he recalls. "I was a big shot, on top of the world. I spent not only my own money, but everybody else's I could get my hands on—I bought six suits at a time, a lot of stupid unnecessary things. I usually left home and set up my own apartment." But in between the highs, there were frightening plunges into depression. "I feared getting out of bed, and was anxious to get into bed at night because I could block out the horror of my daily life." For the last three years, Schwartz has been free of his illness, thanks to daily doses of lithium carbonate. (p. 53)

This excerpt reveals one of the ways a drug can be used to treat mental illness. Like the nutritional approach, the drug approach assumes that psychological problems often have a biochemical basis. In this section we will review chemotherapy as a form of psychotechnology.

What is Chemotherapy?

In the broadest possible sense, **chemotherapy** may be defined as the use of drugs to treat either organic or mental illnesses. In this section, our concern is with mental illnesses. Chemotherapy used against psychological-emotional problems is itself a subclass of a larger subject, **psychopharmacology**—the study of how drugs affect psychological and emotional processes. When the knowledge from psychopharmacology becomes applied, then we speak of

Chemotherapy may be defined as the use of drugs to treat either organic or mental illnesses.

chemotherapy. Our concern in this chapter is with technology, which implies applications of general knowledge.

The use of chemotherapy to treat people's ills is not new. This chapter opened with a quotation from *The Egyptian* designed to reveal the antiquity of psychotechnology. Similarly, records of chemotherapy can be traced to the time of the pharaohs. One of the most famous medical documents in history is the *Papyrus Ebers*. It was compiled in Egypt around 1500 B.C., and it summarizes the knowledge of physicians and priests about treating various illnesses. A list of "chemicals" from the *Papyrus Ebers* is frightening indeed to the modern mind! The list includes: The excretion of animals, teeth crushed in honey, rotten meat, the blood of lizards, and other readily available organic substances. From the time of the ancient Egyptians to the present, humankind has used drugs in many ways. A complete presentation would itself make a long book. Let us content ourselves with a few illustrations.

Galen is one of the most famous physicians in history. A Greek scientist, he lived and worked about a century after the days of Christ. His teachings had a tremendous impact on medicine, lasting for many centuries. Our interest in Galen here is in his use of chemotherapy. In a sense, he was the father of the modern prescription drug that contains more than one ingredient. Galen combined various drugs to form mixtures called **galenicals**. The authority of today's physician to prescribe drugs descends from the prestigious practices of the great Galen.

The ancient Eastern world has a history of drug use for the treatment of illnesses. For centuries, Hindu healers have used the roots of the plant *Rauwolfia serpentina* to treat both organic and psychological problems. **Reserpine**, a drug sometimes used today against psychotic disorders, is extracted from the serpentina plant (Kline, 1974). In the Americas, Indians fought malaria by ingesting the juice from the bark of the cinchona tree. They chewed cocoa leaves for greater strength when confronted with difficult tasks; cocoa leaves contain cocaine.

Our drug chronicle has been brief. But you can see that drug use is nothing new. The great nineteenth-century physician Sir William Osler once commented, "A desire to take medicine is, perhaps, the great feature which distinguishes man from other animals."

Kinds of Drugs Used in Chemotherapy

The four principal kinds of drugs used in chemotherapy for psychological problems are (1) antipsychotic agents, (2) sedative-hypnotic agents, (3) antidepressants, and (4) stimulants.

Antipsychotic Agents Antipsychotic agents are drugs used to combat the effects of psychotic disorders. This class of drugs is used extensively. It is estimated that about four million prescriptions are written for **chlorpromazine (Thorazine)** in a given year (Graedon, 1980). (Don't be confused by the fact that two names are often given for a drug. The first name, uncapitalized, is the **generic** or proper chemical name. The second name, capitalized, and in parentheses, is the trade name. Trade names are given because they are popularized and are often the only name you will associate with the drug.)

Chlorpromazine is used so extensively because of its great calming effect on mental patients. Physical restraints and heavy sedation with barbiturates was the order of the day in mental hospitals of yesteryear. Chlorpromazine's greatest value is thus with patients who are prone to violence. But do not be misled: None of the drugs herein discussed, including chlorpromazine, are cures for psychotic reactions. They make patients more manageable and, in some cases, more amenable to psychotherapy.

There are several other antipsychotic agents in addition to chlorpromazine. We will identify three of the most common: haloperidol (Haldol), lithium, and reserpine (Serpasil). **Haloperidol** is a useful antipsychotic agent because it is sometimes found to be less toxic than chlorpromazine. **Lithium** is particularly useful in cases of affective or mood disorders. Alternating manic and depressive episodes are sometimes regulated with the help of lithium. **Reserpine** is of historical interest because it was one of the first antipsychotic agents to win recognition and wide use. This took place in the early 1950s. But reserpine is seldom used today because of undesirable physical side effects and because the other drugs identified above have proven themselves more effective agents.

It is hypothesized that antipsychotic agents are effective because they regulate the action of neurotransmitters in the brain. A **neurotransmitter** is a chemical substance released when a neuron "fires." Chlorpromazine appears to regulate the action of **dopamine**, one of the brain's principal neurotransmitters. Lithium appears to regulate the action of **norepinephrine**, another important neurotransmitter (Julien, 1978).

Sedative-Hypnotic Agents   The principal physiological effects of sedative-hypnotic agents is to depress the action of brain-arousal mechanisms. Small doses of sedative-hypnotic agents make a person drowsy and sometimes somewhat less reserved in social situations. Let us discuss two general kinds of sedative-hypnotic agents: **barbiturates** and **antianxiety agents**.

Some well-known trade names for barbiturates are Nembutal, Seconal, and Pentothal. Primarily, barbiturates are used as sedatives. They are prescribed for neurotic reactions ranging from anxiety to insomnia. They are also sometimes prescribed for high blood pressure when it is suspected that the high blood pressure is associated with chronic anxiety.

Turning to the antianxiety agents, some well-known trade names are Miltown, Equanil, Librium, and Valium. The antianxiety agents are referred to as the **minor tranquilizers** in contrast to the **major tranquilizers**, the earlier discussed antipsychotic agents. As their name indicates, the antianxiety agents are used to treat anxiety and other "neurotic" disorders. Their use is

Drawing by Richter; © 1982 The New Yorker Magazine, Inc.

extensive. It is estimated that somewhat more than seventy-five million prescriptions per year are written for such agents (Graedon, 1980).

Antidepressants   Antidepressants are drugs prescribed to reduce the symptoms of some depressive disorders in adults. There are two basic classes of antidepressants: (1) Triyclics and (2) Monoamine oxidase (MAO) inhibitors. In different ways, both kinds of drugs have the effect of increasing the levels of norepinephrine in the central nervous system. Thus the effects associated with antidepressants are much like those associated with stimulants. Indeed, some books classify antidepressants along with stimulants. However, it is probably best to think of stimulants and antidepressants as belonging to two different classes because antidepressants do not elevate mood in nondepressed persons. Stimulants, on the other hand, tend to elevate one's mood even if it seems to be already appropriate. Also, unlike many stimulants, antidepressants seem to be nonhabit-forming (Wender and Klein, 1981). This is not to say that antidepressants are without side effects, however.

Stimulants   Stimulants are drugs that tend to increase one's alertness. A moderate dose of a stimulant may temporarily make a person feel stronger, more capable, in a better mood, and optimistic about the future. An exces-

Caffeine and nicotine, both stimulants, are found in coffee and cigarettes.

sive dose of a stimulant may produce an anxiety reaction or a transient psychotic reaction. The widespread use of drugs is illustrated by the fact that **caffeine** and **nicotine**, both stimulants, are found in coffee and cigarettes. **Cocaine**, mentioned earlier, is also a stimulant. An interesting historical note is that Freud went through a brief period of enthusiasm for the use of cocaine, proclaiming its marvelous ability to elevate mood and increase strength. His enthusiasm was brief when he discovered that some cocaine users become addicts.

One of the principal kinds of stimulants used in chemotherapy are the **amphetamines**. Their chemical structure resembles the neurotransmitter norepinephrine, and they tend to mimic its action. Well-known trade names for amphetamines are Benzedrime, Dexedrine, and Methedrine. The principal clinical uses of amphetamines are for the treatment of narcolepsy, hyperkinesis, and obesity. One can clearly see the value of amphetamines in the treatment of narcolepsy. The narcoleptic individual tends to fall asleep at inappropriate times; a stimulant helps the person to stay awake.

In the case of **hyperkinesis**, the logic is a bit more obscure. The hyperkinetic child is already too active. How can a stimulant help him or her? The stimulant seems to have a paradoxical effect. The relationship between arousal and stimulation appears to be an inverted U. Stimulation increases arousal, *but only to a point*. An arousal "crest" is reached, and more stimulation brings the arousal level down. Thus, odd as it seems, a hyperkinetic child may very well be "tranquilized" with a stimulant. Following this logic, it may be noted that caffeine can also be used to treat hyperkinetic children. Some physicians prescribe that such children drink coffee and take amphetamines.

A substantial amount of reservation exists among people interested in mental health about the wide use of amphetamines for the treatment of hyperkinesis (Hughes & Brewin, 1979). As noted earlier, hyperkinetic symptoms may be caused by more than one factor. Critics of chemotherapy argue that the effects of a drug may mask important symptoms, thus allowing an underlying illness to get worse. Others, such as Feingold, feel that taking a hyperkinetic child off artificial food flavors and colors is preferable in many cases to prescribing amphetamines. Peter Schrag, an editor of the *Saturday Review*, and Diane Divoky, an editor of *Learning* magazine, argue in their book *The Myth of the Hyperactive Child* (1975) along the following lines:

By early 1975 between 500,000 and 1,000,000 American children and adolescents were taking amphetamine-type drugs and other psychostimulants by prescription. . . . A small percentage of those children suffer from some diagnosable medical ailment sufficiently serious to warrant chemotherapy. Most do not; they are being drugged, often at the insistence of schools or individual teachers, to make them more manageable. (p. xiii)

Amphetamines have also found large-scale use in the treatment of obesity. They act as appetite suppressants, thus helping the person to stay on a diet. They also give the taker a feeling of well-being and they combat anxiety. Some overweight people are said to eat as a result of negative emotional states, such as anxiety and depression. Thus the "lift" obtained from an amphetamine may work against tendencies to eat associated with low moods. However, there are problems. After several weeks of usage, a tolerance builds up to the drug, and its appetite suppressant qualities are lost. Larger doses are required to obtain the desired effect. Although there is some question about the degree to which amphetamines are addictive, it certainly seems that some users develop a psychological dependence on them. And this is certainly undesirable. All in all, it can be argued that the beneficial effects of amphetamines for weight control are short-lived. They are probably of little value for the long-range control of obesity.

Chemotherapy and Psychosomatic Illnesses

Psychosomatic illnesses are literally "mind-body" disorders. The word "psychosomatic" comes from two Greek words: *psyche*, meaning mind or soul, and *soma*, meaning body. A practical definition of a psychosomatic illness is that such an illness is either caused by psychological-emotional factors or greatly aggravated by them. In popular language, "Your mind can make you sick."

By now, most people have heard it said that ulcers can be psychosomatic. In addition to ulcers, the list of psychosomatic illnesses is long indeed. In

6.3   CONTEMPORARY RESEARCH: SIDE EFFECTS OF DRUG THERAPY

Although drug therapy has its advantages, it also has its costs. There are some risks associated with taking many medications, and these risks must be weighed against potential benefits. Quite a bit of research has been conducted on drug side effects. The material presented below presents some examples of important drug side effects, and is adapted from several sources (i.e., Julien, 1978; Silverman & Simon, 1979; Wender & Klein, 1981).

Antipsychotic agents often have an unwanted effect on muscle action. Spasms, stiffness, convulsions, problems in swallowing, and tremors provide examples. If large doses of anti-psychotic agents are taken for several years, involuntary facial movements may result. In some cases, these involuntary facial movements may persist even when the drug is discontinued. Other side effects sometimes associated with antipsychotic agents are: yellowing of the whites of the eyes or skin (jaundice), changes in blood pressure, abnormal heart rates, greater susceptibility to irritation by the sun, and feelings of diminished energy.

One of the principal uses of barbiturates—the treatment of insomnia—is currently subject to review. Some researchers believe that the "hangover symptoms" of barbiturates the morning after are too high a price to pay for the night's sleep. It is argued that the side effects of frequent barbiturate usage include listlessness and prolonged depression. A well-known researcher on sleep is William C. Dement, widely recognized for his investigations of rapid-eye-movement (REM) sleep. He and his co-authors comment (1975, p. 46):

Almost every sedative, if used regularly, will aggravate the insomnia that it is intended to cure. Anyone who has become dependent on drugs for sleep may need to go through a carefully managed withdrawal program and endure a string of restless, even miserable nights.

None of These Diseases by physician S. I. McMillen (1973) a list of fifty-one illnesses are given a psychosomatic label. Disorders of the digestive system, the circulatory system, the genitourinary system, the nervous system, the glands of internal secretion, the muscles and joints, the eyes, and the skin may all be complicated by psychological-emotional factors. Also, various allergic disorders are often thought of as psychosomatic.

What is the appropriate treatment for the long list of psychosomatic illness? One answer has been chemotherapy. Ulcer patients are often given an antianxiety agent because it is believed that anxiety aggravates ulcers. An-

You will recall that it is estimated that somewhat more than seventy-five million prescriptions per year are written for anti-anxiety agents. Some pharmacologists argue that all sedative-hypnotic agents, including the antianxiety agents, are subject to abuse and addiction. Others argue that many people operate automobiles and other machinery with the false idea that a "tranquilizer" allows one to remain completely clearheaded. Such is not the case. Antianxiety agents tend to affect alertness and vigilance. Some critics also noted that a substantial number of persons use the antianxiety agents in irresponsible ways. For example, it is not uncommon for excessive drinkers to combine alcohol with an antianxiety agent, thus making the user even less alert and vigilant.

Monoamine oxidase (MAO) inhibitors, belonging to the class of antidepressants, have caused sudden high blood pressure in a few persons when taken with certain aged cheeses (e.g., Camembert, cheddar, and Stilton). Red wines, pickled herring, and sardines are also foods to be avoided with MAO inhibitors. (A patient taking an MAO inhibitor is supplied with a more detailed list.)

Amphetamines, belonging to the class of stimulants, have a number of unwanted side effects. They seem to be subject to abuse, probably because some people find them addictive. Persons with hardening of the arteries, heart disease, high blood pressure, thyroid disease, or glaucoma may find the symptoms associated with their conditions aggravated when taking amphetamines. Other difficulties sometimes associated with the use of amphetamines include euphoria, muscle spasms, headache, diarrhea, itching, and diminished sexual drive.

Drug therapy seems to have its proper place in the treatment of mental disorders. However, common sense requires that adverse side effects, such as some of those indicated in this box, should not be ignored.

other illustration is provided by **primary hypertension**, high blood pressure of unknown origin. About 85 percent of all high blood pressure falls into this category. It is estimated that about twenty million American suffer from primary hypertension. Presently, this condition is usually treated with **antihypertensive agents**, drugs that tend to have the effect of reducing blood pressure. Similar statements can be made about other psychosomatic illnesses. Current practice places a heavy reliance on drug treatment.

The question arises, "If we are willing to accept the assertion that your mind can make you sick, would it not be logical to accept the converse assertion that your mind can make you well?" Of course, that is the thesis underlying much of this book. Psychologists work on the assumption that behavioral strategies, those that contribute toward greater adjustment and growth, can act as counterforces against psychosomatic disorders. Advocates of counseling and psychotherapy feel that these approaches may afford better long-run treatment of psychosomatic illness than chemotherapy (see the Applied Exploration at the end of this chapter).

Opiates and Hallucinogens

Our concern with opiates and hallucinogens is not so much with their addictive potential or possible abuse, but with their role in chemotherapy. An **opiate** is a narcotic agent, a drug that has a two-way action: (1) sedation and (2) pain relief. Well-known opiates are opium, heroin, morphine, codeine, and methadone. In moderate doses, several of the opiates produce euphoria, a sense of well-being. In *Confessions of an English Opium-Eater*, published in 1822, author Thomas DeQuincey writes, "Here was a panacea . . . for all human woes; here was the secret of happiness, about which philosophers had disputed for so many ages" (p. 179). You can see why some people have mistakenly believed that opium was a cure for their mental problems. Opiates sometimes play a proper role in the relief of pain and are appropriate for other specific medical purposes. But the sad fact is that they are not useful for the responsible treatment of mental illness.

A **hallucinogen** is a drug that tends to alter conventional perception and thought. Sometimes these drugs are called **psychotomimetic agents**, drugs that "mimic" psychotic reactions. Still another name for these drugs is psychedelic agents. The psychiatrist Humphry Osmond coined the word "psychedelic" to suggest a mind-manifesting action, an expanding of consciousness and an enlarging of vision. It is apparent that "psychotomimetic" is a negative label and that "psychedelic" is a positive label. The labels themselves reveal the controversy that has surrounded the use of hallucinogens. Familiar hallucinogens are lysergic acid diethylamide (LSD), psilocybin, mescaline, and cannabis (marijuana).

There was, during the late 1950s and early 1960s, quite a bit of interest in hallucinogens as adjuncts to psychotherapy. LSD was used to treat alcoholics, the depression brought about by terminal illnesses, and other kinds of problems. A number of favorable reports were published. During the 1960s, however, LSD was also taking on negative associations and receiving a bad press. Many people disapproved of Timothy Leary and others who spoke in positive terms about hallucinogens. Terms such as *bum trip* and *flashback* came into prominence. In the absence of responsible guidance, panic states and psychotic reactions were sometimes reported. The bad press rubbed off on researchers, and experiments with hallucinogens as potential psychotherapeutic tools all but stopped. By 1969 the *Annual Review of Medi-*

cine had little good to say about LSD as a means of looking within one's self.

A small amount of research with the use of psychedelic agents in connection with psychotherapy still goes on. There are still a number of psychiatrists today who feel that drugs may be potent enhancers of experience. For example, psychiatrist Claudio Naranjo, in *The Healing Journey* (1973), tells of his research with psychedelic drugs. He describes two classes of drugs: feeling enhancers and fantasy enhancers. **Feeling enhancers** augment emotional responses. **Fantasy enhancers** increase imaginative capacities. Thus Naranjo speaks of these drugs as psychedelic or mind-manifesting, but not hallucinogenic; they do not produce sensory delusions. Naranjo writes:

If both the agony and the ecstasy of drug experiences have a potential for psychological healing, it is important for us to know the place and promise of each in the treatment of an individual and the best way to deal with each when it occurs. . . . (p. 13)

Naranjo notes that there is a widespread tendency to see drug experiences and psychotherapy as unrelated. He and a relatively small number of researchers make a case for the use of psychedelic drugs in psychotherapy. There is little professional enthusiasm for that point of view, however. At present, chemotherapy for psychological disorders seldom includes the use of psychedelic agents.

In brief, there are five kinds of **psychopharmacological agents**, drugs that affect perception, thought, and emotion: (1) antipsychotic agents, (2) sedative-hypnotic agents, (3) stimulants, (4) opiates, and (5) hallucinogens and psychedelics. It should be noted that although hallucinogens and psychedelics are grouped in the same formal class, some researchers (e.g., Naranjo) assert that not all psychedelics are hallucinogenic. Of the drugs in the five classes cited, those in the first three classes are the principal ones used in the treatment of mental illnesses and other psychological disorders.

BIOFEEDBACK: UNIFYING MIND AND BODY

Imagine an accomplished yogi sitting in a psychophysiological laboratory. Electrodes are attached to his body. An electrocardiogram unfolds a moment-to-moment record of his heart beats. He states that he can consciously control the pumping action of his heart. The yogi focuses his attention, and the EKG shows that his heart is fibrillating rapidly, making it unable to pump blood. He has made good his claim.

Is the preceding description merely a speculative scenario? No; the event actually took place in a laboratory supervised by Elmer Green, a physiological psychologist at the Menninger Foundation (Green & Green, 1977). The yogi was Swami Rama from India, and for years he had been practicing meditation and self-control of the body. But what the yogi was able to do seems to be within the capacities of most people. Self-control of various visceral responses of the body is possible with a procedure known as biofeedback.

What Is Biofeedback?

Biofeedback is a procedure by which a subject can learn to bring physiological processes under voluntary control; this is facilitated by providing the subject with high-quality, moment-to-moment information about the state of such processes. In practice, the information—or feedback—is provided by electronic devices that augment biological signals (see Figure 6.1). The principal response measures that have been used in biofeedback research are (1) the electroencephalogram (EEG), which is associated with "brain waves"; (2) the electrocardiogram (EKG) and other measures associated with the heart's behavior; (3) the electromyograph (EMG), which is associated with muscle tension; (4) the galvanic skin response (GSR), which is associated with emotional responses; and (5) skin temperature, which is associated with the dilation and constriction of small blood vessels.

On a more informal level, biofeedback represents an exciting breakthrough in human-machine systems. For the first time human beings can learn to "play" organs of the body much like a musician can play a piano. Biofeedback has been described with such phrases as **electronic yoga**, **visceral learning**, and **mind over body**. Biofeedback in its present form did not make its appearance on the psychological horizon until the late 1960s. When it did appear, it generated a substantial amount of interest among scientists as well as the general public.

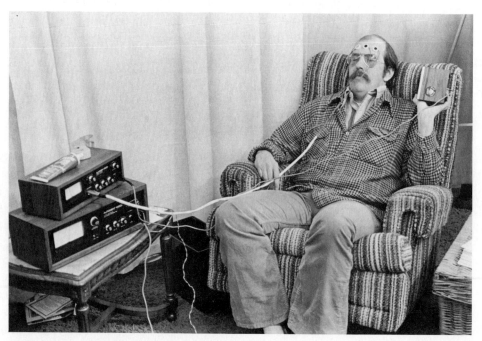

Biofeedback training is a procedure by which a person can learn to bring physiological processes under voluntary control.

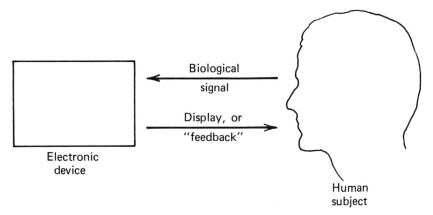

FIGURE 6.1   A schematic illustration of the basic structure of biofeedback training.

The basic principle on which biofeedback is based has been known to psychologists for years. The early learning theorist, Edward L. Thorndike, called the principle **knowledge of results**, which states that learning is greatly facilitated if learners are provided with information about the outcomes of their actions. Imagine yourself sitting blindfolded before a typewriter. Assume that you don't know how to type. You practice, but your practice means nothing because you can't associate keys with letters. Say that a teacher is willing to call out each letter as you strike it. Could you learn the keyboard now? Of course, because you are obtaining knowledge of results. The knowledge of results allows you to shape your behavior, dropping out those responses that do not contribute to your learning goal and keeping in those that do. In a sense, we have all been "blind" when it comes to having knowledge of results about the actions of organs of our body. We have not been able to control them voluntarily because we couldn't "see" (or "hear," or otherwise sense) what they were doing.

A traditional distinction in physiology and psychology has been the distinction between the somatic and the autonomic nervous system. The **somatic nervous system** is said to control the muscles attached to the skeleton. Thus such actions as walking, moving a hand, turning the head, and so forth are thought of as voluntary. We can will these actions, and most of us are able to acquire rather precise control over them. On the other hand, the **autonomic nervous system** is said to control the smooth muscles associated with the body's internal organs and endocrine glands. Such internal events as heart rate, blood vessel changes, gastric juice secretion, and thyroxine production are thought of as involuntary. It is usually said that we cannot will these events, and most of us live our whole lives with no conscious control over them.

At present the whole distinction between what is voluntary and what is involuntary is breaking down. One of B. F. Skinner's accomplishments was to demonstrate that much behavior classified as voluntary could just as well be classified as involuntary. Operant conditioning deals with the conditioning of overt movements, visible actions, the kinds of behavior usually thought of as voluntary. Many people consequently felt that Skinner's work downgraded the importance of conscious control, or what we refer to as the human will. Now biofeedback makes its appearance and says, "Yes, the distinction between voluntary and involuntary is arbitrary. People can gain control over so-called involuntary processes." Thus biofeedback upgrades the importance of conscious control, or the human will.

Let us conduct a thought experiment to illustrate how voluntary control over a visceral reaction can be acquired. Imagine yourself sitting in a chair in a biofeedback laboratory. Before you is a television screen. Electrodes have been pasted to your body; the electrodes convey information about heart activity to an EKG apparatus; the data are quickly analyzed by a computer; and then heart-rate information is projected on the television screen. The televised picture provides you with high-quality information about heart-rate activity. A moving dot and a line across the middle of the screen are the essential elements in the picture. When the dot is moving above the line, your heart rate is above a previously established standard. When the dot is moving below the line, your heart rate is below the standard. Your task is to be able to move the dot from above the line to below the line, or vice versa, at will.

You stare at the display in dismay. You do not have the slightest idea how to control your heart rate, and you express your feeling to the experimenter in charge. The experimenter gives you gentle assurance that most people can develop some internal strategy for getting the dot to move at will. It is a matter of trial and error, and that is why the feedback is so important. So you look at the dot, concentrate, and various thoughts and images come and go. They seem to have only a minimal connection with the display on the screen. Little by little, however, you begin to feel that something is happening. By the end of the session, it seems that you have acquired some modicum of control over the movement of the dot.

Say that you return to the laboratory twice a week for a period of time. After five or ten sessions, it is quite clear that something is happening. Perhaps within ten or twenty sessions you begin to feel quite adept. You can often "drive" the dot at will. You have acquired a degree of voluntary control over your heart rate.

The preceding example was hypothetical. But similar research has been conducted by Peter Lang (1970) of the University of Wisconsin. He has taught a number of subjects to control heart rate. Such research has great promise. Persons suffering from heart problems may be able to relieve some of their symptoms with the help of biofeedback training. There have already been some clinical applications, but so far these have been relatively limited in number.

Biofeedback Research

One of the first reports of a successful biofeedback study dealt with the instrumental conditioning of heart rate in rats. The experiment was conducted by experimental psychologists Neal Miller and Leo DiCara, and it was reported in 1967. In the experiment, heart rate was the instrumental response and electrical stimulation to a rat's pleasure center was the reinforcer. Some of the rats learned to speed up their heart rates for the electrical stimulation; others learned to slow them down.

This pioneer demonstration of the reality of visceral learning was not produced easily. To rule out the possibility that the rats were controlling heart rate indirectly through changes in breathing or muscular activity, the rats were injected with curare, a drug that paralyzes skeletal muscles. The results were clear. The rats were able to attain direct voluntary control over heart rate. Indeed, so powerful was the direct control that seven out of forty rats trained to slow down their heart rates died a sudden death. On hearing these results, a student in one of my psychology classes exclaimed, "What next? Now there are even yogi rats!"

DiCara and other researchers working with Miller have gone on to show that rats can acquire voluntary control of a spectrum of visceral responses, including urine flow and systolic blood pressure. They have also demonstrated that salivation in dogs, usually thought of as an involuntary response, can be instrumentally trained and brought under voluntary control. (It should be noted that there has been some controversy over the methodology and the conclusions of the Miller and DiCara research.)

It would certainly seem that if rats and dogs can take advantage of biofeedback, so can human beings. And this is, of course, the case. One of the first reports of biofeedback research with human beings was the alpha rhythm studies conducted by Joseph Kamiya (1970). Kamiya, at the time a psychologist at the Langley Porter Neuropsychiatric Institute in San Francisco, first trained human subjects to recognize their own alpha rhythms. The **alpha rhythm** is one of several brain-wave patterns. The term "brain wave" is informal usage for the electroencephalographic records (EEG) produced by changing electrical potentials of the brain. There are several prominent frequency bands. These are designated by letters of the Greek alphabet, including **alpha, beta, delta,** and **theta.** The terminology can be slightly confusing because *alpha* is the first letter of the Greek alphabet, but it is ranked second in terms of cycles per second in the four waves just noted.

This is the order in terms of cycles per second:

1. The **beta rhythm** occurs at the rate of about fourteen cycles per second or more and is associated with alertness and high arousal.
2. The **alpha rhythm** occurs at the rate of about eight to fourteen cycles per second and is associated with mental relaxation and what has been described as "passive alertness."

3. The **theta rhythm** occurs at the rate of about four to eight cycles per second and is associated with a reverie-fantasy state in which mental imagery is high.
4. The **delta rhythm** occurs at the rate of about four cycles per second or less and is associated with deep sleep (see Figure 6.2).

After Kamiya discovered that people could reliably recognize alpha states, he wondered if they could learn to increase their production of the alpha rhythm. The task given the experimental subjects was to maintain the sound of a tone. When subjects were in an alpha state, the tone was on; when subjects slipped out of the alpha state, the tone went off. The majority of subjects were able to learn the voluntary control of the alpha rhythm. Kamiya had verified with objective data what meditators have claimed for generations: It is possible to develop self-control of mental states. One of the exciting things about EEG-biofeedback is that the typical subject can make rapid progress in the direction of voluntary mental control, accomplishing in months what might take years without the aid of the biofeedback equipment. This finding has led popularizers to speak of "instant Zen" and the like. (Zen is discussed in Chapter 8.)

But make no mistake. Reasonable researchers, such as Kamiya, make no rash claims for EEG training. For now, it can be said that the alpha state does seem to be associated with a kind of quiet awareness without many visual images. As such, learning how to produce the alpha rhythm at will can be useful in helping a person learn how to relax.

One of the questionable things about alpha training is that it has spawned the production of home units for self-supervised learning. The value of such units, advertised for sale for a few hundred dollars, is dubious. For example, the problem of "noise" or incorrect information in the system is considerable. The movements of the eyes, the wrinkling of the brows, and so forth also

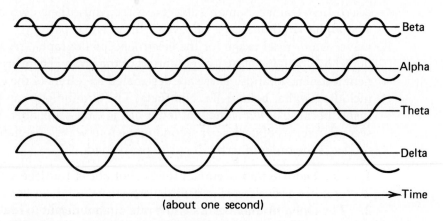

FIGURE 6.2   A schematic illustration of the differences in cycles per second among beta, alpha, theta, and delta rhythms.

produce changing electrical potentials of the muscles; these may give false signals that are misinterpreted. Many persons who are convinced that they are masters of alpha control are simply deceiving themselves.

Relaxation is associated with biological signals other than the alpha rhythm. Indeed, the alpha rhythm may not be the best measure of relaxation. A more direct measure is the **electromyograph** (EMG), a record of muscle tension. Starting in the early 1960s, Thomas Budzynski, an electronics engineer and psychologist, and Johann Stoyva, a psychophysiologist with a special interest in relaxation techniques, have worked together at the University of Colorado Medical School. They have combined autogenic training with EMG feedback; **autogenic training** is a method of inducing relaxation developed in Germany in the 1920s. The method calls for subjects to give themselves suggestions that they are feeling less fatigued and less tense. It is an autosuggestive method. Budzynski and Stoyva (1969) have found that the combined results of autogenic training and biofeedback can be impressive.

It appears from the research of Budzynski and Stoyva that anxiety and deep muscle relaxation are antagonistic responses. If a person is deeply relaxed, it is hard for that person to simultaneously feel anxious. The two researchers have found that an important muscle associated with deep relaxation is the **frontalis**, the forehead muscle. It is a relatively difficult muscle to learn to control voluntarily. If a subject does learn to control it, however, he or she generally gets a spread of relaxation involving the rest of the head and the upper part of the body. Working with a substantial number of subjects over a period of years, Budzynski and Stoyva have been able to help subjects find relief from anxiety, tension headaches, and other woes that have no organic basis.

Tension headaches are not the same as migraine headaches. A tension headache appears to be caused by excessive muscle contraction. A migraine headache is probably caused by temporarily enlarged blood vessels, and this condition produces a pulsing pain. At the Menninger Foundation, Elmer Green (mentioned earlier in connection with the Swami Rama) Alyce Green, and E. Dale Walters (1970) have been conducting research on the relief of migraine. Their method involves skin temperature as the feedback measure. In a typical experiment, a subject sits with a highly sensitive thermometer taped to one hand. The thermometer provides information to a biofeedback device, and the device provides the subject with a visual display that gives skin temperature readings to one-tenth of a degree. Using autosuggestion and the information from the machine, the subject learns voluntary control over skin temperature. After a substantial amount of training, it is not at all unusual for a subject to be able to voluntarily alter the skin temperature of a particular hand by several degrees.

What does this have to do with migraine headaches? If the skin temperature goes up, it means that the subject is enlarging the blood vessels in the hand. When the blood vessels in the hand enlarge, the blood vessels in the

6.4 APPLICATION: CLINICAL USES OF BIOFEEDBACK TRAINING

Biofeedback training offers substantial promise in the area of clinical applications. Indeed, a number of clinical uses of biofeedback training have already been made (Feuerstein & Skjei, 1979). The following are a few of the possibilities gleaned from selected biofeedback literature (Pelletier, 1979; Brown, 1980; Calvin & Ojemann, 1980).

1. It has already been noted that subjects can learn to control their heart rates. This capacity can be of value in treating persons with **cardia arrhythmias**, odd patterns in the usual pumping action of the heart.

2. We have also already noted that biofeedback training can be useful in treating headaches, both the tension and the migraine varieties.

3. Primary hypertension, high blood pressure of unknown origin, was discussed in the section of chemotherapy. High blood pressure is usually treated with drugs. It is hoped that biofeedback techniques will eventually lead to a reduction in the use of antihypertensive agents, replacing drugs with voluntary blood pressure control.

4. Ulcers are believed to be associated with anxiety. If chronic anxiety can be reduced with EEG training or muscle relaxation techniques, the ulcer sufferer may sustain substantial benefits.

5. The EEG has been useful for years in diagnosing epilepsy. There is now the hope that EEG training may be useful in reducing the severity of some epileptic conditions. It appears that by gaining self-control over their brain waves, some epileptic patients can learn to abort seizures.

muscles surrounding the head constrict. The migraine was caused by temporarily enlarged blood vessels in the head muscles; thus raising the skin temperature of the hand brings about relief from the migraine. The Greens have reported promising results using the skin temperature method for treating the pain of chronic migraine. There is evidence that once the subject learns voluntary control of skin temperature, the learning persists for quite some time without the support of the machine. Thus the sufferer is not constantly dependent on the laboratory equipment for relief. This last statement applies not only to skin temperature control, but to biofeedback learning in general.

Biofeedback research has blossomed and expanded on many fronts and it is beyond the scope of this book to present summaries of the many biofeedback studies that have been conducted. But the picture is already clear in many ways. Biofeedback has tremendous practical implications, particularly in the area of treating psychosomatic disorders.

6. It is widely held that asthma is complicated by episodes of anxiety and other emotional factors. Biofeedback training, by giving the sufferer greater self-control over emotional states, may alleviate some of the more severe symptoms associated with asthma.

7. Spastic colitis, a painful and sometimes dangerous condition in which the colon undergoes involuntary contractions offers possibilities for biofeedback training. Again, biofeedback techniques allow the subject to gain voluntary control over autonomic functions traditionally thought of as beyond the reach of the conscious will.

It is clear that biofeedback training offers a large range of possible clinical applications. Many conditions that have been treated by psychosurgery and drugs may eventually fall within the domain of biofeedback technology. This trend, although weak now, is expected to grow as we learn more about biofeedback training and as improvements in the electronic devices continue.

The use of biofeedback techniques, when possible, seems to be advisable over psychosurgery or drugs. Biofeedback training has more than one advantage over other treatment modalities. It is certainly not as drastic as psychosurgery. It does not bring with it the problems of addiction and unwanted side effects associated with chemotherapy. And, finally, biofeedback training allows sufferers to play the part of **active agents** in their own therapy; this is of great value for self-esteem. They are not the passive victims of their illnesses. Instead, with the aid of the biofeedback technology, they can assert themselves against their ailments.

CRITIQUE

Somewhat more than one hundred years ago, the English poet and essayist Charles Colton said, "Tyrants have not yet discovered any chains that can fetter the mind." With the advent of psychotechnology, Colton's statement becomes outdated. A tyrant can control the "mind" via its physical organ, the brain. Let us examine some of the problems associated with psychotechnology.

1. The principal problem is the one expressed in the opening paragraph of this section: the problem of **uninvited behavior control**. This is the biggest single specter raised by psychotechnology. Drugs and electrical stimulation to the brain represent the two most powerful forms of psychotechnology, and it is feared that ESB and drugs can be used against people as well as for people. As techniques of behavior control become increasingly potent, the

question arises: Who will control the controllers? There is no easy answer to this question. ESB in particular has been the target of attacks by worried journalists, who see it as the potential right arm of an Orwellian Big Brother. The following frightening commentary appears in *The Second Genesis* by Albert Rosenfeld (1969), science editor of *Saturday Review*:

It has been suggested that a dictator might even implant electrodes in the brains of infants a few months after birth—and they would never know that their thoughts, moods, feelings, and all-around behavior were not the results of their own volition. Where then is free will, and individual responsibility? (p. 229)

Delgado, ESB's most outstanding spokesman, disagrees. He indicates that the complexities of electrode implants and the problem of individual differences in reactivity make it unlikely that ESB on a grand scale as an agent of social or political control will ever be practiced. He feels that ESB will be restricted mainly to clinical uses. Nonetheless, fears persist.

2. Physiological and chemical treatments of psychological disorders tend to take less of a professional person's time than does psychotherapy. It is faster and seemingly more efficient to shock, drug, or cut a person than to help that person tease apart the complexities of inner conflicts, maladaptive habit patterns, or faulty styles of social interaction. Critics of psychotechnology argue that its methods grossly oversimplify the human condition and that psychotechnology makes "things" of people by viewing them only in biological terms. The living individual is reduced to a kind of high-grade puppet that can be pushed and pulled by electricity and drugs. This in turn can lead to monetary abuses by individuals in private practice. They can charge high fees for remedies that take up little of their professional time and run large numbers of patients through their psychotechnological turnstiles with little regard for each patient's individual personhood.

3. In spite of years of experience with electroconvulsive therapy (ECT), there is still serious debate among psychiatrists about its value. It is true that a majority of psychiatrists consider ECT a valuable therapeutic tool. But a large and vocal minority of psychiatrists, supported by many psychologists and ex-patients, insist that ECT is barbaric. The mixed feelings about ECT are illustrated by these two letters, both of which appeared in *Psychology Today* (December 1975):

Letter 1   *I came home after ECT completely disoriented and frightened. I lived in a three-room apartment and couldn't remember where my vacuum cleaner was. I needed to be shown how to use make-up and how to cook. I played a violin all through my school years, won a medal in fact, but I can't even read music now. This memory loss would be only temporary I was told, but it has lasted 16 years.*

Letter 2   *I was so depressed that I couldn't even pull together a successful suicide plan and after all the horror stories I had heard about ECT from psychologists, I agreed to have it and thought for sure I would die on the table. It seemed as good a way to go as any. After the treatments were over, though, I found I no longer wanted to die. Thus I call the treatments very effective and successful for me.*

What is the answer? There is no such thing as *the* answer. ECT may be helpful or harmful, depending on a host of variables, not the least of which is individual differences in psychiatric patients. Presumably, in the hands of a responsible and qualified psychiatrist, ECT has a proper place among various modes of therapy.

4. Megavitamin therapy, potentially a promising avenue of investigation, has failed to establish its thesis with a large percentage of mental health professionals. The main problem seems to be that most of the research conducted on megavitamin therapy has been conducted by "true believers," people who are anxious to find what they set out to find. The experiments have usually been poorly designed, often lacking adequate controls. The results of megavitamin therapy are often mixed with the results of psychotherapy, ECT, drugs, and vocational rehabilitation. When dramatic "mind cures" are announced, it is impossible for the unbiased observer to decide whether megavitamin therapy was the essential factor in the patient's improvement.

5. If used judiciously, there is little question that drugs can play a proper role in therapy. Chemotherapy has been of particular value in treating the more severe forms of mental problems, the psychotic reactions. Antipsychotic agents have played a big role in reducing the population sizes of overcrowded mental hospitals. Since the advent of chemotherapy, there has been less reliance on ECT and physical restraints to control difficult patients. Thus chemotherapy is in its own way contributing to the more humane treatment of mental patients. In the case of neurotic reactions, character disorders, and hyperkinetic children, however, the picture is less clear. The drugs used to treat these conditions are often addictive and may have harmful physical side effects. Opponents of chemotherapy believe that when drugs are used to control the conditions cited, the underlying problems often get worse. They argue that the real difficulty is masked and often goes untreated. The antidrug voices say that answers to problems in living seldom come in convenient bottles. It may be of some value to note that emotions are reactions to life situations. In bad situations, they are alarm signals. People know through "gut reactions" that something is wrong. Their emotions confirm the knowledge of their intellects that a business is failing, a marriage is unhappy, or that one cannot communicate with one's adolescent children. The commonsense approach is to alleviate the intensity of the emotional reaction by doing something about the life situation. In a sense, the use of a drug has us short-circuiting this process. It numbs us to the situation, providing us with a way of not giving the normal biological response. This may be desirable in persons who are overreactive. But the optimal response to a chronic destructive emotion is to take some realistic action to change a negative life situation into a more positive one.

6. There are even a few dark clouds in the blue sky of biofeedback. As already noted, a gullible public often wastes its money on next-to-worthless equipment of questionable reliability. One practical difficulty with biofeedback training is that it is time consuming, requires a motivated subject, and also requires an interested biofeedback-oriented therapist. In the actual world of day-to-day clinical work, these conditions are not particularly easy to meet. Many people with psychosomatic complaints want something done to them; they don't want to do something to themselves. They see their problems as afflictions that are visited on them, not as stress reactions to difficulties in coping with the challenges of existence. Unless a substantial amount of time is invested in reeducating such individuals prior to biofeedback training, the biofeedback training in and of itself is likely to be of slight value. Another problem with biofeedback training is the tendency to regress to prior behavior patterns. Although the capacity for voluntary control of autonomic responses is a fact, and although there is obviously some persistence of learning in the absence of the machine's support, there will usually be a slow loss of benefits gained. Several sets of retraining sessions over a period of years may be required before the learning can be regarded as more or less permanent.

In an address given at the California Institute of Technology, Albert Einstein said, "Why does this magnificent applied science, which saves work and makes life easier, bring us so little happiness? The simple answer runs: Because we have not yet learned to make sensible use of it." Einstein's observation is also pertinent to the area of applied science here called psychotechnology. It is obvious to thinking persons that psychotechnology is neither good nor bad in and of itself. It can possibly improve the quality of human life if, as Einstein notes, we can learn to make sensible use of it.

SUMMARY

1. Psychotechnology suggests a wide domain of exploration in which the orthodox distinctions among psychology, the physical sciences, and the biological sciences become blurred. Specifically, in this book the study of **psychotechnology** is defined as including the following subjects: psychosurgery, nutrition and behavior, drugs, and biofeedback.
2. **Trepanning**, making a perforation in the skull, is an ancient art.
3. There are three principal forms of **shock therapy**: (1) Metrazol therapy, (2) insulin coma therapy, and (3) electroconvulsive therapy.
4. The **lobotomy** is a surgical procedure in which the connections between the frontal lobes of the cortex are severed from the subcortex.
5. **Electrical stimulation of the brain (ESB)** is a procedure in which electrodes are implanted in selected areas of the brain.

6. ESB researchers have discovered what might be called "pleasure centers" and "pain centers" in the brain.

7. A **stimoceiver** is an electrode-radio unit.

8. The range of potential applications of ESB is quite great, and includes localization of tumors, treatment of Parkinson's disease, treatment of pain, control of severe mental disturbances, control of tremors, and treatment of anorexia nervosa.

9. Nutrition is a factor affecting the behavior of the organism.

10. One of the principal ways of categorizing foods is to identify them as proteins, carbohydrates, and fats.

11. There is evidence that a protein intake inadequate in **tryptophan**, one of the essential amino acids, can adversely affect the levels of a neurotransmitter in the brain such as serotonin.

12. The principle of **protein complementarity** states that one protein can supplement another.

13. A condition of chronic low blood sugar, or **hypoglycemia**, can produce symptoms that mimic certain mental disorders.

14. **Orthomolecular psychiatry** is an approach to mental health in which it is deemed important that mental patients receive the "right molecules." In practice, this refers to **megavitamin therapy**, a regimen that prescribes massive doses of selected vitamins for a patient.

15. It is asserted by researchers such as Feingold that artificial food flavors and colors may induce hyperactive behavior in children.

16. **Chemotherapy** is the use of drugs to treat either organic or mental illnesses. **Psychopharmacology** is the study of how drugs affect psychological and emotional processes.

17. The four principal kinds of drugs used in chemotherapy for psychological problems are: (1) antipsychotic agents, (2) sedative-hypnotic agents, (3) antidepressants, and (4) stimulants.

18. Antipsychotic agents include **chlorpromazine (Thorazine)**, **haloperidol (Haldol)**, **lithium**, and **reserpine (Serpasil)**.

19. There are two general kinds of sedative-hypnotic agents: barbiturates and antianxiety agents.

20. Some well-known trade names for barbiturates are Nembutal, Seconal, and Pentothal.

21. Some well-known trade names for antianxiety agents are Miltown, Equanil, Librium, and Valium.

22. Stimulants tend to increase one's alertness. They include caffeine, nicotine, cocaine, and amphetamines.

23. Drugs are often used to treat psychosomatic illnesses.

24. An **opiate** is a narcotic agent with a two-way action: (1) sedation and (2) pain relief.

25. A **hallucinogen** tends to alter conventional perception and thought.

26. In sum, there are five kinds of **psychopharmacological agents**, drugs that affect perception, thought, and emotion: (1) antipsychotic agents, (2) sedative-hypnotic agents, (3) stimulants, (4) opiates, and (5) hallucinogens and psychedelics.

27. **Biofeedback training** is a procedure by which a subject can learn to bring physiological processes under voluntary control.

28. The principal response measures that have been used in biofeedback research are: (1) the electroencephalogram (EEG), (2) the electrocardiogram (EKG), (3) the electromyograph (EMG), (4) the galvanic skin response (GSR), and (5) skin temperature.

29. The basic principle on which biofeedback training is based has been known to psychologists for years. Thorndike called the principle **knowledge of results**.

30. The term "brain wave" is informal usage for the electroencephalographic records (EEG) produced by changing electrical potentials of the brain. These are designated by letters of the Greek alphabet, including **alpha**, **beta**, **delta**, and **theta**.

31. Biofeedback training offers substantial promise in the area of clinical applications. A few of the possibilities include treatment of: (1) **cardia arrhythmias**, odd patterns in the usual pumping action of the heart, (2) headaches, (3) primary hypertension, (4) ulcers, (5) epilepsy, (6) asthma, and (7) spastic colitis.

Applied Exploration

BEHAVIORAL MEDICINE: PSYCHOLOGY AGAINST ILLNESS

There are few physicians in the history of medicine more admired than Sir William Osler (1849–1919), the first professor of medicine at Johns Hopkins Hospital in Baltimore. Known widely as a humanist, he gave this advice to young students entering the practice of medicine: "Care more for the individual patient than for the special features of the disease." We can see in Osler's comment the core of behavioral medicine: *Treating the patient as a whole person*. Although behavioral medicine is regarded as both a contemporary and exciting trend, which it is, it is also in another sense quite old. The father of medicine, Hippocrates, said more than two thousand years ago, "Wherever the art of medicine is loved, there also is a love of humanity." When we consider that this remark reveals a great concern for the welfare of the individual, we see that the credibility of behavioral medicine has its roots in the practices of ancient times.

Behavioral medicine represents a logical extension and application of behavioral science, including psychotechnology, to organic disorders. The applied aspect of behavioral medicine is quite evident; most of us are concerned about keeping our health and restoring it when we are ill.

What Is Behavioral Medicine?

You already know that the core of behavioral medicine is treating the patient as a whole person. But now a formal definition is in order. **Behavioral medicine** is the application of psychological principles and methods to the treatment of organic disorders. It is the logical complement of **somatic therapy** in psychiatry, which is the application of biological principles and methods to the treatment of mental disorders. Behavioral medicine is a rapidly growing field of interest, and is represented in hospitals, clinics, private practice, and medical schools.

One of the reasons for the growing interest in behavioral medicine is the changing nature of the kinds of illnesses physicians are called on to treat. In 1900 most people died of infectious diseases, not chronic ones. Since 1900 the death rate for infectious diseases has steadily fallen. And the death rate for chronic diseases has steadily risen (Rachman & Philips, 1980). Chronic diseases such as heart disease, cancer, diabetes, ulcers, obesity, kidney disease, emphysema, and others are the very diseases most influenced by behavioral factors such as stress, eating choices, and general life-style. Let's take a look first at the role that stress plays in illness.

Stress and Illness

Boris is a hard-driving insurance sales agent. He often works twelve hours a day, seldom takes a vacation, is impatient with his wife and children, lives by the clock, talks rapidly and aggressively, has difficulty relaxing, and in general leads a fast-paced life. At the age of forty-six he has a heart attack. Does his behavior have anything to do with his heart attack? Is it possible that self-inflicted stress due in part to Boris' own choices and decisions has somehow induced or aggravated coronary artery disease? There is evidence to suggest that the answer to both questions is "yes." Cardiologists Meyer Friedman and Ray H. Rosenman (1974) have conducted research supporting the commonsense notion that driven persons tend to have a higher incidence of heart disease. The behavior pattern of people such as Boris is called **Type A**. A second behavior pattern called **Type B** is characterized by less time urgency, playing just for the sake of playing, and an ability to relax without guilt. Persons with the Type B pattern seem to suffer from less heart disease than those with the Type A pattern. There is a high level of acceptance that Type A behavior is linked to heart disease (Pelletier, 1979). For example, the Psychological Corporation of America publishes a test called the *Jenkins Activity Survey* designed to yield a profile of Type A behavior. The test can be used to screen for potential heart disease victims. It can also be used by physicians and therapists counseling heart patients to evaluate changes in self-inflicted stress.

The relationship between stress and illness is well documented, and does not rest only on the research on personality factors in heart disease. Researchers R. H. Rahe and T. H. Holmes (1966) developed the concept of **life change units (LCUs)**, and have been able to show that life changes in either a positive or a negative direction can be stressful. Examples of LCUs are 100 for the death of a husband or wife, 50 for marriage, and 11 for a traffic ticket. More than 150 LCUs in a two-year period tends to predict negative health changes in the subject being studied.

Probably the most famous researcher on stress and illness is Hans Selye (1979). For many years he has conducted research on animals, and is responsible for the idea of the **general adaptation syndrome** (see Figure 6.3). When an animal is subjected to chronic stress it responds with a three-stage pattern: (1) an alarm reaction, (2) a stage of resistance, and (3) a stage of exhaustion. In the stage of exhaustion, the animal dies prematurely. (It is important to make a distinction between stress and a stressor. **Stress** is defined by Selye as wear and tear on the body. A **stressor** is the agent that produces stress such as a high-pitched whistle or chronic cold.) There seems to be little doubt that in modified form the general adaptation syndrome is applicable to human beings. We, like animals, can use up our resources and die prematurely if we experience more stress than we can handle. The stress can come from the environment, or, as already indicated, it can be self-inflicted.

The term **psychosomatic illness** has become quite familiar. You will recall that it means mind-body disease, and suggests the role that behavior, temperament, anxiety disorders, and attitude may play in getting sick. Examples of illnesses often classified as partly or primarily psychosomatic include ulcers, backaches, headaches, asthma, allergies, and arthritis. Perhaps the term *psychosomatic* leaves something to be desired. The patient is likely to protest, "You mean it's all in my head?" The word tends to perpetuate an ar-

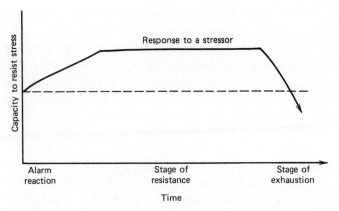

FIGURE 6.3 Basic pattern of Selye's general adaptation syndrome.

bitrary mind-body division. It is probably better to think in terms of stress-induced or stress-aggravated illness. it then becomes evident that stress is simply a factor that must be taken into account in the complete understanding of the illness in question.

Some researchers have been bold enough to suggest that stress may even play a role in cancer. For example, O. Carl Simonton and Stephanie Matthews-Simonton (1978) have suggested that chronic stress adversely affects the body's immune system. This in turn impairs the body's ability to fight off cancer cells. The Simontons argue that cancer patients often have a history of responding to life's problems by feeling hopeless and "giving up." The Simontons combine conventional cancer therapy with a psychological approach. The psychological approach (Simonton & Simonton, 1979, p. 129) consists of relaxing deeply and "visualizing the cancer cells being destroyed either by treatments or by some other mental images." The Simontons report good results with their methods. Others question the validity of their results. In either case, their work is provocative and suggestive of some of the areas that may be explored by behavioral medicine.

Pain Management

One of the most unwelcome features of chronic diseases is that they are often accompanied by chronic pain. There is pain associated with breathing in lung cancer, emphysema, and asthma. Patients with arthritis feel pain in their joints. Heart patients often suffer from **angina pectoris** or pain in the chest area. Other patients suffer from frequent headaches or backaches, sometimes of unknown origin. All of these disorders require some sort of approach to pain management. Drugs and surgery are often used to relieve chronic pain. Behavioral medicine seeks to give the sufferer greater personal control over pain. Several behavioral interventions can be used with varying degrees of success.

Biofeedback   Biofeedback training has already been discussed earlier in this chapter. As you will recall, it has been found useful in the treatment of both tension and migraine headaches. Using biofeedback training to relax certain muscles can reduce the pain associated with some backaches. Biofeedback training used to reduce high blood pressure may in turn alleviate some of the pain associated with angina pectoris.

Hypnosis   Hypnosis has a long, controversial, and colorful history. One of its early advocates was Franz Anton Mesmer who in the eighteenth century used it to "cure" various diseases, diseases which we today identify as conversion disorders (see the appendix). In 1958 the Council on Mental Health of the American Medical Association gave a favorable evaluation of hypnosis. So hypnosis is "respectable." There is little doubt that it can be used to induce anesthesia; surgery, tooth extractions, and childbirth can take place under hypnosis (with suitable and trained subjects). Hypnosis can also be used to bring relief from chronic pain. This can be done by using hypnosis to induce relaxation. It can also be done by using hypnotic suggestions to minimize the intensity of pain sensations.

Relaxation Methods   Relaxation methods are sometimes said to be **hypnoidal**, meaning they are somewhat like hypnosis. Two relaxation methods have received a good deal of attention. These are: (1) progressive relaxation, and (2) meditation (Feuerstein & Skjei, 1979). **Progressive relaxation** was introduced by Edmund Jacobson, a physician, in 1908. It involves a step-by-step approach to relaxation, in which conscious contraction and relaxation of sets of muscles is alternated. Deep relaxation becomes more readily obtained with practice. **Meditation** can be induced by focusing on a mental device such as the word "one" or "peace." More is involved in meditation than this, of course (see the Applied Exploration toward the end of Chapter 8). Herbert Benson (1979) of the Harvard School of Medicine uses meditation to induce the **relaxation response**, a response said to be antagonistic to stressful flight-or-fight reactions (again see the Applied Exploration toward the end of Chapter 8).

Modifying Thoughts   Modifying thoughts is a method associated with both cognitive behavior modification and cognitive therapy. If one is stuck with the automatic thought "It hurts. I can't stand it," it augments the sensation of pain. Some relief might be obtained by voluntarily thinking "It's not so bad. I can take it." Patients can be taught to identify thoughts that either increase or decrease pain, using this information to cope with pain. One technique calls for the patient to reinterpret pain, to try to perceive it as a ticklish or numb feeling instead of a hurting sensation. Sometimes a dramatic reduction in the number of pain-relieving pills required by a patient is achieved through the modification of thoughts.

Why do behavioral interventions often offer some relief from pain? One explanation is that they induce a change in thought, attitude, or perception that stimulates the brain to produce endorphins (Calvin & Ojemann, 1980). **Endorphins** are a type of neurotransmitter, and exist naturally in the human body. They function somewhat like opiates. Indeed the very word **endorphin** is a contraction of the words *endogenous* (i.e., growing from within) and *morphine*. Because endorphins occur naturally, they have none of the undesirable side effects of prescription drugs, nor is a drug dependence fostered. So there are excellent reasons for continuing to seek behavioral interventions in the management of pain.

Self-Control

Samantha is a diabetic; nonetheless, she continues to eat candy bars and drink soft drinks—items loaded with sugar. Timothy suffers from emphysema; his physician has advised him to stop smoking. Yet Timothy continues to smoke almost two packs a day. People such as Samantha and Timothy aggravate the severity of their chronic illnesses by their own behavior. It has been found that a certain percentage of people are prone to engage in **indirect self-destructive behavior** (Farberow, 1980). Indirect self-destructive behavior may be thought of as a form of slow suicide; the individual in question either is unaware or doesn't seem to care about the consequences of his or her behavior. Such people don't usually admit that they are suicidal. If the patient in question also suffers from a chronic illness, such as Samantha or Timothy, there exists a scenario for disaster. Behavioral medicine in such cases can be practiced in the form of effective counseling or psychotherapy

On a more helpful note, some patients with chronic illnesses may not have deep-rooted self-destructive tendencies. But their eating habits, drinking habits, and general life-style aggravate their illnesses. These patients can benefit from the kinds of behavioral self-modification strategies discussed in Chapter 3, "Behavioral Psychology." For example, heart patients are often advised to restrict their intake of fats, particularly animal fats. If a person has been eating a lot of butter, bacon, and steak, this can be rather difficult to do. The application of standard methods for modifying habits can often be quite helpful.

The whole area of the self-control of behavior plays a very important part in behavioral medicine.

In brief, the core of behavioral medicine is treating the patient as a whole person. A formal definition of behavioral medicine is: the application of psychological principles and methods to the treatment of organic disorders. Research has shown that stress, including self-inflicted stress, may be an important factor in some illnesses. Pain management without drugs can sometimes be obtained by behavioral interventions such as biofeedback training, hypnosis, relaxation methods, and modifying thoughts. The self-control of behavior also plays a very important part in behavioral medicine.

Existential-humanistic psychology asserts that as conscious beings we are capable of voluntary action and self-determination.

Chapter 7

EXISTENTIAL-HUMANISTIC PSYCHOLOGY: THE SEARCH FOR AUTHENTICITY

Overview

OUTLINE

KEY QUESTIONS

What is existential-humanistic psychology?
Like cognitive psychology (see Chapter 4), existential-humanistic psychology asserts that human consciousness is important. You will recall that cognitive psychology places its accent on the importance of the thinking process. In contrast, existential-humanistic psychology places its accent on the willing process, our capacity as human beings to make decisions and choices. It asserts that as conscious beings we are capable of voluntary action and self-determination.

How do the principles of existential-humanistic psychology relate to adjustment and growth?
According to existential-humanistic psychology, individuals shape themselves. We are thus responsible for our own adjustment and growth. We are challenged by existential-humanistic psychology to adjust, not to arbitrary norms set by our culture but to our own internal standards.

Imagine that you are watching an animated cartoon. Coyote is chasing Road Runner, is deceived, and runs off a cliff. Coyote continues running, oblivious to the fact that he has lost his support. Suddenly he stops, looks down, appears puzzled, and runs a few more steps. Then he looks down again , and his expression changes as he becomes aware that he is running on thin air. At this point he begins falling. This sort of thing is standard fare for animated cartoons. The cartoon seems to be saying that reality is defined by consciousness, that something is not real until we are aware of it. One almost believes that Coyote can run on the air as long as he thinks he is running on a road. This illustrates the tremendous implicit importance generally attached to consciousness. Although we seldom verbalize it, we take it for granted that awareness has enormous significance. This is a principal assertion of existential-humanistic psychology: Consciousness counts.

Existential-humanistic psychology has been called a Third Force in psychology (Goble, 1971). The reason for this label is that the two dominant forces in psychology in this century have been psychoanalysis and behaviorism. Both, each in its own way, downgrade the importance of consciousness. Recall Freud's famous statement that the mind is an iceberg, that the unconscious domain is much larger and more significant than the conscious domain. The individual only thinks that consciousness is important. In actuality, invisible forces rule one's life, not one's conscious mind. The radical behaviorist denies the importance of consciousness. If it is there, it is only a side effect of the fact that we are reacting organisms. Consciousness has no causative value. It can't make anything happen. Existential-humanistic psychology categorically denies the validity of the way that psychoanalysis and radical behaviorism look at consciousness.

Existential-humanistic psychologists ask these questions: How do you experience your life? Do you experience it as ruled by unconscious forces? Do you experience it as a set of conditioned responses? To these questions, most of us would answer "Of course not." How then do you experience your life? If you experience your life as a self-aware human being capable of taking action and making decisions, then trust this experience. Believe in this first-hand information before you believe in the theories of psychoanalysis and behaviorists. Existential-humanistic psychologists agree that we are organisms, that we react, and that many of the insights of psychoanalysis and behaviorism make sense. However, they assert that we are conscious human beings and that we act as well as react.

EXISTENTIALISM: CREATING YOURSELF

To appreciate the present status of existential-humanistic psychology, it i important to know something about the philosophical movement th spawned it: existentialism. Existentialism is not a philosophy; it is a m ment within philosophy. Its broad current includes several kinds of e tialism. Let us use the word **existentialism** to refer to a general point of view in philosophy that places greater value on subjective experience than an objective data. The existentialist says that what you actually experience within yourself is far more important than what any expert can tell you about yourself.

Roots of Existentialism

Who was the first existential philosopher? The question defies a categorical answer. Some say it was Saint Thomas Aquinas because he said man has a free will. Others say it was René Descartes because he said, "I think, therefore I am!" Thus both men in their own way emphasized the importance of human consciousness. There can be no doubt that there was some thread of existentialism in these early philosophers. The modern existential movement, however, is generally regarded to have begun with the writings of Sören Kierkegaard somewhat more than one hundred years ago. Kierkegaard, a resident of Denmark, has been nicknamed "the lonely Dane" because his musings had a gloomy quality. He is a significant figure in the history of philosophy because he turned philosophy on its proverbial head. European philosophy in Kierkegaard's day was under the influence of such men as Immanuel Kant and Georg Hegel. These men were highly organized thinkers and constructed grand systems of philosophy. They were attempting to describe objectively the essence of human nature and our place in the universe. Kierkegaard in effect asked the impertinent question "What does all of this have to do with me?" He disputed the value of orthodox philosophy, arguing that on a personal level it did little to relieve anxiety and that it left the most important questions about the human condition unanswered.

Two ideas stand out like bright lights in Kierkegaard's works: (1) the importance of the individual and (2) the significance of personal emotions. Kierkegaard asserted that a single person is important, that one has importance in and of oneself, that one's unique characteristics should be valued. Kierkegaard was disconcerted that society was progressing in the direction of stamping out individuality, of placing too much value on the "agreeable person" who is a good member of the team. Kierkegaard fought the idea of conformity with a passion, indicating that an increasingly organized and complex society was making people behave like well-regulated ants in an ant colony. His fear was that this trend was destroying the inner life, the very soul, of the individual.

The second idea, the significance of personal emotions, runs like a black thread through Kierkegaard's works. The thread is black because he was concerned with the "dark" emotions—anxiety and depression. Kierkegaard felt that anxiety and depression were more than neurotic symptoms; they were an inevitable part of the human condition. As we face the future, who cannot feel anxiety? As our illusions are shattered, who cannot feel depressed?

One of Kierkegaard's principal works is titled *Fear and Trembling and Sickness unto Death*, which illustrates the tremendous importance he attached to the emotion of anxiety. Although Kierkegaard did not believe that complete relief from the dark emotions was possible, he did believe that they could be alleviated to some extent by **authentic living**: by pursuing a life in which one is true to oneself as an individual, not pledging false allegiance to the values and standards arbitrarily imposed by other people or one's culture. Kierkegaard said that for his tombstone he would prefer only these words: *The individual*.

Kierkegaard was the fountainhead from which modern existentialism sprang. Let me briefly outline a few of the developments in existential thought following Kierkegaard. The concepts represented by these developments reside behind today's existential-humanistic psychology. My sketch will focus on the ideas of three individuals: Friedrich Nietzsche, Martin Heidegger, and Jean-Paul Sartre. It is not my purpose to present a coherent exposition of the thought of these men, but merely to pluck out of their works those ideas that have been adopted as core ones by contemporary existential-humanistic psychology.

The German philosopher Friedrich Nietzsche, writing shortly after Kierkegaard, also placed great importance on the individual. Indeed, he glorified and celebrated the potentialities of the individual with his idea of the superman, a person with the strength and the will to rise above the gray existence of the masses. Nietzsche felt that life is not worth living unless one has heroic values; the superman is a person with a sense of mission in life, a feeling that there are great things to be accomplished.

Kierkegaard asserted that the individual as an individual has great value.

Associated with the idea of the superman is Nietzsche's concept of the **will to power**, an inborn tendency in all of us to gain ascendency over others. The will to power springs from biological evolution, the struggle of each animal to survive in competition with other animals. Charles Darwin expressed this idea with the phrase **survival of the fittest**. Nietzsche adopted Darwin's formulations and made them part of his philosophy of life. Only the fit deserve to survive, said Nietzsche. Thus in many people the will to power is blocked and destroyed by other people and/or the larger culture. Nietzsche scorned such persons, admiring the "lone wolf" who could preserve his or her individuality against great odds. We will see that Nietzsche's concept of the will to power plays an important part in the psychology of Alfred Adler, an important precursor of existential-humanistic psychology.

With the appearance of Martin Heidegger, also a German philosopher, existential philosophy took a turn in the direction of greater complexity. It is generally agreed that Heidegger's thought is extremely sophisticated. Much of it is opaque to the person with a limited background in philosophy. Heidegger's most significant book is *Being and Time*, first published in 1927. Let us comment on only two ideas in Heidegger's thought, the idea of Being and Being-in-the-world. You will note that the word **Being** is capitalized. This is done to indicate that Being is a concrete reality, not an abstraction. To Heidegger, the most important thing about a person is the simple fact that one exists. One exists *before* one is anything else. Heidegger argues also that this is the way we experience our lives. We are always conscious of Being, or existence itself, prior to all other experiences. To illustrate, let us say that you are tasting an ice-cream cone. Residing behind the fact that you are *tasting* the ice-cream cone is the fundamental fact that you *are* tasting the ice-cream cone. The word *are* is a form of the verb *to be*. Thus Being is fundamental to experience and is primary.

Working forward from the crude concept of Being, Heidegger introduces the more complex concept of Being-in-the-world. This concept is captured in German with the single word **Dasein**. In English, *Dasein* must be rendered by the clumsy four-letter hyphenated form. Heidegger says that we not only have Being; we have *Dasein*. We are "thrown" here on this planet in a particular place and time; this is our human condition of Being-in-the-world. And we are challenged to make the best of it. It is as if each person is a Robinson Crusoe, cast away on an island. He must survive and make do with what he finds. Robinson Crusoe could have been thrown by the sea onto a better island. But he was not. Thus he has to work within the constraints of his actual condition. There is no point in asking a blind Fate "Why didn't I land on a better island?"

Similarly, individuals must work within the constraints of their own particular Being-in-the-world. It is their responsibility to make the most of themselves within the conditions of their lives. For Heidegger, the human condition offers possibilities, but not unlimited ones. Possibilities are limited by one's particular *Dasein*, one's particular set of circumstances. The crucial point is this: If people do not make the most of their possibilities within the framework of realistic constraints, they will eventually fall into existential despair, a state of great disappointment with themselves. Essentially, Heidegger has returned us once again to the idea of authentic living.

The writings of Jean-Paul Sartre (1956), a French existential philosopher, became influential after World War II. The destruction and waste of the great struggle among nations suggested to thinkers such as Sartre that the other side of Being is **Nothingness**. Nothingness is capitalized, like Being, to suggest that it also represents a concrete reality. Without Nothingness to provide it with definition, there could be no Being. Individuals are confronted, says Sartre, with a constant choice between Nothingness and Being. They can choose the road of nonexistence, plunging themselves ever deeper into a meaningless dead-end existence. Or they can consciously choose to give value to their actions, to decide that their individual lives have meaning—and thus nurture their Being (see Table 7.1). This was a stark choice for Sartre and other existential thinkers. They saw many of their friends commit suicide or select the slow suicide of alcoholism and/or purposeless living. Sartre and other existentialists could see no rational purpose to life. They believed in no Higher Purpose or value-giving God. Thus they faced a blank wall and thought that perhaps their suicidal friends were not particularly irrational.

The choice they faced is essentially the choice between life and death. Sartre decided to choose life, to affirm his existence. Why? The choice is based on Being against Nothingness. Sartre says that man has **Being-for-itself**, implying that the individual has a right to exist simply because one exists, not because one serves the purposes of others or of God. In other words, life has **intrinsic value**; it is an end in itself. Others have argued that life is not worth living unless it has **extrinsic value**, suggesting that one's existence must

TABLE 7.1   ORIGINS OF EXISTENTIAL THOUGHT

A Key Personality	A Key Idea
Saint Thomas Aquinas	Human beings have a free will.
René Descartes	We know that we exist because we think.
Sören Kierkegaard	Anxiety and depression are more than neurotic conditions; they are an inevitable part of the human condition.
Friedrich Nietzsche	Human beings have an inborn will to power.
Martin Heidegger	We are "thrown" here on this planet in a particular place and time; this is our *Dasein* or Being-in-the-world.
Jean-Paul Sartre	Persons can consciously choose to give value to their actions, to decide that their individual lives have meaning.

contribute to some larger dimension of meaning. Sartre opposes this view, asserting that a life is worth living even if it is only for itself.

Sartre says that individuals have freedom, that they are conscious, and that they can make real choices. We are very unlike things and animals. They have Being-in-itself, meaning that they cannot change their given characteristics. They are what they are, and they cannot create or mold themselves into new images. Humans, on the other hand, having Being-for-itself, can create themselves by their own hands. Individuals, unlike things and animals, have no given qualities; "Existence comes before essence," writes Sartre. This means that for a given person one *is* before one is *anything*. Because one is conscious and has the capacity for choice, the person can mold himself, even change his character. If we take Sartre seriously, he is saying, "Life isn't something that happens to you. The quality of your life and the very nature of your personality are your responsibility."

Influence on Psychology

At this point it might be well to make a distinction between existential psychology and humanistic psychology. Until now we have been using the hyphenated form existential-humanistic psychology, and we will return to this form as the preferred one as we progress. But to understand why the form is hyphenated, why the two words *existential* and *humanistic* have been joined, it might be well to suggest the different connotations of two words.

Existential psychology is a direct outgrowth of existential philosophy, inspired primarily by the writings of such men as Kierkegaard, Nietzsche, Heidegger, and Sartre. The aim of existential psychology is to help the individual move from a negative state of existence into at least a more or less neutral one.

Humanistic psychology, a current development in psychology, is a combined outgrowth of existential psychology and the traditional achievement orientation of the United States. Humanistic psychology stresses the positive side of life, personal growth, maximizing one's talents and potentialities. Existential psychology tends to stop at the neutral line; humanistic psychology boldly crosses it and stresses the significance of positive factors in human existence. Both psychologies, however, stress the importance of consciousness, the capacity for choice, the reality of responsibility. Both deal with the subjects of existence and the quality of human life.

Before American humanistic psychology bloomed, the seed of European existential psychology was transplanted to these shores. The existential orientation of psychology was introduced to the United States about twenty years ago with the publication, in 1958, of *Existence: A New Dimension in Psychiatry and Psychology*. Prior to that time, existential themes were virtually unknown in American psychology. The principal editor of *Existence* was Rollo May, and he has become a prominent existential psychologist in his own right. *Existence*, and books like it, made American psychologists aware of the thinking of two individuals in particular; Ludwig Binswanger and Medard Boss, both of whom can be properly thought of as pioneers of existential psychology.

Binswanger was a personal friend of Freud; but he gradually moved away from psychoanalysis and developed an approach of his own that is called **Daseinsanalysis**, or the analysis of Being-in-the-world. When working with a disturbed person, Binswanger (1963) does not give major emphasis to the past, to childhood experiences, and the like. He is more interested in helping the person understand his or her way of experiencing reality *now*. Thus the analysis is an analysis of one's present existence, not an analysis of the psyche or personality. An anecdote may help to clarify the similarities and differences between *Daseinsanalysis* and psychoanalysis. Binswanger gave a talk in 1936, commemorating Freud's eightieth birthday. In the talk, Binswanger noted that Freudian psychology overemphasized the view of a human as an animal, that it tends to forget that there is an "upper story" to the human mind, a level concerned with religion and the arts. Freud wrote to Binswanger a warm and somewhat tongue-in-cheek reply in which he indicated that humans have always known they possess a spiritual side and that Freud's task was to reveal to humans the importance of biological forces.

Like Binswanger, Boss (1963) is also concerned with Being-in-the-world. It is clear that both men were greatly influenced by Heidegger's philosophy. One of Boss's principal interests is **guilt**. To the orthodox psychoanalyst, guilt is the result of violating an injunction of the superego. The superego is acquired via the socialization process, and it punishes us for acting on or being tempted to act on our animal urges. Boss feels this is a superficial view of guilt. He certainly agrees that such guilt exists, but he suggests that a more basic kind of guilt can be identified: existential guilt.

Existential guilt refers to the kind of guilt one experiences when one does not fulfill one's possibilities in life. It is the feeling that one's life is being wasted. The guilt is very deep under such conditions. The standard that one should not waste one's life is not acquired from authority figures; it is not a part of a learned superego. Boss maintains that it is inborn, an indivisible portion of the fabric of human existence. Thus existential guilt is not neurotic, and it cannot be analyzed away. A person suffering from existential guilt can reduce it only by beginning to act on possibilities, by making the most of what he or she has to work with.

The American psychologist Rollo May has augmented and clarified existential themes for students of behavior and experience in this country. In *Existential Psychology*, May (1960) contrasts the existential approach with other approaches in the following manner:

The existentialist emphasis in psychology does not . . . deny the validity of conditioning, the formulation of drives, the study of discrete mechanisms, and so on. It only holds that we can never explain or understand any living human being on that basis. And the harm arises when the image of man is exclusively based on such methods. There seems to be the following "law" at work: the more accurately and comprehensively we can describe a given mechanism, the more we lose the existing person. The more absolutely and completely we formulate the forces or drives, the more we are talking about abstractions and not the living human being. For the living person . . . transcends the given mechanism and always experiences the "drive" or "force" in his unique way. The distinction is whether the "person has meaning in terms of the mechanism" or the "mechanism has meaning in terms of the person." The existential emphasis is firmly on the latter. (p. 14)

At the risk of oversimplifying, existential psychology says that a person has unconscious motives, drives, and habits, but they do not necessarily have the person! Augmenting this point in one of his principal works, *Love and Will*, May (1969) makes a distinction of some value between the concepts **driven** and **driving**. The orthodox psychoanalyst sees a human being as a driven creature, controlled by unconscious forces. The existential psychologist sees a human being as potentially a driving creature, the agent of his or her own destiny. The lament of Rollo May is that so many people in today's world have lost their driving capacity and have fallen prey to the impersonal forces that make them into rather pathetic driven creatures.

This section has elaborated on the meaning of existential psychology. American humanistic psychology will be more completely described when we review the work of Abraham Maslow and Carl Rogers later in this chapter. However, as already noted, there is no essential distinction to be made between existential psychology and humanistic psychology. Existential psychology represents the dark side, and humanistic psychology represents the bright side, of the same general domain: human existence. Indeed, no less an authority than May, in the preface to the second edition of *Existential Psychology*, notes that existential psychology is not a separate school in itself. He says, "It is allied to the new 'Third Force' psychology, so that most initiates in the field speak of 'existential-humanistic' psychology, the two words hyphenated" (p. vi).

INDIVIDUAL PSYCHOLOGY: THE WILL TO POWER

It is becoming increasingly conventional to think of Abraham Maslow as the father of American humanistic psychology. His writing gained increasing popularity in the late 1950s and the 1960s, and he was clearly a leading voice of the Third Force. However, more than thirty years before the advent of Third Force psychology, Alfred Adler was expressing ideas that today we could classify in the existential-humanistic domain. Thus Adler was an important precursor of contemporary themes in psychology, and his contributions should not be overlooked.

Who Was Alfred Adler?

It is traditional to classify Alfred Adler as one of the founders of depth psychology. Usually he is associated with Freud and Jung. It is true that in his early professional years Adler worked together with Freud and Jung and was a member of Freud's weekly discussion groups. But within a few years, Adler broke with Freud and the psychoanalysts over questions of theory and established his own approach. That approach, called individual psychology, emphasizes the uniqueness of the individual and the individual's capacity to direct his or her own life (Adler, 1927). It does not emphasize the significance of unconscious mental processes; it refuses to see the person as a helpless victim of invisible forces. Thus Adler is not properly classified as a depth psychologist, and for this reason was not discussed in Chapter 2. He is included in this chapter on existential-humanistic psychology because the principal theme in Adler's writings is a stress on the importance of consciousness in human existence.

Adler was born in 1870, the second son of a successful merchant. He spent his childhood and most of his professional life in Vienna, Austria. In the 1930s he emigrated to the United States; he died in 1937 in Scotland while on a lecture tour. His initial medical specialty was ophthalmology. His observations while working with persons with eye defects contributed to the formulation of two of his important principles: inferiority and compensation. He noted that patients with a visual problem (e.g., difficulty in focusing without the aid of corrective lenses), or an organ inferiority, often put their eyes to better use than persons with no defects. For example, a patient might become an excellent reader and a scholar. This is the principle of compensation at work. One needs to prove to oneself that one is competent as a person in spite of a physical defect. The range of Adler's observations in time went far beyond these beginnings. For example, he eventually came to observe that inferiority feelings could be based on *imagined* defects as well as real ones.

Adlerian psychology has been quite influential. There is an American Society of Adlerian Psychology, and it has branches in a number of major cities. There is also a journal, the *American Journal of Individual Psychology*, which disseminates the thought and research of Adlerians. In a book published five years before his death, *What Life Should Mean to You* (1932), Adler offers the following descriptions of individual psychology:

In Individual Psychology . . . we are considering the psyche itself, the unified mind; we are examining the meaning which individuals give to the world and to themselves, their goals, the direction of their striving, and the approaches they make to the problems of life. (p. 48)

The quotation has a modern ring to it and quite clearly establishes that Adler's vision of the scope of psychology was similar to that proclaimed by contemporary existential-humanistic psychology.

The Will to Power

Initially, Adler was impressed by the writings of Nietzsche and his concept of the will to power. Adler argued that the will to power was the basic theme in human existence. He thus set himself against the Freudians, who were at the time proclaiming the importance of sexuality. Adler said that all of us have an inborn will to power. If the will to power is not frustrated, it is the driving force behind the development of autonomy and skills. The child "would rather do it himself." He grabs the spoon out of his mother's hand and tries to feed himself. This is the raw will to power at work. Unimpeded, it is a natural drive in the direction of competence. If the will to power is not distorted by arbitrary demands, it will play a positive role in normal development. The will to power resides behind what Adler called **superiority striving**, a striving to make the most of oneself. In normal persons, superiority striving leads to self-improvement. In neurotic persons, superiority striving leads to the wish to dominate others.

The frustration of the will to power leads to the **inferiority complex**, which is a set of beliefs about oneself, all revolving about a central core. For this reason Adler used the word *complex*. He wanted to indicate that there was more than one aspect to a negative self-image. If one thinks of oneself as stupid, one may also see oneself as unable to learn mathematics, as uncreative, as unattractive to the opposite sex, and so forth. One will avoid situations in

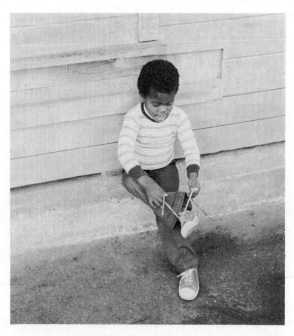

According to Adler, if the will to power is not frustrated, it is the driving force behind the development of autonomy and skills.

which one is required to display any intelligence at all. For example, one might keep putting off taking a driver's examination, convinced that one will fail. The core of the complex is the basic belief in one's own stupidity. Revolving around the core like a set of moons are other negative beliefs, and these make up the elements of the complex.

How does the frustration of the will to power lead to the inferiority complex? Say that a preschool child expresses a wish to dress himself, comb his own hair, wash his own hands, and so forth. Most preschoolers will demonstrate a desire to learn how to perform these tasks, and this is a natural expression of the will to power. The child wants to take the initiative, become more responsible for himself. Adler believed that this is an inborn tendency in children. But say that a particular child has a mother who is a "perfectionist." After the child dresses himself, she comments, "You look sloppy. Here, let me tuck your shirt in. And let me pull up your pants." After the child washes his hands, she says, "You'll never learn how to wash your hands. They're still filthy. Here, hold them out while I go over them again with the washcloth." Instead of making the child responsible for his own appearance and requesting that he repeat unsatisfactorily performed behaviors, she arbitrarily takes over and reduces the child to a passive role. Under such conditions, if continued, the child will gradually form the idea "I'm incompetent," "I'm not coordinated," or some similar idea.

The core idea of a complex is just that, an *idea*. It does not necessarily reflect reality, but an abstraction about reality. The child may not in fact be incompetent or uncoordinated, but he imagines that he is. Thus the negative idea becomes part of the self-image. An imagined defect can be as devastating as a real defect. Note the similarity between the words *imagine* and *image*; they are derived from the same root. One's self-image is thus what one imagines to be true about oneself, not necessarily what is true. This, Adler felt, is one of the great tragedies of human existence. Great numbers of people without actual inferiorities have inferiority complexes. These complexes are in large part derived from the way one was perceived and treated by one's parents. Relationships with peers, particularly during the highly formative grammar school years, also have much to do with self-image formation, however.

The existence of an actual inferiority or of an inferiority complex does not necessarily imply the defeat of the individual. On the contrary, if the flame of the will to power has not been completely extinguished in a person, the principle of compensation will begin to operate. A person will strive to offset real or imagined defects. It has already been mentioned how someone with an eye defect might go on to become an excellent reader and scholar. Many other examples of compensation can be given. Raymond is shorter than average; he takes up body-building. Sally is a somewhat plain girl, or thinks she is; she takes a course in makeup and one in self-improvement. Marla feels she is doing poorly in mathematics in college; she spends triple time on her math course and earns an A. All these individuals are compensating, struggling to overcome inferiority complexes of various kinds and degrees. Adler applauded their efforts. He said that one of the great things about human beings is their capacity to turn a minus into a plus.

Goals and Style of Life

Ask a student, "Why are you going to college?" Say that the answer is "Because I want a B.A." Notice that the student replies in terms of a goal, an event that resides in the future. This is typical of human beings. They explain their behavior in terms of goals, not the events of the past. Adler said that for human beings, a future event is perceived as causing the present action. From an objective point of view, this is inaccurate. The future cannot reach backward in time and cause things to happen in the present. But from a *subjective* point of view, the frame of reference from which life is actually lived, the future is real and has causative power. Adler felt that this was the way the behavior of the person had to be understood, in terms of the person's inner experience of the world.

Adler thus proposed a doctrine of **fictional finalism**. The word "finalism" suggests that a future event is used to explain a present event. The word "fictional" is used because from an objective point of view, the *future is not real*. It may never come to be. The future is a soap bubble that may pop at any instant. A person could die at any hour, and one who feels rich with future might be suddenly bankrupt. It is intolerable to constantly think this way, and we thus construct a fictional future. Adler developed this idea from his reading of the German philosopher Hans Vaihinger's book *The Philosophy of As If*.

As we strive toward goals, we develop a style of life. The **style of life** is made up of the unique set of strategies the individual develops to cope with situations and attain goals. As such, one's style of life develops early and is often fairly well set by grammar school years. One of Adler's methods for ascertaining a person's style of life was to ask for the person's earliest memory. He says, in *What Life Should Mean to You* (1932):

The first memory will show the individual's fundamental view of life; his first satisfactory crystallization of his attitude. It offers us an opportunity to see at one glance what he has taken as the starting point for his development. I would never investigate a personality without asking for the first memory. Sometimes people do not answer, or profess that they do not know which event came first; but this itself is revealing. (p. 75)

Adler tells of a woman who said that her first memory is that of her father buying two ponies when she was three years old, one for her and one for her older sister. The older sister, who was about six years old, led her pony triumphantly down the street. The woman recalls, "My own pony, hurrying after the other, went too fast for me and trailed me face downward in the dirt. It was an ignominious end to an experience which had been gloriously anticipated." Adler notes that the woman's life-style was characterized by the suspicion that she was always behind others. The theme of her existence was "I am always at the back, I must try to get ahead. I must surpass the others. If any one is ahead of me I am endangered. I must always be the first."

Adler believed that each of us has a style of life. Some poeple are overly aggressive. Like the woman in the example, they feel they must constantly strive to be first. Some people are passive. They feel they can attain their goals by being parasites, by "freeloading" off others. Jim thinks he can best attain his goals in life by being a "good sport," by joining clubs and being sociable. Helen thinks she can best attain her goals in life by being a "lone wolf," by keeping to herself and maintaining cool human relations. There are many life-styles, and all of them can be understood in terms of the person's psychological goals.

Social Interest and the Creative Self

As Adler grew older, his thinking mellowed. His early writings emphasized the will to power and the principle of compensation. In his later years, he placed greater emphasis on two concepts: (1) social interest and (2) the creative self. The concept of **social interest** asserts that humans are basically gregarious, that there is an inborn drive in the direction of companionship. More than this, inborn social interest is the fundamental source of the desire to make a contribution to the welfare of humanity. Of course, there are people who do not manifest social interest. These people, contended Adler, suffer from some form of psychopathology. Their personality development has been stunted and distorted. Normal persons care about their fellows and want to feel that their lives play some meaningful part in the larger story of humankind.

It is important to stress that Adler's concept of social interest is at variance with psychoanalytic and behavioristic theory. Psychoanalysis sees social interest as part of the superego; as such, it is a thin veneer over animal impulses. Behaviorism sees social interest as a result of conditioning; in various ways we are reinforced for being concerned about other people. Thus both psychoanalysis and behaviorism tend to define social interest as something that is *acquired*. Adler, on the other hand, sees social interest as *natural*, as a built-in part of the human personality.

With his concept of the creative self, Adler clearly entered the domain that we today call humanistic psychology (Pevan, 1980). The concept of the **creative self** suggests that individuals are, to a large extent, the shapers of their own personality and their own destiny. People not only react, they act.

7.1 CONTEMPORARY RESEARCH: LOCUS OF CONTROL

Adler's concept of the creative self foreshadowed a contemporary concept, locus of control. **Locus of control** may be defined as *where* an individual perceives the principal determinants of his or her behavior coming from. Some people feel they are pawns of fate, that the controlling sources of their behavior are external. Chance, luck, the System, destiny, red tape, the company, and so forth seem to make things happen to them. Other people feel that the controlling sources of their behavior are internal. Decision, will, intention, setting goals, autonomy, and so forth are perceived as realities. (These are the people manifesting what Adler called a creative self.)

What evidence exists to support the observations made above? Julian Rotter (1966) pioneered a testing procedure called the Rotter Internal-External Scale. The *Rotter Internal-External Scale* allows a psychologist to determine the principal locus of control in a given person. The scale consists of a set of questions with which a subject may agree or disagree. For example, how would you answer the questions presented below? (These are not the questions on the actual test.)

1. I can't get ahead in life because it seems that I never get a decent break.
   Agree.   Disagree.
2. The way to be a success is to know the right people.
   Agree.   Disagree.
3. I believe that you can attain most of your goals in life if you just approach them one step at a time.
   Agree.   Disagree.

The human vocabulary contains such words as *will, volition, spontaneity, self-determination, intention,* and *voluntary.* Adler would have said that these words exist for good reason. They describe realities of human experience and, as such, cannot be discredited by labeling them "unscientific" or "subjective." Of course, Adler was not the first person to say that voluntary action is a reality. We have already seen that Saint Thomas Aquinas, Jean-Paul Sartre, and others expressed similar views. Indeed, almost two thousand years ago the Greek philosopher Epictetus asserted that the mind is self-contained, and he is credited with having said, "No one can rob us of our free will." Thus Adler was in good company. He and a number of other thinkers were the forerunners of today's Third Force psychology.

4. Most people who are wealthy inherited their money.
    Agree.   Disagree.
5. If you study hard for examinations, you will get high grades.
    Agree.   Disagree.
6. If you are determined to do it, you can break a bad habit.
    Agree.   Disagree.
7. Most marriage problems can be overcome if the couple makes a sincere effort to work at their marriage.
    Agree.   Disagree.
8. Relatives and friends often present obstacles, keeping you from doing things in your own way.
    Agree.   Disagree.

Agree answers with questions 1, 2, 4, and 8 suggest an external locus of control. *Agree* answers with questions 3, 5, 6, and 7 suggest an internal locus of control. (These items, as already noted, are not the ones on the actual test. Your own responses to the items are not to be taken as a valid measure of locus of control. The items are included merely for purposes of illustration.)

It appears that, on the whole, it is better to have a primarily internal locus of control. Martin Seligman (1975) points out that people who feel helpless and depressed define their locus of control as external. People who feel hopeful and optimistic define their locus of control as internal. A number of research reports support these conclusions (Yalom, 1980).

THE SELF-ACTUALIZATION PROCESS: MAXIMIZING HUMAN POTENTIALITIES

On the opening page of Chapter 1 the following question appeared: Are you making the most of your talents and potentialities as a human being? The challenge posed by this question was the prime concern of Abraham Maslow. He was intensely interested in the self-actualization process. He defined self-actualization as an inborn tendency to make the most of one's possibilities as a person.

Maslow had a substantial impact on psychology. As you already know, he is sometimes thought of as the father of American humanistic psychology.

For a number of years, Abraham Maslow was the guiding light of Third Force psychology.

He was born in 1908 and died in 1970. For a number of years Maslow was the guiding light of the Third Force, articulating the importance of understanding human behavior in terms of awareness, choice, and responsibility as opposed to unconscious motivation and conditioned responses. The *Journal of Humanistic Psychology* was established in 1961, and there is also an Association of Humanistic Psychologists.

Human Motivation

In *New Pathways in Psychology,* Colin Wilson (1972) reports the story of a young woman who came to see Maslow with a personal problem. The time was 1938, during the Depression. She had a job as an assistant personnel manager in a chewing-gum factory, and she was earning fifty dollars a week. During the Depression this was considered quite a good income, and she was supporting the members of her unemployed family with it. The girl complained of insomnia, lack of appetite, disturbed menstruation, and sexual frigidity. She was extremely depressed, bored with life, and said that she was unable to enjoy anything.

In Maslow's discussions with the girl, it became evident that she felt her life was being wasted. She had been an outstanding psychology student in college. Maslow suggested to her that she was frustrated and angry because she was not being her own very intelligent self. He told her that her talents and capacities were motivations in their own right, that they represented needs. The proposal Maslow made was that she pursue graduate studies in the evening, working toward her higher purposes in life. The girl was able to follow Maslow's suggestions, and he reports that she became more alive, happier, and that most of her physical symptoms disappeared. This anecdote illustrates the concept of self-actualization in action. The girl was in the doldrums because she was not making the most of herself.

According to Maslow (1954), there is a hierarchy of motives (see Figure 7.1). Imagine a ladder with basic physiological needs on the bottom rung and the motive for self-actualization at the top of the ladder. Self-actualization does not become a pressing need until the "lower" needs are satisfied. The six rungs on our imaginary ladder are as follows:

1. *Basic physiological needs.* These include such needs as food, air, water, temperature, elimination, rest, and pain avoidance.
2. *Stimulation needs.* Stimulation needs include the need for activity in general, exploration and manipulation of the environment, and novelty-seeking behavior.
3. *Safety needs.* Human beings seek security from the hazards of their environments, as do all organisms. For example, it is natural to wear something warm or to look for a shelter when it is cold.

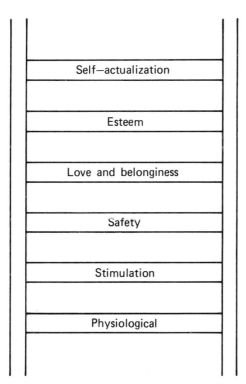

FIGURE 7.1 Maslow's hierarchy of motives is like a ladder.

4. *Love and belongingness needs.* We want the affection of relatives and friends. Also, we usually wish to identify with one or several social groups, such as a family, a faculty, a fraternity, a sorority, a club, or a church.

5. *Esteem needs.* We tend to seek status and careers that have prestige. In addition, we are motivated in the direction of self-esteem, wanting a good opinion of ourselves.

6. *Self-actualization.* Maslow felt that this was the highest need on the scale. Self-actualization has already been defined as an inborn tendency to make the most of one's possibilities as a person. Sometimes the metaphor of a seed is used to get across the idea of self-actualization as Maslow meant it. Say that the seed for a particular flower is planted in hard soil, receives insufficient water, and doesn't get enough sunshine. The plant that grows from the seed will be stunted, and inferior flowers will bloom. On the other hand, assume that the seed is planted in excellent soil, receives an adequate amount of water and sunshine. The plant will be lush and green, and beautiful flowers will bloom. An optimal environment has allowed the plant to maximize its potentialities. Similarly, if the lower needs of the person are not met, his or her personality development will be stunted. Like the plant seed, the seed of the personality needs adequate nurturance to free one to become the best self one can become.

The concept of self-actualization implies that each person has an essential inner nature. Maslow believed that the impulses arising from this inner nature are **instinctoid**, meaning similar to an instinct. He said that they were intrinsic, given, and natural. But he also believed that even though the inner core of the self is biologically based, or instinctoid, it is weak. He notes that it can all too easily be overcome or repressed. Learning, fear, cultural expectations, and disapproval may dampen or distort the self-actualizing tendency. Maslow comments, in *Toward a Psychology of Being* (1962):

Authentic selfhood can be defined in part as being able to hear these impulse-voices within oneself, i.e., to know what one really wants or doesn't want, what one is fit for and what one is not fit for, etc. It appears that there are wide individual differences in the strength of these impulse-voices. (p. 179).

Maslow made a distinction between deficiency motivation and growth motivation. He sometimes spoke of deficiency-needs in contrast to being-needs. Deficiency-needs are represented by the basic needs for food, water, safety, belongingness, love, respect, and self-esteem. They are activated by deficits. Maslow compared them to empty holes in one's existence that must be filled for the sake of health. Being-needs emerge when the deficiency-needs are met; the being-needs are aspects of the basic need for self-actualization. To illustrate, a person may feel that he has an important mission in life.

He chooses a certain career, works long hours, lives in a certain part of the world—all because of his feeling that he has a call to do a particular sort of thing with his life. This individual's sense of mission is a being-need, and it is part of his larger need for self-actualization.

It is also important to realize that self-actualization is a *process*, not an end state. Self-actualization represents growth and becoming. Thus it is proper to speak of self-actualizing persons, but not self-actualized persons. There is always room for more growth. As long as the person is living, as long as he or she has being, there is space for more becoming. The human personality is never a complete project. Only a fool would smugly announce, "Well, I'm self-actualized now. At last I'm perfect."

Characteristics of Self-Actualizing Persons

Maslow felt that psychologists over the years had paid a great deal of attention to defining and understanding psychological sickness, but that not enough attention had been paid to the concept of psychological health. Thus he studied healthy personalities in an effort to ascertain their core attributes. It should be stressed that Maslow believed self-actualization was a positive force, a growth force, in human nature. Self-actualizing people are healthy. The concept of the healthy personality and the self-actualizing person are essentially synonymous in Maslow's writing.

Maslow published several lists of the characteristics of self-actualizing persons; the number of items on the list varied from ten to fifteen. As he himself willingly admitted, he was groping with the concept of self-actualization himself, seeking the best ways of articulating it. In *Toward a Psychology of Being* (1962), he published a list of thirteen characteristics of psychologically healthy people:

1. Superior perception of reality.
2. Increased acceptance of self, of others and of nature.
3. Increased spontaneity.
4. Increase in problem-centering.
5. Increased detachment and desire for privacy.
6. Increased autonomy, and resistance to enculturation.
7. Greater freshness of appreciation, and richness of emotional reaction.
8. Higher frequency of peak experiences.
9. Increased identification with the human species.
10. Changed (the clinician would say, improved) interpersonal relations.
11. More democratic character structure.
12. Greatly increased creativeness.
13. Certain changes in the value system. (p. 23)

We could go over the list item by item, attempting to define and illustrate exactly what Maslow meant by each statement. He did not mean anything

7.2 CONTEMPORARY RESEARCH: BURN-OUT

The importance of self-actualization is well-illustrated by the phenomenon of burn-out. The relationship of the self-actualization process to the concept of burn-out will become clear as burn-out is described and why it takes place.

Burn-out is used to describe a state of mental demoralization and emotional exhaustion. Psychoanalyst Herbert J. Freudenberger (1980) has made a study of burn-out, and his research suggests certain identifying characteristics in a person who is in the process of burning out. Here are some of the principal ones:

1. Tiring more easily than usual.
2. Working harder and harder and accomplishing less and less.
3. Becoming increasingly irritable.
4. Feeling invaded by a sadness one can't explain.
5. Becoming increasingly cynical and disenchanted.
6. Seeing close friends and family members less frequently.
7. Feeling too busy to do even routine things such as making phone calls or reading reports or sending out Christmas cards.
8. Suffering from more physical complaints than usual (e.g., aches, pains, headaches, or a lingering cold).
9. Feeling disoriented when the activity of the day comes to a halt.
10. Being unable to laugh at a joke about oneself.

exactly by each statement, however. He was trying to present a global sketch, to suggest in a few bold strokes the outlines of the healthy personality. Although Maslow wrote extensively about the healthy personality, his writing consisted of expansive discourses, not limiting essays. Thus we will miss the whole concept of self-actualization if we try to look at the list through a microscope. We have to stand back from the list and receive a general impression from it. The general impression we receive is that Maslow was describing a person who is *alive* in the fullest sense of the word.

There is only one technical term on Maslow's list that is unique to his thought: the reference to peak experiences (item 8). A peak experience takes place when a person has a wonderful moment in life, a moment of ecstasy, rapture, or creativity. Such an experience is an emotional high point, and that is why the word peak is used. In addition, the moment is imbued with meaning. One is suddenly "hit" by a book or a painting. Or one suddenly realizes that he or she is really in love. A parent watching a child take his first steps may suddenly feel that life is indescribably mysterious. Sometimes peo-

Why do people experience burn-out? There are probably a set of important determinants such as the fast pace of an industrial society, the demands of an authoritarian employer, stressful work conditions, and so forth. However, one very important determinant seems to be the personality of the person who suffers from burn-out. Indeed, it might be possible to argue that burn-out isn't something that happens to people as if hit by an outside destructive force. They burn themselves out. Freudenberger says that burn-out is associated with overachievement, compulsively striving toward very high goals. He writes (1980):

When trouble sets in, it is usually a result of overcommitment or overdedication, and that, in turn, is almost always an indication that the person's goals have been externally imposed. Somehow, he embarked on his present course because it was expected of him. Or because a standard was set quite early which the individual accepted before he was equipped to think it through. He was never the authentic source of his choices, and consequently, they afford little real satisfaction. (pp. 19–20)

The message seems to be clear. The person subject to burn-out is very often a compulsive striver. As Freudenberger points out, this individual is striving after goals that have been externally imposed. The self-actualizing person, in contrast, is the authentic source of his or her own choices. Consequently this person will find work meaningful, play satisfying, and be resistant to burn-out.

ple "cry for happiness." They are so carried away by joy, their experience is so moving, that they find themselves sobbing. Maslow believed that the peak experience is a growth experience. Because it is meaningful, it helps the individual to gain a broader perspective on life.

In brief, Maslow presented an optimistic view of the nature of human beings. He saw us as having an inborn self-actualizing tendency. Although the tendency can be repressed and distorted, there is hope. Many individuals become self-actualizing, and Maslow passionately wished that as society improves, as human understanding increases, more and more persons will become self-actualizing. He spoke enthusiastically of a **synergic society**, a society in which people cooperate for mutual advantage. He felt that our society is at best only average in terms of synergy. It was his hope that the future would bring a society with greater synergy, thus making it possible for more and more individuals to become self-actualizing personalities.

Maslow has inspired more than one thinker. For example, the psychologist Wayne Dyer dedicated his best-selling book *The Sky's the Limit* (1980) as follows: "To the memory of Abraham H. Maslow—the original pathfinder in the study of man's potental for greatness."

CLIENT-CENTERED COUNSELING: BECOMING A PERSON

One day I asked one of my psychology classes to answer this question: What does the phrase becoming a person mean to you? I asked for brief responses in writing, and the following are some of the answers:

Becoming a person, to me, means being aware of what is going on inside me, understanding myself, so I know what to do to improve myself. It means developing as fully as I possibly can.

Finding out about yourself, and being yourself, not what you think other people expect you to be. Showing one's true feelings.

Being able to make my own decisions. Having my own profession that I enjoy doing. I feel this question should be becoming your own individual.

To mature in every sense of the word. To know ourselves in order to understand somebody else.

I think the phrase becoming a person means to know yourself, what your potentialities and goals are, and to try with all your strength—both physical and mental—to reach your aims. Becoming a person also means to stand on your own feet or to carry your load—sort of independent.

On Becoming a Person is the title of a book by Carl Rogers (1961), the principal exponent of client-centered counseling. Let us compare the student responses with the meaning Rogers attaches to the phrase "becoming a person." In the book, he tells about his work at the Counseling Center of the University of Chicago. He worked with people who presented a variety of problems. He speaks of the student who is failing in college, the wife who is disturbed about her marriage, the individual who is on the edge of a psychotic disorder, the professional who spins sexual fantasies that interfere with working efficiently, the bright student who is afraid he is inadequate, the parent upset by a child's behavior, and so forth. Rogers says he could go on and on citing specific cases of personal problems, but he indicates that there is a theme running through all the problems. He states that he has come to believe that there is perhaps only one problem:

As I follow the experience of many clients in the therapeutic relationship which we endeavor to create for them, it seems to me that each one is raising the same question. Below the level of the problem situation about which the individual is complaining—behind the trouble with studies, or wife, or employer, or with his own uncontrollable or bizarre behavior, or with his frightening feelings, lies one central search. It seems to me that at bottom each person is asking, "Who am I, really? How can I get in touch with this real self, underlying all my surface behavior? How can I become myself?" (p. 108)

Rogers goes on to point out that as the individual grows, he begins to drop the false fronts, or the masks, or the roles, with which he has faced life. Rogers says, "He appears to be trying to discover something more basic, something more truly himself" (p. 109). We thus see that the formal meaning attached by Rogers to the phrase "becoming a person" is similar to the intuitive meanings expressed informally by members of the psychology class. The central theme is expressed by such familiar and informal phrases as *finding yourself, being real,* and *growing up.* The very familiarity and informality of such phrases suggests that the task of becoming a person is one that all of us face.

Rogers was for a number of years a professor of psychology at the University of Chicago where he established the Counseling Center. He was president of the American Psychological Association from 1946 to 1947. Rogers was born in 1902 and is still active as a psychologist (Kirschenbaum, 1979). He is currently associated with the Center for Studies of the Person at La Jolla, California.

Personality Theory

Person to Person is a book written by Rogers and writer Barry Stevens (a woman). The book opens with these remarks by Stevens (1971):

In the beginning, I was one person, knowing nothing but my own experience.

Then I was told things, and I became two people: the little girl who said how terrible it was that the boys had a fire going in the lot next door where they were roasting

Rogers says that as individuals grow they begin to drop the false fronts, or the masks, or the roles, with which they have faced life.

apples (which was what the women said)—and the little girl who, when the boys were called by their mothers to go to the store, ran out and tended the fire and the apples because she loved doing it.

So then there were two of I.

One I always doing something that the other I disapproved of. Or other I said what I disapproved of. All this argument in me so much.

In the beginning was I, and I was good.

Then came in other I. Outside authority. This was confusing. And then other I became very confused because there were so many different outside authorities. (p. 1)

The quotation is useful in that it illustrates important concepts in Rogers's theory of personality. Rogers postulates the existence of two selves in many of us. These two selves are the self-concept and the ideal self. The **self-concept** may be defined as the way the person sees himself. It consists of the attributes he perceives himself as having. For example, a woman may feel that she is quite bright, not very creative, fairly popular, friendly, moderately religious, and so forth. These traits make up her self-concept. The self-concept can range from very negative to very positive. Thus on an informal level we speak of some people who have a "bad" self-concept and of others who have a "good" self-concept.

In contrast to the self-concept, there is the ideal self, the self one feels one would like to be or ought to be. It is the "higher" self, the self of one's dreams and aspirations. The ideal self presents goals and standards of behavior. If moderate, these have motivational value to the person. If impossibly high, they will play an important role in personality disturbances.

According to Rogers, the important thing for the person is not so much the external objective world; it is the internal subjective world. The term **phenomenal field** is used by Rogers to refer to the world as the *individual perceives it*. The concept of a phenomenal field is taken from the writings of existential philosophers. Recall that they placed greater importance on subjective evaluations than on objective data. **Phenomenology**, the study of the way individuals perceive and construct their own version of reality, plays an important part in the tradition residing behind Rogers's formulations. It was Immanual Kant who made the distinction between a noumenon and a phenomenon. He said that a **noumenon** refers to a thing in itself, a part of the external reality. A **phenomenon** refers to the appearance of a thing in the mind, an aspect of human experience.

The self-concept and the ideal self reside in the domain of phenomena, the world of experience. The important thing about these two selves is not their questionable status; it is that they are ideas in the human mind. As such, they have a powerful influence on emotions and behavior. Although the self-concept and the ideal self are subjective, Rogers argues that they can be measured and evaluated. He used a method devised by William Stephenson (1953) called the Q technique.

Imagine that you are a subject in a study of personality utilizing the Q technique. The researcher hands you a set of cards. On the cards are such self-reference statements as "I tend to be shy," or "I like to socialize," or "I am very ambitious," and the like. You are instructed to sort the cards into categories, ranging from "Very unlike me" to "Moderately like me" to "Very much like me." An evaluation of your Q-sort is made, and this represents your self-concept.

Now you are given the same set of cards again, but this time with different instructions. You are instructed to sort the cards into similar categories on the basis of *how you would like to be.* The evaluation of this Q-sort represents your ideal self.

At this point the researcher can make a measurement of the magnitude of agreement between your self-concept and your ideal self. Rogers refers to this measurement with the word **congruence**. Rogers felt that congruence between the self-concept and the ideal self is identified with psychological health. If a person's idea of who he is bears a great similarity to what the person wants to be, that person will be relatively self-accepting and at peace with himself. If, on the other hand, there is **incongruence**, a large gap between the self-concept and the ideal self, that person will manifest the kinds of reactions generally associated with psychological sickness.

An important concept in Rogers's formulations is the need for **self-regard**, the need to have a reasonably positive estimate of oneself. When there is substantial incongruence between the self-concept and the ideal self, self-regard will be low. Rogers thus formulates a motivational tendency in the direction of increasing self-regard. If this is so, why are there so many people with low self-regard? The answer is that many barriers may stand in the way of a positive motivational tendency. There may be emotional conflicts, odd ideas, residual inferiority feelings from childhood, the interference of family, the influence of society, and so forth.

In spite of the barriers, Rogers is an optimist about personal growth. Like Maslow, Rogers also speaks of a self-actualizing tendency, a disposition within the individual to "discover himself," to "become real," or, as already noted, "to become a person." Leo F. Buscaglia, an educator with a humanistic orientation, says the following about Rogers' approach to personal growth (1978):

He feels that the adult good life is more than just a fixed state of reduced tension or a homeostatic condition to be aspired to and in which one can be comfortable functioning in a complex society. He sees maturity not as an actualization or a state of fulfillment, but rather as a process which is forever changing and developing. (p. 42)

Yes, Rogers *is* an optimist. However, he is a *practical* optimist, and he is concerned with these questions: How may the barriers to personal growth be removed? What conditions foster self-actualizing tendencies? Let us now examine Rogers' way of answering these questions.

Counseling

We can gain an understanding of how Rogers believes personal growth is fostered by familiarizing ourselves with his approach to counseling. Rogers sees the counseling situation as a slice of life itself. The relationship between a client and a therapist is not a patient-doctor relationship in which the patient passively submits to something that is done by the healer. On the contrary, the relationship should be a person-to-person relationship in which the therapist talks *with* the client. It is for this reason that Rogers uses the word **client** instead of *patient.* He wants to indicate that the client is not sick in any organic sense, that psychological "sickness" is of a different nature than physical sickness.

The name that Rogers prefers for his approach to counseling is **client-centered counseling**, which indicates that the person is the subject of interest, not the person's symptoms and problems. An older name (no longer in vogue) for client-centered counseling was **nondirective counseling**. That name is still instructive because it reveals something about the Rogerian approach. Client-centered therapists do not give explicit advice to their clients about how to conduct their lives or how to solve a personal problem. The person is not directed to do this or that. Client-centered therapists refrain from trying to be all-seeing and all-knowing wizards. Instead, they adopt the position that in the final analysis the client and only the client is the expert about his or her life. After all, only the client has all the information about his or her existence. Only the client lives life from the inside. The role of the therapist is to create a human relationship in which clients feel they can safely explore their inner worlds.

To create this atmosphere of psychological safety, Rogers recommends that the therapist provide the client with **unconditional positive regard;** that is, the person himself must not be judged by the therapist. If the client feels that his character is being evaluated, he will put on a false front or perhaps leave therapy altogether. A judgmental approach on the part of the therapist shuts off the capacity of the person to reveal deeper concerns. You will recall that low self-regard is typical of persons who seek counseling. Rogers feels that this low self-regard is itself the result of the way the person was treated in the past. Parents, teachers, and other authority figures often act as if the child has no intrinsic value as a person unless the child behaves as they say he or she ought to behave. Thus they do not give the child unconditional positive regard. On the contrary, their regard is *conditional.* "I will love you if you act the way I want you to act" is frequently the message that comes across to the child. People who have had a long history of being acceptable to others only on their conditions will tend to manifest a substantial incongruence between their self-concept and their ideal self. The Rogerian therapist gives unconditional positive regard during the counseling sessions as a partial antidote for the person's earlier experiences.

Another important condition for successful counseling is **empathic understanding** (Rogers, 1980). Rogers says that empathic understanding takes place when the therapist can sense the client's world as if it were his or her own. Rogers notes, however, that the as-if quality must never be lost by the therapist. The therapist must sense the client's emotions without getting bound up in them. Empathic understanding is fostered by two processes: reflection and clarification. **Reflection** takes place when the therapist repeats fragments of what the client has said with little change, conveying to the client a nonjudgmental understanding of his statements. **Clarification** occurs when the therapist abstracts the core or the essence of a set of remarks by the client. Of course, reflection and clarification are not techniques that can be applied mechanically, or they will backfire. The therapist's interest in the client must be genuine, or none of Rogers's methods will work.

The following excerpt from one of Rogers's cases is instructive. The client is a Mrs. Oak, described by Rogers as a housewife in her late thirties who is having problems in her marriage and in her family relationships. The dialogue is taken from a portion of a taped interview from her thirteenth session with Rogers (*On Becoming a Person*, 1961, p. 81). (*Note:* the client uses the word "thing" to make a general reference to the process of therapy.)

Client: Well, I made a very remarkable discovery. I know it's—(laughs) I found out that you actually care how this thing goes. (Both laugh) It gave me the feeling it's sort of well—"maybe I'll let you get in the act," sort of thing. It's—again you see, on an examination sheet, I would have had the correct answer, I mean—but it suddenly dawned on me that in the—client-counselor kind of thing, you actually care what happens to this thing. And it was a revelation, a—not that. That doesn't describe it. It was a—well, the closest I can come to it is a kind of relaxation, a—not a letting down, but a—(pause) more of a straightening out without tension if that means anything. I don't know.

Therapist: Sounds as though it isn't as though this was a new idea, but it was a new experience of really feeling that I did care and if I get the rest of that, sort of a willingness on your part to let me care.

Client: Yes.

Several observations may be derived from the dialogue. In Rogerian therapy, the client does most of the talking; the therapist acts as a sounding board for the client's thoughts and feelings. The client is allowed to express ideas in a trial-and-error manner, searching for her own best way to arrive at a psychological position. The primary purpose of the therapist's remark was clarification; he briefly summarized the client's position. And he did it in a warm way that conveyed to the client empathic understanding.

To summarize the Rogerian approach to becoming a person, the approach asserts that there is an impulse within the individual to "become real" or to "find himself." The person seeks to reduce any incongruency that may exist between his self-concept and his ideal self. This impulse is at root a self-actu-

alizing tendency, similar to the one postulated by Maslow. If the self-actualizing tendency is allowed to blossom, the individual will develop self-regard,
he will respect himself as a person. The conditions that tend to foster the un-
distorted growth of the person are unconditional positive regard and empathic understanding. These conditions are important in both the family atmosphere and in counseling settings.

THE SEARCH FOR MEANING: EXISTENCE AND VALUES

The European psychiatrist Viktor Frankl agrees with Maslow and Rogers
that self-actualization is important. But he asks the hard questions, "Is there
a 'higher' motive than self-actualization? Or does the human being exist for
self-actualization? Is it the purpose of existence?" Frankl asserts that it is a
mistake to regard self-actualization as the highest motive of humans. He says
that to do so is to confuse being with meaning. He writes (1967) that "meaning must not coincide with being; meaning must be ahead of being. Meaning
sets the pace for being. Existence falters unless it is lived in terms of transcendence toward something beyond itself" (p. 12). Thus Frankl believes there is
a motive that is one step above self-actualization: the will to meaning.

Frankl is thought of as an existential psychiatrist, and he has taught and
lectured extensively in the United States. A number of his ideas were formulated out of his experiences as a concentration-camp prisoner in Nazi Germany. *Man's Search for Meaning* (1962) is based on Frankl's experiences, and
a cornerstone of his way of thinking is to resist all efforts to dehumanize persons.

The Will to Meaning

A phrase sometimes used to describe our modern world is "changing times."
Traditional values are up for grabs. For example, we hear people questioning
orthodox models of marriage. Alternate life-styles, such as open marriage,
contract cohabitation, and swinging are being examined seriously. Without
cataloging the details, it is rather clear that today's society is not particularly
tradition-oriented. There has been an increasing emphasis on thinking for
oneself and living autonomously. This emphasis is not necessarily to be de-
nounced. For a substantial number of people, however, it has played an important role in an increasingly pervasive **nihilism**—the view that nothing, including existence, is of any value. Frankl's system of thought, logotherapy,
sets itself against nihilism.

Logotherapy asserts that human beings, unlike animals, have an inborn
will to meaning. The **will to meaning** is an impulse that motivates us to do
things that make sense to us in terms of our place in the larger scheme of
things. We seek to live not only for ourselves, but to contribute something of
worth to other people and to the world we live in. Although it is evident that

the individual's existence is to a certain degree an end in itself, it is more than that. It is also a means to an end, an agent of a bigger destiny than its own. For example, it is typical that responsible parents are as concerned with the welfare of their children as with their own welfare. Indeed, it is not at all uncommon for parents to be more concerned about their children than they are about themselves. Such parents see themselves as having a meaning to fulfill in life: making a success of raising their children.

If a person's will to meaning is frustrated, he finds himself in an **existential vacuum**, which may be described as the feeling that one's life is a void. In the song "What Kind of Fool Am I," the singer proclaims that he is an "empty shell." This phrase aptly captures the essence of the existential vacuum. The person who can see no purpose to life, who thinks that all values are absurd, is said to be suffering from **existential neurosis**. Frankl argues that an existential neurosis arises from a faulty worldview, a dead-end way of looking at the process of living.

Frankl's fear that nihilism and in turn existential problems are on the rise in our culture is shared by more than one thinker. Social psychologist Philip G. Zimbardo (1980, p. 71) notes in an article called "The Age of Indifference" that a growing group of individuals, particularly the children of American affluence, appear to be "passively accepting a way of life that they view as empty and meaningless. The syndrome includes a constricted expression of emotions, a low threshold of boredom, and an apparent absence of joy in anything that is not immediately consumable; hence the significance of music, drugs, alcohol, sex, and status-symbol possessions."

The tenets of logotherapy are intended to point a way out of the dead end created by existential problems. These are the three principal tenets:

1. Humans have an inborn will to meaning.
2. Humans have a free will.
3. Life has meaning.

You are already familiar with the first tenet, the assertion that humans have an inborn will to meaning. Let us turn our attention to the second and third tenets. The view that humans have a free will has a long tradition, reaching back to Saint Thomas Aquinas and beyond. But the view lost favor among pyschologists during the rise of psychoanalysis and behaviorism. These orientations saw behavior in strictly cause-and-effect terms. Tough-minded determinists make no allowance for free will. They say that this is tantamount to proclaiming that the will is an unmoved mover. In contrast, Frankl notes that the freedom of the will is a firsthand experience, and as such can hardly be denied. He comments, in *The Will to Meaning* (1969), "Man's freedom is no freedom from conditions but rather freedom to take a stand on whatever conditions might confront him" (p. 16). Thus we must act within constraints. If Frankl is correct, however, we can make real choices and real decisions within the constraints of our particular life situation. It is

One of the principal tenets of logotherapy is that life has meaning.

his contention that the human quality of a human being must not be disregarded and neglected, that the "machine model" and the "rat model" (understanding the behavior of human beings in terms of the behavior of rats) are woefully inadequate.

The third tenet of logotherapy, that life has meaning, calls attention to the importance of values. Frankl says that values are real, that they actually exist. They are not merely created or invented to satisfy the will to meaning. He puts it this way in *The Doctor and the Soul*:

If I see a lit lamp, the fact that it is there is already given along with my perception of it, even if I close my eyes or turn my back to it. In the perception of an object as something real is already contained the implication that I recognize its reality independently of its perception by myself or anyone else. The same is true of the objects of value perception. As soon as I have comprehended a value, I have comprehended implicity that this value exists in itself, independently therefore of whether or not I accept it. (p. 33)

If accepted, this view of values restores great dignity to human existence. Life is *not* "a tale full of sound and fury, told by an idiot, signifying nothing." On the contrary, life can be seen as a great adventure, filled with challenges, and imbued with high purpose. Joseph B. Fabry, Frankl's biographer and himself a logotherapist, says (1980, p. xi), "The search for meaning is a never-ending attempt to make sense of life in spite of apparent chaos and arbitrariness." This is the view of the human condition proposed by Frankl.

Kinds of Values

Frankl says that there are three kinds of values:

1. Creative values
2. Experiential values
3. Attitudinal values

Creative values are those that are realized by productive action. The clearest example is provided by people who feel they have a calling or a mission in life. They perceive their actions as having objective importance. To illustrate, imagine a scientist who works long hours seeking a cure for a dreaded childhood disease. Assume that he is not the kind of person who questions the value of life. He loves children and hates to see them in pain. Providing them with relief from suffering is a real value to him. Such a person does not work long hours because it gives him any immediate pleasure or personal reward. His eyes are set on higher sights. He dreams of the day when his discoveries can reduce human misery. Such a person is in the process of realizing a creative value.

Of course, one does not have to have a profession or an exalted calling to realize creative values. Anyone doing an ordinary job who takes his or her work seriously, and who sees it as a worthwhile contribution, is realizing a creative value. Some examples are the parent who serves nutritious meals, the auto mechanic who renders honest service, and the farmer who lovingly tends the fields.

Experiential values are those that are realized by being open to impressions from the world. Frankl gives as examples surrendering to the beauty of nature or of art. He says, in *The Doctor and the Soul* (1955):

Imagine a music-lover sitting in the concert hall while the most noble measures of his favorite symphony resound in his ears. He feels that shiver of emotion which we experience in the presence of the purest beauty. Suppose now that at such a moment we should ask this person whether his life has meaning. He would have to reply that it had been worth while living if only to experience this ecstatic moment. (p. 35)

Attitudinal values are those that are realized by taking a courageous stance toward limiting conditions. A person may face an unpleasant destiny, a destiny that must be accepted. Examples are the person whose business is going bankrupt, the patient who knows he has a terminal illness, the prisoner in a concentration camp. Even in extreme situations, when it is not possible to realize either creative or experiential values, the realm of attitudinal values re-

7.3 APPLICATION: DISCOVERING VALUES IN EXISTENTIAL-HUMANISTIC PSYCHOLOGY

You will recall that Frankl says that values are real, that they actually exist. He also indicates that although they actually exist, they often have to be discovered by the individual through the individual's own thought or effort. Taking this approach, what personal values can we find in existential-humanistic psychology, the general subject of this chapter? The following are a few possibilities.

1. One of the principal values of existential-humanistic psychology is that it reminds us of our humanity. It thus imbues life with a depth and richness of quality that goes far beyond the limited range of early academic psychology.

2. The existential-humanistic approach teaches us to respect our own experience. Our anxiety, anger, or joy is not explained away by psychological jargon. Feelings are taken to be real, and there is an insistence on their validity. We are advised to respect our own feelings and the feelings of others.

3. The stress placed on the importance of the individual by existential-humanistic psychology is important. The person is not reduced to an element in a category. Instead, each person is seen as having a universe

mains open. Frankl says that the measure of the person's fulfillment is given by the dignity he or she displays in suffering. If people can retain their humanity under the harshest of conditions, their lives will continue to have meaning.

To illustrate the importance of attitudinal values, Frankl tells of an old doctor who consulted him in Vienna. The doctor had been depressed ever since the death of his wife. Frankl asked him what would have happened if he had died first and his wife would have had to survive without him. The old man replied that this would have been terrible, that his wife would have suffered very much. Frankl then said, "You see, Doctor, such a suffering has been spared her, and it is you who have spared her this suffering; but now you have to pay for it by surviving and mourning her." Frankl reports that the old man perceived his condition in a new way. He saw that his suffering was meaningful.

In brief, Frankl asserts that life has meaning, that the will to meaning is inborn, that we have the free will to realize values in various ways, and that the frustration of the will to meaning plunges the person into an existential

within himself, a universe of thought and feeling. The value of one life is seen as immeasurable.

4. If we accept the idea that we have at least a partial free will, this can have a bracing effect on our existence. With such acceptance, life is not perceived as something that merely happens to us. This view says that we are, to a certain extent, in the driver's seat and that we can shape our own destinies. We are seen, not as the passive victims of fate, but as the authors of our own future.

5. The Third Force in psychology gives us positive images about the way life can be. It speaks of the self-actualizing person and the person who is leading a meaningful life. These images have a pace-setting quality.

6. Although existential-humanistic psychology is grounded in the dark mood of early existential philosophy, it has risen above its own origins. It points upward to a life beyond the gray zone of mundane existence. It says that life can be meaningful and joyful. Contemporary existential-humanistic psychology sounds an optimistic note about the possibilities of human existence.

7. Existential-humanistic psychology asserts that it is our responsibility to make the most of our possibilities. It challenges us to become the "best and the brightest" that we may become. It says that we can consciously choose to live a life that is rich and rewarding.

vacuum. Thus, for Frankl, one of the built-in challenges of existence is the directive that we should take an affirmative stance toward life, not allowing ourselves to fall victim to those forces that would rob life of its intrinsic meaning.

RADICAL PSYCHOLOGY: OF MENTAL ILLNESS AND ALIENATION

Why are so many people finding it hard to lead meaningful lives in the modern world? Frankl would reply in terms of the breakdown of traditions and the failure of people to use free will and to realize values. **Radical psychology**, a counterculture movement within psychology, goes a step further than Frankl. It asserts that most existential suffering is caused by oppressive aspects of familiar social institutions (Maglin, 1980). Its attacks are leveled against the family, marriage, the school, the church, and the Establishment in general. Many of radical psychology's criticisms are overstated, are too categorical, and have a hysterical quality. Nonetheless, a number of interesting points are made by radical psychology, and it quite definitely has something important to say about adjustment and growth.

Is Mental Illness a Myth?

Contemporary radical psychology owes a debt to the psychiatrist Thomas Szasz. His book *The Myth of Mental Illness* (1961) dropped like the proverbial bombshell, somewhat more than twenty years ago, in the midst of orthodox psychologists and psychiatrists; it challenged many unexamined assumptions about "mental illness." In *The Myth of Mental Illness*, Szasz says that so-called mental illness is a metaphor used to describe people who do not "fit in" with established social patterns and who manifest various problems in living. Such people are labeled "sick," as if they have physical afflictions. It should be noted that Szasz is not talking about psychological disturbances resulting from organic causes. He is speaking of *functional* disturbances, those that have no evident physical basis. People having such disturbances, insists Szasz, are not sick at all and should not be so labeled.

Szasz hastens to point out that although he maintains mental illness does not exist, he does not wish to suggest that the various behavior patterns to which the label is attached do not exist. They are real; people do have difficulties in coping with life. The question thus arises: Whose agent is the psychiatrist, psychologist, or mental health worker? Are they the agents of the sufferer helping him or her to constructively work out problems in living? Or are they the agents of relatives, the school, the military services, a business organization, or a court of law? Szasz answers that all too often "therapists" are the agents of these other entities: They do not seek to adjust the person to himself, to those values that are of deepest importance to the person. The therapist thus cannot really be a factor in the sufferer's personal growth.

One of Szasz's principal quarrels is with institutional psychiatry, as distinguished from contractual psychiatry. **Contractual psychiatry** is voluntary. The sufferer seeks help, feels distressed, and may find relief. When practiced with intelligence, contractual psychiatry is of value to the individual. **Institutional psychiatry** is involuntary. It is imposed on those who deviate from established norms of behavior. Szasz thus sees it as oppressive, unfair, and the enemy of the person. Institutional psychiatrists are not necessarily on the side of the person; they are more clearly on the side of the group. In a relatively recent book, *The Second Sin*, Szasz notes that "much of what now passes as psychiatry is also force and fraud—the so-called psychiatric physician trying to coerce others by pretending to be a healer combating a pestilential epidemic" (p. 78).

Szasz is not alone in his quarrel with institutional psychiatry. For example, Jonas Robitscher, a professor of law and behavioral sciences, in his book *The Powers of Psychiatry* (1980) explores some of the abuses of psychiatry. These include superficial examinations, committing patients too quickly, holding them in institutions too long, and overmedicating them. And Peter Conrad (1980), a sociologist, notes that the defining and labeling of deviant behavior as a medical problem, an illness, transforms deviance from *badness* to *sickness*. What this has led to is the medicalization of deviance and the establishment of psychiatry, a medical speciality, as an agent of social control. The question arises in the reflective mind: Is this an appropriate use of medical knowledge? Critics of institutional psychiatry answer *no*.

Antipsychiatry and Alienation

The counterculture movement against institutional psychiatry has acquired the label **antipsychiatry**. The movement has gathered quite a bit of momentum in the past few years. Of course, antipsychiatrists are not against psychiatry per se. Indeed, they are often practicing psychiatrists themselves, and therefore the label may be somewhat confusing. Antipsychiatrists are against many current psychiatric practices. They are for an existential-humanistic approach to patients' problems, an approach in which an effort is made to understand patients' worldviews.

A principal champion and poetic spokesman for antipsychiatry is the British psychiatrist Ronald D. Laing. His writings have a compelling quality, and he has served as a fountainhead of inspiration for the antipsychiatry movement. Laing is not a grand-scale social revolutionary. He is interested in producing what he terms microrevolutions, significant modifications in family patterns and institutional psychiatry. It is Laing's hope that the effect of these changes will spread and have a beneficial effect on society in general.

Laing indicts the family as the prime source behind psychological disturbances. He asserts that people are often driven into madness by a false benevolence and fake kindness exuded by well-meaning parents. In *The Politics of Experience* (1967), he writes:

From the moment of birth, when the Stone Age baby confronts the twentieth-century mother, the baby is subjected to these forces of violence, called love, as its mother and father, and their parents and their parents before them, have been. These forces are mainly concerned with destroying most of its potentialities, and on the whole this enterprise is successful. By the time the new human being is fifteen or so, we are left with a being like ourselves, a half-crazed creature more or less adjusted to a mad world. This is normality in our present age. (p. 58)

In a book of free verse poems called *Knots*, Laing (1970) writes in the first person, attempting to capture the mood of the child experiencing a psychological tangle.

My mother loves me.
I feel good.
I feel good because she loves me.
I am good because I feel good.

I feel good because I am good.
My mother loves me because I am good.
My mother does not love me.
I feel bad.
I feel bad because she does not love me.
I am bad because I feel bad.

I feel bad because I am bad.
I am bad because she does not love me.
She does not love me because I am bad. * (p. 9)*

If this mental maze makes little sense to you, that is precisely the point. It makes as little sense to the child in the family, and yet somehow the child must cope with it.

Laing uses the phrase the **mystification of experience** to describe what happens to the child: He is spellbound, believing that his way of seeing the world is wrong and that he must adjust somehow to the world as others tell him it is. To a lesser extent, Laing argues that the school and other traditional institutions do violence to the growing child's experience of himself. The person who succeeds in coping with the double-bind messages of the family and society in general becomes **self-alienated**. This means that his or her personality is torn apart and that two selves form out of one. In *The Divided Self*, Laing (1965) argues that the "adjusted" person in our society must present a false outer self and repress the real inner self.

If the person cannot manage to become "well adjusted," the other option is to become alienated from others. The person begins to behave oddly, and starts to deviate from established norms of behavior. If the deviations are too severe, the person acquires labels such as **psychotic** or **schizophrenic**. Laing feels that these labels are just that, labels. They are brands that a society places on its psychological untouchables. Laing much prefers the older word **madness** to the clinical labels, thus suggesting the anger and frustration of the disturbed person in contrast to the person's presumed pathology.

Like Szasz, Laing does not see the "psychotic" patient as sick. He does not have a disease; instead, disease becomes dis-ease. The "crazy" person lacks ease in his way of being-in-the-world; he is not comfortable with his way of existing.

E. Fuller Torrey (1980), a critic of the psychiatric establishment and himself a psychiatrist, asks and answers this question: Does psychiatry have a future? He answers:

The major reason that psychiatry has no future as a medical specialty is that it will have no patients. Those people now called "psychiatric patients" will be divided into two groups and reassigned. Those who truly have diseases of the brain will eventually be annexed by neurology, and those who do not will be considered under the

*Copyright 1970 by the R. D. Laing Trust. Reprinted by the permission of the publisher, Random House, Inc., New York.

[Margin handwritten note: Radical psychologists blame social institutions for man's problems & alienation]

jurisdiction of education. With nobody left to call a patient, psychiatry will wither and die. (p. 5)

The antipsychiatrist looks forward to the day when Torrey's prediction comes true. Most psychiatrists, of course, feel that psychiatry continues to have a future as a medical specialty.

In brief, the radical psychologist does not see the disturbed person as sick in any conventional sense. The person's "disease" is dis-ease, a lack of comfort with his or her way of being in the world. The source of the dis-ease is viewed as the influence of the family and other social institutions. Underlying the person's discomfort are two kinds of alienation: (1) self-alienation and (2) alienation from others. To overcome alienation and achieve psychological wholeness, the radical psychologist asserts that the sufferer must be allowed to change and grow in his or her own way.

THE GESTALT APPROACH: GETTING IT ALL TOGETHER

Like radical psychology, the Gestalt approach identifies self-alienation as a common existential problem. Frederick S. Perls, the father of Gestalt therapy, often spoke of the fragmentation of the personality. He felt that inner splits were common, that most people living in Western society are "neurotic." Perls used the word **neurotic** in a general, nonclinical sense to indicate his contention that most people today are "dead" inside. When Perls speaks of "the neurotic" in his writings, it is almost as if he is speaking of Everyperson.

In the foreword to *Man, the Manipulator* by psychologist Everett L. Shostrom, Perls writes (1968):

Modern man is dead, a puppet. This corpse-like behavior is a part of every modern man. He is deliberate and without emotions—a marionette. He is reliable, but without live intentions, wishes, wants, and desires. He controls and manipulates others and is caught in the web of his own manipulations. (p. vii)

Unlike the radical psychologists, Perls was not particularly interested in tilting against social institutions, blaming them for the individual's state of self-alienation. Instead, Perls's principal concern was to devise constructive ways to help the individual return to being alive and being fully human.

Perls was sometimes described as a "bad boy" because he was an iconoclast, willing to impolitely poke holes in the theories of other thinkers and sometimes behaving in a rude fashion (Gaines, 1979). No one can doubt that he was "fully alive." The title of his own autobiography, *In and Out the Garbage Pail* (1969b), reveals the ambivalence he had about his own behavior. His wife, Laura, once described him as a cross between a prophet and a bum, and Perls agreed with her description. Toward the latter part of his life, Perls was associated with the Esalen Growth Center in California. Although he worked in groups, his groups were not **encounter groups**, groups in which people communicate with each other. Perls did individual therapy in a group setting; the person in the group encountered himself. Perls acquired the affectionate nickname Fritz, and that is the title of an irreverent biography of Perls by psychiatrist Martin Shepard (1975). Perls died in 1970 at the age of seventy-six.

Paper People and Wholeness

In his last book, *The Gestalt Approach and Eye Witness to Therapy*, Perls writes, "The idea of Gestalt therapy is to change paper people to real people" (p. 188). Perls was fond of metaphor, and he used the phrase paper people to describe people who lack inner vitality, people for whom life is a lackluster affair with little zest, joy, or meaning. Unfortunately, as already noted, Perls was convinced that most individuals living in the modern world are paper people.

What can be done to help paper people? Perls's answer is: They must be restored to wholeness. Inner fragmentation between various aspects of the personality is what makes people go dead inside. A prime example of inner fragmentation is the split between the **top dog** and the **underdog**, two different aspects of the personality. Perls called these the two clowns of the personality because they play a self-torture game on the stage of human fantasy. The top dog is similar to Freud's concept of the superego and Berne's concept of the Parent. It tends to be righteous, authoritarian, and a bully, and it is fond of issuing such phrases as "You should," "You ought," and "If you don't, then . . ." The underdog bears a closer resemblance to Berne's concept of the Child than it does to Freud's concept of the id. The underdog tends to play the crybaby. It tries to "win by losing," using such strategies as apology, defensiveness, cussing, whining, and the like. There is little peace for the person as long as he continues with a personality fragmented into top dog and underdog.

The way to end the war between top dog and underdog is not for one of them to become the victor. This will not happen. It is an illusion that one or the other can win. And for this reason, in the neurotic person the struggle between the two often goes on for a lifetime. The way out of the dilemma is for the two to make a truce, to make concessions to each other, to recognize that the demands of each are legitimate in their own way. Perls had clients role-play each part, speaking sometimes as top dog and sometimes as underdog. The two "clowns" thus entered into a dialogue with each other and tried to work out a truce.

We can now appreciate why Perls called his approach Gestalt therapy. The German word *Gestalt* can be roughly translated as "organized whole." The classical school of Gestalt psychology, associated with the names of Max Wertheimer, Wolfgang Köhler, and Kurt Koffka, studied human sensory processes in terms of organized wholes in perception. It asserted that our rich perceptual world cannot be explained by reducing Gestalten, organized wholes in experience, into parts-processes (e.g., individual color sensations of specific pitch sensations). To illustrate, a melody is the same melody played in different keys. Thus the melody is not explained in terms of its "parts," specific pitch sensations. It must be understood at a higher level of organization. In contrast to common sense, the Gestalt is *first* in perception and gives to the parts their qualities within the Gestalt. It is not the parts that give a particular quality to the Gestalt.

Gestalt therapy bears only slight resemblance to early Gestalt psychology. Basically, Perls borrowed the word **Gestalt** to suggest his idea that a paper person becomes real by integrating fragmented parts of his or her personality into organized and meaningful wholes. The early Gestaltists also spoke of the principle of **closure**, a tendency for a Gestalt to want to finish itself in perception. For example, a 340-degree arc tends to *not* be defined that way in perception. Instead, it is usually seen as a circle with a gap in it. The tendency to see the finished figure, the Gestalt, is quite strong. Perls worked forward from this principle and spoke of **unfinished business**. The neurotic person is constantly mulling over old problems that have never been satisfactorily resolved. For example, he may harbor resentments toward his parents, still bearing out-of-date grudges. He struggles toward closure, and this aspect of the struggle is a sign of psychological health. But he cannot achieve closure because of what Perls termed the **impasse**.

The impasse is a psychological block, a form of self-induced blindness that keeps the individual from seeing the true nature of his or her problem. It is one of the many ways a person may keep himself from "being real." He is being a phony with himself, kidding himself. The only way to deal with the problem is through **awareness**. According to Perls, the person needs to see how he is stuck. Once he sees how he is stuck, he can deal with the impasse.

Say that John is stuck in an unhappy marriage. This is the impasse. He pretends to himself, however, that the marriage is not unhappy. The pretense is supported by being in love with a fantasy, an idea of what the marriage and his wife should be like. This is the basis of the blaming game, in which his wife is told in various ways that she should be different, that she should change. John complains and criticizes, but he never faces the bald fact: "I'm unhappy in my marriage." He tries to get around this fact. If John faces the stark reality of his unhappiness, he is in a position to do something about it. He may seek marriage counseling, divorce his wife, or do something else. But he will never take any action if he remains at the fantasy level.

According to Perls, the only way to deal with an impasse is to go through it. Paper people try to go around impasses, never facing them squarely. They are thus on an endless psychological merry-go-round. They are filled with unfinished business, incomplete Gestalten in the form of resentments,

An impasse in life may be supported by being in love with a fantasy, an idea of what life should be like.

chronic complaints, and unresolved ambitions. Perls says that real people, people who are psychologically whole, face their problems and take constructive action.

Gestalt Techniques

Perls, in conjunction with a number of colleagues such as R. F. Hefferline, Paul Goodman, Abraham Levitsky, and Laura Perls, formulated a number of **Gestalt techniques**. These are techniques used to help individuals integrate fragmented parts of themselves and to recognize the nature of impasses in their lives (Fagan & Shepherd, 1970). A basic principle running through the Gestalt techniques is what Perls called the **principle of the now**. The client is instructed to stay in the "here and the now," to speak in the present tense as much as possible. For example, if a client is narrating the story of something that happened in the past, he might say, "My father slapped me, and I ran out of the house." Instead, he is asked to say, "My father slaps me, and I run out of the house." Thus he is encouraged to relive his memories, not merely relate them. The aim is to avoid what Perls called **aboutisms**, bland intellectualizations about one's existence.

There is quite a formidable list of Gestalt techniques, and it is beyond the scope of this book to list and discuss all of them. Let us content ourselves with discussing three techniques: (1) dialogue, (2) playing the projection, and (3) concentration.

Dialogue   Dialogue is used to help an individual deal with splits in the personality. The most obvious split is the one between top dog and underdog. The person is encouraged by the Gestalt therapist to verbalize a dialogue between his top dog and his underdog. This helps the person to comprehend clearly the demands of each and may make evident the ways a compromise can be reached.

Assume that a young mother named Marian is verbalizing the conflict between her top dog and her underdog. Marian's top dog says, "Marian, you've got to stop taking college classes and thinking about a career as an illustrator. Your husband and your children come first. Stay home and do your duty! Don't be selfish!" Her underdog replies, "But what about me? I have feelings too! I feel like I'm going to die and just wither up to nothing inside if all I'm going to do with my life is cook, clean, and take care of children!" After a series of such expressions, Marian may spontaneously express the following thought, a thought that reconciles opposites: "I see now that I don't have to make a choice between expressing myself and being a responsible mother. I've been trying to carry a full college load, and I've been feeling guilty about Tom and the kids—the way they've been eating, and the house has been a mess. So top dog is halfway right. But underdog is halfway right too. I'm just not going to sit home and be a drudge. I'm going to carry a half-load and keep plugging away, developing my talent for drawing and painting."

The split between top dog and underdog is not the only possible split in the human personality. Other splits that might exist are those between the feminine self and the masculine self, the introverted self and the extroverted self, the aggressive self and the passive self, and so forth. Any of these divided selves can participate in the Gestalt technique of dialogue.

Playing the Projection   The technique called "playing the projection" is of particular value in helping a person integrate the meaning of a dream. Perls believed that the elements of a dream that appear as nonself, as things or as other people in the dream, are in actuality projections, alienated parts of the self. As an example, Perls was working with a woman named Linda in one of his dreamwork seminars. Linda reported a rather long dream in which she watched a lake drying up. She said that she felt there should be a treasure at the bottom of the lake, but there was only an old license plate. The following exchange is from *Gestalt Therapy Verbatim* (1969a):

Fritz. Will you please play the license plate.

Linda. I am an old license plate, thrown in the bottom of the lake. I have no use because I'm no value—although I'm not rusted—I'm outdated, so I can't be used as a license plate . . . and I'm just thrown on the rubbish heap. That's what I did with a license plate, I threw it on a rubbish heap.

Fritz. Well, how do you feel about this?

Linda (quietly). I don't like it. I don't like being a license plate—useless.

Fritz. Could you talk about this. That was such a long dream until you come to find the license plate. I'm sure this must be of great importance.

Linda (sighs). Useless. Outdated . . . The use of a license plate is to allow—give a car permission to go . . . and I can't give any more permission to do anything because I'm outdated . . . (p. 86)

Through the technique of playing the projection, Linda was able to discover what Perls referred to as the "existential message" of the dream, that at a profound level of her being she felt useless and outdated. Perls asked Linda to play the lake, and as Linda went deeper into the dream she discovered another existential message, the message that there was still hope in her life. The exchange between Perls and Linda ends as follows:

Fritz. . . . On the surface, you find something, some artifact—the license plate, the artificial you—but then when you go deeper, you find the apparent death of the lake is actually fertility . . .

Linda. And I don't need a license plate, or a permission, a license in order to . . .

Fritz (gently). Nature doesn't need a license plate to grow. You don't have to be useless, if you are organismically creative, which means if you are involved.

Linda. And I don't need permission to be creative . . . Thank you. (p. 87)

Concentration   The Gestalt technique called "concentration" requires that the person focus on the here and now. One of Perls's clients, a man who stuttered, was asked by Perls what he felt in his throat when he stuttered. He replied that he felt like choking himself. Perls gave the man his arm, asking him to choke it. The man was thus able to concentrate on his anger, bringing it into the center of his awareness. As he got in touch with his anger, he began to speak loudly without a stutter. Perls comments (1969a), "I showed him he had an existential choice, to be an angry man or be a stutterer" (p. 80).

The concentration technique can be used to help overweight people. Many overweight persons eat rapidly, gobbling their food with little conscious awareness of what they are eating. The concentration technique requires that they slow down, taste their food, masticate it thoroughly, and swallow one mouthful before placing more food in the mouth. Some overweight people feel that they are spellbound by food. The concentration technique helps them "break the bubble." Eating with awareness helps them feel less spellbound.

Being Real

The phrase Perls used to describe authentic living was **being real**. Although he was responsible for developing a number of Gestalt techniques, he said that they were merely tools of somewhat limited value. The important thing to Perls was not technique; it was "not being a phony." He detested phoniness on any level, as he indicates by this short poem (1969a):

A thousand plastic flowers
Don't make a desert bloom
A thousand empty faces
Don't fill an empty room* (p. 2)

One of the important distinctions Perls made was between self-actualization and self-image actualization. Perls believed in self-actualization, in the importance of making real one's talents and potentialities. He felt that many people were on a "bum trip," however. They were not actualizing themselves; they were actualizing an *image*, something that had been "laid on them" by other people. The person who is trying to live out a life planned by parents or by other authority figures is not actualizing himself; the person is actualizing his image of what they expect him to become. This is another way in which a person may fail to be real.

Perls indicated that being real could be divided into two domains: (1) being real with yourself and (2) being real with others. He was against manipulative relationships in which one person attempts to con or use the other person. This is, of course, a familiar theme in existential-humanistic psychology and is not unique to Perls. Perhaps the best expression of the importance of being real with others is found in the theologian Martin Buber's phrase, the **I-thou relationship**. The I-thou relationship recognizes that the other individual is a real person, that he or she has feelings and a personal world view. This is contrasted with the **I-it relationship**, a relationship in which the other individual is reduced to a thing or an object in the first person's environment. According to Perls, the fake person who chooses a manipulative life-style pays a heavy price for his use of other people. He forsakes the aliveness and spontaneity of a real relationship for the control and deadness of a deceptive one.

With the death of Perls in 1970 Gestalt therapy lost much of its energy and impetus as a singular approach to adjustment and growth. However, its philosophy and methods have been integrated into other approaches and settings, particularly into transactional analysis, the expressive arts therapies (i.e., painting, music, and dance), and group workshops (James & Jongeward, 1971; Kovel, 1976; Feder & Feder, 1981).

**Gestalt Therapy Verbatim.* Copyright 1969 by Real People Press. Reprinted by permission of Real People Press, Lafayette, Calif.

7.4 APPLICATION: AVOIDING POSSESSIVENESS IN HUMAN RELATIONSHIPS

Perls was an enemy of possessiveness in human relationships. He was aware of the tendency of some persons to dominate and overcontrol others. You will recall that this tendency was evident in the kinds of games identified in Chapter 5, the chapter on transactional analysis. It is not at all unusual for one person to feel that he or she owns the other person. Perls hated the feeling of being owned, and described some of his own personal struggles in his autobiography, *In and Out the Garbage Pail* (1969b). He expressed his feelings in a poem called the *Gestalt Prayer.* The poem has become quite famous, and has been reproduced on posters, plaques, and in greeting cards. Here is what the poem says:

I do my thing, and you do your thing.
I am not in this world to live up to your expectations.
And you are not in this world to live up to mine.
You are you, and I am I.
And if by chance we find each other, it's beautiful.
If not, it can't be helped. *

The *Gestalt Prayer* has received its share of criticism. For example, Perls' wife Laura, herself a Gestalt therapist, is quoted in *Fritz* (Shepard, 1975, p. 4) as saying that she finds herself "rather unhappy about it. Particularly the last sentence, for it abdicates all responsibility to work on anything." Taken too literally, the *Gestalt Prayer* gives permission to simply walk away from a friendship or a marriage without making the least effort to preserve it. Certainly Laura Perls is correct when she asserts that we should not be so cavalier about our human relationships. It is often possible to work on a relationship that is in trouble and in turn to improve it. If someone you care about is being too possessive toward you, your alternatives are not limited to taking it or walking away. You can explore ways of becoming more assertive and more effective in your dealings with the other person.

On the other hand, the *Gestalt Prayer* does have its positive side. Between the lines it says, "Nobody owns anyone else in this world. No one has a right to manipulate anyone else. And some relationships are too far gone to save. Under such circumstances they should be realistically terminated."

*Copyright 1969 by Real People Press. Reprinted by permission of Real People Press, Lafayette, Calif.

In brief, the basic aim of Gestalt therapy is aptly summarized by the phrase "getting it all together." The Gestalt approach seeks first and foremost to integrate fragmented parts of the self into an organized and meaningful whole. Gestalt techniques can be of some value. But more important, wholeness requires a philosophy of life in which the person places a prime value on being real, on leading an authentic life.

CRITIQUE

Although existential-humanistic thought represents a rich vein of psychological ore, it is not pure gold. Indeed, psychologists who have a strong psychoanalytic or behavioristic orientation would argue that although existential-humanistic psychology glitters attractively, much of its content is fool's gold. As usual, extreme positions are seldom correct. The existential-humanistic point of view has much to recommend it. A number of reservations can be expressed, however.

1. The two principal approaches running contrary to existential-humanistic thought are the psychoanalytic and behavioristic schools of thought. So let us allow them their say first. The orthodox psychoanalyst would say of existential-humanistic psychology, "Its principal difficulty is that it attempts to completely discredit the significance of unconscious motives. It makes the conscious mind king. This is absurd in view of what we know about people from years of observation. We have all kinds of clues—slips of the tongue, everyday errors, and dreams—that suggest to us that there is an important unconscious level to life that cannot be discounted."

The radical behaviorist would say of existential-humanistic psychology, "It is completely unscientific, denying the importance of laboratory research and experimental work in psychology. In particular, it has little to say about the learning process, the single most important process underlying human behavior. Existential-humanistic psychologists seldom talk about conditioned responses and habits, and when they do they tend to brush them away as if they had no real significance in determining behavior. The convinced existential-humanistic psychologist reminds me of an ostrich. He thinks that because he sticks his head in the sand of his own ideas and refuses to look at the learning process, it will go away. What folly!"

2. Sometimes the existential-humanistic psychologist talks about the human will as if it were absolutely free. Reading Frankl, for example, one feels that he has not progressed much past the thinking of Aquinas in regard to the powers of the will. Even if the freedom of the will is granted, serious thinkers would be unwilling to say that there are not many constraints on its action.

3. There are contradictions within the existential-humanistic tradition. To illustrate, Sartre says that we create our own personalities, that an individual does not have an inborn essence. On the other hand, Maslow, speaking of self-actualization, suggests that each person has an inborn set of talents and

potentialities that can be looked at as a "seed." This seed, if nurtured, will blossom into the real self. Thus Sartre says that we do not have an inborn essence, and Maslow says that we do. It is not our task here to attempt to resolve contradictions. But it is important to note that the threads of existential-humanistic thinking are of different colors and make up a variegated fabric.

4. Existential-humanistic psychology stresses the importance of the subjective point of view. We live our lives from the inside, and this internal frame of reference is asserted to be more valid than an external one. Traditional academic psychology disagrees. Humans are not only subjects, but they are the objects of their own study. The scholarly orientation in psychology has held for years that, to a large extent, human behavior can be studied as objectively as the motions of planets or the movements of atoms. Of course, neither the subjective nor the objective point of view needs to be adopted as the one true point of view. The two views may be regarded as complementary, together forming a meaningful whole.

5. The existential-humanistic approach returns us to a philosophical-speculative kind of psychology. The rise of scientific psychology has been a long struggle against nebulous concepts. Existential-humanistic psychology is replete with such misty ideas as *Being,* the *will,* the *creative self, consciousness, self-actualization, authentic living,* and so forth. Although these are powerful ideas, they are also somewhat hazy. As such, they do not easily give rise to testable hypotheses. To a large extent, existential-humanistic psychology consists of a set of assertions not really amenable to scientific validation.

6. Radical psychology overstates its case. It presents too harsh an attack on such age-old institutions as marriage, the family, and the school. Certainly, there are problems with institutions. But one would almost think from reading the radical psychologists that minds are being destroyed haphazardly, that almost everyone is mad or self-alienated. These contentions seem doubtful to more cautious thinkers.

7. If leading an authentic life, or "being real," is made into an absolute value, it may lead to various sorts of practical problems in daily living. Such familiar notions as being polite, have good manners, and telling a white lie may be branded as unauthentic. Yet, may persons find it difficult to function without some sort of facade, some set of pretenses. Also, it is possible for some persons to use "being real" as an excuse for leveling insults at others. Such people fail to see that they are scapegoating aggressions and that the concept of authentic living has become a rationalization for their actions.

These comments do not exhaust the possible list of problems we might identify within the existential-humanistic approach. They do, however, point out the general direction that additional criticisms might take.

The formulations of existential-humanistic psychology make up a rather large tent capable of covering a large conceptual territory. The region included is so wide that neither psychoanalytic nor behavioristic formulations are totally rejected. They are merely subsumed and included in a world view having a larger scope. Tough-minded psychologists will resent being smothered by the affectionate inclusion of the tender-minded existential-humanistic psychologists. But included they will be.

In brief, existential-humanistic psychology says that we are conscious beings, that we are capable of voluntary action, that we can shape our own destinies, and that we are capable of growing and becoming authentic persons. It asserts that we did not choose to be in this world, but we can choose to make the best of it. Some years ago the author William Henley ended his poem *Invictus* with these words: "I am the master of my fate; I am the captain of my soul." Henley's stirring lines portray the essential theme in existential-humanistic psychology: Individuals shape the quality of their own existence.

SUMMARY

1. Existential-humanistic psychology places its accent on the **willing process**, our capacity as human beings to make decisions and choices.
2. Existential-humanistic psychology has been called a Third Force in psychology. The other two dominant forces in psychology in this century have been psychoanalysis and behaviorism.
3. **Existentialism** refers to a general point of view in philosophy that places greater value on subjective experience than on objective data.
4. Two ideas stand out in Kierkegaard's works: (1) the importance of the individual and (2) the significance of personal emotions.
5. Nietzsche wrote of the **will to power**, an inborn tendency in all of us to gain ascendency over others.
6. Heidegger formulated the concept of **Dasein**, meaning Being-in-the-world.
7. Sartre asserts that the human being has **Being-for-itself**, that human life has intrinsic value.
8. Binswanger developed an approach called **Daseinsanalysis**, or the analysis of Being-in-the-world.
9. Boss indicates that **existential guilt** refers to the kind of guilt one experiences when one does not fulfill one's possibilities in life.
10. Adler's approach is called **individual psychology**.
11. Adler stressed the importance of such concepts as the will to power, the inferiority complex, compensation, personal goals, fictional finalism, the style of life, social interest, and the creative self.
12. For a number of years Maslow was the guiding light of the Third Force, articulating the importance of understanding human behavior in terms of awareness, choice, and responsibility.

13. Maslow formulated a hierarchy of motives with physiological needs occupying the bottom position and self-actualization occupying the top position.
14. Maslow published a list of thirteen characteristics of psychologically healthy people. The general impression we receive from the list is that Maslow was describing a person who is *alive* in the fullest sense of the word.
15. According to Rogers, the process of becoming a person revolves around such questions as: "Who am I, really? How can I get in touch with this real self, underlying all my surface behavior? How can I become myself?"
16. Rogers postulates the existence of two selves in many of us. These two selves are the **self-concept** and the **ideal self**.
17. The name that Rogers prefers for his approach to counseling is **client-centered counseling. Unconditional positive regard** and **empathic understanding** are key aspects of client-centered counseling.
18. Frankl believes that there is a motive that is one step above self-actualization; that motive is the **will to meaning**. The will to meaning is an impulse that motivates us to do things that make sense to us in terms of our place in the larger scheme of things.
19. The three principal tenets of **logotherapy** are: (1) humans have an inborn will to meaning, (2) humans have free will, and (3) life has meaning.
20. Frankl indicates that there are three kinds of values: (1) creative, (2) experiential, and (3) attitudinal.
21. **Radical psychology**, a counterculture movement within psychology, asserts that most existential suffering is caused by oppressive aspects of familiar social institutions such as the family, marriage, the school, the church, and the Establishment in general.
22. Szasz says that so-called mental illness is a metaphor used to describe people who do not "fit in" with established social patterns and who manifest various problems in living.
23. The counterculture movement against institutional psychiatry has acquired the label **antipsychiatry**.
24. A principal champion for antipsychiatry is the British psychiatrist Laing. Laing indicts the family as the prime source behind psychological disturbances.
25. Perls, the father of Gestalt therapy, felt that inner splits in the personality were common, that most people living in Western society are "neurotic."
26. Perls used the phrase **paper people** to describe people who lack inner vitality, people for whom life is a lackluster affair with little zest, joy, or meaning.

27.   Perls and his coworkers formulated a number of **Gestalt techniques,** techniques used to help individuals integrate fragmented parts of themselves and to recognize the nature of impasses in their lives. Three of these techniques are: (1) dialogue, (2) playing the projection, and (3) concentration.
28.   The phrase Perls used to describe authentic living was **being real.**

Applied Exploration

SELF-ESTEEM: FEELING GOOD ABOUT YOURSELF

In an autobiographical novel called *The Green Years* the author A. J. Cronin tells how as a boy he checked out a book from the public library titled *The Cure of Self-Consciousness.* He writes (1945, p. 191):

Taking up this volume I opened it at Exercise Ten.
   "Place yourself calmly before a looking-glass," I read. "Fold your arms and gaze at your reflection steadily. Then, narrowing your eyes, give yourself a fearless stare. You are strong, composed, cool." Without question I was cool. "Next, take a deep breath, exhale firmly and repeat three times, in a low yet potent voice, 'Julius Caesar and Napolean! I will! I will! I will!' "
   I obeyed the instructions implicitly—although my eyes watered and their green hue disheartened me a little. I even took a torn-out sheet of exercise book, printed in bold letters the words "I WILL" and pinned it on the wall where it would see my fearless stare whenever I awoke.

Cronin was born in 1896, and the above incident took place when he was about fifteen—about seventy years ago. So you can see there is nothing new about the search for such attributes of the self as confidence or esteem.

The Concept of Self-Esteem

The concept of self-esteem plays an important part in humanistic psychology. It is seen by humanistic psychologists as a significant aspect of a fully functioning or self-actualizing person. You will recall that Maslow places the need for esteem only one step below self-actualization in his hierarchy of motives. We seek the esteem of others, meaning we want to have them regard us as having worth or value. And we also seek self-esteem. **Self-esteem** may be simply defined as looking on oneself as having worth or value. Celia Halas and Roberta Matteson, both psychologists, write (1978, pp. 36–37), "If you feel good about yourself, you have high self-esteem. If you feel bad about yourself, you have low self-esteem. The difference between high and low self-esteem is as simple as that."

"Hi, there, the me nobody knows!"

Drawing by H. Martin; © 1971 The New Yorker Magazine, Inc.

One of the earliest and best ways of grasping the psychological processes involved in self-esteem was offered around 1890 by William James, often referred to as "the dean of American psychologists." James presented the following formula:

$$\frac{\text{Success}}{\text{Pretensions}} = \text{Self-esteem}$$

In this formula, *success* refers to one's actual accomplishments or attainments. *Pretensions* refers to expectations or goals. And self-esteem has already been defined.

James' formula very lucidly brings forth the important insight that self-esteem is *subjective*, that it is a private or personal evaluation. For example, you might have a low opinion of yourself. And yet your family and friends might have a high opinion of you. James' formula show how this is so.

Say that Forrest has set the goal for himself of becoming a physician. So his expectation, or pretension, concerning a vocation is quite high. Things don't go as Forrest anticipates, and he does not become a physician. He goes into paramedical work and becomes an inhalation therapist. In the area of

If you feel good about yourself, you have high self-esteem.

vocation, Forrest has a low opinion of himself. He feels embarrassed by the fact that he is not a physician. Although the people he works with, including physicians, hold him in high esteem, Forrest's private self-evaluation is at variance with theirs.

The way in which James' formula works can be clarified by introducing a rating scale. Let's say that both success and pretensions can range from 1 to 5. 1 = very low, 2 = low, 3 = moderate, 4 = high, and 5 = very high. Now let's attach these numbers to the case of Forrest, imagining that Forrest himself is making the ratings. For pretensions he gives himself a 5, very high. For success he gives himself a 3, moderate. Substituting in James' formula, we have the following:

$$\frac{3}{5} = .60$$

The decimal fraction .60 is the value for self esteem, and it is obviously below what it might be. One or unity would represent optimal self-esteem. For instance, Helen also aspires to be a physician. And she achieves her goal. Imagine that Helen is rating herself; for pretensions she gives herself a 5, very high. But for success she also gives herself a 5, very high. So for Helen we have the following:

$$\frac{5}{5} = 1$$

Helen has connected. She has high self-esteem in the area of her vocation because there is no gap between her pretensions and her success.

It is evident from the application of James' formula that it is not necessary to attain great success to have an optimal level of self-esteem. If one has a moderate set of pretensions, or expectations, and also has moderate success, the result will be high self-esteem. Nicole marries with the unrealistic expectation that her marriage will be "perfect," that she and her husband will never argue. When the success of her marriage is moderate, she begins to suffer from feelings of inadequacy and low self-esteem. Giselle, on the other hand, marries with the realistic expectation that marriage does not necessarily imply "living happily ever after." She expects that there will be rough spots and some problems in communication with her husband. When the success of the marriage is moderate her self-esteem remains high.

Self-esteem is an important aspect of one's self-concept. If we say that someone has a "good" self-concept, we generally mean that he or she also has high self-esteem. Conversely, if we say that someone has a "bad" self-concept, we generally mean that he or she also has low self-esteem. It is in such significant areas as vocation, love and marriage, grades in school, physical appearance, and so forth that most of us slide up and down on the self-esteen continuum.

The concept of self-esteem appears in the work of psychologists other than Maslow and James. A few examples from prior chapters may be recalled. Freud spoke of the **ego ideal**, a subagent of the superego. The ego ideal sets an individual's level of aspiration ("pretensions" in James' terms). If a person fails to live up to the image contained in the ego ideal, the person will suffer from low self-esteem. Karen Horney said that many of us have an **idealized self**, a perfectionistic image of what we feel we ought to become. Failure to attain in reality this perfectionistic image can lead to low self-esteem. A similar view is expressed by Albert Ellis when he says that low self-esteem is often the result when one lives life by a doctrine of perfectionism. The "I'm not OK—you're OK" life position in transactional analysis represents a shorthand way of describing low self-esteem, combining it with the feeling that the subject holds others in higher esteem than he holds himself. And earlier in this chapter Adler's concept of the inferiority complex was discussed. So there is ample concern among psychologists about the importance of understanding self-esteem.

Egotism and Self-Esteem

Sometimes when people first encounter the concept of self-esteem in psychology they confuse it with the idea of egotism. **Egotism** refers to conceit and boasting. When we think of a person who has a swell-head, who struts and swaggers, who shows off, we are thinking of an egotist. Such behavior is often a cover for low self-esteem, a defense against it. Or the person may in some cases simply have an overinflated sense of self-worth, suffering from a personality disorder. In either case, egotism is not what is meant by high self-esteem. The person with high self-esteem has a quiet and realistic sense of self-worth—often appearing relatively modest.

There seems to be little doubt that self-esteem is both important and desirable. Research suggests that people with high self-esteem set moderate and realistic goals. If these goals are achieved, then they raise their sights. In contrast, persons with low self-esteem tend to either seek exalted and unrealistic goals or to go the other way and set their sights much too low (Atkinson, 1957; Bradshaw, 1981). Also, people with low self-esteem are often self-destructive (Farberow, 1980). So we clearly see that self-esteem has little to do with egotism or other negative features of the personality. The picture that emerges when we think of a person with high self-esteem is a positive one.

Ways to Improve Self-Esteem

You are probably convinced by now that high self-esteem is desirable. So the question becomes: How can self-esteem be enhanced or improved? Bringing together a spectrum of psychological viewpoints, there seems to be four basic approaches to the problem. These may be identified as (1) direct suggestion, (2) increase success, (3) decrease expectations, and (4) stop rating oneself.

Direct Suggestion   Direct suggestion may take the form of either suggestion from others or autosuggestion. Another person gives you a pep talk, tells you that you look particularly well, or offers you praise. A therapist may say to a client, "You are OK, you know. You really are!" All of these kinds of inputs from others may have a direct impact on self-esteem and give it a boost.

The opening example for this exploration in which the author A.J. Cronin tried to overcome self-consciousness by looking in a mirror and saying "Julius Ceasar and Napolean! I will! I will! I will!" provides an example of auto-suggestion. Around the turn of the century the French hypnotist Emile Coué recommended that people repeat to themselves daily, "Every day in every way I am getting better and better."

Claire Costales, a recovered alcoholic, indicates in the book *Alcoholism* that building self-esteem was an important part of helping herself. She describes the way in which she used direct suggestion (Costales & Berry, 1980, p. 90):

I talked to myself. Instead of letting ugly, unrealistic thoughts run around in my head, I would tell myself how happy I was going to be now that I had stopped drinking. I would say, "Claire, you are strong and you can do anything you set your mind to."

I would scold myself when I put myself down in any way and would praise myself, out loud, for the things I was accomplishing. "Hey, Claire, congratulations.

You made it through the day without taking a drink. You really know what you're doing with your life. You're in charge of it now." Things like that.

I'd look at myself in the mirror for at least a few minutes every day and pick out physical attributes I liked about the way I looked.

Direct suggestion takes a frontal approach, attempting to improve self-esteem by the quickest and most straightforward means. A critic of the method might say, "Direct suggestion is of little lasting value. Saying good things to yourself about yourself wears off quickly unless reinforced by positive consequences. Maybe it's OK to get things started. But more is needed than suggestion. One needs to get out and actually do things if you want to become a winner." This brings us quite naturally to the next method.

Increase Success   Making an effort to increase success is probably the most common way in industrialized countries to increase self-esteem. We are used to being achievement-oriented and striving toward goals. Concepts such as "rags to riches," "making it," "getting a good job," "getting an education," "getting promoted," and "playing to win" are woven into our way of life.

However, as we see from James' formula, success alone is not enough. Drew is a life insurance sales agent. Last year he earned about $50,000. The other agents in his office think he "has it made." But Drew expected to earn $60,000 last year, and privately he thinks, "I'm losing my touch. I lost a lot of easy sales." And his self-esteem is suffering. When his wife wants to take a ride to the beach on Saturday, he says, "I can't. I've got three important calls to make." When his son asks him to go to a scout meeting, he refuses with the explanation, "I've got a prospect I've got to talk to." He's working hard, his self-esteem is low, and he's not getting much fun out of life. Allan Fromme, a clinical psychologist says (1981, p. 124), "For a good world image, success is important. For a good self-image, the enjoyment of self is important." Drew's objective success and low self-esteem illustrates Fromme's point.

Fromme's point and the example of Drew are not meant to discredit the importance of achievement and striving toward goals. There isn't much satisfaction in a steady stream of failures. But there also isn't much satisfaction in a success that is below one's expectations. In fact, such a "success" is a success only in the external world's terms, not in one's inner, or psychological, world. Thus more than one philosopher, thinker, and therapist has given attention to a third possibility, decreasing expectations.

Decreasing Expectations   Looking for ways to decrease expectations, to reduce pretensions and desires, is the traditional way to reduce personal suffering advocated by Eastern wisdom and oriental philosophy. It is the way of Buddhism (see Chapter 8). However, it is also the way of the Western philosophy known as **stoicism**, a viewpoint that seeks to develop indifference to pleasure or to pain. Epictetus, a Greek stoic philosopher who lived almost two thousand years ago, said, "Bear and forbear." In other words, learn to put up with adversity.

Applying the above philosophy to the example of Drew's self-esteem, the recommendation to Drew would be to decrease his expectations. Maybe he is setting his financial goals unrealistically high. He should ask himself, "Is it worth it? Why do I have to always make more money every year? Can I learn to be satisfied with what I can earn by working forty hours a week?" If Drew can look at things differently, change his viewpoint, and bring his level of aspiration into better line with his actual abilities, he will sense a rise in self-esteem.

Stop Rating Oneself   You will recall that Albert Ellis says there is no answer to the question, "What am I worth?" (see Chapter 4). He says we should stop rating ourselves. This has already been explained in the section on rational-emotive therapy, and will not be elaborated on again. Self-esteem is likely to rise if one ceases to be one's own judge.

The last two ways of improving self-esteem identified, voluntarily decreasing one's expectations and stopping the rating of oneself, are much easier said than done. It is difficult to revise one's level of aspiration in a downward direction. And it only makes sense if the level of aspiration is too high. It is equally difficult to not rate oneself. We are so used to criticism and praise that these aspects of our life have become second nature. The last two approaches to self-esteem may be thought of as belonging to the ways of the sage, or wise person. They require a fairly high level of self-awareness and emotional maturity.

Summarizing, the concept of self-esteem plays an important part in humanistic psychology. Self-esteem may be simply defined as regarding oneself as having worth or value. William James presented a formula in which he showed that self-esteem is related to actual success and pretensions (i.e., expectations). Other psychologists have expressed similar views concerning the nature of self-esteem. Egotism is not to be confused with self-esteem. Egotism refers to conceit and boasting. There are four basic approaches to the problem of improving self-esteem. These are: (1) direct suggestion, (2) increase success, (3) decrease expectations, and (4) stop rating oneself.

The insights and techniques represented within the body of transpersonal psychology are often called "ways of liberation."

Chapter 8

TRANSPERSONAL PSYCHOLOGY: OF BLISS AND COSMIC AWARENESS

Overview

OUTLINE

KEY QUESTIONS

What is transpersonal psychology?

Transpersonal psychology represents a blend of Eastern philosophy, esoteric knowledge, and Western psychology. It draws heavily from such traditions as Yoga and Zen. We may thus characterize transpersonal psychology as "mental science" in contrast to tough-minded behavioral science. The approach is sometimes described as intuitive in comparison to rational.

How do the principles of transpersonal psychology relate to adjustment growth?

The insights and techniques represented within the body of transpersonal psychology are often called "ways of liberation." The individual is shown that much of one's suffering as a human being is needless. Escapes from the chains of anxiety, tension, depression, anger, and petty ambition are revealed. Advocates of transpersonal psychology hold out the promise of finding serenity, bliss, and ecstasy. Opponents of transpersonal psychology reject it with such phrases as "hazy mysticism" and "cloudy occultism."

Transpersonal psychology is being called a Fourth Force in psychology because it is bringing a new look to orthodox psychological thinking. Interest in transpersonal psychology is anything but new, however. For example, *Lost Horizon* by novelist James Hilton was published in 1933, more than forty years ago. The book is still in print and is now in its seventy-ninth printing! And two motion pictures have been made from the novel. *Lost Horizon* tells the story of Hugh Conway and his involuntary journey to the valley of Shangri-La, an enchanted place, hidden deep in the Himalaya mountains of Tibet. The residents of Shangri-La age very slowly and live for centuries. The High Lama of Shangri-La is described as spending most of his time in clairvoyant meditation, seeing into the future of the world. He also has powers of telepathy. The task the High Lama sets for Shangri-La is the preservation of things of beauty and important knowledge against the destruction of a future great war. *Lost Horizon*, although a novel, is rich in Eastern philosophy—perhaps this accounts for its perennial popularity.

The years of popularity enjoyed by *Lost Horizon* are small, however, when contrasted with the span of the centuries. The history of Yoga, for example, can be traced to the *Upanishads*, sacred Hindu texts, dated about 400 B.C. (Prabhavananda & Manchester, 1957). But what of the Western world? Is not the mystical way of thinking relatively new to its residents? The answer is no. One of the founders of Western philosophy, Plato, was a mystic. Writing also around 400 B.C., Plato said that the mind has an intuitive power. It can grasp reality directly without the aid of the sense organs. But it must be admitted that this aspect of Plato's thought was not augmented by the philosophers who followed him.

The mystical tradition in the Western world was kept alive for centuries not by philosophers, but by devout religious practitioners. There is, for example, a definite tradition of Christian mysticism. A few of the names that are usually cited in connection with this tradition are Dionysius the Areopagite, Meister Eckhart, Jan van Ruysbroeck, Saint Teresa of Avila, and Saint John of the Cross (Stace, 1960).

A **mystic** is a person who believes that through the use of intuition he or she can have a direct experience with Ultimate Reality. Sometimes this Ultimate Reality is called God. Others refer to it as the All, the One, the Eternal, the Supernatural, the Transcendental World, and so forth. There is a distinct similarity in the reports of mystics when they come "back to Earth." They consistently report the mystical union with Ultimate Reality to be a blissful and ecstatic experience. It is said that they more than intellectually realize, they actually know, that the distinction between one's self and the rest of the universe is an arbitrary construction of time-bound mortals.

Coming closer to the present, the American essayist-poet-philosopher Ralph Waldo Emerson can be cited as a forerunner of transpersonal psychology. Writing in New England about one hundred years ago, Emerson's philosophy came to be known as "transcendentalism." He preached the doctrine of **pantheism**, a belief system that asserts that there is no distinction between the universe and God. Pantheism says that God is not a being, but Being itself. It should be noted that this view is essentially the same one that underlies the Yoga and Zen traditions.

The first major figure in modern psychology to recommend a transpersonal approach was Carl Jung. As you already know, Jung was one of the giants of twentieth-century psychological thinking and a principal founder of depth psychology. As noted in Chapter 2, Jung was a scientist; but he was also a mystic. Jung had a great respect for Eastern philosophy. In *Autobiography of a Yogi* by Paramahansa Yogananda (1974), Jung is quoted as follows:

Quite apart from the charm of the new and the fascination of the half-understood, there is good cause for Yoga to have many adherents. It offers the possibility of controllable experience and thus satisfies the scientific need for "facts"; and, besides this, by reason of its breadth and depth, its venerable age, its doctrine and method, which include every phase of life, it promises undreamed-of-possibilities. (p. 264)

In spite of Jung's enthusiasm for Yoga and other Eastern disciplines, Western psychology remained hostile to Oriental ways of thought. Indeed, Freud spoke with disdain of the "black mud of occultism." In spite of the hostility of tough-minded psychologists, transpersonal psychology has made slow but steady inroads into academic psychology. Quasi-respectability was achieved when Abraham Maslow founded, with Anthony Sutich, the *Journal of Transpersonal Psychology*. This event occurred just one year before Maslow's death and suggests that he was moving into a broader domain of thought than the one represented by existential-humanistic psychology. The Journal identifies some of its concerns as *metaneeds, ultimate values, unitive consciousness, ecstasy, mystical experience, bliss, transcendence of the self, oneness,* and *cosmic awareness.*

If existential-humanistic psychology may be identified as a Third Force in psychology, let us again note that transpersonal psychology is a Fourth Force. Transpersonal psychology, hailed as the newest star on the psychological horizon, is in actuality the reappearance of one of the oldest stellar bodies in the philosophical firmament: the star of mental science. Let us begin our exploration into transpersonal psychology by familiarizing ourselves with one of its basic themes, the doctrine that we live in a world of appearances.

PERCEPTION: THE SPELL OF MAYA

A *Star Trek* episode called "The Menagerie" tells the story of a cripled starship captain who chooses to return to an unusual alien planet. The inhabitants of the planet are master hypnotists, capable of creating illusions so strong they are taken for reality. He decides to live out the rest of his life on the planet, being restored in his mind to physical health. He prefers the illusion to the reality. On a deeper level, the episode asks the philosophical question: What is reality? If an illusion is so strong that it shuts out all other experience, does it become reality?

The Doctrine of Maya

Eastern philosophy maintains that all of us, like the injured starship captain, live in a kind of waking dream, taking our perceptions for reality. This is the doctrine of maya. In the *Zen Dictionary* compiled by scholar Ernest Wood (1957), the following definition of **maya** is given:

An old Hindu and especially Vedantic teaching, referring to the creation of all manifest things, of both the mind and the body, from ignorance, through the two processes of (1) veiling and reality, and then (2) building on the basis of the veiling by projection. The product—the whole world of body and mind—is then called maya. The word maya *is often translated "illusion," which is not to be confused with "delusion." Strictly, in modern terms, it seems very closely related to the idea of relativity or relative truth, which is never really correct. (p. 80)*

Edward Albertson (1969), author of *Spiritual Yoga for the Millions*, says that maya is not so much untruth, as it is our limited view of the truth. We experience reality through limited sense organs and mistakenly take our experiences for reality itself. He tells the following anecdote to clarify his point:

Once at a museum exhibition I saw a device which gave a superlative illustration of maya. The whole thing was contained in a six-foot-high cabinet, the front of which was blank except for a narrow vertical slot opening into the interior. A plate which could be moved down along this slot had a small hole in it, giving a limited view of what was going on, or seemed to be going on, behind it. As the machine was activated, the little opening descended, and one could see through it what appeared to be a blue light revolving about a red one, much like a miniature planet revolving around a sun.

Then I was invited to step around to the side of this device, which was entirely covered by a sheet of glass, according a full view of the cabinet's insides. Nothing was in motion, absolutely nothing at all. There were only two neon tubes—a blue one in the form of a spiral, and a straight red one standing in the center of that blue spiral. What had caused me to think there was motion occurring inside that cabinet? My own limited view of the proceedings. Once I had become illumined—that is, once I had seen the whole device in its entirety and without limitation—the truth became clear. (pp. 22–23)

The doctrine of maya thus says that the world we experience is our mental construction, not reality itself (see Figure 8.1). Behind the world of experience stands the real world—unchanging, eternal, infinite. The world of experience might be compared to the countless items that can be made from a vast amount of clay. The clay itself is impersonal, formless, and has no character.

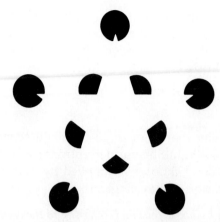

FIGURE 8.1 The doctrine of maya says that the world is our mental construction. Is there a star in this picture? Or is it constructed out of our acts of perception?

But from the featureless clay all kinds of interesting objects can be made. The One, the All, is like the featureless clay. It resides behind everything. We take the momentary patterns of the clay for eternal forms, when in fact they are merely temporary appearances out of the clay.

Another way of understanding maya is to define it as our classification and measurement schemes. Indeed, maya is derived from the Sanskrit root *matr-*, which means "to measure." Human beings speak of things as being big and small, heavy and light, good and bad, right and wrong, and so forth. The doctrine of maya says that measurement and classification may be necessary to function and deal with the world. We should not, however, confuse our classification schemes with reality itself. Classification chops up reality into arbitrary parts, chops the flow of events into bits and pieces, and creates dualities where none exist. For example, are there right and wrong deeds? Common sense would answer of course. But what of the classic case of the poor man who steals milk and bread to feed his starving children? Was he right or wrong? He was wrong to break the law. But he was right to feed his starving children. The dilemma is created by maya, by the way we chop up the world into dualities such as good and bad. Eastern philosophy would not force us to make a logical choice.

The major value of the doctrine of maya resides in what it has to say about human suffering. If we take the doctrine seriously, all suffering occurs because the person attaches himself to maya instead of reality. He takes his personal world of experience for the All. He is spellbound by his own expectations, learnings, and values. He thinks that his finite world of perception is Everything, and this leads to all kinds of negative emotional reactions. There is the feeling that "things must go my way. It is essential!" Naturally, things do not always go the way the person wishes, and then there is frustration, anger, and disappointment. We are attached to our property, our jobs, our marriages, our parents, our children, our loves, our hopes, our plans, and so forth. And yet these are all aspects of maya. None of them, including ourselves, are permanent. Everything appears momentarily out of the universal

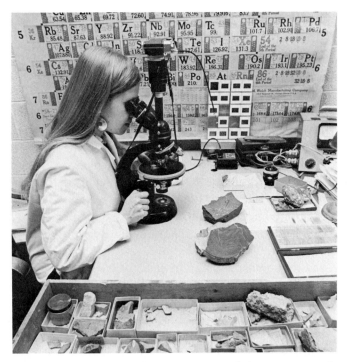

One way of understanding maya is to define it as our classification and measurement schemes.

"clay," and everything will once again merge into it. All experiences and appearances are temporary. Thus Eastern philosophy asks "Why be troubled?" It advises "Relax and do not attach yourself to maya."

The World View of don Juan

If, as the doctrine of maya teaches, the everyday reality of the average person is illusion, it is possible that there are other "realities." This is precisely the point of view espoused in a series of widely read books by University of California anthropologist Carlos Castaneda. *The Teachings of don Juan: A Yaqui Way of Knowledge* (1968), *A Separate Reality* (1971), and other books by Castaneda tell of his adventures with a Yaqui Indian from northwestern Mexico. Castaneda refers to him as "don Juan." Don Juan is a *brujo*, meaning a sorcerer, medicine man, and curer. Castaneda became don Juan's apprentice and for a number of years explored the secrets of Mexican sorcery. Peyote (referred to by don Juan as Mescalito), mushroom powder, and psychotropic mixtures were used by don Jaun to open the doors of perception to other realities.

A distinction is made in the Castaneda books between ordinary reality and nonordinary reality. **Ordinary reality** is the consciousness of the average individual; it refers to the consensual world, the one that most of us agree on.

8.1 APPLICATION: THE ART OF SEEING AND CONTROLLED FOLLY

An important theme in the Castaneda books is the doctrine of *seeing*, and it is closely related to what has already been said about reality. Don Juan tells Castaneda that the average person merely looks, but the "man of knowledge" *sees*. Responding to things in terms of their surface appearance is what don Juan means by merely looking. Responding to events in terms of a larger space-time perspective is what don Juan means by seeing. The art of seeing can be used to exercise what don Juan refers to as **controlled folly**, a deliberate shifting of one's attention beyond the immediate event when one faces a personal disappointment.

For example, say that a businessman loses all of his savings in a stock market crash. If he merely looks at the situation, he is despondent. Some people have been known to commit suicide during such a period of despair. But if he practices controlled folly, he will see that there may be many tomorrows, that his health is still good, that his wife still loves him, and so forth. If he is really skilled at controlled folly, he might even laugh at his misfortune. Thus he is a "fool" in a sense, but a *wise* fool.

Don Juan's idea of seeing as opposed to looking is similar to the Eastern idea of "piercing the veil of maya." It seems that the esoteric teachings of Indian sorcerers and the doctrines of Eastern philosophy together suggest that freedom from much psychological-emotional suffering is possible. Release from suffering requires that the individual be made aware of the fact that he or she lives in a psychological soap bubble of his or her own making.

It is the reality of everyday society, of one's culture. **Nonordinary reality** appears when the person is in an altered state of consciousness. It is a strange psychological domain described by Castaneda (1971) as "incomprehensible and impossible to interpret by means of our everyday mode of understanding the world" (p. 18). According to don Juan, it takes an unusual person, a "warrior," to be able to enter and leave nonordinary reality successfully. Thus Castaneda's ability to face his experiences in nonordinary reality with will and courage became a test to his mettle as a person.

One of Casteneda's ventures into nonordinary reality involved a meeting with a strange creature called the guardian:

I was looking at an unbelievably enormous animal. It was brilliantly black. Its front was covered with long, black, insidious hair, which looked like spikes coming through the cracks of some slick, shiny scales. The hair was actually arranged in tufts. Its body was massive, thick and round. Its wings were wide and short in comparison to the length of its body. It had two white, bulging eyes and a long muzzle. This time it looked more like an alligator. It seemed to have long ears, or perhaps horns, and it was drooling.

. . . It made a wide circle before stopping in front of me; its mouth was wide open, like a huge cavern; it had no teeth. It vibrated its wings for an instant and then it charged at me. It actually charged at my eyes. I screamed with pain and then I flew up, or rather I felt I had ejected myself up, and went soaring beyond the guardian, beyond the yellowish plateau, into another world, the world of men, and I found myself standing in the middle of don Juan's room. (pp. 158–160)

And what, in ordinary reality, was the guardian? Merely a tiny gnat! When Castaneda discussed this with don Juan, the sorcerer pointed out that in nonordinary reality the gnat actually became the guardian, and it could have killed Castaneda. Even in terms of conventional psychological formulations, don Juan's assertion is plausible. It is easy to imagine that experiences in altered states of consciousness might produce emotional shocks strong enough to induce death. Voodoo deaths, in which tribal members expire from a witch doctor's curse, provide another example of the way an individual's particular construction of reality may induce tragedy. This is why don Juan warned Castaneda that only the brave dare enter the world of nonordinary reality. And it is also why Castaneda needed the steady support, wisdom, and experience of don Juan to guide him safely into and out of the other world.

The Study of Perception

The age-old doctrine of maya has its counterpart in orthodox psychology. You are already familiar with the term **phenomenal world**, the world as perceived, from the chapter on existential-humanistic psychology. This is a familiar idea in Western philosophy and psychology. It can readily be traced all the way back to Plato's famous allegory of the person imprisoned in a cave. The person sees shadows on the wall projected from outside the cave and mistakenly takes these for reality. Plato used the allegory to suggest that we are forced to construct a limited reality, a psychological world, from the small bits of data available to us from Reality itself. As noted in Chapter 7, a similar formulation can be found in the writings of the philosopher Immanuel Kant.

Students of perception sometimes distinguish between sensation and perception. **Sensation** refers to the raw data of experience. In the case of vision, thes might be patches of color and brightness. **Perception** refers to the meaningful whole organized out of the raw data. The bits and pieces of sensation are organized, like the bits and pieces of a jigsaw puzzle, into a coherent pattern. Thus when looking at a painting of a landscape, we do not see a random jumble of colors, but the water and the woods.

Perceptions also differ among individuals, however. A basic finding derived from experiments in perception is that motives, expectancies, and attitudes affect perception. Thus David might look at a particular painting in an art gallery and say, "It is beautiful." His companion, Deborah, might look at the same painting and say, "It is ugly." They might even start arguing about whether the painting "is" beautiful or ugly. But they are not debating the "isness" of the painting. They are merely having incongruent perceptions. If they can really appreciate this, their pointless debate might end quickly.

Over and over in the research on perception, we encounter the idea that the person constructs his or her own reality. This is true even in the domain of tough-minded research. For example, one conceptual model for understanding perception is the Tanner-Swets theory of visual detection. W. P. Tanner, Jr., and J. A. Swets (1954) found that subjects required to identify visual signals in laboratory experiments report many false positives and false negatives. A **false positive** occurs if the subject says, "A light flashed," when in fact no light flashed at all. A **false negative** occurs if the subject says, "I see no light," when in fact a light flashed. Here is the important point: Both false positives and false negatives change as a function of the subject's motives and expectancies. If the subject has a good reason to see or not see a light flash, or if past experience has led the subject to believe that a light will or will not flash, the subject's perception is directly altered. In more dramatic terms, the subject misses things that are clearly evident and "hallucinates" things that are not there. In short, a wide spectrum of formulations, including Eastern philosophy, the teachings of don Juan, Platonic doctrine, and experimental psychology, suggest that the individual constructs his or her psychological world. As philosopher-author Joseph Pearce says in *The Crack in the Cosmic Egg* (1971, p. 2), "we represent the world to ourselves, and respond to our representations."

YOGA: AN ANCIENT MENTAL SCIENCE

The aim of Yoga is to carry the person beyond maya into a perfect union with the All. Indeed, the word Yoga is derived from **yuj**, a Sanskrit root meaning "to yoke." Literally, Yoga means that the individual self is yoked with the Divine Self, thus attaining a sense of oneness with all creation and a state of cosmic awareness. To the cynic, it is amusing that Yoga is a contemporary rage, one of the "in" things to be doing, one of the fads of modern times. In actuality, this "new" technique is one of the oldest kinds of "mental science" known to the human race.

Yoga is easily traced to 200 B.C. and the writings of the great teacher Patanjali (Rama, 1979). Raja Yoga, or Royal Yoga, is associated with Patanjali, and is described in the next section. A **yogi** is one who practices Yoga; the term suggests that he has attained a certain level of expertise. A **swami** is a

Yoga is one of the oldest kinds of "mental science" known to the human race.

master; the word connotes one who has attained mystical union with the All. The holy Swami Order has existed in India for more than one thousand years.

Types of Yoga

Yoga is a complex discipline with a variety of techniques. All the techniques have the same general aim—spiritual growth—but they operate in different ways. In *Awakening* by scholar C. William Henderson (1975), the specific methods are described as follows:

They can be likened to the separate cars, buses, trucks, and motorcycles on any highway. The road leads in the direction you want to go, but the vehicles get you there. There are many of these yoga vehicles. Some are similar, some overlap, and a few are the same things going under different names. (p. 121)

The variety of techniques exist to deal with the realities of human temperament. We all have different personalities; thus the different types of Yoga appeal to different people. For example, an action-oriented person might find that he is unsuited for sedentary meditation. He might, however, be suited for *Karma Yoga*. Let us identify five basic types of Yoga: (1) **Raja Yoga**, (2) **Jnana Yoga**, (3) **Karma Yoga**, (4) **Bhakti Yoga**, and (5) **Hatha Yoga**.

Raja Yoga   Raja Yoga is "Royal" Yoga and is the oldest form of Yoga. It is the one that demands a substantial amount of sedentary meditation. Meditation, as conceived by Raja Yoga, is a skill that requires long hours of intense concentration. The mind of the unskilled meditator is like an unfocused lens. The sun shines through it, but there is no pinpoint of light. The skilled yogi, however, learns to focus the lens of his mind, making consciousness into a small ray of intense energy. This ray "burns" through the veil of maya and carries the yogi into ecstatic union with the All.

At the level of daily living, Raja Yoga may hold some promise as a method to facilitate learning. Sheila Ostrander, Lynn Schroeder, and Nancy Ostrander (1979), authors of *Superlearning*, describe experiments on memory training. Some of the experiments used Raja Yoga exercises to aid both relaxation and concentration, and the exercises appeared to be quite helpful to learners.

Jnana Yoga   Jnana Yoga suggests that harmony with the Infinite can be acquired through self-knowledge. The individual examines himself, his motives, his ambitions, his emotions, and so forth. He gives up practices of self-deception, a kind of inner maya that keeps him from knowing himself completely. Jnana Yoga is similar to the teachings of depth psychology, particularly the teachings of Carl Jung. A disciple of Eastern philosophy might say that such men as Freud and Jung rediscovered in their own way and in their own words the ancient practice of Jnana Yoga.

Karma Yoga   Karma Yoga asserts that self-realization can be attained by leading a responsible life, by being of service to other people. The decent person who is doing his work and raising his children is living according to the principles of Karma Yoga. The idea of **selfless action**, action that has no obvious external reward for the individual, is the core of Karma Yoga. Frankl's logotherapy bears a strong resemblance to Karma Yoga.

Bhakti Yoga   The emphasis of Bhakti Yoga is on devotion. We thus have the image of a person who prays, who chants, who adores his **guru**, his spiritual teacher on Earth. The key concept in Bhakti Yoga is fervent worship, which suggests that practicing great reverence for the All is one way that mystical union can be achieved.

Hatha Yoga   Hatha Yoga is perhaps the most popular form of Yoga in the Western world (see Table 8.1). Its purpose is to help the individual attain better physical health. This is accomplished through a variety of methods. There are **asanas**, postures that are essentially isometric or "static" exercises; these are designed to strengthen the muscles of the body. There is **pranayama**, or Yogic breathing; this is designed to capture for the body **prana**, or vital energy, believed by yogis to be in the air we breathe. There are also rec-

TABLE 8.1   TYPES OF YOGA

Type	A Key Feature
Raja Yoga	Meditation requiring long hours of intense concentration.
Jnana Yoga	Attaining harmony with the Infinite through self-knowledge.
Karma Yoga	Attaining self-realization by leading a responsible life.
Bhakti Yoga	Practicing great reverence and devotion.
Hatha Yoga	Training the body as a means of attaining a higher level of spiritual development.
Integral Yoga	Seeks to combine the best features of the other five types of Yoga.

ommendations for correct eating and cleansing of the body. Hatha Yoga is based on the premise that the human being has three aspects: body, mind, and spirit. The thesis is that mental and spiritual growth requires a healthy body. Thus the true yogi does not get "stuck" at the Hatha Yoga level; he does not become preoccupied with physical culture for its own sake. For him it is a mere stepping-stone to higher levels of development.

In addition to the various Yogas just described, there is Integral Yoga. **Integral Yoga** was conceived by the Indian sage Sri Aurobindo, and it seeks to combine the best elements of the five principal Yoga systems (Chaudhuri, 1965).

Mental-Spiritual Growth

According to Yoga philosophy, mental-spiritual growth takes place via a set of seven stages. These stages are represented by *chakras*, Sanskrit for "disks." The **chakras** are said to be wheellike patterns of energy located at various places in the body. A poetic language is used to describe the process of psychological awakening. A female serpent called the Kundalini is said to be asleep at the base of the spine of the ordinary person. Yogic techniques are designed to awaken the Kundalini, and she slowly ascends from the first *chakra* to the seventh *chakra*. The seven chakras are (1) the root, or basic, chakra, located at the base of the spine; (2) the spleen chakra; (3) the navel chakra; (4) the heart chakra; (5) the throat chakra; (6) the brow chakra; and (7) the crown chakra, located on the top of the head. It should be understood that it might take a number of years of Yogic study and practice before the Kundalini reaches the crown chakra.

When the Kundalini reaches the crown chakra, the yogi experiences *samadhi*. In *Yoga Sutras* by Rammurti Mishra (1963), a Sanskrit scholar, the following definition of **samadhi** is given:

State of superconsciousness; highest state of existence; identification of mind with Supreme Consciousness; state of union of individual consciousness with Cosmic Consciousness. (p. 532)

Thus *samadhi* is the supreme goal of Yogic training. Phrases such as "torrential bliss," "blessed experience," and "ecstatic union" are used to describe *samadhi*. In his later years, the Swami Paramahansa Yogananda wrote a poem called *Samadhi*. Here is a brief excerpt from the poem as it appears in his *Autobiography of a Yogi* (1974, p. 171):

I, in everything, enter the Great Myself.
Gone forever: fitful, flickering shadows of
    mortal memory;
Spotless is my mental sky—below, ahead,
    and high above;
Eternity and I, one united ray.
A tiny bubble of laughter, I
Am become the Sea of Mirth itself. *

Although *samadhi* is the goal of Yogic training, the yogi is urged to return from *samadhi* and show others the way of mental-spiritual growth. The danger of *samadhi* is presented in Yoga philosophy by telling the story of the salt doll who wanted to discover the depth of the ocean. Obviously, the doll melted into the ocean and never came back. In other words, the yogi should not get "hooked" on *samadhi*. He has a responsibility to his fellow human beings.

It should be understood that the ascension of the Kundalini may be accepted as a case of poetic license. A student of Yoga does not necessarily believe that a real serpent rises from the base of the spine. When Perls spoke of paper people, he did not mean that if snipped such persons would not bleed. The Kundalini and the paper person are metaphors used to get across concepts. In fact, Maslow's formulation of a hierarchy of motives rising in stages from basic drives to self-actualization is remarkably similar to the rise of the Kundalini from the root chakra to the crown chakra.

Yoga and Paranormal Phenomena

Yoga takes paranormal phenomena for granted. In the *Autobiography of a Yogi*, Yogananda (1974) speaks of materializations, astral projection, and clairvoyance as matter-of-factly as a Western person might speak of making a telephone call or watching television. To the yogi, the common view that we live in a universe limited by the three dimensions of space and the one dimension of time is just another case of maya. The example is given by Swami Vishnudevananda (1960) of a ship sailing on the ocean. It can travel in only two dimensions: longitude and latitude. Assume that the captain of the ship is unfamiliar with air travel. An airplane appears overhead. Then it "disappears." Much to the captain's amazement, he finds the airplane at his destina-

8.2 CONTEMPORARY RESEARCH: STUDYING PARANORMAL PHENOMENA

The existence of paranormal phenomena is an unsettled question within the profession of psychology. There is a body of experimental work on **psi abilities**, capacities of the mind asserted to transcend its normal limits. The traditional psi abilities include clairvoyance, precognition, telepathy, and psychokinesis. **Clairvoyance** is said to be the capacity to perceive objects or events present elsewhere (e.g., "seeing" something in a distant place). **Precognition** is said to be the capacity to perceive objects or events in the future (e.g., "knowing" that someone is going to win at the races next week). **Telepathy** is said to be the ability of one mind to know directly the thoughts and ideas of another mind (e.g., a person "reads" your mind and tells you that you are thinking of going to see a particular movie this evening). Clairvoyance, precognition, and telepathy all belong in the general category **extrasensory perception (ESP)**, said to be the ability of the mind to know something about events external to oneself without the use of vision, hearing, taste, touch, or smell.

Psychokinesis (PK) stands alone as a psi ability. It is said to be the ability of the mind to directly affect matter. For example, a gambler may try to make a pair of dice come up seven through mental influence. In the science-fiction movie *The Empire Strikes Back*, Luke Skywalker, the hero, learns to lift a small spaceship out of a bog by concentrating his mental energy.

The pioneer psychologist in the area of research on ESP and PK was J. B. Rhine. His findings are available in the *Journal of Parapsychology* and in his books, including his most famous, *The Reach of the Mind* (1947). Rhine was convined of the reality of psi abilities and presented various experiments with statistical analyses to support his contentions.

More recently, in a book called *Learning to Use ESP* (1976), Charles Tart of the University of California at Davis reports on a series of telepathy experiments. Tart applied the principles of operant conditioning to the learning of telepathic ability. He designed "telepathy trainers," machines capable of giving subjects feedback on their telepathic "hits." Tart reports that ESP can possibly be learned through reinforcement, much like other skills.

The research on parapsychology is extremely difficult to evaluate objectively. There are all sorts of problems in experimental design, fine points of statistical analysis, and experimenter bias that enter in to discredit the research in the minds of the scientific community (Gardner, 1981). The case in favor of the existence of paranormal phenomena has *not* been made in the halls of academic psychology. At present, it can only be said that a large number of psychologists keep an open mind about parapsychology. They do not give it categorical rejection or categorical acceptance.

tion. The airplane has traveled in the third dimension—a dimension unknown to the captain. Thus its behavior seemed incredible and paranormal. Similarly, the yogi believes that the **astral body**, a "second" body made of a finer matter than the ordinary body, can travel in higher dimensional planes. Extrasensory perception and other paranormal phenomena are understood in such terms.

Instead of making much of paranormal phenomena, we find that the serious yogi tends to discount them! He discounts them not because he supposes they are not real, but because he feels they interfere with mental-spiritual growth. In other words, they are a trap. They tend to appear before the Kundalini reaches the seventh *chakra*. If the novice becomes distracted by his supernormal mental powers, he may be delayed in reaching *samadhi*. Yoga warns that even if psi abilities are real, they are hardly ends in themselves.

Yoga sees itself as having a responsibility to humanity. In the *Autobiography of a Yogi*, Yogananda writes:

The Western day is nearing when the inner science of self-control will be found as necessary as the outer conquest of Nature. The Atomic Age will see men's minds sobered and broadened by the now scientifically indisputable truth that matter is in reality a concentrate of energy. The human mind can and must liberate within itself energies greater than those within stones and metals, lest the material atomic giant, newly unleashed, turn on the world in mindless destruction. (p. 265)

Yoga seeks to improve the human condition by inner transformation. Swami Kriyananda, a follower of Yogananda, says (1977, p. 150), "Without inner transformation, any outer improvement in the human lot would be like trying to strengthen a termite-ridden building with a fresh coat of paint."

Briefly, Yoga teaches that it is possible to pierce the veil of maya and attain mystical union with the All. This produces a state of bliss known as *samadhi*. Several kinds of Yoga exist, but they are not thought of as mutually exclusive. As an ancient science, Yoga teaches that it is possible to attain tremendous levels of inner self-control over the body and the mind. It should be understood, however, that the techniques of Yoga are merely instruments in the whole scheme. The real purpose of Yoga is spiritual growth.

ZEN: THE ENLIGHTENED LIFE

Like Yoga, Zen seeks to break the spell of maya. But there are important differences between Yoga and Zen. Yoga is "upward bound." It takes the person into the psychological stratosphere. It is truly transpersonal in that it takes the person "out" of himself. Zen, on the other hand, is "down to Earth." It returns the individual to himself. This is evident in that a prime goal of Zen is to see into one's own true nature. In Zen poetry, one finds a love of and a closeness to the Earth itself—to the land, the trees, the flowers, the animals, the rivers, and so forth. Zen holds that our true nature is *not* divided from Nature itself. We are part of Nature. More than a part of Nature, we are an

Zen is down to earth.

indivisible aspect of Nature. Ringing Western phrases such as "the conquest of space" are nonsense to the Zen mind. They are artificially pit human beings against the universe.

Use of the single word Zen is technically incorrect. The proper term is Zen Buddhism, a meditative approach to Buddhism. But Zen Buddhism is a sufficiently unique school of thought that informal usage allows the single word Zen to stand alone. Zen is a Japanese word derived from the Chinese word Ch'an, meaning "meditation." Ch'an itself is derived from the Sanskrit word for meditation, *Dhyana*. Thus the core meaning of Zen is simply meditation. Zen was brought to Japan, where it flourished, about eight hundred years ago by traveling monks. There are presently about twenty thousand Zen temples in Japan.

The Tao and the Four Noble Truths

Because Zen is derived from **Taoism**, the ancient religion of China, and also from Chinese Buddhism, it would be well to examine these roots of Zen. In the words of the Great Chinese sage Lao-tzu:

There are ways but the Way is uncharted;
There are names but not nature in words:
Nameless indeed is the source of creation . . .

These words are said to have been written in the fourth century B.C. A paraphrase of the quotation is offered by the Eastern Scholar R. B. Blakney (1955):

None of the ways observed or described by us, in which things happen or events occur, is the Master Way by which nature works. No word or name can disclose nature's deepest secret. Creation began in an event which is not identified and therefore has no name. (p. 53)

The Tao is thus the Way, the Master Way, of existence. It is inexorable in its course, and it must be accepted. Taoism teaches that there is nothing we can do to change it. Like a great river, it carries everything along in its forceful flow. Deep acceptance of the Tao is said to be the key to tranquility and a nonartificial life. Jean S. Bolen (1979, p. xii), a psychiatrist and author of *The Tao of Psychology*, says that acceptance of the Tao represents a "path with heart," a way we can "live in harmony with the universe."

Another root of Zen is the set of Four Noble Truths proposed by Chinese Buddhism. It should be understood that Buddhism and its variant, Zen, are psychologies as well as religions. As earlier noted, they are "ways of liberation." They aim to free human beings from unnecessary suffering. The Four Noble Truths are intended to contribute to this goal:

1. The First Noble Truth is the simple admission that suffering exists. Human beings experience pain, despair, frustration, and decay of the body. These are inevitable.
2. The Second Noble Truth is that suffering originates with excessive desire. A person may want too much sexual activity, too much money, too much food. Also, the Second Noble Truth asserts that some people have too strong a desire to save their own souls. Such spiritual craving is also seen as a source of suffering.
3. The Third Noble Truth is that suffering can be eliminated. This can be done by getting rid of excessive desire. By focusing on the reality of the Tao, the inevitability of the great cycle of birth, growth, and decay, one can gain a great perspective. One sees that excessive desire is folly in terms of the great course of existence.
4. The Fourth Noble Truth is that there is an Eightfold Middle Path between excessive desire and excessive self-denial. In *Selling Water by the River*, a manual of Zen training by the Abbess Jiyu Kennett (1972), the following eight aspects of the Middle Path are designated: (1) right understanding, (2) right thought, (3) right speech, (4) right action, (5) right livelihood, (6) right effort, (7) right mindfulness, and (8) right concentration (p. 10). The Middle Path is essentially the path of moderation.

The teachings of Taoism and Buddhism are the underpinnings of Zen, and contemporary Zen still incorporates these basic orientations. They are implicit themes in all the Zen literature.

The World View of Zen

It is easy to be glib about Zen. But serious students of Zen quote the words of Lao-tzu:

Those who know do not speak;
Those who speak do not know.

Assume that you pick up a small book titled *What is Zen?* by no less an authority than D. T. Suzuki (1972), one of the principal persons responsible for awakening the Western mind to the possibilities in Zen. This is what you find on the opening page:

You ask, "What is Zen?"
   I answer, "Zen is that which makes you ask the question, because the answer is where the question arises. The answerer is no other than the questioner himself."
   "Do you then mean that I am Zen itself?"
   "Exactly. When you ask what Zen is, you are asking who you are, what your self is. It is for this reason that the Zen masters often tell you not to ask where the donkey is when you are right on it, or not to seek for another head when yours has been on your shoulders ever since you were born. It is the height of stupidity to ask what your self is when it is this self that makes you ask the question."
   Now, you know what Zen is, for it is Zen that tells you what your self is, and that that self is Zen. This now saves you from asking such a stupid question. (p. 1)

Do you feel vaguely disgusted, insulted, and confused? You read on and soon feel like throwing the book away. That is the whole point! When Suzuki says you should not "seek for another head," he simply means *think for yourself*. He is asking you, "Why turn to me or to any other authority for ideas about right living? You have a head. Use it!" Zen seeks to teach by example, and Suzuki is perfectly willing to turn you away from him if this will contribute to your self-sufficiency.

Zen has a great mistrust of abstract thinking, the forte of the Western rational mind. In a book called *Zen Buddhism and Psychoanalysis*, co-authored with Erich Fromm and Richard DeMartino (1970), a book much less obscure than the one already cited, Suzuki clarifies the Zen mistrust of analytical thought. He quotes a *haiku*, a seventeen-syllable poem, written about three hundred years ago by Basho, a great Japanese poet:

When I look carefully
I see the nazuna blooming
by the hedge! (p. 1)

The *nazuna* is a wild plant, the sort that most people might not even notice as they walk by. The poem does not seem to be much of a poem at all by Western standards, hardly the work of a great poet. But Suzuki points out that the poem is intended to convey a depth of feeling and an appreciation for nature just as it is. Basho has an emotional reaction to the *nazuna*—per-

8.3   CONTEMPORARY RESEARCH: ZEN AND THE BRAIN'S RIGHT HEMISPHERE

Zen scholar D. T. Suzuki (1972) summarizes the world view of the Western mind with such words as analytical, discriminative, differential, inductive, individualistic, intellectual, objective, scientific, generalizing, conceptual, schematic, impersonal, power-wielding, and self-assertive. In contrast, the world view of Zen is described with such words as synthetic, totalizing, integrative, nondiscriminative, deductive, nonsystematic, dogmatic, intuitive, subjective, spiritually individualistic, and socially group-minded. Suzuki writes in the tradition of Eastern philosophy, and does not connect his observations with recent research on the structures and functions of the brain. However, it is quite possible to do so.

Two important structures in the brain are the **left cerebral hemisphere** and the **right cerebral hemisphere**. Seen from above, each hemisphere looks somewhat like half of a melon. The **corpus callosum** connects the two structures and permits communication between them. The corpus callosum is sometimes deliberately severed in human beings by neurosurgeons in an effort to control life-threatening epileptic seizures. Roger W. Sperry (1967) and his associates at the California Institute of Technology conducted early investigations of the thinking and perception of persons with a severed corpus callosum. A substantial amount of research on the differing functions of the

haps admiration or a transient sense of joy—and he records the feelings. Suzuki contrasts Basho's poem with a superficially similar poem by the Western poet, Alfred, Lord Tennyson:

Flower in the crannied wall,
I pluck you out of the crannies;—
Hold you here, root and all, in my hand,
Little flower—but if I could understand
What you are, root and all, and all in all,
I should know what God and man is.

The difference between the minds of Basho and of Tennyson is indeed great. Tennyson cares nothing for the flower itself—his act must kill the flower. He is interested in understanding the world he lives in, grasping it intellectually. Consequently, he both destroys and alienates himself from that world. Basho is interested in appreciating the world he lives in; thus he does

two hemispheres, some of it on intact brains, has been carried out since Sperry's initial investigations (Restak, 1979). Certain findings appear to be consistent.

The evidence suggests that the left cerebral hemisphere is the dominant one in verbal and analytic modes of thought. For example, say that you engage in the following train of thought: "I don't want to go to Tom's birthday party unless Mary goes. I think she's going. I guess I'll go too." Research suggests you relied on your left brain to process the statements and reach a conclusion.

The right cerebral hemisphere is the dominant one in spatial and nonverbal modes of thought. For example, say that you are asked to define a spiral staircase. Neurologist David Galin (1979) points out that you might say a few words haltingly, and then make a twirling gesture with an upraised finger. He notes that the complex concept spiral staircase can be handled more easily by a visual-kinesthetic representation than a verbal one.

Critics of Western education and child-rearing practices say that we have overemphasized left brain modes of thought. It is their belief that to make people more integrated and more creative we should give somewhat more attention to right brain modes of thought. It is said that the right brain's function is **holistic**, that it brings elements together into an organized whole. If this is so, and it seems to be, it is not a function that should be slighted. Zen training seems to be one of the ways discovered by the human race to integrate and enhance the functions of the brain's right hemisphere.

not set himself against it. Tennyson's approach is used to symbolize the approach of Western rational thought. Basho's approach is used to symbolize the approach of Zen.

Principles of Zen

Perhaps we can make the world view of Zen more explicit by formulating some of the teachings of Zen in the form of principles. Three principles will be specified: (1) the principles of no-thingness, (2) the principle of no-twoness, and (3) the principle of no-mind. These principles would probably not be abstracted formally from the flow of Zen, as we have done, by a Zen master interested in instructing a student. The listing of principles is itself a categorizing process toward which Zen is indifferent. Thus let us proceed with at least the awareness that our procedure does some violence to the Zen way of thinking.

The Principle of No-thingness   As we look about the world, we see the familiar environment of things, objects of perception. We see pencils, cups, tables, houses, cars, and so forth. Zen teaches that these are not things, but abstractions we have made from the great flow of the Tao. It is our perceptual processes that create the world of things. They are psychological constructions, created by our sense organs. There was a time when they were not. There will be a time when they are not. Things merely appear and disappear out of the current of existence. It is thus a form of maya to think that the world is made up of hard, enduring objects. The same can be said of ourselves. We are not things. We too appear and disappear, produced by and swallowed up by the Tao. It is thus folly to attach too much importance to material possessions or to the "ultimate" possession—life itself. For life itself will dissolve into the river of the Way.

The same thinking is applied by Zen to the ego, the conscious self. It is not a thing either, but a construction abstracted from space-time events. Not being a permanent thing, the Zen view would make no assertions about the survival of the ego after one's death. A Zen koan, a "puzzler" or thought-provoking paradox used to foster enlightenment, asks: "Where does your fist go when you open your hand?" The word *fist* is a noun and seems to refer to a thing. Yet the "thing" disappears merely by opening the hand! And yet we see, from our larger frame of reference, that nothing was lost. Indeed, there never actually existed a "thing" called the fist in and of itself. Similarly, Zen teaches that to ask "Where does the ego go after death?" is like asking about the fist. The ego is not a thing in and of itself any more than the fist is. It doesn't "go" anywhere. There is only a change of form. The human ego, says Zen, is a temporary organization emerging briefly from the restless changes of existence itself.

Alan Watts, author of *The Way of Zen* (1957) and a number of other books about Eastern ways of thought, offers the following example to illustrate how the Zen view of the ego fits into the principle of no-thingness. We say the ocean makes waves. The word *wave* is treated in English as a noun, a thing. (You will recall that a noun is defined as a person, place, or thing. A wave is not a person or a place; thus ordinary English grants it the status of a thing.) We say, "The wave travels to the shore" or "The wave breaks on the shore." Watts notes, however, that this usage is inaccurate. If we reflect a moment, we can easily appreciate that the wave is not a thing. It is in fact nothing, an organization of water into a temporary form. In like fashion, suggests Watts, the universe produces egos. He converts the nouns to verbs, thus suggesting processes instead of things. It is now possible to say, "As the ocean *waves*, the universe *egos*."

The Principle of No-twoness   Zen teaches that most dichotomies are false. They are another aspect of maya. We speak of mind and body, good and bad, tall and short, right and wrong, and so forth. In reality, asserts Zen, members of a duality are aspects of each other. There can be no mind without the body, no good without bad, no tall without short, and no right without wrong. So-called opposites have a complementary relationship, creating each other. They are merely two faces of the same coin. Returning to the subject of the ego or the self, Zen says that it is a mistake to make a subject-object dichotomy between oneself and the world. The Western mind is trained to think in terms of the I "in here" and the world "out there." To illustrate its position, Zen invokes the image of the moon-in-the-lake. Take away the moon, and there is no moon-in-the-lake. Take away the lake, and there is no moon-in-the-lake. The moon-in-the-lake requires the moon and the lake. The phenomenon vanishes if either is removed. Similarly, the person-in-the-world phenomenon requires both the person and the world. The person and the world are aspects of each other. Zen thus sees the division between people and nature as arbitrary.

The Principle of No-mind   The principle of no-mind asserts that it is possible to think too much. Again, in Zen we encounter the mistrust of abstract thinking and analytical thought. The Zen goal is to act spontaneously without too much reflection, analysis, and unnecessary cogitation. The psychologically "stuck" person is the person who must overthink everything. Such persons put great faith in their rational faculties. They think if they can gather all the facts, ponder long enough, and be sufficiently logical, they will always make the right decision. Zen says that this is another aspect of maya, the illusion that the conscious mind is sufficient to light the darkness of the maze of existence. Zen, instead, advises us to live with a stronger sense of intuition, to base our decisions at least as much on nonverbal feelings as articulated thoughts.

The principle of no-mind should not be misunderstood as advising rash action. Zen does not see itself as giving license for foolhardy behavior. On the contrary, Zen is simply arguing that some persons are too inhibited. Such persons need to let go of their death grip on their intellects and act more spontaneously. When one is on a mental merry-go-round, Zen advises that one simply jump off! In other words, it says, "Take action! Act now! Even if the decision is the 'wrong' one, it is better than mental paralysis and psychological self-torture."

A bit of perspective can be gained on the principle of no-mind by realizing that Japan is a tradition-oriented culture. The no-mind advice can be of value to persons who are too culture-bound and, in consequence, too inhibited— the kind of person clinical psychology would call "neurotic." In a society that puts out the heavy hand of tradition to keep its members "in line," there may be a high incidence of neurosis. But the principle of no-mind would not be helpful for persons at the opposite end of the pole, persons clinical psychology would place in the category of "personality disorders." Such individuals are impulsive, and they do not need no-mind. They need more mind!

In actuality, the Zen principle of no-mind can be correctly understood in terms of the Middle Way of the Four Noble Truths of Buddhism. There is an optimal way of behaving between excessive inhibition and excessive excitation. This optimal way is known as **spontaneity**. Subjectively, spontaneity might be described as the inner feeling that one has the capacity to take right action without undue strain. The spontaneous person trusts himself and his capacity to make decisions.

Methods of Awakening

It is not enough, according to Zen, to know about nothingness, no-twoness, and no-mind. Intellectual understanding is fine, but the person who has only intellectual understanding is not in fact awakened. He or she must be "hit" by these ideas like the proverbial ton of bricks. If and when this happens, the person experiences **satori**. *Satori* may be thought of as a sudden awakening in which the spell of maya is cast off. One not only realizes intellectually the things we have been talking about in the past few pages; one directly knows that they are so. In Western psychology, we would refer to *satori* with the word **insight**. *Satori*, or insight, suggests an abrupt "seeing into" the heart of a problem. Everything "clicks" into place, and one thinks, "Ah hah! I've got it!"

An analogy may enhance our understanding of *satori*. *Satori* is like a flash of lightning that illuminates a dark landscape. The flash may last for only an instant, but we never forget what we saw during that instant. Similarly, what a person "sees" during *satori* is preserved, brought back to ordinary experience as it were, and may change the person's life forever. Of course, a person may experience *satori* more than once—just as lightning can flash again. But the *satori* experience is not one that can be sustained for long. And an awakened person does not live in a state of constant *satori*.

There are two principle methods of inducing *satori*. The first mode is advocated by the Soto school of Zen, which advocates a gradual approach to *satori*. *Satori* may be a "flash" in which a person is changed in an instant. But in Soto Zen, there is a slow buildup to the "moment of Truth." Soto Zen places its emphasis on Za-Zen, which is seated meditation in an approved posture. During Za-Zen the novice is instructed to look into his own nature, to meditate upon himself, with no particular goal in mind. It is expected that under such conditions all sorts of thoughts will pass through the mind and that little by little the meditator will come to see that distinctions between the inner and the outer world are like the moon-in-the-lake. He may strive after *satori* in utter frustration for months or for years. But *satori* cannot be willed. Perhaps at a certain point he stops trying to make it happen and just allows matters to take their course. When he least expects it, *satori* may occur. It happens of its own accord, spontaneously, from the depths of his being. About two-thirds of the Zen temples in Japan are Soto temples.

Satori is like a flash of lightning that illuminates a dark landscape.

The other principal mode of inducing *satori* is advocated by the Rinzai school of Zen. It emphasizes the *koan*. According to Thomas Hoover (1980), author of *The Zen Experience*, the *koan* is the most discussed and least understood teaching concept of the East. Basically, the **koan** is a paradoxical question used to hasten the arrival of *satori*. It is designed to create a psychological double bind. Hours and hours of meditation on a *koan* "blows the mind" and may result in sudden illumination or *satori*. (The Soto school also uses the *koan* occasionally. But its principal advocate is the Rinzai school.) It is interesting to note that the renowned physicist Neils Bohr taught that there is no progress without paradox (Overbye, 1981). Bohr is reported to have said, "A great truth is a truth whose opposite is also a great truth."

There are many *koans*; about 1700 different ones are used. Here are a few examples:

What is the sound of one hand clapping?

What was your original face before you were born?

A girl is crossing the street. Is she the younger or older sister?

When you are working, where is your true self?

When the student has meditated long enough on *koans*, he sees that they are nothing but tangles of words. He is brought to the realization that words are traps, the agents of maya. Reality itself is beyond words and must be

8.4   APPLICATION: LIVING AN ENLIGHTENED LIFE

According to Zen, you do not have to join a religious order to live an enlightened life. Zen beams its message out to the world. Its philosophy is designed to bring enlightenment to persons in all walks of life. This is not to say that most people who read about Zen achieve enlightenment. As we have already seen, there is a vast difference between enlightenment itself and learning about enlightenment on an academic level. Nonetheless, Zen need not be understood as an esoteric practice reserved for a few reclusive monks in Japanese monasteries. As noted previously, it is a "way of liberation" from unnecessary human suffering. As such, it has general value.

Let's set up a hypothetical person, the *enlightened person*, a person who has achieved *satori* in Zen terms. The image is created to get across an idea, the idea of the enlightened life. Actual persons might come close to or depart far from the image; but the image gives us a standard against which to measure behavior. The enlightened person could be almost anybody doing anything. This individual would not have to have a high-status position, have a profession, make a lot of money, or be highly creative. The enlightened person would have no exalted goals. He or she would have only realistic ambitions, not burning ones; such people would not be what has been described as a *workaholic*, someone addicted to the activities associated with one's job or vocation (Machlowitz, 1980). The enlightened person would have overcome the opposites of success and failure. These too, according to Zen, are aspects of maya.

The enlightened person would be able to cry and to laugh, to play and to work. But he or she would not get "stuck" in various emotional states or behaviors. One would not, for example, suffer from chronic depression, anger, or anxiety. Another characteristic of the enlightened person would be spontaneity, an optimal trait between excessive inhibition and excessive excitation.

To illustrate, a person who has a problem with alcohol may be straining to resist it. Jack is on the wagon, he won't touch a drop. This represents the extreme pole of excessive inhibition. Jack pays a price for not drinking, feeling

comprehended and acted on at a nonverbal level. In a well-known *koan*, the Zen master shows a student a stick. He says, "If you say this is a stick, I will hit you with it. If you say it is not a stick, I will hit you with it." The master's words seem to create an impossible double bind. The student may say, "It is a staff," thinking he is clever by assigning a different label to the stick. Much

tense and disgruntled. Then Jack falls off the wagon. He drinks too much, has no self-control. This represents the opposite end of the pole, excessive excitation. Contrast the behavior of the problem drinker with the behavior of a person, Jenny, who does not have a problem. Jenny's feeling about alcohol is "I can take it or leave it." Sometimes she drinks and sometimes she refuses a drink. Jenny drinks in moderation spontaneously, without "willpower" or effort. If Jenny could behave with similar spontaneity in all domains of her life, she would be an enlightened person.

What about the moral and ethical behavior of the enlightened person? Would an enlightened person live what is generally called a "decent" life? The answer is that for the enlightened person the general rules of everyday conduct would remain about the same as for persons in general. He or she would fit in with the general culture and not fight it. The person would not be vigorously pro-Establishment, nor vigorously anti-Establishment. The ideas of the conservatives and radicals, the ideas of all people, are simply more strands in the web of maya. The enlightened person would not, therefore, be sold on the Absolute Truth of any particular moral-ethical code. He or she would regard social conventions as significant local customs. As a consequence, the person would observe them. He or she would practice the dictum, "When in Rome do as the Romans do." Practical, reality-oriented, interested in surviving, and having a reasonable desire to enjoy life, the enlightened person would spontaneously follow the general behavioral norms of the culture without particular effort.

The picture we have painted of the enlightened person is not in the Western tradition of the hero. The enlightened person would be amused by a character such as Cervantes' Don Quixote, the self-proclaimed rescuer, forever tilting at windmills. The enlightened person does not seek psychological mountains to climb; such individuals are not interested in Great Tasks in life. They are more interested in a plain philosophy, such as "live and let live." They would feel a kinship with the Italian folk saying *"Che sera, sera,"* meaning "What will be, will be." They accept the fact that the Tao, the great river of existence, flows on inexorably and that we can have only a small effect on its direction.

to his surprise, the master hits him with the stick! The *koan* is properly understood if the student takes the stick away from the master and simply breaks it. A nonverbal response solves the seemingly impossible paradox.

Rinzai Zen uses the koan along with Za-zen, seated meditation, to facilitate the internal processes that bring the student to *satori*. When the aspirant really knows, as opposed to intellectual understanding, that subject-object dichotomies (dualisms) are false, that they are forms of maya created by the way human beings use words, he or she is enlightened.

Although Rinzai Zen is usually thought of as a faster approach to *satori* than is Soto Zen, both schools emphasize the importance of a period of meditation and training. In an entertaining book called *Zen Without Zen Masters*, meditation teacher Camden Benares (1977, p. 44) has this comment to make about abrupt enlightenment: "It's quite a bit like the overnight success in show business: it's frequently preceded by years of hard work." And Philip Kapleau (1979, p. 49), author of *Zen Dawn in the West*, writes, "Strictly speaking, every kind of awakening is sudden in the sense that it occurs abruptly, like water coming to a boil; what is 'gradual' is the long training that usually precedes it."

OUT-OF-BODY EXPERIENCES: STAR ROVING

Jack London, the author of such classic novels as *The Call of the Wild* and *The Sea Wolf*, wrote a lesser-known novel called *The Star Rover*. In this book, the story is told of a prisoner named Darrell Standing who escapes the suffering of a straitjacket by projecting his personality out of his body. He roves to the stars and relives past lives. The book was published in 1915, which suggests that reports of out-of-body experiences have been around a long time. Of late there has been a renewed wave of interest in out-of-body experiences. Let's take a closer look at these experiences and their possible relevance to adjustment and growth.

Causes and Description

As noted above, there is nothing new about out-of-body experiences. Indeed, the word **ecstasy** is derived from Greek roots meaning literally "standing outside oneself." We sometimes also speak of "being beside oneself" and "being transported." Out-of-body experiences have been reported in various cultures and go by such names as **travelling clairvoyance** and **astral projection** (Tart, 1977).

Out-of-body experiences can be caused in various ways. One source of such experiences is a near-death encounter. A **near-death encounter** may include a state of severe shock or a temporary clinical death. A temporary clinical death takes place when a physician considers a person to be clinically dead and the same person is subsequently resuscitated. (It is possible to debate whether or not these persons were "really" dead and what we want the word *dead* to mean.) Out-of-body experiences caused by near-death experiences have a spontaneous quality; they are uninvited and often quite a surprise to the individual who has one of them. An example of such an out-of-body experience is described by physician Raymond A. Moody (1975):

A man is dying and, as he reaches the point of greatest physical distress, he hears himself pronounced dead by his doctor. He begins to hear an uncomfortable noise, a loud ringing or buzzing, and at the same time feels himself moving very rapidly through a long tunnel. After this, he suddenly finds himself outside of his own physical body, but still in the immediate physical environment, and he sees his own body from a distance, as though he is a spectator. He watches the resuscitation attempt from this unusual vantage point and is in a state of emotional upheaval.

After a while, he collects himself and becomes more accustomed to his odd condition. He notices that he still has a "body," but one of a very different nature and with very different powers from the physical body he has left behind. Soon other things begin to happen. Others come to meet and to help him. He glimpses the spirits of relatives and friends who have already died, and a loving warm spirit of a kind he has never encountered before—a being of light—appears before him. This being asks him a question, nonverbally, to make him evaluate his life and helps him along by showing him a panoramic, instantaneous playback of the major events of his life. . . (pp. 21–22)

A second source of out-of-body experiences is the mystic tradition. Techniques such as meditation or other methods designed to induce an altered state of consciousness can sometimes cause an out-of-body experience. Robert S. de Ropp (1979), a biochemist who has spent many years studying the teachings of mystics, describes one of his own out-of-body experiences while reclining at night on a beach in California:

Ascending out of the body I rose on the bird of time above the Californian shore. Reflected light, bouncing off the moon, illuminated the earth. On such trips I became aware of my body lying there by the beach, a speck no bigger than a grain of sand. Sometimes the bird of time journeyed so far that I wondered if I would be able to return. What would happen to my speck of a body without the "I am"? But there was a thread like the string of a kite between me and the body, and always it wound me back. (p. 388)

Charles T. Tart (1978), a psychologist interested in paranormal phenomena, identifies five characteristics of out-of-body experiences. He writes:

The typical experience usually contains some combination of the following elements: (1) floating; (2) seeing one's physical body from the outside; (3) thinking of a distant place while "outside" and suddenly finding oneself there; (4) possessing a nonphysical body; and (5) being absolutely convinced that the experience was not a dream. (p. 134)

You will recall that the yogi believes that the astral body, a "second" body made of a finer matter than the ordinary body, can travel in higher dimensional planes. This belief corresponds to Tart's item 4. There seems to be no question that out-of-body experiences are, under certain conditions, common enough. Now these questions arise: What do they mean? How can we explain them? The two questions are, as we will see, closely related.

Meaning and Explanation

Like the experience of *samadhi* in yoga or *satori* in Zen, an out-of-body experience is transpersonal in nature. The individual seems to be closer in some way to nature or the universe. The barrier between the ego and the external world is to some extent overcome. This enlarged view of existence seems to give many a sense of comfort, a feeling of being "at home" in the universe. For many, out-of-body experiences reinforce a belief in the survival of the soul after biological death, and this adds to their feelings that life has meaning, purpose, and continuity. As Frankl notes (see Chapter 7), the conviction that life has meaning is an antidote to despair and demoralization. So, in some cases, people who have had out-of-body experiences feel that life is imbued with greater richness.

There are two principal ways to explain out-of-body experiences, and they affect the meaning we attach to such experiences. The first principal way is **dualism**, the view that a human being is made up of a body and a soul. Dualism is an ancient and venerated principle in both philosophy and orthodox religion. For example, the Greek philosopher Plato postulated the dual nature of human existence more than two thousand years ago. If there is in fact both a body and a soul, there is some plausibility to the idea that the soul can leave the body under certain conditions and also survive the body's biological death.

The second principal way to explain out-of-body experiences is through **scientific rationalism**, the view that all events and experiences are part of the natural world. According to scientific rationalism, out-of-body experiences are essentially kinds of hallucinatory phenomena, perceptual illusions created by an altered state of consciousness. To the scientific rationalist, an out-of-body experience is important in that it has a kind of subjective or personal reality; but it has no objective or external reality.

Believers in the objective reality of out-of-body experiences assert that the individual can perceive events in a remote location from the body. If this is so, it would tend to support the position of dualism. However, Andrew Neher (1980), a psychologist who has conducted research on the physiology of altered states of consciousness, says, "studies have found that the vast majority of subjects cannot perceive events in a distant place during an out-of-body experience, even though they feel certain they are doing so." Thus research on one aspect of out-of-body experiences seems to support the viewpoint of scientific rationalism.

The significance of out-of-body experiences is quite profound if one accepts dualism and mysticism. Such experiences add to and deepen the sense of meaning in existence. On the other hand, the significance of out-of-body experiences from the viewpoint of scientific rationalism is that they are a kind of psychological defense mechanism against the feeling that life has no meaning or that death brings oblivion. In either case, out-of-body experiences are of considerable interest and merit further study.

Tart (1978, p. 150) notes that out-of-body experiences "are not mysterious happenings beyond the pale of scientific investigation. With a proper respect for the phenomena and the persons who experience the phenomena, the advantages of scientific investigation can be gained, adding a valuable facet to our quest for understanding the nature of man."

In brief, out-of-body experiences involve such sensations as floating and seeing one's physical body from the outside. One source of such experiences is a near-death encounter. A second source of out-of-body experiences is the mystic tradition: techniques such as meditation or other methods designed to induce an altered state of consciousness can sometimes cause an out-of-body experience. The two principal ways to explain out-of-body experiences are *dualism* and *scientific rationalism*. An out-of-body experience is transpersonal in nature, making the individual seem to be closer in some way to nature or the universe.

CRITIQUE

There are few domains of psychological investigation that evoke more passionate claims and counterclaims than transpersonal psychology. Speaking of "Eastern science" in *The Psychology of Consciousness*, Ornstein (1972) comments, "there is no other area of human experience, save perhaps sexuality, about which so much garbage has been written" (p. 116). And Ornstein tends to be favorably disposed toward transpersonal psychology! Let us survey a few of the reservations that may be expressed about the field of transpersonal psychology.

1. Faultfinders readily level many put-downs of transpersonal psychology. It is accused of being replete with fuzzy thinking, useless ideas, and idle speculation. It is said that the transpersonal approach is based on personal experience not amenable to the experimental method, that the transpersonal approach is hostile to Western science and its research methods. It is feared by some that transpersonal psychology represents the potential destruction of all that academic psychology has worked so hard for—objectivity in behavioral study.

2. Censurers of the transpersonal approach can become particularly vocal when they speak of the claims made in favor of paranormal phenomena such as extrasensory perception or psychokinesis. These "abilities" are seen as absurd. The censurer claims that there is really no hard evidence in favor of psychic powers. There are only colorful anecdotes and experiments of doubtful validity.

3. The skeptic takes a negative view of the claim made by mystics that their minds penetrate past the world of appearances and arrive at a perception of the True Reality. To the skeptic, mystical experiences are hallucinatory phenomena similar to those experienced during sensory deprivation. The doctrine of **empiricism**, a key doctrine in Western philosophy and science, states that we can know about the world only through our sense organs. The mystical approach and the empirical approach are highly incompatible.

4. The orthodox thinker says that transpersonal psychology tends to take the individual away from involvement with the world. If the view that everything is maya is taken to its logical conclusion, then life as we know it is a mere illusion and, in consequence, rather meaningless. Even loving one's spouse or one's child are maya. For some, the Eastern view would seem to make of life a cruel joke. The view that all experience is maya is said to be reminiscent of the thinking of certain demoralized early existential philosophers who saw everything as absurd and unreal.

5. Looking at the negative side of Yoga, its goal of **samadhi**, the identification of mind with Supreme Consciousness, hardly seems to be a worthwhile end in and of itself. If the person who "trips out" does not bring something back of value for others, it merely seems that superconsciousness is a form of self-indulgence. There are yogis who spend several hours a day in an ecstatic state, and one wonders if they are not "hooked" on *samadhi* somewhat like drug users might be addicted to a particular drug. It is true that the Yoga tradition warns against the misuse of *samadhi*. Nonetheless, it would appear that for some the warning is not enough.

6. Cynics note that much of what esoteric disciplines have to say is known to Western science in different language. They take the attitude that there really isn't much that is new beneath the sun. Students of experimental psychology and perception know the psychological world is our construction. The philosophy of modern science teaches that so-called things or perceptual objects are space-time events. (Recall that this point was also made by Korzybski, as noted in Chapter 4.) Maslow, Rogers, Perls, and others—like Zen—speak in favor of spontaneous behavior. Thus the cynic may yawn on hearing the ideas of transpersonal psychology and ask, "So what else is new?"

7. Zen says that concepts represent maya. Yet Zen cannot do without concepts itself. Against dualism, it nonetheless sets up its own dualisms, such as the enlightened versus the unenlightened person. If dualisms are arbitrary, then there are just persons—neither enlightened nor unenlightened. If you were to challenge a Zen master with this observation, he might smile and answer, "You are right." But if this is so, there is nothing to seek because the division between the *satori* experience and ordinary perception is also arbitrary. "Quite so," the Zen master might agree. And you are nowhere—like a dog chasing its own tail. This sense-nonsense approach of Zen leaves many

an initial enthusiast in a totally baffled state. The critic of Zen feels that a philosophy that purports to be down to Earth and back to Nature should be direct and unequivocal. Zen seems to lack the very attributes it claims to have.

8. Advocates of transpersonal psychology often seem to smugly act as if "we know something you don't know." They frequently appear to be playing the game of "Mine is better than yours." Pretentious posturing plays no role of value in human adjustment and personal growth and reduces transpersonal psychology to a fad. The superficial cultist may use transpersonal psychology as a put-down of the way people in the Western world traditionally think and behave. This is more a criticism of the way some people respond to transpersonal psychology than it is a criticism of transpersonal psychology itself. The venerable traditions of such disciplines as Yoga and Zen would appear to deserve better than the vapid attention of dilettantes.

In brief, at one end of the pole is the tough-minded psychologist with an anti-intuitive and proanalytical stance. At the other end of the pole is the tender-minded thinker with a pro-intuitive and antianalytical stance, declaiming in favor of transpersonal psychology. It is difficult to reconcile the two stances in a meaningful way. Nonetheless, some meeting of the minds, some type of compromise is necessary between the two orientations. What is needed is balance, not blind enthusiasm for, or categorical rejection of, transpersonal psychology.

In a hard world of physical danger, disease, war, overpopulation, and other maladies, transpersonal psychology is at once the oldest and the newest star on the psychological horizon. It represents the reappearance, in the Western world, of the star of mental science. In a hard world, perhaps there is a place for unorthodox/subjective "soft" transpersonal psychology.

SUMMARY

1. Transpersonal psychology represents a blend of Eastern philosophy, esoteric knowledge, and Western psychology.
2. Transpersonal psychology is sometimes called a "Fourth Force" in psychology.
3. A **mystic** is a person who believes that through the use of intuition he or she can have a direct experience with Ultimate Reality.
4. The first major figure in modern psychology to recommend a transpersonal approach was Carl Jung.
5. The *Journal of Transpersonal Psychology* identifies some of its concerns as metaneeds, ultimate values, unitive consciousness, ecstasy, mystical experience, bliss, transcendence of the self, oneness, and cosmic awareness.
6. The doctrine of **maya** says that the world we experience is our mental construction, not reality itself.

7. A distinction is made in the Castaneda books between **ordinary reality** and **nonordinary reality**.

8. The exercise of what don Juan refers to as **controlled folly** requires that one shift one's attention beyond the immediate event.

9. The term **phenomenal world** is used to refer to the world as perceived.

10. The Tanner-Swets theory of visual detection suggests that perception can be altered by motives and expectancies.

11. The aim of Yoga is to carry the person beyond maya into a perfect union with the All.

12. The textbook identifies five basic kinds of Yoga: (1) **Raja Yoga**, (2) **Jnana Yoga**, (3) **Karma Yoga**, (4) **Bhakti Yoga**, and (5)**Hatha Yoga**.

13. The **chakras** are said to be wheellike patterns of energy located at various places in the body.

14. **Samadhi** is the supreme goal of Yogic training. Phrases such as "torrential bliss," "blessed experience," and "ecstatic union" are used to describe *samadhi*.

15. Yoga takes paranormal phenomena for granted.

16. The research on paranormal phenomena is extremely difficult to evaluate objectively.

17. A prime goal of Zen is to see into one's own nature.

18. The **Tao** is the Way, the Master Way, of existence. Like a great river, it carries everything along in its forceful flow.

19. One of the roots of Zen is the set of Four Noble Truths proposed by Chinese Buddhism.

20. Zen has a great mistrust of abstract thinking, the forte of the Western rational mind.

21. Suzuki summarizes the world view of the Western mind with such words as analytical, discriminative, differential, inductive, and so forth. The world view of Zen is described as synthetic, totalizing, integrative, nondiscriminative, and so forth.

22. The textbook identifies three principles of Zen: (1) nothingness, (2) no-twoness, and (3) no-mind.

23. **Satori** may be thought of as a sudden awakening in which the spell of maya is cast off.

24. There are two principal modes of inducing *satori*. The first mode is advocated by the Soto school of Zen, which advocates a gradual approach to *satori*. The other principal mode of inducing *satori* is advocated by the Rinzai school of Zen, which emphasizes the use of the koan.

25. The **koan** is a paradoxical question designed to create a psychological double bind.

26. The **enlightened person**, according to Zen, has overcome the opposites of success and failure.

27. The word **ecstasy** is derived from Greek roots meaning literally "standing outside oneself."

28. **Out-of-body experiences** have been reported in various cultures and go by such names as **travelling clairvoyance** and **astral projection**.

29. One source of out-of-body experiences is a **near-death encounter**. A second source of out-of-body experiences is the mystic tradition.

30. The two principal ways to explain out-of-body experiences are **dualism** and **scientific rationalism**.

31. An out-of-body experience is transpersonal in nature, often making the individual seem to be closer in some way to nature or the universe.

Applied Exploration

MEDITATION: THE SERENE MIND

In both the Yoga and the Zen traditions, meditation plays a key role. In Yoga, meditation is used to achieve *samadhi*. In Zen, meditation is used to achieve *satori*. In both cases, meditation is used as a tool to break through the veil of maya. Behind maya is presumed to reside the domain of reality itself as opposed to the world of appearances. The goal of meditation is to gain at least temporary entry into the domain of reality itself. In *Meditation*, Watts (1974) writes:

The art of meditation is a way of getting into touch with reality. And the reason for meditation is that most civilized people are out of touch with reality. They confuse the world as it is with the world as they think about it, talk about it, and describe it. For on the one hand there is the real world and on the other a whole system of symbols about that world which we have in our minds. These are very, very useful symbols; all civilization depends on them. But like all good things, they have their disadvantages, and the principal disadvantage of symbols is that we confuse them with reality in the same way as we confuse money with actual wealth, and our names, ideas, and images of ourselves with ourselves. (p. 5)

Roger N. Walsh and Frances Vaughan (1980, p. 136), editors of *Beyond Ego*, a book of articles on transpersonal dimensions in psychology, say, "Basically, meditation can be described as any discipline that aims at enhancing awareness through the conscious directing of attention."

For centuries, human beings have sought ways of finding islands of serenity in the often stormy sea of human existence. Advocates of meditation claim that it can momentarily lift its practitioner out of the mundane world of everyday affairs to a calm place in his or her own mind, a place that has always been there but has been undiscovered. When the meditator "returns"

For centuries, human beings have sought ways of finding islands of serenity in the often stormy sea of human existence.

to the world, the person returns with a more serene mind. It is claimed that, as a consequence, he or she functions more efficiently than the average person.

Advocates of meditation cite research indicating that it may be of substantial benefit in the treatment of stress-induced, or "psychosomatic" diseases (Benson, 1979; Pelletier, 1979). This point was touched on briefly in the Applied Exploration at the end of Chapter 6, "Behavioral Medicine." You will also recall that it has been asserted by some investigators that the meditative techniques associated with Yoga may facilitate learning (Ostrander, Schroeder, & Ostrander, 1979). Thus the potential practical applications of meditation are quite large in scope.

Kinds of Meditation

There is more than one kind of meditation. I will specify four types. But before I deal with specifics, let me make the general observation that there is a common thread running through all the modes of meditation: **concentration**, the focusing of one's attention on a limited range of stimuli. In *The Psychology of Consciousness*, psychologist Robert Ornstein (1972) notes that meditators often refer to the successful achievement of the focusing of attention as "one-pointedness of mind" (p. 125).

The four kinds of meditation that will be reviewed are (1) intellect-oriented meditation, (2) feeling-oriented meditation, (3) body-oriented meditation, and (4) action-oriented meditation. The four types are adapted from *How to Meditate* by psychologist Lawrence LeShan (1974). It should be understood that the four kinds of meditation are not mutually exclusive and that they overlap to a large degree.

Intellect-oriented Meditation   In intellect-oriented meditation, the meditator gives attention to something that stimulates or challenges thinking capacities. The Zen *koan* provides a classic example. But isn't this paradoxical? Isn't the aim of Zen meditation to reach a state of *satori*, a no-mind state beyond the intellect and abstract thinking? "Of course," agrees the Zen master. "However, we use thought to annihilate thought. We use concepts to destroy concepts." It is much like fighting fire with fire.

Another example of intellect-oriented meditation is the approach of the Indian sage J. Krishnamurti. In one of his books, *Think on These Things*, Krishnamurti (1964) provides a list of more than one hundred thought-provoking questions at the back of the book. Examples are:

It is true that society is based on acquisitiveness and ambition; but if we had no ambition would we not decay?

Discontent prevents clear thinking. How are we to overcome this obstacle?

Why do we want to live in luxury?

It is presumed that by sincerely pondering these and similar questions at length, the meditator will find himself becoming progressively illuminated about his relationship to existence. This illumination will empty the mind of arbitrary conceptual content and bring about a state that Krishnamurti calls the **silent mind**, an aware state in which one watches thoughts flow through the conscious mind without discriminating "between them in terms of value, importance, or rightness." (Holroyd, 1980, p. 53)

Feeling-oriented Meditation   In feeling-oriented meditation, the meditator gives attention to an emotion-laden symbol. Traditionally, the symbol has usually been one with religious associations. For example, a Christian might meditate on the Holy Cross and its personal meaning. A member of an Eastern religion might meditate on a *mandala*, a venerated circular pattern. Or one might meditate on a *mantra*, a sacred word or chant. The symbol acts as a focusing device for one's attention. As attention wanders, the meditator brings it back to the symbol. This kind of meditation, feeling-oriented meditation, is the one most usually associated with states of bliss, such as *samadhi*.

Transcendental meditation, discussed later, is derived from the feeling-oriented meditation in which a mantra is used.

Body-oriented Meditation   In body-oriented meditation, the meditator usually gives attention to an autonomic process. For example, one may count breaths, focus on pulse rate, or concentrate on the position of one's body. Hatha Yoga is a form of body-oriented meditation. Body-oriented meditation, like any of the varieties of meditation, may lead an individual to an altered state of consciousness. In addition, body-oriented mediation may lead the individual to acquire greater self-control over autonomic processes—the kind of self-control aimed at by biofeedback training.

Action-oriented Meditation   In action-oriented meditation, the meditator concentrates attention on a behavior pattern. *Tai Chi Chuan* provides one example of action-oriented meditation. A Chinese art, it requires that the individual perform a habitual movement consciously and deliberately. To illustrate, instead of just lifting one's arms over one's head, the meditator might lift them in slow motion, thus augmenting a sense of behavioral awareness. This is clearly another way of reclaiming for the voluntary domain that which has been "lost" in the involuntary domain.

Another example of action-oriented meditation is provided by the Zen tradition. In *Method of Zen*, Eugen Herrigel (1960), a European student of Zen, writes:

It is astonishing and, for the European, almost inconceivable how much time the Japanese spend in restraining and controlling gestures which can at most be regarded as aesthetic faults. Say someone slams the door in a temper. In the East this is not taken as the expression of a forceful personality, nor is it regarded as a lapse which should not be taken seriously. Anyone who does such a thing will not, like the European, deem it justified by the situation, or excuse himself by saying that his feelings ran away with him. He will go back to the door, open it, close it softly, and say to it: "I beg your pardon." Thereafter he will take care how he shuts doors. (p. 32)

The theme of concentration on actions is similarly reflected in Zen archery, swordsmanship, flower arranging, painting, and the Japanese tea ceremony. All these represent different aspects of action-oriented meditation.

Transcendental Meditation

As already noted, transcendental meditation (TM) is derived from feeling-oriented meditation in which a mantra, a sacred word or chant, is used. TM, a Yogic technique, was brought to the widespread attention of Americans by the Maharishi Mahesh Yogi. Adam Smith (1975), author of *Powers of Mind* says (1975, p. 126), "Transcendental Meditation is the McDonald's of the meditation business." It is estimated that about one million people have learned the TM technique (Bloomfield & Kory, 1978). There is a Maharishi International University in Iowa. And the Students International Meditation Society (SIMS) has been active on college campuses.

No less an authority than Hans Selye, a pioneer researcher on stress-induced diseases, wrote an approving foreword to the best-selling *Transcendental Meditation: Discovering Inner Energy and Overcoming Stress* by physician Harold Bloomfield and two co-authors, Michael Cain and Dennis Jaffe (1975). Selye concludes his foreword with this enthusiastic endorsement of TM:

In all, I feel that TM will enjoy immediate success and offer the general public a most effective explanation of how pure awareness and creative intelligence, combined with what medical science has taught us about the bodily effects of stress, can help humanity face "the crisis of modern life." (p. xii)

What happens during transcendental meditation? The authors of *Transcendental Meditation* answer the question thus:

A person allows his mind to experience a relaxed and enjoyable state which draws his attention inward. He experiences a state in which the mind becomes very quiet, but extraordinarily alert. Though sense impressions, feelings or thought may be present during TM, meditators report brief or sometimes extended periods of "blank awareness," "being awake inside with nothing going on," "not being asleep, but not being aware of anything in particular." . . . When a meditator allows his attention to shift inward, he experiences quiet levels of the mind in which he becomes increasingly aware of the unbounded nature of his awareness in the absence of objects. This state, which will be termed pure awareness, consists of nothing more than being wide awake inside without being aware of anything except awareness itself. (p. 11)

The state referred to as pure awareness is induced by mentally reciting a mantra, usually in rhythm with one's normal breathing. The mantra acts as a focusing device, aiding concentration. As the meditator repeats the mantra, his attention will drift from it. He is instructed to gently bring his wandering attention back to the mantra. An analogy may be made by taking a child for a walk in the park. The child will stray from the main path, running toward the swings, chasing a butterfly, and so forth. The understanding adult will return the child to the main path without anger or force. Similarly, as the attention wanders from the mantra, the meditator, without anger or force, simply returns his attention to the mantra. In anywhere from five to fifteen minutes, the meditator will begin to experience "pure awareness."

TM is usually practiced twice a day for ten to twenty minutes per session almost anywhere; in a bus station, in a waiting room, riding on a train, and so forth. The state described as pure awareness is induced more easily with practice. The experienced meditator slips into it rather easily. Being basically alert and awake, the practitioner of TM can come out of the state easily and at will. TM is an altered state of consciousness, but it is not sleep. This point is elaborated later.

Advocates of TM detach it from any philosophical, theological, or religious overtones. The assertion is that one can practice TM whatever one's world view. It does not contradict any dogma or the teachings of any religious organization. Thus TM enthusiasts say it can be practiced by anyone and have beneficial results. Members of SIMS see TM as a gift from the East, a gift that can free its recipients from stress-induced diseases. It is also asserted that the beneficial effects of TM will in the long run free many persons from a dependence on such drugs as antihypertensive agents and antianxiety agents.

Teachers of TM associated with the Maharishi's movement warn against learning TM from a book without the assistance of a qualified guide. It is asserted that a suitable mantra cannot be personally selected by the novice. The "vibrations" may not be right for the particular individual and may have an adverse effect on his or her nervous system. Others argue that this is a dubious contention and that almost any pleasant word or sentence can be used as a mantra. In any case, large numbers of people are practicing some version of TM. It behooves us to ask: To what extent are the TM claims valid? Let us now explore the answer to this question.

The Relaxation Response

The principal value claimed for TM is that it helps to combat stress-induced, or "psychosomatic," diseases. The argument is that the complexities of modern civilization produce psychological conflicts that result in nervous tension, anxiety, chronic anger, and so forth. It is presumed that these primitive reactions often have no adequate outlet. Unreleased, the person suffers. In the following statement taken from Smith's *Powers of Mind* (1975), he speaks of *pterodactyls*, flying reptiles that existed during the Mesozoic era. He makes the reference as a loose metaphor to suggest that our forebears faced various dangers we do not face. But we are still programmed with their primitive fight-or-flight reactions. In a modern setting, in the absence of a clear physical danger, the primitive internal mechanism can cause trouble:

Minds. The trouble is minds, not organic medicine, not some germ that comes flying through the air looking for a home. This is Dr. Hans Selye, sixty-eight years old, the distinguished dean of stress medicine. Stress is "a physiologic response inappropriate to the situation." Misfired signals between mind and body. The physiologic response is the caveman's response when the shadow of a pterodactyl falls over him. Adrenal secretions increase and muscles tense and the coagulation chemistry gets ready to resist wounds. Fight or flight. But what pterodactyl is this? They tell you: the market is down twenty points, or the vice-president wants to see you, or, the whole operation is going to be shut down and moved to Chicago. Blam, pterodactyl time. Gives you, says Dr. Selye, headaches, insomnia, high blood pressure, sinus, ulcers, rheumatism, cardiovascular and kidney disease. And more. (p. 5)

Does TM give relief from the adverse effects of the primitive fight-or-flight reaction? The question has been studied by Herbert Benson, associate professor of medicine at the Harvard Medical School, and his answer is a qualified yes. TM does seem to have beneficial effects. It appears to unlock a mechanism Benson (1975) calls the **relaxation response**, an innate pattern that is antagonistic to the fight-or-flight reaction. By calling up the relaxation response, the individual to some degree neutralizes the effects of the primitive fight-or-flight reaction.

Benson's research clearly suggests that TM is not sleep. During sleep, oxygen consumption falls about 8 percent below normal, and it requires about four or five hours to reach this stage. During meditation, oxygen consumption falls from 10 to 20 percent, and this tends to occur within the first three minutes of meditation. Another difference between sleep and meditation noted by Benson is that alpha waves increase during meditation but are not associated with sleep. Alpha waves seem to be associated with alert relaxation. The finding that meditators produce a large percentage of alpha waves lends further credence to the TM claims. Benson also notes that blood lactate decreases during meditation. This is considered significant because it is purported that a high level of blood lactate is associated with anxiety. Sleep, notes Benson, is not meditation; and meditation is not sleep. The one cannot replace the other. Each has a different function and a different value.

Benson is not, however, particularly enchanted with the rituals associated with TM. He has had persons meditate on the word *one*, selected arbitrarily, and has found the same physiological changes as those produced by persons meditating upon a mantra especially selected for them by a TM trainer. Benson feels that his laboratory research has simply validated age-old wisdom, that it has produced no innovations in and of itself. Stripping the relaxation response of any religious, cultic, or mystical associations, Benson says that four conditions are helpful in bringing forth the relaxation response: (1) a quiet environment; (2) a mental device, used to shift one's attention to a constant stimulus; (3) a passive attitude, an attitude in which one "lets" relaxation happen rather than "makes" it happen; and (4) a comfortable position.

Benson warns that although a little meditation may be beneficial, a lot of meditation may be harmful. Excessive elicitation of the relaxation response for prolonged periods of time may produce hallucinations similar to those experienced during sensory deprivation. Such adverse side effects do not seem to occur, says Benson, among those who meditate for ten or twenty minutes at a time twice a day.

Benson asserts in his book *The Relaxation Response* (1975) that the relaxation response is a natural gift, that anyone can turn it on and use it. He concludes, "We could all greatly benefit by the reincorporation of the Relaxation Response into our daily lives. At the present time, most of us are simply not making use of this remarkable, innate, neglected asset" (p. 125). Benson (1979) indicates that regular elicitation of the relaxation response can help to alleviate symptoms associated with excessive anxiety and may be beneficial in the lowering of high blood pressure.

Briefly, meditation is an ancient technique. Its practitioners have variously claimed that it is a tool for achieving *samadhi*, *satori*, and serenity. There are several kinds of meditation. All of them, however, require concentration and the focusing of attention on a limited range of stimuli. Through meditation it appears possible to call forth an innate relaxation response. The relaxation response appears to be antagonistic to the fight-or-flight reaction and, as such, may be useful in combating stress-induced diseases.

Is there a Royal Road to better living?

Chapter 9

SYNTHESIS: IS THERE A PATHWAY OF PATHWAYS?

Overview

OUTLINE

Is there a pathway of pathways leading to greater adjustment and personal growth? **Systematic thinkers**, advocates of one particular school of thought, answer yes. The Royal Road to better living is the one that they speak and write about. On the other hand, there are **eclectic thinkers**, represented in psychology by those who pick and choose from various schools of thought those conceptions that seem of particular value. The eclectic psychologist does not completely reject or embrace any one mode of thinking about adjustment and growth. Although the majority of psychologists are somewhat dissatisfied with eclecticism, they feel that it is the only realistic stance to take toward a field that is as profuse with ideas as psychology. Thus the consensus statement of contemporary psychology is: No, there is no single pathway that is the pathway leading toward greater adjustment and personal growth.

Eclecticism has much to recommend it. But it also has its pitfalls. Psychologists Ernest Hilgard and Gordon Bower (1966, p. 13) warn that if opposing points of view are presented as equally plausible, a choice between them may seem to be completely arbitrary. They note that a person may fall into a vapid eclecticism, relying on the general formula "There's much to be said on all sides." The desire to avoid a vapid eclecticism is contained in the following statement by N. H. Pronko (1980, p. iv), a psychologist with a behavioral orientation: "As for my own position, I rejected from the outset a neutral eclecticism that attempts to organize incompatible or contradictory theories into a seemingly coherent system." Warnings against a vapid or neutral eclectism have merit.

On the other hand, the choice is not between being systematic or eclectic. A *dynamic*, as opposed to vapid, eclecticism is possible. The individual may have strong leanings, personal preferences, and biases and still be generally eclectic in his or her approach to psychology. There is room for passion and conviction within an eclectic position. An illustration of how a psychologist can have a dynamic eclectic orientation is provided in an autobiographical sketch by Paul T. Young (1972), one of the deans of American psychology:

In the current social unrest and turmoil over problems of war and peace, exploding populations, poverty, pollution of the environment, crime and violence, revolution, and others, I am sure that one must view human nature as it actually is—partly rational, partly emotional, partly dominated by habit, partly spiritual. . . . My approach to behavioral problems has been eclectic and multi-disciplinary. (p. 352)

Young clearly identifies himself as an eclectic, but he is not bland in his approach to psychology. He was the winner of the Distinguished Scientific Contribution Award of the American Psychological Association in 1965, and he expresses strong biases:

I have never abandoned the concept of consciousness. I continue to believe that the science of psychology has a unique responsibility to analyze and interpret subjective phenomena such as perceptions, mental images, the experiences of memory and thought, the awareness of feelings, and emotions. (p. 339)

Like Young, as you survey the seven pathways toward adjustment and growth discussed in this book, you need not fall into a vapid eclecticism. In terms of you, the individual, all approaches are not equally valid. One approach will click for you; another approach will leave you cold. It is natural to have preferences for one way of thinking over another. Only by following the conceptions that directly appeal to you will you be able to usefully employ those conceptions. As already noted, the eclectic position does not completely reject or embrace any one approach. Nonetheless, differences in emphasis, in which one approach is greatly favored over another, are possible.

RECURRENT ADJUSTMENT-GROWTH ISSUES

Although an eclectic orientation recognizes the valid distinctions among the seven pathways discussed in this book, it should be noted that the pathways crisscross, overlap, and are not totally distinct from each other. Psychologists representing different schools of thought often say similar things with different words. Freud's id, Berne's Child, and Perl's underdog are similar concepts. Assertiveness training in behavioral psychology is similar to the concept of authentic living, or "being real," in existential-humanistic psychology. Korzybski's view of "things" as space-time events is paralleled in the Zen principle of no-thingness. Many other specific parallels could be easily drawn. But let us draw away from specific parallels.

Let us, instead, take a giant step backward so that we can view the pathways as if from a great distance. Details now fade, but broad general patterns emerge. We see that there are certain recurrent adjustment-growth issues, issues that cut across all the pathways. Like two-edged swords, the issues tend to present themselves as pairs of opposites: (1) freedom versus determinism, (2) unconscious versus conscious, (3) motives and habits versus thought and will, and (4) group similarities versus individual differences. The issues will be briefly sketched and then a unifying statement will be made.

Freedom versus Determinism

The philosophy of **determinism** asserts that all behavior is caused. It is caused by genetic factors, motives, learned responses, or some other specifiable source. This orientation does not allow for human freedom. If accepted, determinism relieves individuals of Ultimate Responsibility for their lives. They did not choose their genetic structure, biological drives, conditioning experiences, situation of life, and so forth. They are the "victim" of forces beyond their control. In contrast, the opposing orientation, known as **voluntarism**, asserts that free will is a reality, that we can make real choices, and that we are not the pawns of fate.

Unconscious versus Conscious

A powerful and influential contention is that our behavior is determined largely by unconscious mental processes. Psychoanalysis amplified this contention and made it into the keystone of its system. In view of the fact that for a number of years psychoanalysis dominated the psychological landscape along with behaviorism, the significance of unconscious factors cannot be dismissed lightly. The counterorientation is the contention that consciousness is both real and powerful and that its reality and power make a difference. This second view finds its strongest expression in cognitive psychology and existential-humanistic psychology.

Motives and Habits versus Thought and Will

The two great "mechanical" forces underlying human behavior are motives and habits. They are mechanical in that they represent both involuntary and automatic action. Our basic drives are said to arise from deep sources within ourselves. These are our primary motives. Our secondary drives, or learned motives, are acquired by conditioning. Many of our behaviors are also acquired by conditioning and are said to be habits. Also, our perceptions of the world are colored by our motives and our habits. We would seem to be "locked in" to a fixed set of behaviors by the two giant processes of motivation and learning.

Determinism asserts that all behavior is caused. In contrast, voluntarism asserts that free will is a reality, that we are not the pawns of fate.

Although motivation and learning are accepted as significant processes, two opposing conceptions are often brought forth as principal counterprocesses: thinking and willing. It is said that we can think, that we have the capacity to reflect, to analyze, and to solve problems. For example, psychologists favorably disposed to cognitive psychology assert that thought to some degree can modify the impact of motives and habits. It is also said that we can will; that we are not only driven creatures, but that we can at least sometimes be driving human beings. Existential-humanistic psychologists expound this point of view. (As noted in Chapter 7, the "driving" example was given by Rollo May.)

Group Similarities versus Individual Differences

Systematic thinkers tend to favor the view that the similarities among individuals are more important than the differences among them. This view tends to "swamp out" the particular person. The person's idiosyncrasies, interests, specific talents, and unique potentialities are reduced to "error variance" in an experiment. The grand goal is to organize data into parsimonious theoretical statements. The living individual, seeking information about adjustment and growth, often cares little for the elegant theories of the systematist, however. This individual is looking for practical information that will help the person cope with problems and deal effectively with the challenges of life. Thus he or she is attracted to views that assert that individual differences are more important than the similarities among individuals. The person wants to know what is applicable to his or her particular life situation, and tends to be favorably disposed to views that respect his or her unique personhood.

A Unifying Statement

Pairs of opposites such as the ones presented in the previous pages are not easily reconciled. They represent broad points of view, not scientifically testable hypotheses. And because they are recurrent issues, we are probably best off if we learn to live with the tension of their bipolarity. It is an old observation that opposing conceptions define each other. Alan Watts (1974) says in *Meditation*, "I have a friend who was born blind. She has no idea what darkness is" (p. 49).

Ancient Eastern philosophy understands pairs of conceptual opposites in terms of **yin** and **yang**, the negative and positive aspects of the world (see Figure 9.1). Such dualities as right and wrong, light and darkness, and good and bad are not seen as realities in themselves, but as the products of the thinking-perceiving process. Similarly, pairs of opposites, such as determinism versus freedom, can be seen as contrasts instead of mutually exclusive agents. This is a difficult model to accept. We are well trained in either-or

FIGURE 9.1 Ancient Eastern philosophy understands pairs of conceptual opposites in terms of yin and yang.

thinking, and it would seem that a choice must be made. But it is well to remind ourselves that we are merely striving to make a choice among *concepts*, ways we imagine reality to be, not reality itself. This point is as ancient as the writings of Lao-tzu and as contemporary as the modern philosophy of science. Let us now elaborate this last point.

OF TRUTH AND MODELS

The modern philosophy of science teaches that our various scientific theories are not Truth. They could be Truth only if each one was reality itself. They are statements about reality. Thus they have the status of conceptions. That is why contradictory conceptions can stand for centuries—they are each a glimpse from a particular angle of whatever reality "is." This last point is implicit in Plato's allegory of the cave (Chapter 8), in general semantics, in Kantian philosophy, in the doctrine of empiricism, in the yin and yang of Eastern philosophy, in the doctrine of maya, and in the experimental study of perception. This is why, although we may yearn for the one True Pathway toward a better life, we must content ourselves with the lesser achievement of finding incomplete and sometimes contradictory pathways. We grasp reality not directly, but through our conceptions about it. Our conceptions are the building blocks of what philosophers of science call "models."

Kinds of Models

What is a model? A model is something that represents the real thing. For example, a model of a jet airliner suggests to us what the actual airplane is like; but it is clearly not the airplane itself. Similarly, psychological models represent real processes, but must not themselves be confused with the actual processes. In the sciences, including psychology, three kinds of models are used: (1) physical models, (2) ordinary language models, and (3) mathematical models.

Physical Models   A physical model is made out of wood, metal, glass, or some other substance. Say that Professor Elizabeth C. brings into a psychology class a clear glass bowl. She pours water into the bowl and says, "Let the waterline represent the division between the conscious mind and the unconscious mind. The entire container and its contents represent the mind." Now she drops a few Ping-Pong balls into the container, and they float. "The floating balls are like conscious ideas." She then drops some small stones into the water, and they sink. "These are like repressed ideas." The demonstration continues. Professor C. is using a crude physical model to represent certain aspects of depth psychology. Of course, more sophisticated physical models can be built. An example of advanced physical model-building is provided by using computers to simulate processes of the central nervous system. As we watch the computer mimic nervous-system action, we may acquire new insights about actual biological processes.

Ordinary Language Models An ordinary language model is made out of words, sentences, and concepts. The "substances" that make it up are the symbols by which human communication is possible. The great danger of ordinary language models is that they do not seem to be models at all. They seem to be the Truth itself. Physical models are clearly not the things they represent. But a theory of psychology, such as psychoanalytic theory, can be widely held—even by relatively sophisticated persons—as a reality. Clear thinking demands that we recognize language models as symbolic conceptions about behavioral processes, not as the processes themselves.

The bulk of this book has been made up of elaborations on numerous ordinary language models. One of the harshest criticisms we can make of almost all the models is that they use the language of truth, implicitly suggesting that the model in question is not a model, but "the real thing." The majority of theorists do not say, "Here is a useful conception." Instead, they say, "This is the way it is." This seemingly trivial distinction is the source of endless confusion, making us feel that we have to take sides when none have to be taken.

Mathematical Models A mathematical model, like an ordinary language model, is made out of symbols. Numerals, used to represent quantities, and operators, used to manipulate sets of numerals, are the principal symbols used in mathematical models. For example, $2 + 3 = 5$ is a mathematical model. The 2, the 3, and the 5 represent quantities. They are not quantities in and of themselves, only symbols. (The underlying quantities represented by symbols are called numbers in contrast to the numerals, which are merely marks on paper.) The plus sign and the equals sign are operators. They "operate" on the numerals and transform them into other forms.

Just as ordinary words can be used to represent behavioral processes, mathematical equations can be used to mimic these same processes. A substantial amount of work has been done, for example, on mathematical models for learning. **Stochastic processes**, probability processes in which events are neither wholly dependent on nor wholly independent of past occurrences, can be elegantly represented by mathematical models. *Stochastic Models for Learning* by Robert Bush and Frederick Mosteller (1955) provides one example of how it is possible to build a mathematical model that simultaneously incorporates the contrasting concepts of determinism and voluntarism into a single formula.

Mathematical models have not played a large part in the psychology of adjustment and growth. Because they do not communicate their meanings in familiar terms, they are of little direct value to the general reader. Also, mathematical models tend to deal with a limited range of behavioral phenomena. They focus on **molecular**, or "small," behaviors as opposed to **molar**, or "big," behaviors, the wide-ranging response patterns to the problems and challenges of daily living discussed in prior chapters. Of the three kinds of models discussed in this section—physical, ordinary language, and mathematical—the one that is overwhelmingly favored as the favorite mode of presenting adjustment-growth pathways is the ordinary language model.

Allegories

Allegories are useful devices for conveying ideas in a richer form. It is all well and good to understand intellectually that ordinary language models are not the Truth, only ways of apprehending it. Nonetheless, this abstract understanding may fail to hit home in any significant way. That is why authors often turn to such devices as allegories to illustrate their meanings in more concrete form.

Perhaps the most famous allegory used to distinguish between the concepts that we have about reality and reality itself is Plato's formulation of the prisoner in the cave. The prisoner sees only shadows and takes these appearances to be the world itself. Plato's allegory was referred to in Chapter 8. Another well-known allegory used to convey essentially the same point is "The Blind Men and the Elephant" by John Godfrey Saxe:

It was six men of Indostan
To learning much inclined,
Who went to see the elephant
(Though all of them were blind),
That each by observation
Might satisfy his mind.

The First approached the elephant,
And happening to fall
Against his broad and sturdy side,
At once began to bawl:
"God bless me! But the elephant
Is nothing but a wall!"

The Second, feeling of the tusk,
Cried: "Ho! What have we here
So very round and smooth and sharp?
To me 'tis mighty clear
This wonder of an elephant
Is very like a spear!"

The Third approached the animal,
And happening to take
The squirming trunk within his hands,
This boldly up and spake;
"I see," quoth he, "The elephant
Is very like a snake!"

The Fourth reached out his eager hand,
And felt about the knee:
"What most this wondrous beast is like
Is mighty plain" quoth he;
" 'Tis clear enough the elephant
Is very like a tree."

The Fifth, who chanced to touch the ear,
Said "E'en the blindest man
Can tell what this resembles most;
Deny the fact who can,
The marvel of an elephant
Is very like a fan!"

The Sixth no sooner had begun
About the beast to grope,
Thus, seizing on the swinging tail
That fell within his scope,
"I see," quoth he, "The elephant
Is very like a rope!"

And so these men of Indostan
Disputed loud and long
Each in his own opinion
Exceeding stiff and strong
Though each was partly in the right,
*And all were in the wrong!**

Like the blind men approaching the elephant, each explorer into the domain of psychology comes with a different vision of reality depending on one's preconceptions, the quality of one's data, and the particular aspect (or aspects) of behavior one chooses to study. That is why there is no single adequate psychology of adjustment and growth, but a *set* of psychologies. Each psychology has value in its own right; none is completely correct or completely incorrect. Again, an intelligent eclecticism is demanded. The individual must pluck the best from each formulation in terms of his or her unique interests and needs.

---

*Copyright by John G. Saxe. Reprinted by permission of the publisher, Houghton Mifflin Co., New York, N.Y.

PSYCHOLOGICAL HEALTH

Chapter 1 had a section titled "When Adjustment Fails." We have come full circle now, and it is fitting for the book to close with a section on psychological health. Let us stop a moment to ponder the fact that we also approach psychological health through concepts, the mental models we construct about it in our minds. Thus one person's idea of psychological health may not square with another person's. Forewarned, let us explore some possibilities.

Informal Conceptions

In a loose sense, almost everybody "knows" what psychological health is. The problem is to articulate it. Many informal expressions exist to describe persons who have psychological health: "He's really got it all together." "She's got a clean act." "Tom is really an OK person." "Mary really understands herself." "Bill knows where he's going in life and how he's going to get there." "I've never met a happier, more optimistic person than Nancy." "Harry is a person with a lot of wisdom."

I asked students in an introductory psychology class to write brief re-

In a loose sense, we all "know" what psychological health is.

sponses to the following question: "What is your conception of psychological health?" Unedited, here are a few of the responses:

Being able to deal with life and the mental problems it can bring. Finding solutions to problems dealing in health. The state of mind can have a psychological effect on your health.

To me this means the state of mind that you're in. How well you deal with people and occurrences in the world around you. Also, how you deal with the worlds other people tend to live in. People that are in good psychological health are able to be at ease and deal well with what goes on or comes along. But those in bad psychological health are kind of lost and confused with what's happening.

How healthy one's mind is in terms of outlook on life, how he views himself and others. Being aware of the natural world and things beyond our reason. Keeping an open mind, not closed on fears, mainly of human nature. Realizing our mortality. Always striving for the "Right way to live."

It is the balance or imbalance of a person's emotional habits—how well they can adjust to certain things that happen in everyday life.

Being able to adapt yourself to life. Adjusting to your social and business pressures, etc. Functioning: no matter what the circumstances or situations.

The students who wrote those responses were not advanced psychology students. Their replies were written during their third week of instruction,

"You don't need another book about how to be happy. You _are_ happy."

Drawing by Weber; © 1981 The New Yorker Magazine, Inc.

and represent commonsense views of psychological health. As such, they are quite congruent with views of psychological health set forth by professional psychologists. Keep the student responses in mind as we turn to a more formalized presentation of the concept of psychological health.

A Unifying View

A unifying view of personality appreciates that no one attribute is the key attribute of psychological health. The human personality is complex, consisting of a set of attributes. Moreover, the set of attributes tends to take on different patterns in different individuals. It would seem reasonable to assert that there is no one unique pattern that represents psychological health. The concept of psychological health must certainly allow for individual differences in human beings. Having said this, let me—with some trepidation—abstract from the seven pathways, the major psychologies presented in this book, the implicit attributes associated with psychological health. Keep in mind that the statements listed are sweeping abstractions and, as such, will simultaneously have the advantage of great power and the disadvantage of being much too general. Psychologically healthy persons tend to manifest the following characteristics:

1. *Insight.* Healthy persons have a substantial amount of insight into their motivational structures. They are not the slaves of forbidden desires and repressed wishes. A minimum of self-deception is practiced.
2. *Positive habits.* Healthy persons are more or less free of "bad" habits. They have established a set of "good" habits. It might also be argued that healthy persons are able to modify, extinguish, or break habits when they are motivated to do so.
3. *Clear thinking.* Healthy persons have a great capacity for reality-oriented clear thinking. They are more rational than irrational, allowing for the notion that a bit of irrationality can itself be of some value for psychological health. Also, healthy persons can use their capacity for clear thinking to cope constructively with their emotions. Thus they are not at the mercy of chronic anxiety, anger, or depression.
4. *Effective communication.* Healthy persons have the ability to communicate effectively. They are able to state their desires and feelings without putting down another person. It is presumed that the capacity for effective communication is of particular importance in highly significant interpersonal relationships—those involving parents, children, husbands, wives, and close friends. Communication skills enhance the likelihood that intimacy, or emotional closeness, will emerge and endure between two persons.
5. *Physical well-being.* Healthy persons have organic as well as psychological health. The supposition is that we are organisms and that any division we might care to make between mind and body is arbitrary. It

takes a well-balanced biochemical state within the brain and nervous system to produce what people call "a healthy mind."

6. *Authentic living.* Healthy persons are, on the whole, able to lead authentic lives. They feel that they are not wasting their lives, that they are making the most of their talents and potentialities. Also, they have a well-defined sense of values. Living in terms of their values, they feel that life is meaningful and worth living. Similarly, they feel that they are in charge of their own existence, that they have the capacity to will their own behavior.

7. *Larger vision.* Healthy persons have what might be called "larger vision." They do not view their lives in small or petty terms. They see themselves as part of the grand sweep of existence. They usually have a strong identification with humankind, feeling an empathy for these famous lines by the English poet John Donne: "No man is an island, entire of himself. Every man is a piece of the continent, a part of the main."

These, then, are the attributes we may associate with psychological health as derived from the seven principal orientations toward human adjustment and personal growth presented in this book. A somewhat longer or shorter list might be presented. No pretense is made that this list is final or definitive. Indeed, you would do well to turn back to Chapter 7 and reread the list of attributes Maslow gave for self-actualizing persons. His conception of psychological health and the one presented in this chapter are similar.

We adjust to external demands and may grow as persons throughout our lives. There is no such person as the individual who is well adjusted once and for all. If such a person existed, he or she would be a robot or one of Perls's paper persons. There is, similarly, no such human being as the self-actualized person, the person who has fulfilled every talent and potentiality. There are, instead, self-actualizing people, people who keep alive the "growing tip" of their personalities. In short, adjustment and personal growth are dynamic processes.

SUMMARY

1. **Systematic thinkers** advocate one particular school of thought. **Eclectic thinkers** pick and choose from various schools of thought those conceptions that seem of particular value.

2. Eclecticism need be neither vapid nor neutral. A *dynamic* eclecticism is possible.

3. The seven pathways discussed in this book crisscross, overlap, and are not totally distinct from each other.

4. Four recurrent adjustment-growth issues are identified in the textbook. These are (1) freedom versus determinism, (2) unconscious versus conscious, (3) motives and habits versus thought and will, and (4) group similarities versus individual differences.

5. The philosophy of **determinism** asserts that all behavior is caused. In contrast, the opposing orientation, known as **voluntarism**, asserts that free will is a reality.
6. Psychoanalysis contends that our behavior is determined largely by unconscious mental processes. The counterorientation, expressed in both cognitive psychology and existential-humanistic psychology, is that consciousness is both real and powerful and that its reality and power make a difference.
7. Although motivation and learning are accepted as significant processes, two opposing conceptions are often brought forth as principal counterprocesses: thinking and willing.
8. Systematic thinkers tend to favor the view that similarities among individuals are more important than differences among them. The living individual seeking information about adjustment and growth is attracted to views that assert that individual differences are more important than group similarities.
9. Ancient Eastern philosophy understands pairs of conceptual opposites in terms of **yin** and **yang**, the negative and positive aspects of the world. Pairs of opposites can be seen as contrasts instead of mutually exclusive agents.
10. The modern philosophy of science teaches that our various scientific theories are not Truth, but statements *about* reality.
11. Our conceptions about reality are the building blocks of what philosophers of science call "models." Three kinds of models are used in science: (1) physical models, (2) ordinary language models, and (3) mathematical models.
12. A **physical model** is made out of wood, metal, glass, or some other substance.
13. An **ordinary language model** is made out of words, sentences, and concepts.
14. A **mathematical model**, like an ordinary language model, is made out of symbols. **Numerals**, used to represent quantities, and **operators**, used to manipulate sets of numerals, are the principal symbols used in mathematical models.
15. Both Plato's allegory about the prisoner in the cave and John Godrey Saxe's poem about the blind men and the elephant are used to make a distinction between the concepts that we have about reality and reality itself.
16. Almost everyone has an informal conception concerning the nature of psychological health.
17. A unifying view of personality appreciates that no one attribute is *the* key attribute of psychological health. The human personality is complex, consisting of a set of attributes. Psychologically healthy persons tend to manifest the following characteristics: (1) insight, (2) positive

habits, (3) clear thinking, (4) effective communication, (5) physical well-being, (6) authentic living, and (7) larger vision.
18.   Adjustment and personal growth are dynamic processes.

Applied Exploration

TOWARD A PHILOSOPHY OF LIFE: A PRACTICAL APPROACH

In writing this textbook I have tried, on the whole, to get out of the way. Only in a few places have I used the personal pronoun *I* in addressing you. This is proper. A textbook author has a mission different from the author of a popular psychology book. The textbook author's aim is to give a balanced and fair presentation of major viewpoints and varied findings. The popular author, on the other hand, usually seeks to show you the power of a single viewpoint such as psychoanalysis, transactional analysis, or behavior modification.

I think the time has come to step out of the wings and drop my persona as a completely unbiased textbook author. I would enjoy sharing with you a few observations concerning a philosophy of life—something I consider quite important, and part of your adjustment and personal growth. I don't want to go quite so far as to say that what I am going to present is *my* philosophy of life. The material offered here is not quite that personal. Rather, it is an attempt to describe what seems to me to be a few key aspects of a *workable* philosophy of life—with plenty of latitude for differences in your personality and mine.

What follows below is based on my research in both psychology and philosophy, and my experience as a classroom teacher, professional psychologist, and human being.

It seems to me that every human being both has and *needs* a philosophy of life. And just what *is* this strange existential creature that I keep calling a philosophy of life? There's no mystery. It is simply the *set of assumptions that guide your life*. The assumptions may be spoken or unspoken, understood clearly or dimly perceived. But they are there. And they count.

Some assumptions are life-enhancing. Others are life-detracting. Let's focus on some assumptions that will help you answer for yourself a perennial question asked by speculative philosophy: "What is the good life?"

Autonomy

As indicated earlier in Chapter 9, a recurrent adjustment-growth issue is freedom versus determinism. Although the issue itself is by no means completely resolvable, there is good evidence to suggest that persons who assume they have some degree of inner freedom are better off for making the assumption. A feeling of inner freedom contributes to what psychologists call **autonomy**, a sense of self-direction in life. Various metaphors are used to get this idea across. We speak of "pulling your own strings" or "pushing your own buttons." Or we can speak more simply of taking charge of your own life.

The research of Julian Rotter (1966) on locus of control reinforces the importance of a sense of autonomy in one's life. Rotter's research indicates that people tend to locate control of their lives either within themselves or outside of themselves. People with an internal locus of control tend to feel that they run their own show, that they are in charge of their own lives. People with an external locus of control tend to feel that they are pawns of fate. They feel that luck, other people, the government, or some other external agent runs their lives. Researcher Martin E. P. Seligman (1975) points out that people who feel helpless and depressed tend to think that their futures are out of their hands. They define the locus of control as external.

So you can see that the issue of freedom versus determinism is more than an idle issue in a textbook. The assumption you adopt concerning the issue tends to affect the quality of your life.

Hope

The concept of hope is closely linked to the issue of freedom of versus determinism. As indicated above, people with a strong sense of autonomy tend in general to have a hopeful attitude toward life.

A philosophy of life is the set of assumptions that guides your life.

Hope is the expectation that things will turn out well. It is very similar to the concept of **optimism**. The person who is an optimist tends to look on the bright side of things. It must be realized that in some situations there is no particular rational basis for either hope or optimism. Nonetheless, it can be argued, whether it is rational or irrational, hope helps to see people through their darkest moments. When people hope, they see a light at the end of the tunnel instead of darkness. It is the capacity to hope that carries people through the stress of war, economic upheaval, marriage problems, and similar difficulties. Physician Arnold A. Hutschnecker (1981, p. 11), author of *Hope*, opens his book with these words, "Hope sustains life. Hopelessness causes death."

Love

"Love makes the world go 'round" is a popular phrase, indicating the importance of love in human existence. The word **love** has more than one meaning. It can refer to the strong sexual attraction that one person feels for another. In this case it is probably best to speak of *erotic love*. Or it can refer to any sense of devotion or affection that is felt for another person. So it is possible to speak of a parent's love for a child.

There are those who are cynical about love. They say that love is an illusion, that it wears off, that it has no reality. There is no point in debating here the truth or untruth of such assertions. But it is important to note that when one feels this way it is not life-enhancing. On the other hand, when one feels that love is real and that there is love in one's life, then life is imbued with greater significance and meaning. In short, love is a human value of great importance. To return to the opening phrase, one author, Franklin P. Jones, said, "Love doesn't make the world go 'round. Love is what makes the ride worthwhile."

The Good Universe

On the whole, adjustment and growth is fostered by a belief in what I call the **good universe**. The idea of the good universe can take the traditional form of a belief in the God of the Western world. It can also include acceptance of the teachings of an orthodox religion. Or it may take a less conventional form. For example, physicist Freeman Dyson (1979, p. 250) says, "I do not feel like an alien in this universe. The more I examine the universe and study the details of its architecture, the more evidence I find that the universe in some sense must have known that we were coming." He goes on to indicate that the universe is an unexpectedly hospitable place for living creatures to make their home in.

It is not the truth or untruth of the idea of the good universe that is the issue here. It is easy enough to contest traditional ideas or statements such as Dyson's. If one is willing to look at everything from the viewpoint of cold logic, there is inevitably another side to every belief coin. The question is simply this: Do people seem to be better off for assuming as a part of their philosophy of life that the universe is in some way "good"? The answer seems to be yes.

Positive Versus Negative

It would be possible to go on citing other assumptions that appear to be life-enhancing. But by now I think you get the idea. Whenever confronted with an assumption about existence that has both a positive and a negative aspect, it seems to foster both adjustment and growth to pick the positive aspect. Sometimes this is done more or less unconsciously. Sometimes it is a matter of values learned in childhood. And sometimes one makes a deliberate choice. In any event, as I have said before, it is not so much a question of true or false as it is a question of *what will work*. My own observation, and conviction, is that positive assumptions about the nature of existence *do* work to foster psychological health.

I do not pretend that what I have offered here is a complete philosophy of life. As the title of the section indicates, I have tried to aim you *toward* a philosophy of life, not give you one ready-made. You have to arrive at your own philosophy of life or it probably won't mean much. But I have tried to give you a few arrows pointing in the right direction.

The Good Life

Let's return to that perennial question asked by speculative philosophy, "What is the good life?" Obviously there is no categorical answer to this question. In a sense, this entire book is an attempt to give a partial answer. Certain things are clear. The good life is not rooted to a particular kind of place—such as a commune or a kibbutz or a farm or the Big City. Nor is the good life tied to a particular time—such as the Good Old Days or the Age of Aquarius or the Golden Future. The good life may be found in various times and places because healthy personalities determine the good life.

Also, there are no absolute criteria for the good life. It is not possible to say that personal happiness can be found by having three children or a new car or $100,000 in the bank or a profession or any other explicit symbol of success. The criteria for the good life are largely subjective. They are determined by the individual's unique personality; they depend on what he or she finds to be rewarding, meaningful, and gratifying. The philosopher Bertrand Russell commented, "The good life is one inspired by love and guided by knowledge" (Egner, p. 17). This was his definition of the good life, and it allows for a broad range of personal interpretation. Perhaps Russell's definition will do. In any event, it is my hope that this book in some way contributes to a good life for you.

Appendix

CLASSIFYING MENTAL DISORDERS: AN INTRODUCTION TO THE DIAGNOSTIC CATEGORIES IN DSM-III

OUTLINE

Two friends are having a conversation about a third friend:

"I understand she had a nervous breakdown and they had to put her in a mental hospital."

"Well, did she go insane?"

"No. She just had a nervous breakdown."

Neither of the two diagnostic categories used in this casual conversation—*nervous breakdown* and *insane*—are to be found in the official classification system used by the American Psychiatric Association. The familiar label **nervous breakdown** has no formal status at all. It is just a wastebasket term that can mean anything from a psychotic disorder to an anxiety disorder. It tells us very little. And the word **insane**, although having historical meanings such as mentally deranged or demented, is not a part of the contemporary clinical language either. It is correctly used in a legal framework only, having to do with diminished capacity to take responsibility for one's actions.

In view of the fact that about one in ten people will receive a psychiatric diagnosis such as *organic mental disorder, schizophrenic disorder, adjustment disorder,* or *personality disorder* at some point in their lives, it pays all of us to have some basic knowledge of what these terms mean.

Let's hasten to add that just because one in ten people will receive a psychiatric diagnosis that *not* one in ten of us "goes crazy." "Going crazy" is another popular term that has no accurate clinical or psychiatric meaning. Keep in mind that the mental disorders we are going to discuss in this section cover a large range of human problems—many of which require no hospitalization (or only a brief stay).

HISTORICAL BACKGROUND

The attempt to classify behavioral patterns and to attach labels to these patterns goes far back in history. You will recall from Chapter 1 that Hippocrates spoke of four basic kinds of personality types: sanguine, melancholic, choleric, and phlegmatic.

430

The father of contemporary attempts to classify mental disorders was the German psychiatrist Emil Kraepelin (1856–1926). For example, he made popular the term **dementia praecox** for what we today call a schizophrenic disorder. (The term *dementia praecox* roughly translates into "early or youthful madness.") Kraepelin used the term **manic-depressive psychosis** for a mental disorder characterized by wide swings in emotional states from elation to depression.

One of the most popular terms ever used to describe a pathological mental or emotional state is **neurosis**. Freud and other psychoanalysts have written at length about neurotic conditions, discussing their causes, symptoms, and treatment. A neurotic disorder in traditional terms is characterized by a core of anxiety. (However, the core of anxiety may be masked by symptoms designed to control it and keep it from consciousness.)

There has been in recent times a disenchantment with blanket references to neurotic disorders. A consensus of the clinical and psychiatric community feels that such references are too broad, too all-inclusive. The term **neurotic disorders** has fallen on hard times—perhaps because of overuse. The contemporary nomenclature discussed below includes the neurotic disorders under five categories: **affective**, **anxiety**, **somatoform**, **dissociative**, and **psychosexual** disorders. But the blanket term neurotic disorders itself does not presently exist as an official diagnostic category recognized by the American Psychiatric Association.

It is outside the scope of this book to present a detailed history of all the steps leading to the present classification system. Essentially what has happened is that clinicians and psychiatrists have gradually through a process of trial-and-error arrived at a set of descriptive terms on which there is a fairly high level of agreement. There has been plenty of debate. And a certain proportion of therapists are unhappy with the present classification system. For example, some therapists would have liked to see the term *neurotic disorder* retained as an official term.

The most widely accepted classification system for mental disorders is published in *The Diagnostic and Statistical Manual of the American Psychiatric Association (Third Edition)*. This is quite an awkward title, and it is conveniently abbreviated *DSM-III*. It represents the results of a team that worked on the revision of psychiatric nomenclature for a number of years. The American Psychiatric Association is the oldest national medical society in the United States. (It was founded in 1844.) Its classification system is taken as a highly responsible effort to arrive at a standard terminology for classifying mental disorders.

THE DSM-III CATEGORIES

The *DSM-III* approach to classifying mental disorders is quite sophisticated, and involves making an assessment of a troubled person's problems on the basis of five possible aspects. These aspects are called "axes," and the classification system is said to be **multiaxial**, meaning that more than one feature or dimension of adjustment is taken into consideration when a diagnosis is made.

Axes 1 and II contain the basic classification of mental disorders, and are the bases for the clinical terms identified and described below. Axes III, IV, and V refer to aspects of adjustment and health that may have an impact on the course of a mental disorder such as the individual's physical health, the severity of stressful conditions in his or her life, and the kinds of adjustment the individual has been making in the past year. Axes III, IV, and V recognize that these kinds of factors may play an important part in a diagnosis. But such factors do not make up the central diagnosis. A principal diagnosis is made on the basis of either Axis I or Axis II. Here is the way that these two axes are described in *DSM-III*:

Axis I: Clinical Syndromes, Conditions Not
          Attributable to a Mental Disorder
          That Are a Focus of Attention or
          Treatment and Additional Codes.

Axis II: Personality Disorders and Specific
          Developmental Disorders.

If the above descriptions of the two axes don't make too much sense as they stand, that is understandable. Clarification of the overall scheme will result as each specific diagnostic category is discussed below. In order to understand the basic diagnostic categories it will not be necessary to belabor the distinctions between axes. (The reference to the word *code* in connection with Axis I above has to do with the fact that DSM-III assigns a code number to diagnostic categories. This is for insurance and statistical purposes, and will not be of further concern in this presentation.)

Let's now review the seventeen principal diagnostic categories used in DSM-III. In each category there are a number of subcategories. It would be impractical to detail all the subcategories. The *Quick Reference to DSM-III* itself contains 267 pages! We will have to content ourselves with an identification of the principal categories and selected examples.

1. **Disorders Usually First Evident in Infancy, Childhood, or Adolescence**. One example of a disorder included in this category is an **attention deficit disorder with hyperactivity**. Children with this disorder are inattentive, not seeming to listen to adults. They are impulsive and may frequently act before thinking. They are hyperactive, meaning they excessively run about, have difficulty staying seated, may move about a great deal during sleep, and seem in general to be always "on the go." Other disorders in category 1 in-

clude **mental retardation, conduct disorders,** and **anxiety disorders of childhood or adolescence.**

2. **Organic Mental Disorders.** These are mental disorders involving an actual brain disturbance. Possibilities include brain damage, biochemical imbalances, and hormonal imbalances. An example of a disorder included in this category is **dementia.** Individuals with dementia display a loss of intellectual abilities; to qualify as dementia the loss must be sufficiently severe that it interferes with one's social life or vocation. Other characteristics of dementia include loss of memory and impaired ability to think in abstract terms. Other disorders in category 2 include **delirium, organic delusional syndrome, organic hallucinosis,** and **organic personality syndrome.**

3. **Substance Use Disorders.** These disorders include the maladaptive use of various drugs. An example of a disorder in category 3 is **alcohol abuse.** Alcohol abuse is characterized by what *DSM-III* calls "a pattern of pathological alcohol use." This pathological pattern may include a daily need for a drink, the inability to regulate drinking, and periods when the individual goes "on the wagon." The pattern is often complicated by missing work, losing one's job, and legal problems. Other substance use disorders include **barbiturate or similarly acting sedative or hypnotic abuse, opioid abuse, cocaine abuse, phencyclidine (PCP) or similarly acting arylcyclohexylamine abuse, cannabis abuse,** and **tobacco dependence.**

4. **Schizophrenic Disorders.** These disorders are characterized by delusions (false ideas), hallucinations (the perception of something that has no actual presence), incoherence, and illogical thinking. (These are the disorders most often associated with popular and slang words such as "mad," "crazy," "screwy," "cracked," and "out-of-your-mind.") One example of a disorder in category 4 is a **schizophrenic disorder, disorganized type.** This subcategory is characterized by incoherent talk, random and disorganized delusions, and silly behavior. The person's speech and behavior seems to have no "rhyme or reason." Other schizophrenic disorders include **catatonic type** and **paranoid type.** A stupor and/or mutism (not talking) are often associated with the catatonic type. Delusions of being persecuted, of being a great person, or of jealousy often go with the paranoid type.

5. **Paranoid Disorders.** These disorders are not to be confused with the schizophrenic disorder, paranoid type. The main difference is that in the paranoid disorders the delusions are more well organized than in the schizophrenic type. And in the paranoid disorders there are no obvious hallucinations. An example of a disorder in category 5 is **paranoia.** Paranoia is characterized by an ongoing and stable set of delusions lasting for at least six months. The delusions have to do with persecution. The individual may insist, "Someone is trying to poison my food." Other subcategories include **shared paranoid disorder, acute paranoid disorder,** and **atypical paranoid disorder.**

6. **Psychotic Disorders Not Elsewhere Classified**. The title of this category is self-descriptive and basically tells you what it is. An example of a disorder in category 6 is a **brief reactive psychosis**. The pattern of a brief reactive psychosis might run as follows: Something very distressing happens to an individual (for example, the end of a love affair). Shortly after the individual displays psychotic symptoms including delusions and hallucinations. The symptoms last no more than two weeks, and in a relatively short time period the individual in question returns to a more or less normal level of functioning. Other disorders in category 6 include **schizophreniform disorder**, **schizoaffective disorder**, and **atypical psychosis**. (These labels, of course, have no meaning without definitions and examples. They are included merely to give you some appreciation of the large range of diagnostic categories in *DSM-III*.)

7. **Affective Disorders**. Affective disorders are disturbances of emotion or mood. An example of a disorder in this category is **major depression**. Major depression is characterized by a lack of interest in most familiar activities. There seems to be no pleasure left in life. Words such as *sad, blue, hopeless, low,* and *irritable* are associated with the condition. The person is said to be "down in the dumps." Other signs of a major depression include: poor appetite, sleep disturbances, decreases in sexual drive, loss of energy, feelings of worthlessness, slowed thought processes, and a preoccupation with death and suicide. Other affective disorders include **manic episode**, **bipolar disorder**, and **cyclothymic disorder**.

8. **Anxiety Disorders**. The quality we call **anxiety** is communicated by words such as *apprehension, tension,* and *uneasiness*. The kind of anxiety central to an anxiety disorder is said to be of a neurotic quality—there is no external basis for the anxiety. The person is afraid without a reasonable basis. One example of an anxiety disorder is **agoraphobia**. Agoraphobia is characterized by a fear of public places. There is frequently an avoidance of crowds, tunnels, bridges, and public transportation. The individual with this disorder wants to be in a position to escape or get help if suddenly incapacitated by anxiety. Persons with agoraphobia often stay very close to home, and in some cases may even make themselves house prisoners. Other anxiety disorders include **social phobia**, **panic disorder**, and **obsessive compulsive disorder**.

9. **Somatoform Disorders**. Somatoform disorders are disorders having to do with the body. (**Soma** is the Greek word for body.) One example of a disorder in this category is **conversion disorder**. Classical psychoanalytic theory holds that in this kind of disorder anxiety is converted into a physical symptom such as blindness, deafness, or paralysis. However, the physical difficulties have no organic basis; they are the expression of a psychological conflict. Other disorders in category 9 include **psychogenic pain disorder** and **hypochondriasis**.

10. **Dissociative Disorders**. Dissociative disorders are often characterized by a loss of integrity of the conscious self or ego. There are disturbances in one's sense of identity. An example in category 10 is **psychogenic amnesia**. A person suffering from this disorder may be unable to recall central personal information. The loss of memory concerning one's identity is so great that it cannot be thought of as an ordinary lapse. Another example in category 10 is **multiple personality** in which the individual manifests two or more personalities. Other dissociative disorders include **psychogenic fugue** and **depersonalization disorder**.

11. **Psychosexual Disorders**. These are disorders having to do with disturbances of the sexual aspects of human behavior. An example in category 11 is **transsexualism**. Transsexualism is characterized by a feeling that one's actual gender is inappropriate. The physical male may, for example, wish to be a woman. In order to qualify as transsexualism the feelings expressed must have been continuous for at least two years. Other examples in category 11 include **fetishism, transvestism, pedophilia, exhibitionism, sexual masochism, sexual sadism, inhibited sexual desire, inhibited female orgasm, inhibited male orgasm**, and **premature ejaculation**.

12. **Factitious Disorders**. These disorders are those in which a patient voluntarily produces a physical or psychological symptom. This would seem to be malingering. But the disorder is somewhat more complex than that. It seems that the individual wants to assume the patient role and mimics the symptoms of an actual disorder. Persons with factitious disorders may, for example, even be willing to submit to surgery in order to play out the self-assumed patient's role. An example in category 12 is a **factitious disorder with physical symptoms**. The individual may complain of a sickness such as heart disease and may play out the role of heart patient with several hospitalizations. The other major kind of factitious disorder is **factitious disorder with psychological symptoms**.

13. **Disorders of Impulse Control Not Elsewhere Classified**. As the title of category 13 suggests, these are disorders in which the individual has a difficult time controlling an inclination to behave in an irresponsible way. An example is **pathological gambling** in which the individual gambles chronically to the point that the stability of family life and vocation are disrupted. Other disorders in category 13 include **kleptomania, pyromania, intermittent explosive disorder**, and **isolated explosive disorder**.

14. **Adjustment Disorder**. These are disorders involving a maladaptive reaction to stressful conditions in one's life. Usually the individual's ability to function in either social or vocational settings is impaired. In order to be thought of as an adjustment disorder the reaction must be excessive and beyond what might be normally expected in response to life's frustrations. An example of an adjustment disorder is an **adjustment disorder with disturbance of conduct**. This disorder is characterized by behaviors such as tru-

ancy, vandalism, reckless driving, fighting, or not meeting one's legal responsibilities. Other disorders in category 14 include **adjustment disorder with depressed mood**, **adjustment disorder with anxious mood**, and **adjustment disorder with work (or academic) inhibition**.

15. **Psychological Factors Affecting Physical Condition**. This diagnostic category is used with the individual who is suffering from an actual illness, and that illness is in turn aggravated by a psychological factor. For example, let's say that the individual in question is a woman who is suffering from rheumatoid arthritis. Assume that her marriage is breaking up and she is going through a transient depression. It is possible that her emotional reactions to her life situation might aggravate the symptoms of her arthritis. There are no subcategories under category 15.

16. **Personality Disorders**. This is one of the most difficult of the diagnostic categories to characterize in any overall way. However, if we think of behaviors that are immoral, impulsive, illegal, irresponsible, or just plain irritating to others we will be more or less on the right track. Persons with personality disorders often experience little subjective distress and don't necessarily see themselves in need of assistance and/or therapy. An example of a personality disorder is the **narcissistic personality disorder**. Individuals with this disorder exhibit an excessive sense of self-importance and exaggerate their achievements. They may be preoccupied with fantasies of unlimited success, power, brilliance, beauty, or ideal love. They often require constant attention and admiration. And they resist criticism. Other kinds of personality disorder include **histrionic personality disorder**, **antisocial personality disorder**, and **passive-aggressive personality disorder**.

17. **Conditions Not Attributable to a Mental Disorder That Are the Focus of Attention or Treatment**. As the name of this category suggests, there are conditions associated with problems of adjustment that cannot be classified as mental disorders. Nonetheless, these conditions may require some attention or treatment. Obviously, this is a kind of catch-all category that does not lend itself to a common psychological or behavioral theme. An example of a condition in category 17 is **malingering**. Malingering involves the voluntary production of either physical or psychological symptoms. This may be done to avoid a duty or to avoid work. It may also be done with a goal in mind (e.g., to defraud an insurance company). Other conditions included in category 17 include **borderline intellectual functioning**, **academic problem**, **occupational problem**, **uncomplicated bereavement**, and **noncompliance with medical treatment**.

CRITIQUE

It is possible to find fault with any classification system, and the one presented by *DSM-III* is no exception. Even clinical psychologists and psychiatrists who generally approve of *DSM-III* may find fault with it. Here are examples of the kinds of criticisms that can be made of *DSM-III*:

1. There are too many diagnostic categories. Categories cease to be useful when they multiply. The principal value of categories is to summarize and to organize. Perhaps many of the diagnostic categories overlap too much. A clinician's decision that a particular individual is suffering from a compulsive personality disorder (in category 16) and *not* an obsessive compulsive disorder (one of the anxiety disorders in category 8) may be to some extent arbitrary. A behavioral psychologist might say, "We've given a lot of fancy clinical names to a lot of odd behaviors. But we really don't need so many fancy names."

2. It might be better to speak of **behavioral disorders** instead of mental disorders. The term *mental disorder* still carries with it a strong social stigma or disgrace. And certainly not all the disorders in *DSM-III* are primarily mental in nature. Alcohol abuse, tobacco dependence, social phobia, inhibited sexual desire, and personality disorders all sound more like behavioral disorders than mental disorders. The broader term *behavioral disorder* could easily include mental disorders as a kind of subcategory.

3. It might have been a good idea to retain a broad general category called **neurotic disorders**. The five categories affective, anxiety, somatoform, dissociative, and psychosexual disorders could have been included under this category. The term *neurotic disorders* still retains a substantial amount of meaning for many clinical psychologists and psychiatrists.

It would be possible to level additional criticisms. But the present aim is simply to illustrate that *DSM-III*, like any human instrument, is not necessarily perfect. If not perfect, *DSM-III* does have its strong points as well as its weak ones. And it might be well to identify some of its strong points. On the positive side, we can say of *DSM-III* that:

1. It makes every effort to be precise. Categories are carefully defined and diagnostic standards are carefully described.

2. It does not cater to anyone's pet theory of mental disorders. It attempts to be descriptive, not theoretical. It doesn't say that neurotic anxiety is due to an unconscious conflict between the id and the superego. This might make a psychoanalyst happy but would irritate a behavior therapist who might comprehend anxiety in terms of conditioning and learning. Thus *DSM-III* respects different theoretical orientations toward behavioral and mental disorders.

3. It uses the word **disorder** in preference to either the words *illness* or *reaction*. This is a step in the right direction. The word **illness** may be more of a metaphor than a fact when used to describe mental disorders. And the word **reaction** suggests in a too limiting way that mental disorders are responses to life's frustrations. The broader word *disorder* recognizes

that some problems may be **endogenous** (i.e., arising from within the individual).

SUMMARY

In brief, we can rely on *DSM-III* as representing the best collective judgment of a qualified group of mental health professionals. It makes every effort to be precise, it avoids taking sides on theoretical issues, and it does not oversimplify the nature of mental disorders. In the interests of clear communication among both laypersons and mental health professionals there is quite a bit of virtue in adopting the diagnostic language recommended by *DSM-III*.

Glossary

Abnormal behavior. Literally, behavior that is away from the norm or average. Usage usually refers to maladaptive behavior patterns.

Abreaction. An emotional release involving the "reliving" or vivid recall of painful emotional experiences.

Activation-synthesis hopothesis. A hypothesis suggesting that dreams represent an attempt to make sense out of uncoordinated and contradictory messages arising from somewhat arbitrary central nervous system activity.

Active listening. Listening in such a way that one decodes the emotional message behind a set of surface words and reflects this decoded message back to the speaker.

Actual self. As formulated by Horney, a compromise self made between the idealized and true selves. The actual self is the self that is brought forth and presented to the world at large.

Adjustment. Successfully adapting to one's environment; establishing a harmonious relationship with the environment.

Adult ego state. In transactional analysis, that aspect of one's personality capable of making decisions, planning ahead, and taking reality into account.

Alienation. The feeling that one is an outsider. A psychological state in which the individual does not feel a sense of belonging or identification with either nature or other human beings.

All-or-nothing thinking. A kind of thinking tending to sort all events and experiences into two categories. Can also be called "either-or thinking" or "black and white thinking."

Alpha rhythm. An electroencephalographic pattern occurring at the rate of about eight to fourteen cycles per second.

Amphetamines. Various kinds of stimulants with a structure closely resembling the brain's own norepinephrine.

Amygdalae. Two almond-shaped brain structures located near the hypothalamus. They appear to play an important role in the experience of pain.

Anal-expulsive character. In Freudian theory, a personality structure underlying such behaviors as being disorderly, defiant, cruel to others, or "making a mess."

Anal-retentive character. In Freudian theory, a personality structure underlying such behaviors as being stingy, excessively orderly, and holding back affection.

Anal stage. In Freudian theory, the second psychosexual stage. This second psychosexual stage is estimated to last from about eighteen months of age to the third year of life.

Analytic therapies. Modes of psychotherapy that employ the concept of an unconscious mental life, making the assumption that an analysis or interpretation of one's motivational structure will bring about insight into the roots of a psychological-emotional problem.

Anima. In Jungian theory, an archetype of the self representing one's female personality.

Animus. In Jungian theory, an archetype of the self representing one's male personality.

Anorexia nervosa. Chronic lack of appetite without apparent organic basis. A person suffering from anorexia nervosa finds food repugnant, and it is believed that this active rejection of food is associated with emotional conflicts.

Anthropomorphism. Assigning human qualities to organisms or entities that are not human.

Antianxiety agents. Kinds of sedative-hypnotic agents widely prescribed to treat chronic anxiety. Also known as the minor tranquilizers.

Antihypertensive agents. Drugs used to combat chronic high blood pressure.

Antipsychiatry. A counterculture movement opposed to institutional psychiatry.

Antipsychotic agents. Drugs used to combat the effects of psychotic reactions. Also known as the major tranquilizers.

Antivitalism. Doctrine asserting that the existence of life can be explained without such concepts as the soul or a "vital energy." Antivitalism holds that life is explained by the interaction of known electrochemical reactions.

Apperception. Similar to the concept of subliminal perception, the ability of an organism to record an event without conscious awareness.

Apperceptive mass. A mental reservoir consisting of all of our ideas and all of our past experience.

Archetype. In Jungian theory, an enduring pattern in the mind derived from centuries of similar experiences by members of the human race. The equivalent of instincts in animals.

Asanas. Various postures used in Hatha Yoga.

Assertiveness training. A program of learning designed to increase a person's competence in dealing with other human beings.

Astral body. According to Yoga, a "second" body made of finer matter than the ordinary body. Yoga teaches that the astral body can travel in higher dimensional planes.

Authentic living. Pursuing a life in which one is true to oneself as an individual, not pledging false allegiance to the values and standards arbitrarily imposed by other people or one's culture.

Autogenic training. An autosuggestive method of inducing relaxation developed in Germany in the 1920s.

Automatic thoughts. Thoughts that appear spontaneously and are very rapid, coming and going quickly.

Autonomic nervous system. The subsystem of the entire nervous system that controls the smooth muscles associated with the body's internal organs and endocrine glands. It is traditionally said to function on an involuntary basis.

Autonomy. Self-directed behavior. In the context of transactional analysis, gamefree and scriptfree living.

Avoidance conditioning. A form of conditioning in which an organism learns on cue to avoid contact with a particular kind of stimulus.

Axes. As used in the framework of *DSM-III*, features or dimensions of adjustment taken into consideration when a psychiatric diagnosis is made. The *DSM-III* classification system is said to be *multiaxial*, and includes five axes of concern.

Barbiturate. Kind of sedative-hypnotic agent. A drug that acts as a sedative, depressing the brain's arousal mechanisms.

Basic anxiety. According to Karen Horney, the underlying feeling that one is alone and helpless in a hostile world.

BCP psychology. As formulated by Glasser and Powers, an approach to psychology utilizing insights derived from cybernetics. B, C, and P stand for behavior, control, and perception.

Behavior therapies. Modes of psychotherapy that emphasize the importance of action in contrast to the concept of insight. Behavior therapies stress the extinction and/or modification of conditioned responses and habits.

Behavioral disorders. Maladaptive patterns of behavior. Has roughly the same meaning as **mental disorders**.

Behavioral medicine. The application of psychological principles and methods to the treatment of organic disorders.

Being. According to Heidegger, Being is the simple fact that a person or thing exists. Heidegger capitalizes Being in order to stress that existence is a concrete reality, not an abstraction.

Being-for-itself. As formulated by Sartre, the right of a human being to exist simply because the person exists, not because the person serves the purposes of others or of God.

Being-in-itself. According to Sartre, the kind of existence associated with things and animals. Existing without the ability to change given characteristics.

Being-in-the-world. As formulated by Heidegger, existing as a person on this planet in a particular place and time.

Being needs. As formulated by Maslow, various aspects of the need for self-actualization.

Beta rhythm. An electroencephalographic pattern occurring at the rate of about fourteen cycles per second or more.

Bhakti Yoga. Kind of Yoga in which mystical union with the All is achieved by the means of fervent worship.

Biofeedback training. A procedure by which a subject can learn to bring physiological processes under voluntary control.

Body-oriented meditation. Kind of meditation in which the meditator gives attention to an autonomic process such as breathing.

Broken record. In assertiveness training, a skill that involves calm repetition of one's position.

Burn-out. A state of mental demoralization and emotional exhaustion. The person suffering from burn-out tends to be irritable, uninterested in sexual activity, cynical, and disenchanted.

Catastrophic thinking. As formulated by Ellis, a tendency to overgeneralize in which a single negative instance of a phenomenon is used by the subject to predict total disaster.

Chakras. According to Yoga, wheel-like patterns of energy located at various places in the body.

Chemotherapy. Type of somatic therapy for mental illness. Various kinds of drugs are given to patients with the aim of altering their thought processes, perceptions, and moods.

Child ego state. In transactional analysis, a set of emotional "recordings" carried forward from childhood.

Chlorpromazine. Antipsychotic agent with a great calming effect on agitated mental patients.

Choleric. A temperament that is easily excited to anger.

Client-centered counseling. Form of counseling advocated by Rogers in which the individual person is the subject of interest, not the person's symptoms and problems.

Clinical antidepressants. Various kinds of stimulants that facilitate the production of norepinephrine.

Closure. As formulated by Gestalt psychology, the tendency of an incomplete figure to form an organized whole in perception.

Cocaine. A stimulant obtained from coca leaves.

Cognitive behavior modification. A learning procedure aimed at reshaping thoughts, beliefs, and perceptions (i.e., cognitions).

Cognitive dissonance. As formulated by Festinger, the lack of harmony between at least two conscious ideas. The theory of cognitive dissonance postulates that individuals are motivated to reduce dissonance.

Cognitive psychology. The psychology of conscious mental processes, including thinking, knowing, perceiving, and reasoning.

Cognitive therapies. Therapies stressing the importance of clear thinking. They assume that maladaptive behaviors are caused by irrational ideas and cognitive distortions.

Cognitive triad. According to Beck, a set of three conscious elements associated with depression. The three elements are (1) a negative conception of the self, (2) a negative interpretation of life, and (3) a nihilistic view of the future.

Collective unconscious. In Jungian theory, an impersonal psychological level made of universal psychological patterns shared by the entire human race.

Compensation. An ego defense mechanism used to defend against feelings of inferiority. Striving to demonstrate that one is competent in areas where there is some question about one's competence.

Complementary transaction. A transaction free of conflict. On a transactional analysis diagram, the lines representing the transactions are parallel.

Concrete operations. As formulated by Piaget, it refers to a stage of cognitive development lasting from about the age of seven to the age of twelve. An intermediate stage of mental development in which the child elaborates his or her capacity for symbolic thought and becomes more flexible in thinking.

Conditioned inhibition. In Hull's learning theory, a learned tendency not to respond to a conditioned stimulus. Conditioned inhibition is antagonistic to the conditioned response.

Conditioned response. A learned response. A response arising from a learned response potential.

Conditioned stimulus. A stimulus to which there exists in the organism a learned response potential.

Congruence. As used by Rogers, it refers to the degree of agreement between one's self-concept and one's ideal self.

Conscience. In Freudian theory, a subagent of the superego. The conscience sets up inhibitions, restraints within the individual against taking certain kinds of actions.

Contamination. In transactional analysis, encroachment by the Parent or the Child ego states into the psychological territory of the Adult ego state.

Contiguity. In Guthrie's learning theory, the presentation to an organism of two stimuli at the same time.

Continuous reinforcement. Reinforcement in which there is a one-to-one relationship between the instrumental response and the reinforcer.

Contractual psychiatry. As formulated by Szasz, a kind of psychiatry in which the sufferer voluntarily seeks help, feels distressed, and may find relief.

Covert operant. An operant hidden within the individual. Such an operant is not subject to public inspection.

Creative self. According to Adler, the capacity of an individual to shape his or her own personality and destiny.

Crossed transaction. A transaction in which there is conflict between two or more people. On a transactional analysis diagram, the lines representing the transactions cross.

Cybernetics. The science that deals with the control of systems (e.g., computers).

Dasein. According to Heidegger, Being-in-the-world. Existing as a person on this planet in a particular place and time.

Daseinsanalysis. As formulated by Binswanger, the analysis of Being-in-the-world.

Defense mechanisms. A set of psychological devices by which the ego distorts its perception of reality in favor of the fantasy-oriented wishes of the id.

Deficiency-needs. As formulated by Maslow, basic needs for food, water, safety, belongingness, love, respect, and self-esteem.

Delta rhythm. An electroencephalographic pattern occurring at the rate of about four cycles per second or less.

Delusion. A perception on the part of a given individual that most of us would reject as "untrue."

Dementia praecox. Another term for a schizophrenic disorder. The term was introduced by Kraepelin and literally means "early or youthful madness." It is considered outdated, and is no longer a part of recommended psychiatric nomenclature.

Demonology. The viewpoint that maladaptive behaviors are caused by evil spirits.

Depth psychology. The psychology of unconscious mental processes.

Determinism. The doctrine that all behavior is caused.

Discriminative stimulus. In instrumental learning, a stimulus that provides an organism with information that an operant act is presently paying off or not paying off.

Displacement. An ego defense mechanism in which the ego allows the individual to place on one stimulus an emotional reaction that properly should be placed on another stimulus.

Dopamine. One of the principal neurotransmitters.

Down's syndrome. A physical condition linked to genetic factors; associated with mental retardation. Also known as *mongolism.*

Drama triangle. As formulated by Karpman, the assertion that in a large percentage of games there is a triangular relationship between the participants such that they play the social roles of Persecutor, Rescuer, and Victim. Also known as the *game triangle.*

Dream work. In Freudian dream theory, the distortion of the latent content into a symbolic manifest content that is relatively innocent to the conscious mind.

Drive. In learning theory, conceptualized as a source that energizes the behavior of an organism.

Drive-reduction theory. The hypothesis that

habits are reinforced when they reduce the intensity of drive states within the organism.

DSM-III. The *Diagnostic and Statistical Manual of the American Psychiatric Association*, Third Edition.

Dualism. The philosophical position that the body and the soul (including the mind) are two distinct and different substances.

Dynamic psychology. Roughly synonymous with depth psychology. Any psychology that assumes there are unconscious psychological forces and that ideas within the mind push and shove each other about.

Dynamism. According to Harry Stack Sullivan, a behavioral pattern similar to a habit or a trait. The concept of dynamism stresses habitual reactions to other people.

Eclectic. Selecting from a variety of theories, schools, and methods. Seeing value in more than one point of view.

Ego. In Freudian theory, the *I* or the conscious center of the personality. The ego is said to be reality-oriented.

Egocentric. The inability to see any point of view but one's own. Perceiving the world as revolving about one's self.

Ego-ideal. In Freudian theory, a subagent of the superego. The ego-ideal sets an individual's level of aspiration, presenting him or her with a mental picture of what should be done with life.

Ego state. As formulated by Berne, the actual experience of acting like a child, a parent, or an adult.

Ego strength. Primarily a psychoanalytic concept. A person with a high level of ego strength is well-oriented in time and space, knows the practical limits of his or her capacities, and in general is able to cope effectively with the challenges of life.

Egotism. A tendency to be selfish, self-centered, conceited, and boastful.

Electra complex. A term sometimes used to suggest the female counterpart of the Oedipus complex in males.

Electrical stimulation of the brain. A form of psychosurgery in which electrode implants are placed deep within the paleocortex ("old brain"), making it possible to apply small amounts of electric current to selected brain regions.

Electroconvulsive therapy. A kind of shock therapy in which electric current is used to induce a seizure.

Electromyograph. A record of momentary muscle tension.

Electroshock therapy. Type of somatic therapy in which a brief pulse of electricity is sent through the frontal portion of the brain. Used primarily for psychosis and extreme depression.

Elicited behavior. Behavior in which a particular stimulus produces a predictable response.

Emitted behavior. Behavior that does not appear to be a response to a readily identifiable external stimulus.

Emotional trauma. A painful psychological experience.

Empiricism. A philosophical doctrine asserting that all of human knowledge is based on experience acquired via the sense organs.

Encounter groups. Groups in which people exchange thoughts and feelings for the purpose of maximizing human potentialities. Emphasis is on relatively normal people becoming more authentic and self-actualizing.

Endorphins. Neurotransmitters that function somewhat like opiates. They exist naturally in the human body.

Erogenous zones. Sometimes referred to as erotogenic zones. Zones that are particularly rich in nerve endings responsive to touch. These are the oral, anal, and the genital areas.

Erotic love. The strong sexual attraction that one person feels for another.

Exhibitionism. The act of exposing one's body (often the genitals) in public places.

Existential guilt. Kind of guilt one experiences when one does not fulfill one's possibilities in life.

Existential-humanistic psychology. An orientation toward psychology that asserts the importance of human consciousness. An accent is placed on the willing process, our capacity as human beings to make decisions and choices.

Existential position. A stance we take toward ourselves, our relationships with others, and life itself.

Existential therapies. Modes of psychotherapy that emphasize the importance of making the most of one's life. What is analyzed in the existential approach is the relationship of the person to existence itself.

Existential vacuum. As formulated by Frankl, the feeling that one's life is a void, that existence is empty of meaning.

Existentialism. A very general point of view in philosophy that places greater value on subjective experience than on objective data.

Experimental neurosis. The deviant response pattern of an organism that cannot make an adequate discrimination between two conflicting conditioned stimuli.

Extinction. In conditioning theory, learning to stop responding to the conditioned stimulus.

Extroverted attitude. In Jungian theory, a tendency to have a dominant interest in the outside world as opposed to the inner world of thought and the mind.

Fantasy. An ego defense mechanism in which the ego allows the individual to indulge in imaginary wish-fulfilling experiences.

Feeling enhancers. Psychedelic agents that are said to augment emotional responses.

Feeling-oriented meditation. Kind of meditation in which the meditator gives attention to an emotion-laden symbol.

Feeling talk. As formulated by Salter, a systematic assertive skill in which the person more openly expresses feelings.

Fictional finalism. As formulated by Vaihinger and elaborated by Adler, the doctrine that one's imagined future determines one's present actions.

Fixation. In Freudian theory, refers to the libido or part of the libido becoming permanently attached to one of the infantile levels of psychosexual development.

Fogging. In assertiveness training, a skill that teaches acceptance of manipulative criticism by the strategy of superficially agreeing with a critic.

Formal operations. As formulated by Piaget, refers to the last stage of cognitive development. Characterized by the appearance of high-level cognitive capacities.

Free association. Used as a way of probing the unconscious mental processes of a patient in psychoanalysis. The patient is asked to relax and tell the therapist anything that comes to mind.

Functional hypoglycemia. Hypoglycemia without apparent organic basis.

Game. As formulated by Berne, refers to a set of manipulative transactions between at least two people.

General adaptation syndrome. As identified by Selye, a typical reaction pattern of organisms subjected to chronic stress. Involves stages of alarm, resistance, and exhaustion.

General semantics. An approach to adjustment and growth that places great emphasis on the importance of improving our language environment.

Genital stage. In Freudian theory, the final stage of psychosexual development. It is estimated that this stage begins at approximately the twelfth or thirteenth year of life, and there is no psychosexual stage beyond it.

Gestalt. A German word with such meanings as pattern, configuration, and organized whole.

Gestalt techniques. In Gestalt therapy, various methods of helping the individual integrate fragmented parts of the self and to recognize the nature of personal impasses.

Grand mal seizure. A large convulsion manifested by the epileptic person.

Habit. In learning theory, conceptualized as a learned response pattern.

Hallucinogen. A drug that alters conventional perception and thought.

Hatha Yoga. Kind of Yoga used to help the individual attain better physical health. The most popular form of Yoga in the Western world.

Hedonism. As an explanation of human behavior, the view that pleasure and pain are the main factors in human motivation.

Higher-order conditioning. Learning to respond to a second conditioned stimulus in which the learning is reinforced by a first conditioned stimulus, not by an unconditioned stimulus.

Holism. The doctrine that an organism is an organized whole that cannot be meaningfully divided into parts.

Hypnotism. From the Greek word *hypnos*, meaning sleep. A state with a superficial resemblance to sleep in which a subject tends to be more suggestible than usual.

Hypoglycemia. A pathological condition in which the individual suffers from chronic low blood sugar.

I-it relationship. A relationship in which the subject reduces the other individual to a thing or an object in the subject's environment.

I-message. A communication skill in which one takes responsibility for a feeling instead of projecting it or blaming it on another person.

I-thou relationship. As formulated by Buber, a relationship in which the subject recognizes that the other individual is a real person with feelings and a world-view of his or her own.

Id. In Freudian theory, the primitive and basic portion of the personality.

Ideal self. The self that one feels he or she would like to be or ought to be.

Identification. An ego defense mechanism in which the individual associates his or her ego with the ego of an admired person.

Identity. A sense of continuity as a person. The feeling that one knows who one really is. Association of the self with one's social roles.

Implosive therapy. A form of behavior therapy in which a client adapts to fearful stimuli by experiencing anxiety at very high levels.

Individual psychology. Approach toward psychology formulated by Adler. Individual's capacity to direct his or her own life.

Individuation process. In Jungian theory, a process of inner psychological growth. A tendency in the direction of self-realization and wholeness.

Inferiority complex. As formulated by Adler, a set of negative beliefs about oneself, all revolving about a central core.

Insight. In psychoanalytic theory, becoming aware of a previously unconscious idea or motive. Also, gaining greater understanding of a personal problem.

Instinctoid. Term used by writers such as Jung and Maslow to suggest inborn behavioral tendencies in human beings that bear distinct similarities to instincts in animals.

Institutional psychiatry. As formulated by Szasz, a kind of psychiatry in which the sufferer has psychiatric treatment imposed on him or her.

Instrumental conditioning. Learning that certain actions will produce certain results. Performing in such a way as to obtain reinforcers.

Intellect-oriented meditation. Kind of meditation in which the meditator gives his or her attention to something that stimulates or challenges thinking capacities.

Intimacy. Psychological or emotional closeness. In transactional analysis, refers to gamefree emotional exchanges between people.

Introverted attitude. In Jungian theory, a tendency to have a dominant interest in the inner world of thought and the mind as opposed to the outside world.

Jnana Yoga. Kind of Yoga in which harmony with the Infinite is acquired through self-knowledge.

Knowledge of results. In the psychology of human learning, the principle that learning is facilitated if one knows the results of what one is doing. Similar to the concepts of reinforcement and feedback.

Koan. In Zen, a "puzzler" or thought-provoking paradox used to foster enlightenment.

Latency stage. In Freudian theory, the fourth stage of psychosexual development. It is estimated that the latency stage lasts from about the sixth year of life to about the twelfth year. During the latency stage there is no conscious interest in sexuality.

Latent learning. Learning that takes place without reinforcement and lays dormant until it is ready to be used.

Latent level. In Freudian dream interpretation, it refers to what the dream is about, what the dream means. The deep or real layer of the dream.

Law of effect. As formulated by Thorndike, the view that actions leading to a state of satisfaction are learned by the organism.

Libido. In Freudian theory, the energy that makes the mechanisms of personality go. Freud felt that this energy was both psychological and sexual in nature.

Life change units (LCUs). As formulated by Rahe and Holmes, a unit of measurement assigning a numerical value to stressful changes in one's life. These changes can be in either a positive or a negative direction.

Limen. The threshold of consciousness.

Lobotomy. A surgical procedure in which the connections between the frontal lobes of the cortex are severed from the subcortex.

Long-range hedonism. As formulated by such thinkers as Ellis and Mowrer, the view that it is better to maximize one's total happiness over a lifespan than to live only for the pleasure of the moment.

Madness. A nonclinical term for psychotic reactions.

Major tranquilizers. Various kinds of drugs used to combat psychotic reactions.

Mandala. In Eastern religions, a venerated circular pattern.

Manifest level. In Freudian dream interpretation, refers to the surface features of a dream.

Mantra. A sacred word or chant used in meditation for the purpose of facilitating concentration.

Maya. In Eastern philosophy, the doctrine that the perceived world is an illusion veiling reality.

Meditation. Concentration of thought and attention. In Eastern philosophy, meditation is used to achieve mystical union with the All. In the West, meditation may be used with the lesser goal of finding greater serenity and peace of mind.

Megavitamin therapy. Prescribing massive doses of selected vitamins for a sufferer. Megavitamin therapy is applicable to both physical and psychological ailments.

Melancholic. A moody and easily depressed temperament.

Mental disorders. Maladaptive patterns of behavior. Used in *DSM-III* to describe and classify such patterns.

Minimal brain damage. A condition in which damage to the nervous system is so slight that the individual in question seems to be organically normal.

Moderate behaviorism. Agrees with the general behavioristic view that behavior, not consciousness, is the subject matter of psychology. However, asserts that thinking, a covert and not directly observable process, is a kind of behavior.

Mysticism. The doctrine that through the use of a power of the mind such as intuition it is possible for a human being to have a direct experience with God or Ultimate Reality.

Negative reinforcer. A reinforcer that precedes an instrumental action. In such a case the instrumental action is a means of avoiding or escaping from the negative reinforcer.

Neo-Freudians. Psychoanalysts who disagree with some of the important concepts in Freudian theory, offering in their place concepts of their own. The neo-Freudians do, however, accept the basic concept of an unconscious mental life.

Neurosis. In traditional terms, an emotional disorder often characterized by anxiety, restlessness, nervous tension, phobias, obsessive-compulsive patterns, and depression. The term is no longer used to identify a single principal diagnostic category in *DSM-III*. Instead, contemporary nomenclature associates the concept of neurosis with five categories: affective, anxiety, somatoform, dissociative, and psychosexual disorders. Consequently, the word *neurosis* standing alone has neither a formal nor a precise meaning.

Neurotransmitters. Chemical substances capable of either exciting or inhibiting the activity of an adjacent neuron. They act as message carriers.

Nihilism. The view that nothing, including existence, is of any value. A doctrine of scepticism in which the denial of our capacity to know anything for certain is made a central principle.

Nondirective counseling. An older name, no longer in vogue, for client-centered counseling. Suggested that the client-centered therapist does not give explicit advice to a client about how to conduct his or her life or how to solve a personal problem.

Nonordinary reality. According to don Juan, the world that appears during special states of altered consciousness.

Norepinephrine. A hormone produced by the adrenal glands. When found in the nervous system, it acts as a transmitter substance between neurons.

Nothingness. As formulated by Sartre, the other side of Being.

Noumenon. The thing-in-itself, the reality.

Oedipus complex. In Freudian theory, a set of conflicting ideas associated with a core incest fantasy during early childhood toward the parent of the opposite sex.

Operant behavior. Any behavior that produces a change in the external environment. Virtually synonymous with instrumental behavior.

Opiate. A narcotic with the dual actions of sedation and pain relief. In moderate doses, it produces euphoria or a sense of well-being.

Oral character. In Freudian theory, a personality structure underlying such oral gratifications as excessive talking, smoking, and eating.

Oral stage. In Freudian theory the first psychosexual stage, lasting from birth to between twelve and eighteen months of age.

Ordinary reality. According to don Juan, the world as perceived by the average individual, the consensual world.

Orthomolecular psychiatry. Kind of psychiatric practice in which the psychiatrist prescribes that the mental patient follow a sound nutritional regime. Often the psychiatrist prescribes massive doses of selected vitamins.

Out-of-body experience. An experience in which the individual feels that the self has become detached from the physical body. Also referred to as *travelling clairvoyance* and *astral projection*.

Oversocialized. As formulated by Eysenck, it refers to a person who is too concerned with the letter of the law, too inhibited, and correct to a fault.

Overt behavior. Behavior that is observable by two or more individuals.

Pantheism. A doctrine that asserts there is no distinction between the universe and God.

Parent ego state. In transactional analysis, a set of value-oriented "recordings" carried forward from childhood, consisting of a number of "oughts" and "shoulds."

Partial reinforcement. Reinforcement in which the instrumental response is successful in producing the reinforcer only some of the time.

Partial reinforcement effect. A phenomenon in which organisms manifest greater resistance to extinction when trained under conditions of partial reinforcement than when trained under conditions of continuous reinforcement.

Peak experience. As formulated by Maslow, the experience associated with a wonderful moment in one's life—a moment of ecstasy, rapture, or creativity.

Perceptions. The organized wholes constructed by the individual out of the raw data of experience.

Perceptual-conscious. In early writings of Freud, the "surface" of the mind; the portion of the mind in moment-to-moment contact with reality.

Persona. In Jungian theory, an archetype of the self representing one's public self or social mask.

Personal growth. As used in this book, synonymous with the concept of self-actualization. Developing one's talents and potentialities.

Personal unconscious. Concept introduced by Carl Jung to distinguish the Freudian unconscious from Jung's formulation of a collective unconscious. The personal unconscious consists of an individual's repressed ideas based on his or her unique personal experiences.

Personality. A more or less stable set of traits, habits, and motivational predispositions characteristic of a particular individual.

Personalization. In the framework of cognitive therapy, a tendency of one person to take responsibility for another person's failures, lack of success, or otherwise disappointing behavior.

Phallic character. In Freudian theory, a personality structure associated with unresolved conflicts over masturbation and incest wishes. It is asserted that the person with a phallic character structure is unable to give others real love, only synthetic love.

Phallic stage. In Freudian theory, the third psychosexual stage. This third psychosexual stage is estimated to last from about the third year to the sixth year of life.

Phenomenal field. The world as the individual perceives it.

Phenomenology. The study of the way the individual perceives and constructs his or her own version of reality.

Phenomenon. The appearance of a thing in the mind, things as perceived.

Placebo effect. The capacity of almost any treatment "to please" the patient or client and to elicit a temporary improvement.

Positive reinforcer. A reinforcer that follows an instrumental action.

Prana. A vital energy believed by yogis to be in the air we breathe.

Preconscious. In early writings of Freud, the portion of the mind just below the conscious surface; similar to the popular psychology concept of "the subconscious mind."

Pregenital sexuality. In Freudian theory, the sexual life of infants and children. Sensuous gratification received through erogenous zones in the early years, forming the foundation for genital or adult sexuality.

Premature ejaculation. Ejaculating too quickly. A condition in which the male attains his orgasm before the female attains hers.

Preoperational thought. Thinking that is stimulus-bound, anthropomorphic, and egocentric.

Primary hypertension. High blood pressure of unknown origin.

Primary impotence. A condition in which a male has never been able to have an erection adequate for sexual intercourse.

Primary orgasmic dysfunction. A condition in which a woman has never had an orgasm, and seems unable to have one.

Primary process. According to Freudian theory, the mental process used by the id; the process by which ideas have nonrational connections.

Principle of no-mind. In Zen, the teaching that too much conscious thought may interfere with spontaneous action.

Principle of no-thingness. In Zen, the teaching that the objects of perception are not things, but abstractions we have made out of the current of existence.

Principle of no-twoness. In Zen, the teaching that most dichotomies are false.

Progressive relaxation. As introduced by Jacobson, a step-by-step approach to relaxation in which conscious contraction and relaxation of sets of muscles is alternated.

Projection. The tendency to perceive the external world in terms of our personal motivational structure. As an ego defense mechanism, a tendency to see our failures and shortcomings as arising from external sources.

Projective tests. Personality tests based on the assumption that an individual's response to an ambiguous stimulus reveals a great deal about his or her unconscious mental life.

Psi abilities. Mental capacities asserted to transcend the mind's normal limits. Telepathy and extrasensory perception would be examples of psi abilities.

Psyche. Greek world for soul. Also used in psychology to signify the mind and/or the personality.

Psychedelic agents. Synonymous with psychotomimetic agents. Drugs that produce an experience in the taker similar to the experience of a psychotic reaction.

Psychic determinism. The point of view that all mental events have a cause.

Psychoanalysis. Refers to both a theory of personality and a kind of psychotherapy. Based on Freud's thinking with an emphasis on the importance of unconscious aspects of mental life.

Psychological functions. In Jungian theory, the processes by which the conscious mind orients itself toward the outer world and the inner world. Jung designated four psychological functions: thinking, feeling, sensation, and intuition.

Psychological testing. The giving of standardized tests of intelligence, personality, aptitude, or interest.

Psychomotor epilepsy. A form of epilepsy in which the patient is conscious during a seizure, but lacks voluntary control over his or her actions.

Psychopharmacology. The study of how drugs affect psychological and emotional processes.

Psychosocial development. Development of the human personality based on a child's relationship with significant other persons in his or her life.

Psychosomatic illness. An illness that is either caused by psychological-emotional factors or greatly aggravated by them.

Psychosurgery. Type of somatic therapy for mental illness. A broad term that includes lobotomy and electrical stimulation of the brain.

Psychotherapy. Treatment of emotional and behavioral disorders by psychological methods.

Psychotomimetic agents. Drugs that produce an effect that is said to "mimic" or copy the experience of a psychotic disorder.

Pubococcygeus muscle (PC muscle). A muscle surrounding the vaginal channel. Undergoes wavelike contractions during the female orgasm.

Radical behaviorism. The point of view that behavior cannot be explained by making references to consciousness. (In its most extreme form, the existence of consciousness is denied.)

Radical psychology. A counterculture movement within psychology that asserts that most existential suffering is the result of oppressive aspects of familiar social institutions.

Raja Yoga. "Royal" Yoga, the oldest form of Yoga. In Raja Yoga, meditation is used to pierce the veil of maya in order to attain ecstatic union with the All.

Rational-emotive therapy. As formulated by Ellis, an approach to adjustment and growth in which the client is encouraged to replace irrational ideas with rational ones.

Rationalization. An ego defense mechanism in which a cover motive replaces a real motive when the real motive is unacceptable to the ego.

Reaction formation. An ego defense mechanism in which a repressed thought or feeling is converted into its conscious opposite.

Reactive inhibition. In Hull's learning theory, a temporary fatiguelike process that acts to suppress a conditioned response.

Reciprocal inhibition. In systematic desensitization, the use of relaxation to counteract anxiety.

Recognition hunger. In transactional analysis, the need to have others confirm one's presence and existence.

Regression. An ego defense mechanism in which the individual exhibits behavior patterns that brought comfort at an earlier age.

Reinforcer. A stimulus that increases the probability of occurrence of a certain class of behavior.

Relaxation response. As formulated by Benson, an innate pattern that is antagonistic to the fight-or-flight reaction.

Repression. A process by which a psychological force opposes certain ideas and shoves them "down" into the nether territory of the unconscious.

Reserpine. A drug extracted from the Rauwolfia serpentina plant. The drug is sometimes used to treat psychotic disorders.

Resistance. A concept used in psychoanalysis to indicate mental blocks that thwart honest self-disclosure. Also used to indicate the unwilling-ness of a patient to accept a psychoanalytic inter-pretation.

Respondent behavior. Term used by Skinner to identify behavior associated with classical condi-tioning. Refers to behavior elicited by known stimuli.

Reward. As distinguished from a reinforcer in learning theory, a reward is defined in terms of what the giver of the reward subjectively believes to be of value to another organism.

Rinzai Zen. A school of Zen Buddhism utilizing the *koan* or paradoxical question as a device for hastening the arrival of satori or illumination.

Samadhi. The supreme goal of Yogic training. Experience of great bliss associated with mystical union with God, the All, or Ultimate Reality.

Satori. In Zen, a sudden awakening in which the spell of maya is cast off.

Scientific rationalism. The view that all events and experiences are explainable in terms of proc-esses associated with the natural world.

Scripts. In transactional analysis, an unconscious life plan.

Secondary impotence. A condition in which a male has an inadequate erection for intercourse twenty-five percent or more of the time.

Secondary process. According to Freudian the-ory, the mental process used by the ego; the pro-cess by which we are in contact with reality, think logically, and make rational decisions.

Sedative-hypnotic agents. Chemical substances that depress the action of brain arousal mecha-nisms.

Self-actualization. As formulated by Goldstein, striving toward becoming a complete person. As elaborated by Maslow, an inborn tendency to make the most of one's possibilities as a person.

Self-alienated. As formulated by Laing, a person-ality that is torn apart. A psychological situation such that a false outer self represses a real inner self.

Self-concept. The way that one sees oneself, con-sisting of the attributes an individual perceives himself or herself as having.

Self-esteem. Regarding oneself as having worth or value. Self-esteem can be thought of as a gra-dient ranging from low to high.

Self-realization. As formulated by Horney, the making of an optimal compromise between the inner urgings of the true self and the demands of the idealized self.

Self-regard. As formulated by Rogers, it refers to the need to have a reasonably positive estimate of one's self.

Sensations. The raw data of experience underly-ing organized perceptions. For example, patches of color and brightness are some of the sensa-tions making up the organized perception of a landscape.

Sexual response cycle. As formulated by Masters and Johnson, a four-stage cycle including (1) ex-citement, (2) plateau, (3) orgasm, and (4) resolu-tion.

Shadow. In Jungian theory, an archetype of the self representing the animal side of one's person-ality. Similar to Freud's concept of the id.

Shock therapies. Therapies in which the treat-ment involves sending the organism into a state of shock by either electrical or chemical means.

Situational orgasmic dysfunction. A condition in which a woman rarely has an orgasm with her sexual partner.

Social interest. According to Adler, an inborn drive to be gregarious and also concerned about the welfare of other human beings.

Somatic nervous system. The subsystem of the nervous system that controls the muscles at-tached to the skeleton. Traditionally, said to be under one's voluntary control.

Somatic therapies. Therapies applied directly to the body for the purpose of alleviating the effects of mental illness.

Soto Zen. A school of Zen Buddhism advocating a gradual approach to satori. Emphasis is placed on seated meditation.

Spontaneous recovery. The reappearance after a

rest period of a conditioned response previously extinguished.

Stimulants. Drugs that tend to increase one's alertness, quickening central nervous system arousal mechanisms.

Stimulus-bound. As formulated by Piaget, refers to a child's thinking when he or she makes evaluations on the basis of one and only one outstanding aspect of a stimulus situation.

Stimulus generalization. Progressive decrements in the magnitude of a conditioned response on either side of an original conditioned stimulus value. The capacity of an organism to detect similarities and differences among a set of conditioned stimuli.

Stimulus hunger. The craving for some kind of sensory input.

Stochastic processes. Probability processes in which events are neither wholly dependent on nor wholly independent of past occurrences.

Stress. As formulated by Selye, the sum of all nonspecific changes caused by function or damage. Also, the rate of wear and tear on the body.

Stressor. That which produces stress. A condition that can activate the general adaptation syndrome. Not to be confused with stress itself.

Stroke. In transactional analysis, any act that recognizes the presence of another person.

Structural analysis. In transactional analysis, structural analysis is the study of how the three ego states—Parent, Adult, and Child—relate to each other in a single individual.

Structure hunger. The craving for "something to do" or "somewhere to go."

Sublimation. In Freudian theory, a process in which direct sexual expression of libido is repressed and reappears in modified form as a general interest in the wider world.

Superego. In Freudian theory, that aspect of the personality orienting itself toward abstract concepts of good and bad, right and wrong, decency and indecency. The superego is said to be morality-oriented.

Superiority striving. According to Adler, a striving to make the most of oneself.

Swami. A Yoga master.

Synapse. The gap between two neurons.

Systematic desensitization. A learning procedure by which an individual learns to adapt to anxiety-arousing and fear-arousing stimuli. In systematic desensitization, the noxious stimuli are presented in a hierarchy from most noxious to least noxious.

Systematic thinkers. Advocates of one particular school of thought such as psychoanalysis or behaviorism.

Tabula rasa. As formulated by the philosopher John Locke, the view that the mind at birth contains no inborn ideas.

Tao. In Chinese thought, the fundamental principle of life. The Way, the Master Way, of existence.

Taoism. The ancient religion of China.

Theta rhythm. An electroencephalographic pattern occurring at the rate of about four to eight cycles per second.

Top dog. As formulated by Perls, an aspect of the human personality tending to be righteous, authoritarian, and a bully.

Transaction. According to Berne, the unit of social intercourse in which there is some sort of communicative give and take between at least two persons.

Transactional analysis. As formulated by Berne, an approach to adjustment and growth that emphasizes the positive value of nonmanipulative communication.

Transcendental Meditation. A Yogic technique brought to the widespread attention of Americans by the Maharishi Mahesh Yogi. In Transcendental Meditation, the meditator focuses on a *mantra* as a means of attaining a state of pure awareness.

Transference. In psychoanalytic theory, the transfer by patients of feelings held in childhood toward their parents to the therapist.

Transpersonal psychology. An orientation toward psychology representing a blend of Eastern philosophy, esoteric knowledge, and Western psychology. "Mental science" in contrast to tough-minded behavioral science.

Transpersonal psychotherapy. A kind of psychotherapy aiming to help individuals reach a high state of personal development variously called liberation, enlightenment, individuation, wisdom, or certainty.

True self. As formulated by Horney, the self that one was "born to become." That self maximizing one's unique abilities, interests, and aptitudes.

Type A behavior. As described by Friedman and Rosenman, a behavior pattern characterized by a high level of time urgency, aggressive competitiveness, and an inability to relax and enjoy life.

Type B behavior. As described by Friedman and Rosenman, a behavior pattern characterized by a lack of time urgency and the presence of an interest in the process of living.

Unconditional positive regard. As formulated by Rogers, an orientation on the part of the therapist in which the client as a person is not judged by the therapist.

Unconditioned response. A response that is not learned. A response arising from a presumably inborn response potential.

Unconditioned stimulus. A stimulus to which there exists in the organism an unlearned response potential.

Unconscious mind. In early writings of Freud, a domain of the personality not accessible to the conscious ego.

Voluntarism. The doctrine that free will is a reality.

Will to meaning. As formulated by Frankl, an inborn impulse that motivates us to do things that make sense to us in terms of our place in the larger scheme of things.

Will to power. As formulated by Nietzsche and elaborated by Adler, the contention that there is an inborn tendency in all of us to gain ascendency over others.

Workaholics. Persons addicted to the activities associated with their jobs or vocations.

Yang. In Eastern philosophy, the name given to positive aspects of the world.

Yin. In Eastern philosophy, the name given to negative aspects of the world.

Yoga. A world-view associated with East Indian philosophy. Yoga teaches that it is possible for the person to go beyond maya or perceptual reality and achieve perfect union with God or Ultimate Reality.

Yogi. One who practices Yoga. The term suggests that the practitioner has attained a certain level of expertise.

Za-zen. As advocated by Soto Zen, seated meditation in an approved posture.

Zeitgeist. A German word referring to the dominant mood or way of thinking typical of a particular culture or time period.

Zen Buddhism. A meditative approach to Buddhism in which a prime goal is to see into one's own true nature.

References

Abrahamson, E. M., and Pezet, A. W. *Body, Mind, and Sugar*. New York: Pyramid Books, 1971.

Adler, A. *Practice and Theory of Individual Psychology*. New York: Harcourt, Brace & World, 1927.

_____. *What Life Should Mean to You*. London: George Allen & Unwin, 1932.

Alberti, R. E. "Assertive Behavior Therapy." In *The Psychotherapy Handbook*. R. Herink (Ed.). New York: The New American Library, 1980, 47–49.

_____, and Emmons, M. L. *Your Perfect Right*. San Luis Obispo, Calif.: Impact, 1978.

Albertson, E. *Spiritual Yoga for the Millions*. Los Angeles: Sherbourne Press, 1969.

Alexander, F. F., and Selesnick, S. T. *The History of Psychiatry*. New York: New American Library, 1968.

Allport, G. As quoted in Hall, C. S., and Lindzey, G., *Theories of Personality* (3rd ed.). New York: John Wiley and Sons, 1978.

American Psychiatric Association. *A Psychiatric Glossary* (5th ed.). Washington, D.C.: American Psychiatric Association, 1980.

American Psychiatric Association. *Diagnostic and Statistical Manual of Mental Disorders* (3rd ed.). (*DSM-III*). Washington, D.C.: American Psychiatric Association, 1980.

Ansbacher, H. L., and Ansbacher, R. R. *The Individual Psychology of Alfred Adler*. New York: Harper & Row, 1964.

Aronson, E. "The Rationalizing Animal." *Psychology Today*, 6 (1973), 46–52.

_____. *The Social Animal* (3rd ed.). San Francisco: W. H. Freeman, 1980.

Atkinson, J. W. "Motivational Determinants of Risk-Taking Behavior." *Psychological Review*, 64 (1957), 359–372.

Azrin, N. "Pain and Aggression." In *Readings in Psychology Today* (2nd ed.). Del Mar, Calif.: CRM Books, 1972.

Bach, G. R. and Deutsch, R. M. *Stop! You're Driving Me Crazy*. New York: Berkley Books, 1979.

Bassin, A. "Reality Therapy." In *The Psychotherapy Handbook*. R. Herink (Ed.). New York: The New American Library, 1980, pp. 553–557.

Bateson, G. "Breaking Out of the Double Bind." As interviewed in *Psychology Today* by D. Goleman, 12 (1978), 42–51.

Beck, A. T. *Cognitive Therapy*. New York: The New American Library, 1976.

Becker, W. C., and Becker, J. W. *Successful Parenthood*. Chicago: Follett Publishing Co., 1974.

Beier, E. G. and Valens, E. G. *People-Reading*. New York: Warner Books, 1975.

Beltz, S. *How to Make Johnny Want to Obey*. Englewood Cliffs, N.J.: Prentice-Hall, 1971.

Benares, C. *Zen Without Zen Masters*. Berkeley, Calif.: And/Or Press, 1977.

Bennet, E. A. *What Jung Really Said*. New York: Schocken Books, 1966.

Benson, H. *The Relaxation Response*. New York: William Morrow, 1975.

_____. *The Mind/Body Effect*. New York: Berkley Books, 1979.

Berne, E. *Games People Play*. New York: Grove Press, 1964.

_____. *Principles of Group Treatment*. New York: Grove Press, 1966.

_____. *What Do You Say after You Say Hello?* New York: Grove Press, 1972.

Binswanger, L. *Being-in-the-World*. New York: Harper & Row, 1963.

Blakney, R. B. *The Way of Life: Lao-tzu*. New York: New American Library, 1955.

Bloomfield, H. H., Cain, M. P., and Jaffe, D. T. *Transcendental Meditation: Discovering Inner Energy and Overcoming Stress*. New York: Delacorte Press, 1975.

_____, and Kory, R. B. *The Holistic Way to Health and Happiness*. New York: Simon and Schuster, 1978.

Bolen, J. S. *The Tao of Psychology*. New York: Harper & Row, 1979.

Boss, M. *Psychoanalysis and Daseinsanalysis*. New York: Basic Books, 1963.

Bradshaw, P. *The Management of Self-Esteem*. Englewood Cliffs, N.J.: Prentice-Hall, 1981.

Brown, B. *New Mind, New Body*. New York: Harper & Row, 1974.

_____. *Supermind*. New York: Harper & Row, 1980.

Bruner, J. S., Goodnow, J., and Austin, G. *A Study of Thinking*. New York: John Wiley & Sons, 1956.

Bry, A. (Ed.), *Inside Psychotherapy*. New York: New American Library, 1972.

Budzynski, T., and Stoyva, J. "An Instrument for Producing Deep Muscle Relaxation by Means of Analog Information Feedback." *Journal of Applied Behavior Analysis*, 2 (1969), 231–237.

Bugelski, B. R., and Graziano, A. M. *The Handbook of Practical Psychology*. Englewood Cliffs, N.J.: Prentice Hall, 1980.

Burns, D. D. *Feeling Good*. New York: William Morrow, 1980.

Buscaglia, L. F. *Personhood*. Thorofare, N.J.: Charles B. Slack, 1978.

Bush, R. R., and Mosteller, F. *Stochastic Models For Learning*. New York: John Wiley & Sons, 1955.

Calvin, W. H., and Ojemann, G. A. *Inside the Brain*. New York: New American Library, 1980.

Castaneda, C. *A Separate Reality*. New York: Simon & Schuster, 1971.

———. *The Teachings of don Juan: A Yaqui Way of Knowledge*. New York: Ballantine Books, 1968.

Chase, S. *The Tyranny of Words*. New York: Harcourt, Brace & World, 1966.

Chaudhuri, H. *Integral Yoga*. Wheaton, Ill.: Theosophical Publishing House, 1965.

Clark, M. "Coping with Depression." *Newsweek*, January 8, 1975.

Conrad, P. "On the Medicalization of Deviance and Social Control." In *Critical Psychiatry: The Politics of Mental Health*. D. Ingleby (Ed.). New York: Pantheon Books, 1980.

Costales, C., and Berry, J. *Alcoholism*. Glendale, Calif.: G/L Publications, 1980.

Craighead, W. E., Kazdin, A. E., and Mahoney, M. J. *Behavior Modification: Principles, Issues, and Applications*. Boston: Houghton Mifflin, 1976.

Crichton, M. *The Terminal Man*. New York: Alfred A. Knopf, 1972.

Cronin, A. J. *The Green Years*. Boston, Mass.: Little, Brown, 1945.

Delgado, J. M. R. *Physical Control of the Mind: Toward a Psychocivilized Society*. New York: Harper & Row, 1969.

———, Miller, N. E., and Roberts, W. W., "Learning Motivated by Electrical Stimulation of the Brain." *American Journal of Physiology*, 179 (1954), 587–593.

Dement, W. C. et al. "Sleeplessness, Sleep Attacks and Things That Go Wrong in the Night." *Psychology Today*, 9 (1975), 45–50.

DeQuincey, T. *Confessions of an English Opium-Eater*. New York: E. P. Dutton & Co., 1907. (First published in 1822.)

deRopp, R. S. *Warrior's Way*. New York: Delta, 1979.

Dollard, J., and Miller, N. *Personality and Psychotherapy*. New York: McGraw-Hill Book Co., 1950.

Dunlap, K. *Habits: Their Making and Unmaking*. New York: Liveright, 1932.

Dusay, J. M. *Egograms*. New York: Bantam, 1977.

Dyer, W. *The Sky's the Limit*. New York: Simon and Schuster, 1980.

Dyson, F. *Disturbing the Universe*. New York: Harper & Row, 1979.

Egner, R. E. (Ed.), *Bertrand Russell's Best*. New York: New American Library, 1958.

Ehrlich, P. R. *The Population Bomb*. New York: Ballantine Books, 1968.

Ellis, A. *Humanistic Psychotherapy: The Rational-Emotive Approach*. New York: Julian Press, 1973.

———, and Harper, R. A. *A Guide to Rational Living*. Englewood Cliffs, N.J.: Prentice-Hall, 1961.

Estes, W. K. "Experimental Study of Punishment." *Psychological Monographs*, 57 (1944), 1–40.

Eysenck, H. J. *Sense and Nonsense in Psychology*. Baltimore: Penguin Books, 1957.

———. "The Effects of Psychotherapy: An Evaluation." *Journal of Consulting Psychology*, 16 (1952), 310–324.

———. *The Effects of Psychotherapy*. New York: The International Science Press, 1966.

Fabry, J. B. *The Pursuit of Meaning*. New York: Harper & Row, 1980.

Fagan, J., and Shepherd I.L.(Eds.), *Gestalt Therapy Now*. New York: Harper & Row, 1970.

Faraday, A. *Dream Power*. New York: Berkley Medallion Books, 1973.

Farberow, N. L. "Indirect Self-Destructive Behavior: Classification and Characteristics." In

The Many Faces of Suicide. N. L. Farberow (Ed.). New York: McGraw-Hill, 1980, pp. 15–27.

_____. *The Many Faces of Suicide*. New York: McGraw-Hill, 1980.

Feder, E., and Feder, B. *The Expressive Arts Therapies*. Englewood Cliffs, N.J.: Prentice-Hall, 1981.

Feingold, B. F. "An Interview." *People Weekly* (December 8, 1975).

_____. *Why Your Child Is Hyperactive*. New York: Random House, 1974.

Fensterheim, H., and Baer, J., *Don't Say Yes When You Want To Say No*. New York: David McKay, 1975.

Festinger, L. *A Theory of Cognitive Dissonance*. Stanford, Calif.: Stanford University Press, 1957.

Feuerstein, M., and Skjei, E. *Mastering Pain*. New York: Bantam, 1979.

Fine, R. *A History of Psychoanalysis*. New York: Columbia University Press, 1979.

Fitzgerald, E., trans. *Rubáiyát of Omar Khayyám*. New York: Grosset and Dunlap, 1946.

Fordham, F. *An Introduction to Jung's Psychology*. Baltimore: Penguin Books, 1966.

Forman, L. H. and Ramsburg, J. S. *Hello Sigmund, This Is Eric!* Kansas City: Sheed Andrews and McMeel, 1978.

Frank, J. *Persuasion and Healing*. Baltimore: Johns Hopkins Press, 1961.

Frankl, V. E. *Man's Search for Meaning*. Boston: Beacon Press, 1962.

_____. *Psychotherapy and Existentialism*. New York: Washington Square Press, 1967.

_____. *The Doctor and the Soul*. New York: Alfred A. Knopf, 1955.

_____. *The Will to Meaning*. New York: The New American Library, 1969.

Freed, A. *T.A. for Tots*. Sacramento, Calif.: Jalmar Press, 1973.

Freeman, L. *Freud Rediscovered*. New York: Arbor House, 1980.

Freeman, W., and Watts, J. W. *Psychosurgery in the Treatment of Mental Disorders and Intractable Pain*. Springfield, Ill.: Charles C. Thomas, 1950.

Freud, S. *The Ego and the Id*. London: Hogarth Press, 1923.

_____. *The Interpretation of Dreams*. London: Hogarth Press, 1900.

_____. "The Unconscious," in *A History of the Psycho-Analytic Movement, Papers on Metapsychology and Other Works*. London: Hogarth Press, 1915.

Freudenberger, H. J., and Richelson, G. *Burn-Out*. New York: Doubleday, 1980.

Friedberg, J. *Shock Treatment Is Not Good For Your Brain*. San Francisco: Glide Publications, 1976.

Friedman, M., and Rosenman, R. H. *Type A Behavior and Your Heart*. New York: Knopf, 1974.

Fromm, E. *The Anatomy of Human Destructiveness*. New York: Holt, Rinehart & Winston, 1972.

_____. *Greatness and Limitations of Freud's Thought*. New York: Harper & Row, 1980.

_____, Suzuki, D. T., and DeMartino, R. *Zen Buddhism and Psychoanalysis*. New York: Harper & Row, 1970.

Fromme, A. *The Book for Normal Neurotics*. New York: Farrar, Straus, and Giroux, 1981.

Gaines, J. *Fritz Perls*. Millbrae, Calif.: Celestial Arts, 1979.

Galin, D. "The Two Modes of Consciousness and the Two Halves of the Brain." In *Consciousness: Brain, States of Awareness, and Mysticism*. D. Goleman and R. J. Davidson (Eds.) New York: Harper & Row, 1979.

Gardner, H. "Hello Up There, Dr. Q." *Human Behavior* (January 1975) vol. 4, pp. 24–29.

Gardner, M. "A Skeptic's View of Parapsychology." In *Psychology 81/82*. T. H. Carr and H. E. Fitzgerald (Eds.). Guilford, Ct.: The Dushkin Publishing Group, 1981, 70–71.

Gaylin, W. *Feelings*. New York: Harper & Row, 1979.

Gerald, M. C. *Pharmacology*. Englewood Cliffs, N.J.: Prentice-Hall, 1974.

Gibran, K. *The Voice of the Master*. New York: Citadel Press, 1958.

Ginott, H. G. *Between Parent and Child*. New York: Avon Books, 1969.

Glasser, W. *Reality Therapy*. New York: Harper & Row, 1965.

_____. *The Identity Society*. New York: Harper & Row, 1972.

_____, and Zunin, L. M. "Reality Therapy," in R. Corsini (Ed.), *Current Psychotherapies*. Itasca, Ill.: F. E. Peacock Publishers, 1973.

_____. *Stations of the Mind.* New York: Harper & Row, 1981.

Goble, F. *The Third Force.* New York: Pocket Books, 1971.

Goldiamond, I. "Self-control Procedures in Personal Behavior Problems." reprinted in Gazzaniga, M.S., and Lovejoy E. P., (Eds.), *Good Reading in Psychology.* Englewood Cliffs, N.J.: Prentice-Hall, 1971.

Gordon, T. *Parent Effectiveness Training.* New York: Peter H. Wyden, 1970.

Graedon, J. *The People's Pharmacy* (2nd ed.). New York: Avon, 1980.

Green, E. E., and Green, A. M. *Beyond Biofeedback.* New York: Delacorte Press, 1977.

_____, Green, A. M., and Walters, E. D. "Voluntary Control of Internal States: Psychological and Physiological." *Journal of Transpersonal Psychology,* 2 (1970), 1–26.

Greenberg, R. P., and Fisher, S. "Testing Dr. Freud." *Human Behavior,* 9 (1978), 28–33.

Guthrie, E. R. *The Psychology of Learning.* New York: Harper & Row, 1935.

Halas, C., and Matteson, R. *I've Done So Well—Why Do I Feel So Bad?* New York: Ballantine Books, 1978.

Hall, C. S. *The Meaning of Dreams.* New York: McGraw-Hill Book Co., 1966.

Harris, T. *I'm OK—You're OK.* New York: Harper & Row, 1967.

Hayakawa, S. I. "How Words Change Our Lives," in *Symbol, Status, and Personality.* New York: Harcourt, Brace & World, 1963.

Heath, R. G. "Electrical Self-stimulation of the Brain in Man." *American Journal of Psychiatry,* 120 (1963), 571–577.

_____. "Modulation of Emotion with a Brain Pacemaker: Treatment for Intractable Psychiatric Illness." *J. of Nervous and Mental Disease,* 165 (1977), 300–317.

Heidegger, M. *Being and Time.* New York: Harper & Row, 1962.

Henderson, C. W. *Awakening.* Englewood Cliffs, N.J.: Prentice-Hall, 1975.

Herrigel, E. *The Method of Zen.* New York: Random House, 1960.

Hilgard, E R., and Bower, G. H. *Theories of Learning* (3rd ed.). New York: Appleton-Century-Crofts, 1966.

Hilton, J. *Lost Horizon.* New York: William Morrow, 1933.

Hilts, P. J. *Behavior Mod.* New York: Harper's Magazine Press, 1974.

Holroyd, S. *The Quest of the Quiet Mind: The Philosophy of Krishnamurti.* Wellingborough, Northamptonshire, Great Britain: The Aquarian Press, 1980.

Homme, L. *How to Use Contingency Contracting in the Classroom.* Champaign, Ill.: Research Press, 1970.

Hoover, T. *The Zen Experience.* New York: New American Library, 1980.

Horney, K. *The Neurotic Personality of Our Time.* New York: W. W. Norton & Co., 1937.

_____. *Our Inner Conflicts.* New York: W. W. Norton & Co., 1945.

Hudspeth, W. J. "Sugar and a Fad Disease: A Case of Mistaken Identity." *Psychology Today,* 14 (1980), 120.

Hughes, R., and Brewin, R. *The Tranquilizing of America.* New York: Warner Books, 1979.

Hull, C. L. *Principles of Behavior.* New York: Appleton-Century-Crofts, 1943.

Hutschnecker, A. A. *Hope.* New York: G. P. Putnam's Sons, 1981.

James, M. and Jongeward, D. *Born to Win.* Reading, Mass.: Addison-Wesley Publishing Co., 1971.

James, W. *The Principles of Psychology.* New York: Henry Holt, 1890.

Johnson, W. *People in Quandaries.* New York: Harper & Row, 1946.

Julien, R. M. *A Primer of Drug Action.* San Francisco: W. H. Freeman, 1978.

Jung, C. G. *Memories, Dreams, Reflections.* New York: Holt, Rinehart & Winston, 1972.

_____. *Two Essays on Analytical Psychology.* Princeton, N.J.: Princeton University Press, 1953.

Kamiya, J. "Conscious Control of Brain Waves." *Readings in Experimental Psychology Today.* Del Mar, Calif.: CRM Books, 1970.

Kaplan, H. S. *The New Sex Therapy.* New York: Brunner-Mazel, 1974.

Kapleau, P. *Zen Dawn in the West.* New York: Doubleday, 1979.

Karpman, S. B. "Fairy Tale and Script Drama Analysis." *Transactional Analysis Bulletin,* 7(1968), 39–43.

Kelly, G. A. *The Psychology of Personal Constructs.* New York: Norton, 1955.

Kennett, J. *Selling Water by the River.* New York: Random House, 1972.

Kierkegaard, S. *Fear and Trembling and Sickness unto Death*. New York: Doubleday, 1954.

_____. *Kierkegaard Anthology*. New York: Modern Library, 1959.

Kiester, E. "Images of the Night." *Science 80*, 1 (1980), 36–43.

Kinsey, A. C., Pomeroy, W. B., Martin, C. E., and Gebhard, P. H. *Sexual Behavior in the Human Male*. Philadelphia: W. B. Saunders, 1948.

_____, Pomeroy, W. B., Martin, C. E., and Gebhard, P. H. *Sexual Behavior in the Human Female*. Philadelphia: W. B. Saunders, 1953.

Kirschenbaum, H. *On Becoming Carl Rogers*. New York: Dell, 1979.

Kline, N. S. *From Sad to Glad*. New York: Ballantine Books, 1974.

Koestler, A. *The Ghost in the Machine*. New York: Macmillan, 1967.

Korzybski, A. *Science and Sanity* (4th ed.). Lakeville, Conn.: International Non-Aristotelian Library Publishing Co. 1958.

Kovel, J. *A Complete Guide to Therapy*. New York: Pantheon Books, 1976.

Krishnamurti, J. *Think on These Things*. New York: Harper & Row, 1964.

Kriyananda, Swami. *The Path*. Nevada City, Calif.: Ananda Publications, 1977.

Laing, R. D. *Knots*. New York: Random House, 1970.

_____. *The Divided Self*. London: Penguin Books, 1965.

_____. *The Politics of Experience*. London: Penguin Books, 1967.

Lang, P. "Autonomic Control." *Psychology Today*, 3 (1970), 37–41.

Lappé, F. M. *Diet for a Small Planet*. New York: Ballantine Books, 1971.

Lazarus, R. S., and Launier, R. "Stress-related Transactions Between Person and Environment." In *Perspectives in Interactional Psychology*. L. Pervin and M. Lewis (Eds.). New York: Plenum, 1978.

Lehrman, N. *Masters and Johnson Explained*. Chicago, Ill.: Playboy Press, 1976.

LeShan, L. *How to Meditate*. Boston: Little, Brown & Co., 1974.

Lesser, M. *Nutrition and Vitamin Therapy*. New York: Grove Press, 1980.

Liebman, J. L. *Peace of Mind*. New York: Simon & Schuster, 1946.

Loftus, E. *Memory*. Reading, Mass.: Addison-Wesley, 1980.

London, J. *The Star Rover*. New York: Macmillan, 1915.

London, P. *Behavior Control*. New York: Harper & Row, 1969.

Lubar, J. F. "Electrical Stimulation of the Brain." In *The Encyclopedia of Psychology*. Guilford, Conn.: DPG Reference Publishing, 1981, pp. 94–95.

Ludwig, E. *Doctor Freud*. New York: Manor Books, 1973.

Machlowitz, M. *Workaholics*. Reading, Mass.: Addison—Wesley, 1980.

Maglin, A. "Radical Therapy." In *The Psychotherapy Handbook*. R. Herink (Ed.). New York: New American Library, 1980.

Mahoney, M. J. "Cognitive-Behavioral Therapies." In *The Psychotherapy Handbook*. R. Herink (Ed.). New York: The New American Library, 1980, 94–96.

Martin, G., and Pear, J. *Behavior Modification: What It Is and How to Do It*. Englewood Cliffs, N.J.: Prentice-Hall, 1978.

Martin, R. R., and Poland, E. Y. *Learning to Change*. New York: McGraw-Hill, 1980.

Maslow, A. H. *Toward A Psychology of Being*. Princeton, N.J.: D. Van Nostrand Co., 1962.

_____. *Motivation and Personality*. New York: Harper & Row, 1954.

Masters, W. H., and Johnson, V. E. *Human Sexual Response*. Boston: Little, Brown and Company, 1966.

Maugham, W. S. *Of Human Bondage*. New York: Doubleday & Co., 1915.

May, R. *Love and Will*. New York: Dell Publishing, 1969.

_____ (Ed.), *Existential Psychology*. New York: Random House, 1960.

_____, Angel, E., and Ellenberger, H. F. (Eds.), *Existence: A New Dimension in Psychiatry and Psychology*. New York: Basic Books, 1958.

McMillen, S. I. *None of These Diseases*. Old Tappan, N.J.: Fleming H. Revell, 1973.

Meehl, P. E. "Schizotaxia, Schizotypy, Schizophrenia." *American Psychologists*, 17 (1962), 827–838.

Meichenbaum, D. *Cognitive–Behavior Modification*. New York: Plenum, 1977.

Meininger, J. *Success Through Transactional Analysis*. New York: Grosset & Dunlap, 1973.

Miller, N. E., and DiCara, L. V. "Instrumental Learning of Heart-Rate Changes in Curarized Rats: Shaping and Specificity to Discriminative Stimulus." *Journal of Comparative and*

Physiological Psychology, 63 (1967), 12–19.

Mishra, R. S. *Yoga Sutras.* New York: Julian Press, 1963.

Moody, R. A. *Life After Life.* New York: Bantam, 1975.

Naranjo, C., *The Healing Journey.* New York: Ballantine Books, 1973.

Neher, A. *The Psychology of Transcendence.* Englewood Cliffs, N.J.: Prentice-Hall, 1980.

Neihardt, J. G. *Black Elk Speaks, Being the Life Story of a Holy Man of the Oglala Sioux.* Lincoln: University of Nebraska Press, 1961. NYT-56 (1939).

Nietzsche, F. *The Portable Nietzsche.* New York: Viking Press, 1954.

Norman, D. A. *Human Information Processing.* New York: Academic Press, 1977.

Notterman, J., Schoenfeld, W.N., and Bersh, P. J. "Conditioned Heart Rate Response in Human Beings During Experimental Anxiety." *Journal of Comparative and Physiological Psychology,* 45 (1952), 1–8.

Oden, T. C. *Game Free: The Meaning of Intimacy.* New York: Dell Publishing Co., 1974.

Olds, J., and Milner, P. "Positive Reinforcement Produced by Electrical Stimulation of Septal Area and Other Regions of the Rat Brain." *Journal of Comparative and Physiological Psychology,* 47 (1954), 419–427.

Ornstein, R. E. *The Psychology of Consciousness.* New York: Penguin Books, 1972.

Ostrander, S., Schroeder, L., and Ostrander, N. *Superlearning.* New York: Delta, 1979.

Overbye, D. "Messenger at the Gates of Time." *Science 81,* 2 (1981), 61–67

Overstreet, H. A. As quoted in *The Great Quotations.* New York: Pocket Books, 1967.

Passwater, R. *Supernutrition.* New York: Dial Press, 1975.

Pauling, L. C. "Orthomolecular Psychiatry." *Science,* 160 (1968), 265–271.

_____, and Hawkins, D. *Orthomolecular Psychiatry.* San Francisco: W. H. Freeman, 1973.

Paulson, T. *Assertion Training Syllabus.* Pasadena, Calif.: Fuller Graduate School of Psychology. Unpublished manuscript, 1974.

Pavlov, I. P. *Selected Works,* edited by K. S. Kostoyants. Moscow: Foreign Language Publishing House, 1955.

Pearce, J. *The Crack in the Cosmic Egg.* New York: Julian Press, 1971.

Pelletier, K. R. *Holistic Medicine.* New York: Delacorte Press, 1979.

Penfield, W., and Rasmussen, T. *The Cerebral Cortex of Man.* New York: Macmillan, 1950.

Perls, F. S. *Gestalt Therapy Verbatim.* Lafayette, Calif.: Real People Press, 1969a.

_____. *In and Out the Garbage Pail.* Lafayette, Calif.: Real People Press, 1969b.

_____. *The Gestalt Approach and Eye Witness to Therapy.* Palo Alto, Calif.: Science & Behavior Books, 1973.

Pevan, D. "Adlerian Psychotherapy." In *The Psychotherapy Handbook.* R. Herink (Ed.). New York: New American Library, 1980, 9–12.

Piaget, J. *The Language and Thought of the Child.* New York: Harcourt, Brace & World, 1926.

Prabhavananda, Swami, and Manchester, F. (Eds.), *The Upanishads.* New York: New American Library, 1957.

Premack, D. "Toward Empirical Behavioral Laws: 1. Positive Reinforcement." *Psychological Review,* 66 (1959), 219–233.

Pronko, N. H. *Psychology From the Standpoint of an Interbehaviorist.* Monterey, Calif.: Brooks/Cole, 1980.

Rachlin, H. *Behaviorism in Everyday Life.* Englewood Cliffs, N.J.: Prentice-Hall, 1980.

Rachman, S. J., and Philips, C. *Psychology and Behavioral Medicine.* Cambridge: Cambridge University Press, 1980.

Rahe, R. H., and Holmes, T. H. "Life Crisis and Major Health Change." *Psychosomatic Medicine,* 28 (1966), 774.

Rama, Swami. *Lectures on Yoga.* Honesdale, Pa.: The Himalayan International Institute of Yoga Science and Philosophy, 1979.

Reik, T. As quoted in E. P. Freeman, "Theodor Reik, A Conversation." *Psychology Today,* 5 (1972), 47–50.

Restak, R. M. *The Brain.* New York: Doubleday, 1979.

Rhine, J. B. *The Reach of the Mind.* New York: William Sloane Associates, 1947.

Robitscher, J. *The Powers of Psychiatry.* New York: Houghton Mifflin, 1980.

Rogers, C. *On Becoming a Person.* Boston: Houghton Mifflin Co., 1961.

_____. *A Way of Being*. Boston: Houghton Mifflin, 1980.

_____, and Stevens, B. *Person to Person*. New York: Pocket Books, 1971.

Rosenfeld, A. *The Second Genesis*. New York: Vintage Books, 1969.

Rosenfeld, I. *Second Opinion: Your Medical Alternatives*. New York: The Linden Press, 1981.

Rotter, J. B. "Generalized Expectancies for Internal Versus External Control of Reinforcement." *Psychological Monographs*, 80 (Whole No. 609), 1966.

_____. "Trust and Gullibility" *Psychology Today*, 14 (1980), 35–42.

Rubins, J. L. *Karen Horney: Gentle Rebel of Psychoanalysis*. New York: The Dial Press, 1978.

Rush, A. J., "Cognitive Therapy." In *The Psychotherapy Handbook*. R. Herink (Ed.). New York: The New American Library, 1980, 91–93.

Rycroft, C. *The Innocence of Dreams*. New York: Pantheon Books, 1979

Salter, A. *Conditioned Reflex Therapy*. New York: Farrar, Straus & Giroux, 1949.

Sartre, J. P. *Being and Nothingness*. New York: Philosophical Library, 1956.

Saunders, J., and Ross, H. M. *Hypoglycemia*. Los Angeles, Calif.: Pinnacle Books, 1980.

Saxe, J. G. "The Blind Men and the Elephant," in A. L. Alexander (Ed.), *Poems That Touch the Heart*. New York: Doubleday & Co., 1956.

Schaefer, H. H., and Martin, P. L. *Behavioral Therapy*. New York: McGraw-Hill, 1969.

Schrag, P., and Divoky, D. *The Myth of the Hyperactive Child*. New York: Pantheon Books, 1975.

Seligman, M. E. P. *Helplessness*. San Francisco: W. H. Freeman, 1975.

Selye, H. "Stress: The Basis of Illness." In *Inner Balance*. E. M. Goldwag (Ed.). Englewood Cliffs, N.J.: Prentice-Hall, 1979, pp. 28–58.

Shepard, M. *Fritz*. New York: E. P. Dutton, 1975.

Shevrin, H. "Glimpses of the Unconscious." *Psychology Today*, 13(1980), 128.

Shostrom, E. L. *Man, the Manipulator*. New York: Bantam Books, 1968.

Silverman, H. M. and Simon, G. I. *The Pill Book.*New York: Bantam, 1979.

Simonton, O. C., and Simonton, S. M. "Stress, Self-Regulation, and Cancer." In *Inner Balance*. E. M. Goldwag (Ed.). Englewood Cliffs, N.J.: Prentice-Hall, 1979, pp. 121–138.

_____, Simonton, S. M., and Creighton, J. *Getting Well Again*. Los Angeles: J. P. Tarcher, 1978.

Skinner, B. F. *About Behaviorism*. New York: Alfred A. Knopf, 1974.

_____. *Beyond Freedom and Dignity*. New York: Alfred A. Knopf, 1971.

_____. *The Behavior of Organisms*. New York: Appleton-Century-Crofts, 1938.

_____. *Walden II*. New York: Macmillan, 1948.

Smith, A. *Powers of Mind*. New York: Random House, 1975.

Smith, G. W. *Hidden Meanings*. Millbrae, Calif.: Celestial Arts, 1977.

Smith, M. J. *When I Say No, I Feel Guilty*. New York: Dial Press, 1975.

Snyder, M. "Self-Monitoring Processes." In *Advances in Experimental Social Psychology, Vol. 12*. L. Berkowitz (Ed.). New York: Academic Press, 1979.

Solomon, R. L. "Punishment." *American Psychologist*, 19 (1964), 239–263.

Sperry, R. W. "The Great Cerebral Commissure." In *Psychobiology: The Biological Bases of Behavior*. J. L. McGaugh, N. W. Weinberger, and R. E. Whalen (Eds.). San Francisco: W. H. Freeman, 1967.

Stace, W. *The Teachings of the Mystics*. New York: New American Library of World Literature, 1960.

Stampfl, T. G., and Levis, D. J. "Essentials of Implosive Therapy: A Learning-Theory-Based Psychodynamic Behavioral Therapy." *Journal of Abnormal Psychology*, 72 (1967), 496–503.

Steiner, C. *Games Alcoholics Play*. New York: Ballantine Books, 1971.

_____. *Scripts People Live*. New York: Grove Press, 1974.

_____. *Healing Alcoholism*. New York: Grove Press, 1979.

Stephenson, W. *The Study of Behavior*. Chicago: University of Chicago Press, 1953.

Stone, I. *The Passions of the Mind*. New York: Doubleday & Co., 1971.

Storr, A. *The Art of Psychotherapy*. New York: Methuen, 1980.

Sullivan, H. S. *The Interpersonal Theory of Psychiatry*. W. W. Norton & Co., 1953.

Sulloway, F. J. *Freud: Biologist of the Mind*. New York: Basic Books, 1979.

Suzuki, D. T. *What Is Zen?* New York: Harper & Row, 1972.

Szasz, T. S. *The Myth of Mental Illness.* New York: Harper & Row, 1961.

———. *The Second Sin.* New York: Doubleday, 1974.

Tanner, W. P., Jr., and Swets, J. A. "A Decision-Making Theory of Visual Detection." *Psychological Review,* 61 (1954), 401–409.

Tart, C. T. *Learning to Use ESP.* Chicago: University of Chicago Press, 1976.

——— Introduction to *Journeys Out of the Body.* R. A. Monroe (Author). New York: Doubleday, 1977.

———. "A Second Psychophysiological Study of Out-of-the-Body Experiences in a Gifted Subject." In *Mind Beyond the Body.* Middlesex, England: Penguin Books, 1978.

Taylor, R. L. "Electroconvulsive Treatment (ECT): The Control of Therapeutic Power." *The Thin Edge: A Mental Health Newsletter for San Bernardino County* (November 1975), 1, 4–7.

Thorndike, E. L. *Animal Intelligence.* New York: Macmillan, 1911.

Toffler, A. *Future Shock.* New York: Bantam Books, 1971.

Tolman, E. C. *Purposive Behavior in Animals and Men.* New York: Appleton-Century-Crofts, 1932.

Torrey, E. F. (A reply appearing in the letter column of *Psychology Today*.) *Psychology Today,* 15 (1980), 12.

———. "Does Psychiatry Have a Future?" In *Psychiatry at the Crossroads.* J. P. Brady and H. K. H. Brodie (Eds.). Philadelphia, Pa.: W. B. Saunders, 1980, 4–13.

Vaihinger, H. *The Philosophy of As If.* Trans. by C. K. Ogden. New York: Harcourt, Brace, 1925.

Viscott, D. S. *The Making of a Psychiatrist.* Greenwich, Conn.: Fawcett Publications, 1972.

Vishnudevananda, Swami. *The Complete Illustrated Book of Yoga.* New York: Julian Press, 1960.

Walker, S., III. "We're Too Cavalier about Hyperactivity." *Psychology Today* 8 (1974), 43–48.

Walsh, R. N., and Vaughan, F. (Eds.), *Beyond Ego.* Los Angeles: J. P. Tarcher, 1980.

Waltari, M. *The Egyptian.* New York: G. P. Putnam's Sons, 1949.

Watson, J. B. "What Is Thinking?" In *Good Reading in Psychology.* Gazzaniga, M. S. and Lovejoy, E. P. (Eds.). Englewood Cliffs, N.J.: Prentice-Hall, 1971.

Watts, A. *Meditation.* New York: Pyramid Communications, 1974.

———. *The Way of Zen.* New York: Random House, 1957.

Wender, P. H. *The Hyperactive Child.* New York: Crown Publishers, 1973.

———, and Klein, D. F. *Mind, Mood, and Medicine.* New York: Farrar, Straus, & Giroux, 1981.

Williams, R. J. *Nutrition Against Disease.* New York: Pitman Publishing Corp., 1971.

Williams, R. L., and Long, J. D. *Toward a Self-Managed Life Style.* Boston: Houghton Mifflin, 1975.

Wilson C. *New Pathways in Psychology: Maslow and the Post-Freudian Revolution.* New York: New American Library, 1972.

Wolman, B. B., (Ed.), *Dictionary of Behavior Science.* New York: Van Nostrand Reinhold Co., 1973.

Wolpe, J. *Psychotherapy by Reciprocal Inhibition.* Stanford, Calif.: Stanford University Press, 1958.

———. *The Practice of Behavior Therapy.* New York: Pergamon, 1974.

———. *Our Useless Fears.* Boston: Houghton Mifflin, 1981.

Wood. E. *Zen Dictionary.* Rutland, Vt.: Charles E. Tuttle Co., 1957.

Woollams, S. and Brown, M. *The Total Handbook of Transactional Analysis.* Englewood Cliffs, N.J.; Prentice–Hall, 1979.

Yalom, I. D. *Existential Psychotherapy.* New York: Basic Books, 1980.

Yogananda, P. *Autobiography of a Yogi.* Los Angeles: Self-Realization Fellowship, 1974.

Young, P. T. "An Eclectic in Psychology." In *The Psychologists.* T. S. Krawiec (Ed.) New York: Oxford University Press, 1972.

Yudkin, J. *Sweet and Dangerous.* New York: Peter H. Wyden, Inc., 1972.

Zilbergeld, B., and Evans, M. "The Inadequacy of Masters and Johnson." *Psychology Today,* 14 (1980), 29–43.

Zimbardo, P. G. "The Age of Indifference." *Psychology Today,* 14 (1980), 71–76.

Photo Credits

Chapter 1
Opener: Bob Fuschetto/Photo Researchers. Page 3: Joan Liftin/Archive Pictures. Page 8: Elizabeth Crews. Page 10: Joel Gordon. Page 17: Smithsonian Institution National Anthropological Archives. Page 25: Charles Harbutt/Archive Pictures.

Chapter 2
Opener: Ron Church/Photo Researchers. Page 33: Courtesy of GTE. Page 38: Max Halberstadt. Page 42: Culver Pictures. Page 51: Elizabeth Crews. Pages 66 and 73: The Bettmann Archive. Page 82: Courtesy of Karen Horney Clinic, New York City. Page 95: Nina Howell Starr/Photo Researchers.

Chapter 3
Opener: Alan Carey/Image Works. Page 108: Arthur Grace/Stock, Boston. Page 109: Culver Pictures. Page 110: Michael Weisbrot and Family/Image Works. Page 127: Sam Falk/Monkmeyer Press. Page 133: Drawing by Jack Tippit, permission to reprint, *Parade* Magazine. Page 137: Culver Pictures. Page 147: Betsy Cole/Stock, Boston. Page 156: Chester Higgins/Rapho-Photo Researchers.

Chapter 4
Opener: Thomas Hopker/Woodfin Camp. Page 170: Elizabeth Crews. Page 176: Left, The Bettman Archive; right, Photo Trends. Page 181: Courtesy of Albert Ellis. Page 191: Thomas S. England/Photo Researchers. Page 193: Dick Hyman/Rapho-Photo Researchers. Page 204: William Carter/Photo Researchers.

Chapter 5
Opener: Joel Gordon. Page 208: United Press International. Page 213: Joel Gordon. Page 225: Alice S. Kandell/Photo Researchers. Page 238: Jean-Claude Lejeune/Stock, Boston. Page 248: Joel Gordon. Page 254: Paul Fortin/Stock, Boston.

Chapter 6
Opener: Cary Wolinsky/Stock, Boston. Page 264: Museum Boymans-van Beuningen de Rotterdam. Page 268: Courtesy of Dr. James Olds, California Institute of Technology. Page 275: Beryl Goldberg. Page 280: Donald Dietz/Stock, Boston. Page 284: Christa Armstrong/Rapho-Photo Researchers. Page 290: Peter Menzel/Stock, Boston.

Chapter 7
Opener: Susan Lapides/Design Conceptions. Page 313: Alan Carey/Image Works. Page 320: Elizabeth Crews. Page 326: The Bettmann Archive. Page 333: Arthur Tress/Photo Researchers. Page 340: Elizabeth Crews. Page 350: Springer/Bettmann Film Archive. Page 361: Chester Higgins/Rapho-Photo Researchers.

Chapter 8
Opener: Jock Pottle/Design Conceptions. Page 373: Frederik D. Bodin/Stock, Boston. Page 377: Joel Gordon. Page 383: Lynn Lennon/Photo Researchers. Page 391: David R. Frazier/Photo Researchers. Page 402: Frederik D. Bodin/Stock, Boston.

Chapter 9
Opener: Joe Munroe/Photo Researchers. Page 415: Owen Frank/Stock, Boston. Page 421: Anestis Diakopoulos/Stock, Boston. Page 427: Donald Dietz/Stock, Boston.

Name Index

Subject Index